THE ESSENTIAL
TAGORE

THE ESSENTIAL
TAGORE

RABINDRANATH TAGORE

Edited by
Fakrul Alam *&* Radha Chakravarty

THE BELKNAP PRESS *of* HARVARD UNIVERSITY PRESS

Cambridge, Massachusetts
London, England

First Harvard University Press paperback edition, 2014

Pages 816–817 constitute an extension of the copyright page.

Library of Congress Cataloging-in-Publication Data
Tagore, Rabindranath, 1861–1941.
　[Selections. English. 2011]
　The essential Tagore / Rabindranath Tagore ; edited by Fakrul Alam and
Radha Chakravarty.
　　p.　cm.
　　Includes bibliographical references and index.
　　ISBN 978-0-674-05790-6 (cloth : alk. paper)
　　ISBN 978-0-674-41704-5 (pbk.)
　　1. Tagore, Rabindranath, 1861–1941—Translations into English.
I. Alam, Fakrul.　II. Chakravarty, Radha.　III. Title.
　　PK1722.A2　2011
　　891′.448409—dc22　　2010051635

 *To Nazma and Pinak*

CONTENTS

viii

ix

x

Poetry as Polemic

Whatever the unborn and the dead may know, they cannot know the
beauty, the marvel of being alive in the flesh.

D. H. Lawrence, *Apocalypse*

*I*BEGAN TO FEEL PUT OFF by Tagore in my late teens, around the time
I discovered Indian classical music, the devotional songs of Meerabai,
Tulsidas, and Kabir, not to speak of the work of the modernists. I was
also—to place the moment further in context—reading contemporary
European poetry in translation, in the tremendous series edited by Al
Alvarez, the Penguin Modern European Poets. My father knew of my
promiscuous adventurousness when it came to poetry, and, in tender
deference to this, he (a corporate man) would buy these books from
bookshops in the five-star hotels he frequented, such as the mythic Nal-
anda at the Taj. Among the poets I discovered through this route of priv-
ilege was the Israeli Dan Pagis, of whom the blurb stated: "A survivor of
a concentration camp, Dan Pagis possesses a vision which is essentially
tragic." I don't recall how my seventeen-year-old self responded to Pagis,
but I do remember the poem he is most famous for, "Written in Pencil in
the Sealed Railway-Car." Here it is in its entirety:

> here in this carload
> i am eve
> with abel my son
> if you see my other son

cain son of man
tell him i

The resonance of the poem escaped me at the time: this history was not mine. What struck me were the qualities I found most attractive when I was seventeen—metaphysical despair; deliberate irresolution. I mention the poem because I think it figured as a subtext to a difference of opinion I had with my uncle when my parents and I visited him in London in 1979. My uncle, a bachelor and an executive in shipping, was the most shameless propagandist for Tagore I have ever met, and his enthusiasm only furthered my dislike for the Bengali poet. Walking around Belsize Park, he would tell me that Tagore was the greatest poet the world had ever seen, surpassing everybody, including "the poets of the *Bhagavad Gita.*" (Homer and Shakespeare didn't even merit a mention.) I countered with the name of my favorite poet, T. S. Eliot, flag-bearer of a certain kind of twentieth-century despondency especially attractive to teenagers, and spoke too of Meera's devotionals, saying I preferred the latter to Tagore's lyrics. "You somehow feel," I said, "that there's a real urgency and immediacy about her songs. They could have been scribbled upon a prison wall." I was probably invoking Pagis here, and also having a go at Tagore's premeditated and loving craftsmanship. Many poets—besides, of course, philosophers—have insisted that there are things that are more important than poetry, especially in the face of trauma; for poets, this disavowal is, in fact, a respectable literary strategy. Even an adolescent detractor could tell that, to Tagore, *nothing* was as important as poetry.

My uncle attempted to indoctrinate me each time I went to London in the 1970s. In his eyes, Tagore was an amazingly contradictory agglomeration of virtues and characteristics. "If Tolstoy was a sage whose heart bled for mankind," said my uncle, "then Rabi Thakur was a greater sage. No one has felt more pity for man's sorrows." He spoke of him in the semifamiliar, affectionate way of the Bengali *bhadralok,* as if Tagore were a cherished acquaintance—"Rabi Thakur"—and not hieratically, as "Gurudev," the appellation Gandhi had conferred on him (as, in turn, Tagore had reportedly conferred "Mahatma" on Gandhi). He sometimes hummed Tagore's more popular and plangent lines ("My days wouldn't remain in the golden cage / those many-coloured days of mine" and "I know, I know that the prayers that went / unanswered in life haven't been lost") mainly to express his sadness: for he was a man who loved company, and family, but had oddly chosen to be alone, and an expatriate. Then, the mood would change abruptly. Tagore, according to my uncle, was a "tennis player"—this odd metaphor was deployed to suggest, I think, a series of departures: the breaking away of Tagore's family, starting with his great-grandfather Nilmoni Tagore, from its conservative Brahminical roots; Tagore's own breaking out from his "aristocratic," landed past into modernity, art, individualism, and, of course, glamorous mystique. The latter, presumably, is what Tagore, the celebrity poet, and the tennis player had in common—besides finesse and control.

My uncle was as much in awe of Tagore's looks as he was of his work—both were, in fact, impossible to disentangle from one another. Despite his immemorial, world-denying air from his forties onward, Tagore and everything associated with him—his handwriting; the interiors he inhabited, with their new "ethnic" design; the habitations he constructed for himself in Santiniketan; the paintings created out of manuscript corrections—had an air of provisionality and experiment. They emanated from a man taking his cue from, or experiencing resonances with, a number of sources and excitements—tribal arts and crafts; the devotional-mystic music of Bengal; the dance traditions of neighboring regions, like Manipur; Shelley; the *Upanishads;* Paul Klee. All this translated, in the public domain, into the personality and the appearance themselves—the commanding but ineffable, and somehow wholly contemporary, presence of the "world poet." It was this image that held my uncle in thrall. "'People who compare me with Shakespeare should realize that I had to make a leap of five hundred years to write as I do,' said Rabindranath," reported my uncle calmly. There was a remonstrative edge to his words, though, for his identification with Tagore was fierce. "All men who repeat one line of Shakespeare *are* William Shakespeare," said Jorge Luis Borges; all Bengalis of a certain generation were, at one point or another, Tagore. And, of course, there are many Tagores, as you will discover in this volume. The phrase *renaissance man* does not capture the restless energy and vitality with which he—a colonial subject—journeyed toward different genres in the manner of one learning, mastering, and finally altering new languages. He undertook each genre as an exploration: the revealing (in all kinds of ways) letter-writing of the young man; the shadowy microcosm contained in the plays; the great novels and stories; the often deeply original but underrated essays; the paintings that emerged almost by accident—from manuscript corrections—when he was a much older man. The act of journeying and the element of chance were (as I discovered later) both crucial to Tagore.

For the versatility I've just mentioned, Tagore is occasionally compared to Goethe. I see him as being closer to another German, Josef Beuys, as someone who wants not only to address or to influence the world around him, but to rearrange and reorder it—creatively, radically, sometimes physically. As a consequence, Tagore was interested not only in literature but in book design, apparel, and the decorative and cultural aspects of our drawing rooms. Indeed, Buddhadeva Bose, writing about a visit to the Tagore household, mentions how subtly innovative and experimental (and finely judged) both the food and the decor were. Tagore's urge to experiment was relentless; and we can't really pretend that what he did within the covers of a book and what he did outside it emerge from two wholly divergent impulses. Beuys refuses to distinguish between the text and the world that is his immediate material and, in many ways, dissolves the frame around the artwork; Tagore, too, frequently refuses to make the same distinction. This volume's songs, poems, stories, extracts from his novels, reflections on literature and politics and on his frequent and exhausting travels, and even instances of his sui generis humor shouldn't be read as his "writings" alone, but seen in conjunction with Tagore's larger interest—evident in almost all he did—in intervening in and reshaping his surroundings. His school, Santiniketan, served as a hothouse and a laboratory for this creative experiment. In important ways, Santiniketan—indeed, the many-pronged, all-embracing Tagorean project—was a precursor to Beuys's vision of "total art" and "social sculpture," and a successor to the Wagnerian *Gesamtkunstwerk,* the art-performance in which every form of art is incorporated. Yet Tagore's impulse needs to be distinguished from Wagner's messianic vision.

Tagore was absorbed in the everyday, the domestic, and his modernist love of the momentary.

Naturally, my uncle had a view on Tagore's metamorphic effect: "Let's say you were to set a murder mystery in the early twentieth century, and the murder had been committed by someone who grew up before Tagore became famous. Let's say a manuscript page was the single available clue. You'd catch the murderer just by looking at the handwriting, because Bengali handwriting changed forever after Tagore." Moreover, "Words like *Keatsian* and *Wordsworthian* describe a literary style associated with that particular poet," he pointed out, for he had read a great deal. "Only *Rabindrik*"—the Bengali adjective derived from Tagore's first name—"encompasses an entire generation, an outlook, that came into being with the poet's work." For my uncle, this was a matter of intransigent pride. For the very original poets who followed Tagore in the Bengali language, the legacy was a mixed one. "It was impossible to write like Rabindranath, and it was impossible not to write like Rabindranath," said Buddhadeva Bose. When, in fact, I quoted and cited the great post-Tagorean poets I particularly loved, like Jibanananda Das or Bose, to my uncle, he was completely immune to their music: "I've heard it all before. Don't you see none of this would be possible without Rabindranath?" Thus my uncle, an idiosyncratic but sensitive reader, deliberately echoed a vulgar undertone of a particular form of Bengali romanticism—that Tagore was a historical pinnacle, after which everything was a kind of decline, and every writer a latecomer. This view precluded any further fruitful discussion between my uncle and myself, though that didn't stop either of us.

There was another dimension to these conversations in London. My uncle knew, as I think I must have, that the dismantling of Tagore's reputation as a serious poet had started early—soon after the Nobel Prize in 1913—and that, by the seventies, very little survived of that reputation in the West, or, for that matter, anywhere outside the cocoon of Bengal. The rise itself had been at once astonishing and suspect, impossible without the interconnectedness of the world from the nineteenth century onward, and points to the dangers and benefits of the sort of global fame we've now become familiar with. In my introduction to the *Picador/Vintage Book of Modern Indian Literature,* I'd said that Tagore was probably the world's "first international literary celebrity"; an Indian reviewer, who must have immediately concluded I was celebrating the fact, said my claim was "risible." An English poet who taught at Oxford said the dubious honor might belong to Byron. People have forgotten how startling Tagore's incursion was into the various languages of the twentieth century. Martin Kaempchen points out that he was Germany's first bestseller; Jiménez's translations made him a cult in the Spanish-speaking world; this is not to invoke his renown in China, Japan, Russia, Eastern Europe, and the United States. This fame was a product, largely, of Tagore's English-language, Nobel-Prize–winning *Gitanjali;* the English *Gitanjali* is perhaps one of the earliest examples of how capitalism fetishizes the book. To use the word *celebrity,* then (rather than terms like "high critical standing"), isn't inappropriate, as Tagore's presence was felt so predominantly outside the field of literature, as it still is—except in the forgotten sphere of Bengali literature. And to recover Tagore today as a poet and writer must entail some sense of the Bengali language becoming a realm of literary possibility.

Looking back today to the middle of the nineteenth century, we feel compelled to admit that something exceptional occurred with the emergence of Bengali as a literary language. Disturbingly, we still know very little of this moment, partly because an easeful way of looking at colonial history (according to which modernity comes from elsewhere, bringing with it certain genres and practices) has saved us from engaging too strenuously with the question of how and why things changed when they did. For instance, I don't think we still have a proper genealogy of the word *sahitya,* which we've been using for more than a century to mean "literature" and "literary tradition" in the modern, secular sense, and not to mean, as it once did in the Indian languages, "literary content" or "literary meaning." Tagore's own etymological gloss on the word asks us to look at its root, *sahit* ("to be with"), thereby turning literature into a social, companionable thing. It is fairly certain, though, that *sahitya,* as we understand it, is not a timeless Indian verity (for that, we should perhaps look up the word *kavya*) but a contingent, humanist construct, just as "Indianness" and the modern Bengali language are. It is also certain that the emergence of Bengali encompassed more than nationalism. It became—in lieu of English—a respectable vehicle for cosmopolitan self-expression by the 1860s. It is the latter development that failed in Ireland and Wales with regard to Gaelic and Welsh, and nationalism alone (of which there was no shortage in Ireland) didn't succeed in turning those languages into viable literatures or prevent them from becoming, essentially, curios. In Ireland, it is the English language that became the medium through which the modern formulated his or her ambivalence and self-division, so giving Irish literature and diction its shifting registers in English. Gaelic, largely associated with identity and nation, became, with a few striking exceptions, an unusable artifact. Something quite different and exceptional happened in Bengali colonial modernity. The Bengali language emerged from not only a conviction about identity but an intimation of distance, from not just the wellspring of race but disjunction and severance. These essentially cosmopolitan tensions always animate Tagore's language.

I used the word *curio* deliberately, in order to recall Buddhadeva Bose's unfair but revealing attack on Indian poets writing in English in the 1960s, in which he accused them of producing, by choosing not to write in the mother-tongue, not poems but "curios." In one sense, Bose is right. It is the English language that has risked becoming, over and over, a sort of Gaelic in India: not because, as Bose would have it, it was a foreign or colonial tongue, but because, like Gaelic, it bore too notionally the burden of identity and nationality. The relative and paradoxical freedom from this burden in the emergence of modern Bengali gave it its special air of play and potential. In other, fundamental ways, Bose was wrong. The poets he attacked had based their achievement on a cunning with which they had sabotaged and complicated the possibility of a pan-Indian tradition; they too were writing, in their way, in a vernacular. In fact, it was the long poem that Bose held up as the great exemplary Indian English poem, *Savitri* by Sri Aurobindo, that the shrewd Nissim

xxii

Ezekiel pointed out as the actual curio for, presumably, its faux high cultural atmosphere of the Orient as well as its emulation of the English canon (it was composed in iambs). It should be pointed out that Tagore's English translation of *Gitanjali* would be—for Indian poets writing in English like Ezekiel, A. K. Ramanujan, Arvind Krishna Mehrotra—yet another Gaelic artifact to bypass or circumvent. In his brief memoir "Partial Recall," Mehrotra quotes, with little indulgence toward his youthful self, from the ambitious and sonorous pastiche of that *Gitanjali* which he produced as a teenager.

The fact that Literature—specifically English Literature—was a university discipline first invented for the colonies is fairly well-known today. In the 1880s, English Literature became an object of study leading to a degree at the University of Calcutta, well before any such development had taken place elsewhere, let alone Oxford or Cambridge. But the incursion of English and European literary texts into Bengal had begun a century earlier. The study of literature cannot be seen simply as an instrument of imperialist pedagogy from 1820s onward (when it first surfaces as a taught discipline in Calcutta). By the early nineteenth century, Bengalis, especially when naming literary and cultural societies, were reflecting on what literature, or, in Bengali, *sahitya,* might be—great texts of all kinds, or a different way of approaching and valuing texts? A significant historical narrative is contained in the evolution of the word *sahitya* into its present-day meaning. What seems pretty sure is that it was not a word just lying around, ready to slip into its contemporary, secular role. Nor is it a simple translation of the word *literature,* though it means much the same thing from the middle of the nineteenth century onward. That is, it is neither a purely Indian (whatever that may be) or colonial term, but one that keeps abreast of these dichotomies until they start to waver. Tagore, in his first essay on the subject in 1889, defines it in negatives: "The essence of literature does not allow itself to be trapped within a definition. It is like the essence of life: we know what it cannot exist without, but what it is we do not know." These are the words of a poet who has come into his own at a cusp in history. Perhaps the specificity of Tagore's problem, and the duress of the historical moment he's speaking in and of, would become clearer if the key word were left untranslated: "The essence of *sahitya* does not allow itself to be trapped," and so on. But the translator, Sukanta Chaudhuri, doesn't do so because he presumes Tagore has already leaped toward the sense in which that word operates today; and, in part, he's right. By 1889, Tagore's readers have definitely begun to recognize the literary, in spite of the strangeness of the sentences I have quoted. Yet one must keep in mind the strangeness of the time. Tagore's complex and difficult position as a modern Indian, a colonial subject, an elite cosmopolitan, an inheritor and inventor of Eastern civilizational values, and a progeny of the Enlightenment allows him to partake of the exclusive secular ethos of literature but also to view it from the outside, as a process. You feel more than once as you gaze back on that crucial period that you are over-familiar with its outlines, and also that you are only on the verge of understanding it.

Tagore has been such a fountainhead of nationalist pride, such a static emblem ever since one can remember that we forget that he was clearly aware, as a writer, of living in a unique and transformative time. There is, in Tagore, a constant acknowledgment of the power of the past, and of the canonical riches of Indian tradition, and constant inquiry about the terms in which these are available to us. In this, he is different from either the Hindu reformers or the Indian nationalists, for whom tradition has an integrity and wholeness, and is a given to be improved upon or invoked in the services of politics and identity. For Tagore, tradition is at once contemporary and immediate, and inaccessible and disjunctive. As a result, contrary emotions permeate his great essay on the fourth-century Kalidasa's poem on the rainy season, *Meghadutam* (*The Cloud-Messenger*):

> From Ramgiri to the Himalayas ran a long stretch of ancient
> India over which life used to flow to the slow, measured mandra-

kanta metre of the *Meghadutam.* We are banished from that India, not just during the rains but for all time. Gone is Dasharna with its groves hedged with ketaki plants where, before the onset of the rains, the birds among the roadside trees fed on household scraps and busily built their nests, while in the jaam copse on the outskirts of the village, the fruit ripened to a colour dark as the clouds.

The intimation of contemporaneity here is astonishingly suburban; it has to do with nature, yes, but nature viewed from the point of view of the town and the ebb and flow of domesticity: the "household scraps" the birds feed on, the ripening jaam that will be collected and brought home to the family. Kalidasa is not a naïve poet; he is a court sophisticate, an urban sensibility, already viewing the natural at one remove. The loss experienced here, then—"We are banished from that India, not just during the rains but for all time"—is a double, even a multiple, one. From which India, exactly, are we banished? This paradox—to do with immediacy, recognizability, and absolute inaccessibility—is also the subject of Tagore's own poem, *Meghdut,* which records the experience of re-reading Kalidasa's eponymous poem. Tagore's poem, filled with images of human activity and habitation, describes how the reader comes to inhabit Kalidasa's world as he reads and becomes an exile from it once the poem is over.

Tagore's fascination and absorption in heritage could have made him an elegist, or a poet who turned from the physical life of the present to contemplate the ruins of the past. This trajectory was, to a certain extent, T. S. Eliot's. But, oddly, this is not the case. Tagore's way of suggesting that he lives in a unique moment in history is to embrace change as a fundamental constituent of existence—indeed, as a crucial constituent of diction, imagination, and craft. "In order to find you anew, I lose you every moment/ O beloved treasure." In this line from a song and others like it, Tagore embraces accident. He weds contingency to the modernist's love of the moment, the here and now. The latter—as in the Joycean epiphany—heightens the quotidian: Tagore's welcoming of contingency introduces an element of risk to the epiphany and the image. He introduces the possibility of *any* imaginable consequence, including an intuition of the divine. Tagore's apotheosis of his historical moment, his here and now, is not a surreptitious celebration of the colonial history into which he was born, but a recognition of the fact that no historical period can be contained within its canonical definition. Accident and chance ensure that its outcomes are unpredictable and life-transforming.

This embrace of life, of chance, of play, makes Tagore stand out in the intellectual and moral ethos of late romanticism and modernism—an ethos with which Tagore shares several obsessions (time, memory, the moment, the nature of reality, poetic form), but whose metaphysics he constantly refutes. By *metaphysics* I mean a system whereby value and meaning have their source elsewhere, somewhere beyond the experienced world—whether it is European civilization, antiquity, the Celtic twilight, or some other lost world. The present, severed from its organic resources in that past, becomes degraded and splintered, and yet continues to be haunted, even burnished, by what it has lost. I think Tagore is deeply interested in this metaphysics in the context of Bengal, and it runs through his songs, with their momentary scenes, encounters, and revelations, where any hint of transcendence is qualified by the temporal and the fragmentary. This metaphysics is partly invoked as incantation in the refrain from the poem *"Balaka,"* or "The Wild Geese": *"Hethha noi, hethha noi, onno konokhane!"* ("Not here, not here—elsewhere!") But there is also—in the same oeuvre, often in the very same songs and poems—the Tagore of whom I have become more and more aware, the near-contemporary of Nietzsche's, who, like the latter, makes a break with that "elsewhere" and constructs a sustained argument against it in song, and in the terms that life and desire give him: "I've become infinite: / such is the consequence of your play. / Pouring me out, you fill me / with new life once again." This, in many ways, is an astonishing and audacious assertion, all the more striking for being entirely self-aware about its audacity (this is a tonal characteristic Tagore shares with Nietzsche). The oeuvre is full of such assertions, running counter to both romanticism's backward glance and his own "Not here, not here" refrain. It marks him out, like D. H. Lawrence, as a writer embodying a radical historical break. The lines I have tried to reproduce in English are among the most difficult to translate from the work of this largely untranslatable poet. They (in Tagore's own English) are also among his most famous, being the opening lines of the first song in the English *Gitanjali*. In Tagore's English prose-poem version: "Thou hast made me endless, such is thy pleasure." All sorts of echoes adorn the next two lines in Tagore's English—"This frail vessel thou emptiest again and again . . ." and "This little flute of a reed thou hast carried over hills and dales"—placing the song now in the context of a psalmlike, New Testament sweetness ("this frail vessel") and now in an English arcadia ("little flute of a reed . . . hills and dales"). The words are removed, in effect, from the radical moment they inhabit in the Bengali. The original—*"Amare tumi ashesh kore-chho / emoni leela taba"*—is remarkable, as I've said, on many levels. The word *leela* can be translated as divine play: Hindu philosophy sees divine play as childlike and solipsistic, and the creation and destruction of the universe, and of man, among its various corollaries. Tagore translates the word as "pleasure," to denote the primacy of delight and desire, rather than moral design, in divine creation. Among the unintended, almost inadvertent, results of that play, the song has it, is man's immortality, or "infinity" (my word), or "endlessness" (Tagore's). And so the centrality of the human is bestowed upon her or him by divinity, certainly, but not by design or according to a legible purpose. In this way, Tagore introduces the notion of chance and coincidence into the story of man's emergence, and removes the human narrative from its familiar logical movement (an ascent or a decline) from the past to the present, from tradition to modernity.

Radical claims abound in the songs and poems. Also in the *Gitanjali* is the song beginning (in my translation): "To the festival of creation I have had an invitation: / Blessed, blessed is human life!" In Tagore's English prose-poem, though, the song's declaration is more modest: "I have had my invitation to this world's festival, and thus my life has been blessed." This is almost Christian, a muttering of grace. The Bengali is far more unsettling: it has "human life" *(manab jiban)* instead of the prayerful "my life." It is more triumphal. Again, alongside the celebration of the occurrence of life and consciousness is the deliberate celebration of contingency. An invitation is always a bonus and a gift; you can't really expect it or plan for it or demand it. And, once more, the two lines, with their narrative of cause and effect, are structured at once to invoke logic and to mock it. In the earlier song, Tagore writes as if he knows that the self's infinity or endlessness should be a natural consequence of divine play, while also knowing very well there is absolutely no logical reason for the one to lead to the other. In the second song, the progression, from discovering the invitation to the festival of existence to the assertion that human life is "blessed" *(dhanya),* is presented seamlessly, although we know there is actually no good reason why the second should follow from the first. (In the English version, which adds a "thus" that is absent in the Bengali, the progression in the first line is far more acceptable.) But why should divine play lead to the speaker's belief in his own infinitude? Why should his being invited to earthly existence be a cause of joy for all human life? There's a logical structure to the way these statements develop, but it is a structure that conceals a deep arbitrariness. The second song strongly implies, in its movement from the first line to the second in Bengali, a "thus" or "therefore" or *"tai,"* without being able to quite justify or explain that powerful implication. The English translation, by adding a "thus" and substituting "human life" with "my life," simply dispenses with that mysterious tension and diminishes the audacity of the opening. We, as listeners of the Bengali song, are moved and unsettled, but we ask, in the end, for no justification: it is almost as if we know that, in Tagore's world, anything is possible.

Much of Tagore's work, then, is preoccupied with—indeed, mesmerized by—coincidence and possibility. It is a preoccupation that seems to go against the closure and yearning of "Not here, not here, elsewhere," because one can never predict when or where that moment of possibility will occur. One of the songs I have translated for this volume, "The sky full of the sun and stars, the world full of life, / in the midst of this, I find myself—/ so, surprised, my song awakens," is, again, a paean to coincidence. It is also a refutation of metaphysics, of a higher purpose (whatever that might be), according to whose design existence or consciousness might find its proper meaning and arrangement. I have translated Tagore's word *bismaye* as "surprised," though it could plausibly be rendered as "in wonder." The role of the naïve or nature poet, or even a certain kind of romantic, is to wonder at the real, at the universe, but the speaker in the song is not just transfixed by the beauty of the universe but by the happenstance that's brought him to it: "in the midst of this, I find myself." This is what gives to the poet-mystic's *bismay* (his sense of wonder) the element of the unexpected, of surprise—the surprise of the time-traveler (expressed in the poem *Meghdut*) moving between worlds and phases of history. Tagore's peculiar lyric voice, with its curiously urgent apotheosis of the world, its constant note of arrival, can be partly understood through the trope of science fiction (one of whose recurrent themes is the sudden advent into new universes), or through the notion of rebirth and return, or both. This is an odd but powerful, and revealing, characteristic in the foremost artist to have emerged from a background of Brahmo reformism and the Bengali Enlightenment.

Tagore's recurrent metaphors of time-travel, return, and arrival, and the fact that the great protagonist of his songs and poems is a figure determinedly committed to journeying toward life and birth, were picked up by two great Bengali artists who came after him: the poet Jibanananda Das and the filmmaker Ritwik Ghatak. Das (1899–1954), who, after his untimely death in an accident with a tram, has come to be seen as the outstanding Bengali poet after Tagore, and whose personality—solitary, disturbed—is the antithesis of the older poet's, sensed that Tagore was the principal writer of his time of the will to, and desire for, life. Without remarking upon this in so many words, he took on this mantle himself, but expressed himself far more equivocally, if no less forcefully. Das's time-traveler, in his poem "Banalata Sen," moves through epochs and civilizations, arriving at last in a modern drawing room in Bengal, in a journey during which both mythic and ordinary place-names are made strange:

> For thousands of years I roamed the paths of this earth,
> From waters round Ceylon in dead of night to Malayan seas.
> Much have I wandered. I was there in the gray world of Asoka

And Bimbisara, pressed on through darkness to the city of
  Vidarbha.
I am a weary heart surrounded by life's frothy ocean.
To me she gave a moment's peace—Banalata Sen from Natore.
  (trans. Clinton B. Seely)

The irrepressible Tagorean energy, the irresistible will to arrive—"in the
midst of this, I find myself—/ so, surprised, my song awakens"—has
faded here but not vanished. Das gets his habit of repeating ancient place
names from Tagore as one of the ways in which the traveler orders his
journey while commemorating past arrivals; here is Tagore in his epony-
mous essay on Kalidasa's poem, "The *Meghadutam*": "Avanti, Vidisha,
Ujjayini, Vindhya, Kailas, Devagiri, the Reva, the Shipra, the Vetravati."
But Das's speaker experiences a fatigue that the radical Tagorean protag-
onist didn't know. Das's hero, or antihero, must press on, despite his
"weary heart": he has inherited, perplexingly, the same life-urge. Das too
is a great poet of the will to live—precisely because his view of it is darker,
and far more qualified. His protagonist desires to be born despite being
conscious that birth is not an unmixed blessing. This is Das's troubling
modulation upon the Tagorean idea of the "invitation" to earthly exis-
tence, as a result of which "human life" is "blessed":

Drawn to the Earth's ground, to the house of human birth
I have come, and I feel, better not to have been born—
yet having come all this I see as a deeper gain
when I touch a body of dew in an incandescent dawn.
  (*"Suchetana," trans. Joe Winter*)

In the first two lines of this famous stanza, Das has a familiar Sophoclean
moment; but, in the third and fourth lines, he's come round to the Ta-
gorean belief that arrival and return create their own article of faith; the
body becomes an incarnation of the will ("I touch a body of dew"); in
Tagore's words, "I've pressed upon each blade of grass on my way to the
forest." Again and again, Das will be of two minds about this matter,
about withdrawing from the cycle of life or, taking his cue from his great
precursor, returning to it:

When once I leave this body
Shall I come back to the world?
If only I might return
On a winter's evening
Taking on the compassionate flesh of a cold tangerine
At the bedside of some dying acquaintance.
("Tangerine," *trans. Clinton B. Seely*)

For Tagore, withdrawal was out of the question. "In the midst of this, I find myself," he'd said in the song. In the poem "Liberation" *("Mukti"),* he put it elegantly but with directness: "Liberation through renunciation—that's not for me"; and, later, "To shut / in penance, the senses' doorway—that's not for me." We can connect this to the Buddhist thought that deeply attracted Tagore; but if we place it in the context of his oeuvre, of the modernity he lived in, and the modernism he was always ambivalent about, we must put him in the lineage of Nietzsche, Whitman, Lawrence, and others who made a similar rebuttal of negation. Actually, looking again at the poem *"Balaka"* ("The Wild Geese"), in which the admonitory refrain "Not here, not here, elsewhere" occurs, I find it lit not so much by a desire for "elsewhere" (the foundational desire of metaphysics) but, again, by the subversive urge for life itself. The poet is standing after sunset before a landscape of hills and deodar trees, near the river Jhelum, when, unexpectedly, the sudden transit of a flock of geese flying transmogrifies the observer and his vision of nature. The Tagorean landscape is often orchestral, participatory, musical, synchronic, but not Wordsworthian, with the "still, sad music of humanity"; it is alive, but not in an anthropomorphic sense. In another, early poem, *"Jete nahi dibo"* ("I Won't Let You Go"), all of nature, as the speaker departs from home and family on a long absence involving work, echoes his daughter's final words to him in an actively participatory way, in what can only be called an orchestral threnody:

What immense sadness has engulfed
The entire sky and the whole world!
The farther I go the more clearly I hear
Those poignant words, "Won't let you go!"

From world's end to the blue dome of the sky
Echoes the eternal cry: "Won't let you go!"
Everything cries, "I won't let you go!"
Mother Earth too cries out to the tiny grass
It hugs on its bosom, "I won't let you go!"
　　(*trans. Fakrul Alam*)

This is not anthropomorphism; it is the landscape agitated by the life-urge, and making a vocal, direct intervention. In "The Wild Geese," Tagore revisits and revises his vision:

It seemed that those wings
　　　　Bore away tidings
　　Of stillness thrilled in its innermost being
By the intensity of motion . . .
　　(*trans. Fakrul Alam*)

And again:

　　　　　　　. . . The grass fluttering its wings
　　On the earth that is its air—
　　　　Underneath the darkness of the soil
　　　　　Millions of seeds sprouting wings
　I see today

From Tagore, the filmmaker Ritwik Ghatak (1925–1976) got his sense of the landscape being not just a serene, indifferent, permanent background to human endeavor, as in the Brueghel painting of Icarus's fall described wryly by W. H. Auden in his "Musée des Beaux Arts," but as a multivocal, orchestral entity actively involved in the desire for existence. So, at different points of time in Ghatak's films, the landscape appears to move and listen; it is aware of the protagonist, just as the protagonist is partly conscious of it being conscious of him. Ghatak's great modulation upon "The Wild Geese" and its cry—as well as the cry "I won't let you go"—occurs toward the end of *Meghe Dhaka Tara* (The Cloud-Covered Star), his most fraught and painful film. Nita, once the breadwinner of a family of East Bengali refugees displaced by migration, is now terminally ill with tuberculosis. She has been transferred by her brother, Shankar, from their house in Calcutta to a sanatorium in the hill-station, Shillong. Anil, now a successful singer, comes to visit her; the two figures are surrounded by an astonishing panorama. As she listens to him talk about their younger sister's mischievous child, Nita bursts out without warning, "Dada, I *did* want to live!" Crushed, attempting to placate and silence her, Anil responds with "Idiot!" (Indeed, there is something comic, even imbecilic, about the life-urge and its insistent simplicity; which is why we, on occasion, shake our heads in consternation at Tagore and Whitman and Lawrence and Ghatak—all very different kinds of artists, admittedly.) In a series of rapid frames, we witness the landscape congregating from various angles and echoing her words, "I so love life, dada! I *will* live!" This is the primordial Tagorean "message" ("I felt the message of those beating wings") of a near-heretical faith; ironicized by Ghatak, seen unflinchingly for its heresy, but not made meaningless. This faith contains an acknowledgment of death and "elsewhere," but also an answer and a refutation.

Death and life share the quality of being contingent, accidental: we don't know when and how they will happen, or even, really, why they do. (This would have been pretty clear to Tagore, who lost his muse and sister-in-law Kadambari Devi when he was twenty-two—she had died by her own hand—and then, over the years, his wife and two of his children.) Tagore's work is less about universals, absolutes, and unities (though it *is* also about these) than about the role of chance governing the shape of the universe and of the work itself, taking the form of a sustained meditation: "In order to find you anew, I lose you every moment / O beloved treasure." Contingency preoccupied him all his life. In 1930, when he had a couple of meetings with Albert Einstein, he opened the dialogue enthusiastically with, "I was discussing with Dr. Mendel today the new mathematical discoveries which tell us that in the realm of infinitesimal atoms chance has its play; the drama of existence is not absolutely predestined in character." Einstein replies with a dampener: "The facts that make science tend toward this view do not say goodbye to causality."

This famous, over-publicized conversation can be read in a number of ways. Einstein clearly sees Tagore as a "poet" in the "high" cultural western sense, but still more as an eastern sage, and is dry and cautious as a result. He—not Tagore—keeps bringing up the word *religion* in a mildly defensive, mildly accusatory manner. Einstein, responsible for a shatteringly disorienting theory that would forever change philosophy and the humanities, not to speak of the sciences, forecloses, in response to Tagore, that strand of insight, and becomes a conventional scientist-empiricist: for "that," he says, "is my religion." Tagore, in the course of the two slightly anxious, circular conversations, appears in various fluid incarnations: as a romantic poet, talking about beauty and truth; as a transcendentalist; a believer in the absolute; a propagandist for universal man. We have dealt with him in these guises in the last one hundred years of discussions about Tagore; no doubt we will again, one hundred and fifty years after his birth. But Tagore's secret concern with life, play, and contingency keeps resurfacing in his part of the dialogue; he might well have believed that this powerful undercurrent would provide common ground with the German. Einstein, though, pushes the interaction toward a more conservative dichotomy: that of the romantic, the man of religion, or the metaphysician with his purely subjective response to the universe, on the one hand, and the scientist with his empirical and objective vantage point, on the other.

For me, there are two great lineages in poetry from the upheavals of the nineteenth century onward: the metaphysical, or the poetry of the beautiful (sometimes anguished) fragment made radiant by the light of the vanished old world and of bygone value; and the polemical, sounding the note of constant, occasionally arbitrary, arrival and return, disrupting not just linearity, as the former does, but causality. I think Tagore belongs deeply, if only partially, to the first category, and I have written before of his songs in this light. But, increasingly, I believe his great power derives from being essentially in the second camp, from denying, like Whitman and Lawrence, that there is any need to apologize for life and its accidental provenance. One characteristic of the writers in the first camp is how they practice their art and their criticism in distinct domains, and, in a sense, detach themselves from the "meaning" of their artistic work, like Joyce's fingernail-paring author-god, or James's evolving "figure in the carpet," upon which the narrator will deliberately not elaborate. The polemicists, on the other hand, not only immerse themselves in the thrust of their work with every fiber of their being—"a man in his wholeness wholly attending," as Lawrence said of poetry—but in every sphere of activity they undertake, as Tagore did. This is why they seem open to deciphering and are more vulnerable to misunderstanding.

I had begun by mentioning my adolescent impatience with Tagore and my enthusiasm for Dan Pagis's poem about the Holocaust. I still admire that poem—in fact, more than I did when I was seventeen—for its craft, tragic exactness, and its shrinking shape informed by Adorno's stark dictum that poetry is no longer tenable after Auschwitz. Adorno's admonition, however, has a history older than the horrors of the twentieth century: it comes from a metaphysical belief that, on many levels, life (and, as a result, its chief expression, language) is too fragile to wholly justify itself. Tagore is still the great poet in our age of life's inherent and inexhaustible justification—this is what he is actually conveying to Einstein—but his argument is plainest in the songs and poems. Accustomed as we are to the luminosity of elsewhere, to the backward glance, to action and outcome with a cause, and less accustomed to the joy of unforeseen arrival (which, after all, rapidly wanes into alienation), encountering Tagore has to be an unsettling experience—but one through which we also come to recognize our deepest unspoken urges and beliefs incarnated in the most surprising and incomparable language.

AMIT CHAUDHURI

THE ESSENTIAL
TAGORE

ফাগুলাল

সে সকলের আগে এগিয়ে গেছে।

বিশু

কোথায় গেছে? নন্দিনী!

ফাগুলাল

সে চলে গেছে মুক্তির পথে।

বিশু

তবে আর দেরি কেন ফাগুলাল!

ফাগুলাল

বিশুভাই, চল।

বিশু

ধুলোয় পড়ে?

ফাগুলাল

এই রক্তকরবীর কাঁকন তার ডান হাত থেকে খসে পড়েছে।

বিশু

এই তার শেষের দান। তার রাখীবন্ধন। চল তবে।

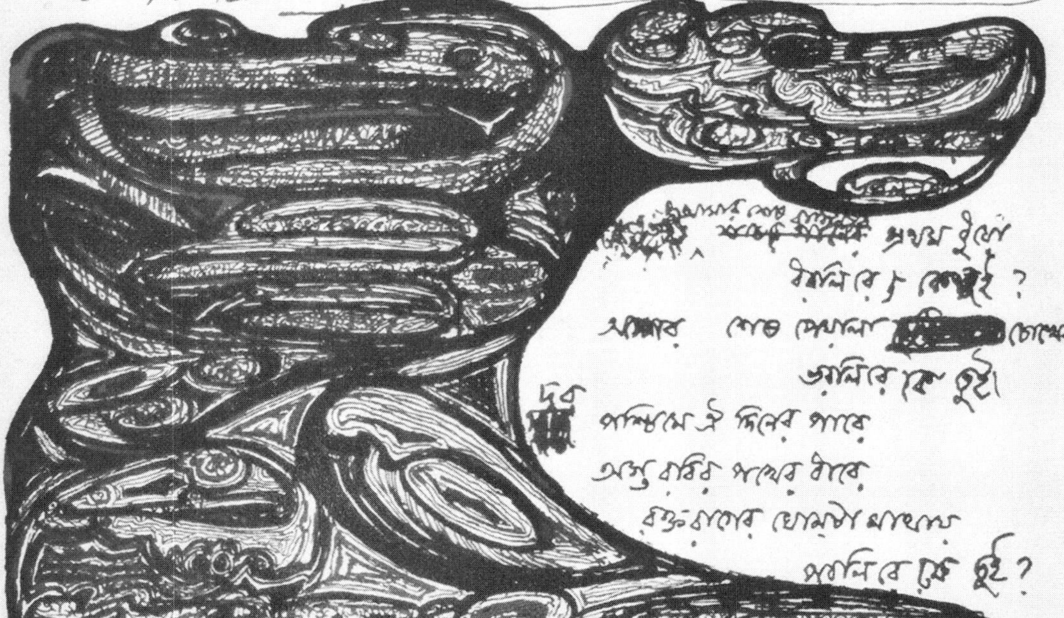

প্রথম তুমি
ভুলালি রে কে তুই?
আমার শেষ পেয়ালা চোখের জ
ভরালি রে কে তুই।
পশ্চিমে ঐ দিনের পারে
অস্তরবির পথের ধারে
রক্তরাগের ঘোমটা মাথায়
ডাকলি রে কে তুই?

Introduction

WHEN RABINDRANATH TAGORE passed away in 1941 he left behind thousands of pages of poetry, prose, plays, essays, letters, humorous pieces, autobiographical writings, and travel literature. An astonishing number of these works remain of interest to twenty-first century readers and highlight his importance in the contemporary world. This volume explores the essential Tagore, offering a selection of his works from the many genres with which he experimented and collecting them in one volume. In letter #92 in *Chhinnapatra (Torn Leaves)*, Tagore confesses that though poetry has been for him "a kind of secret and forbidden delight," he has also found pleasure in writing short fiction, writing "in the form of a diary or some such genre," as well as producing polemical pieces. He affirms that it is "very important to cross swords with our people on social issues," although this offers him a pleasurable dilemma: "I don't want to disappoint any of my Muses." He realizes that "in literature, my sense of duty isn't concerned with what brings the most benefit to the world, but with what I can do best." He describes his growing awareness that he not only is good at poetry but also has a talent for theater, and for composing songs and essays on controversial issues such as child marriage or differences in education. Even painting attracts him, he says, though he admits that it seems beyond his capacity when he is writing the *Chhinnapatra* letters. In short, although he apparently devoted himself to poetry, what was essential for his creative spirit was the urge to branch out in all directions.

The Essential Tagore offers a comprehensive view of Tagore's infinite variety and incomparable genius in a single volume, for it is only when we get a broad view of Tagore's creative practice that we can begin to appreciate the extent of his achievement and understand why he remains relevant and open to reinterpretation, even as we reach his sesquicentenary year.

His Life and Works

Rabindranath Tagore was born in the Jorasanko house of the Tagores on 7 May 1861. The family had first settled down in this Kolkata house in the 1780s because of Rabindranath's great grandfather Nilmoni Tagore, who had profited like his elders from his close association with the East India Company. But the Tagore family became really prominent in the city because of Rabindranath's grandfather Dwarkanath Tagore. He was reputed to be fabulously wealthy and well connected with the East India Company. He was a leading light of the city's cultural and religious life, famous for his extravagance and his progressive ideas. A close friend of the celebrated reformer Raja Rammohon Roy, he was also associated with the reformist Brahmo Samaj and with educational initiatives such as the Hindu College. These men and some of their contemporaries initiated a movement that came to be known as the Bengal Renaissance, during which western enlightenment values and cultural texts galvanized a people seemingly bent on leading moribund lives.

Tagore's father Debendranath became the head of the family after the death of Dwarkanath. Unlike Dwarkanath, Debendranath was spiritually inclined and devoted to the austere and monotheistic Hinduism embodied in the *Upanishads*. He saw to it that the children grew up in an atmosphere that combined Bengali traditions with western culture. He also ensured that his father's excesses would not be repeated in the Jorasanko house, prescribing reformist ideas and a regime of prayers instead. Given to meditation, discipline, and frugality, he revived the family fortunes and set up a retreat in land he owned close to the little town of Bolpur, calling it Santiniketan or the place of peace. Hailed as the "Maharshi" or great sage, he also wrote a book of sermons.

Rabindranath was the youngest of Debendranath's fourteen children. Heirs to the grandfather's reformist zeal and their father's work ethic and devotional practices, several of these children grew up and distinguished themselves through their professional and cultural attainments. Dwijendranath, the eldest of Tagore's brothers, was a poet, philosopher, and nationalist. Debendranath's second son Satyendranath, on the other hand, became somewhat Anglicized after his visit to England, where he had successfully completed his education to become the first Indian recruited to the Indian Civil Service. He was proficient in English, Sanskrit, and Bengali and wrote in all three languages. A sister, Swarnakumari, earned fame as the first Bengali female novelist. Her success indicates the impact of modernization on some upper-class Bengali Hindu women. But the brother who had the greatest influence on Rabindranath was Jyotirindranath Tagore. He painted, played different musical instruments, edited a newspaper, and produced farces and plays that he had written and translated. He ensured his siblings' participation in the productions staged in the Jorasanko house. From 1874, Tagore also took lessons in art. His early drawings, from 1874 to 1883, are preserved in the manuscript "Malati Puthi" in the Tagore Museum (Rabindra Sadan) at Santiniketan. Even after he discontinued his lessons in art, Tagore continued to experiment with sketches and doodles. In these early attempts, we can trace the origins of his later paintings, and his urge to express in the visual medium what he could not say in words.

Tagore did not get much of a formal education; he hated the mechanical teaching he had encountered in all three schools he was sent to and became a lifelong critic of joyless learning by rote. Ultimately, he was taught by his father (when he could spare the time), his older siblings, and private tutors, but took early to learning on his own. Indeed, he was often left on his own, for though his father loved the children and took the twelve-year-old Tagore along with him on a particularly memorable trip to the Himalayas and elsewhere, he was away frequently on business or in religious retreat. Tagore's mother, Sharada Devi, was also busy managing her many children and a large, bustling household. She died when Rabindranath was fourteen years old. Tagore was left with his siblings and servants to give him company when he sought it. But when Jyotirindranath married Kadambari Devi in 1868, Tagore found a companion who was not only close to him in years but also in temperament. The two gradually became very intimate.

Growing up in a large family where so many of his siblings were involved in literary work, art, and theater, Tagore turned to writing early in life. He found stimuli for his writing in the activity in the Jorasanko house and its environs, and in his reading. He was soon recognized as a phenomenal talent by his siblings, elders, and family friends, who included him in their literary activities. He was only thirteen when he composed a verse translation of *Macbeth* and had a poem published anonymously in a local paper. In 1875, the fourteen-year-old Tagore read a patriotic poem publicly at the well-attended cultural-religious festival known as Hindu Mela and then had it published in the reputable newspaper *Amrita Bazar Patrika;* in the same year he composed his first song for Jyotirindranath's play *Sarojini* and contributed a long narrative poem called *Banaphul (The Wild Flower)* to a periodical. He was soon contributing literary criticism to magazines. In 1877 he made his stage debut, playing the lead role in Jyotirindranath's Bengali version of Molière's *Le Bourgeois Gentilhomme* in a production staged at Jorasanko. The next year he became a regular contributor to *Bharati,* a monthly journal edited by his eldest brother Dwijendranath with the help of Jyotirindranath. It contained poems, literary criticism, Tagore's first long story, "Bhikharini," and a novel titled *Karuna* that he did not manage to finish. But the most audacious of the precocious Tagore's literary endeavors in his sixteenth year was a cycle of poems that he eventually published under a pseudonym in 1884 as *Bhanusingha Thakurer Padavali.* Written in an archaic style, this was his attempt to do what Thomas Chatterton had done with his pseudo-medieval poems, but unlike the English poet's works, which brought him infamy, Tagore gradually welded his cleverly crafted lyrics to music, and as songs they became classics of *Rabindrasangeet.*

Tagore was blossoming as a writer in Bengali, but Debendranath had not given up on his desire to give his talented son a "proper" education. In 1878, therefore, he sent Tagore to stay for a while in Ahmedabad with his second brother Satyendranath, who was at that time the district judge of the city. The idea was to prepare Tagore for England, where he could get the schooling required to follow Satyendranath's footsteps and eventually join the Indian Civil Service. En route, Tagore stayed for a while in Mumbai with the Anglicized family of a Marathi physician, Atmaram Dadoji Panduram. He became a close friend of their daughter Ana, later dedicating some poems to her. He then went to school in Bristol, England, where he lived with Satyendranath's wife and children, one of whom, Indira Rani Chaudhurani, became a confidante to whom he would write some of his most famous letters. Tagore was then sent to study English literature at University College London, but once again he proved temperamentally unable to stick to a formal course of studies. The trip to England, however, exposed him to contemporary British culture and led to some sparkling letters which he first published in *Bharati* and then in a book, *Europe Prabasir Patra* (1881).

Returning to India in 1880, Tagore plunged into creative work. As he said in *Boyhood Days:* "The fountain of my music now began to play" (62). The next year he composed a set of devotional songs for the Brahmo Samaj; wrote his first musical play, *Valmiki Pratibha,* and played the lead role of Valmiki, the author of the first Indian epic, *Ramayana;* published the verse play *Rudrachanda* and the long poem *Bhagnahriday;* gave his first public lecture titled "Music and Feeling" in Calcutta Medical College; and published a number of prose essays and reviews, as well as *Europe Prabasir Patra.* His writings from 1881 onward bore the imprint of his exposure to England, for he would often mingle western musical elements with Bengali forms and reveal the influence of the English Romantic and Victorian poets in his lyrics, plays, and verse narratives, even when the subjects were derived from Indian myth, legend, and history.

In 1882 Tagore helped Jyotirindranath set up Saraswat Samaj, a kind of academy of Bengali letters, which would become the Bangiya Sahitya Parishad ten years later. Such organizational activity showed a side of Tagore which became even more prominent as the years went by, for he would take the lead in transforming the course of Bengali letters in the future. There was a kind of literary nationalism at work with the Tagore brothers; they were dedicated to creating a new Bengal through their cultural activities. But this year was most memorable for a quasi-mystical experience that Tagore underwent when he was staying with Jyotirindranath and Kadambari Devi at their Kolkata house. The experience,

5

recorded in the poem "The Fountain's Awakening," is significant because it seemed to be a clear call to Rabindranath to "flood the world" with his poems and songs, articulating his sense of wonder through his writing.

Tagore was married off to the ten-year-old Mrinalini Devi in 1883 by Debendranath. The marriage proved to be a happy one. The couple had three daughters and two sons. Mrinalini supported her husband steadfastly in her literary and cultural endeavors until her death in 1902. For his part, Tagore involved her in his affairs, even putting her on stage in one of his productions.

The year 1884 proved to be very unhappy for Tagore; his beloved sister-in-law Kadambari Devi committed suicide in April. Apparently, she and Jyotirindranath had drifted apart because of his many preoccupations, and the newly married Rabindranath also had little time for her. The death of Kadambari was one of the most tragic events in Tagore's life. His triangular relationship with Jyotirindranath and Kadambari had been intense and complex, and he brooded on her death seemingly for the rest of his life. He would compose songs and poems about her, and the relationship became the source for his famous story "The Broken Nest." Even toward the end of his life, he was haunted by her memory and expressed his grief in his paintings and poetry.

Despite the shock of Kadambari's death, however, Tagore continued to compose songs, poems, plays, and prose works at a prodigious rate, and to take on new responsibilities. In 1884 he became secretary of the Adi Brahmo Samaj, which claimed to be the original branch of the reformist sect. He always took his religious duties seriously; the idea of divinity in man and nature permeated his life and writings. He composed music for events of the Samaj and sang at their meetings. He wrote and delivered sermons regularly then and in Santiniketan later.

Tagore was also becoming part of the nationalist tide that was now flooding India. He composed patriotic poems and engaged in controversies in print over religious and social issues to assert his vision for the future of the country. A short trip to England in 1890 seemed to have made him only more critical of colonial rule.

In 1890, Debendranath gave Tagore the responsibility of running the family estates in East Bengal. Tagore made Shilaidaha (now part of

Kushtia, Bangladesh) his base. He had to travel extensively to visit his family's far-flung holdings in this deltaic land. It will be no exaggeration to say that the experience changed him decisively. For the first time, perhaps, Tagore, essentially city-bred till then, gained full exposure to the countryside and came into close contact with rural people. For the first time, too, he undertook managerial duties on a scale that immersed him in work with ordinary men and women and also involved him directly in economic and public affairs. As a consequence, new elements entered his writings. His verse now was steeped in his awareness of the natural world, while his short fiction and prose took a turn away from romance, history, and legend to focus on the quotidian. He also picked up folk tunes and became familiar with the *bauls,* wandering minstrels with a philosophy based on mysticism, religious tolerance, and esoteric rites. Tagore was now poised to become a great writer.

In 1891 Tagore made his debut as a writer of short stories. In the same year, he and his nephew Sudhindranath Tagore started editing the monthly *Sadhana.* With characteristic energy and inventiveness, Tagore inundated the magazine with fiction, criticism, essays, and other literary compositions. He would eventually become its sole editor and make it the vehicle of some of his best work of the period. His widening circle of interests became evident as he now began to write about education, the importance of using Bengali, the tyranny of colonial rule, Hindu-Muslim relations, folk culture, and rural development. *Sadhana* ceased publication in 1895, but Tagore would find outlets for his creative energy and burgeoning interests in a succession of short-lived periodicals such as *Bharati* and *Bangadarshan,* which he began editing in 1898 and 1901, respectively.

By the end of the nineteenth century it was clear that Indians would not be content with anything less than self-rule. Tagore became increasingly nationalistic and anti-British in his work, and promoted the virtues of self-reliance. This was the period when Tagore wrote a series of patriotic songs that were then taken up by others. When Bengal was partitioned in 1905 and the Swadeshi movement was launched, these songs were sung all over the country. Tagore's contributions to the movement also included essays and lectures criticizing colonial education, and poems like the ones collected in *Katha* (*Lays and Ballads,* 1900) celebrating Indian heroes of the past. He set up a weaving school in Kushtia and an agricultural school in Patisar, both parts of his estate, with the aim of encouraging self-reliance and improving agriculture. He also tried to implement his ideas about the kind of education that would inculcate Indian values and privilege the vernacular by establishing a school on his father's Santiniketan estate. For this school he drew inspiration from the *tapovanas* or the ancient schools of India that were located in forests or meditation groves.

The new century, however, introduced a series of personal tragedies for Tagore. Mrinalini Devi died in 1902, followed by one of his daughters in 1903 and his father in 1905. But the culminating tragedy for him was the death of his dear son Samirindranath in 1907. Tagore coped with these tragedies in two contrasting ways. On the one hand, he took recourse to prayer and meditation, expressing his emotions in some intensely personal and spiritual writings; on the other hand, he focused on building his school, teaching, managing his estate, and participating in the ongoing anti-Partition movement in Bengal. However, he eventually became alienated from the movement because of the violent turn it took; this would be symptomatic of his attitude to the nationalist movement in subsequent decades. Although always critical of British rule, he distanced himself from the excesses of nationalism in India and elsewhere. Tagore opposed colonial oppression, yet he remained receptive to the influence of western culture and regarded the interaction between civilizations as a positive force.

Tagore's literary work almost always continued unabated despite his personal problems and heavy involvement in public affairs. The first collected edition of his poetry, *Kavyagranthavali,* came out in 1896, and his first collection of short stories, *Galpaguchchha,* in 1900. The poetry he had written thus far was collected in the nine volumes of *Kavya-Grantha,* published in 1903 and 1904; his works in prose, including his comedies and skits, were published in sixteen volumes between 1907 and 1909 as *Gadya Granthavali.*

His writings were noted in Bengal not for their bulk but for their variety, subject matter, topical interest, and innovative nature. For exam-

8

ple, *Sonar Tari* (*The Golden Boat,* 1892) signaled a distinctive turn toward the symbolic in Bengali poetry. "The Lord of Life," from his 1896 collection *Chitra,* created controversy over his very personal concept of religion. His serialization of his novel *Chokher Bali* (1903) marked a decisive moment in the history of the Bengali novel because of the way it delved into the minds of men and women. *Gora* (1907), a novel of ideas, saw him boldly engaged in negotiating the strong ideological currents of the time. The skits collected in *Vyangakautuk* (1906) mocked Brahmin and upper-class pretensions and delighted audiences. Prose pieces he wrote at this time such as "The Problem and the Cure" were seized on by nationalists who were also singing his patriotic songs. If Bengali readers had initially been merely curious about this prodigy or bemused by his rather dilettantish image, by the first decade of the century they were beginning to regard him as a major talent. He was by then quite visible at cultural events and on political occasions. He was requested to preside over the Bengal Literary Conference held in 1907 and the Bengal Provincial Conference in 1907. A public reception given to him in Kolkata in January 1912 in a belated commemoration of his fiftieth birthday confirmed his emergence as one of the leading writers in Bengal.

However, the world outside Bengal knew little or nothing about Tagore's works. A couple of his short stories and poems had been translated into English and published in *The Modern Review,* but this was a Kolkata journal and limited in its impact. Some Bengali admirers living in England translated some of his poems and stories and reported that they were well received there, but their impact was also limited. These admirers felt that Tagore's presence in England would make a difference, and so invited him there. He also attracted the attention of the London-based painter Sir William Rothenstein, who had visited the Jorasanko house of the Tagores.

Tagore therefore decided that the time had come to launch himself in England. He sailed for England for the third time in May 1912—his second trip there in April 1891 was aborted in Madras because of the illness of a fellow traveler. This time he carried a notebook containing translations of mostly spiritual prose poems. He had begun translating them while convalescing in Shilaidaha and took advantage of the sea voyage to polish them further. Arriving in London in June 1912, he handed the notebook containing over a hundred prose poems to Rothenstein. Excited by the poems, the painter sent copies of the notebook to W. B. Yeats, Stopford Brooke, and others. He also arranged a reading of Tagore's poems on 30 June where, among others, Yeats, Brooke, Ezra Pound, and Ernst Rhys heard him read some poems and sing a few of them. Other readings and receptions followed; soon, at least a section of literary London was abuzz with his work. Tagore's plays *The King of the Dark Chamber* and *The Post Office* were performed some weeks later. Thus by the time he left London for the United States in October to visit his son Rathindranath, who was studying agriculture at the University of Illinois, Tagore left behind a host of distinguished English and expatriate admirers.

Indefatigable in his efforts to promote Tagore, Rothenstein persuaded the India Society to publish 750 copies of the 103 prose poems after Yeats had done some light editing. Tagore called the collection *Gitanjali (Song Offerings)*. When this edition was sold out, Rothenstein persuaded Macmillan to publish the collection, along with an enthusiastic introduction contributed by Yeats. The reviews were mostly very appreciative. An anonymous reviewer of the *Times Literary Supplement* welcomed the poems for their "harmony of emotion and idea," so wanting in European writing. The reviewer added, "As we read the pieces we seem to be reading the psalms of a David in our time" (cited in Kripalani, p. 233).

When Tagore arrived in the United States, his fame had preceded him in at least a few poetic circles, not a little due to Pound's exuberant response. He had seen to it that six of Tagore's poems were published by Harriet Monroe in the influential periodical *Poetry*. Monroe also invited Tagore to Chicago. The saintly looking poet with his almost transcendental verse was invited to lecture on his spiritual beliefs at Illinois, at Chicago, and at Harvard. His lectures were subsequently published in *Sadhana* (1913); they enhanced his reputation as the kind of meditative and soothing poet war-strained westerners needed to read. Three other translations of his verse were published the same year. Though the translations did not match the quality of the English writings of the previous year, they did not dent his reputation. On the contrary, the number of Tagore admirers kept increasing dramatically in the parts of England and the United States that he had visited.

Still, in November 1913 the news that Tagore had won the Nobel Prize surprised almost everyone. He was the first Asian to win the prize, and his fame was based on a slim volume of verse. He had been nominated for the prize by Thomas Sturges Moore, but he was considered a long shot at most—Thomas Hardy and Emile Faguet had appeared to be the favorites. Tagore was awarded the prize mostly due to the efforts of the Swedish poet Verner von Heidenstam, who had declared on reading the English *Gitanjali:* "I was deeply moved when I read them and I do not remember having read any lyric writing to equal them during the past twenty years or more" (cited in Kripalani, 242). Per Hallstrom, another member of the Selection Committee, whose response was also decisive, noted, "What Nobel in his innocence believed that we could do each year—present a new genius to the world—is something we are now free to do, for once" (cited in Dutta and Robinson, *Myriad-Minded Man,* 186).

The Nobel Prize made Tagore a celebrity in India and internationally. Indians were delighted that they had a poet whom the world had acclaimed; Bengalis henceforth called him *viswa kabi* or "the world poet." The British administration also felt they had to honor him; he was knighted in 1915. Tagore was gratified by the award, but rather alarmed at the adulation that followed; never again would he enjoy the privacy to which he was accustomed. Everyone seemed to have great expectations of him—Indians, the British literati, and the western reading public. Even countries where English was not spoken sought him out and wanted readings or translations of his works. Moved by his poems, writers as famous as André Gide in France and Zenobia Jiminez in Spain translated his works. He was now world famous.

Tagore took his new role seriously. At home he remained involved in the struggle against British rule and the movement for self-reliance, while abroad he was in great demand as the sage of the east. He felt strongly that humanity had to come together nationally and globally, overcoming barriers erected by those who were short-sighted, jingoistic, and chauvinistic. The violence of the First World War and the nationalist movement in India distressed him. He felt drawn toward Gandhi's message of nonviolence and self-reliance, becoming progressively more outspoken in denouncing the repressive measures adopted by the British in India. Tagore and Gandhi met for the first time in Santiniketan on 6 March 1915. They took a liking to each other that would grow over the years despite the many and sometimes marked differences in their outlooks about the route India should take to independence.

Tagore embarked on his fourth tour of the world in May 1916. His first major stop was Japan, where he delivered lectures on the dangers of nationalism. He felt that Japan had adopted an overtly aggressive posture and was perversely bent on imitating the imperial outlook of the West as well as its worship of the machine. He continued lecturing in the same vein during the extended tour of the United States that followed. These lectures would be published in 1917 in a book called *Nationalism*. Criticized roundly at that time in Japan and the United States for its trenchant critique of nationalism and the excesses of capitalism, it has subsequently proved to be one of his most appreciated books in English. In 1919, Tagore rejected his knighthood in protest against the Amritsar massacre in which over 400 Indian protesters were brutally mowed down by British troops.

Despite his many overseas tours and public commitments at home, Tagore continued to produce quality work in Bengali, demonstrating that his desire to innovate and his dread of repeating himself had not deserted him. In 1916 he published two complex novels, *Ghare Baire (The Home and the World)* and *Chaturanga (Quartet)*. The former is about human relationships torn apart by ideological conflicts and the latter tracks the insidiousness of desire. In *Balaka (The Flight of Geese),* a collection of poems, Tagore rejects inertia and expresses his craving for change. In 1917 he initiated a literary revolution of sorts by writing the first short story in *chaltibhasha* or colloquial Bengali.

Tagore's most important initiative in the years after the Nobel Prize was the establishment of Visva-Bharati, an institution that he would build over the years to bring East and West together and promote knowledge that was intercultural and humanistic. In the first two months of

1919 he undertook a lecture tour in South India where he tried to raise money for this venture. Later that year he founded departments of Indology and Fine Arts in Santiniketan and started to teach in them. In 1920 he set out on his fifth foreign tour to raise funds for his projected university. In this extended trip lasting over a year, he traveled across the European continent and the United States, lecturing to raise funds and resources. The climax of the tour perhaps was his Nobel Lecture, presented to members of the Swedish Academy at Stockholm eight years after he won the prize. Visva-Bharati officially opened as a university on 23 December 1921. Tagore had already allocated his property and the interest from the Nobel Prize to the Santiniketan school; henceforth the prize money itself, the copyright fees of his Bengali works, and a lot of his energy would be devoted to sustaining the institution and expanding its sphere of activities.

Tagore's long tour of the West was not a monetary success. He did, however, manage to attract the attention of many leading intellectuals—especially in continental Europe, where he would tour again in 1926—but noticed a marked decline of popular interest in his literary works in the West. He even detected a certain amount of resentment in England and America. As early as 1913, with the appearance of *Sadhana: The Realization of Life,* Tagore's philosophical stance drew criticism from the Anglo-American press. *The Nation* in New York accused him of "flabby mysticism," and the *Spectator* in Britain detected "a fatal flaw of insincerity" in Tagore's "most seemingly elevated utterances." *Nationalism* (1917) received a mixed response in America and England, with some reviewers focusing on Tagore's abstract mysticism, some dwelling on his exotic image, and others calling him a neo-Hindu who did not really understand politics. To many western readers, Tagore's poetry appeared exotic but incomprehensible, like "a Persian carpet or a Japanese print" (Aronson, 14).

Several explanations can be offered for this situation: many in the English-speaking world had not taken kindly to his rejection of the knighthood and his denunciation of the nexus between capitalism, jingoism, imperialism, and nationalism; he had rushed into print too many translations of his work without vetting them to ensure the kind of standards he had set for *Gitanjali;* and fashions in literature had changed drastically among war-weary Europeans now resigned to life in a wasteland, in the era later labeled "high" modernism. Tagore's books did not go completely out of print in the West, and he continued to attract some new readers there, but the popularity he had enjoyed for a while after the Nobel Prize all but dissipated. He now found pockets of admirers in the English-speaking world and his books gradually became part of the niche book market. In mainland Europe, interest in Tagore and demand for translations of his work persisted for a while, and his impact continued to be felt in the Far East and Latin America for a long time.

Tagore's sixth foreign tour took him to China and Japan in 1924. Large crowds greeted Tagore in Beijing and other Chinese cities, confirming his belief that he was reviving the ancient contact between India and China that Buddhist missionaries had initiated in ancient times. His public lectures did not go unopposed, though. A leaflet in Chinese, circulated at his second lecture in Beijing, declared: "Dr. Tagore would have nationality and politics abolished, replacing them with the consolation of one's soul. These are a refuge and a source of aesthetic joy for the sluggards, but not for us. We cannot but oppose Dr. Tagore, who upholds these things which would shorten the life of our nation" (cited in Dutta and Robinson, 1995, 251).

Tagore was friendly with the Japanese art historian and curator Okakura Tenshin, whom he had met in Kolkata in 1902. Okakura, a champion of Japan's cultural heritage, drew Tagore's attention to civilizational links between India and the rest of Asia. During his visits to Japan in 1916, 1924, and 1929, Tagore was struck by the beauty of their traditional culture, but repelled by the evidence of industrialization and the growing commercialism that he saw there. His critique of Japan's nationalism met with growing hostility in Japan, and in 1938, he would exchange public letters with Japanese poet Yone Noguchi in which the two of them would express their mutual disagreement on the issue of Japan's military interventions in Korea and China.

Tagore's growing international reputation led to invitations to visit other countries as well. In 1922 he visited Sri Lanka. In 1924 he set out for Peru, but because he felt sick en route, he ended up spending a few months in Argentina instead. On his way back from Argentina, he returned via Italy to India. In 1927 he toured Southeast Asia. Leonard Elmhirst, the English agricultural economist and Tagore's close associate in his rural reconstruction projects, noted that the impact Tagore had on Chinese intellectuals was considerable: "It was not until he had met with the scholars at Peking that the Chinese progressives suddenly realized how much common ground they shared with Tagore. Like Dante and Chaucer in their own day and age, Tagore and Hu Shih were both determined to use the vernacular of their peoples as the ordinary medium for literary expression rather than some classical dialect that had been the monopoly of a limited group of literati" ("Personal Memories of Tagore" in *Rabindranath Tagore: A Centenary Volume,* 21). Tagore's lectures in China and Japan focused on Asian unity and the need to go beyond western materialism and concepts of development.

In 1926, Tagore again visited Italy, where he was well received by Mussolini and feted by the public. Later, however, he realized the dangers of fascism, and came out against it in letters written to C. F. Andrews and Carlo Formichi, an Italian scholar who had been sent to Santiniketan earlier by the Italian government. In Argentina the ailing Tagore met the Argentinean publisher and promoter of art Victoria Ocampo and accepted her offer to stay in her house until his health was restored. With her Tagore developed one of his most intimate relationships. It was at her home that he wrote some very fine poems and began transforming his doodles into works of art. Later, when he took to painting seriously, she would prove to be not only a muse but also an impresario, helping organize his international debut as a painter in Paris in 1931.

Throughout the 1920s, during his foreign trips and in the years he spent at home, Tagore continued to take his creative work in newer directions, drawing upon his experiences of other cultures. For instance, the tours of the decade resulted in travelogues about his trips to Japan (*Japan-Jatri,* 1919). His reflections on his visits to the West and Java were published in one volume as *Jatri* (1929). Perhaps because of his exposure to modernism, he experimented with prose poems—as in the collection titled *Lipika* (1922)—and wrote quite a few poems in free verse. Increasingly, he tended to tone down the music in his lyrical poems as if to bring himself closer to modern poetry. The volume of poetry titled *Purabi* shows the impact of his encounter with Ocampo. In his plays, too, he strove for a fusion of eastern and western traditions in works such as *Roktokorobi* (1926). His trip to Indonesia so impressed him that he incorporated elements of Balinese dance-drama in the plays he composed and choreographed toward the end of the 1920s. He would even send someone to the island so that the intricacy of Balinese batik work could be replicated in Santiniketan's arts and crafts institutions. Tagore was always receptive to change. He drew inspiration from his travels abroad as well as within India. He experimented with indigenous traditions such as the classical music of north or south India, or the Manipuri dance traditions of northeast India. Always, he would take only what he needed and follow his own path, refusing to be overwhelmed by any one literary style or movement. *Shesher Kabita* (*Farewell Song,* 1929), his last major work of the decade, for instance, is a novel that shows his complex take on modernity, acknowledging modernism wryly, yet ambivalent in his response to it.

In the 1930s Tagore's productivity did not lessen, though his health declined steadily. He reduced the number of his overseas tours but continued to be creative, writing even from a sickbed or in convalescence. In addition to his writings in prose and verse and his social, cultural, and educational commitments and political interventions, he somehow found the time to paint hundreds of pictures. He also composed and choreographed several dance dramas and musical plays.

The decade opened with another extended tour of Europe and North America, the highlights of which were his first painting exhibition in Paris on 2 May 1930, his delivery of the Hibbert Lectures at Oxford and Manchester, published as *The Religion of Man* (1931), his visit to Russia in September, which he recorded enthusiastically in *Russiar Chithi* (*Letters from Russia,* 1931), and the reception he was awarded by President Hoover in Washington, D.C., in December. In 1932 he traveled to Iran. He wrote about his experience of the land of Hafiz—his father's favorite poet—in the travelogue *Japan-Parasye* (*Travels in Japan and Persia,* 1936). His last overseas trip would be to Sri Lanka in 1934. After this tour he became too frail for extended visits to other lands, despite his wanderlust.

In 1931 his seventieth birthday was observed by his admirers at home and abroad through a public reception in Kolkata on 11 May and with the publication of the *Golden Book of Tagore* in December. The numerous essays and felicitations sent for the massive volume from all corners of the world indicated the extent to which Tagore had become a celebrity and a revered figure. His seventy-second birthday was celebrated with almost equal enthusiasm by Iranians, for Tagore was then touring Persia. Tagore himself, however, found his birthdays a time for contemplation, as indicated in the brooding poem "Panchishe Baisakh" ("The Twenty-fifth of Baisakh"), composed for his birthday in 1935.

In fact, Tagore in his seventies had other things to brood about, nationally and internationally. At home, Indians were mobilizing against the British, and the "Quit India" movement had developed a momentum of its own. Time and again, it went out of control; people were becoming restive and Hindu-Muslim relationships had deteriorated. Tagore dreaded this fratricidal situation as well as the violence that had accompanied anti-British agitation for decades, but he now felt that things were going from bad to worse. He wrote with urgency on the topics of Hindu-Muslim relations and feudal practices in contemporary India. As before, he criticized British policies publicly but did not spare nationalist excesses. As on the eve of the First World War, he started to brood about the tense situation in Europe that appeared to be taking the European continent to the brink of another war. Outbreaks of Japanese aggression in the Far East distressed him. When war broke out in the West and the East and the whole world was in a conflagration stoked by hatred and the lust for power, Tagore delivered his final birthday message, tinged with despair at the turn humanity had taken, in May 1941. The English version was titled "Crisis in Civilization." Tagore concludes by declaring that despite signs everywhere of the ruins of "a proud civilization," he would not "commit the grievous sin of losing faith in Man" and "would rather look forward to the opening of a new chapter in history after the cataclysm is over and the atmosphere rendered clean with the spirit of service and sacrifice." He continued to affirm his faith in mankind through his writings and his institutions and reform schemes until the very end. Indeed, though the physical discomforts of age increased at the end of the 1930s, he wrote comic and even nonsense verse for children, such as the ones contained in *Khapchhada* (*Out of Sync,* 1937), *Chharar Chhabi* (*Pictures in Rhyme,* 1937), *Shey* (*He,* 1937), and *Prahasani* (*The Smiling One,* 1939). Even as he lay dying, he composed poetry. His last poem, "On the Way to Creation," dictated immediately before a surgical intervention that could not revive him, expresses his hope for those who opted for the right way and reaffirms his faith in God's plan:

> But you haven't benighted the truly great.
>   His heart is illumined with your star;
>   Its passages are forever clear.
>   His simple faith keeps it ever bright.
>   Let him appear deviant from outside; inside he is
> ever straight.
>   That is what he takes pride in.
>   People say he has been deceived.
> But he has embraced truth
>   Cleansing his innermost being by its light.
>   Nothing can deceive him.
> He brings the ultimate prize
>   To his own treasure-hoard.
> He who withstands deceptions effortlessly
>   Gathers from your own hands
>   The unremitting right to peace.

Tagore's Reputation in the World

Tagore's international reputation depended mainly on translations of his works into English. From 1909 to 1912, as mentioned earlier, *The Modern Review* in Kolkata had been publishing translations of Tagore's works, especially his poems. Many of these were by Roby Dutt and Ajit Chakravarti. Enthused by these translations, William Rothenstein urged Tagore to produce more. Tagore now wished to translate his works himself, articulating his dissatisfaction with the work of other translators. Instead of metrical translations of his poems and songs, he favored prose renderings. When he translated *Gitanjali,* he opted for prose poems with Biblical cadences, "ahistorical and more fluid in form and intent than any English literary model would allow" (Amit Chaudhuri, "Rabindranath Tagore: the English *Gitanjali,*" *The Daily Star,* vol. 4, no. 333, 8 May, 2004). In 1912, the India Society published the English *Gitanjali,* providing Tagore with the impetus to undertake more translations of his own work. In 1913, Macmillan published three volumes of Tagore in English: *Gitanjali, The Gardener,* and *The Crescent Moon. Fruit-Gathering* (1916) and *Lover's Gifts and Crossing* (1918) followed thereafter. Translations of Tagore's plays, short stories, epigrams, lectures, and autobiographical writings were also published. Tagore now came to be known as a bilingual poet. His reputation was established with the success of *Gitanjali,* which Rothenstein did a great deal to promote. Ezra Pound praised the work highly, comparing its simplicity to that of the New Testament, and lauding its "distinctly Oriental" beauty. Pound's remarks reflect Tagore's general image in the West as a mystic and an Oriental, a "latter-day Wise Man from the East" (Lago and Warwick, eds., *Rabindranath Tagore's Perspectives in Time,* 1989, p. 5). The English *Gitanjali* was praised by critics in India as well. Buddhadeva Bose has called the English version of the book "a miracle of translation"—the miracle being "not that so much has survived," but that "the poems are re-born in the process, [and] the flowers bloom anew on a foreign soil" (*An Acre of Green Grass,* 15). Bose even finds "moments when the translation surpasses the original."

By the 1920s, however, Tagore's translations were beginning to lose their charm, and his mystic appeal faded for westerners; the magic of the *Gitanjali* years had dissipated. Tagore's reception in non–English-speaking countries varied. His work was translated by three poets who later won the Nobel Prize—André Gide, Juan Ramón Jiménez, and Boris Pasternak. He visited Germany in 1921, and again in 1926 and 1930. German writers who responded to Tagore included Bertolt Brecht, who at sixteen wrote an enthusiastic review of *The Gardener* and praised *The*

Home and the World in his diary; Rainer Maria Rilke, who showed interest in Gide's translation of *Gitanjali* but refused publisher Kurt Wolff's request that he translate the work into German; Hermann Hesse, who described Tagore as "a quiet, noble dreamer who spends his days, remote from the world, in poetic worship, and whose Indian-ness is tinged with the influence of European literature"; and Stefan Zweig, who in his letters to Romain Rolland praised Tagore's writings, especially the "serenity" and "beauty" of his poems (Kaempchen, 21–64). In 1932, Tagore met French scholar and artist Alain Daniélou, who was so inspired by *Rabindrasangeet*, Tagore's collection of songs, that he spent several decades transcribing them for voice and piano in the western musical tradition.

When Tagore traveled to China in 1924, he received a mixed reception. The crowds there were effusive, because his writings had already been translated into Chinese by admirers like Chen Duxiu and Shen Yanbing. Xu Zhimo, a young poet, had been so inspired by *The Crescent Moon* that he became one of the founders of the Xinyueshe (The Crescent Moon Society) in 1923, and in 1925 launched a monthly journal in collaboration with his poet friend Wen Yiduo called *The Monthly Crescent Moon.* But Tagore's speeches met with opposition from certain political quarters, as mentioned earlier. In 1983, Zhang Guangliang of the Institute of South Asian Studies of the Chinese Academy of Social Sciences at Beijing published a volume entitled *Lun Taige'er (On Tagore),* containing articles on Tagore by various Chinese scholars and political activists written between 1921 and 1924.

Among Russians, too, Tagore found admirers like the painter Nicholas Roerich and the theater director Konstantin Stanislavsky, and translators such as the Nobel laureate Ivan Bunin and Leo Tolstoy's son Ilya Tolstoy. Most of his works available in English were translated into Russian by the late 1920s. *Gitanjali* itself had been translated into Russian (from English) several times. In Persia and Iraq, Tagore found himself well received and accepted as a poet, though the crowds knew little about his work. In Teheran, he was lauded as "the greatest star shining in the eastern sky" (Dutta and Robinson, 1995, 317).

Tagore's international reputation during his lifetime was thus a fluctuating mixture of fame, indifference, criticism, and adulation.

Though his English writings were substantial, his image as a writer and thinker depended primarily on translations. While the English *Gitanjali* remains a unique creative work in its own right, most of these translations fail to do justice to Tagore's original writings in Bengali. The poems often lack lyricism, and the English is archaic, removed from everyday life. Tagore himself was aware of this. As his letters and conversations reveal, he was not very confident about his own command of English and far from complacent about English translations of his work. He also tried to make his works accessible to readers in the West by toning down the Indianness of his works. As a result, these translations often lack the sparkle and the cultural specificity of the originals.

After *Gitanjali,* the subsequent volumes of translations seemed designed to perpetuate the image of Tagore as a seer and a mystic poet. Edward Thompson, the author of *Rabindranath Tagore: Poet and Dramatist,* noted that Tagore had "avoided his boldest, strongest poems or watered [them] down to prettiness" (quoted in Buddhadeva Bose, *Kabi Rabindranath,* 1966, p. 120). Also, the translations adopted the same monotonous style, making it appear that Tagore's poetry lacked variety. According to Ana Jelnikar, Tagore's critique of imperialism displeased his English audience. Besides, the *Gitanjali* style, acceptable to early modernist readers, might have seemed too mannered to readers used to a "high modernist" idiom. While translating his poems, Tagore also condensed many of them, reducing some to mere paraphrases of the original and needlessly truncating others, making them appear disjointed and confused. According to Sisir Kumar Das, "What escaped Tagore's notice in the uninterrupted flow of production of his works in English was not only the growing monotony of style and diction of the translations but also the unimaginative selections and arrangements" (23).

Tagore himself seemed to have realized by 1921 that he had done himself a disservice. "Like a coward, I avoided all complexities in my translations; as a result they have become emaciated," he confessed to Edward Thompson in a letter written that year. With the publication of *The Collected Poems and Plays* in 1936, Tagore's reputation in England and America was tarnished for generations. Not all the translations in that volume were Tagore's own. Many were insipid, and the collection did not reflect his versatility. The publisher, however, spread the impression that all the works were originally in English. The book has remained in print, amplifying the damage to Tagore's reputation across decades. Careless editing by publishers also complicated matters. Macmillan, for instance, published their edition of *Gora* in English with errors that Tagore found "ludicrous" because of their hurry to go into print (letter to Thomas Sturges Moore, 20 May 1924; Dutta and Robinson, 2005, 311). These flawed translations did much to tarnish Tagore's literary image outside India, leading many readers to wonder why he had been found worthy of the Nobel Prize.

Tagore's own conflicted personality also contributed to the fluctuations in his reputation. Arguing that Tagore's literary persona became secondary to his public image in later life, Nirad C. Chaudhuri says: "during the last thirty years of his life there existed two Tagores, one true and the other false. This dichotomy was at the root of the tragedy [of] his later life" (634). Sankha Ghosh describes Tagore's whole life as a balancing act between two images, claiming that Tagore wanted his own countrymen to view him as a remote, alien figure, while to the rest of the world, he projected himself as the quintessential Indian (Ghosh, *Nirman Ar Srishti* [Santiniketan: Visva-Bharati, *c.* 1982], 192).

In his own country, especially in Bengal, Tagore was very often out of step with the trends of his time, arousing adulation among his followers and derision among those skeptical about his talent. He was almost always in the eye of a storm, stirring up as much opposition as he inspired admiration. His withdrawal from active support of the Swadeshi movement, for example, and his differences with Gandhi made him a controversial figure. Ashis Nandy, referring to Tagore's evolving views on nationalism, calls him a "dissenter among dissenters" (xi). By the 1920s, some younger writers in Bengal were contesting Tagore's supremacy, accusing him of blocking the path to modernity with his lack of innovation, though some of them, like Buddhadeva Bose, continued to admire him, admitting later that they were overshadowed by his towering genius. Considering Tagore's waning reputation at home and abroad, Nirad C. Chaudhuri predicted despondently: "Tagore is likely to remain only a hagiographical legend in Bengal and a forgotten historical figure elsewhere: or the lost great man of India for future generations of men" (*Thy Hand, Great Anarch!,* 597).

Yet Tagore's memory persists in the public imagination, and his image refuses to be consigned to oblivion. In 1961, his birth centenary sparked a revival of interest in his works in some parts of the Bengali- and English-speaking world, and marked the publication of several books that attempted to reappraise his genius. In his introduction to the Sahitya Akademi publication *Rabindranath Tagore: A Centenary Volume 1861–1961* (1961), Jawaharlal Nehru comments, "This great and highly sensitive man was not only a poet of India, but also a poet of humanity and of freedom everywhere, and his message is for all of us" (xvi). Humayun Kabir, in the Tagore Birth Centenary number of the *Calcutta Municipal Gazette,* gives Tagore credit for being the first to promote federalism and nonalignment, premised on ideas of difference and multiplicity ("Tagore Was No Obscurantist," 122–125).

Although general public interest in Tagore has declined in recent years, his work continues to inspire artists and intellectuals from different parts of the world. Tagore's intellectual legacy and his relevance for our times is being increasingly recognized. Edward Said, for instance, admires Tagore for being the model postcolonial intellectual, who never allows his critical sense to be clouded by his patriotism (41). In "Literary Witness in a World of Terror: The Inward Testimony" (a lecture delivered in Kolkata in November 2008), Nadine Gordimer draws attention to Tagore's experiments with the modern psychological novel. Martha Nussbaum cites Tagore in her critique of nationalism. Ghulam Murshid's Bengali text *Rabindrabiswe Purbabanga, Purbabange Rabindracharcha* (*East Bengal in Tagore's World and Tagore in East Bengal,* 1993) offers an overview of Tagore's relationship with East Bengal, now Bangladesh. Reminiscing about her childhood days in Santiniketan, Mahasweta Devi points out the contemporary relevance of Tagore's ecological concerns: "We were taught in our school in Santiniketan that every animal, every cat, every bird, had a right to live. From childhood, we were taught to care for nature, not to break a single leaf or flower from a tree" (introduction to *The Land of Cards,* viii). Amartya Sen, in "Tagore and His India," lauds Tagore's championing of freedom of thought. Amit Chaudhuri, in his essay "Two Giant Brothers: Tagore's Revisionist Orient," in *Clearing a Space: Reflections on India, Literature and Culture* (2008), describes Tagore as a writer who dismantles the western opposition of nature and culture: "for Tagore, nature is *the* site of civilization, refinement, and of certain ideals of the secular Enlightenment, such as the ideal of living in harmony with the world: and it's a specifically Indian location for these things" (134). Tagore's life continues to attract biographers, from Krishna Dutta and Andrew Robinson's *Rabindranath Tagore: The Myriad-Minded Man* (1995) and Prashantakumar Pal's nine-volume *Rabijibani (The Life of Tagore)* to Uma Das Gupta's *My Life in My Words* (2006).

Despite Tagore's fluctuating reputation, there has also been a steady stream of translations of his works into English, and over the years, their volume has grown significantly. William Radice's *Rabindranath Tagore: Selected Poems* (1985) is one of the most sustained and successful attempts by a non-Bengali to render the poet's verse into English. Radice's book contains only forty-eight poems, though, and cannot be regarded as representative of Tagore's vast oeuvre. He leaves out Tagore's songs and his last poems (from the volume *Shesh Lekha*) because he finds them untranslatable. Radice's subsequent translations, published for instance in *Selected Stories* (1991), *Particles, Jottings, Sparks: The Collected Brief Poems of Rabindranath Tagore* (2004), and the twin volumes *The Post Office* and *Card Country* (2009), confirm his position as one of Tagore's major translators. While Radice translates as a native speaker of English, Ketaki Kushari Dyson, an Indian scholar, critic, poet, and linguist based in England, draws upon her bilingual resources as a translator. *I Won't Let You Go: Selected Poems* (1992) would be a comprehensive representation of Tagore's verse in English, but it excludes many of Tagore's most famous poems (such as "Nirjharer Swapnabhanga"). In *The Gitanjali of Rabindranath Tagore* (1998), Joe Winter attempts, with mixed success, to restore rhyme and meter to the poems, in order to recapture the music of the original Bengali. *Rabindranath Tagore: Final Poems* (2001) is the product of the collaboration between the American poet Wendy Barker and Saranindranath Tagore, a Bengali academic who also happens to be Tagore's descendant. In their translations of Tagore's last poems, Barker and Saranindranath "use ordinary American colloquial diction" and "fresh language in English" (xiv).

With the lapse of copyright in 2001, Tagore's works once again came into the limelight, this time through the efforts of translators and publishers eager to make his writings available to the public in new, more modern ways. Some publishers have been republishing old translations in new packaging. Others, notably Oxford University Press and to an extent Penguin and Rupa, have been experimenting with a series of new translations aimed at the twenty-first-century reader. *Rabindranath Tagore: Three Plays* (2001), translated by Ananda Lal; *Rabindranath Tagore: Selected Writings for Children* (2002), edited by Sukanta Chaudhuri; *Of Love, Nature, and Devotion: Selected Songs of Rabindranath Tagore* (2008), translated by Kalpana Bardhan; and Reba Som's *Rabindranath Tagore: The Singer and His Song* (2009) are instances of modern translation that seek to remain faithful to the original without sacrificing readability. Several of Tagore's novels and short stories, and some of his autobiographical writings, have also been retranslated. Cumulatively, the impact of these translations has been considerable, but the majority of Tagore's writings still await the attention they deserve. Also, most of these translations are from Bengali into English; the importance of translating Tagore's works into other world languages has not yet been fully apprehended. There continue to be attempts to adapt or translate Tagore's works into other languages, not directly from Bengali but via English, but it still remains for truly bilingual translators to address Tagore's work directly, without the mediation of English.

Today, Tagore continues to command respect and recognition across the globe among those who recognize his contemporary relevance. In India, Sahitya Akademi, for instance, has announced that his novel *Gora* will be translated into twenty-one Indian languages because of its position as a major text of modern Indian literature. In 2008, *The University of Toronto Quarterly* devoted a special issue to Rabindranath Tagore, and editors Richard and Kathleen O'Connell in their perceptive introduction took fresh stock of Tagore's significance for the world today. Worldwide, preparations are under way to celebrate the 150th anniversary of Tagore's birth. Even in China, where the response to him was always ambivalent, the observance of this occasion will be marked with great fanfare. The German scholar Martin Kaempchen, based in Santiniketan, continues to work with the Sriniketan project, which Tagore initiated with the vision of empowering the socially underprivileged by turning cottage industries and handicrafts into a livelihood for them. Stage and screen adaptations of Tagore's works continue to draw audiences; in the sixties and seventies, Satyajit Ray and Tapan Sinha made several famous film versions of Tagore texts. More recently, Rituparno Ghosh's Bollywood film *Chokher Bali* (2003) in Hindi was a commercial success. Yet, despite these niches of Tagore-related activity, his achievements as a writer, thinker, and reformer remain largely forgotten.

Tagore Anthologies—Past and Present

This is not the first Tagore anthology, of course, for throughout the past century there have been attempts to anthologize Tagore's work in meaningful ways. The first book to present a selection of Tagore's works in the English language was Macmillan's *Collected Poems and Plays of Rabindranath Tagore* (1936). This volume remained in print for a long while, but it probably did more harm than good to the poet's reputation, for it gave the impression that it had brought together all of Tagore's writings in English, although it had left out much of his best work in the language. This volume also created the misleading idea that Tagore wrote entirely in English, since the text nowhere identifies itself as a collection of translated pieces.

Tagore's birth centenary in 1961 was the occasion for *A Tagore Reader*, the first real attempt to represent some of his best work in an English-language anthology. It was edited by the distinguished Bengali poet Amiya Chakravarty. Within 400 pages or so, Chakravarty aimed to represent Tagore's achievement through selections from his travel writing, letters, short stories, plays, autobiographical works, recorded conversations, fables, verse, and essays on politics, education, art, literature, religion, and morality. Chakravarty prefaced each section with brief but helpful comments on the writings and their contexts, based on his own intimate knowledge of Tagore and his works. Chakravarty relied for the most part on Tagore's own translations or translations approved by him, hence the contemporary reader may find much of the writing old-fashioned. Also, because he included many of Tagore's conversations, letters, and speeches that are widely available in English, Chakravarty was left with insufficient space for significant works that had not yet been translated from Bengali. Still, the anthology did serve its purpose. As the Rupa reprint of 2003 notes on its dust-jacket, the book is "a fairly comprehensive view of Tagore's contribution to our times."

During the centennial celebration in 1961, *Towards Universal Man* was published by Asia Publishing House. This volume brought together eighteen of Tagore's essays on social, economic, political, and educational subjects. When it was published, many intellectuals of the western world acknowledged that they had had no idea of the extent and influence of Tagore's ideas on modern India. Encouraged by the reception of the volume, the Tagore Commemorative Volume Society then commissioned the publication of *Poems of Rabindranath Tagore* (1966), an anthology edited by the distinguished Indian litterateur Humayan Kabir. Containing translations of 101 poems by Tagore chosen by leading Indian poets and translators of the period, the volume is a model of good taste and collaborative zeal. It was reprinted in 2005 jointly by Visva-Bharati and UBS publishers in a volume enhanced by the addition of twenty beautiful color reproductions of Tagore's paintings. Together, the two volumes demonstrated the significance of bringing a large group of translators together to represent Tagore comprehensively and attractively for a new generation of readers, without resorting to translations many decades old. In 1964, Visva-Bharati brought out the anthology *Boundless Sky*, a selection of Tagore's works that includes stories, poems, and prose writings.

Another work that seeks to represent Tagore's many-sided genius in a single book is *Rabindranath Tagore: An Anthology* (1997). Edited by Krishna Dutta and Andrew Robinson, this useful volume brings together the work of Tagore the dramatist, travel and letter writer, essayist, novelist, poet, and writer of autobiographical pieces in around four hundred pages. However, as the editors acknowledge, "a third of the pieces in the book were written in English, two-third[s] in Bengali" ("Note on the Translations," 17). Of the two-thirds originally written in Bengali, more than half, as in the Chakravarty volume, are translations done by Tagore or other translators whose work he had approved. Though the editors inform us that they revised many of the translations in reprinting them, a basic problem remains: at times, the translations can strike a contemporary reader as dated.

To be sure, anyone looking for fresh translations of Tagore can now turn to the Oxford Tagore translations. Oxford University Press's Indian wing has assembled a skillful group of translators based in India who have translated some of Tagore's important work. The first volume of the series, published in 2000, is devoted to the short stories. The second volume, a collection of Tagore's writings on literature and language, published in 2001, is the work of Sukanta Chaudhuri and Sisir Kumar Das. The third, from 2002, brings together some of his most delightful work for children, and the fourth, launched in 2004, presents a selection of the poems. The first, third, and fourth volumes were edited by Chaudhuri. The series also includes Kalpana Bardhan's translations of Tagore songs in *Of Love, Nature, and Devotion* (2008), and *Selected Writings on Education and Nationalism* (2009), edited by Uma Das Gupta. The cumulative aim of the Oxford Tagore series volumes is to demonstrate Tagore's relevance to our world, and the range and quality of his writing.

There have been other noteworthy attempts to collect Tagore's writings in anthologies to make them accessible to English language readers. *The Tagore Omnibus Volume 1* (New Delhi: Penguin, 2005) is a collection of Tagore's novels, and the four volumes of *The Rabindranath Tagore Omnibus* (2003–2009), published by Rupa, are collections, across genres, of reprinted versions of some of Tagore's well-known works. Another recent example is *The Sky of Indian History: Themes and Thoughts of Rabindranath Tagore* (2010). Compiled and edited by S. Jeyaseela Stephen, the volume aims to bring together the most important of Tagore's writings on Indian and world history and his thoughts on historiography.

No critical survey of anthologies of Tagore's works in English can be complete without mentioning the four-volume Sahitya Akademi collection, *The English Writings of Rabindranath Tagore.* The first three volumes, edited by Sisir Kumar Das, devoted to the poems, plays, stories, essays, lectures, conversations and interviews, were published between 1994 and 1996. The fourth volume, another miscellany published in 2007, was edited by Nityapriya Ghosh. Together, these collections, amounting to well over three thousand pages, make *The English Writings of Rabindranath Tagore* a truly monumental work. However, these volumes only include Tagore's writings in English or translations that he had commissioned and vetted in his lifetime. As many of these translations do not represent him at his best, the four volumes of *The English Writings of Rabindranath Tagore,* though extensive and indispensable to the Tagore specialist, have little appeal for general readers.

In Search of the Essential Tagore

Anthologies of Tagore's works attempt to encompass his genius, but also reveal the difficulty of compressing into a single volume his vast and variegated talent. Editors are compelled to make hard choices, their selections often dictated as much by subjective preference as by popular perceptions and changing literary fashions. Although individual pieces in these collections highlight particular aspects of Tagore's work, they do not always achieve an adequate overview of his creative and intellectual achievement. They also tend to leave us with only a hazy impression of the man behind the writings.

When we began work on *The Essential Tagore,* therefore, we were aware that we were taking up a daunting challenge. Our anthology is inspired by the desire to explore Tagore's core concerns, to examine the motivating impulses behind his evolution as a man and as a creative artist, and to share our quest for the "best of Tagore" with contemporary readers across the world. "The essential Tagore" is a phrase that editors Mary Lago and Ronald Warwick first use in their introduction to their collection of essays, *Rabindranath Tagore: Perspectives in Time* (1989). The phrase underscores the need to probe beneath surfaces for the deeper, less visible aspects of Tagore's genius. It is impossible, though, to pinpoint the "essential" quality of a writer so versatile, mercurial, dynamic, and self-contradictory. For while poetry remained his primary passion, Tagore experimented with multiple genres throughout his career. Paradoxically, it was this constant urge to discover new ways of expressing himself that remained the most "essential" impulse behind his work. *The Essential Tagore* is therefore a title that expresses the spirit of inquiry underlying our exploration of Tagore's life, work, and legacy, rather than an attempt to place a label on his achievements.

Our selections cover a broad spectrum of Tagore's writings, including autobiography, letters, poetry, songs, prose, drama, novels, short stories, and humor and travel literature. The headnotes to separate sections are intended to contextualize our selections and provide a brief overview of Tagore's work in particular genres. A few pieces in the anthology are originally written in English or translated by Tagore himself. They draw attention to his role as a bilingual writer and foreground his practice as a translator—a facet of his creativity often overlooked when appraising his literary achievement. The bulk of our collection, though, consists of modern translations intended for a contemporary audience. Although a few of these are reprinted from recent publications, most of the translations were commissioned specially for *The Essential Tagore.* Instead of the rather archaic, stilted translations of the earlier versions, our contributors, in tune with the spirit of this book, have attempted lucid, idiomatic English translations that will make Tagore's writings accessible for a new generation of readers.

Our translators are located in different parts of the world, including Bangladesh, different parts of India (Santiniketan, Kolkata, Delhi, Ahmedabad), the United Kingdom, and the United States. Instead of expecting them to conform to a single, prescriptive style of translation, we have encouraged a diverse and flexible approach, with the aim of demonstrating the varied directions in which Tagore translations have evolved after the lapse of copyright in 2001. Tagore, our collection shows, can be translated in multifarious ways.

We have also avoided italicizing Bengali words, weaving them into the translations so that their meaning is either briefly indicated within the text or made apparent from the context in which they occur. This helps preserve the local flavor of the original sources, making the reader aware of the cultural ethos in which Tagore's works are rooted. Although there is a Glossary at the end of the book, we have deliberately kept it to a minimum, allowing the translations to speak for themselves. We have used simple, phonetic Sanskrit spellings for non-English words, barring a few instances (as in the name "Jokkhopuri" in the translation of *Roktokorobi,* where the translator felt it was important to retain the Bengali pronunciation of certain words). These variations in spelling reflect our effort to highlight through translation the fault lines that exist between local, national, and global readings of Tagore's work.

Choosing what to include in our anthology has proved extremely difficult, for we wanted to strike a balance between well-known items and ones that languish unknown or neglected. While some items in *The Essential Tagore* have been translated many times over, others (such as the poem from *Pushpanjali*) have never been translated before. From the English *Gitanjali,* we have included some of Tagore's own translations, which Yeats had deleted from the manuscript; but alongside, we have also used some recent translations of other poems from the same collection. These variant translations underscore the richness of this extraordinary text, which continues to lend itself to reinterpretation a century after it was first composed.

Tagore's poems, essays, and short stories have often been anthologized, but we have focused also on some neglected genres, such as humor. Tagore's satires, farces, and children's verse illuminate how misleading is his popular image in the West as the mystic from the East. His wry wit and the sharpness of his satire contrast starkly with the emotional intricacies of his verse and the intellectual drift of much of his prose. Tagore's genius as a novelist is also underrated; we have used extracts from four other significant works that establish his claim: *Gora, Connections, Farewell Song,* and *Four Chapters.* Tagore's autobiographical writings and his letters show us the man behind the public mask. Yet even these personal writings can be elusive, the gaps and silences in them sometimes more revealing than the words. Tagore, as some of his most perceptive critics recognize, was a fractured, complex personality, often at war with himself, and his writings became the arena where these internal struggles were enacted.

Although our book is divided into ten sections, the divisions between genres are not watertight, for Tagore's creative spirit ranged freely across boundaries. Some of his poems, for instance, are also songs, and some songs can be read as poems. The plays in this anthology are punctuated by songs. Two of the letters appear in the "Prose" section, and Tagore himself chose to print them in his collections of prose. The "Humor" section includes poems, farces, and prose. The sections of the book thus reinforce each other and indicate the essential unity underlying the variegated surface of Tagore's writings. For example, a poem such as "My Little Plot of Land" has much in common with the essay on the tenant farmer. Tagore's critique of imperialism in his prose pieces echoes the ideas expressed in *Chhinnapatra (Torn Leaves)*, *Chhinnapatrabali (Letter Fragments)*, "The Black Ant's Remarks," and *The Kingdom of Cards*. His concern for the plight of women in Indian society is as apparent in our selections from his poems as in the short stories and the extracts from his novels.

Accompanying the selections from Tagore's writings are a few illustrations. These highlight Tagore's artwork, some places and people associated with his life, and his impact on contemporary cultural practices. There are also some unusual Tagore portraits by artists from Bangladesh, India, and Sri Lanka. Interestingly, even his doodles often blur generic boundaries, occupying the middle ground between writing and drawing, and turning the written page into a work of art. We hope therefore that the selections in *The Essential Tagore* will give our readers a sense of the underlying connections between the diverse facets of Tagore's genius, even while highlighting his inner conflicts and contradictory impulses. It is not for nothing that his biographers Dutta and Robinson have described him as a "myriad-minded man"!

Attempting to capture the range and depth of Tagore's literary output in a single volume is a formidable task, and it brings home to us the importance of his legacy. For while it remains crucial to understand Tagore in relation to the time and place that he inhabited, he was also in many ways a pioneer, and ahead of his times. Across genres, Tagore's central concerns come across with remarkable cogency: his love of nature and spirituality; his broad humanism; his anxiety about social inequities; his divided feelings about the relationship between East and West; his visionary approach to education; his emotional entanglements; and his passion for life, art, and literature. His engagement with these issues must be understood in relation to the socio-historical context as well as the personal circumstances that produced them. Yet, it is remarkable how much of Tagore's work continues to have a bearing on questions that concern us today. His thoughts on education, rural reconstruction, secularism, environment, man-woman relationships, gender, art, politics, literature, and religion give us much to think about in relation to our own world in the twenty-first century. His insight into basic human instincts and passions continues to amaze us, and his broad humanism, his sympathy for all forms of life, and his breadth of vision remain a model of inspiration in our increasingly divided world. Our quest for the essential Tagore points in these directions.

An anthology such as this one is of course necessarily incomplete, for in trying to compress all the diverse aspects of Tagore's achievement into a single volume, we are compelled to make do with a broad outline and satisfy ourselves only with having provided relevant signposts to map a terrain that still remains to be more fully explored. All the same, if this collection inspires readers across cultures to ask fresh questions about this towering literary giant whose legacy lives on in his works, our collaborative effort will, we hope, reaffirm his stature as a leading thinker, writer, and social reformer of international significance. The quest for the essential Tagore is not over, for with every new generation of readers in a changing world, the process of exploration and discovery must begin all over again. That is the Tagore magic.

Autobiography

"It is not easy to know oneself. It is difficult to organize life's various experiences into a unified whole," muses the seventy-year-old Tagore in *Atmaparichay* (*Self-Recognition*, 1943), a collection of six introspective essays published posthumously. Although he did not write a formal autobiography, many of his lectures and writings are attempts to reconstruct the narrative of his personal development as a man and as a writer. Impelled by the desire to understand himself and his environment, Tagore is also self-conscious about the image he wants to present to the world.

In 1912, Tagore published *Jibansmriti,* with black-and-white sketches by his nephew Gaganendranath Tagore. Surendranath Tagore's English translation of the work, *My Reminiscences,* was published by Macmillan in 1917. Here Tagore describes the early years of his life; his experiences of loneliness, love, and loss; and his emergence as a poet. In the process, he also introduces us to his family circle and paints a grim picture of the formal education against which he rebelled. With disarming simplicity, the text captures a child's-eye view of a mysterious, fascinating world in which fantasy blends seamlessly with reality. In the passage describing his first encounters with death, the poignancy of grief proves to be liberating, offering a new, deeper insight into the beauty of life.

In April–May 1924, invited by Liang Chi-Chao, president of the University Lecture Association of Peking, Tagore delivered a series of lectures in China, which were later published as *Talks in China* (1925). "Autobiographical," from this collection, is Tagore's attempt to contextualize his life in relation to the broad historical trends of the time, and the personal and family influences that shaped his spirit in his formative years. In this piece, Tagore makes it clear that despite the many roles life has imposed on him, it is as a poet that he wants to be remembered.

In "My School," a lecture published in *The Modern Review* in

1931, Tagore speaks of his other passion: the mission to revolutionize education by rearing young minds in harmony with nature. He describes the trauma of his own schooldays, his sense of liberation when he finally left school at thirteen, and the germination of his vision of a new form of education through his experiments with the school at Santiniketan. Here, as in his other autobiographical writings, his key concern is freedom of the mind.

Chhelebela (Boyhood Days) was published in 1940, shortly before Tagore's death. Requested by Nityanandabinod Goswami, a literary scholar and teacher at Santiniketan, to write something for young readers, Tagore embarked on this delightful account of his childhood and adolescence, describing his experiences from his earliest recollections up to the time of his first visit to England in 1878. With an episodic structure that depends more on associations of memory than on chronological sequence, this impressionistic narrative captures the child's wonder at the world around him and also offers a vivid picture of life during those times. He observes, but often feels excluded from, the sphere of adult activities, and thinks himself abandoned to a lonely and loveless existence. This solitariness is both a source of anguish and the wellspring of his creativity, for he compensates for his drab outer life by withdrawing into a vivid inner world created by his imagination. There are no ghosts in *My Reminiscences,* but in *Boyhood Days,* nature is a living presence, and magical spirits lurk around every corner. In his preface to *Boyhood Days,* Tagore says: "Some features of this book's contents may be found also in *Jibansmriti,* my memoirs, but that has a different flavour—like the contrast between a lake and a waterfall. That was a story, while this is birdsong; that belongs to the fruit basket, this to the tree." (*Boyhood Days,* 4).

My Reminiscences and *Boyhood Days* should not be read as a truthful account of Tagore's childhood, for not all details in these texts are factually accurate. Biographers point out, for instance, that the Tagores had two houses in Jorasanko, not one, and that the young Robi was not denied adequate clothing as he claims. Such distortions, gaps, and silences hint at Tagore's reticence about certain private matters, such as tensions within the joint family, and his desire to underscore his loneliness, for

38

which the lack of clothing becomes a metaphor. These memoirs are therefore best understood as "memory pictures," or literary reconstructions of the past in which imagination and sentiment play as great a role as factual detail: "I do not know who has painted the pictures of my life imprinted on my memory. But whoever he is, he is an artist. He does not take up his brush simply to copy everything that happens; he retains or omits things just as he fancies; he makes many a big thing small and small thing big . . . In short, his task is to paint pictures, not to write history" (*My Reminiscences,* 17). Tagore's autobiographical writings blur the distinction between fiction and history. That is their special charm.

Autobiographical

I was born in 1861: that is not an important date of history, but it belongs to a great period of our history in Bengal. You do not know perhaps that we have our places of pilgrimage in those spots where the rivers meet in confluence, the rivers which to us are the symbols of the spirit of life in nature, and which in their meeting present emblems of the meeting of spirits, the meeting of ideals. Just about the time I was born the currents of three movements had met in the life of our country.

One of these movements was religious, introduced by a very great-hearted man of gigantic intelligence, Raja Rammohan Roy. It was revolutionary, for he tried to re-open the channel of spiritual life which had been obstructed for many years by the sands and debris of creeds that were formal and materialistic, fixed in external practices lacking spiritual significance.

There was a great fight between him and the orthodox who suspected every living idea that was dynamic. People who cling to an ancient past have their pride in the antiquity of their accumulations, in the sublimity of time-honored walls around them. They grow nervous and angry when some great spirit, some lover of truth, breaks open their enclosure and floods it with the sunshine of thought and the breath of life. Ideas cause movement and all movements forward they consider to be a menace against their warehouse security.

This was happening about the time I was born. I am proud to say that my father was one of the great leaders of that movement, a movement for whose sake he suffered ostracism and braved social indignities. I was born in this atmosphere of the advent of new ideas, which at the same time were old, older than all the things of which that age was proud.

There was a second movement equally important. A certain great man, Bankim Chandra Chatterjee who, though much older than myself, was my contemporary and lived long enough for me to see him, was the first pioneer in the literary revolution which happened in Bengal about that time.

Our self-expression must find its freedom not only in spiritual ideas but in literary manifestations. But our literature had allowed its creative life to vanish. It lacked movement and was fettered by a rhetoric rigid as death. This man was brave enough to go against the orthodoxy which believed in the security of tombstones and in that perfection which can only belong to the lifeless. He lifted the dead weight of ponderous forms from our language and with a touch of his magic wand aroused our literature from her age-long sleep. What a vision of beauty she revealed to us when she awoke in the fullness of her strength and grace.

There was yet another movement started about this time in my country which was called National. It was not fully political, but it began to give voice to the mind of our people trying to assert their own personality. It was a voice of indignation at the humiliation constantly heaped upon us by people who were not oriental, and who had, especially at that time, the habit of sharply dividing the human world into the good and the bad according to what was similar to their life and what was different.

This contemptuous spirit of separateness was perpetually hurting us and causing great damage to our own world of culture. It generated in the young men of our country distrust of all things that had come to them as an inheritance from their past. The old Indian pictures and other works of art were laughed at by our students in imitation of the laughter of their European schoolmasters. . . .

The spirit of revolt had just awakened when I was born and some people were already trying to stem the tide. This movement had its leaders in my own family, in my brothers and cousins, and they stood up to save the people's mind from being insulted and ignored by the people themselves.

We have to find some basis that is universal, that is eternal, and we have to discover those things which have an everlasting value. The national movement was started to proclaim that we must not be indiscriminate in our rejection of the past. This was not a reactionary movement but a revolutionary one, because it set out with a great courage to deny and to oppose all pride in mere borrowings.

These three movements were on foot and in all three the members of my own family took active part. We were ostracized because of our heterodox opinions about religion and therefore we enjoyed the freedom of the outcaste. We had to build our own world with our own thoughts and energy of mind. We had to build it from the foundation, and therefore had to seek the foundation that was firm.

We cannot create foundations, but we can build a superstructure. These two must go together, the giving of expression to new life and the seeking of foundations which must be in the heart of the people themselves. Those who believe that life consists in change because change implies movement, should remember that there must be an underlying thread of unity or the change, being unmeaning, will cause conflict and clash. This thread of unity must not be of the outside, but in our own soul.

As I say, I was born and brought up in an atmosphere of the confluence of three movements, all of which were revolutionary. I was born in a family which had to live its own life, which led me from my young days to seek guidance for my own self-expression in my own inner standard of judgment. The medium of expression doubtless was my mother tongue. But the language which belonged to the people had to be modulated according to the urging which I as an individual had . . .

The impertinence of material things is extremely old. The revelation of spirit in man is truly modern: I am on its side, for I am modern. I have explained how I was born into a family which rebelled, which had faith in its loyalty to an inner ideal. If you want to reject me, you are free to do so. But I have my right as a revolutionary to carry the flag of freedom of spirit into the shrine of your idols,—material power and accumulation. . . .

42

II

When I began my career I was ridiculously young; in fact, I was the youngest of the writers of that time who had made themselves articulate. I had neither the protective armor of mature age, nor that of a respectable English education. So in my seclusion of contempt and qualified encouragement I had my freedom. Gradually I grew up in years, for which, however, I claim no credit. Gradually I cut my way through derision and occasional patronage into a recognition in which the proportion of praise and blame was very much like that of land and water on our earth.

If you ask me what gave me boldness, when I was young, I should say that one thing was my early acquaintance with the old Vaishnava poems of Bengal, full of the freedom of meter and courage of expression. I think I was only twelve when these poems first began to be re-printed. I surreptitiously got hold of copies from the desks of my elders. For the edification of the young I must confess that this was not right for a boy of my age. I should have been passing my examinations and not following a path that would lead to failure. I must also admit that the greater part of these lyrics was erotic and not quite suited to a boy just about to reach his teens. But my imagination was fully occupied with the beauty of their forms and the music of their words; and their breath, heavily laden with voluptuousness, passed over my mind without distracting it.

My vagabondage in the path of my literary career had another reason. My father was the leader of a new religious movement, a strict monotheism based upon the teachings of the Upanishads. My countrymen in Bengal thought him almost as bad as a Christian, if not worse. So we were completely ostracized, which probably saved me from another disaster, that of imitating our own past.

Most of the members of my family had some gift—some were artists, some poets, some musicians and the whole atmosphere of our home was permeated with the spirit of creation. I had a deep sense, almost from infancy, of the beauty of nature, an intimate feeling of companionship with the trees and the clouds, and felt in tune with the musical touch of the seasons in the air. At the same time I had a peculiar susceptibility to human kindness. All these craved expression, and naturally I wanted to give them my own expression. The very earnestness of my emotions yearned to be true to themselves though I was too immature to give their expression any perfection of form.

Since then I have gained a reputation in my country but a strong current of antagonism in a large section of my countrymen still persists. Some say that my poems do not spring from the heart of the national traditions; some complain that they are incomprehensible, others that they are unwholesome. In fact, I have never had complete acceptance from my own people, and that too has been a blessing; for nothing is so demoralizing as unqualified success.

This is the history of my career. I wish I could reveal it to you more clearly through the narration of my own work in my own language. I hope that will be possible some day or other. Languages are jealous. They do not give up their best treasures to those who try to deal with them through an intermediary belonging to an alien rival. You have to court them in person and dance attendance on them. Poems are not like gold or other substantial things that are transferable. You cannot receive the smiles and glances of your sweetheart through an attorney, however diligent and dutiful he may be. . . .

III

My religion essentially is a poet's religion. Its touch comes to me through the same unseen and trackless channels as does the inspiration of my music. My religious life has followed the same mysterious line of growth as has my poetical life. Somehow they are wedded to each other, and though their betrothal had a long period of ceremony, it was kept secret from me. Then suddenly came a day when their union was revealed to me.

44

At that time I was living in a village. The day came with all its drifting trivialities of the usual commonplace. The ordinary work of my morning had come to its close and before going to take my bath I stood for a moment at my window, overlooking a market place on the bank of dry river bed. Suddenly I became conscious of a stirring of soul within me. My world of experience in a moment seemed to become lighted, and facts that were detached and dim found a great unity of meaning. The feeling which I had was like what a man, groping through a fog without knowing his destination, might feel when he suddenly discovers that he stands before his own house.

I remember the day in my childhood when, after the painful process of learning my Bengali alphabet, I unexpectedly came to the first simple combination of letters which gave me the words: "It rains, the leaves tremble." I was thrilled with the delight of the picture which these words suggested to me. The unmeaning fragments lost their individual isolation and my mind revealed in the unity of a vision. In a similar manner, on that morning in the village, the facts of my life suddenly appeared to me in a luminous unity of truth. All things that had seemed like vagrant waves were revealed to my mind in relation to a boundless sea. From that time I have been able to maintain the faith that, in all my experience of nature or man, there is the fundamental truth of spiritual reality.

(From "Autobiographical," *Talks in China,* 1925)

From *Reminiscences*

I

Contact with the outer world was virtually impossible for me no doubt, but perhaps for that very reason, I found it easy to relish the joys of the open air. If one has too many resources, the mind becomes lazy. It remains totally dependent on outward things, forgetting that it is the celebration of inner life that matters more in the festival of happiness. This is the first lesson human beings learn in their infancy. At that stage, their resources are meager and insignificant, but they need no more than that to make them happy. But the unfortunate child who has a limitless supply of playthings finds that his play is ruined.

It would be quite an exaggeration to describe the green patch in our inner quarters as a garden. A pomelo tree, a jujube tree, a hogplum tree and a row of coconut palms were its main features. At the center was a paved circular terrace. Through its cracks, grass and sundry creepers had encroached and planted their flags of conquest. Those flowering plants, refusing to die even if neglected, never protesting against the gardener's indifference, would blossom dutifully and uncomplainingly, as best they could. In the northern corner was a dhenkighor, a rice-threshing shed where the inhabitants of the antahpur, the secluded women's quarters, would sometimes assemble to attend to household needs. Acknowledging that rural customs in Kolkata had utterly lost their battle for survival, this dhenkighor silently hid its face and vanished one day. I don't believe that the paradise inhabited by Adam, the first human being, was better designed than this garden of ours. For the paradise of the earliest humans had no outward décor; it had not tried deliberately to cover itself. Ever since they first tasted the fruit of the tree of knowledge, humans have developed a growing need for adornment and ornamentation, a need that will persist until they manage to digest that fruit completely. In that respect, the garden within our house was paradise to me; for me, it was enough. I well remember how, on a Sharat dawn in early autumn, I would come out into the garden as soon as I awakened. A dewy aroma from the grass and foliage would waft to my nostrils, and the morning, with its gentle, fresh sunshine, would peep over the eastern wall, beneath the shivering coconut fronds.

To the north of our house lay another piece of land, which to this day we describe as the Golabari. This name proves that sometime in the remote past, the place was used as a granary for the year's stock of grain. Town and country would share a resemblance those days, like young siblings; but now, it is hard to detect any similarity between the brother and his elder sister.

On holidays, if I got the chance, I would repair to the Golabari. It wouldn't be accurate to say that I went there to play. It was the place, rather than the prospect of play, that had a greater attraction for me. It's hard to say why. Perhaps because it was a solitary, abandoned area in a corner of the house, it seemed strangely mysterious to me. It was not our living area, nor a room that we used, nor did it have any practical utility. Located outside the building, bearing no marks of everyday use, it was an unattractive, redundant, abandoned piece of land. No-one had even planted flowering shrubs there. Hence, in that desolate, barren space, a boy's mind could indulge his wishful fantasies unhindered. Whenever I managed to escape there somehow, through some loophole in my guardians' discipline, it would feel like a holiday.

There was another place in the house, but till today I have not been able to ascertain its location. A playmate of mine, a little girl my own age, would call it Rajar Bari, the King's Palace.[1] "I went there today," I would hear her say sometimes. But I never had the good fortune of accompanying her there. It was an extraordinary place: the possibilities for play there were amazing, and the playthings equally exquisite. Apparently it was somewhere very close to us, on the ground floor or the level above, but it always remained beyond our reach. "Is the Rajar Bari outside our house?" I often asked the little girl. "No," she would reply, "it's inside this very house." Perplexed, I would wonder where it might be located, for I had seen all the rooms in the house, after all! I had never even asked who the king might be. The location of his kingdom remains undiscovered till today. One has only gathered that the king resides within one's very own home.

1912
(From "Ghar o Bahir," *Jibansmriti*)
Translated by Radha Chakravarty

2

Meanwhile, several deaths occurred in our family. Until now, I had never come face to face with death. When Ma passed away, I was very young. She had been ailing for a long time, and I had not even realized when her illness became life-threatening . . . When I woke up in the morning to hear the news of Ma's death, I could not absorb the full meaning of the event. Emerging into the outer veranda, I saw her ceremonially bedecked body lying on a bed placed in the courtyard. But that body bore no sign to indicate that death was a terrible thing. The face of death which I beheld that day in the early morning light was as calm and beautiful as a peaceful sleep . . .

But my acquaintance with death in my twenty-fourth year was a permanent one. Merging its pain with the grief of every successive bereavement since then, it has continued to weave a long garland of tears . . .

I was unaware then of the slightest lack anywhere in my life; there seemed no loophole in its tightly woven fabric of laughter and tears. Nothing was visible beyond it, hence I had accepted it as the ultimate truth. And then death suddenly arrived from somewhere. In a single instant, it tore away one end of this very visible fabric of life. How bewildered I felt now! All around me, the trees, earth, water, sun and moon, planets and stars, remained as real as before; and yet, the person more real to me than all of them, the one so closely in touch with my body and soul, my mind and heart, had vanished so easily in a single instant, just like a dream. Now, gazing at the whole world, I began to wonder: what sort of self-contradiction is this! How will I reconcile what remains with what is gone?

From this gap in my life, a bottomless dark revealed itself, drawing me towards it, day and night. . . . When a seedling is fenced into a dark space, its sole effort is to somehow escape that darkness, to emerge into the light, stretching upwards as if on tiptoe, as far up as possible. Likewise, when death suddenly imprisoned my heart inside a dark nothingness, my entire being struggled desperately, day and night, to penetrate that darkness and come out into the light of existence. But when the darkness conceals the way out of darkness, can there be any sorrow greater than that?

And yet, through this unbearable grief, from time to time, I felt the touch of a sudden joyous breeze. I was surprised at it . . . I had been forced to give up the one I had clung to for support. Seeing this as a loss, I suffered agony; but simultaneously, perceiving it as a sort of liberation, I experienced a vast sense of peace. . . .

Viewed through that sense of detachment, the loveliness of nature appeared even more profoundly entrancing . . . Death had created the distance that is required for one to see the world whole, and to see it in all its beauty. From my position of detachment, I gazed at the image of the world etched against the vast backdrop of death, and realized that it was exquisitely beautiful.

1912
(From "Mrityushok," *Jibansmriti*)
Translated by Radha Chakravarty

From *Boyhood Days*

I

I was born in Kolkata of the olden days. Raising clouds of dust, hackney carriages would speed through the city, the horses' skeletal frames lashed by cord-whips. There were no trams, no buses, and no motorcars. Those days, life followed a leisurely pace, spared the breathless pressure of work. Having inhaled a stiff dose of tobacco, chewing paan, the babus would leave for office, some in palanquins or palkis, others in shared carriages. The well-to-do would ride carriages emblazoned with their family titles, the leather hoods overhead resembling half-drawn veils. In the coach-box rode the coachman, turban tilted at an angle, and at the back were two grooms, no less, yak-tail fly-whisks swinging from their waistband, startling the pedestrians with their street-cry: *"Heinyo!"* Women, too shy to ride in carriages, ventured out in the stifling darkness of closed palkis. Never, in sunshine or in rain, would they shield their head with an umbrella. If a woman was seen in the long loose chemise or even shoes, she would be accused of aping the mem-sahibs, a sign of utter brazenness. If ever a woman came face to face with a man from another family, her veil would instantly descend over her countenance, down to the very tip of her nose, and she would turn her back on him, biting her tongue in shame. They went out in closed palkis, just as they lived behind closed doors at home. The wives and daughters of elite families would travel in palkis covered with an additional pall made of thick diamond-patterned linen. The palkis looked like walking graves. Accompanying the palki on foot would be a bodyguard, the darwanji, armed with a lathi. The darwans were supposed to remain stationed at the portico, guarding the main entrance to the house; to finger their beards; to deliver money to the bank and women to their paternal homes; and on auspicious days, to take the lady of the house for her holy dip in the Ganga, closed palki and all. When hawkers came to the door with their display-boxes, our darwan Shiunandan also received his share of the profits. And there was the driver of the hired carriage; if dissatisfied with the bakhra, or his share of the spoils, he would engage in a ferocious quarrel in front of the main gate. Our pehelvan or strongman, sweeper Shobharam, would from time to time contort his body to practice wrestling moves, exercise with heavy weights, pound hemp for his drink, or consume a horseradish, leaves and all, with great relish. We would go up close and scream "Radhey-Krishna!" into his ear. The more he protested, throwing up his hands, the more stubbornly we persisted. This was his strategy for hearing us pronounce the names of his family deities.

49

The city, those days, had neither gas, nor electricity; when kerosene lamps appeared, we were amazed at their brilliance. At dusk, the attendant would go from room to room lighting castor-oil lamps. Our study was illuminated by a sej, a lamp with a double wick in a glass bowl.

In the dim, flickering light, our tutor, Mastermoshai, taught us the *First Book of Pyari Sarkar.* I would yawn, then become drowsy, and afterwards, rub my eyes to stay awake. I was repeatedly reminded that Mastermoshai's other pupil, Satin, was a gem of a boy, extraordinarily serious about his studies. He would rub snuff in his eyes to ward off sleep. As for me? The less said the better. Even the terrible prospect of remaining the only illiterate dunce among all the boys would not keep me alert. At nine in the evening, half-asleep, my eyes heavy with drowsiness, I would be set free.

The narrow passage from the public area to the inner quarters of the house was screened by venetian blinds, and lit by dim lanterns suspended above. Crossing it, I felt sure I was being followed. A shiver would run down my spine. Those days, you stumbled upon ghosts and spirits in stories and rumors, in the nooks and crannies of people's minds. Every so often, the nasal wail of the shankchunni, the nocturnal spirit, would cause some maidservant to collapse in a fainting fit. That female ghost was the most temperamental of all, and she had a weakness for fish. There was also an unknown standing figure, straddling the dense almond-tree to the west of the house, and the third floor cornice. There were many who claimed to have sighted that apparition, and no dearth of people who believed in the story. When my elder brother's friend laughed off the matter, the servants of the house were convinced that he knew nothing about religious faith. Just wait till the spirit wrung his neck one day, that would put an end to all his learned wisdom! Those days, the air was filled with terror, which had spread its net so wide that just to place one's feet under the table was enough to make one's flesh crawl.

There were no water-taps, then. In the months of Magh and Phalgun, on bankhs or shoulder-borne yokes, bearers carried kolshis, rounded water-pitchers filled with water from the Ganga. Inside a dark chamber on the ground floor, in row upon row of enormous water vessels, the year's supply of drinking water would be stored. It was a well-known fact that the spirits who secretly inhabited those damp, gloomy spaces on the lower floor, had huge, gaping mouths, eyes in their chests, ears like kulos—the flat U-shaped baskets used for husking puffed rice—and feet that faced the wrong way. As I crossed those ghostly shadows to reach the private garden of the house, my heart would heave in terror, adding wings to my feet.

Those days, at high tide, the waters of the Ganga would flood the channels that lined the streets. From my grandfather's times, a share of those waters was reserved for our pond. When the sluices were opened, the foaming tide would descend like a waterfall, with a babbling sound. The fish would try to swim against the current. Clinging to the rails of the southern balcony, I would gaze at the scene in fascination. But the days of the pond were numbered. One day, cart-loads of rubbish were thrown into it. As soon as the pond was filled up, it was as if the mirror reflecting the green shadows of the province had vanished. The almond tree remains, but there is no trace now of that ghostly spirit, though there is still space enough for him to straddle.

Now we have more light, both indoors and out.

The palki belongs to my grandmother's era. Its proportions are large and generous, cast in the royal mould. Each pole is designed for the shoulders of eight bearers. Gold bangles on their wrists, thick gold hoops on their ears, clad in red short-sleeved quilted jackets called mirjais, those bearers, with all the wealth and luxury of the bygone days, have faded away like the many-hued clouds of sunset. This palki was embellished with colorful designs, some of which have worn away. It is stained in places, the coir stuffing spilling out of the upholstery. Like a discarded item struck off from today's inventory, it lies abandoned in a corner of the verandah outside the khatanchikhana, the ledger-room. I was then about seven or eight. I had no useful role to play in this world; and that old palki, too, had been dismissed from all forms of useful employment. That was why I felt such a deep affinity with it. As if it was an island in the sea, and on holidays, I was Robinson Crusoe, lost to the world, concealed behind the palki's closed doors to elude the oppressive surveillance that surrounded me.

Those days, our house was full of people, and degrees of familiarity were not clearly demarcated. All around us was the hustle and bustle of male and female attendants deployed in different quarters of the household: Pyari the maid, crossing the front yard, on her hip a dhama or large rattan basket laden with vegetables; Dukhan the bearer, fetching water from the Ganga in pitchers suspended from the bankh balanced on his shoulder; the weaver-woman, making for the inner quarters of the house, to peddle saris designed with the latest borders; Dinu the salaried goldsmith who served our family, pumping the hissing bellows in the room beside the alley, heading for the ledger-room to claim his payment from Kailash Mukhujje, the man with the quill-pen tucked behind his ear; in the courtyard, the dhunuri, fluffing the cotton stuffing of old quilts, to the clanging sound of his bow-shaped cotton-gin. And outside, the doorman Mukundalal, rolling about on the ground, practicing wrestling grips with the blind pehelwan, noisily slapping his thighs before performing twenty or twenty-five push-ups in quick succession. And a crowd of beggars waiting, hoping for their regular portion of charity.

As time advanced, the sunlight grew harsh, the bell in the portico announced the time; but inside the palki, the day refused to keep track of the passing hours. In there, it was the noontime of those bygone days, when the danka, the large kettle-drum at the palace-gate, would signal the end of the public audience, and the king would depart for his daily bath in sandalwood-scented water. One afternoon, on a holiday, my supervisors had dozed off after their daytime meal. I was alone. The immobile palki sped through the terrain of my mind, borne by loyal minions made of air. The path they traversed had been carved out from my own whims and fancies. On that route the palki traveled, to faraway lands bearing names gleaned from books. Sometimes, the journey would take the palki into deep forests, where tiger eyes gleamed, and the flesh crept in fear. With me was hunter Biswanath. *Bang!* went his gun, and it was all over. All was still.

Then, at some point, the palki transformed into a mayurpankhi, a magical boat shaped like a peacock. It floated on the ocean, no sign of land anywhere. In regular rhythm, the oar hit the water, *splash! splash! splash!* Up and down, swaying and heaving, the waves rose and fell. "Watch out! Watch out! Storm ahoy!" cried the sailors. At the helm was oarsman Abdul, with his pointed beard, shaven upper lip, and bald pate. I knew him. From the river Padma, he fetched tortoise eggs and hilsa fish for Dada, my elder brother.

He told me a story once. One day late in the month of Chaitra, he was out fishing in his dinghy when there was a sudden summer thunderstorm, a kalboishakhi. It was a terrible storm; the boat was about to sink. Gripping the tow rope in his teeth, Abdul dived into the water and swam to the sandbank, tugging the boat ashore.

I did not like a story that ended so quickly. The boat didn't even sink, and he survived so easily—this was no story at all!

"What happened next?" I kept prodding him.

"What a to-do there was, then!" he replied. "I found myself face-to-face with a wolf. What enormous whiskers he had! During the storm, he had climbed onto the pakur tree on the other shore, near the market. A gust of wind, and the tree fell into the Padma. Our friend the wolf was adrift in the rushing torrent. Gasping for air, he reached the sandbank and clambered ashore. As soon as I saw him, I wound my rope into a noose. The creature confronted me with the glare of his huge, bulging eyes. All that swimming had whetted his appetite. The sight of me made his bright-red tongue begin to water. He knew many folks inside out, but he didn't know Abdul. "Come, my little one!" I called out. The moment he reared up on his hind legs, I flung the noose round his neck. The harder he struggled to free himself, the tighter the noose became, making his tongue hang out.

53

"Did he die, then, Abdul?" I enquired anxiously, at this point.

"No power on earth could allow him to die!" Abdul assured me. "With the river in flood, I had to get back to Bahadurganj, didn't I? Tying him to the dinghy, I got the wolf-cub to tow the boat a distance of at least twenty crosh—about ten miles. He moaned and groaned, I prodded his belly with the oar, and in an hour and a half, he'd covered the distance of a ten-to-fifteen-hour journey. Don't ask what happened next, baba, for you will not get a reply!"

"Very well," I agreed, "so much for the wolf. Now, tell me about the crocodile?"

"I've often seen the tip of his nose jutting out above the water," replied Abdul. "Stretched out on the sloping river-shore, basking in the sun, he seems to have a hideous smile on his face. With a gun, I could take him on. But my license has expired. A funny thing happened, though. One day, Kanchi bedeni the snake-catcher was scraping split bamboo with the curved blade of her da, her baby goat tethered by her side. Sneaking up from the river, the crocodile grabbed the baby goat by the leg and began to drag it away, towards the water. In a single leap, the bedeni was astride the crocodile's back. Using her da, she struck blow upon blow on that giant reptile's neck. Relinquishing the baby goat, the creature sank into the water."

"And then?" I cried, in agitation.

"Reports of what happened next have sunk to the bottom of the river," replied Abdul. "It will take a long time to retrieve the information. I shall send a scout to find out what happened, and bring you the details when we meet again."

But he hasn't come back since. Perhaps he has gone to find out what happened.

So much for my travels within the palki. Outside the palki, I sometimes played the schoolmaster, with the verandah railings for pupils. They were silent with awe. There would be the occasional naughty ones, not interested in lessons at all. They would grow up to be coolies, I would warn them. Beaten black and blue, they would still show no sign of giving up their pranks. It wouldn't do to let the mischief end, after all: for that would put an end to my game.

There was one more game I played, with Singhimama, my wooden lion. Tales of animal-sacrifices performed on prayer-days had convinced me that sacrificing my lion would be an event of great magnitude. Many were the blows I rained upon his neck with a twig. I had to make up the mantra, of course, for no puja is complete without that:

Singhimama, off with your head!
At Andibose's shrine I strike you dead!
Ulkut dhulkut dum dum dum
Walnut balnut whack-whack-whack
Crack-crack-crack!

Almost all the words here were borrowed. Only "walnut" was my own. I had a weakness for walnuts. From the word "whack," it will be apparent that my scimitar was made of wood. And "crack" suggests that the scimitar was none too strong.

1940
(From *Chhelebela*)
Translated by Radha Chakravarty

My School

When I was young, as usual, I was sent to school. Some of you may have read from the translation of my autobiography about the misadventure I had when I began my career as a student in a school. It was a terribly miserable life, which became absolutely intolerable to me. At that time I did not have the capacity to analyze the reason why I suffered, but then when I grew up, it became quite clear to me what it was that hurt me so deeply to be compelled to attend my class in that school where my parents sent me.

I have my natural love for life, for nature, and for my surroundings where I have my dear ones; and to be snatched away from these natural surroundings with which I had all my inner deeper life of relationship, and to send me an exile, to the school, to the class with its bare white walls, its stare of dead eyes, frightened me every day. When I was once inside these walls, I did not feel natural. It was absolutely a fragment torn away from life and this gave me intense misery because I was uprooted from my own world and sent to surroundings which were dead and unsympathetic, disharmonious and monotonously dull.

It could not be possible for the mind of a child to be able to receive anything in those cheerless surroundings, in the environment of dead routine. And the teachers were like living gramophones, repeating the same lessons day by day in a most dull manner. My mind refused to accept anything from my teacher. With all my heart and soul I seem to have repudiated all that was put before me. And then there were some teachers who were utterly unsympathetic and did not understand at all the sensitive soul of a young boy and tried to punish him for the mistakes he made. Such teachers in their stupidity did not know how to teach, how to impart education to a living mind. And because they failed, they punished their victim. And this was how I suffered for thirteen years of my life.

And then I left school when I was thirteen and in spite of all the pressure exerted on me by my elders, I refused to go to my studies in that school.

Since then I have been educating myself and that process is still being carried on. And whatever I have learned, I have learned outside the classes. And I believe that was a fortunate event in my life—that avoiding the schoolmaster when I was still young. And whatever I have done in later life, if I have shown any special gift or originality, I feel certain it was owing to the fact that I was not drilled into a kind of respectable education, which generally all good boys, good students, have to submit to.

And it went on like that. I took to my own work. I retired in a solitary place near the Ganges and a great part of my life I lived in a house-boat, writing my poems, stories and plays; dreaming my dreams.

I went on till I gradually became known to my own countrymen and claims were made on me from all parts of my country for writings and for various kinds of help. But I kept to my solitude for the greater part of my days. It is very difficult for me to say what it was, how the call came to me to go out of my isolation of literary life and be among my fellow-beings and share their life and help them in their living.

And it is also a surprise to me how I had the courage to take upon myself to start an educational institution for our children, for I had no experience in this line at all. But I had confidence in myself. I knew that I had very profound sympathy for children, and about my knowledge of their psychology I was very certain. I felt that I could help them more than the ordinary teachers who had the delusion to think that they had proper training for their work.

I selected a beautiful place, far away from the contamination of town life, for I myself, in my young days, was brought up in that town in the heart of India, Calcutta, and all the time I had a sort of homesickness for some distant land somewhere, where my heart, my soul, could have its true emancipation. Though I had no experience of the outer-world, I had in my heart great longing to go away from my enclosure of those walls and from that huge, stony-hearted step-mother, Calcutta. I knew that the mind has its hunger for the ministrations of nature, mother-nature, and so I selected this spot where the sky is unobstructed to the verge of the horizon. There the mind could have its fearless freedom to create its own dreams and the seasons could come with all their colors and movements and beauty into the very heart of the human dwelling.

And there I got a few children around me and I taught them. I was their companion. I sang to them. I composed some musical pieces, some operas and plays, and they took part in those plays. I recited to them our epics and this was the beginning of this school. I had only about five or six students at that time.

People did not have any confidence in a poet and they had a right to doubt my confidence in bringing up the children and truly educating them in their orthodox fashion. And so I had very few students to begin with.

My idea was that education should be a part of life itself and must not be detached from it and be made into something abstract. And so when I brought these children around me, I allowed them to live a complete life. They had perfect freedom to do what they wished, as much liberty as was possible for me to give them. And in all their activities I tried to put before them something which would be interesting to them. I tried to arouse their interests in all things, in nature's beauty and the surrounding villages and also in literature, through play-acting, through listening to music in a natural manner, not through merely class teaching.

They knew when I was employed in writing some drama and they took an intense interest as it went on and developed, and in the process of their rehearsal they got through a great deal more of reading of literature than they could through grammar and class-teaching. And this was my method. I knew the children's mind. Their subconscious mind is more active than the conscious one, and therefore the important thing is to surround them with all kinds of activities which could stimulate their minds and gradually arouse their interests.

I had musical evenings—not merely music classes, and those boys who at first did not have any special love of music, would, out of curiosity, listen to our songs outside of the room, and gradually they too were drawn into the room and their taste for music developed. I had some of the very great artists of our land and while they went on with their work, the boys could watch them and saw day by day how those works developed.

An atmosphere was created and what was important, this atmosphere had provided the students with a natural impulse to live in harmony with it.

(From a lecture published in *The Modern Review,* January 1931)

57

2

Letters

THROUGHOUT HIS LIFE, Tagore communicated with family, friends, public figures and professional associates through letters that constitute a veritable treasure trove of social commentary, self-revelation, philosophical meditation, and literary creativity. Unlike other literary genres, letters occupy the borderline between public and private worlds. Tagore's letters reveal facets of his personality that do not emerge from his formal writings and speeches. His Bengali letters are available, mainly in the *Chithipatra* series and a few other collections published by Visva-Bharati. The Bengali journal *Desh,* published from Kolkata, continues to print his unpublished correspondence in its special issues. Although many of his letters in English have been compiled by Krishna Dutta and Andrew Robinson *(Selected Letters of Rabindranath Tagore)*, C. F. Andrews *(Letters to a Friend)*, Mary Lago *(Imperfect Encounter: Letters of William Rothenstein and Rabindranath Tagore, 1911–1941)*, Ketaki Kushari Dyson *(In Your Blossoming Flower Garden)*, and Uma Das Gupta *(A Difficult Friendship: Letters of Edward Thompson and Rabindranath Tagore, 1913–1940)*, most of them still remain unpublished.

Some of the earliest letters Tagore wrote were from England, during his first visit there as a student, from 1878 to 1880. Immature, spontaneous responses to his first exposure to a foreign culture, these letters, included in *Europe Prabasir Patra,* later proved embarrassing, and he retracted some of the statements made in them.

From 1887 to 1895, Tagore wrote letters from East Bengal, as he traveled through the countryside, very often by boat, sometimes accompanied by family, but usually alone. His brother's daughter, Indira Devi, copied some of the letters into two exercise books and presented them to her uncle. Tagore further revised these letters, giving them a narrative turn, and his son Rathindranath, along with Nagendranath Gangulee, published them as *Chhinnapatra (Torn Leaves)* in 1912. In this collection, the first eight letters were written to his friend Srishchandra Majumdar, and the rest to Indira Devi. Nirad C. Chaudhuri describes these letters as "great works of literature," expressing Tagore's "character and personality with unadorned truth" (*Thy Hand, Great Anarch!* 602). An English translation of *Chhinnapatra,* titled *Glimpses of Bengal,* was published in 1920. *Chhinnapatrabali (Letter-Fragments),* published in 1960, includes only the letters to Indira Devi, in their fuller form, with an additional 107 letters that were left out of the earlier edition.

Tagore wrote to a wide range of recipients. In his personal letters, he expressed his moods and emotions much more directly than in his official correspondence. His letters to his young wife Mrinalini Devi, written between 1890 and 1901, were published in volume 1 of the *Chithipatra* series. They reveal a mixture of tenderness and affection, tinged often with a desire to shape her personality. His letters to the young girl Ranu (later Lady Ranu Mookerji) were published in 1930 as *Bhanusingher Patrabali,* and those to Nirmalkumari Mahalanobis (the wife of scientist Prashanta Mahalanobis, one of Tagore's travel companions during his Europe tour in 1926) appeared in *Pathe O Pather Prante.*

Tagore corresponded with public personalities and literary figures across the world, including Mahatma Gandhi, Albert Einstein, Bertrand Russell, W. B. Yeats, Woodrow Wilson, Yone Noguchi, and Ezra Pound. His letters address an astonishing variety of subjects. In the letter to the scientist J. C. Bose, he muses on poetry, science, and human life in relation to the cosmos. To Myron B. Phelps, he writes about the evils of the caste system, East-West relations, and the need for a revitalized, more egalitarian society in India. In the letter to C. F. Andrews, he comes out against the idea of noncooperation as a mode of nationalist protest against British rule, and dwells on the implications of the zamindari or landowning system to which he belongs—concerns also voiced in his fiction and prose writings.

In his letters, we see Tagore as a man often assailed by self-doubt. The letter to Edward Thompson, written in response to his biography of Tagore, is steeped in anxiety about the seduction of fame, which can breed complacency. The letters to William Rothenstein, Robert Bridges, and James Drummond Anderson, included here, express Tagore's concern about his limited command of English, his thoughts on translation, and his sensitivity to the reception of his works abroad. To Romain Rolland, he writes of the "civil war" in his heart, between his solitary instincts as a poet and his urge to collaborate with others as a social activist and philanthropist.

Some of Tagore's most significant interventions in political history were in the form of letters. Perhaps his most famous letter is the one addressed to Lord Chelmsford, in which he rejects his knighthood in reaction to the massacre of innocent Indians in Jallianwallah Bagh in Amritsar in 1919. In the letter to Pulinbehari Sen, he explains the context in which he composed the song "Janaganamana Adhinayaka," the national anthem of India. Everywhere, his secular, humanitarian approach is apparent. In the letters to Gandhi and to Mahadev Desai included here, for instance, he critiques the exclusionary practice of worship in temples, and shows his openness to religions other than his own.

Tagore's letters vary in style according to the subject, context, and addressee. Some letters bear a strong autobiographical and confessional vein, some read like journal entries, and others paint word-pictures, offer capsules of philosophy, or are full of passionate argument. The letters often cross generic boundaries. Some, for instance, belong in the genre of travel literature, and are represented in the appropriate section of this volume. Others, like the letters to Kanti Chandra Ghosh, Kazi Nazrul Islam, and Sufia Kamal, are prefaces to books, sometimes written in verse. Tagore used the epistolary form even in his fiction, as in the story "The Wife's Letter."

It would be a mistake, though, to read Tagore's letters as a factual record of his life and thoughts, for many of them are examples of conscious self-fashioning. A number of the letters are significant for their literary rather than documentary value, registering his always acute and sensitive responses to what was happening around him, and sometimes transcending the factual to reflect a visionary perspective. Tagore's letters, expectedly, are not as consciously structured as his more formal literary writings. Full of digressions and pensive musings, they traverse the space between the private man and his public persona.

From *Torn Leaves*

NO. 10

To Indira Devi
Shilaidaha
[November 1889]

Our boat has docked at a sandbank facing Shilaidaha. The sandbank is vast and desolate. One cannot see its end—only the contour of the river appears here and there; sometimes the sand mirages as a river—no villages around, no human beings, no trees, no grass—for variety, only the wet and cracked black soil at places, or dry white dust. If one looks towards the east, one sees the endless blue above and endless grey below; the sky is empty, the earth too; sparse dry hard emptiness below, and an insubstantial liberal emptiness above. Such desolation cannot be seen anywhere. A sudden glance at the west reveals the placid lap of the little river, the steep bank on the other side; trees and huts—giving the appearance of a strange dream in the light of the evening sun. As if one bank of the river sees creation while the other sees cataclysm. The reason the light of the evening sun has been evoked here: we usually choose the evening for a stroll and the picture of the evening remains etched in our mind. Living in Calcutta, one forgets how beautiful the earth really is. It's only when one lives here that one realizes how uncommon and sublime are the events that take place in our universe—such as the daily sunsets amid the trees along the little river, or the silent emergence of thousands of stars above the solitary and silent sandbanks every night. What a great book it is that the sun so leisurely unfolds every dawn, and what strange runes are scribbled on the leaf that the sun slowly turns above the sky from the west in the evening—and this skimpy river and this sandbank stretching to the horizon and that neglected edge of the world beyond the other shore that spreads like a picture—what huge, hushed lonesome place of learning is this! Let that be. These words sound much like "poetry" in the capital city, but here, they are never out of place. In the evening boys who have been allowed out on the sandbank romp across to one side with their companions. I go to another side, while the two women trek to yet another. The sun meanwhile drops below the horizon, the golden glimmer in the sky dissolves, and everything around becomes indistinct in the gathering darkness. Eventually the slim shadow emerging by my side tells me that the slender crescent moon has begun to cast its light bit by bit—the pale moonlight falling on the pale sand below creates a different kind of confusion in the eyes—I just have to imagine where the sand, the water, the earth or the sky lies. Everything gets into a tangle, giving the feel of an unreal, mirage-like world. Yesterday, after wandering on this illusory shore for a long while I went back to the boat, and saw that except for the boys, no one had returned. I sat still on a chair, and began reading a book on a very hazy subject, *Animal Magnetism,* under hazy lamplight. But nobody still seemed to have returned. So I placed the book face down on the bed and came out. From the top of the boat I could see no trace of any black head anywhere—everything around was pale and desolate. I shouted with all my strength: "Bolu!" My hollow voice travelled in all ten directions, but no one responded. I felt my heart sink a bit, like a big open umbrella suddenly collapsing. Gafur came out with a light. Prasanna followed him; the boatmen too came out. We divided into groups and went in several directions. I kept calling "Bolu, "Bolu" from one end—Prasanna too went on calling "Chhoto Ma" from another—now and then the boatmen shouted "Babu, Babu." In the silent night the desert was filled with our anguished voices. But no one answered. Once or twice Gafur shouted from afar "There she is!" and then corrected himself "No," "Not really." Imagine the state of my mind! And you can only begin to imagine it all if you conjure up the whole picture—the silent night, the pale moonlight, the solitary, silent empty sandbank, the flickering light of Gafur's swinging lantern in the distance, periodic distressed calls from different directions and their vacant echoes. All kinds of apprehensive thoughts flashed through my mind. If at times I thought Bolu might have stepped into quicksand, at other times I kept thinking she might have fainted or had been struck by some other affliction; sometimes I felt in my imagination the horror created by the thought of wild beasts. I began to feel that "those who are unable to protect themselves, unworriedly bring danger for others." As I hardened myself against women's liberation, there was a hue and cry to the effect that Bolu had mounted the slope to go to the other side of the river and had got stuck there. The boat was rowed to the other bank, the boat-lady returned to the boat. She kept saying "I won't go out with you ever again." Everyone was apologetic, tired, distressed, so my well-meaning, palatable words of admonition remained unuttered—even the next morning when I got up, I didn't have the resolve to be angry.

NO. 14

Patisar

6 Magh 1891

I have tied my boat in a secluded place quite far from my kachhari which I use as my office. Here, there is no clutter or clamor; one may find it in the marketplace, may be, along with sundry other items, but not here. Besides, where I have reached now, no human faces can be seen. All around a huge empty field gives a look of desolation—the paddy has been harvested and only the stubble remains, overwhelming the whole field. Yesterday, at the end of the day, towards sunset, I went out for a walk in the field. The sun gradually took a blood-red hue and disappeared behind the last horizon line. How can I describe the inexplicable beauty that flushed the world! Far away, near the farthest edge of the horizon, a cluster of trees lay in a circle—the place appeared so graceful that I thought that was where Evening has its abode; there she loosens her crimson sari-edge, carefully lights up her evening star, sits waiting in her private solitude like a bride, her hairline decked in vermilion, and, stretching her legs out, strings a garland of stars, humming a dream. On the whole stretch of the endless field fell a shadow—a soft sadness—not tears, but something like the feeling of moist heaviness under the long eyelashes of an unblinking eye. One may even imagine that Mother Earth was living here in a human settlement with her children amid much noise and going about her household chores—but wherever there was some empty space, a spell of quietness, or a bit of open sky, she was divulging her great heart's indifference and revealing the sadness in her heart. Only in such a place could one hear her deep sighs. One doubts if any place in Europe ever offers the unbounded, clear skies and the interminably stretching plain lands one sees in India. That is why the Indian nation has been able to discover the infinite indifference of this great world. That is why our Purabi and Todi ragas express the desolation of the heart of this wide world—not anyone's private grief. There is a side to the world which is diligent, affectionate and limited but it didn't have the scope to influence us with that mood. Rather, it is the world's solitary, rare and infinite mood that has made us so indifferent. That is why when the strings of the violin strum the mirh of the Bhairavi raga, Indians feel a pull in their hearts. Last evening, the secluded field resonated with raga Purabi, and I was the only soul wandering around for miles, while another living being stood as if self-possessed near the boat with a stick in his hand and wearing a turban. On my left, the small river meandered along the channel lying between steep banks and went out of sight after a while. There was not even a trace of a wave in it; only the evening glow stuck at it for some time like a dying smile. The field was as immense as was the solitude. There were only the birds—forming a class of their own—who build their nests in the ground. As darkness thickened, one of these birds began to tweet distrustfully, chirping all the more as I frequented the neighborhood of its nest. In a while the moon of the dark phase began to give out a tiny glow—with my head bowed in thought I began to walk along the narrow foot-trail on the edge of the field near the river.

NO. 15

The time of the day is perfect for lazing around. No one to rush me, no crowd of tenants or crunch of work yet. Everything seems to be peaceful, unhurried, lonely—as if there is nothing in the world called "urgent"—as if it is all the same whether one takes a bath or decides not to—the habit among the people of Calcutta to take their meals on time appears to be an old superstition here. The mood of this place reflects that un-hurried pace. There is a small river here, but it has hardly any current. Spreading its limbs among the tangle of watercress and moss, the river lies supine and seems to ask itself, if it is alright not to flow, why bother? The tall grass and aquatic weed that have grown in its placid water would lie still the whole day if the fishermen didn't cast their nets. Five or six large boats remain moored in a row, and on top of one, a boatman lies napping in the sun, wrapping himself head to toe in a piece of cloth. Atop another, someone is braiding a rope. And basking in the sun, near the oar, is a middle-aged man with a bare torso who squats, gawking at our boat for no reason. On the bank, people of different descriptions dawdle unsurely towards a destination—why, no one knows. No one knows why someone sits on his heels, hugging his knees, or someone else stands casting an uncertain look at nothing in particular. Only a small flock of ducks shows a semblance of activity—they squawk rather loudly and with increasing enthusiasm dip their heads into water, pulling them up at once and shaking them violently. It seems as if the ducks are out to discover the dark mysteries of the underwater world, and shoving their long necks every minute and then withdrawing them, shout "nothing there—nothing." The days here bask lazily in the sun for twelve hours, and for the remaining twelve hours they wrap themselves up in a pro-found darkness and sleep soundlessly. Here, looking at the wide world outside, one feels like gently rocking the thoughts that cross the mind, and humming a tune while the eyes from time to time turn lazy or heavy with sleep—like a mother in winter sitting with her back to the sun the whole day with her child in her lap, rocking him, and singing a tune in a hushed voice!

NO. 23

Chuhali / on the waterway
16 June 1891

We are moving full sail down the middle of the Jamuna. On my left are fields where cows are grazing, towards the south the shoreline disappears from view. The strong current of the river is loosening chunks of earth from the banks which collapse with a persistent crash. The strange thing is that, except for our boat, there is no second boat in sight in the entire expanse of this huge river—all around can be heard the lapping sound of surging water and the whistling wind. Yesterday, towards the evening, we moved the boat on a sandbank—this river is actually a tributary of the little Jamuna. On one side of the river, a nearly unending stretch of white sand, unrelieved by any human presence; on the other, green crop land, and far away, a village. How do I repeat myself when I describe how amazingly beautiful the evening is on the river, in the field, in the village! One can only feel its vastness, its peace and its profundity in tranquility—to describe it is to become restless. Gradually, when everything around became indistinct in the dark, only the line of water could be distinguished from the shore line and the trees and the huts dissolved into each other to compose a hazy world that lay in a wide sweep in front of my eyes. I felt as if all this was nothing but the manifestation of the spectacular fairy world of our childhood—when this scientific world hadn't formed fully, the process of creation had just begun, the whole world had been wrapped in the gloom of dawn in a palpable, terrifying stillness—when in the illusory land beyond the seven seas and thirteen rivers the exceedingly beautiful princess lay in eternal rest, when the prince and the minister's son were roaming the vast stretches of wilderness with an impossible resolve—as if this silent riverside belonged to that far distant and forgotten world, enchanted and illusive in some state of semi-consciousness. And I can even imagine that the prince who is roaming the evening world with an impossible resolve is me—this small river is one of those thirteen, and the seven seas remain to be traversed—things are still far off; so many events, so many quests still remain—on many unknown shores, on many unfamiliar strands so many moonlit nights still keep waiting for their turn—and then, after so many journeys, so many tears, so much heartache my words may cease, the proverbial leaf fold itself—suddenly it might seem that all the while I was just telling a tale, but that now the tale has ended, it is midnight, time for all children to go to sleep.

NO. 26

Shajadpur
22 June 1891

70

What more can I say about the wonderful moonlit nights here? Of course, it's not my design to say that the place this letter is meant to reach doesn't see such nights—I have to admit that there too, the light of the moon silently extends its sway over the big field, over that church steeple and the silent trees in front. But there, you have five other things besides the light of the moon—here I have nothing else before me but the silent night. I can't tell you what boundless peace and beauty I see in the heart of the night, sitting all by myself. There are some people who grow restless and keep asking "why can't we apprehend all that the world says," and there are others who become agitated saying "why can't we express all that we feel in our hearts"—But in the process, all that the world has to say remains with the world, and the hearts' utterance remain locked within. I rest my head on the window frame—the wind, as if it is the affectionate hand of nature, gently strokes my hair with its fingers, the water flows with a lapping sound and moonlight shines on, and many a time my eyes "overflow with involuntary tears." Sometimes, unfeigned feelings of hurt or an affectionate word releases a gush of tears. Despite the lifelong grievance we have against nature for our unsatisfying life, whenever she shows her loving face, that grievance melts and turns into teardrops. Nature then begins to caress us more and more and we hide our faces in her bosom with redoubled passion.

NO. 52

Shilaidaha
Wednesday, 2 Asadh 1299

Yesterday, on the first day of Asadh, the monsoon had its coronation amid much fanfare. The day was very hot, but towards afternoon the sky became dark with thick clouds.

Yesterday, I thought that on the first day of monsoon, it was better to get wet than spend the day inside a dark well. The year '99 would never come twice in my life—and come to think of it, out of the total number of years that we live, how many times do we see the first of As-adh? If all those new Asadh days add up to thirty, one would say it's been quite a life. After *Meghdoot* had been written, the first day of Asadh as-sumed a special significance, at least for me. I often think how each day a new day dawns in my life—some steeped in the hues of the rising or set-ting sun, some in the shimmering blue of reflecting clouds; some cheer-ful like white flowers in the light of the full moon—how very fortunate I am! Are these any less precious! After Kalidasa welcomed the first day of Asadh a thousand years ago, in my life too, every year the first day of As-adh dawns with all its treasure filling the entire sky—it is the same first Asadh day belonging to the ancient poet living in ancient Ujjayani, as well as to hundreds of men and women of different ages with their hap-piness and pain, separation and union. Each year sees the disappearance one more time of that ancient, great first day of Asadh from my life. Eventually a time will come when fortune will not preserve even a single one of these celebrated days of Kalidasa, of *Meghdoot,* the first day of the Indian monsoon—for me. When I ponder over this possibility, a desire grows in me to look closely at the world again; to consciously greet each sunrise in my life and say goodbye to each sunset like I would to a good friend. If I were of saintly character I could imagine that life is perishable, and, therefore, instead of wasting it everyday, spend it doing good work and reciting the Lord's name. But that is not my nature—and so from time to time I ask myself, why can't I gather all those enchanting days and nights that are vanishing from my life! All these colors, this light and shade, this silent splendor spreading to the end of the sky, this peace and grace filling up all the empty spaces between heaven and earth—is there any end to the spectacle! How vast is the ground of festivity! And how meager is the response of our hearts to this feast! Do we live at such dis-tance from the world? The light of a star reaches this earth from millions of miles away, traversing millions of years through endless darkness, but stops short at our hearts—as if our hearts lie even farther, millions of miles away. The brilliant mornings and nights drop into the ocean like gems coming unstrung from the torn necklace of a housewife, but none drops in our midst! That magical sunset I saw on the still waters of the Red Sea on my way to England—where has it gone? But it was my good fortune that I saw the sunset, it was my good fortune once again that one more evening didn't go to waste because I chose not to neglect it. No other poet in the world except me has witnessed that miraculous sunset among all the endless days and nights. Its colors are still there in my life. Such days are like precious treasures. A few days I spent in the garden of Peneti, a few nights on the roof of that three-storied building, a few rainy days on the western and southern verandas, a sunset and a moonrise on the Sinchal peak in Darjeeling—these are some of the nuggets of time that I have preserved as if in a file. When in my childhood I used to linger on the roof in moonlit spring nights, I felt as if the moonlight was overflowing like the white foam of some wine drowning me in strong intoxication. But the people of the world where I have come to live must be strange characters or else why are they erecting rules and walls day and night, lest their eyes see something, and why are they erecting screens with such care? The creatures of this world are really strange. It's a surprise that they haven't already put enclosures around flowering plants or erected a canopy under the moon. What sights of the world can these willfully blind ones see as they ride in enclosed palanquins!

If the afterworld conforms to our desires and is in accordance with our austere devotional practices, then may I take my leave from this world that lies wrapped in a cover, and be born in a joyful world of generous unbounded beauty. Only those who are really unable to immerse themselves in beauty scorn beauty merely as a wealth of the senses. But those who have plumbed its indescribable depths know that beauty is something that lies beyond the ultimate power of the senses; if we enter its world with all our heart, let alone with all our eyes and ears, there cannot be any end to our longing.

I have been moving in the avenues of the city dressed as a gentleman, exchanging polite words with impeccable gentlemen and in the process, spending a useless life. I am uncivilized and rude in my heart—isn't there any exceedingly beautiful chaos anywhere for me? A joyful fair of some desperate people? But wait—what am I saying!—this is how poetic heroes speak, delivering a three to four page soliloquy on conventionality and considering themselves greater than the denizens of human society. Honestly, I am embarrassed to say these things. But the truth they contain has been suppressed by the babel of ages. Everyone in the world speaks solemnly, and I am at their forefront. I realize that truth all of a sudden.

> N.B.: I managed to forget what I really wanted to say. Don't be afraid—I won't take four more pages to do so—what I wanted to say is just this—it rained quite heavily in the afternoon of the first of Asadh.

NO. 69

Balia
Tuesday, February 1893

No, I don't feel like travelling anymore. What I desire most is to chat for a while and then sit in a corner all by myself. There are two sides to India—on the one side are the householders, and on the other, hermits; some don't stir out from the corners of their houses, some do not have a house at all. I feel the presence of both types of Indians within myself. The house-corner pulls me, the world outside also beckons me. I feel the urge to go on long travels, and, just as well, when I am tired and confused, I begin to crave for a nest. Just like a bird: the little nest is good enough for me to live in, and the huge sky to spread my wings. The corner I love most is where I can compose my mind. My mind tends to work tirelessly within its own inward spaces, but in a crowd, its enterprise gets rudely repulsed at every step—so much so that it becomes restless—and keeps pecking at me as if from inside a cage. In a moment of solitude, it can think as it wishes, can look around, can articulate its feelings the way it likes. It wants uninterrupted leisure day and night—just as the Creator sits alone amidst his creation, my mind too wants to rule over its world of thought alone.

NO. 70

Cuttak
10 February 1893

74

A grotesque-looking Englishman lives here, who has a huge nose, cunning eyes, a foot-length chin, clean-shaven face, coarse voice: a fully grown John Bull. There is strong resentment everywhere against the government's attempt to interfere in our jury system. The Englishman forced the topic into his conversation with Mr. B_____ and picked up an argument. The moral standard of this country is low, he said; the people here do not have much faith in the sacredness of life; they are not fit to become members of a jury. What impression do people like him have of us!—this man who comes as an invited guest to a Bengali's house, sits among other Bengalis, and doesn't hesitate to speak in such a fashion. When I moved from the dining table to a corner of the drawing room, I felt as if a shade had spread in front of my eyes, as if the whole expanse of great India was lying before me, and I was sitting at the head of my sad motherland bereft of any glory—I can't tell you what a massive melancholy possessed my whole heart. Yet, the whole thing was fraught with ambiguity—Memsahib in her evening dress, and the hum of laughter and small talk in English within my hearing. How real is our eternal India to me—and how empty and hollow this sweet English laughter is, this English small talk at the dinner table!

NO. 73

Balia
March 1893

The boat I am using is a small one. But its chief end appears to be to humble the vanity of a tall person like me about his height. If I inadvertently raise my head a little, a wooden plank of the boat gives it a huge whack—which suddenly sinks my spirit. That's why I've been going about with a bowed head since yesterday. In addition to all the pain and hurt fate has in store for me, now, each time I try to stand up, I invite new afflictions. That however, is something I don't mind much; but last night the mosquitoes just wouldn't let me sleep. This I think is positively unfair.

Meanwhile, the days are heating up after the spell of winter; the sun is getting hot, even as a cool damp breeze is blowing through the boat window and caressing my back. Today, there is no special concession for winter or civilization; my baize chapkan and choga—coat and long coat—hang suspended from a hook. No bell rings to usher in a well-dressed valet, saluting and waiting for me to order. I am enjoying an unclean ease and comfort of incivility. The birds warble and on the shore, the leaves of two big banyan trees rustle in the wind—the trembling water reflects the sunlight inside the boat: the day progresses in such a leisurely fashion. While I was in Cuttak I could very much feel how precious time was and the haste of civilized human society as I saw the hurry of school children and Mr. B_____ rushing to the Court. But here, time has no puny divisions, but only the two large markers—day and night.

NO. 75

Cuttak
6 March 1893

And then I listened to the Englishman's songs, I too sang for him, clapped, and received his applause. But this applause that we get—does it really find a place in our hearts? Isn't it a gratification of some curiosity? Is it a fact that whatever I like, they also like? And, what they don't like, is really not worth liking? If that is so, why should I be so happy, hearing their claps? If we begin to put an extra value to an Englishman's applause, then we have to forsake many good things of our country, and accept many bad things of theirs. Then we might feel embarrassed to go out without wearing socks, but won't feel embarrassed about putting on their dance costumes. We don't hesitate to flout our own etiquette, but are willing to embrace many of their age-old, impolite manners without batting an eyelid. We will discard our own achkan—short coat—as an imperfect dress, but will put on our head with all humility a horrible looking cap from their country. Either knowingly or unknowingly we keep on casting our lives according to the directives of the applause, and make it very small. I address myself and say, "O earthen pot, keep away from that bell-metal pot; if it gets angry and hits you, you'll turn into smithereens; and if it pats you on the back even out of affection, you'll crack and sink to the fathomless depths—therefore, listen to Old Aesop's advice: Keep your distance. That's the essence. Let the bell-metal pot stay in a big house and here, in this modest house, a modest pot like me may have its utility—but if it shatters itself, it will neither have a big house, nor a small one, but will be reduced to just plain earth. In that case, perhaps the owner of the big house will pick up the shards and keep them near the cabinet of his drawing room—only as a curiosity—but surely, it is more worthwhile to reign sovereign in the room of a village housewife."

NO. 80

Shilaidaha
8 May 1893

Poetry is my long-time sweetheart—indeed, we probably got engaged when I was Rathi's age. From then on, the base of the banyan tree near our pond, the garden inside the house, the undiscovered rooms in the ground floor of the house, the whole outside world, and the rhymes and the fairytales I heard from the female servants created a world of enchantment inside me. It is very difficult to express the feelings of my singular shadowy mind, but this much I can say—I had, by then, already exchanged garlands with Poetic Fancy. But I have to admit that the lady is hardly auspicious; if anything, she never brings good luck. I can't say she doesn't give happiness, but when it comes to comfort, she has nothing to do with it. Whoever she embraces, she gives intense pleasure for a while, but then the embrace becomes so tight that she seems to suck all the blood out of his heart. The person she selects—the luckless one—finds it impossible to pitch himself in the middle of domestic life as a householder and stay placid and relaxed. But I have pawned my real life to her. Whether I write for *Sadhana*[1] or look after my estate, whenever I begin to write a poem, I enter into what is my eternal, true self—I quite realize that this is where I belong. It is possible to indulge in many falsities in life, either knowingly or unknowingly, but I never lie in my poems—it is the only sanctuary of all the profound truths of my life.

NO. 84

Shelidah
16 May 1893

I take a bath after six-thirty in the evening. This gives me a cool and clean feeling. Afterwards, I walk on the sandbank along the edge of the river for an hour, then tug our new jolly boat to the middle of the river, make a bed on its top deck, and lie down on my back in the gathering darkness with a cool breeze blowing. Sh___ sits nearby and prattles on. The sky above is spangled with stars. Looking at the spectacle almost every day, I wonder if I will ever be born again under such a star-studded sky! Will I, ever again, lie down on a bed atop this jolly boat on such a peaceful evening, on this placid Gorai river, in this beautiful corner of the land of Bengal, in such a mood! I might not get back such an evening in any of my reincarnations again! Who knows what profound changes will take place then—and what would be the state of my mind in those births. I may get many such evenings, but not one of them will ever lie spreading her hair on my bosom, so silently and with such profound love. What is more, will I be the same person then! Strangely enough, what I fear most is being born again somewhere in Europe. For, in that place, it is not possible to cast your spirit upward and laze in indolence—that, to all Europeans, is an abomination. I might have to work heart and soul in a factory, or in a bank, or in a Parliament. Just as the city streets there are paved in brick for the ease of traffic, the minds of the people, and their habits too, are cast in concrete for them to be fit to conduct business—leaving no space for a tender leaf of grass or a plant to grow. Very ship-shape. But I can't say why, compared to that, my fancy-loving, idle and self-indulgent mind containing the whole wide sky within doesn't appear to be something I have to be ashamed of. Lying down on my jolly boat, I can never deem myself to be any less insignificant than those active people of the world. On the contrary, if I got down to business resolutely, I might have appeared small compared to those youthful, oak-tree felling people.

NO. 92

Shajadpur
30 Asadh 1893

Nowadays, writing poetry has become for me a kind of secret and forbidden delight. I haven't, however, written a line for next month's *Sadhana*. While the editor is sending periodic reminders, nearby, the Aswin-Kartik double issue of *Sadhana* waits with empty hands, looking at me with reproachful eyes, and making me take refuge in the inner courtyards of my poetry. Everyday I say to myself: "just one more day"—but soon the days pile up. I can't really decide what my real task is. Sometimes I feel I can write a great many short stories and write them quite well too, and find pleasure in doing so. At other times, I feel that the moods and feelings that cross my mind cannot be written down in poetry; it is better to record them in the form of a diary or some such genre. Perhaps this is more productive and pleasurable as well. Sometimes it is very important to cross swords with our people on social issues, and when no one else is doing so, I must take this unpleasant task upon myself—and at other times I think, what the heck, let the world oil its own machine—I'd rather leave everything, and sitting by myself in my own little corner, do something that comes naturally to me—play with rhymes and rhythms and compose brief poems. Just as a vainly passionate young woman doesn't want to let go any of her lovers, I too have a similar dilemma. I don't want to disappoint any of my Muses—but this only adds to the burden of my work, and perhaps, in the long run, I'll fail to get a proper hold on any of them. Even in the real discipline of literature, sense of duty has its sway, but it is a bit different from the sense of duty in other disciplines. In literature, my sense of duty isn't concerned with what brings the most benefit to the world, but with what I can do best. This may be true for all other disciplines of life. As far as my wits tell me, it is poetry where I have the greatest competence. But the flames of my hunger want to spread everywhere in the world outside and inside my mind. When I get down to compose a song, I feel I should keep doing this one particular task; but when I indulge in a bit of acting, it becomes such an addiction that I begin to believe that this is a field where one may spend a lifetime. And again, when I get busy with "Child Marriage" or "Differences in Education," I tend to see such work as the best preoccupation in life. And yet again, putting aside all modesty, I may honestly admit that I have always cast the covetous look of a forsaken lover at the discipline called painting which is now beyond my power as the age for an engagement with it is gone. Like other Muses, painting too doesn't submit herself so easily— her unflinching vow seems to be: unless one is totally exhausted plying the brush, one cannot receive her favor. It is therefore most advantageous for me to live with poetry alone—I believe she has yielded herself most to me—she has been my devoted and long-time companion since my childhood.

Regarding the question that has been raised about a silent or voiceless poet, my view is that although the intensity of feeling may be the same among the voiced and the voiceless, real poetic genius is something else. It is not the power of language alone, but the ability to create. Feelings, in the hand of a poet, assume spectacular shapes through invisible, unselfconscious skills. This creative power is at the root of poetic genius. Language, mood and feelings are only its tools. Someone has the words, someone has the feelings, someone else has both the words and the feelings; but there is another one who has the words, feelings and the creative power—only this person can be called a poet. The first three may be voiced or voiceless, but they are not poets. One or two of them may at best be called imaginative or reflective. But then, they too are quite rare in this world, and the poet's thirsty soul forever pines for them.

After this introduction, it will be easier for me to explain my poem "Jaal Phela" ("Casting the Net"). If I had the poem with me, I could have read it again to understand its meaning better before trying to explain it. Still, I have a vague notion about what the poem is about. Imagine someone standing near the sea of the dawn of his life and looking at the sunrise. That sea may be in his own mind, or the world out there, or the sea of thoughts and moods in between the two—the poem however doesn't state any of this clearly. Whatever that may be, the man looks at that unparalleled spectacle of the fathomless sea and thinks: why not cast my net into these mysterious waters and see what I can collect? He then casts his net wide into the sea. The net begins to haul a wealth of exquisite items—some dazzling like a smile, some radiant like a tear drop, some flushed like bashfulness. The man keeps casting his net with great pleasure throughout the day; he drags from the bottomless depth all sort of mysteries and piles them up on the shore. And he spends the whole livelong day in this manner. In the evening, he decides he has done enough for now; he would rather carry his finds to someone. Who this someone is, the poem doesn't make explicit. That someone could be his beloved, or his motherland. But the one who would receive his rare offerings hasn't seen them before. The man thinks: what could these be? Are these really necessary? Would these help drive away want? What could be their value if he takes them to the marketplace for assessment? In other words, these are not science, philosophy, history, geography, economics, sociology, theology or theory—these are only some colorful ideas and moods. Even then he can't tell which one goes by what name or description. Indeed, the person he gives the gems to, culled from the bottomless sea with his net through a day's labor queries, what are these? The wielder of the net himself is repentant—he says to himself, what I've collected isn't anything special; I've only cast my net and pulled. I haven't been to the market, haven't spent any money, didn't have to pay anyone even a pennyworth of tax or tariff. He feels a bit embarrassed and sad, and collects all the gems, sits down at his door and throws them onto the road one by one. The next day, some passers-by pick up those precious gems and take them to their homes here and abroad. I think the person who wrote this poem felt that his domestic chore-loving, inner dwelling-bound motherland and his contemporary readers wouldn't be able to decipher the thoughts of his poems; they are simply unaware of his value; therefore, for now, all these gems are thrown on to the road—you will neglect them, I too will neglect them, but at the end of the night, posterity will pick them up and take them in different directions. But will that assuage the net wielder's feeling of regret?

Whatever the case might be, I don't think anyone should object to the poet relishing the pleasurable feeling that posterity, like a woman on a love tryst, is slowly approaching the poet throughout the long night, and might even turn up at his door at the end of the night. I don't exactly recollect what that poem about the temple meant. I guess it is about a real temple. In other words, when, sitting in a corner and immersing one's gods in some false fancy, and, in the process, driving one's own mind into an intense abnormal state—if, at such a moment, a bolt of doubt splinters those age-old false walls, then, suddenly, the splendor of nature, the light of the sun, and a joyful chorus sung by the people of the world stream inside to take the place of charms and incantations, incense and lamp—and then only I will realize that only this is real prayer and the gods are going to be pleased with it.

NO. 120

Patisar
10 September 1894

A day in the month of Bhadra—not much of a wind blowing, the sagging sail of the boat hanging loose—and the boat moving at a slow and lazy pace with complete disinterestedness. In this huge weed-filled watery world, in the bright autumn sun, I sit on a wooden chouki with my legs stretched on another and hum the tune of a song. As soon as I evoke even the semblance of a note of Ramkeli or any other morning raga, an all-pervading compassion begins to melt and turn the world around tearful, and to me all these ragas seem to be music that belongs to the whole sky and the whole world. This is an illusion, a magical spell. There is no end to all the scattered words that I add to the humming tunes of mine. How many of these one-line songs have accumulated throughout the day, and how many I have thrown away! Sitting on this chouki, it is beyond my power for now to take more than the effortless slothfulness that gets into me as I move on to taste the golden sunlight with my eyes, and lightly touch the tenderness of the moss floating on the water. I remember the two or three lines that I recited throughout the morning in rather ordinary Ramkeli. I may quote them as an example:

> Come, O you, inside my heart in ever new likeness
> (O my eternally new one!)
> Come as scent, color and melody!
> Come, O you, wherever I cast my eyes
> Come inside my closed enchanted eyes!

(Extracts from *Chhinnapatra*)
Translated by Syed Manzoorul Islam

From *Letter-Fragments*

NO. 1

Darjeeling
September 1887[2]

Have only just landed up at Darjeeling. Beli *behaved* very well on the way. Didn't cry very much. Although she did shout and create a disturbance, also ululated, also turned her hands around and called out to the birds, although one couldn't see where the birds were. There was a huge amount of disorder while boarding the steamer at Shara-ghat. Ten o'clock at night—hundreds of bags and things, two coolies, five women, and only one man. After crossing the river we managed to get on to a small train which had four sleepers while we (including Makhan) were six human beings. The women and some of the things were loaded on to the *ladies' compartment*—that statement sounds brief, but the act itself was not exactly similarly precise. There was a huge amount of running around and calling and shouting involved—still, Na-didi says I didn't do a thing. That is, that a full-grown man such as myself, accompanying five women, should have done a great deal more of calling and shouting and running around, and should have sometimes got off here or there on the *platform* to stride around spouting Hindustani. That is, it would have been much more appropriate for me to have become the image of what happens when an entire man gets entirely incensed—that would have been much manlier. Na-didi was not a little *disappointed* to see my cool demeanor. But in these two days I have opened so many boxes and closed them again and shoved them underneath benches and then pulled them out again from aforesaid place, and I have gone around after so many boxes and things tied up in cloth bundles, and so many of these boxes and bundles have followed me around like a curse, so many have been lost and so many found again, and so many not found again and then so much effort having tried and still trying to retrieve those not found again, that no twenty-six year old son of civilized parents has had such things written in his destiny. I have developed a veritable box-*phobia*—when I see a box, my teeth start chattering. When I look all around me and all I see are boxes, only boxes, small, big, medium, light and heavy, wooden and tin and animal-leather and cloth—one on top, one below, one on the side, one behind—then all my ordinary strength to call and shout and run around ebbs away—and then if you see my vacant gaze, drawn face and poor aspect you will think I am no less than a coward—therefore Na-didi's opinion of me is quite correct—fallen in the midst of this variegated diversity of boxes, I was not myself. Tell Suren to draw a picture of me in this state. Anyway. After that I got into another compartment and lay down. That compartment had two Bengalis in it. They had come from Dhaka—the moment you saw them you thought of them somehow as Dhakai—one of the two had a head almost completely bald and speech that was extremely skewed—he asked me, "Was your father on Darjeeling?" If Lakkhi had been there she would have had an appropriate answer; perhaps she would have said: "He was on Darjeeling, but Darjeeling was feeling cold then, so he has gone home now." My reflexes couldn't supply me with such Bengali.

From Siliguri to Darjeeling, Sarala's continuous wonder-struck *exclamations.* "O my, how wonderful" "how amazing" "how beautiful"—she kept nudging me and saying, "Rabimama, look, look." What to do, I must look at whatever she shows me—sometimes trees, sometimes clouds, once an invincible blunt-nosed mountain-girl, or sometimes so many things at the same time that the train leaves it all behind in an in-

83

stant and Sarala is unhappy that Rabi-mama didn't get to see it, although Rabi-mama is quite unrepentant. The train kept on going. Beli kept on sleeping. Forests, hilltops, mountains, streams, clouds and a vast number of flat noses and slant eyes began to be seen. Progressively it became wintry, and then there were clouds, and then Na-didi developed a cold, and then Bar-didi began to sneeze, and then shawls, blankets, quilts, thick socks, frozen feet, cold hands, blue faces, sore throats, and, right after, Darjeeling. Again those boxes, those bags, that bedding, the same bundles. Luggage piled on luggage, bearers upon bearers. Getting all the things kept in the *brake,* identifying them, loading them on the heads of the bearers, showing the receipt to the sahib, arguing with the sahib, not finding things, and then making various arrangements to find those lost things—all this took about six hours, by which time Na-didi and company had got into their conveyance, gone home, wrapped themselves in shawls, reclined on sofas and were thinking to themselves that Rabi is not really very manly.

Calcutta

16 September 1887

31.5.1294

NO. 6

Shazadpur

January 1890

So it was that in the afternoon I put on my pagri, put my name on a card, got into my palanquin and set off as the zamindar-babu. The sahib was dispensing justice from the veranda of his tent, the police spies on his south side. Those seeking justice were waiting around on the grounds, the fields, under the trees—the palki was put down right in front of his nose, so the sahib politely seated me on a chair. Laddish type, hint of a moustache, very bleached hair with some patches of black in between— all in all he turned out to be very strange looking, one would suddenly think him an old man, yet the face was very immature. Exchanged a vast

amount of pleasantries with the sahib; said to him, "come and have din-
ner with me tomorrow evening." He said, "I'm leaving for another place
today to arrange for *pig-sticking*." (I was secretly elated) Said I'm very
sorry to hear that. Sahib said, "I return on Monday." (To hear which I
was terribly crestfallen) I said, "Then make it on Monday." He was in-
stantly agreeable. Anyway, I sighed and reminded myself that Monday
was still some distance away, and reached home. The skies became dark
with terrible clouds—immense storm, pounding rain. Didn't feel like
touching a book, impossible to write, the mind became terribly restless,
what in poetic language one would say is a feeling of something missing,
some desired one absent, and not to be found anywhere near, etc. I paced
through this room and that—it had become dark, the thunder had a roll-
ing sound, flash upon flash of lightning, the wind was whistling through
the air and seemed to take hold of the low tree in front of our veranda
and shake it by its beard—in no time at all our dry pond filled up almost
completely . . . I feel like writing another one like that, but perhaps there
is nothing more to write. Anyway, while wandering around in this man-
ner, it suddenly struck me that it was my duty to ask the magistrate to
shelter in my house in this storm. Wrote a letter, "Sahib, you shouldn't
leave for pig-sticking in this weather—although you are the son of a sa-
hib, it is impossible for the species who live on land to reside in tents,
therefore if you think dry land is a good thing, then do come and take
shelter with me." After sending off the letter, when I went to oversee the
room, I saw the room had two bamboo hammocks with mattress, pil-
lows and dirty quilts hanging on them—the servants' tobacco, smoked
tobacco-cake, charcoal dust, two wooden chests, also theirs, a worn out
quilt, a cover-less oily pillow and a blackened cane mat, also theirs, a
piece of torn jute and on top of it a variety of filth—some . . . boxes with
the remnants of broken things such as a rusted kettle lid, a bottomless
broken iron oven, a very dirty zinc sheet, some . . . stems of glasses, shat-
tered glass from a broken lantern, a dirty candlestick, two *filters,* a *meat
safe,* some liquid jaggery in a *soup-plate* thickened with layers of dust,
many broken and whole plates, a number of dirty, wet, black dusters—in
one corner, a bucket to wash plates in, Gofur Mian's dirty kurta and old

velvet *skull cap,* a weather-beaten, ant-eaten, mirror-less *dressing table* adorned with water marks, oil marks, milk marks, jaggery marks, black marks, *brown* marks, white marks and many colored marks—its broken mirror kept leaning somewhere else against a wall, its cavities filled with dust, toothpicks, napkins, old locks, bottoms of broken glass tumblers and *soda water bottle* wires, some bed stands, sticks and rice, one broken-legged *wash-stand stand,* a terrible smell, the walls stained and with some nails driven in here and there—upon seeing this state of affairs, I was completely astounded.—"Call everybody, bring the nayeb, call the khajanchi, find some coolies—bring the broom, bring water, set up the ladder, untie the cord and the bamboo sticks, pull down the pillows, the quilt, the covers, pick up the pieces of broken glass bit by bit, dislodge the nails one by one, hey, what are all of you doing standing there open-mouthed, take, take these things away one by one—o my god, broken, they've broken everything—bang, crash, boom—three lanterns broken to bits—pick them up piece by piece." The dust-laden broken baskets and torn mats I pulled down and threw away with my own hands—five or six cockroaches and their families emerged from under them and scattered all over the place. They had been living with me as part of my extended family—living off my jaggery, my bread, and the varnish off my very own burnished new shoes. The sahib wrote, "I'm coming right now, am in grave danger." "Hey, he's here, he's almost here—hurry up." After which—there comes the sahib. Quickly dusting off my hair and beard, I become quite the gentleman, and behaving as if I had no work at all at hand, as if I had been sitting around at ease the entire day, I sit down with him in the hall. With the occasional smile and much waving of hands I begin to chat with the sahib in a most relaxed manner. The thought of what had become of the sahib's bedroom kept pushing its way into my mind from time to time. Went and saw that it had somehow managed to pass muster. Perhaps the night might even pass peacefully, unless those homeless cockroaches tickle the soles of his feet at night. The sahib said, "I'll leave tomorrow morning for shikar." I didn't raise any objection. In the evening, the paik, scared of the sahib, came and reported that his tent had been torn to pieces in the storm. His kachhari tent too was destroyed in the rain, so the plan to hunt other animals had to be put on hold, and he had to remain stationary at the zamindar-babu's for now.

Calcutta

28 January, 1890

10.10.1293

NO. 17

Shazadpur
February 1891

On some days, the postmaster of this place comes over occasionally in the evenings and begins to chat with me, telling me many stories about the letters coming and going in the mail. The post office is on the ground floor of this bungalow of ours—it's very convenient, we get our letters the moment they arrive. I quite enjoy the stories the postmaster tells. He keeps narrating all sorts of the most amazing stories in a completely serious manner. Yesterday he was saying, the people in this part of the country have such an extreme faith in the Ganga that, when a relative dies, they grind the bones and keep it, and then when they meet someone who has drunk Ganges water, they feed him those ground bones mixed in a paan, and think that some part of their relative has at last found the Ganga. I began to laugh, and said, "This is a story, perhaps?" He thought over it quite seriously and admitted, "Sir, that could be the case."

Calcutta

10 February, 1891

29.10.1297

NO. 23

Shazadpur
23 June 1891
10.3.1298

These days I quite enjoy the afternoons, Bob.[3] All around it is very quiet in the sun—the mind becomes very capricious, I take a book in hand, but don't feel like reading. A kind of smell of grass emanates from the river bank where the boat is tied, and from time to time, you feel the hot breath of the earth upon your body—it is as if this living, heated up earth is breathing upon you from very close up, and perhaps my breath too is grazing its body. The short stalks of the rice plants tremble in the breeze—the ducks descend upon the water and continuously dip their heads into it and clean the feathers upon their backs with their beaks. There is no other sound, except when the water, pushing at the boat, makes it slowly lean over until the boat's steps and cable keep making a tender, soft sound. Not very far away there is a ferry ghat. All sorts of people have collected under the banyan tree to wait for the ferry, the moment the boat arrives, they quickly get up—I like to watch this coming and going of boats over a length of time. There is a village market on the other bank, which is why there is such a crowd on the ferry boats. Some carry a bundle of grass, some a basket, some have a sack on their shoulder as they go to the market and return from the market; these two small villages on either side of this small river and between them, on this somnolent afternoon, this little bit of work, this little flow of human life, proceeding very slowly. I was sitting and thinking, why are the fields, the river banks, the sky, the sun of our country bathed in such a deep melancholy? The reason might be that in our country, it is nature that one notices the most—cloudless skies, borderless fields, the sun beating down—in the midst of this man seems very insignificant—men come and go like the ferry boat from this side to that, one hears their faint indistinct murmur, one sees their small crossings in life's market in the hope of small joys and sorrows—but in this vast, spread out, endless, indifferent natural world, how small, how brief, how full of futility these indistinct murmurs, these snatches of song, this constant activity and work seems. In this idle, drowsy, peaceful, aimless world of nature there is such a large, beautiful, careless and generous peace to be seen, and in comparison with that, one sees such a continuously trying, belabored, harassed, minute disquiet in one's self, that, gazing at the shadowy blue line of the trees on the distant shore one becomes quite preoccupied. "Sitting all day in the shade with the sound of the trees in the breeze" etc. Where nature is nervous and shrouded in cloud and mist and snow and darkness, there man is very lordly—there man thinks that all his wishes, all his efforts will be permanent, adding his signature to all his own work, he looks toward posterity, builds monuments, writes autobiographies, and even builds stone houses for everlasting remembrance over dead bodies—many of these signs are broken later and many names forgotten, but nobody notices this because nobody has the time.

89

Calcutta

1891

NO. 62

Shazadpur

29 June 1892

26.3.1299

I had written to you that yesterday at *7 pm* I would set up an *engagement* with the poet Kalidasa. Just when I had lit the lamps and pulled my arm-chair up to the table and was quite ready, in the place of the poet Kalidasa, the postmaster of this place turned up. A living postmaster has far greater claim than a dead poet—I couldn't say to him, "why don't you leave now, I have some urgent work with Kalidasa"—even if I had said so, he would not have understood what I meant. Consequently Kalidasa had to vacate his chair for the postmaster and slowly take his leave. I have a particular connection with this man. When the post office was located in this bungalow itself and I used to see him everyday, then, sitting on the first floor one afternoon, I had written that story about the postmaster, and when that story appeared in the *Hitabadi* then our postmaster babu had referred to it and spread a great many modest smiles all around. Anyway, I quite like the man. He chatters on with his stories, and I sit quietly and listen. He has quite a good sense of humor, so he can liven up things very quickly. After a whole day spent quietly by myself, sometimes when you come into contact with a living person of this type, then life can start up again. He was talking about our munsef babu. Hearing the story and watching his mimicry, I laughed continuously until I was quite tired. The story is this: one day, all of a sudden, the munsef babu saw Shiva in the trunk of a tree. On the first day he saw Shiva, the next day it was Kali, after that it was Radha-Krishna etc.—the entire pantheon of gods and goddesses had suddenly come down to live under the banyan tree at Shazadpur. He was catching hold of everybody and saying—"Look! Look! Don't you see it! There's the eyes! There's the tongue!" All those who are his clients or are indebted to him were able to see it as required, and those who were not dependant on him in any way could see nothing at all. Our postmaster belonged to the latter group. On days when the goddess is worshipped with kheer and jackfruit, those are the days he can see—but the moment the kheer is finished he asks the munsef, "Which one are you calling the eyes, mister?" The munsef says, "Can't you see? There they are on top!" The postmaster says with great gravity, "Oh I see! That was just the part I thought was the head!" Some days the munsef says to him, "Look here, mister, have you noticed something? Today during the ringing of bells at arati something came and sat on the tree and then two or three drops of water fell from above!" The postmaster replies, with a face like a very simple person, "Oh yes, the tree was moving for sure." The ground around that tree has been paved—the munsef worships there day and night, the conch shell is being blown, a sanyasi sits there and smokes ganja and closes his eyes and says, "There she is—I can see Kali Mai." On top of that one or two people go and faint over there, and make prophetic pronouncements in that state. Various kinds of trickery have started there. The postmaster was saying, "When the Magistrate comes to your *zamindari* you go and see him, and so many gods have found their way to the shade of the banyan tree—you really should go and *pay a visit*." I too think I should go and see the fun for myself. Anyway, if this entertainment continues for very long then Shazadpur might become a place of pilgrimage. We stand to profit from that. After the postmaster left, I sat down with *Raghuvamsa* once more the same night. I was reading about Indumati's swayamvar. The rows of thrones in the court were occupied by well-dressed good looking rajas when Indumati came and stood in their midst to the sound of conch shells and the bugle horn, dressed in bridal clothes, holding the hand of Sunanda. It is such a pretty picture to imagine! After that Sunanda is introducing them to her one by one, and Indumati is touching each one's feet without love and moving on. This touching of feet is so beautiful! To touch the feet of those who you are rejecting to show your respect and humility is so appropriate! It is much better than the proud English-woman's arrogance. Indumati is a mere slip of a girl, all the others are kings and much older than her—if she had not wiped away the obvious rudeness of the fact that she was leaving all of them behind with a pretty and humble *pranam* then the scene would not have been beautiful. But as it was getting very late, I had to go to sleep before she could put the garland around Aja's neck—that is why yesterday side by side with Priya's wedding, Indumati's wedding could not be concluded.

Kolkata
1 July 1892

NO. 77

Cuttack
February 1893

In the first place you know I can't stand these Indian Englishmen. They normally look down on us, have not an iota of *sympathy* for us, and on top of all that, to *exhibit* one's self to them is for me truly painful. So much so, that I don't have the slightest inclination to enter even their places of amusement, theatres and shops (except for Thacker's shop). It rankles in my mind to think that however big a cow is born in an English home, he feels he is superior to every person in our country. Until they accept that we have something in us, every time we approach them, we have to do so with servility or we have to feel humiliated. Sometimes I feel unbearably angry with the people of our country! Not because they aren't getting rid of these Englishmen, but because they don't do a thing about anything at all—they can't show their superiority in a single re-spect. They don't even have that aim in their minds—all they do is pick up the peacock feathers the English have plucked and tuck it into their tails and keep dancing around in this strange fashion—they don't feel the slightest shame or lowliness in doing so. They don't want to teach our countrymen anything, look down on our country's language, and are indifferent to anything that the Englishman is unaware of—they think that if they join both hands together and form Congress and plead with the Government they are going to become big people. My personal opinion is that until we can do something for ourselves it is better for us to remain in exile. After all, since we really do deserve such indignity, with what plea should we protect our self-respect in front of others? Will it do to only learn how to shake our tails in exactly their manner? When we establish ourselves in the world, when we can contribute to the work of the world, only then shall we be able to smile and talk with them. Until then it is better to hide away and shut up and keep doing our own work. The people of our country think it is just the opposite—whatever is done with interiority, whatever has to be done privately, they think that is unimportant, and that which is momentary and transient, which is only gesture and ornament, that is what they are inclined towards. Ours is the most wretched country. It is very difficult here to keep one's strength of mind. There is no one to really help you. You cannot find anybody with whom one can exchange a few words and feel alive within ten or twenty miles—nobody thinks, nobody feels, nobody works; nobody has any experience of a great work or a life worth living; you will not be able to find a mature humanity anywhere. All these people seem to be wandering around like ghosts. They eat, go to office, sleep, smoke, and chatter and chatter like complete idiots. When they speak of feeling they become sentimental, and when they speak of reason they become childish. One feels a real mental thirst to be in the company of a real humanity, one wishes for a give and take, an argumentation and quarrel of ideas. But there are no real flesh and blood strong and solid men to be found—all are phantoms, floating in a disconnected way with this world. I don't think there is anybody lonelier and more isolated in this country than the man who has one or two *ideas* in his head. I don't know how this train of thought has got going—but this is my most heartfelt complaint. Much of the disenchantment of life is from this lack of humanity.

Sholapur
February 1893

NO. 79

Cuttack
10 February 1893

It is the lame man who finds the ditch. As it is I can't stand these *Anglo-Indians,* and on top of that yesterday I had special occasion to be acquainted with their crude behavior. The Principal of the college here is an uncouth Englishman—huge nose, crafty eyes, one and a half foot of jaw, clean shaven, heavy voice, a strangulated pronunciation that cannot articulate the letter "r"—all in all a most complete and whole specimen. He really had it in for our people. You know, I think, of the huge outcry all around against the Government's attempt to take in hand the jury system in our country. This man forced the subject upon us and began to argue with B. . . babu. Said the *moral standard* in this country was *low,* people here did not have enough belief in the *sacredness of life,* they are not fit to be in a jury. How shall I describe to you how I was feeling! My blood boiled, but I could not find any words. Lying in bed so many things came to my mind, but at that time I became completely dumb. Just think of it, Bob, to be invited to a Bengali's house, to sit among Bengalis and not to feel abashed to speak in this manner—what do they think of us! And why! Forget about *sympathy,* those who don't even think it is necessary to behave politely with us, why do we go to them and smile and smile, and brush up against them, and take it upon ourselves to ally our honor to a marriage with them, Bob? The moment we feel the slightest handshake of a favor on their part, why immediately are our entire selves transformed into a mass of *jelly,* trembling and wobbling from top to toe? Ooh, how proud they are, how scornful! And as for us, what poverty, what lowliness! It is bad enough to swallow the insults and keep quiet, but on top of that to go and sidle up to them and ask for their affection—I feel that is the lowest point one can reach. Let us pull this wretched, insulted, scorned Bharatvarsha of ours to our hearts, let us try to mend and to forgive all her faults, all her weaknesses, all her poverty—let us not push her away from our hearts because all her thoughts and ways are not in sync with our minds! If our own country keeps us at

94

a distance because of some mistaken orthodoxy then why do we instantly move away without a word, and when the sahibs openly beat us with brooms and kick us a hundred times, still the diehard party cannot be evicted from under their feet or from their doors. Where they do not allow us to wear shoes we take off our shoes and go, where they do not allow us to raise our heads high there we bow our heads in a salaam and enter, where our fellow people are not allowed entry we disguise ourselves as sahibs and turn up. They don't want us to go and sit in their meetings, to participate in their amusements, to contribute to their work—but still we try, we hawk our wares, we find an opportunity, we try and please them by keeping our own people at a distance, by participating in criticizing our own race, by agreeing in every insult to our country—we feel we are saved if we can just be near them in any way possible. I don't want to pretend to be an *exception,* but if you have no respect at all for our race, then I don't want to act civilized and become your pet. With all the love in my heart, I will stay among my people and do what is my duty—you will never hear of it or see it. I don't expect even an inch of your scraps, your bits of affection—I kick it away. Your affection is to me what the pig is to the Muslim. It makes me lose my religion—really lose it—an insult to one's soul is what really makes one lose caste—it destroys your standing in a moment—after that what pride can I retain! Let us not give any respect at all to those who buy exterior glory by destroying their own pride in their hearts. I will never be ashamed to call the most miserable farmer in the most ramshackle hut one of my own people, but if I ever feel tempted to mix with those who dress in phit-phat style and go about in *dogcarts* and call us *niggers,* however uplifted and civilized they may be, then let me be beaten soundly on the head with a shoe. Yesterday my head and my heart were hurting so that I could not sleep all night—I kept tossing and turning in my bed. When I went and sat in one corner of that drawing room, it all appeared like a shadow to my eyes—it was as if I could see in front of me all of this great country spread out before me, as if I was sitting at the side of this unhappy, humble and wretched motherland—such a vast disconsolate feeling overwhelmed my whole heart—what can I say? Yet in front of me were memsahibs in *evening dress* and in my ear was the murmur of English conversation and laughter—all in all such discordance! How true was my eternal Bharatvarsha to me, and this dinner table, with its sugary English smiles and English polite conversation, how empty, how false, how deeply untrue! When the mems were talking in their low sweet cultivated voices then I was thinking of you, oh wealth of my country. After all, you are of this Bharatvarsha.

95

Sholapur
16 February, 1893

NO. 142

Shilaidaha
10 August 1894
26.4.1301

Last night, not very late, I was woken by the sound of water. A great tumult and powerful restlessness had suddenly come to the river. Perhaps all of a sudden a new tide of water had arrived. This sort of thing happens almost everyday. I'm sitting for some time when suddenly I see the river has awoken with a gurgling splashing sound and there is a great celebration all around you. If you put your foot on the planks of the boat you can clearly feel what a variety of forces run untiringly underneath it—some of it trembles, some stumbles, some inflates, some falls with a thud. Exactly as if I have my finger on the pulse of the land. Last night at midnight such a restless joy suddenly came and increased the dance of the pulse rate quite a bit. I sat for a long time on the bench by the window. There was a very misty light, which made the entire maddened river seem madder. Occasional clouds in the sky. The shadow of a great big flickering star lengthened upon the water till quite far out, trembling and shivering like a shuddering piercing sorrow. Both banks of the river lay unconscious, shrouded in indistinct light and a deep sleep. In its middle, a sleepless mad restlessness flowed on in full force and disappeared. If you wake up and sit like this in the middle of the night, in the midst of such a scene, you feel as if you and the world are somehow in some way made anew, as if the world of daylight and commerce with men becomes completely untrue. Again, waking up this morning, how far away and indistinct that world of my night seems to have become. For man, both are true, yet both are terribly divided. It seems to me as if the world of the day is European music—in its tuneful and out of tune moments, in its parts and its whole—like a forceful tremendous tangle of harmony, and the world of the night is our Indian music, a pure, tender, deep and unmixed ragini. Both move us, yet both are opposed to each other. There is nothing to be done about it, there is a division, a tremendous opposition, right at the root of nature, everything is divided between king and queen. Day and night, variety and entirety, expressiveness and eternity. We Indians live in this kingdom of night. We are overwhelmed by that which is timeless and whole. Ours is the song of personal solitude, Europe's is that of crowded accompaniment. Our music takes the listener outside of the limits of man's everyday vicissitudes to that lonely land of renunciation that is at the root of the entire universe, while Europe's music dances variously to the tunes of the rise and fall of humanity's happiness and unhappiness.

Satara

15 August 1894

(Extracts from *Chhinnapatrabali*)
Translated by Rosinka Chaudhuri

To Mrinalini Devi

Kolkata, December 1900

Bhai Chhuti,

Do I have no right to your states of mind in the evening? Do you think I am concerned only with your daytime moods? Do you think my eyes too veer away from your mind and set the moment the sun sets? Why didn't you write to me describing all the thoughts and feelings that crossed your mind? The letters you wrote me over the last few days leave me somewhat puzzled. Of course I can't analyze it to pinpoint what it is, but a curtain of some kind tends to conceal it. Never mind! Engaging in a discussion of the finer aspects of the heart is not a profitable enterprise. I think it is better to accept everything in a straightforward manner.

Neetu is better today. He has a slight fever. Pratap babu is of the opinion that it may ease off altogether after the new moon. In his opinion he should be sent to Madhupur immediately after the remission of fever. I've decided that's what I'll do. The condition of his enlarged liver has considerably improved and the pain is much less severe now.

Last night I dreamt that you were cross with me and were scolding me for everything under the sun. Since a dream is but a dream, we could certainly do with good dreams—there are plenty of real troubles in the world when you are awake—but the situation becomes virtually unbearable if illusory dreams also bring on illusory troubles. This morning too, I was feeling none too good as the memories of those dreams got me down. Besides, the whole place was crawling with people this morning. I had a mind to do the write-up for the 7th of Poush, but didn't get a chance to put pen to paper. Just managed to scribble two *Naibedya* poems this morning in the bathroom.

Rabi

(From *Chithipatra,* vol. 1)
Translated by Subhransu Maitra

To Jagadish Chandra Bose

6 Asadh, 1309 (*circa* 1902)
Santiniketan
Bolpur

Friend

Asadh has arrived—but Asadh's familiar dense clouds are not to be seen. That's why we wait, mouths agape. Here fields stretch out into the distance—nowhere is there anything to block one's view. Nowhere else do clouds have such a vast playing field. It was here that the poet Jaidev described a monsoon night in the tamal forest in ringing rhymes. Jaidev's birthplace is six miles from here—Chandidas's birthplace isn't far either. It would be an excellent thing to be able to kidnap and bring you here one monsoon. At times it strikes me, as in a flash of illumination, that we think too much of our work—we give speeches, we write, we are in a breathless flurry of activity, we unleash stratagems to liberate the country—all this is ultimately rubbish. As a result, life remains fragmented, scattered, incomplete. Love is for all time; peace is eternal. The pity is that humans have to travel beyond a temporary distraction, a short-lived unpleasantness, in order to approach this final conclusion. This is how life comes to a close. And then where are you and where am I! A sense of wholeness sparkles like a mirage perpetually ahead of us on this endless road. What is it that drives us thus? At times I feel like rebelling, throwing aside all my work, sitting with you face to face and filling my heart to the brim. But when the road beckons, I can't sit still, wretch that I am. I start running again, perpetually running! I'm caught in an endless whirl. The whole world is a whirling tangle. It keeps turning as if that motion itself is its fit conclusion. Humanity too is spinning and spinning, turning and turning—where does this all end? This is why the Buddha was so desperate to free himself from this tangle. But unless all are free, it is impossible for one being to gain liberty. One has to keep spinning, torturously, painfully, in this human whirlwind, for this life and for all the lives to come. According to your science, in a corner of the sky, the earth, spinning on its axis, sparkles to life in a tumult of innumerable stars— doesn't some wise scientist say this? In the middle of this spinning circle lie countless other circles—circles of stars, solar circles, circles of planets, beings' lifecycles—only outside of this circle lies stillness and peace. One holds out one's arms to this stillness, but the tremendous pull of the world tugs one back into its endlessly spinning vortex. Love offers us a hint of calm and fullness within this spinning circle. If two hearts sit face to face, the raucous sound of the world's wheels is diminished for a moment. Then one can forget for a while gain and loss, joy and sorrow, sin and virtue, the endless argument of victory and defeat.

But at the moment of your scientific conquest of the world such poetic mewls are not in order. Now the clamor of war drums is in order! Let the heart's utterances remain within the heart.

Plant your flag of victory in Germany and America. Don't hurry back. I shall perhaps be able to help you in a month or two—I've made the necessary arrangements. We won't call you back just now. First finish your work. Then we will spend a long evening together, lighting a lamp, drawing up our armchairs.

A Japanese student has come to Santiniketan to learn Sanskrit. He's an awfully good chap. He's become very close to us all. Your friend Mira has entranced him with a daily gift of flowers. She's learned a few words of Japanese from him as well. If these developments are not to your liking do not hesitate to protest.

Your Robi

(From *Chithipatra,* vol. 6)
Translated by Shormishtha Panja

To Myron H. Phelps[4]

Santiniketan
4 January 1909

My dear Sir,
I am exceedingly gratified to receive your very kind letter and to know of your desire for our welfare.

In regard to the assistance you expect from me, I am afraid that as I have never been used to express myself in the English language I shall not be able to give an adequate or effective idea of what I feel to be the truth about our country. However, I shall attempt as best I may to give you an outline of my views, more as a response to your message of goodwill than with the hope of rendering any help in your friendly endeavors.

One need not dive deep, it seems to me, to discover the problem of India; it is so plainly evident on the surface. Our country is divided by numberless differences—physical, social, linguistic, religious; and this obvious fact must be taken into account in any course which is destined to lead us into our own place among the nations who are building up the history of man. The trite maxim "History repeats itself" is like most other sayings but half the truth. The conditions which have prevailed in India from a remote antiquity have guided its history along a particular channel, which does not and cannot coincide with the lines of evolution taken by other countries under different sets of influences. It would be a sad misreading of the lessons of the past to apply our energies to tread too closely in the footsteps of any other nation, however successful in its own career. I feel strongly that our country has been entrusted with a message which is not a mere echo of the living voices that resound from western shores, and to be true to her trust she must realize the divine purpose that has been manifest throughout her history; she must become conscious of the situation she has been instrumental in creating—of its meaning and possibilities.

It has never been India's lot to accept alien races as factors in her civilization. You know very well how the caste that proceeds from color takes elsewhere a most virulent form. I need not cite modern instances of the animosity which divides white men from Negroes in your own country, and excludes Asiatics from European colonies. When, however, the white-skinned Aryans on encountering the dark aboriginal races of India found themselves face to face with the same problem, the solution of which was either extermination, as has happened in America and Australia, or a modification in the social system of the superior race calculated to accommodate the inferior without the possibility of either friction or fusion, they chose the latter. Now the principle underlying this choice obviously involves mechanical arrangement and juxtaposition, not cohesion and amalgamation. By making very careful provision for the differences, it keeps them ever alive. Unfortunately, the principle once accepted inevitably grows deeper and deeper into the constitution of the race even after the stress of the original necessity ceases to exist.

Thus secure in her rigid system of seclusion, in the very process of inclusion, India in different periods of her history received with open arms the medley of races that poured in on her without any attempt at shutting out undesirable elements. I need not dwell at length on the evils of the resulting caste system. It cannot be denied, and this is a fact which foreign onlookers too often overlook, that it served a very useful purpose

in its day and has been even up to a late age, of immense protective bene-
fit to India. It has largely contributed to the freedom from narrowness
and intolerance which distinguishes the Hindu religion and has enabled
races with widely different culture and even antagonistic social and reli-
gious usages and ideals to settle down peaceably side by side—a phenom-
enon which cannot fail to astonish Europeans, who, with comparatively
less jarring elements, have struggled for ages to establish peace and har-
mony among themselves. But this very absence of struggle, developing
into a ready acquiescence in any position assigned by the social system,
has crushed individual manhood and has accustomed us for centuries
not only to submit to every form of domination, but sometimes actually
to venerate the power that holds us down. The assignment of the busi-
ness of government almost entirely to the military class reacted upon the
whole social organism by permanently excluding the rest of the people
from all the political cooperation, so that now it is hardly surprising to
find the almost entire absence of any feeling of common interest, any
sense of national responsibility, in the general consciousness of a people
of whom as a whole it has seldom been any part of their pride, their
honor, their dharma, to take thought or stand up for their country. This
completeness of stratification, this utter submergence of the lower by the
higher, this immutable and all-pervading system, has no doubt imposed
a mechanical uniformity upon the people but has at the same time kept
their different sections inflexibly and unalterably separate, with the con-
sequent loss of all power of adaptation and readjustment to new condi-
tions and forces. The regeneration of the Indian people, to my mind, di-
rectly and perhaps solely depends upon the removal of this condition.
Whenever I realize the hypnotic hold which this gigantic system of cold-
blooded repression has taken on the minds of our people whose social
body it has so completely entwined in its endless coils that the free ex-
pression of manhood even under the direst necessity has become almost
an impossibility, the only remedy that suggests itself to me and which
even at the risk of uttering a truism I cannot but repeat, is—to educate
them out of their trance.

I know I shall be told that foreign dominion is also one of the
things not conducive to the free growth of manhood. But it must be re-
membered that with us foreign dominion is not an excrescence the forc-

ible extirpation of which will restore a condition of normal health and vigor. It has manifested itself as a political symptom of our social disease, and at present it has become necessary to us for effecting the dispersal of all internal obstructive agencies. For we have now come under the domination not of a dead system, but of a living power, which, while holding us under subjection, cannot fail to impart to us some of its own life. This vivifying warmth from outside is gradually making us conscious of our own vitality and the newly awakened life is making its way slowly, but surely, even through the barriers of caste.

The mechanical incompatibility and consequent friction between the American colonies and the parent country was completely done away with by means of a forcible severance. The external force which in eighteenth-century France stood to divide class from class [could] only be overcome by *vis major* to bring emancipation to a homogeneous people. But here in India are working deep-seated social forces, complex internal reactions, for in no other country under the sun has such a juxtaposition of races, ideas and religions occurred; and the great problem which from time immemorial India has undertaken to solve is what in the absence of a better name may be called the race problem. At the sacrifice of her own political welfare she has through long ages borne this great burden of heterogeneity, patiently working all the time to evolve out of these warring contradictions a great synthesis. Her first effort was spent in the arrangement of vast materials, and in this she had attained a perhaps somewhat dearly bought success. Now has come the time when she must begin to build, and dead arrangement must gradually give way to living construction, organic growth. If at this stage vital help has come from the West even in the guise of an alien rule, India must submit—nay welcome it, for above all she must achieve her life's work.

She must take it as a significant fact in her history that when on the point of being overcome with a torpor that well nigh caused her to forget the purpose of what she had accomplished, a rude shock of life should have thus burst in upon her reminding her of her mission and giving her strength to carry it on. It is now manifestly her destiny that East and West should find their meeting place in her ever-hospitable bosom. The unification of the East which has been her splendid if unconscious achievement must now be consciously realized in order that the process may be continued with equal success and England's contribution thereto utilized to full advantage.

For us, there can be no question of blind revolution, but of steady and purposeful education. If to break up the feudal system and the tyrannical conventionalism of the Latin church which had outraged the healthier instincts of humanity, Europe needed the thought impetus of the Renaissance and the fierce struggle of the Reformation, do we not in a greater degree need an overwhelming influx of higher social ideals before a place can be found for true political thinking? Must we not have that greater vision of humanity which will impel us to shake off the fetters that shackle our individual life before we begin to dream of national freedom?

It must be kept in mind, however, that there never has been a time when India completely lost sight of the need of such reformation. In fact she had no other history but the history of this social education. In the earliest dawn of her civilization there appeared amidst the fiercest conflict of races, factions and creeds, the genius of Ramachandra and Krishna introducing a new epoch of unification and tolerance and allaying the endless struggle of antagonism. India has ever since accepted them as the divine will incarnate, because in their life and teachings her innermost truth has taken an immortal shape. Since then all the illustrious names of our country have been of those who came to bridge over the differences of colors and scriptures and to recognize all that is highest and best as the common heritage of humanity. Such have been our emperors Asoka and Akbar, our philosophers Shankara and Ramanuja, our spiritual masters Kabir, Nanak, Chaitanya and others not less glorious because knit closer to us in time and perspective. They belong to various sects and castes, some of them of the very "lowest," but still they occupy the ever-sacred seat of the guru, which is the greatest honor that India confers her children. This shows that even in the darkest of her days the consciousness of her true power and purpose has never forsaken her.

The present unrest in India of which various accounts must have reached you, is to me one of the most hopeful signs of the times. Different causes are assigned and remedies proposed by those whose spheres of activity necessarily lead them to a narrow and one-sided view of the situation. From my seclusion it seems to me clear, that it is not this or that

103

measure, this or that instance of injustice or oppression, which is at the bottom. We have been on the whole comfortable with a comfort unknown for a long time, we have peace and protection and many of the opportunities for prosperity which these imply. Why then this anguish at heart? Because the contact of East and West has done its work and quickened the dormant life of our soul. We have begun to be dimly conscious of the value of the time we have allowed to slip by, of the weight of the clogging effete matter which we have allowed to accumulate, and are angry with ourselves. We have also begun vaguely to realize the failure of England to rise to the great occasion, and to miss more and more the invaluable cooperation which it was so clearly England's mission to offer. And so we are troubled with a trouble which we know not yet how to name. How England can best be made to perceive that the mere establishment of the *Pax Britannica* cannot either justify or make possible her continued dominion, I have no idea; but of this I am sure that the sooner we come to our senses, and take up the broken thread of our appointed task, the earlier will come the final consummation.

With kindest regards,
Yours sincerely,
Rabindranath Tagore

(From *The Modern Review,* August 1910)

To William Rothenstein[5]

508 W. High Street, Urbana, [Illinois, USA]
15 December 1912

My dear Friend,

I have got the manuscripts you sent to me. Last night I read *The Post Office* before a friendly audience here and it was heartily appreciated. My reputation as a poet is fast spreading here but it has not made my stay here impossible as yet. I am left pretty much to myself. People connected with papers came to me to ask for my portrait and materials [on] my life but I held them at bay—but I believe they had better satisfaction from

Rathi. Rathi has a natural affection for the people here and he does not like to disappoint them.

I have read the review of my book that appeared in the *Athenaeum.* Do you know, that is the kind of criticism I expected all along. It is not hostile, you can even call it appreciative, but you feel that the reviewer is at a loss how to estimate these poems. He has not got a standard by which to judge these productions, quite strange to him. He sees some beauty in them but they arouse no real emotion in him, so he imagines them as cold—he thinks they have no real life blood in them. He cannot believe that they are quiet and simple, not because there is lack of enthusiasm in them but because they are absolutely real. I can assure you they are not literary productions at all they are life productions.

My writings have met with a very generous appreciation in your country. I never could believe it to be possible. So much so that sometimes it oppresses me. That his works should be accepted by men is the highest reward that can come to an artist. Yet we should be strong enough not to have to depend upon it. Reward should not be made a necessity to us. This fame in a foreign land has a strange fascination and I am afraid it was growing upon me; I was unconsciously getting into the habit of expecting it more and more. But I must get out of it. It is like using your own best works as chains to shackle you. I have a poem which I translated when I was in London. I do not know if it is in your collection. I give it below.—

> Free me from bonds of praise and blame of men and guide me only by the beckons of your right hand, my lord. Let all the forces of my life take the one great course, made irresistible by one supreme love, even as the river that ever flows through its boundaries yet ever loses its limits in the sea, led by the hidden call and the inmost impulse of its own.[6]

I send you herewith the translation of a poem, story of which is based upon an episode of the *Ramayana.*[7]

Ever your friend
Rabindranath Tagore

(MS original in Rothenstein Papers, Harvard University)

To Robert Bridges[8]

Kolkata
18 November 1915

Dear Dr Bridges,

106   I am painfully diffident about my English writings and the advices I get
from my friends are so conflicting that I think it wise to leave it to
my publishers to decide for me when any question arises concerning
my English works. Please never think that I have any exaggerated no-
tion of my English style, knowing for certain that it must have blemishes
which I am not competent even to detect and much less to remove. I
never had the advantage of university training and analytically study-
ing your language. Therefore in my attempts at English writing it is dif-
ficult for me to know where I fail or dare to be sure that I have caught
the right expression. If there be any excellence in my translations it is
unconscious, it is like correctly walking in dreams in places which it is
not safe to attempt when wakeful. Indeed I should consider myself fortu-
nate to be able to secure any help from a poet like yourself who is a mas-
ter of all intimate secrets of the musical capacity of your language. Only
thing that makes me hesitate is not being sure [where] the line is beyond
which it is dishonest for a man of my position [to go]. In pure litera-
ture it is very often that the mode of expression is of greater value than
richness of thought. Therefore I feel that in my translations I should be
loath to borrow from my brother artists any thing of real splendor and
appropriate its value for myself. I must appear before the public with all
my natural and accidental limitations excepting about mistakes in gram-
mar and idiom. Henceforth I shall be [a] great deal more careful than
before not merely to keep up my reputation, but to attain my true place,
if there is any chance for me, in your literature. I believe I have had what
is more than enough for me in my own language and I never should be
greedy in trying to scramble for that which is not my true position in
yours.

I know what this war is to you and I bow my head in awe before
your people who are vindicating the divine in man by boundless suf-
fering and heroism. Please let Mrs. Bridges accept my heartfelt sympathy

and reverence whose son is fighting for the cause of liberty in one of the greatest wars in the history of mankind.

Yours very sincerely
Rabindranath Tagore

(MS copy in Bridges Papers, Bodleian Library)

To James Drummond Anderson[9]

Kolkata
14 April 1918

Dear Mr. Anderson

I have greatly enjoyed reading two of my *Gitanjali* poems done into verse by your friend and thank you for sending them to me. It was the want of mastery in your language that originally prevented me from trying English meters in my translations. But now I have grown reconciled to my limitations through which I have come to know the wonderful power of English prose. The clearness, strength and the suggestive music of well-balanced English sentences make it a delightful task for me to mould my Bengali poems into English prose form. I think one should frankly give up the attempt at reproducing in a translation the lyrical suggestions of the original verse and substitute in their place some new quality inherent in the new vehicle of expression. In English prose there is a magic which seems to transmute my Bengali verses into something which is original again in a different manner. Therefore it not only satisfies but gives me delight to assist my poems in their English rebirth though I am far from being confident in the success of my task.

I have asked the editor to send you the Chaitra number of *Shabuj Patra* which contains my lecture on Bengali prosody.[10]

With kindest regards, I am
Yours very sincerely
Rabindranath Tagore

(MS copy at Rabindra Bhavan, Santiniketan)

To Lord Chelmsford[11]

Kolkata
31 May 1919

108

Your Excellency,
The enormity of the measures taken by the government in the Punjab for quelling some local disturbances has, with a rude shock, revealed to our minds the helplessness of our position as British subjects in India. The disproportionate severity of the punishments inflicted upon the unfortunate people and the methods of carrying them out, we are convinced, are without parallel in the history of civilized governments, barring some conspicuous exceptions, recent and remote. Considering that such treatment has been meted out to a population, disarmed and resourceless, by a power which has the most terribly efficient organization for destruction of human lives, we must strongly assert that it can claim no political expediency, far less moral justification. The accounts of the insults and sufferings undergone by our brothers in the Punjab have trickled through the gagged silence, reaching every corner of India, and the universal agony of indignation roused in the hearts of our people has been ignored by our rulers—possibly congratulating themselves for imparting what they imagine as salutary lessons. The callousness has been praised by most of the Anglo-Indian papers, which have in some cases gone to the brutal length of making fun of our sufferings, without receiving the least check from the same authority, relentlessly careful in smothering every cry of pain and expression of judgment from the organs representing the sufferers. Knowing that our appeals have been in vain and that the passion of vengeance is blinding the noble vision of statesmanship in our Government which could so easily afford to be magnanimous, as befitting its physical strength and normal tradition, the very least that I can do for my country is to take all consequences upon myself in giving voice to the protest of the millions of my countrymen, surprised into a dumb anguish of terror.

The time has come when badges of honor make our shame glaring in the incongruous content of humiliation, and I for my part wish to stand, shorn, of all special distinctions, by the side of those of my countrymen who, for their so-called insignificance, are liable to suffer degradation not fit for human beings. And these are the reasons which have compelled me to ask Your Excellency, with due deference and regret, to relieve me of my title of knighthood which I had the honour to accept from His Majesty the King at the hands of your predecessor, for whose nobleness of heart I still entertain great admiration.

> Yours faithfully,
> Rabindranath Tagore

To Charles Freer Andrews[12]

2970 Ellis Avenue, Chicago
5 March 1921

Dear friend, lately I have been receiving more and more news and newspaper cuttings from India giving rise in my mind to a painful struggle that presages a period of suffering which is waiting for me. I am striving with all my power to tune my mood of mind to be in accord with the great feeling of excitement sweeping across my country. But deep in my being why is there this spirit of resistance maintaining its place in spite of my strong desire to remove it? I fail to find a clear answer and through my gloom of dejection breaks out a smile and voice saying, "Your place is on the seashore of worlds, with children; there is your truth, your peace, and I am with you there."[13] And this is why lately I have been playing with meters, with merest nothings. These are whims that are content to be borne away by the current of time, dancing in the sun and laughing as they disappear. But while I play, the whole creation is amused, for are not flowers and leaves never-ending experiments in meter, is not my God an eternal waster of time? He flings stars and planets in the whirlwind of changes, he floats paper boats of ages filled with his fancies on the rushing stream of appearance. When I tease him and beg him to allow me to remain his little follower and accept a few trifles of mine as the cargo of his paper boat, he smiles and I trot behind him catching the hem of his robe. But where am I among the crowd, pushed from behind, pressed from all sides? And what is this noise about me? If it is a song then my own *sitar* can catch the tune and I can join in the chorus, for I am a singer. But if it is a shout then my voice is wrecked and I am lost in bewilderment. I have been trying all these days to find a melody, straining my ear, but the idea of noncooperation, with its mighty volume of sound does not sing to me, its congregated menace of negation shouts. And I say to myself, "If you cannot keep step with your countrymen at this great crisis of their history, never say that you are right and rest of them wrong; only give up your role as a soldier, go back to your corner as a poet, be ready to accept popular derision and disgrace."

Rathi, in support of the present movement, has often said to me that the passion for rejection is a stronger power in the beginning than the acceptance of an ideal.[14] Though I know it to be a fact, I cannot accept it as a truth. We must choose our allies once for all, for they stick to us even when we might be glad to be rid of them. If we once claim strength from intoxication, then in the time of reaction our normal strength is bankrupt, and we go back again and again to the demon that lends us resources in a vessel whose bottom it takes away.

Brahma-vidya in India has for its object *mukti,* emancipation, while Buddhism has *nirvana,* extinction. It may be argued that both have the same idea [under] different names. But names represent attitudes of mind, emphasize particular aspects of truth. *Mukti* draws our attention to the positive, and *nirvana* to the negative side of truth. Buddha kept silence all through his teachings about the truth of the *Om,* the *everlasting yes,* his implication being that by the negative path of destroying the self we naturally reach that truth. Therefore he emphasized the fact of *dukkha,* misery, which had to be avoided and the *Brahma-vidya* emphasized the fact of *ananda* which had to be attained. The latter cult also needs for its fulfillment the discipline of self-abnegation, but it holds before its view the idea of Brahma, not only at the end but all through the process of realization. Therefore the idea of life's training was different in the Vedic period from that of the Buddhistic. In the former it was the purification of life's joy, in the latter it was the eradicating of it. The abnormal type of asceticism to which Buddhism gave rise in India reveled in celibacy and mutilation of life in all different forms. But the forest life of the *Brahmanas* was not antagonistic to the social life of man, but harmonious with it. It was like our musical instrument *tambura* whose duty is to supply the fundamental notes to the music to save it from going astray into discordance. It believed in *anadam,* the music of the soul, and its own simplicity was not to kill it but to guide it.

III

The idea of noncooperation is political asceticism. Our students are bringing their offering of sacrifices to what? Not to a fuller education but to noneducation. It has at its back a fierce joy of annihilation which in its best form is asceticism and in its worst form is that orgy of frightfulness in which human nature, losing faith in basic reality of normal life, finds a disinterested delight in unmeaning devastation, as has been shown in the late war and on other occasions which came nearer home to us. No in its passive moral form is asceticism and in its active moral form is violence. The desert is as much a form of *himsa* as is the raging sea in storm, they both are against life.

I remember the day, during the Swadeshi Movement in Bengal, when a crowd of young students came to see me in the first floor of our Vichitra House. They said to me that if I ordered them to leave their schools and colleges they would instantly obey me. I was emphatic in my refusal to do so, and they went away angry, doubting the sincerity of my love for my motherland. Long before this ebullition of excitement, I myself had given a thousand rupees, when I had not five rupees to call my own, to open a *swadeshi* store and courted banter and bankruptcy. The reason for my refusing to advise those students to leave their schools was because the anarchy of a mere emptiness never tempts me, even when it is resorted to as a temporary shelter. I am frightened of an abstraction which is ready to ignore living reality. These students were no mere phantoms to me; their life was a great fact to them and to the All. I could not lightly take upon myself the tremendous responsibility of a mere negative program for them which would uproot them from their soil, however thin and poor that soil might be. The great injury and injustice which had been done to those boys who were tempted away from their career before any *real* provision was made, could never be made good to them. Of course that is nothing from the point of view of an abstraction which can ignore the infinite value even of the smallest fraction of reality. But the throb of life in the heart of the most insignificant of men beats in the unison of love with the heartthrob of the infinite. I wish I were the little creature Jack whose one mission was to kill the giant abstraction which is claiming the sacrifice of individuals all over the world under highly painted masks of delusion.

I say again and again that I am a poet, that I am not a fighter by nature. I would give everything to be one with my surroundings. I love my fellow beings and I prize their love. Yet I have been chosen by destiny to ply my boat there where the current is against me. What irony of fate is this that I should be preaching cooperation of culture between East and West on this side of the sea just at the moment when the doctrine of noncooperation is preached on the other side? You know that I do not believe in the material civilization of the West, just as I do not believe [in] the physical body. What is needed is the establishment of harmony between the physical and the spiritual nature of man, maintaining of balance between the foundation and superstructure. I believe in the true meeting of the East and the West. Love is the ultimate truth of soul; we should do all we can not to outrage that truth, to carry its banner against all opposition. The idea of noncooperation unnecessarily hurts that truth. It is not our hearth fire, but the fire that burns out our hearth.

While I have been considering the noncooperation idea one thought has come to me over and over again which I must tell you. *Bara Dada* and myself are zamindars, which means collectors of revenue under British Government.[15] Until the time comes when we give up paying revenue and allow our lands to be sold we have not the right to ask students or anybody else to make any sacrifice which may be all they have. My father was about to give up all his property for the sake of truth and honesty.[16] And likewise we may come to that point when we have to give up our means of livelihood. If we do not feel that that point has been reached by us then at least we should at once make ample provision out of our competency for others who are ready to risk their all. When I put to myself this problem the answer which I find is that by temperament and training all the good I am now capable of doing presupposes [a] certain amount of wealth. If I am to begin to earn my living, possibly I shall be able to support myself but nothing better than that. Which will mean not merely sacrificing my money but my mind. I know that my God may claim even that, and by the very reclaiming repay me. Utter privation and death may have to be my ultimate sacrifice for the sake of some ideals which represent immortality. But so long as I do not feel the call or respond to it myself how can I urge others to follow the path which may prove to be the path of utter renunciation? Let the individuals choose their own responsibility of sacrifice, but are we ready to accept that responsibility for them? Do we fully realize what it may mean in suffering or in evil? Or is it a mere abstraction for us which leaves us untouched [by] all the concrete possibilities of misery [for] individuals? Let us first of all try to think [of] them as the nearest and dearest to us and then ask them to choose danger and poverty for their share [in] life.

> With love,
> Ever yours
> Rabindranath Tagore

(MS original at Rabindra Bhavan, Santiniketan)

To Kanti Chandra Ghosh

I was able to take a look at the translations you have made into Bengali of Omar Khayyum's poems before they appeared in print. It is difficult to recast such poems in another language. This is because their primary element is not in their content but in the movement of the mind. That is why Fitzgerald was unable to translate them properly; it is essential to recreate such poems by recapturing the mood in which the original was created.

Your translations made me think of one thing in particular: Bengali poetry is so rich in its stock of words that it can easily express now even the playful element of another language. Your ability as a translator is revealed in the ease with which you have been able to render the liveliness of the original in Bengali rhythms. Poetry is usually like a shy bride who finds her freedom curbed when she has had to forsake the inner sanctum of her home for a new one. In your translations, however, you have managed to dispel her shyness and have even allowed the reader to see her smiling through the veil she has had to wear.

29 Sravan 1326 (*circa* 1920)

(Preface to Kanti Chandra Ghosh's
Rubayat-e-Omar Khayyum, published in Kolkata)
Translated by Fakrul Alam

To Edward John Thompson[17]

Santiniketan
20 September 1921

Dear Thompson

I have just received your book dealing with myself. I believe it is my sensitiveness born of my egotism which makes me shrink from attending to any discussions concerning me. But I have read your book all through. I am sure you have tried to be fair in your estimate of my works. About the comparative merits of my individual productions I myself am undecided though I have my preferences with which I never expect my readers always to agree. In fact as a critic of my own writings my ideas do not often coincide with those of Ajit.[18]

All along my literary career I have run against the taste of my countrymen, at least those of them who represent the vocal portion of my province. It has hardly been pleasant to me, but it has had the effect of making me reconciled to my mental loneliness. In the West—for some little while in England and lately in the continental countries of Europe—the recognition which I met with came to me with a shock of surprise. When a poet's life's works are accepted by his fellow beings it gives him a sense of intellectual companionship with his readers which is precious. But it has a great danger of growing into a temptation—and I believe, consciously and unconsciously I have been succumbing to it with regard to my western readers. But I have this paradox in my nature that when I begin to enjoy my success I grow weary of it in the depth of my mind. It is not through any surfeit of it, but through something in it which hurts me. Reputation is the greatest bondage for an artist. I want to emancipate my mind from its grasp not only for the sake of my art, but for the higher purposes of life, for the dignity of soul. What an immense amount of unreality there is in literary reputation, and I am longing—even while appreciating it like a buffalo the luxury of its mud bath—to come out of it as a *sanyasi,* naked and aloof. A gift has been given to me—this great world—which I can truly enjoy when I am simple and natural. I am looking back to those days of my youth when I had easy access into the heart of this universe—and I believe I shall yet again recover my place there when I am able to sever my mind from the attraction of the literary world which with its offer of rewards tries to standardize creative visions according to criterions distractingly varied and variable.

115

You have spared yourself no trouble in your attempt to understand me, and I am sure your book is the best one that has yet appeared about myself. I must thank you for this—at the same time I wish I could altogether lose the memory of my fame as a poet.

Yours
Rabindranath Tagore

(MS original in Thompson Papers, Bodleian Library)

To Kazi Nazrul Islam[19]

24 Sravan 1329 (*circa* 1922)
Kazi Nazrul Islam

Kalyaniyeshu

> Come, O shining comet! Blaze
> Across the darkness, with your fiery trail.
> Upon the fortress-top of evil days,
> Let your victory-pennant sail.

What if the forehead of the night
Bear misfortune's sinister sign?
Awaken, with your flashing light,
All who lie comatose, supine.

Rabindranath Tagore
Translated by Radha Chakravarty

To Romain Rolland

Santiniketan
28? February 1924

My very dear friend, before I sail for China, the time for which is drawing near, I must thank you for the delight that your letter has given me.

Pearson had an abundant gift of friendship which he freely offered to those, who, because of their obscurity, failed to attract notice. They were like night's background against which his love found its light fully revealed. He was sensitively conscious of the immense value of the individual man, irrespective of his special merits and uses, and this made him keenly suffer whenever that individual was ignored or hurt in consequence of social maladjustment or tyranny of organization. This grew in him to such as extent that he became jealous of all institutions which represented some ideal which had a wide range transcending the limits of the concretely personal. In fact, lately his mind was distracted when Santiniketan outgrew its vocation as a mere educational body belonging to immediate locality, when it tried to respond in its various efforts to what I consider to be the great call of the present age. He was afraid lest our attention should in the least measure be diverted from the children attending our school into a channel for the communication of ideas and formation of a community. I was feeling anxious about him for some time before he died when he grew restless at the apprehension of encroachment of some adventurous ideal into the happy realm of personal service. No doubt idealism is a disturbing factor in all settled forms of life and therefore prosperous people have a vigorous suspicion against it.

There is such a thing as the enjoyment of emotional prosperity where the stimulation to our personal feeling of love is constantly supplied. Pearson found it when he first came here and his own natural instinct of attachment had its full scope among our school children and the neighboring villagers. Then came the idea of Visva-Bharati like a strong breeze, scattering the petals from our ashram-flower, claiming its fruit. Pearson never was fully reconciled to it to the end of his days. Intellectually he had nothing to say against it, but his heart ached—for his mind was like the bee which has nothing to do with the fruit but only with the flower.

I understand this conflict in his mind because I myself have a kind of civil war constantly going on in my own nature between my personality as a creative artist, who necessarily must be solitary, and that as an idealist who must realize himself through works of a complex character needing a large field of collaboration with a large body of men. My conflict is within myself between the two opposite forces in my character, and not, as in the case of Pearson, between my individual temperament and the surrounding circumstance. Both of the contending forces being equally natural to me I cannot with impurity get rid of one of them in order to simplify my life's problem. I suppose a proper rhythm is possible to be attained in which both may be harmonized, and my work in the heart of the crowd may find its grace through the touch of the breath that comes from the solitude of the creative mind.

But unfortunately at the present moment, the claim of the organization is rudely asserting itself, and I do not know to restrain it within bounds. The poet in me is hurt, his atmosphere of leisure dust-laden. I do not wish that my life's sunset should thus be obscured in a murky air of strenuous work, the work which perpetually devours its own infinite background of peace. I earnestly hope that I shall be rescued in time before I die—in the meanwhile I go to China, in what capacity I do not know. Is it as a poet, or as a bearer of good advice and sound common-sense?[20]

With love,
Rabindranath Tagore

(MS copy at Rabindra Bhavan, Santiniketan)

To Sir William Rothenstein[21]

Santiniketan,
26 November 1932

My dear friend,

Your letter has given me deep joy. I have suffered much in life and my grandson's death was one more poignant sorrow for me. He was a lovable boy, and that his fresh young life should be taken away from us was hard indeed to bear. I have now recovered from the shock: experience widens our realization of life which includes death as well.

Persia was a great inspiration to me. It is splendid to find a nation courageously throwing off the stranglehold of inert tradition and relentless foreign exploitation and emerging with fresh and rebellious life into the sunlight and freedom. I felt a stir of new consciousness in the air of Persia, which harmonized so well with the beauty of the land and the great culture of its people.

Coming back to my country I find things worse in India—a deepening gloom which has been relieved by the vigorous reforms set in motion by Mahatmaji's great fast. Not being a politician I cannot presume to devise means and methods which may bring in better days for our peoples but I suffer with them. As you say there is exaggeration on both sides and I shrink from the aggressiveness inevitably produced by litigants both of whom are to blame for the present condition. The party whose voice is smothered by every means at the command of an efficient scientific power naturally attach too much importance to events which are inconsequential when seen in a wide perspective of truth. It is a pity that Sastri whom you rightly praise has been ruled out from the conference in London.

Your letter has the subtle atmosphere of Art evoking many-colored images of reality. Who would leave them for the harsh assertiveness of facts that carry no meaning in themselves and must wait for the inner mind to be related to significance?

You remind me of those early days of *Gitanjali.*

Poets are proverbially vain and I am no exception. Therefore if I cherish even an exaggerated notion of the value of my own poems which are in Bengali I am sure you will half humorously tolerate it. But I am no such fool as to claim an exorbitant price for my English which is a borrowed acquisition coming late in my life. I am sure you remember with what reluctant hesitation I gave up to your hand my manuscript of *Gitanjali* feeling sure that my English was of that amorphous kind for whose syntax a schoolboy could be reprimanded. The next day you came rushing to me with assurance which I dared not take seriously and to prove to me the competence of your literary judgment you made three copies of those translations and sent them to Stopford Brooke, Bradley and Yeats. The letter which Bradley sent to you in answer left no room for me to feel diffident about the merit of those poems and Stopford Brooke's opinion also was a corroboration. These were enthusiastic as far as I remember. But even then I had no doubt that it was not the language but the earnest feeling expressed in a simple manner which touched their hearts. That was [ample] enough for a foreigner and the unstinted praise offered to me by those renowned critics was a great deal more than I could ever expect. Then came those delightful days when I worked with Yeats and I am sure the magic of his pen helped my English to attain some quality of permanence. It was not at all necessary for my own reputation that I should find my place in the history of your literature. It was an accident for which you were also responsible and possibly most of all was Yeats. But yet sometimes I feel almost ashamed that I whose undoubted claim has been recognized by my countrymen to a sovereignty in our own world of letters should not have waited till it was discovered by the outside world in its own true majesty and environment, that I should ever go out of my way to court the attention of others having their own language for their enjoyment and use. At least it is never the function of a poet to personally help in the transportation of his poems to an alien form and atmosphere, and be responsible for any unseemly risk that may happen to them. However, you must own that you alone were to blame for this and not myself. To the end of my days I should have felt happy and contented to think that the translations I did were merely for private recreation and never for public display if you did not bring them before your readers. Please thank Yeats once again on my behalf for the help which he rendered to my poems in their perilous adventure of a foreign reincarnation and assure him that I at least never underrate the value of his literary comradeship. Latterly I have written and published both prose and poetry in English, mostly translations, unaided by any friendly help, but this again I have done in order to express my ideas, not for gaining any reputation for my mastery in the use of a language which can never be mine.

120

It is sad that some of our artists should feel that they have little scope for creative work in our own land. Burman, as far as I know, is still in Tripura state, and there is a danger of his wasting his talents for want of proper stimulation. European art, like European literature has its great message for us, and this can be truly realized only when we have developed our own individuality which can react to it and assimilate it into the living texture of its being. What is fatal for our creative workers is to get into the habit of depending upon the approbation of western critics and trying to come up to their expectations. The standard of critical judgment must be in the artists' own realizations and in the atmosphere which surrounds them. I feel that the present ferment in India's social and cultural life should open up new vistas before our artists, giving them abundant material wherewith to enrich their art. Nanda Lal and others have already felt the need of a new orientation in their technique and subject matter and their recent works show a vigorous departure from traditions and that spirit of creative adventure which you speak of so beautifully.

Ever sincerely yours,
Rabindranath Tagore

(MS original in Rothenstein Papers, Harvard University)

To Mahatma Gandhi

Santiniketan
[March 1933]

Dear Mahatmaji
It is needless to say that I do not at all relish the idea of divinity being enclosed in a brick and mortar temple for the special purpose of exploita-

tion by a particular group of people. I strongly believe that it is possible for simple-hearted people to realize the presence of God in the open air, in a surrounding free from all artificial obstruction. We know a sect in Bengal, illiterate and not dominated by Brahminical tradition who enjoy a perfect freedom of worship profoundly universal in character. It was the prohibition for them to enter temples that has helped them in their purity of realization.[22]

The traditional idea of Godhead and conventional forms of worship hardly lay emphasis upon the moral worth of religious practices[;] their essential value lies in the conformity to custom which creates in the minds of the worshippers an abstract sense of sanctity and sanction. When we argue with them in the name of justice and humanity it is contemptuously ignored for as I have said the moral appeal of the cause has no meaning for them and you know that there are practices and legends connected with a number of our sectarian creeds and practices which are ignoble and irrational.

There is a tradition of religion connected with temple worship, and though such traditions can be morally wrong and harmful, yet they cannot merely be ignored. There the question comes of changing them, of widening their range and character. There can be differences of opinion with regard to the methods to be adopted. From the point of view of the trustees of traditions they are acting according to an inherent sense of property in preserving them as they are, in keeping the enjoyment of idol worship in temples for exclusive groups of people. They not only deny the right of such worship to Christians and Mohammedans but to sections of their own community. Particular temples and deities are their own property and they keep them locked up in an iron chest. In this they are acting according to traditional religion which allows them such freedom, rather enjoins them to act in this manner. A reformer in dealing with such morally wrong traditions cannot adopt coercion and yet as in fighting with other wrong and harmful customs he must exert moral force and constantly seek to rectify them. This fight is necessary. I do not think Tucker[23] makes this point clear.

As to the Santiniketan prayer hall it is open to all peoples of every faith. Just as its doors do not shut out anybody so there is nothing in the simple form of worship which excludes people of different religions. Our religious service could as well take place under the trees, its truth and sacredness would not at all be affected but perhaps enhanced by such a natural environment. Difficulties of climate and season intervene, otherwise I do not think separate buildings are really necessary for prayer and communion with the divine.

I have sent a poem for the *Harijan*—translating it from one of my recent Bengali writings.[24] I do hope it is one in spirit with the ideal of the *Harijan* which I read with much pleasure and interest. There can be no more hopeful sign for India than the fact that her repressed humanity is waking up as a result of the great fast.

With loving regards

Yours sincerely
Rabindranath Tagore

(MS copy at Rabindra Bhavan, Santiniketan)

To Mahadev Desai[25]

Santiniketan
4 January 1937

My dear Mahadeo,

I am not surprised that you should have requested me to explain fully my views with regard to the question of conversion of Harijans to Sikhism. At the very outset, let me tell you that I have not actually advised them to change their religious faith, but pleaded the case of Sikhism if, for reasons well known to all of us, they contemplated such a radical step. I hold the same view with regard to Buddhism as well.

In everyday use, Hinduism is just a way of life, and however great its philosophical and cultural basis may be, that alone will not atone for all the social injustices perpetrated throughout ages, in its name. Our religion divides the society into so many graded groups, and those at the bottom are not only denied bare social justice but are constantly made to feel themselves as less than human. Sanatanists are not very far wrong when they claim that this spirit of division, keeping down a large section of our community, is in the permanent structure of our religion forming the basis of our society, as can be proved by the injunction of our ancient law-givers such as Manu, Parasara and others.

Many of us try to give their texts a civilized gloss but such individual interpretations do not help the victims or touch the social autocrats in their behavior. There are some modern incidents of their defeat such as had happened even so late as in the time of Chaitanya which was quickly followed by reaction, and we cannot be certain that the future of the social reform already achieved by our modern pioneers is permanently assured.

I am hardly concerned about the political aspect of the case. Whether they vote as Hindus or Sikhs is, according to me, of much lesser importance than what affects our humanity and forms our mental attitude towards our fellow beings. Long ago, it is now nearly 25 years, in a poem "Hey Mor Durbhaga Desh" I had uttered my denunciation of the society that has raised itself on the indignity imposed upon the majority of our population in India and made her ready for centuries of defeat and degradation.[26] My cry has been a feeble cry in a wilderness that has obstructed along its history of dense growth the path of light and repeated efforts of those path-markers, who were the predecessors of the present great guide of our nation. Mahatmaji with his phenomenal hold upon the masses has indeed stirred us up but yet I do not know how long we must wait for his teaching to work effectively at the noxious roots in the dark depth of the soil. At the same time we must know that disasters that dog the footsteps of evils do not wait to consult our own time for their mitigation—for medicine which is sluggishly slow in its curative effect is too often overtaken by death.

I do hold the view that Buddhism or Sikhism were attempts from within at the eradication of one of the most intractable social deformities in Hinduism that turns into ridicule our aspiration for freedom. It was indeed a great day not only for the Sikhs but also for the whole of India when Guru Govinda, defying the age-long conventions of the Hindu society, made his followers one, by breaking down all barriers of caste and thereby made them free to inherit the true blessings of a self-respecting manhood. Sikhism has a brave message to the people and it has a noble record. How great would be its effect, if this religion can get out of its geographical provincialism, shed its exclusiveness inevitable in a small community and acquire a nationwide perspective, one can only guess. I do not find anything in [the Sikh] religious practices and creeds which hurts my human dignity. My father often used to offer his worship in Amritsar *gurudwara* where I daily accompanied him but I never could imagine him at the Kali's temple in Calcutta. Yet, in his culture and religion he was a Hindu and in his daily living maintained a purer standard of Hinduism than most of those who profess it by words of mouth and pollute it in their habits. I therefore do not fear that the Harijans' conversion to Sikhism or Buddhism will mean also their neglecting or abandoning Hindu culture.

I felt very happy that Nanda Lal proved once again his great worth. But I never had any doubts about his making Faizpur arrangements an unqualified success.[27]

With loving blessings,

Yours sincerely,
Rabindranath Tagore

(MS copy at Rabindra Bhavan, Santiniketan)

To Sufia Kamal[28]

Almora
[May/June 1937?]

Kalyaniashu,
　　To bid farewell, the forests bring
　　The sun a holy offering,
　　　　A handful of asoka blooms, forlorn.
　　In the final hour, its lingering hint
　　Will infuse the clouds' vermillion tint,
　　　　When Robi, the sun, is gone.

(From the journal *Jayashri*, 1355, circa 1948)
Translated by Radha Chakravarty

To Pulinbehari Sen[29]

You have enquired whether I composed the song "Janaganamana" unbiased by the needs of any special occasion. I realize this question has occurred to you because of the harsh statements originating in various parts of the country concerning this song. Under Fascist ideology, to disagree is dangerous. Very harsh punishment is reserved for it. In our country a difference of opinion is tantamount to a defect of character. Very harsh words are used to condemn it. Many times in my life I have faced this reaction and never have I protested against it. I have decided to reply to your letter not to add fuel to the raging controversy, but to satisfy your curiosity about the composition of the song.

Once, my late friend Hemchandra Mallik, accompanied by Bipinchandra Pal Mahashay, came to me with a request. Their intention was to assimilate the image of Durga with an image of the Motherland as a goddess, and thereby invest the autumnal ceremony of Durgapuja with a new significance and inaugurate a new tradition. Their special plea to me was to compose a prayer for this deity with appropriate fervor and devotion. I remonstrated, saying this devotion would not touch my heart, and would therefore be wrong. If this matter had fallen solely within the literary field, then regardless of my own religious beliefs, I would have had no hesitation. But unsanctioned entry into the area of worship and faith is to be condemned. My friends were not convinced. I composed "Bhubanamana mohini." That the song is not suitable for a sacred pavilion goes without saying. On the other hand one has to admit that the song is also unsuitable for a public gathering of the Indian nation. A non-Hindu will not be able to identify or empathize with it.

A similar incident had occurred in my life once before. That was the year arrangements were afoot to welcome the Emperor of India. A friend of mine, well placed in the imperial administration, earnestly requested me to compose a song of tribute to the Emperor. I was surprised and also rather annoyed.

In reaction, I composed the song "Janagana mana adhinayaka" to announce the triumph of the deity who rules over the destiny of Bharat, who eternally propels travelers down an uneven roads, who is the omniscient guide of the people. Loyal as he was to the government, even my friend realized that no George, whether Fifth or Sixth, could ever be the eternal charioteer of the carriage of human destiny. Strong as his dedication to the government was, he did not lack for intelligence. Today the hostility I encounter due to our differences of opinion is not a matter of concern to me, but the mental aberration of my opponents is a worrying sign.

In this connection, another incident of many years ago comes to mind. Those days the upturned palms of our leaders were raised towards the remote pinnacle of the imperial palace in expectation of a shower of alms. Once a few of them were scheduled to assemble somewhere in the evening. An acquaintance of mine was their messenger. In spite of my strong refusal, he insisted that without my presence their gathering would be incomplete. God has not given me the strength to resist till the end, however rational be the grounds of my refusal. I had to go. Just before I left, I composed the following song:

"Ask me not to sing."

The gathering broke up after this song had been performed. The members present had not been pleased.

After repeated blows, I have come to realize that it is easy to please people if you trim your sails to the wind, and watch the sky. But that is not always the best or the true path. Even for a poet who speaks in many tongues, it is a matter of degradation. In this context I remember a saying of Bhagwan Manu. He said: be aware that glory is poison, and regard blame or infamy as nectar.

1937

Translated by Kalyani Dutta

To Victoria Ocampo

Santiniketan
14 March 1939

Dear Vijaya

How often I feel that your nearness which once was so untrammeled and close, now that it has receded into a hopeless distance, has come poignantly closer to me, its gifts disclosing value that teases the mind by its rarity. Unfortunately the paths that accidentally had reached some preciousness can never be retraced and when the heart longs to own it back it realizes that it is lost for ever. The picture of that building near the great river where you housed us in strange surroundings with its cactus beds that lent their grotesque gestures to the atmosphere of an exotic remoteness, often comes to my vision with an invitation from across an impossible barrier.[30] There are some experiences which are like treasure islands detached from the continent of immediate life, their charts ever remaining vaguely deciphered—and my Argentine episode is one of them. Possibly you know that the memory of those sunny days and tender care has been encircled by some of my verses—the best of their kind—the fugitives are made captive, and they will remain, I am sure, though unvisited by you, separated by an alien language.[31]

With dearest love
Rabindranath Tagore

(MS copy at Rabindra Bhavan, Santiniketan)

To Revd. Foss Westcott[32]

Santiniketan
16 June 1941

My dear Lord Bishop

I thank you for the trouble you have taken to acquaint me with your reaction to my recent reply to Miss Rathbone's open letter. I respect your sentiments and share your conviction that never was mutual understanding more necessary between your people and ours than today. I have, as you are no doubt aware, worked all my life for the promotion of racial, communal and religious harmony among the different peoples of the world. I have also, at considerable personal cost and often at risk of being misunderstood by my own people, set my face against all claims of narrow and aggressive nationalism, believing in the common destiny and oneness of all mankind. I hold many of your people in the highest regard and count among them some of my best friends. Both my faith and my practice during the last so many decades should be ample guarantee that I was not carried away by any racial, religious or merely national prejudice in my recent statement. I have neither the right nor the desire to judge the British people as such; but I cannot help being concerned at the conduct of the British Government in India, since it directly involves the life and well-being of millions of my countrymen. I am too painfully conscious of the extreme poverty, helplessness and misery of our people not to deplore the supineness of the Government that has tolerated this condition for so long. I have nothing against Miss Rathbone personally, and I am glad to be assured by you of her estimable qualities and of her love for our people. But I had hoped that the leaders of the British nation, who had grown apathetic to our suffering and forgetful of their own sacred trust in India during their days of prosperity and success, would at last, in the time of their own great trial, awake to the justice and humanity of our cause. It has been a most grievous disappointment to me to find that fondly cherished hope receding farther and farther from realization each day. Believe me, nothing would give me greater happiness than to see the people of the West and the East march in a common crusade against all that robs the human spirit of its significance.

With kind regards,
Yours sincerely
Rabindranath Tagore

(MS copy at Rabindra Bhavan, Santiniketan)

3

Prose

THIS SELECTION OF TAGORE'S nonfictional prose represents both translations from his Bengali works and selections from his English writings and lectures. Tagore composed voluminously in prose in both languages, and his works in the medium are among his most important legacies. In his lifetime, he published around thirty volumes of essays in Bengali alone, and another ten volumes were published posthumously. His English prose writings, as can be seen from the four-volume folio-sized *English Writings of Rabindranath Tagore,* run to nearly two thousand pages.

In Bengali Tagore used prose not only to write letters, autobiographical pieces, travelogues, and fiction, but also to publish expository, polemical, comical, and satirical pieces on current political and social issues, literature, and the arts. He also penned meditative and even discursive essays on the life of the spirit and humanism. He contributed innumerable occasional essays and reviews to a number of periodicals. His prose writings in Bengali also include the countless speeches, lectures, and radio broadcasts that he gave on all conceivable occasions. As our selections, included under the rubric *Self-Reliance and Other Essays* (1895–1930) and the essay "Statecraft and Ethics" (1907), will indicate, he engaged himself in topical issues and was passionately involved in the debates and controversies of his age. His Bengali prose works also represent his thoughts on history, aesthetics, education, social reform, self-reliance, the economy, politics, colonial rule, East-West and Hindu-Muslim relations, women's empowerment, and rural development. Significantly, it was during the tumultuous events associated with the short-lived partition of Bengal (1905–1911) that he published most frequently in prose—sixteen volumes of his essays came out in the first decade of the twentieth century alone!

Initially, Tagore's Bengali prose was quite conventional. Except for his letters and autobiographical writings, where he stuck to *chaltibha-*

sha, or the language of everyday life, he chose *sadhubhasha,* or formal and elevated language, for his prose writings in the nineteenth century. Though this form of prose is eminently readable and capable of reflecting his agile intellect, his use of it at this stage of his literary career suggests that he was not inclined toward stylistic innovations in prose. But in the works that he published in the new century he began to develop a prose that is much closer to speech. The result is writing that is remarkable for its originality and expressive quality.

132

Buddhadeva Bose, himself adept both in Bengali prose and verse, declares in his essay "Tagore and Bengali Prose" that "the greatest poet in the Bengali language is also supreme in prose." Indeed, Bose adds that modern Bengali prose is Tagore's "creation," for though he had written prose "modestly" toward the end of the nineteenth century, he had decided to change his prose style "radically" in the new century in a deliberate bid to capture the rhythms of speech. As Bose observes, the example of Tagore's use of "the natural rhythm of spoken Bengali" was decisive. Once he "perfected" the use of *chaltibhasha,* there would be no going back to *sadhubhasha* for him and for almost all subsequent Bengali writers of prose (*Tagore: Portrait of a Poet,* 103, 110).

Many of the Bengali essays assembled here are from Tagore's middle period, such as "Self-Reliance" and "Statecraft and Ethics"; these and late works such as "Hindus and Muslims" and "The Tenant Farmer" (1937) reveal the intense emotions generated in him by the plight of people fractured by religion and class. In contrast, his essays on literature, "The Components of Literature" and "The Significance of Literature" (1907), display the author's interest in literary theory as he tries to probe the mysteries of literary creation and account for the nature and significance of writing.

Tagore turned to English prose from the second decade of the twentieth century after the English *Gitanjali* made him a celebrity in the West. Later, the fame generated by the Nobel Prize and the need to raise money for Visva-Bharati embarked him on extended lecture tours in Europe, the United States, Japan, and China. "The Problem of Self," published in *Sadhana, the Realization of Life* (1913), is part of the lectures that he gave at Harvard a few months after the launch of the English *Gitan-*

jali. These lectures, written in the spirit of the poems, articulate his thoughts on the path toward union with the infinite. "Nationalism in the West" is one of four polemical and hard-hitting lectures on what he considered to be the negative course history had taken in the West and in Japan. Published as *Nationalism* (1917), they were decried by many in these parts of the world, though they are perhaps his most often-read prose works outside India now. The Nobel Prize Acceptance Speech (1921) was actually delivered eight years after the award. It shows the poet trying to account for the distinction that had been conferred on him and describing his response to it with sincerity and feeling. The few extracts chosen from *Thoughts from Rabindranath Tagore* (1921) indicate that Tagore could write in an experimental vein in English too. These brief prose excursions, modeled perhaps after Pascal's *Pensées,* are aphoristic but also typify his lyrical-meditative bent. "My Pictures" (1930) first appeared as the catalogue for an exhibition of his paintings held in Birmingham. "Crisis in Civilization" (1941) represents his final thoughts on the conflict engulfing the world as he reached the end of his life. It is also the "authorized" translation of his final public address, completed under his supervision by Kshitish Roy and Krishna Kripalani.

Whether in Bengali or in English, Tagore's prose writings illustrate his wide interests and his passionate engagement with the world. Taken together, they are indicative of his prodigious energy and monumental intellect. He resorted to prose to articulate his evolving views about subjects such as nationalism and race relations. His prose writings nevertheless reflect the voice of a major poet, for his liberal use of figurative language and his insistent rhythms and emotional pitch suggest that the lyrical poet is never far from the prose. Even read selectively, the prose works suggest that his achievement in the genre is substantial and of continuing relevance.

From *Self-Reliance and Other Essays* (1895–1930)

Self-Reliance

While discussing national issues, I have been saying right from the start that we have kept undone all that could have been done, as we spend our days in effortless excitement and recriminations for others. Surely, this is not national duty. We have forgotten our work, so we are busy talking about the work of others. This is a waste of our energy. If we are to achieve "Swaraj" [or self-rule] then we have to prove before we get it that we are capable of doing the work of Swaraj. The area of that work is indeed wide. The love of the country expressed through work for the country does not depend on some external circumstance, it depends upon inner truth. If today that expression is lazy and indifferent, then, if Swaraj comes because of some outside dispensation, it will not be able to remove our mental inertia. This is what I believe. I must not say this even to deceive myself that when our outside obstacle is removed, then our love for the country can be expressed fully and we will devote ourselves to her work . . . Swaraj must come first, only then will come our worship of the country. This Swaraj will be false and meaningless.

1930

(From *"Atmashakti O Samuho,"* Section 13)
Translated by Debjani Sengupta

The Right Way

I received reliable news from a certain place in Barisal that even if "Korkoch" (indigenous) salt is today cheaper than foreign salt at present, the Muslim acquaintances of my correspondent were using the latter, more expensive one. My correspondent also added that they were using foreign salt and cloth not out of necessity but out of obstinacy. In many parts of the country, the scheduled classes were also acting similarly.

A day had come when annoyed about the Partition [of Bengal in 1905] we had vowed to eradicate the use of foreign cloth and salt from the country. We had not thought of anything bigger or further than that.

If you ask me what can be a bigger issue than this, I would say it is this: the reason for anxiety caused by the Partition of Bengal—that reason must be removed. We should do that with all our might rather than express our anger over a small matter.

What are the causes of our unease in the Partition? We have discussed these reasons amongst ourselves often enough. We have also thought that the Government, aware of them, has divided Bengal, so that Bengal divided becomes infirm, handicapped.

In Eastern Bengal, Muslims are a majority. Due to religious and social reasons, the Muslims are more united amongst themselves than the Hindus; so they already possess the main ingredient of strength. They are connected with the Hindus through [a] shared literature, language and education. If Bengal is divided into two according to Hindu and Muslim majorities then, gradually it will be easier to loosen all the other bonds between them.

It is difficult to separate Hindus from other Hindus with a line drawn on a map because there is a social unity between Bengali Hindus; but there is a difference between a Hindu and a Muslim. The extent of that difference has been difficult to ascertain because they have lived closely together, and have been near each other as two groups.

But today, if the King [now] tries to widen that already existing difference to nurture separately the two sides, then as time goes by, without doubt, the distance between Hindus and Muslims will widen. Hatred and jealousy will become rampant amongst the two communities.

The truth is, in this unfortunate country, it is easy to give birth to difference than to unity. The Biharis are our neighbors and we have traded with them for years, yet there is no love lost between Bengalis and Biharis; every Bengali living in Bihar knows this to be true. Educated Oriyas are always eager to stand apart from Bengalis and so are the Assamese. Therefore, the Bengal region, comprising Orissa, Assam, Bihar and Bengal, is made up of inhabitants who have never acknowledged themselves as Bengalis; and nor have the Bengalis ever tried to like the Bihari, the Oriya or the Assamese. Instead, they have always insulted them by looking down upon them.

So, the part of Bengal that is inhabited by people who call themselves Bengali is not a large one; and within this, the geographical part that is fertile, filled with natural resources, with hardy inhabitants whose life-blood has not been drained by famine and malaria, that part comprises mainly of Muslims. The Muslims predominate while Hindus are slowly declining in number in this part.

In such a situation, if Bengal, comprising only of Bengalis, is divided in a way that Muslim-Bengal and Hindu-Bengal are separated, then no other province in India will be as unstable and as estranged as Bangladesh.

In this case, whichever way we may fight the British Raj over the Partition of Bengal and give a call for Boycott to express our anger, what is the real necessity that faces us? It is necessary for us to try our utmost to see that the Partition perpetrated by the Government will not be mirrored by another partition within us.

Instead of doing that, we decided our only duty was towards the Boycott. We were determined to make Boycott successful by any means; so much so that we slowly helped each other move towards another nightmare, a nightmare that would have inevitably come with the Partition.

Impatiently, without considering the wishes and conveniences of people, we began to think of the prohibition against foreign salt and cloth as our ultimate goal, without any regard for consequences. We did not have the patience to wait and to win over our people; we became impatient to show the English the result of *their* actions.

Thus, we began to trample upon the desires and conveniences of our peasantry to make the Boycott a success. The truth of this may not be easy for us to admit, but is certainly difficult for us to repudiate.

The result of all this is that we have managed to alienate one section of our population because of the intensity of our desire. I don't know how far we have succeeded in making them wear clothes of our choice, but we have certainly succeeded in losing their trust. I don't know how successful we were in making the English our enemy, but we have managed without doubt to sow enmity within the country. Certainly, it is true that alienating Muslims and other lower castes over the Boycott has resulted in antagonism in every corner of the country. The reason for this is before we inspired them to work we did not gain their trust; nor did we take any steps to address their lack of faith in us. We have forced them to follow our doctrines, we have used them, but we have not made any attempt to get close to them. Out of the blue, one fine day, we go to their somnolent houses and rouse them from sleep. Naturally they are suspicious and aggressive. We do not draw them close, yet we demand closeness from them. We have angered and annoyed them, an anger only close relations can bear, and thus we have alienated them more than ever before.

This time, after many years, our leaders had left the English political high ground to come and stand at the door of the ordinary people. The people, in turn, were naturally assailed by a question—why were the "babus" so concerned about us, what had transpired?

To speak the truth, our concern for them has never been great in the past, nor is it great now. We did not go to the people saying, "If you wear Swadeshi cloth, it will benefit you; we are concerned about your welfare." We went to them saying "We want to teach the English a lesson. If you do not support us, the Boycott will not be complete; so, even if you do not profit by it, you must wear it."

We have never pondered on or worked for the welfare of the poor and the downtrodden; we have never acknowledged them as our own, and we have never shown them any respect. Now, when we have to suffer losses, we have called them our brothers. Naturally, they have ignored our call.

We get angry when they fail to respond to us. We have always mistreated them; now when we flatter them, it is their pride that stops them from coming under our spell.

Men, who think they are above all others, are impatient about people beneath them. They have no respect for human nature and remain unacquainted with it. For a similar reason even the English get angry when they perceive any obstacle to their plans. When we are high up, and our desires clash with those below us, then it may look like undiluted obstinacy on the part of those who are inferior to us. So, when the proponents of Swadeshi failed to attract the Muslim peasants in Mymensingh and other places, they were extremely offended. Never once did they pause to think that because we have never worked for the welfare of the Muslims or other ordinary people of the country, we couldn't blame them if they are suspicious of our recent overtures of friendship. A brother suffers losses for another brother; but if a stranger comes and calls us "brother" do we let him have a portion of our house? The common folk of our country do not know they are our brothers, and nothing in our actions has ever shown them this sense of brotherhood we are supposed to have for them in our hearts.

Let me reiterate this again. We had gone to the ordinary people of our country not because we loved them but because we wanted to teach the English a lesson. So the word "brother" does not sound like a melody, it comes out instead as a harsh discordant note of hatred for others.

We, the educated folks of the country, have rent the air with the cry "Mother" for the country we love. Our heart's impulses are so full of that word that we often forget that we have not truly realized the mother in our country. We think that through songs and the excitement of our call this mother is manifest everywhere. When the common people do not see this "mother" in their "Swadesh," we become impatient with them. We begin to think it is an act of deliberate blindness on their part or else our enemies have managed to incite them to rebellion. We are not willing to shoulder the guilt and realize that we have failed to establish a true motherland within the country.

The teacher has not taught, he does not have the ability to do so; yet when his pupil fails to answer a question, he raises a hand to strike the student. Surely our present situation is something like that. We have distanced the ordinary people from us, yet when they stay away from us in our times of need, we are annoyed with them. We have used the force we are capable of stirring against those who have never been with us. When after the platitudes of the English-educated "Babus" the ordinary people have refused to budge from the path they have traditionally taken, we are annoyed. We are determined to defeat them, to make them understand what is good for them, even through force. We have reassured ourselves that it is necessary to use force.

It is our misfortune that even though we desire freedom, we really do not believe in it. We do not have the patience to respect the intelligence of others; we only try to terrorize and dominate that intelligence. To invoke the fear of ancestors rotting in hell, or to ostracize someone from the community, setting fire to homes or the nightmare of being beaten up on the road are some of the ways of establishing a slavish mentality in our hearts. When we follow these shortcuts to save labor, we prove once again that we do not know what can be the freedom of mind and action. We think it will be good if we force others to follow what we think is best—if they do so out of free will, excellent; if not, they can be coerced, misleading them through deceit if need be.

Without a doubt, through Boycott, we have taken these shortcuts and have dealt a fatal blow to reason and good judgment. A few days ago, a letter arrived from the provinces saying that in large markets, traders had received a notice stating if they do not comply with the Boycott of foreign goods, their stalls will be set on fire. In some places such notices have been followed by arson. Export of foreign goods was forcefully stopped and customers who were buying such goods threatened. Slowly that enthusiasm has expanded to setting fire to people's homes and killing innocent men.

It is indeed sad that for some of our educated men this kind of oppression is not wrong. They have decided that such terror tactics are necessary for the good of the country. To such men it is useless to speak of justice. They say what is done for the country cannot ever be unjust, and seen to be "adharma." But even to a perverse mind we should repeatedly state that injustice cannot be good for a land and for its people.

I must ask if acts of arson or maltreatment of an unwilling people, forcing them to give up foreign cloth, is not a way in which their entire being is forever made rebellious against Swadeshi. Their hatred of Swadeshi-preaching men is made more permanent through these means!

The lower castes and the Muslim peasants have become impatient and these thoughts run through their minds—"Those who have never loved us, who have been indifferent to us in our misery and dangers, those who treat us as animals socially, when they come to oppress us because of foreign cloth or any other reason we will certainly not tolerate it." Therefore, in spite of great personal loss and hardship, they continue to use foreign materials.

140

  This is the reason why I say that the greatest curse upon the country is not foreign cloth but this quarrel within it. Nothing is worse than one section of the populace enslaving the opinions of another through force and against their will. Even when we chant "Bande Mataram" this will not be the true worship of our motherland; it will simply be an incantation of the words of brotherhood and then committing fratricide. Unity through the use of force is not real unity—terrorizing and writing abusive editorials to force other's opinions is not conducive to national unity.

  All these are symptoms of slavery. Those who go around saying these are for the good of the country only betray to the world their own cursed history of subservience. They also teach this mode of slavery to those whom they try to dominate and terrorize.

If we have any respect for human life, then we will never desire to set fire to any one's home or to beat them up. With patience and understanding we will try to influence their minds and hearts towards goodness and towards justice. Then we shall want not people, we shall not want to see what cloth they wear or what salt they eat. If we want to do good to others, we must work for them, remove artificial barriers between us, and be modest. If we care for human beings, then we must devote ourselves completely to them; we must surrender ourselves to their good and not try to impose our opinions on them or to force them to follow our ideas and doctrines. When the other person understands that I am not trying to enslave him, or not forcing him to do things against his will, he will surely understand I am doing what every human should do unto another. He will understand that with "Bande Mataram" we are worshipping a motherland whose children are the great and the small. Then, we will not insult or demean anyone through our attitudes, words and thoughts whether Muslim or lower caste, Bihari or Oriya, English educated or not—we will not be filled with self-pride . . . To be enthused by a short-lived idea will never light the real fire, it will only be a small blaze. The material we work upon must be—Man. And truth lies in man's intelligence, his heart and his humanity; it is not Swadeshi cloth or indigenous salt. If we insult this humanity every moment and continue to worship mill cloth, we will never receive God's blessings. The result will be exactly the opposite of what we now desire.

(From *"Shodupaye,"* 1909)
Translated by Debjani Sengupta

The Disease and the Cure

Right at the beginning, we must remember a truth. For whatever reason or through whatever means, if we try to retaliate against the English, then they will certainly do something about it. The consequence of their action will not be beneficial to us. This is easy to understand—yet we did not take into account this obvious truth. When we were busy boasting about ourselves we were actually busy paying our respects to the greatness of the English, we did not prove our good sense or our courage by doing so.

Even before the battle had begun we had misjudged our opponent, just as we did not judge carefully our own strengths. Today we lament that the English are secretly inciting the Muslims against the Hindus. If this is true, why should we feel angry with the English? Why should we think that the English lack the brains to try and use whatever means and opportunities they have at their disposal to thwart us? Or feel reassured that they would not do so?

We should really focus on the fact that the Muslims can be incited against the Hindus rather than who incites them. We have to be aware of this fissure within us, not what comes in through it. The hatred that exists between us will be used by our enemy—if not today, then certainly tomorrow; if not by this enemy then certainly by another. So we must condemn the fault and not the enemy.

There is a wrong that exists in this country regarding Hindu-Muslim relations, and it is a wrong that has continued for many hundreds of years. We cannot escape the consequences of this wrongdoing, this sin.

Humans are unaware of a wrong if it is committed habitually. The darkness that exists between Hindus and Muslims has now assumed terrifying proportions. This is good, because this enables us to acknowledge it, to get to know it.

We have come to know it, yet we are not learning any lessons from it. What we have refused to see, God has caught us by our ears and forced us to notice—we blush with shame at that ignominy, but if we ignore that lesson, our shame and sorrow will continue to increase.

Surely there is no need to lie to each other any more now. We will have to acknowledge the barrier that exists between the Hindus and Muslims. Not only are we different, we are also against each other.

We have, for hundreds of years, lived side by side, eaten the same crop from the same field; drunk the water from the same river, shared the same sunlight. We speak the same language, share the same joys and sorrows; but the ordinary human interactions that take place between neighbors have never taken place between us. We have not behaved like brothers. For so long have we nurtured this sin amongst us that even when we have lived with each other for so long, we have been unable to stop this division from growing. God will not be able to forgive us this sin.

We know in many places of Bengal, Hindus and Muslims do not share the same seat; if a Muslim enters the room he is made to sit on a separate seat and the water in the hubble-bubble is changed for fear of pollution.

During an argument, we say that nothing can be done about this, the holy texts must be followed. No holy book states Hindus must hate Muslims. If any sacred text does say that, it will not be able to establish Swadesh or Swaraj in this land. In a country, where hatred of neighbors is taught by religion, where man invites hell's wrath by drinking water from the glass of another, when one race can be saved by humiliating another, then degradations and insults await the people of that country. If one set of people looks down upon another, then they will have to suffer the same humiliations in the hands of others.

Where our humanity is concerned we are very weak—because we do not consider some human beings as part of mankind. We are always engaged in curbing others' rights into minuscule boundaries; we abandon our own people at the hint of the slightest fault and we have never learnt to accept others in amity. We have divided ourselves, and, since we understand difference more than unity, we will never rid ourselves of slavery and piteous humiliation.

Then, we announced the war against the English with "Boycott" and decided to follow the path of Swaraj. In this struggle, we thought all obstacles were outward, and we were strong within. This time, the Almighty has shown us clearly, decisively, our divided state. We have now realized we were the means of our own slavery, and we ourselves the greatest obstacle to our progress. When we began to realize this we began to ask ourselves this question—We must save our country, but from whom? The answer is from our own sins.

. . . We must realize that when the English depart from this land it will not become our motherland again. We must earn our country, through our own efforts. By providing food and shelter, health, happiness and education to our countrymen, we must become their mainstay. We must learn to do the best for the country in times of sorrow and hardship. When we understand this truth in the innermost core of our hearts then we will also realize our country—there will not be any need to give speeches to make people understand the meaning of the word "country." Today, when the English-educated city men go to the illiterate peasant and announce "We are brothers," then the poor man fails to understand the meaning of the term. We had called them "that peasant character"; we had never seen the importance of their happiness or sorrow. When we wanted to know about their lives we had resorted to Government surveys; now these people whom we disdain and avoid, suddenly appear as our brothers today. We tell them to boycott cheap foreign cloth and to get beaten up by the Gurkha brigade. Naturally, they are deeply suspicious of our motives. I have heard a famous Swadeshi preacher describe in East Bengal how he had overheard a Muslim peasant murmur after his resounding speech, "Probably the Babus are in trouble!" The preacher was annoyed but the peasant was right. They were quick to understand the tone in the preacher's honeyed words. When someone wishes to form a relationship from ulterior motives even an inferior person will have no taste for it; however important the motive may be, whether it is Boycott, or Swadeshi or the good of the country. Respectfully as human beings, and lovingly as country-men, if we had remained united, if we had not divided and not alienated ourselves through western education, if we had worked tirelessly for each others' good, then we could have given a call to them in this day of danger and loss. That would have been a truly appropriate gesture.

One day in a public meeting the speaker was expanding upon the benefits of Hindu–Muslim unity. I could not resist stopping myself from saying this was not an occasion to talk of benefits. If two brothers lived together, naturally the benefits were numerous, but that should not be the sole reason for staying together. Circumstances may change, so can the benefits. The only real truth was we lived together because we are the inhabitants of this country; and in sorrow or happiness, we are together as human beings. It is a shame if we are not united, an "adharma." We are the children of the same country—the Almighty has bound us together. If we disregard that bond, through good times and bad, then our humanity has failed us. Between us, our relationship must be of love, not of gain but of selfless devotion—only then can benefits be counted and losses disregarded.

. . . A lot of work is awaiting us. Have we done anything at all? Let us think clearly, truthfully for once and we will realize how far our country has receded from us—how very far! Leave alone the whole of India, just the very thought of the land of Bengal makes us realize how tenuous is our relationship to her. In love, in knowledge, in accomplishments, this Bangladesh is far away from us. How insignificant are our deeds on her behalf—To know her, to give back something to her, to do something for her! Look within your hearts and minds and speak the truth— how deeply indifferent you are to your country! Have her poverty, her sorrow, her beauty, her wealth ever touched our hearts to such an extent that some of us have thought of spending our time and money on her? We, the educated few, and the vast sections of our countrymen remain separate as ever, as if a vast ocean stretches between us. So I say, all our work has remained undone.

(From *"Byadhi O Protikar,"* 1908)
Translated by Debjani Sengupta

145

The King and [His] Subjects

Many amongst us do not know and many more of us refuse to accept that Boycott has been accomplished by hurting one section of our people. If we understand a problem well, we must also have the patience to make others understand it through example and good advice. If we fail to grasp the truth that it is wrong to forcefully impede another person's real rights, it will be impossible to contain all that is incontinent. When we do something wrong in the name of duty, the whole country suffers from its ill-effects. This is why we have rebelled against freedom by doing something wrong in its name; and we have spread the fire of mischief by forcibly trying to unite all who disagreed with our views and who went against our wishes. We have killed diversities in opinions and actions and have termed it national unity. Whatever I say everyone else must say it too, whatever I do everyone must do that—this has killed off the diversity. We have been intimidating to opposing opinions, we have been rudely obscene in our editorials, and we have threatened physical harm to those who dared to say anything different to us. Anonymous letters have been sent to many and even the elderly have not been spared . . .

I have said earlier too that when one does not have the strength to build, one shall perish if one lacks ingenuity. I must say I doubt if this creativity is expressed anywhere in our country. What forces of originality and vision are working within us, to unite us? All we see around are signs of divisiveness, of separation. When this difference is very strong, we are unable to establish our rule or tenets in our own land. So, someone else will govern over us—nothing we do can prevent that from happening. Many amongst us are of the opinion that our lack of freedom is an outward burden in the shape of an alien government, not an internal disease like a headache. When we get rid of this burden we will feel lighter instantly. But this is easier said than done. The English government is not the cause of our slavery; they are a symptom of our own deep-rooted inclination towards slavery.

146

Unfortunately, nowadays we do not have the patience to think about deep-rooted causes. When the question arises how it is possible to establish Swaraj in India, to unite all races into a "Mahajati," then many of us hastily give the example of Switzerland, with many races, yet free!

All these examples may help us to forget the real situation but we will not be able to hoodwink the Almighty. The real argument is not whether Swaraj is possible in a country with diverse races. Diversity is of many kinds—in a family of ten, there are ten different kinds of diversities. The question is if within this diversity real unity exists or not. If Switzerland has been able to achieve unity with diverse races then we see how unity has been able to reign supreme in spite of diversity. Swiss society is ruled by a sense of unity. Our country has diversity but without a true sense of unity. Diversity has taken many shapes of language, race, religion, society and culture, to divide this huge country into smaller and larger units.

Therefore I do not see how we can rest by citing these examples. We cannot say this and satisfy ourselves of truth—if we get rid of the English then Bengali, Marathi, Punjabi, Madrasi, Hindus and Muslims will unite in one body, in one self, in one unit to be free.

Truly speaking, the unity that we see today in India, for which we think fulfillment of our wishes is near, is a mechanical unity. It is not organic. This unity has not come about in our philosophy of life and religion, but foreign rule has brought about this unity externally.

Living things often coalesce when they are put together mechanically. Twigs and branches are artificially propagated in this way by tying two twigs together. Till they unite the outward twine must not be removed. Certainly, this twine is not a part of the tree, so whatever good it may do, it pains the tree to be encircled by it. But when diversity must be enhanced through unity then we must acknowledge that twine. That twine bites deeper than it should—the only remedy to that is to use all our internal might to bring together the two sides, to make them one with life's juices, by putting heart to heart. I am certain, when this unity is complete, the Divine Gardener will remove the external twine. We must acknowledge the outward burden of English rule. Without depending mechanically on it, we must enhance unity with our own hands in this disparate country with our sacrifice, with our devotion, with love. Through creative work and organization this geographical space must be shaped into our motherland. Different people must be made our own through our own efforts.

I have heard many people say the enmity against the English will give us unity. The natural unkindness the English possess against the Oriental races has made them behave with indifference and disrespect, and this has pained and angered everyone throughout the land. As days go by, the searing pain goes deeper into our natures. This diurnal increasing pain is a unifying force bringing together all sections of the population. Many say this enmity must be our mainstay in our fight against the British.

If this is true then when the cause of this enmity leaves, that is, when the English leave the country, then this artificial bond of unity will also snap. Where can we find a second cause of unity? We need not travel far to find another cause, nor do we have to look outside. Our bloodthirsty hatred for each other will wound and tear each other to pieces.

(From *"Raja O Proja,"* 1895)
Translated by Debjani Sengupta

Statecraft and Ethics

All of us know about the incident of the incarceration of Someshwar Das of Allahabad. Such unjust action against an individual is hardly an issue to be taken up by a monthly newspaper. This current matter, however, targets all Indians through an individual. That is why it is necessary to make a few brief comments about it.

The *Pioneer* writes that diverse communities live together in India. To maintain peace between them all is an unpleasant necessity for the British government. Hence, whenever the possibility of strife among these communities arises, the need for a particularly tough measure against it arises as well. Given such situations, however, the incarceration of Someshwar Das cannot be termed a harsh sentence.

The esteemed English newsweekly, *New India,* has very clearly pointed to the inappropriateness of the *Pioneer's* argument. I can see hundreds of examples of how perfunctorily, if at all, the British administrator pays any attention to such instances of British behavior which have contributed to hurting Indian sentiments. Just the other day, when an Englishman forced a respectable Brahmin to carry his footwear for him, even the highest court in the country decided that the matter was extremely inconsequential.[1] Of course, it may be so, but not in quite the same way as put forth by the *Pioneer!* The humiliation of a respectable Brahmin in this fashion is an extremely serious issue for every Indian.

If that be the case, let us try to understand the significance of the incident. For the court, humiliating those communities that are law-abiding—that is to say, the ones that follow the letter of the law without protest—may be a trivial matter. In fact, to unfairly hurt those who will not break peace at any cost, may also be considered a minor issue. But to raise your hand against those who are insensitive, those who make their own rules at will, is a crime of the highest order. Under British rule, the solution to having the tiger and the cow drink water from the same hole is not found by killing the tiger but by breaking the horns of the cow!

However, I cannot get angry at what the *Pioneer* states. Having taken us to be friends, the *Pioneer* has taught us a lesson. After all, it is not as grave a crime to set damp cotton on fire than it is to set gunpowder ablaze. It is simply not possible to consider it a crime to insult those who are ever gentle and compliant. Therefore, though we must protect the law from harm, the law is under no compulsion to protect us. This is the *Pioneer's* considered opinion about us "mild Hindus."

There is another point to be made. In the eyes of the law, there is no inequality between the literate and the illiterate, or the black and the white. But there exists indeed the very serious matter of political need or compulsion, and no matter which way that veers, the law bends accordingly. In this country, the native's blind approbation of the Englishman is a matter of political expediency, and therefore it is impossible to form a critical opinion about it. According to the letter of the law, no doubt the sentence served to the native for his misbehavior toward the Englishman remains absolutely the same as the one served to the Englishman for similar behavior toward the native. The law books also do not include any major thesis on this point. But political necessity considers itself of far greater importance than the letter of the law.

It is beyond any doubt that in the modern Dharmashashtra of the Western civilization, politics occupies the ultimate position while ethical considerations play second fiddle. Only when political ends have been met can Dharma take its place. How insidiously truth and reality get distorted due to political need has been elaborated in an article elsewhere in a volume by Herbert Spencer. That the lawmaker must mould himself according to such political need has indeed been acknowledged even by the *Pioneer*.

Judge William Burkitt has used the word "audacity" to describe Someshwar's behavior. That it is audacious for a native to oppose an Englishman in self-defense is something the judge himself has pointed to. At the same time, we certainly cannot consider the judge as having been very "brave" or as having shown us his humanity through his act of sentencing the same "audacious" individual for his "misdemeanor." In fact, the judge has not displayed any daring whatsoever by trying to be unbiased towards Someshwar in a mindless case. In this particular case, if the one punished has been "audacious," then we can apply absolutely any English adjective to describe the one who has passed the judgment.

But we cannot remain content by simply condemning the result of this case and burying it forever as a trivial matter restricted to a short paragraph in a weekly newspaper. Every single day we learn from all kinds of occurrences that the rule of law, and truth itself, does not go hand in hand with political need at all.

I, however, see no need for us to lose sleep over this fact by cogitating about whether this has proven beneficial or harmful for our rulers. What we really need to worry about is that our mind is slowly becoming forgetful of our highest Dharma and that our regard for truth is gradually getting distorted. We have even begun to grant the ultimate position to necessity. We have begun to accept that it is unnecessary to experience Dharmic doubts in the face of political necessity. So how can we protect ourselves from the lessons learnt of humiliation, from the knowledge that comes along with Dharma? And, what could we depend on if we begin to push aside our Dharma by calling it useless? On the values of a foreign culture? Is that culture the only permanent thing in the entire universe? Unfortunately, for us, only that which bears down on our chests proves to be the most important thing for us in the world—even the Himalayas seem small when compared with it. In the face of this fact, we take utmost pride in the ethics of Western culture, and the ethics of our Dharma cannot stand up to it.

Therefore, whether we like it or not, we have to perforce swallow the lessons the West teaches us. We will, thus, begin to acknowledge Clive, Hastings, Dalhousie, as the pinnacles of perfection; we will not trouble those people who contend with the English on issues involving rights and wrongs; wherever we hear the call to subjugate India we will deem it a question of our prestige and choose to ignore the call of the Divine—all this I accept with bowed head. But what ought we to do when this same "Guru" approaches us to propagate his own morality by dismissing Shivaji's Rashtraniti as not being Dharmic enough? Will we then still accept that the one who writes the word of the law is afraid of the powerful and avoids the ethics of our Dharmashashtra? Ergo, to hell with Shivaji.[2]

(From *"Rashtraniti aar Dharmaniti,"* 1907)
Translated by Chandana Dutta

The Components of Literature

Writing is not done for the pure pleasure of the self. Some people wax poetic and claim that, just as birds sing to amuse themselves, the author's composition is a passionate soliloquy of sorts—which readers eavesdrop to listen in.

I cannot claim with certainty that bird music has no impact on the society of birds. If there is none, be it so; debate on the issue is pointless. Authors, however, write only for readers.

This does not mean that literature is artificial. The mother's milk is for the baby alone. That does not make it less spontaneous.

Two misconceptions regarding literature prevail in some circles: poetry occurs in isolation and it is a product of self-induced passion. Calling people poets because they look at the sky and remain as mute as the sky is like calling an unburned log fire. What lurks in someone's mind intrigues no one. There is a saying that the general public is only after the cake. During a wedding, guests don't like to speculate on the size of the cake in the pantry; they want the slices on their plates.

Self-existing passion is a similar notion in literature. That writing is not for the writer is a self-evident fact, and that is how it should be considered and examined.

Our mind has a natural tendency to be perceived by other minds. We see in nature that all animals struggle to exist and lay their claim to be so perceived. The organism that is able to multiply manifold makes its existence a pronounced one.

Humans struggle to do the same. The difference between animals and humans is this: animals claim their existence in time and space whereas humans do so in mind and time. The mind seeks to possess many minds over the ages.

This personal quest has been in existence from the beginning of time in gestures, in languages, in scripts, in stone inscriptions, in metal weldings, in leather bindings, on tree barks, on their leaves, on paper, in brush strokes, in cuneiforms, in so many scribbles, in so many efforts—from left to right, from right to left, from top to bottom, from one column to another! What are these? What I have thought, what I have felt, will not die. They will flow from mind to mind, from time to time, in other thoughts, in other perceptions. My dwelling, my furniture, my body, my mind, all my personal possessions will leave me, but my thoughts and feelings will find a home in humanity's thought and intelligence.

When from the sands of the Gobi deserts tattered and forgotten scrolls of an extinct civilization emerge, what grief do those unknown letters of an unknown language express! The effort of what time and mind is seeking to access our hearts! He who wrote those letters is no more, the locale that made it possible is no more, but the thoughts and feelings, the desire to be nurtured in human joy and sorrow after ages, may no longer communicate themselves but are gesturing at us with outstretched arms.

The world's greatest emperor Asoka inscribed on the mountain the words that he wanted to be permanently heard. He figured a mountain would never die, never move; it would stand immovable for endless epochs but recite words to travelers of new times. He gave the task of communication to the mountain.

The mountain has carried his message irrespective of time. Where is Asoka, where is Pataliputra, where are the glory days of that blessed India! Yet the mountain is still uttering those words in forgotten letters in an unknown tongue. For ages they have cried in the woods. Those great words of Asoka have invited the human heart with gestures for centuries like a mute. The Rajput went down the road, so did the Pathan, the Mughal, and even the Maratha despite his quick sword and whip—spelling disaster. No one responded to the motions of the mountain. But from an island across the oceans that Asoka never knew—when his craftsmen were inscribing his doctrines on stone slabs, the forest-dwelling druids of that island were expressing the passion of their worship in speechless pillars of rock—came a foreigner after millennia to rescue the language of those silent gestures. The sovereign Asoka's desire became a reality after so many centuries. That desire is no big deal. Even though he was a great king, his likes and dislikes must be made known even to the travelers on the road. His wish has been seeking a home in the human heart, standing by the road for ages. Some on the road looked at the sovereign's earnest desire, some didn't and went on their ways.

This doesn't mean I regard Asoka's doctrines as literature. What this proves is the existence of a primal urge in the human heart. The idols we craft, the paintings we draw, the poetry we write, the stone temples that we build—the relentless effort that is underway everywhere is nothing but the appeal the human heart makes to other human hearts for everlasting recognition.

That which seeks immortality in the human heart usually differs from those efforts which are temporal. For our domestic needs, we plant rice, barley, wheat, and medicinal herbs, but if we want to raise a forest we need seeds of huge vegetations.

Literature's attempt to be immortal reflects a cherished human need. This is why when well-meaning critics worry that useful writing is scarce though the country is awash with plays, novels, and poems, writers don't come to their senses. This is because writing that has practical applications meets immediate need whereas writing with no such value has the potential of greater permanence.

Words of wisdom fulfill their purpose as soon as they become known. In the realm of knowledge, old discoveries are eclipsed by the new. What was unfathomable to scholars yesterday is no longer new even to an immature boy. Truth in a new form leads to a revolution, but truth in a traditional guise does not even surprise. It is indeed astounding that ideas that are familiar even to the ignoramus today plagued scholars once. But feelings of the heart never grow stale though they have been stated many times.

Once known, knowledge needs no further knowing. Fire is hot, the sun round, water liquid—knowing these facts once is enough; someone wanting us to know them again tires our patience. But words of the heart do not exhaust us though we hear them again and again. The fact that the sun rises in the east no longer fascinates us, but the beauty and joy of the sunrise still remain untarnished. Indeed, the more feelings of yore pass onto us through generations the more is their depth enhanced, the more is their appeal.

Therefore, when humanity seeks to keep something personal permanently afresh, it has to do so through words of feeling. This is the reason that literature's primary base is feeling, not knowledge.

Besides, knowledge can be transferred from one language to another. Sometimes moving it from its original work to another work even enhances its lucidity. Its purpose, in fact, is quite effectively served when its subject is exposed by many people in many languages in many ways.

This principle does not apply to words conveying feeling. They cannot separate themselves from the form they assume.

Words of knowledge have to be proven whereas words of feeling have to be spread. To accomplish the latter, one needs hints and gestures, tricks and means. The process is not one of explanation; rather it is one of creation.

A product of these arts and endeavors, the work becomes the body where feelings manifest themselves. The power to give this body life identifies one as a writer. The nature and shape of this body determine the work's appeal to its readers, and the vigor of the work governs its influence in mind and time.

Life's essence resides solely in the body. Unlike water, it cannot be transferred from one container to another. Body and mind quicken each other, becoming one in the process.

Feelings, subjects, and dogmas are the common property of people. If one doesn't express them, then, another will. Writing, on the other hand, represents something completely personal. One's effort never resembles another's. This is why, the writer's true existence can be found in the work and not in feelings, not certainly in the subject matter.

However, the work means simultaneously both itself and the expressed material; still, the method is the writer's own.

An artificial lake can mean both water and a dug-up reservoir of water. But where does the endeavor lie? Water is not a human creation—it is elemental. The measure for making that water available to all for a long time is the deed of great people. Ideas belong to everybody, but arranging them in a special way to please many, as in the work, is the author's achievement.

Thus we see that personalizing feelings and ideas and making them available for all is literature; this is art. Ember is found in many forms in land, water, and air and is commonly available to people. Trees incorporate it by their unique hidden power, and that is how it becomes usable to people. The tree is useful not only for cooking and heating, but also for beauty, shade, and health.

Therefore, it is evident that making an object commonly held by many uniquely one's own and reconstructing it into an object for the common use of many uniquely through a similar process is the goal of literature.

If that is the case, then, matters of knowledge exclude themselves from literature on their own. The reason is that what in English is called *truth* and what in Bengali we name truth—that is, what is accessible to our perception—should be depersonalized by all means. Truth is impersonal, clean, and colorless. The law of gravity is not one thing to me and another thing to another. In truth, there can never be a variety of perceptions.

What is seeking diffusion in other hearts through the music and hue of talented hearts, what cannot be spread in other minds unless formed by our own minds, are the components of literature. Through gestures and hints, feelings and expressions, melody and rhythm, it claims an existence; it is singularly personal; it is not a discovery, nor an imitation; it is creation. Therefore, once published, its shape cannot be altered to suit another situation; its totality depends on its each individual part. When a discrepancy occurs between the two, the literature loses its value.

1907

(From *"Sahitya"*)
Translated by Farhad B. Idris

The Significance of Literature

The world becomes another world in our mind. In this world exist not only the color, shape, sound, and other attributes of the other world, but also our likes and dislikes, our fear and wonder, our pleasure and grief. Our mind, through its various processes, suffuses the outside world differently.

This act of the mind enables us to individualize external reality.

Just as insufficient gastric juice causes indigestion to some, so when one's mind's power is feeble, one's consciousness falls short of integrating the world, is unable to claim it as its own, and fails to invest it with humanity.

There are those vegetative ones whose curiosity extends only to few affairs of the world. Though a part of this world, they are divorced from most of it. Their minds have few crevices, and these are narrow; consequently, they alienate themselves from the world.

There are also those lucky ones whose senses of wonder, love, and imagination are ever alert. They are welcome to nature's halls; and the harp of their heart pulsates with the music of human action.

Through the color and shape of their mind, the external world assumes variegated shapes.

This world is more precious to the imaginative individual than the outside world or the human world. The mind helps this world to become more suitable for access into people's hearts, rendering it unique for consumption.

Thus there is a difference between the outside world and the human world. The human world does not inform us of what is black and white and what is large and small. It tells us of what is dear and vile, what is beautiful and ugly, and what is good and bad in different ways.

This human world has always flowed in our hearts. This stream is old and ever new. Through newer senses and newer perceptions, this age-old flow always assumes unique forms.

But how do we locate ourselves in this flow? How do we preserve it? If this gorgeous world of imagination is not reconstructed with beauty, it creates and wrecks itself continually.

But this thing cannot be allowed to perish. The world of the mind is keen on expressing itself. That is why literature has its lasting appeal among people.

Two issues determine the evaluation of literature. First, how strong is the litterateur's mind in claiming the world? Second, how steady is that power in expressing itself?

A fine coordination between the two does not always exist. Where it does, the result is awesome.

The more worldly the poet's imagination, the more fulfilling is the work for us, and the more expansive does the human world become, enabling us to explore its largesse with depth.

However, aesthetic finesse is also a prized quality of literature. The reason is that even when the medium of that faculty appears relatively weak, the faculty itself is not completely diminished. Instead, it accumulates in language and literature. This enhances the power of expression of humanity itself. People have always been eager to possess it. They confer fame upon those consummate ones who dish it out for them.

How to express the world the mind creates within itself?

It has to be expressed in such a manner that it leads to a mood.

To create this mood, many ingredients are needed.

The work clothes of men are simple. It has to be without frills to be appropriate for work. In civilized society, on the other hand, women's dresses, modesty, and gestures are usually complex.

Women work on the mind. They have to lend their heart as well as appeal to the heart. This is why they can't merely be straight, simple, and unadorned. Men must be proper, but women have to be attractive. It's alright for men to be bold in manners; however, women's conduct must be alluring.

Literature, too, takes recourse to ornaments, allegory, rhymes, suggestions, and indications. Unlike philosophy, it cannot be without embellishments.

To describe the indescribable, the inexpressible has to be preserved in expression. The inexpressible in literature somewhat resembles women's beauty and modesty. It is beyond imitation. It surpasses style and is never clouded by style.

To establish in language what is beyond language, literature primarily combines two things: image and music.

That which cannot be told in words has to be told in pictures. There is no limit to illustrations in literature. Simile, analogy, and allegory enhance feelings. "Eyes follow like birds to see." In this line Balaramdas has said it all. How can mere description capture the eagerness of the roving eye! The tremendous struggle to suggest that the eyesight is flying like a bird is resolved in this image.

In addition, literature obviously uses music in rhyme, diction, and figurative language. That which cannot be said in any way can be said only through music. When meaning is analyzed, even seemingly trivial expression becomes profound. It is music that has the power to make a statement full of sorrow.

Hence image and music are the chief components of literature. An illustration lends a shape to feelings and music gives motion to them. Thus visuals are the body and the music its pulse.

It is not that the human heart alone stores literature. The human personality is such a unique creation that unlike inanimate constructions it is not accessible through our senses. It won't stand up when it is asked to do so. Supremely intriguing, this personality cannot be harnessed like an animal in a cage for analysis.

158

Literature seeks to bring to light even this elusive human character from its secret chamber, which is an extremely difficult task. The task is difficult because that character is not stable, nor consistent. It has many departments, many layers; one cannot reach its ins and outs. Besides, its workings are so subtle, so unpredictable, and so sudden that making it comprehensible is a remarkable feat. Vyasa, Valmiki, and Kalidasa were able to accomplish this in the past.

Now if we want to summarize the subject of literature, we can say that the subject is the human heart and the human personality.

Perhaps including the human personality is redundant here. Basically, literature is the linguistic construct and the music of that protean self tirelessly shaped and resonated by external nature and human personality.

God's joy manifests itself in nature and humanity. The human heart seeks to shape and express itself in literature. This process has no end and is remarkably diverse. Poets are mere instruments of this eternal struggle of humanity.

God's joyous poetry emanates from within itself; humanity's cultural products are a reflection of that force. The happy music of cosmic creation constantly vibrates the harp of the heart.

That song of the self, that creative impulse reverberating in tune with divine creation, is literature. Inspired by the breath of the universe, the heart, like a reed, sings; literature attempts to capture that tune. Literature is not exclusively for the individual, nor is it for the author alone. Literature is divine utterance. Just as external reality ever seeks to express itself, with all its imperfection, so does literature struggle to manifest itself in different regions and languages.

1907

(From "*Sahitya*")
Translated by Farhad B. Idris

The Problem of Self

It is not only in Buddhism and the Indian religion but in Christianity too, that the ideal of selflessness is preached with all fervor. In the last the symbol of death has been used for expressing the idea of man's deliverance from the life which is not true. This is the same as Nirvāna, the symbol of the extinction of the lamp.

In the typical thought of India it is held that the true deliverance of man is the deliverance from *avidyā,* from ignorance. It is not in destroying anything that is positive and real, for that cannot be possible, but that which is negative, which obstruct our vision of truth. When this obstruction, which is ignorance, is removed, then only is the eye lid drawn up which is no loss to the eye.

It is our ignorance which makes us think that our self, as self, is real, that it has its complete meaning in itself. When we take that wrong view of self then we try to live in such a manner as to make self the ultimate object of our life. Then are we doomed to disappointment like the man who tries to reach his destination by firmly clutching the dust of the road. Our self has no means of holding us, for its own nature is to pass on; and by clinging to this thread of self which is passing through the loom of life we cannot make it serve the purpose of the cloth into which it is being woven. When a man, with elaborate care, arranges for an enjoyment of the self, he lights a fire but has no dough to make his bread with; the fire flares up and consumes itself to extinction, like an unnatural beast that eats its own progeny and dies.

In an unknown language the words are tyrannically prominent. They stop us but say nothing. To be rescued from this fetter of words we must rid ourselves of the *avidyā,* our ignorance, and then our mind will find its freedom in the inner idea. But it could be foolish to say that our ignorance of the language can be dispelled only by the destruction of the words. No, when the perfect knowledge comes, every word remains in its place, only they do not bind us to themselves, but let us pass through them and lead us to the idea which is emancipation.

Thus it is only *avidyā* which makes the self our fetter by making us think that it is an end in itself, and by preventing our seeing that it contains the idea that transcends its limits. That is why the wise man comes and says, "Set yourselves free from the *avidyā;* know your true soul and be saved from the grasp of the self which imprisons you."

We gain our freedom when we attain our truest nature. The man who is an artist finds his artistic freedom when he finds his ideal of art. Then is he freed from laborious attempts at imitation, from the goadings of popular approbation. It is the function of religion not to destroy our nature but to fulfill it.

The Sanskrit word *dharma* which is usually translated into English as religion has a deeper meaning in our language. *Dharma* is the innermost nature, the essence, the implicit truth, of all things. *Dharma* is the ultimate purpose that is working in our self. When any wrong is done we say that *dharma* is violated, meaning that the lie has been given to our true nature.

But this *dharma,* which is the truth in us, is not apparent, because it is inherent. So much so, that it has been held that sinfulness is the nature of man, and only by the special grace of God can a particular person be saved. This is like saying that the nature of the seed is to remain enfolded within its shell, and it is only by some special miracle that it can be grown into a tree. But do we not know that the *appearance* of the seed contradicts its true nature. When you submit it to chemical analysis you may find in it carbon and protein and a good many other things, but not the idea of a branching tree. Only when the tree begins to take shape do you come to see its *dharma,* and then you can affirm without doubt that the seed which has been wasted and allowed to rot in the ground has been thwarted in its *dharma,* in the fulfillment of its true nature. In the history of humanity we have known the living seed in us to sprout. We have seen the great purpose in us taking shape in the lives of our greatest men, and have felt certain that though there are numerous individual lives that seem ineffectual, still it is not their *dharma* to remain barren; but it is for them to burst their cover and transform themselves into a vigorous spiritual shoot, growing up into the air and light, and branching out in all directions.

The freedom of the seed is in the attainment of its *dharma,* its nature and destiny of becoming a tree; it is the non-accomplishment which is its prison. The sacrifice by which a thing attains its fulfillment is not a sacrifice which ends in death; it is the casting-off of bonds which wins freedom.

When we know the highest ideal of freedom which a man has, we know his *dharma,* the essence of his nature, the real meaning of his self. At first sight it seems that man counts that as freedom by which he gets unbounded opportunities of self-gratification and self-aggrandizement. But surely this is not borne out by history. Our revelatory men have always been those who have lived the life of self-sacrifice. The higher nature in man always seeks for something which transcends itself and yet is its deepest truth; which claims all its sacrifice, yet makes this sacrifice its own recompense. This is man's *dharma,* man's religion, and man's self is the vessel which is to carry this sacrifice to the altar.

We can look at our self in its two different aspects. The self which displays itself, and the self which transcends itself and thereby reveals its own meaning. To display itself it tries to be big, to stand upon the pedestal of its accumulations, and to retain everything to itself. To reveal itself it gives up everything it has, thus becoming perfect like a flower that has blossomed out from the bud, pouring from its chalice of beauty all its sweetness.

The lamp contains its oil, which it holds securely in its close grasp and guards from the least loss. Thus is it separate from all other objects around it and is miserly. But when lighted it finds its meaning at once; its relation with all things far and near is established, and it freely sacrifices its fund of oil to feed the flame.

Such a lamp is our self. So long as it hoards its possessions it keeps itself dark, its conduct contradicts its true purpose. When it finds illumination it forgets itself in a moment, holds the light high; and selves it with everything it has; for therein is its revelation. This revelation is the freedom which Buddha preached. He asked the lamp to give up its oil. But purposeless giving up is a still darker poverty which he never could have meant. The lamp must give up its oil to the light and thus set free the purpose it has in its hoarding. This is emancipation. The path Buddha pointed out was not merely the practice of self-abnegation, but the widening of love. And therein lies the true meaning of Buddha's preaching.

When we find that the state of *Nirvāna* preached by Buddha is

161

through love, then we know for certain that *Nirvāna* is the highest culmination of love. For love is an end unto itself. Everything else raises the question "Why?" in our mind, and we require a reason for it. But when we say, "I love," then there is no room for the "why"; it is the final answer in itself.

162

Doubtless, even selfishness impels one to give away. But the selfish man does it on compulsion. That is like plucking fruit when it is unripe; you have to tear it from the tree and bruise the branch. But when a man loves, giving becomes a matter of joy to him, like the tree's surrender of the ripe fruit. All our belongings assume a weight by the ceaseless gravitation of our selfish desires; we cannot easily cast them away from us. They seem to belong to our very nature, to stick to us as a second skin, and we bleed as we detach them. But when we are possessed by love, its force acts in the opposite direction. The things that closely adhered to us lose their adhesion and weight, and we find that they are not of us. Far from being a loss to give them away, we find in that the fulfillment of our nature.

Thus we find in perfect love the freedom of our self. That only which is done for love is done freely, however much pain it may cause. Therefore working for love is freedom in action. This is the meaning of the teaching of disinterested work in the Gītā.

The Gītā says action we must have, for only in action do we manifest our nature. But this manifestation is not perfect so long as our action is not free. In fact, our nature is obscured by work done by the compulsion of want or fear. The mother reveals herself in the service of her children, so our true freedom is not the freedom *from* action but freedom *in* action, which can only be attained in the work of love.

God's manifestation is in his work of creation, and it is said in the Upanishad, *Knowledge, power, and action are of his nature,*[3] they are not imposed upon him from outside. Therefore his work is his freedom, and in his creation he realizes himself. The same thing is said elsewhere in other words: *From joy does spring all this creation, by joy is it maintained, towards joy does it progress, and into joy does it enter.*[4] This means that God's creation has not its source in any necessity; it comes from his fullness of joy; it is his love that creates, therefore in creation is his own revealment.

The artist who has a joy in the fullness of his artistic idea objectifies it and thus gains it more fully by holding it afar. It is joy which detaches ourselves from us, and then gives it form in creations of love in order to make it more perfectly our own. Hence there must be this separation, not a separation of repulsion but a separation of love. Repulsion has only the one element, the element of severance. But love has two, the element of severance, which is only an appearance, and the element of union which is the ultimate truth. Just as when the father tosses his child up from his arms it has the appearance of rejection but its truth is quite the reverse.

So we must know that the meaning of our self is not to be found in its separateness from God and others, but in the ceaseless realization of *yoga,* of union; not on the side of the canvas where it is blank, but on the side where the picture is being painted.

This is the reason why the separateness of our self has been described by our philosophers as *māyā,* as an illusion, because it has no intrinsic reality of its own. It looks perilous; it raises its isolation to a giddy height and casts a black shadow upon the fair face of existence; from the outside it has an aspect of a sudden disruption, rebellious and destructive; it is proud, domineering and wayward, it is ready to rob the world of all its wealth to gratify its craving of a moment; to pluck with a reckless, cruel hand all the plumes from the divine bird of beauty to deck its ugliness for a day; indeed man's legend has it that it bears the black mark of disobedience stamped on its forehead for ever; but still all this is *māyā,* envelopment of *avidyā* it is the mist, it is not the sun; it is the black smoke that presages the fire of love.

Imagine some savage who, in his ignorance, thinks that it is the paper of the banknote that has the magic, by virtue of which the possessor of it gets all he wants. He piles up the papers, hides them, handles them in all sorts of absurd ways, and then at last, wearied by his efforts, comes to the sad conclusion that they are absolutely worthless, only fit to be thrown into the fire. But the wise man knows that the paper of the banknote is all *māyā,* and until it is given up to the bank it is futile. It is only *avidyā,* our ignorance, that makes us believe that the separateness of our self like the paper of the banknote is precious in itself, and by acting on this belief our self is rendered valueless. It is only when the *avidyā* is removed that this very self comes to us with a wealth which is priceless. For *He manifests Himself in deathless forms which His joy assumes.*[5] These forms are separate from Him, and the value that these forms have is only what his joy has imparted to them. When we transfer back these forms into that original joy, which is love, then we cash them in the bank and we find their truth.

164

When pure necessity drives man to his work it takes an accidental and contingent character, it becomes a mere makeshift arrangement; it is deserted and left in ruins when necessity changes its course. But when his work is the outcome of joy, the forms that it takes have the elements of immortality. The immortal in man imparts to it its own quality of permanence.

Our self, as a form of God's joy, is deathless. For his joy is *amritam,* eternal. This it is in us which makes us skeptical of death, even when the fact of death cannot be doubted. In reconcilement of this contradiction in us we come to the truth that in the dualism of death and life there is a harmony. We know that the life of a soul, which is finite in its expression and infinite in its principle, must go through the portals of death in its journey to realize the infinite. It is death which is monistic, it has no life in it. But life is dualistic; it has an appearance as well as truth; and death is that appearance, that *māyā,* which is an inseparable companion to life. Our self to live must go through a continual change and growth of form, which may be termed a continual death and a continual life going on at the same time. It is really courting death when we refuse to accept death; when we wish to give the form of the self some fixed changelessness; when the self feels no impulse which urges it to grow out of itself; when it treats its limits as final and acts accordingly. Then comes our teacher's call to die to this death; not a call to annihilation but so eternal life. It is the extinction of the lamp in the morning light; not the abolition of the sun. It is really asking us consciously to give effect to the innermost wish that we have in the depths of our nature.

We have a dual set of desires in our being, which it should be our endeavor to bring into a harmony. In the region of our physical nature we have one set of which we are conscious always. We wish to enjoy our food and drink, we hanker after bodily pleasure and comfort. These desires are self-centered; they are solely concerned with their respective impulses. The wishes of our palate often run counter to what our stomach can allow.

But we have another set, which is the desire of our physical system as a whole, of which we are usually unconscious. It is the wish for health. This is always doing its work, mending and repairing, making new adjustments in cases of accident, and skillfully restoring the balance wherever disturbed. It has no concern with the fulfillment of our immediate bodily desires, but it goes beyond the present time. It is the principle of our physical wholeness, it links our life with its past and its future and maintains the unity of its parts. He who is wise knows it, and makes his other physical wishes harmonize with it.

We have a greater body which is the social body. Society is an organism, of which we as parts have our individual wishes. We want our own pleasure and license. We want to pay less and gain more than anybody else. This causes scramblings and fights. But there is that other wish in us which does its work in the depths of the social being. It is the wish for the welfare of the society. It transcends the limits of the present and the personal. It is on the side of the infinite.

He who is wise tries to harmonize the wishes that seek for self-gratification with the wish for the social good, and only thus can he realize his higher self.

In its finite aspect the self is conscious of its separateness, and there it is ruthless in its attempt to have more distinction than all others. But in its infinite aspect its wish is to gain that harmony which leads to its perfection and not its mere aggrandizement.

The emancipation of our physical nature is in attaining health, of our social being in attaining goodness, and of our self in attaining love. This last is what Buddha describes as extinction—the extinction of selfishness. This is the function of love, and it does not lead to darkness but to illumination. This is the attainment of *bodhi,* or the true awakening; it is the revealing in us of the infinite joy by the light of love.

The passage of our self is through its selfhood, which is independent, to its attainment of soul, which is harmonious. This harmony can never be reached through compulsion. So our will, in the history of its growth, must come through independence and rebellion to the ultimate completion. We must have the possibility of the negative form of freedom, which is license, before we can attain the positive freedom, which is love.

This negative freedom, the freedom of self-will, can turn its back upon its highest realization, but it cannot cut itself away from it altogether, for then it will lose its own meaning. Our self-will has freedom up to a certain extent; it can know what it is to break away from the path, but it cannot continue in that direction indefinitely. For we are finite on our negative side. We must come to an end in our evil doing, in our career of discord. For evil is not infinite, and discord cannot be an end in itself. Our will has freedom in order that it may find out that its true course is towards goodness and love. For goodness and love are infinite, and only in the infinite is the perfect realization of freedom possible. So our will can be free not towards the limitations of our self, not where it is *māyā* and negation, but towards the unlimited, where it is truth and love. Our freedom cannot go against its own principle of freedom and yet be free; it cannot commit suicide and yet live. We cannot say that we should have infinite freedom to fetter ourselves, for the fettering ends the freedom.

So in the freedom of our will, we have the same dualism of appearance and truth—our self-will is only the appearance of freedom and love is the truth. When we try to make this appearance independent of truth, then our attempt brings misery and proves its own futility in the end. Everything has this dualism of *māyā* and *satyam,* appearance and truth. Words are *māyā* where they are merely sounds and finite, they are *satyam* where they are ideas and infinite. Our self is *māyā* where it is merely individual and finite, where it considers its separateness as absolute; it is *satyam* where it recognizes its essence in the universal and infinite, in the supreme self in *paramātman.* This is what Christ means when he says, "Before Abraham was I am." This is the eternal *I am* that speaks through the *I am* that is in me. The individual *I am* attains its perfect end when it realizes its freedom of harmony in the infinite *I am.* Then is its *mukti,* its deliverance from the thralldom of *māyā,* of appearance which springs from *avidyā,* from ignorance; its emancipation in *çantam çivam advaitam,* in the perfect repose in truth, in the perfect activity in good-ness, and in the perfect union in love.

Not only in our self but also in nature is there this separateness from God, which has been described as *māyā* by our philosophers, be-cause the separateness does not exist by itself, it does not limit God's in-finity from outside. It is his own will that has imposed limits to itself, just as the chess-player restricts his will with regard to the moving of the chessmen. The player willingly enters into definite relations with each particular piece and realizes the joy of his power by these very restric-tions. It is not that he cannot move the chessmen just as he pleases, but if he does so then there can be no play. If God assumes his role of omnipo-tence, then his creation is at an end and his power loses all its meaning. For power to be a power must act within limits. God's water must be water, his earth can never be other than earth. The law that has made them water and earth is his own law by which he has separated the play from the player, for therein the joy of the player consists.

As by the limits of law nature is separated from God, so it is the limits of its egoism which separates the self from him. He has willingly set limits to his will, and has given us mastery over the little world of our own. It is like a father's settling upon his son some allowance within the limit of which he is free to do what he likes. Though it remains a portion of the father's own property, yet he frees it from the operation of his own will. The reason of it is that the will, which is love's will and therefore free, can have its joy only in a union with another free will. The tyrant who must have slaves looks upon them as instruments of his purpose. It is the consciousness of his own necessity which makes him crush the will out of them, to make his self-interest absolutely secure. This self-interest cannot brook the least freedom in others, because it is not itself free. The tyrant is really dependent on his slaves, and therefore he tries to make them completely useful by making them subservient to his own will. But a lover must have two wills for the realization of his love, because the consummation of love is in harmony, the harmony between free-dom and freedom. So God's love from which our self has taken form has made it separate from God; and it is God's love which again establishes a rec-onciliation and unites God with our self through the separation. That is

167

why our self has to go through endless renewals. For in its career of separateness it cannot go on for ever. Separateness is the finitude where it finds its barriers to come back again and again to its infinite source. Our self has ceaselessly to cast off its age, repeatedly shed its limits in oblivion and death, in order to realize its immortal youth. Its personality must merge in the universal time after time, in fact pass through it every moment, ever to refresh its individual life. It must follow the eternal rhythm and touch the fundamental unity at every step, and thus maintain its separation balanced in beauty and strength.

The play of life and death we see everywhere—this transmutation of the old into the new. The day comes to us every morning, naked and white, fresh as a flower. But we know it is old. It is age itself. It is that very ancient day which took up the newborn earth in its arms, covered it with its white mantle of light, and sent it forth on its pilgrimage among the stars.

Yet its feet are untired and its eyes undimmed. It carries the golden amulet of ageless eternity, at whose touch all wrinkles vanish from the forehead of creation. In the very core of the world's heart stands immortal youth. Death and decay cast over its face momentary shadows and pass on; they leave no marks of their steps—and truth remains fresh and young.

This old, old day of our earth is born again and again every morning. It comes back to the original refrain of its music. If its march were the march of an infinite straight line, if it had not the awful pause of its plunge in the abysmal darkness and its repeated rebirth in the life of the endless beginning, then it would gradually soil and bury truth with its dust and spread ceaseless aching over the earth under its heavy tread. Then every moment would leave its load of weariness behind, and decrepitude would reign supreme on its throne of eternal dirt.

But every morning the day is reborn among the newly-blossomed flowers with the same message retold and the same assurance renewed that death eternally dies, that the waves of turmoil are on the surface, and that the sea of tranquility is fathomless. The curtain of night is drawn aside and truth emerges without a speck of dust on its garment, without a furrow of age on its lineaments.

We see that he who is before everything else is the same to-day.

Every note of the song of creation comes fresh from his voice. The universe is not a mere echo, reverberating from sky to sky, like a homeless wanderer—the echo of an old song sung once for all in the dim beginning of things and then left orphaned. Every moment it comes from the heart of the master, it is breathed in his breath.

And that is the reason why it overspreads the sky like a thought taking shape in a poem, and never has to break into pieces with the burden of its own accumulating weight. Hence the surprise of endless variations, the advent of the unaccountable, the ceaseless procession of individuals, each of whom is without a parallel in creation. As at the first so to the last, the beginning never ends—the world is ever old and ever new.

It is for our self to know that it must be born anew every moment of its life. It must break through all illusions that encase it in their crust to make it appear old, burdening it with death.

For life is immortal youthfulness, and it hates age that tries to clog its movements—age that belongs not to life in truth, but follows it as the shadow follows the lamp.

Our life, like a river, strikes its banks not to find itself closed in by them, but to realize anew every moment that it has its unending opening towards the sea. It is as a poem that strikes its meter at every step not to be silenced by its rigid regulations, but to give expression every moment to the inner freedom of its harmony.

The boundary walls of our individuality thrust us back within our limits, on the one hand, and thus lead us, on the other, to the unlimited. Only when we try to make these limits infinite are we launched into an impossible contradiction and court miserable failure.

This is the cause which leads to the great revolutions in human history. Whenever the part, spurning the whole, tries to run a separate course of its own, the great pull of the all gives it a violent wrench, stops it suddenly, and brings it to the dust. Whenever the individual tries to dam the ever-flowing current of the world-force and imprison it within the area of his particular use, it brings on disaster. However powerful a king may be, he cannot raise his standard of rebellion against the infinite source of strength, which is unity, and yet remain powerful.

It has been said, *By unrighteousness men prosper, gain what they de-*

sire, and triumph over their enemies, but at the end they are cut off at the root and suffer extinction.[6] Our roots must go deep down into the universal if we would attain the greatness of personality.

It is the end of our self to seek that union. It must bend its head low in love and meekness and take its stand where great and small all meet. It has to gain by its loss and rise by its surrender. His games would be a horror to the child if he could not come back to his mother, and our pride of personality will be a curse to us if we cannot give it up in love. We must know that it is only the revelation of the Infinite which is endlessly new and eternally beautiful in us and gives the only meaning to our self.

(From *"Sadhana,"* 1913)

Nationalism in the West

. . . The truth is that the spirit of conflict and conquest is at the origin and in the centre of the Western nationalism; its basis is not social cooperation. It has evolved a perfect organization of power but not spiritual idealism. It is like the pack of predatory creatures that must have its victims. With all its heart it cannot bear to see its hunting grounds converted into cultivated fields. In fact, these nations are fighting among themselves for the extension of their victims and their reserve forests. Therefore the Western Nation acts like a dam to check the free flow of the Western civilization into the country of the No-Nation. Because this civilization is the civilization of power, therefore it is exclusive, it is naturally unwilling to open its sources of power to those whom it has selected for its purposes of exploitation.

But all the same moral law is the law of humanity, and the exclusive civilization which thrives upon others who are barred from its benefit carries its own death sentence in its moral limitations. The slavery that it gives rise to unconsciously drains its own love of freedom dry. The helplessness with which it weighs down its world of victims exerts its force of gravitation every moment upon the power that creates it. And the greater part of the world which is being denuded of its self-sustaining life by the Nation will one day become the most terrible of all its burdens ready to drag it down into the bottom of destruction. Whenever Power removes all checks from its path to make its career easy, it triumphantly rides into its ultimate crash of death. Its moral brake becomes slacker every day without its knowing it, and its slippery path of ease becomes its path of doom.

Of all things in Western civilization, those which this Western Nation has given us in a most generous measure are law and order. While the small feeding bottle of our education is nearly dry, and sanitation sucks its own thumb in despair, the military organization, the magisterial offices, the police, the Criminal Investigation Department, the secret spy system, attain to an abnormal girth in their waists, occupying every inch of our country. This is to maintain order. But is not this order merely a negative good? Is it not for giving people's life greater opportunities for the freedom of development? Its perfection is the perfection of an egg-shell whose true value lies in the security it affords to the chick and its nourishment and not in the convenience it offers to the person at the breakfast table. Mere administration is unproductive, it is not creative, not being a living thing. It is a steam-roller, formidable in its weight and power, having its uses, but it does not help the soil to become fertile. When after its enormous toil it comes to offer us its boon of peace we can but murmur under our breath that "peace is good but not more so than life which is God's own great boon."

On the other hand, our former governments were woefully lacking in many of the advantages of the modern government. But because those were not the governments by the Nation, their texture was loosely woven, leaving big gaps through which our own life sent its threads and imposed its designs. I am quite sure in those days we had things that were extremely distasteful to us. But we know that when we walk barefooted upon a ground strewn with gravel, gradually our feet come to adjust themselves to the caprices of the inhospitable earth; while if the tiniest particle of a gravel finds its lodgment inside our shoes we can never forget and forgive its intrusion. And these shoes are the government by the Nation,—it is tight, it regulates our steps with a closed up system, within which our feet have only the slightest liberty to make their own adjustments. Therefore, when you produce your statistics to compare the number of gravels which our feet had to encounter in former days with the paucity in the present regime, they hardly touch the real points. It is not the numerousness of the outside obstacles but the comparative powerlessness of the individual to cope with them. This narrowness of freedom is an evil which is more radical not because of its quantity but because of its nature. And we cannot but acknowledge this paradox, that while the spirit of the west marches under its banner of freedom, the Nation of the west forges its iron chains of organization which are the most relentless and unbreakable that have ever been manufactured in the whole history of man.

When the humanity of India was not under the government of the organization, the elasticity of change was great enough to encourage men of power and spirit to feel that they had their destinies in their own hands. The hope of the unexpected was never absent, and a freer play of imagination, both on the part of the governor and the governed, had its effect in the making of history. We were not confronted with a future which was a dead white wall of granite blocks eternally guarding against the expression and extension of our own powers, the hopelessness of which lies in the reason that these powers are becoming atrophied at their very roots by the scientific process of paralysis. For every single individual in the country of the no-nation is completely in the grip of a whole nation,—whose tireless vigilance, being the vigilance of a machine, has not the human power to overlook or to discriminate. At the least pressing of its button the monster organization becomes all eyes, whose ugly stare of inquisitiveness cannot be avoided by a single person amongst the immense multitude of the ruled. At the least turn of its screw, by the fraction of an inch, the grip is tightened to the point of suffocation around every man, woman and child of a vast population, for whom no escape is imaginable in their own country, or even in any country outside their own.

It is the continual and stupendous dead pressure of this inhuman upon the living human under which the modern world is groaning. Not merely the subject races, but you who live under the delusion that you are free, are every day sacrificing your freedom and humanity to this fetish of nationalism, living in the dense poisonous atmosphere of worldwide suspicion and greed and panic.

I have seen in Japan the voluntary submission of the whole people to the trimming of their minds and clipping of their freedom by their government, which through various educational agencies regulates their thoughts, manufactures their feelings, becomes suspiciously watchful when they show signs of inclining toward the spiritual, leading them through a narrow path not toward what is true but what is necessary for the complete welding of them into one uniform mass according to its own recipe. The people accept this all-pervading mental slavery with cheerfulness and pride because of their nervous desire to turn themselves into a machine of power, called the Nation, and emulate other machines in their collective worldliness.

When questioned as to the wisdom of its course the newly converted fanatic of nationalism answers that "so long as nations are rampant in this world we have not the option freely to develop our higher humanity. We must utilize every faculty that we possess to resist the evil by assuming it ourselves in the fullest degree. For the only brotherhood possible in the modern world is the brotherhood of hooliganism." The recognition of the fraternal bond of love between Japan and Russia, which has lately been celebrated with an immense display of rejoicing in Japan, was not owing to any sudden recrudescence of the spirit of Christianity or of Buddhism,—but it was a bond established according to the modern faith in a surer relationship of mutual menace of bloodshedding. Yes, one cannot but acknowledge that these facts are the facts of the world of the Nation, and the only moral of it is that all the peoples of the earth should strain their physical, moral and intellectual resources to the utmost to defeat one another in the wrestling match of powerfulness. In the ancient days Sparta paid all her attention to becoming powerful—and she did become so by crippling her humanity, and she died of the amputation.

But it is no consolation to us to know that the weakening of humanity from which the present age is suffering is not limited to the subject races, and that its ravages are even more radical because insidious and voluntary in peoples who are hypnotized into believing that they are free. This bartering of your higher aspirations of life for profit and power has been your own free choice, and I leave you there, at the wreckage of your soul, contemplating your protuberant prosperity. But will you never be called to answer for organizing the instincts of self-aggrandizement of whole peoples into perfection, and calling it good? I ask you what disaster has there ever been in the history of man, in its darkest period, like this terrible disaster of the Nation fixing its fangs deep into the naked flesh of the world, taking permanent precautions against its natural relaxation?

You, the people of the West, who have manufactured this abnormality, can you imagine the desolating despair of this haunted world of suffering man possessed by the ghastly abstraction of the organizing man? Can you put yourself into the position of the peoples, who seem to have been doomed to an eternal damnation of their own humanity, who not only must suffer continual curtailment of their manhood, but even raise their voices in paeans of praise for the benignity of a mechanical apparatus in its interminable parody of providence?

Have you not seen, since the commencement of the existence of the Nation, that the dread of it has been the one goblin-dread with which the whole world has been trembling? Wherever there is a dark corner, there is the suspicion of its secret malevolence; and people live in a perpetual distrust of its back where it has no eyes. Every sound of footstep, every rustle of movement in the neighborhood, sends a thrill of terror all around. And this terror is the parent of all that is base in man's nature. It makes one almost openly unashamed of inhumanity. Clever lies become matters of self-congratulation. Solemn pledges become a farce,—laughable for their very solemnity. The Nation, with all its paraphernalia of power and prosperity, its flags and pious hymns, its blasphemous prayers in the churches, and the literary mock thunders of its patriotic bragging, cannot hide the fact that the Nation is the greatest evil for the Nation, that all its precautions are against it, and any new birth of its fellow in the world is always followed in its mind by the dread of a new peril. Its one wish is to trade on the feebleness of the rest of the world, like some insects that are bred in the paralyzed flesh of victims kept just enough alive to make them toothsome and nutritious. Therefore it is ready to send its poisonous fluid into the vitals of the other living peoples, who, not being nations, are harmless. For this the Nation has had and still has its richest pasture in Asia. Great China, rich with her ancient wisdom and social ethics, her discipline of industry and self-control, is like a whale awakening the lust of spoil in the heart of the Nation. She is already carrying in her quivering flesh harpoons sent by the unerring aim of the Nation, the creature of science and selfishness. Her pitiful attempt to shake off her traditions of humanity, her social ideals, and spend her last exhausted resources to drill herself into modern efficiency, is thwarted at every step by the Nation. It is tightening its financial ropes round her, trying to drag her up on the shore and cut her into pieces, and then go and offer public thanksgiving to God for supporting the one existing evil and shattering the possibility of a new one. And for all this the Nation has been claiming the gratitude of history, and all eternity for its exploitation; ordering its band of praise to be struck up from end to end of the world, declaring itself to be the salt of the earth, the flower of humanity, the blessing of God hurled with all his force upon the naked skulls of the world of no nations.

I know what your advice will be. You will say, form yourselves into a nation, and resist this encroachment of the Nation. But is this the true advice? that of a man to a man? Why should this be a necessity? I could well believe you, if you had said, Be more good, more just, more true in your relation to man, control your greed, make your life wholesome in its simplicity and let your consciousness of the divine in humanity be more perfect in its expression. But must you say that it is not the soul, but the machine, which is of the utmost value to ourselves, and that man's salvation depends upon his disciplining himself into a perfection of the dead rhythm of wheels and counterwheels? That machine must be pitted against machine, and nation against nation, in an endless bull-fight of politics?

You say, these machines will come into an agreement, for their mutual protection, based upon a conspiracy of fear. But will this federation of steam-boilers supply you with a soul, a soul which has her conscience and her God? What is to happen to that larger part of the world, where fear will have no hand in restraining you? Whatever safety they now enjoy, those countries of no nation, from the unbridled license of forge and hammer and turn-screw, results from the mutual jealousy of the powers. But when, instead of being numerous separate machines, they become riveted into one organized gregariousness of gluttony, commercial and political, what remotest chance of hope will remain for those others, who have lived and suffered, have loved and worshipped, have thought deeply and worked with meekness, but whose only crime has been that they have not organized?

But, you say, "That does not matter, the unfit must go to the wall —they shall *die,* and this is science."

No, for the sake of your own salvation, I say, they shall *live,* and this is truth. It is extremely bold of me to say so, but I assert that man's world is a moral world, not because we blindly agree to believe it, but because it is so in truth which would be dangerous for us to ignore. And this moral nature of man cannot be divided into convenient compartments for its preservation. You cannot secure it for your home consumption with protective tariff walls, while in foreign parts making it enormously accommodating in its free trade of license.

Has not this truth already come home to you now, when this cruel war has driven its claws into the vitals of Europe? when her hoard of wealth is bursting into smoke and her humanity is shattered into bits on her battlefields? You ask in amazement what has she done to deserve this? The answer is, that the West has been systematically petrifying her moral nature in order to lay a solid foundation for her gigantic abstractions of efficiency. She has all along been starving the life of the personal man into that of the professional . . .

Thus, man with his mental and material power far outgrowing his moral strength, is like an exaggerated giraffe whose head has suddenly shot up miles away from the rest of him, making normal communication difficult to establish. This greedy head, with its huge dental organization, has been munching all the topmost foliage of the world, but the nourishment is too late in reaching his digestive organs, and his heart is suffering from want of blood. Of this present disharmony in man's nature the west seems to have been blissfully unconscious. The enormity of its material success has diverted all its attention toward self-congratulation on its bulk. The optimism of its logic goes on basing the calculations of its good fortune upon the indefinite prolongation of its railway lines toward eternity. It is superficial enough to think that all to-morrows are merely to-days with the repeated additions of twenty-four hours. It has no fear of the chasm, which is opening wider every day, between man's ever-growing storehouses and the emptiness of his hungry humanity. Logic does not know that, under the lowest bed of endless strata of wealth and comforts, earthquakes are being hatched to restore the balance of the moral world, and one day the gaping gulf of spiritual vacuity will draw into its bottom the store of things that have their eternal love for the dust.

Man in his fullness is not powerful, but perfect. Therefore, to turn him into mere power, you have to curtail his soul as much as possible. When we are fully human, we cannot fly at one another's throats; our instincts of social life, our traditions of moral ideals stand in the way. If you want me to take to butchering human beings, you must break up that wholeness of my humanity through some discipline which makes my will dead, my thoughts numb, my movements automatic, and then from the dissolution of the complex personal man will come out that abstraction, that destructive force, which has no relation to human truth, and therefore can be easily brutal or mechanical. Take away man from his natural surroundings, from the fullness of his communal life, with all its living associations of beauty and love and social obligations, and you will be able to turn him into so many fragments of a machine for the production of wealth on a gigantic scale. Turn a tree into a log and it will burn for you, but it will never bear living flowers and fruit.

This process of dehumanizing has been going on in commerce and politics. And out of the long birth-throes of mechanical energy has been born this fully developed apparatus of magnificent power and surprising appetite, which has been christened in the West as the Nation. As I have hinted before, because of its quality of abstraction it has, with the greatest ease, gone far ahead of the complete moral man. And having the conscience of a ghost and the callous perfection of an automaton, it is causing disasters of which the volcanic dissipations of the youthful moon would be ashamed to be brought into comparison. As a result, the suspicion of man for man stings all the limbs of this civilization like the hairs of the nettle. Each country is casting its net of espionage into the slimy bottom of the others, fishing for their secrets, the treacherous secrets brewing in the oozy depths of diplomacy. And what is their secret service but the nation's underground trade in kidnapping, murder and treachery and all the ugly crimes bred in the depth of rottenness? Because each nation has its own history of thieving and lies and broken faith, therefore there can only flourish international suspicion and jealousy, and international moral shame becomes anemic to a degree of ludicrousness. The nation's bagpipe of righteous indignation has so often changed its tune according to the variation of time and to the altered groupings of the alliances of diplomacy, that it can be enjoyed with amusement as the variety performance of the political music hall.

I am just coming from my visit to Japan, where I exhorted this young nation to take its stand upon the higher ideals of humanity and never to follow the West in its acceptance of the organized selfishness of Nationalism as its religion, never to gloat upon the feebleness of its neighbors, never to be unscrupulous in its behavior to the weak, where it can be gloriously mean with impunity, while turning its right cheek of brighter humanity for the kiss of admiration to those who have the power to deal it a blow. Some of the newspapers praised my utterances for their poetical qualities while adding with a leer that it was the poetry of a defeated people. I felt they were right. Japan had been taught in a modern school the lesson how to become powerful. The schooling is done and she must enjoy the fruits of her lessons. The West in the voice of her thundering cannon had said at the door of Japan, Let there be a Nation—and there was a Nation. And now that it has come into existence, why do you not feel in your heart of hearts a pure feeling of gladness and say that it is good? Why is it that I saw in an English paper an expression of bitterness at Japan's boasting of her superiority of civilization— the thing that the British, along with other nations, has been carrying on for ages without blushing? Because the idealism of selfishness must keep itself drunk with a continual dose of self-laudation. But the same vices which seem so natural and innocuous in its own life make it surprised and angry at their unpleasantness when seen in your other nations. Therefore when you see the Japanese nation, created in your own image, launched in its career of national boastfulness you shake your head and say it is not good. Has it not been one of the causes that raise the cry on these shores for preparedness to meet one more power of evil with a greater power of injury? Japan protests that she has her *bushido,* that she can never be treacherous to America to whom she owes her gratitude. But you find it difficult to believe her,—for the wisdom of the Nation is not in its faith in humanity but in its complete distrust. You say to yourself that it is not with Japan of the bushido, the Japan of the moral ideals, that you have to deal—it is with the abstraction of the popular selfishness, it is with the Nation; and Nation can only trust Nation where their interests coalesce, or at least do not conflict. In fact your instinct tells you that the advent of another people into the arena of nationality makes another addition to the evil which contradicts all that is highest in Man and proves by its success that unscrupulousness is the way to prosperity,—and goodness is good for the weak and God is the only remaining consolation of the defeated.

Yes, this is the logic of the Nation. And it will never heed the voice of truth and goodness. It will go on in its ring-dance of moral corruption, linking steel unto steel, and machine unto machine; trampling under its tread all the sweet flowers of simple faith and the living ideals of man.

But we delude ourselves into thinking that humanity in the modern days is more to the front than ever before. The reason of this self-delusion is because man is served with the necessaries of life in greater profusion and his physical ills are being alleviated with more efficacy. But the chief part of this is done, not by moral sacrifice, but by intellectual power. In quantity it is great, but it springs from the surface and spreads over the surface. Knowledge and efficiency are powerful in their outward effect, but they are the servants of man, not the man himself. Their service is like the service in a hotel, where it is elaborate, but the host is absent; it is more convenient than hospitable.

Therefore we must not forget that the scientific organizations vastly spreading in all directions are strengthening our power, but not our humanity. With the growth of power the cult of the self-worship of the Nation grows in ascendancy; and the individual willingly allows the nation to take donkey rides upon his back; and there happens the anomaly which must have its disastrous effects, that the individual worships with all sacrifices a god which is morally much inferior to himself. This could never have been possible if the god had been as real as the individual.

180

Let me give an illustration of this point. In some parts of India it has been enjoined as an act of great piety for a widow to go without food and water on a particular day every fortnight. This often leads to cruelty, unmeaning and inhuman. And yet men are not by nature cruel to such a degree. But this piety being a mere unreal abstraction completely deadens the moral sense of the individual, just as the man who would not hurt an animal unnecessarily, would cause horrible suffering to a large number of innocent creatures when he drugs his feelings with the abstract idea of "sport." Because these ideas are the creations of our intellect, because they are logical classifications, therefore they can so easily hide in their mist the personal man.

And the idea of the Nation is one of the most powerful anesthetics that man has invented. Under the influence of its fumes the whole people can carry out its systematic program of the most virulent self-seeking without being in the least aware of its moral perversion,—in fact feeling dangerously resentful if it is pointed out.

But can this go on indefinitely? continually producing barrenness of moral insensibility upon a large tract of our living nature? Can it escape its nemesis forever? Has this giant power of mechanical organization no limit in this world against which it may shatter itself all the more completely because of its terrible strength and velocity? Do you believe that evil can be permanently kept in check by competition with evil, and that conference of prudence can keep the devil chained in its makeshift cage of mutual agreement?

This European war of Nations is the war of retribution. Man, the person, must protest for his very life against the heaping up of things where there should be the heart, and systems and policies where there should flow living human relationship. The time has come when, for the sake of the whole outraged world, Europe should fully know in her own person the terrible absurdity of the thing called the Nation.

The Nation has thriven long upon mutilated humanity. Men, the fairest creations of God, came out of the National manufactory in huge numbers as war-making and money-making puppets, ludicrously vain of their pitiful perfection of mechanism. Human society grew more and more into a marionette show of politicians, soldiers, manufacturers and bureaucrats, pulled by wire arrangements of wonderful efficiency.

But the apotheosis of selfishness can never make its interminable breed of hatred and greed, fear and hypocrisy, suspicion and tyranny, an end in themselves. These monsters grow into huge shapes but never into harmony. And this Nation may grow on to an unimaginable corpulence, not of a living body, but of steel and steam and office buildings, till its deformity can contain no longer its ugly voluminousness,—till it begins to crack and gape, breathe gas and fire in gasps, and its death-rattles sound in cannon roars. In this war, the death-throes of the Nation have commenced. Suddenly, all its mechanism going mad, it has begun the dance of the furies, shattering its own limbs, scattering them into the dust. It is the fifth act of the tragedy of the unreal.

Those who have any faith in Man cannot but fervently hope that the tyranny of the Nation will not be restored to all its former teeth and claws, to its far-reaching iron arms and its immense inner cavity, all stomach and no heart; that man will have his new birth, in the freedom of his individuality, from the enveloping vagueness of abstraction.

The veil has been raised, and in this frightful war the West has stood face to face with her own creation, to which she had offered her soul. She must know what it truly is.

She had never let herself suspect what slow decay and decomposition were secretly going on in her moral nature, which often broke out in doctrines of skepticism, but still oftener and in still more dangerously subtle manner showed itself in her unconsciousness of the mutilation and insult that she had been inflicting upon a vast part of the world. Now she must know the truth nearer home.

And then there will come from her own children those who will break themselves free from the slavery of this illusion, this perversion of brotherhood founded upon self-seeking, those who will own themselves as God's children and as no bondslaves of machinery, which turns souls into commodities and life into compartments, which, with its iron claws, scratches out the heart of the world and knows not what it has done.

And we of no nations of the world, whose heads have been bowed to the dust, will know that his dust is more sacred than the bricks which build the pride of power. For this dust is fertile of life, and of beauty and worship. We shall thank God that we were made to wait in silence through the night of despair, had to bear the insult of the proud and the strong man's burden, yet all through it, though our hearts quaked with doubt and fear, never could we blindly believe in the salvation which machinery offered to man, but we held fast to our trust in God and the truth of the human soul. And we can still cherish the hope, that, when power becomes ashamed to occupy its throne and is ready to make way for love, when the morning comes for cleansing the bloodstained steps of the Nation along the highroad of humanity, we shall be called upon to bring our own vessel of sacred water—the water of worship—to sweeten the history of man into purity, and with its sprinkling make the trampled dust of the centuries blessed with fruitfulness.

(From *Nationalism,* 1917)

The Nobel Prize Acceptance Speech

I am glad that I have been able to come at last to your country and that I may use this opportunity for expressing my gratitude to you for the honor you have done to me by acknowledging my work and rewarding me by giving me the Nobel Prize.

I remember the afternoon when I received the cablegram from my publisher in England that the prize had been awarded to me. I was staying then at the school Santiniketan, about which I suppose you know. At that moment we were taking a party over to a forest near by the school, and when I was passing by the telegram office and the post office, a man came running to us and held up the telegraphic message. I had also an

English visitor with me in the same carriage. I did not think that the message was of any importance, and I just put it into my pocket, thinking that I would I read it, when I reached my destination. But my visitor supposed he knew the contents, and he urged me to read it, saying that it contained an important message. And I opened and read the message, which I could hardly believe. I first thought that possibly the telegraphic language was not quite correct and that I might misread the meaning of it, but at last I felt certain about it. And you can well understand how rejoicing it was for my boys at the school and for the teachers. What touched me more deeply than anything else was that these boys who loved me and for whom I had the deepest love felt proud of the honor that had been awarded to him for whom they had feeling of reverence, and I realize that my countrymen would share with me the honor which had been awarded to myself.

The rest of the afternoon passed away in this manner, and when the night came I sat upon the terrace alone, and I asked myself the question what the reason could be of my poems being accepted and honored by the West—in spite of my belonging to a different race, parted and separated by seas and mountains from the children of the West. And I can assure you that it was not with a feeling of exaltation but with a searching of the heart that I questioned myself, and felt humble at that moment.

I remember how my life's work developed from the time when I was very young. When I was about 25 years I used to live in utmost seclusion in the solitude of an obscure Bengali village by the river Ganges in a boat-house. The wild ducks which came during the time of autumn from the Himalayan lakes were my only living companions, and in that solitude I seem to have drunk in the open space like wine overflowing with sunshine, and the murmur of the river used to speak to me and tell me the secrets of nature. And I passed my days in the solitude dreaming and giving shape to my dream in poems and studies and sending out my thoughts to the Calcutta public through the magazines and other papers. You can well understand that it was a life quite different from the life of the West. I do not know if any of your Western poets or writers do pass the greatest part of their young days in such absolute seclusion. I am almost certain that it cannot be possible and that seclusion itself has no place in the Western world.

And my life went on like this. I was an obscure individual—to most of my countrymen in those days. I mean that my name was hardly known outside my own province, but I was quite content with that obscurity, which protected me from the curiosity of the crowds.

And then came a time when my heart felt a longing to come out of that solitude and to do some work for my human fellow-beings, and not merely give shapes to my dreams and meditate deeply on the problems of life, but try to give expression to my ideas through some definite work, some definitive service for my fellow-beings.

And the one thing, the one work which came to my mind was to teach children. It was not because I was specially fitted for this work of teaching, for I have not had myself the full benefit of a regular education. For some time I hesitated to take upon myself this task, but I felt that as I had a deep love for nature I had naturally love for children also. My object in starting this institution was to give the children of men full freedom of joy, of life and of communion with nature. I myself had suffered when I was young through the impediments which were inflicted upon most boys while they attended school and I had to go through the machine of education which crushes the joy and freedom of life for which children have such insatiable thirst. And my object was to give freedom and joy to children of men.

And so I had a few boys around me, and I taught them, and I tried to make them happy. I was their playmate. I was their companion. I shared their life, and felt that I was the biggest child of the party. And we all grew up together in this atmosphere of freedom.

The vigor and the joy of the children, their chats and songs filled the air with a spirit of delight, which I drank every day I was there. And in the evening during the sunset hour I often used to sit alone watching the trees of the shadowing avenue, and in the silence of the afternoon I could hear distinctly the voices of the children coming up in the air, and it seemed to me that these shouts and songs and glad voices were like those trees, which come out from the heart of the earth like fountains of life towards the bosom of the infinite sky. And it symbolized, it brought before my mind the whole cry of human life, all expressions of joy and aspirations of men rising from the heart of Humanity up to this sky. I could see that, and I knew that we also, the grown-up children, send up our cries of aspiration to the infinite. I felt it in my heart of hearts.

In this atmosphere and in this environment I used to write my poems *Gitanjali,* and I sang them to myself in the midnight under the glorious stars of the Indian sky. And in the early morning and in the afternoon glow of sunset I used to write these songs till a day came when I felt impelled to come out once again and meet the heart of the large world.

I could see that my coming out from the seclusion of my life among these joyful children and doing my service to my fellow creatures was only a prelude to my pilgrimage to a larger world. And I felt a great desire to come out and come into touch with the Humanity of the West, for I was conscious that the present age belongs to the Western man with his superabundance of energy.

He has got the power of the whole world, and his life is overflowing all boundaries and is sending out its message to the great future. And I felt that I must before I die come to the West and meet the man of the secret shrine where the Divine presence has his dwelling, his temple. And I thought that the Divine man with all his powers and aspirations of life is dwelling in the West.

And so I came out. After my *Gitanjali* poems had been written in Bengali, I translated those poems into English, without having any desire to have them published, being diffident of my mastery of that language, but I had the manuscript with me when I came out to the West. And you know that the British public, when these poems were put before them, and those who had the opportunity of reading them in manuscript before, approved of them. I was accepted, and the heart of the West opened without delay.

And it was a miracle to me who had lived for fifty years far away from activity, far away from the West, that I should be almost in a moment accepted by the West as one of its own poets. It was surprising to me, but I felt that possibly this had its deeper significance and that those years which I had spent in seclusion, separated from the life and the spirit of the West, had brought with them a deeper feeling of rest, serenity and feeling of the eternal, and that these were exactly the sentiments that were needed by the Western people with their overactive life, who still in their heart of hearts have a thirst for the peace, for the infinite peace. My fitness was that training which my muse had from my young days in the absolute solitude of the beaches of the Ganges. The peace of those years had been stored in my nature so that I could bring it out and hold it up to the man of the West, and what I offered to him was accepted gratefully.

I know that I must not accept that praise as my individual share. It is the East in me which gave to the West. For is not the East the mother of spiritual Humanity and does not the West, do not the children of the West amidst their games and plays when they get hurt, when they get famished and hungry, turn their face to that serene mother, the East? Do they not expect their food to come from her, and their rest for the night when they are tired? And are they to be disappointed?

Fortunately for me I came in that very moment when the West had turned her face again to the East and was seeking for some nourishment. Because I represented the East I got my reward for my Eastern friends.

And I can assure you that the prize which you have awarded to me was not wasted upon myself. I as an individual had no right to accept it, and therefore I have made use of it for others. I have dedicated it to our Eastern children and students. But then it is like a seed which is put into the earth and comes up again to those who have sown it, and for their benefit it is producing fruits. I have used this money which I got from you for establishing and maintaining the university which I started lately, and it seemed to me, that this university should be a place where Western students might come and meet their Eastern brethren and then they might work together in the pursuit of truth and try to find the treasures that have lain hidden in the East for centuries and work out the spiritual resources of the East, which are necessary for all Humanity.

1921

From *Thoughts from Rabindranath Tagore*

We are like a stray line of a poem, which ever feels that it rhymes with another line and must find it, or miss its own fulfillment. This quest of the unattained is the great impulse in man which brings forth all his best creation. Man seems deeply to be aware of a separation at the root of his being, he cries to be led across it to a union; and somehow he knows that it is love which can lead him to a love which is final.

Last night when the north wind was keen, like a sharp blade of steel, the stall-keepers improvised some kind of shelter with twigs and leaves. With all its flimsiness it was the most important necessity for them, for the time. But this morning, before it is light, we hear them shouting for their bullocks and dragging out from underneath the trees their creaking carts. It is urgently important for them now to leave their shelter.

"I want" has its constant counterweight—"I do not want." Otherwise the monster necessity, with its immovable weight, would crush all existence. For the moment we may sigh at the fact that nothing remains for long, but we are saved from permanent despair at the calamity that nothing moves at all. Things remain and things move—between these two contrary currents we have found our dwelling-place and freedom.

The day breaks in the east, like a bud bursting its sheath to come out in flower. But if this fact belonged only to the outside world of events, how could we ever find our entrance into it? It is a sunrise in the sky of our consciousness, it is a new creation, fresh in bloom, in our life.

Open your eyes and see. Feel this world as a living flute might feel the breath of music passing through it, feel the meeting of creative joy in the depth of your consciousness. Meet this morning light in the majesty of your existence, where it is one with you. But if you sit with your face turned away, you build a separating barrier in the undivided sphere of creation, where events and the creative consciousness meet.

188

To fledgling birds flight in the sky may appear incredible. They may with apparent reason measure the highest limit of their possibilities by the limited standard of their nests. But, in the meanwhile, they find that their food is not grown inside those nests, it is brought to them across the measureless blue. There is a silent voice that speaks to them, that they are more than what they are, and that they must not laugh at the message of soaring wings and glad songs of freedom.

Religion, like poetry, is not a mere idea, it is expression. The self-expression of God is in the endless variedness of creation; and our attitude towards the Infinite Being must also in its expression have a variedness of individuality ceaseless and unending. Those sects which jealously build their boundaries with too rigid creeds excluding all spontaneous movement of the living spirit may keep hoarded their theology, but they kill religion.

With the truth of our expression we grow in truth. The truth of art is in the disinterested joy of creation, which is fatally injured when betrayed into a purpose alien to itself. All the great civilizations that have become extinct must have come to their end through some constant wrong expression of humanity; through slavery imposed upon fellow-beings; through parasitism on a gigantic scale bred by wealth, by man's clinging reliance on material resources; through a scoffing spirit of skepticism robbing us of our means of sustenance in the path of truth.

The question is asked, if life's journey be endless where is its goal? The answer is, it is everywhere. We are in a place which has no end, but which we have reached. By exploring it and extending our relationship with it we are ever making it more and more our own. The infant is born in the same universe where lives the adult of ripe mind. But its position is not like a schoolboy who has yet to learn his alphabet, finding himself in a college class. The infant has its own joy of life because the world is not a mere road, but a home, of which it will have more and more as it grows up in wisdom. With our road the gain is at the end, but with this world of ours the gain is at every step; for it is the road and the home in one; it leads us on yet gives us shelter.

A block of stone is unplastic, insensitive, inert, it offers resistance to the creative idea of the artist. But for a sculptor its very obstacles are an advantage and he carves his image out of it. Our physical existence is an obstacle to our spirit, it has every aspect of a bondage, and to all appearance it is a perpetual humiliation to our soul. And therefore it is the best material for our soul to manifest herself through it, to proclaim her freedom by fashioning her ornaments out of her fetters. The limitations of our outer circumstances are only to give opportunities to our soul, and by being able to defy them she realizes her truth.

The sign of greatness in great geniuses is their enormous capacity to borrow, very often without their knowing it; they have an unlimited credit in the world market of culture. Only mediocrities are ashamed and afraid of borrowing, for they do not know how to pay back their debt in their own coin. Even the most foolish of critics does not dare blame Shakespeare for what he openly appropriated from outside his own national inheritance. The human soul is proud of its comprehensive sensitiveness; it claims its freedom of entry everywhere when it is fully alive and awake.

190

What is this rhythm? It is the movement generated and regulated by harmonious restrictions. This is the creative force in the hand of the artist. So long as words remain in an uncadenced prose form, they do not give us any lasting feeling of reality. The moment they are taken and put into rhythm they vibrate into a radiance. It is the same with the rose. . . . The rose appears to me to be still, but because of its meter of composition it has a lyric of movement within that stillness, which is the same as the dynamic quality of a picture that has a perfect harmony. It produces a music in our consciousness by giving it a swing of motion synchronous with its own. If the picture were to consist of a disharmonious aggregate of colors and lines, it would be deadly still. In perfect rhythm, the art form becomes like the stars which in their seeming stillness are never still, like a motionless flame which is nothing but movement.

The world as an art is the play of the Supreme Person reveling in image-making. Try to find out the ingredients of the image—they elude you, they never reveal to you the eternal secret of appearance. In your effort to capture life as expressed in living tissue, you will find carbon, nitrogen, and many other things utterly unlike life, but never life itself. The appearance does not offer any commentary on itself through its materials. You may call it *māyā* and pretend to disbelieve it; but the great artist, the *Māyāvin,* is not hurt. For art is *māyā,* it has no other explanation but that it seems to be what it is. It never tries to conceal its evasiveness, it mocks even its own definition and plays the game of hide-and-seek through its constant flight in changes.

Music is the most abstract of all arts, as mathematics is in the region of science. In fact, these two have deep relationship with each other. Mathematics as the logic of number and dimension is the basis of our scientific knowledge. When taken out of its concrete associations with cosmic phenomena and reduced to symbols, it reveals its grand structural majesty, the inevitableness of its own perfect concord. But there is also such a thing as the magic of mathematics, which works at the root of all appearances, producing harmony of unity, the cadence of the interrelation of the parts bringing them under the dominion of the whole. This rhythm of harmony has been extracted from its usual context and exhibited through the medium of sound. And thus the pure essence of expressiveness in existence is offered in music. In sound it finds the least resistance and has a freedom unencumbered by the burden of facts and thoughts. It gives it a power to arouse in us an intense feeling of reality, it seems to lead us into the soul of all things and make us feel the very breath of inspiration flowing from the supreme creative joy.

1921

My Pictures

When at the age of five, I was compelled to learn and to repeat the lessons from my text-book, I had the notion that literature had its mysterious manifestations on the printed pages, that it represented some supernatural tyranny of an immaculate perfection. Such a despairing feeling of awe was dissipated from my mind when by chance I discovered in my own person that verse-making was not beyond the range of an untrained mind and tottering handwriting. Since then my sole medium of expression has been words, followed at sixteen by music, which also came to me as a surprise.

In the meanwhile the modern art movement, following the line of the oriental tradition, was started by my nephew Abanindranath. I watched his activities with an envious mood of self-diffidence, being thoroughly convinced that my fate had refused me passport across the strict boundaries of letters.

But one thing which is common to all arts is the principle of rhythm which transforms inert materials into living creations. My instinct for it and my training in its use led me to know that lines and colors in art are no carriers of information; they seek their rhythmic incarnation in pictures. Their ultimate purpose is not to illustrate or to copy some outer fact or inner vision, but to evolve a harmonious wholeness which finds its passage through our eyesight into imagination. It neither questions our mind for meaning nor burdens it with unmeaningness, for it is, above all, meaning.

Desultory lines obstruct the freedom of our vision with the inertia of their irrelevance. They do not move with the great march of all things. They have no justification to exist and, therefore, they rouse up against them their surroundings; they perpetually disturb peace. For this reason the scattered scratches and corrections in my manuscripts cause me annoyance. They represent regrettable mischance, like a gapingly foolish crowd stuck in a wrong place, undecided as to how or where to move on. But if the spirit of a dance is inspired in the heart of that crowd, the unrelated many would find a perfect unity and be relieved of its hesitation between to be and not to be. I try to make my corrections dance, connect them in a rhythmic relationship and transform accumulation into adornment.

This has been my unconscious training in drawing. I find disinterested pleasure in this work of reclamation, often giving to it more time and care than to my immediate duty in literature that has the sole claim upon my attention, often aspiring to a permanent recognition from the world. It interests me deeply to watch how lines find their life and character, as their connection with each other develops in varied cadences, and how they begin to speak in gesticulations. I can imagine the universe to be a universe of lines which in their movements and combinations pass on their signals of existence along the interminable chain of moments. The rocks and clouds, the trees, the waterfalls, the dance of the fiery orbs, the endless procession of life send up across silent eternity and limitless space a symphony of gestures with which mingles the dumb wail of lines that are widowed gypsies roaming about for a chance union of fulfillment.

In the manuscript of creation there occur erring lines and erasures, solitary incongruities, standing against the world principle of beauty and balance, carrying perpetual condemnation. They offer problems and, therefore, material to the *Visvakarma,* the Great Artist, for they are the sinners whose obstreperous individualism has to be modulated into a new variation of universal concord.

And this was my experience with the casualties in my manuscripts, when the vagaries of the ostracized mistakes had their conversion into a rhythmic inter-relationship, giving birth to unique forms and characters. Some assumed the temperate exaggeration of a probable animal that had unaccountably missed its chance of existence, some a bird that only can soar in our dreams and find its nest in some hospitable lines that we may offer it in our canvas. Some lines showed anger, some placid benevolence, through some lines ran an essential laughter that refused to apply for its credentials to the shape of a mouth which is a mere accident. These lines often expressed passions that were abstract, evolved characters that hung upon subtle suggestions. Though I did not know whether such unclassified apparitions of non-deliberate origin could claim their place in decent art, they gave me intense satisfaction and very often made me neglect my important works. In connection with this came to my mind the analogy of music's declaration of independence. There can be no question that originally melody accompanied words, giving interpretation to the sentiments contained in them. But music threw off this bond of subservience and represented moods abstracted from words, and characters that were indefinite. In fact, this liberated music does not acknowledge that feelings which can be expressed in words are essential for its purpose, though they may have their secondary place in musical structure. This right of independence has given music its greatness, and I suspect that evolution of pictorial and plastic art develops on this line, aiming to be freed from an absolute alliance with natural facts or incidents.

However, I need not formulate any doctrine of art but be contented by simply saying that in my case my pictures did not have their origin in trained discipline, in tradition and deliberate attempt at illustration, but in my instinct for rhythm, my pleasure in harmonious combination of lines and colors.

1930

194

Hindus and Muslims

For Kalidas Nag

The rain has been streaming down. That must be why my mind has been sweeping across the fences erected by hundreds of years of human history and has been roaming freely. Like the wind and the wave flowing across the open spaces of the sky and the ocean, the pulse beat and memories of generations have been playing the strains of the *Meghmalhar* raga in me. My sense of responsibility and the rational side of me too appear to have been swept away and I seem to have become part of the rows of mohua and chhatim trees in front of me. They are the aristocrats of the natural world, for they have been thriving on the sun and the showers streaming down from time immemorial. They are not the creation of modern times like men and that is why they are evergreen. Among mankind perhaps it is only the poet who has not totally squandered the patrimony it has received from ancient times because of wastefulness induced by civilizing habits. Only the poet has managed to hold on to something of his primeval self. That is why the trees do not look down on poets as mere mortals despite their aristocratic lineage. This is also the reason why year after year when the rainy season arrives I feel such excitement stirring in me, why I feel so free of all responsibilities and respond to its call to be part of life's playhouse. I seem to be taken over then by the child that resides in my innermost being, by the earliest manifestation of myself. And so whenever the rainy season sets in I begin to compete with the wind, the rain and the trees. I abandon all claims to work and start to compose songs. In a way I am at that time least human; my mind stirs like the grass, shimmers like the leaves. The poet Kalidas observes that on such an occasion even the most content person becomes restless. Contrariness in us then seems to be something that takes us outside the world that we have made for ourselves. Such a disposition takes one back to a far away time when our soul could play unfettered, where our mind had not decided to restrain itself in the hectoring tone of a school teacher. Then even through the very thick pillar of a school one is able to see flowers blooming in the grass and butterflies fluttering in their midst. In any case, this is the season when the thick clouds congregate at midday, casting over everything a shadow, when in fields the wild wind keeps blowing its trumpet, and when sudden restless small streams giggle like truant schoolgirls causelessly breaking out into peals of laughter.

Today is the 7th of the month of Asadh, the 11th day of the waning of the moon, the day when the Anbubanchi festival is supposed to begin. The naming of the event is an apt one, for the whole of nature appears to be reverberating with the sound of water in full flow. In the overcast sky and in the shadow cast by the moon as it approaches its dark period, there is a concert going on, with a score written especially for the occasion. Invited to the musical soiree organized by the trees are the crickets. The toads too have joined this raucous performance. Don't even think for a moment that I don't have a seat in this orchestra. I am not the kind of person to keep mum and not respond to the summons issued by the clouds when they rumble. Like clouds following clouds my songs keep coming forth day after day; they have no special significance, no goal, like the clouds melding light and water and mist and heat for reasons no one knows, they are made out of a potion that has no particular purpose. Just such a mood of composition induced me to sit by the window and hum a tune,

> My mind, stirred by the newly arrived clouds,
> Lilts and sings; my thoughts sway restlessly.

It is just at that point I got your letter, written to me from across the ocean, asking me what I feel is the way out of the Hindu-Muslim conflict bedeviling India. All of a sudden, I am brought back to earth; I am made aware I have work to do for the family that is mankind. It won't do to merely respond to the clouds forming in a tune set in raga *Meghmalhar,* one has to also come up with answers to a question that has cast a dark cloud over human history. That is why I have had to leave the Anbu-banchi congregation folks behind.

The world has two religions whose adherents are markedly different from all other sects—Christianity and Islam. They are not content with following the bent of their own religions; they are also bent on eliminating other ones. It is for this reason they feel that the religion they belong to can only survive by bringing the adherents of other religions into their fold. However, one thing in favor of the adherents of Christianity is that they seem to bear a modern outlook; their mind is not enclosed in the frame of the medieval world. Religious beliefs have not fenced every aspect of their lives. That is why they will not make of their religion an insurmountable barrier in their dealings with the people of other religions. To be "European" is therefore not the same thing as being "Christian." There is no conflict between being a "European Buddhist" and a "European Muslim." But a people who are identified according to religion are bound to be labeled by its beliefs. It is thus impossible to coin a word like "Muslim Buddhist" or a "Muslim Christian" spontaneously. On the other hand, Hindus are in one sense exactly like the Muslims. That is to say, they are completely fenced in by their religion. A superficial distinction between them is that in Hinduism opposing other religions is not an active principle needing an object; with all religions that are not Hindu they exist in a state of *non-violent non-cooperation.* However, because Hindus are enclosed within a rampart erected from birth and religious customs the fortifications hemming them in are even more formidable than those surrounding Muslims. The latter at least acknowledge that their members can interact with each other as equals; Hindus are excessively narrow-minded even in this respect. Also, Muslims will not reject people of other religions by refusing to have anything to do with their food or customs but Hindus tread warily in such instances. That is why during the Khilafat Movement Hindus were not willing to embrace Muslims as closely as Muslims were able to do by inviting them to their mosques and to other places they hold sacred. Custom is a bridge that enables people to interact with each other; it is precisely in their religious practices that Hindus have erected barriers for themselves again and again. Once I began to work as a zamindar I saw that when I had to deal with my Muslim tenants as their landlord I was expected to make them sit only after the cover was removed from the couch! There is no obstacle more formidable that can separate a group of people from another as one which considers the adherents of another religion impure.

It is the fate of the India that two religions like Hinduism and Islam have come together. Though Hinduism doesn't have strong prohibitions, it has formidable customs. In Islam, on the other hand, custom isn't insuperable but religious belief is strong. While one side has a door open, the other side's door is shut! How can the two religions come together then? At one time different nationalities like the Greeks, the Persians and the Scythians mingled freely and lived together in India. But you must remember that this happened before the advent of Hinduism. The advent of the Hindus became an era of reaction—it was the period when the belief of Brahmins was consolidated in the country purposively. Hinduism blocked itself by erecting a wall of custom that was not going to allow anyone to scale it. But one thing was not kept in view—any living thing is going to die if anyone tries to control it by wrapping it up. In any case, the outcome was that at a particular moment of our history after the Buddhist period there was a bid to preserve the purity of the Hindu religion after it had brought races like the Rajputs within its fold to erect a huge fence that would prevent any more alien customs or influences from pervading it. Key to this move was the prohibition and rejection of others. Nowhere else in the world could one see such an obstacle created by means of such an adroit strategy. This obstacle was designed not only to divide Hindus and Muslims. People like you and me who would like to be free through our actions have also been singled out and subject to barriers.

So these are the problems but how are we to solve them? The answer is by changing our mindset and by moving on to a new era of relationships. In the manner in which Europe emerged from the middle ages and entered the modern era through the pursuit of truth and by expanding the frontiers of knowledge, Hindus and Muslims will have to venture forth from the walls hemming them in. If religion is made into a grave and if the entire nation is confined to the past forever there is no way that we can tread on the path to development and there is no possibility of us melding with one another. We will never attain freedom if we fail to demolish the barriers that have been built in our minds. And such massive transformation of minds can only be achieved through education and through arduous struggle to achieve this end. We will have to get rid of the superstition that the cage is bigger than the spread of the wing. Only then will we be able to secure happiness for ourselves. The union of Hindus and Muslims is waiting for that crucial moment of transformation. But there is no reason to take fright at this thought. This is because other nations have already managed to alter themselves through arduous struggle; they have thereby been able to come out of their shells and have been able to stretch their wings. We too must overcome our mental barriers, for if we don't, there will be nothing in the future for us.

1937
(From *Kalantar*)
Translated by Fakrul Alam

The Tenant Farmer

For Pramathnath Chaudhury

Our holy books tell us that the course of worldly life is truly incredible. It originates in the upper sphere but must extend itself to survive. In other words, it cannot stand on its own and must dangle from a height. Reading your book, *The Tenant Farmer,* one realizes that our politics has affinities with this scheme of things. In its origins the Congress, it is obvious, had its roots in the upper echelons of the upper class, but whether for food or shelter, it must sustain itself at that elevation.

Those people whom we deem to be gentlemen had decided that politics amounted merely to sharing the throne of India amongst the princely class and the gentry. Both in war and peace, whether on the public podium or in the newspaper, their weapon in their vision of politics was the English language in all its refinement—sometimes used for supplications in the pathetic vein and sometimes spent in artificial anger expressed in animated tones. And when the country witnesses such arrogance and bluster in its upper sphere, and while its denizens busy themselves in producing such steam, the ordinary people of the country who are close to the soil go on in their eternal ways, living and dying, giving birth, tilling the land, weaving clothes, and producing food for all with the sweat of their brows. The gods who feel polluted when they encounter them in their temples have the masses bend in supplication outside it. And yet these are the people who cry and laugh in their mother tongue and who bear the burden of streams of insults and can only strike their foreheads at their miseries, blaming everything on "fate." The gulf between the politicians who inhabit the stratosphere and the masses at the bottom who suffer so is immense.

But there has been a turnaround in this form of politicking, resulting in a situation not unlike that in which a woman turns her eyes away from her lover because she is upset with him. The people are saying: "We won't see the dark clouds that you keep forecasting, O herald." Once there was time for courtship and assignation, now it is the time for people to feel piqued and for separation. But while there has been a twist in the plot there is no change in the fortune of the players. As empathically as yesterday when they had said "We want," today they say, "We don't want." The political capital that had accumulated is spent in the extravagance of the gentle folks. Little is spent for the welfare of the rural masses. In other words, from the beginning of politics in the modern era we have seen the people at the top practice patriotism by excluding the people of the countryside.

Those at the top who produce such effusions of false love are either owners of estates or factories. And those who provide the words for such effusions are the law merchants. They have no space for the rural masses in their scheme of things, which is to say, they have no space for the country in their scheme of things. As far as they are concerned, that is the land of the dead and of the disembodied. To them, the inhabitants of the land are powerless—either in wielding words or in their resources. If the courts had operated unhindered, the powerful ones would have to call them, but that action would have been undertaken only to stop them from paying their taxes so that they could be disposed of. And those who are at this time being called upon because of their adeptness at targeting them with their bow-strings are being used only to make them shut down shops to observe general strikes and to demonstrate to the powers that are that our political situation is completely askew.

These are the reasons why the fate of the tenant farmer is always put on the back burner. Let the throne be set up, the crown be designed, the scepter kept handy and let Manchester burn—and then there will be time to think about the tenant farmer. The politics of the land must have precedence over its people! And that is why at the outset such a big deal is made about the garb and order to be followed in politics. The amazing thing is that the ordinary person is not seen to be of any consequence in getting ready for the task at hand. The dress that people of another country have made after repeated measurements and adjustments based on their physique and the weather they are accustomed to encountering is seen to be all that is needed to provide work for the tailors of another country. One knows what this outfit is called—the appellations have been memorized from textbooks—for in our factories things must have a name even before the product is given a shape. It is as if all we have to do is close our eyes to image words like "democracy," "Parliament," "Canada," "Australia," "South Africa," "Forms of Government" etc. It is as if you don't need the person before you when you have decided to tailor an outfit which is going to be right for him. We seem to believe that saying that we must have self-rule first and think about the people for whom self-rule is needed later will allow us to enjoy the thing itself hassle-free. In all other parts of the world people have designed a system of rule on the basis of their own genius and according to their own needs and natures. We appear to be the only people in the world who take a date from the calendar and then declare, "We are going to have self-rule on January 1" or some such date as arbitrary as that and then decide that we are going to impose it on the populace from then on. And all the while our masses have to cope with malaria, epidemics, money-lenders, landlords, the police and the constabulary. They have to cope with the noose that will tighten around their necks as they take loans to marry their daughters off, or pay the expenses they will incur for the funeral rituals of their mothers, or come up with the taxes they will have to yield to a social system that has a hundred arms or provide the fees they must give to the lawyer who will help them to stay the all-engulfing summons of the court.

It is for these reasons that I doubt whether our politics has been captured in its essence in your work about our tenant farmers. You are not only declining to put the coach before the horse, you are also trying to thwart the attempt to do so by the elite. You are also trying to find out if the horse they have tried to tie up has been fed properly or valued adequately. Isn't there any one among your friends who have taken it on them to counsel you to say that only when one has got the coach moving can it reach its destination given an auspicious moment? Only then will one be able to find out whether the horse is still capable of moving or not or regardless of whether it is alive or dead. You should have known that contemporary politics is fitted to a timetable; the main objective seems to be to fix up a trunk and put it on the coach. Of course in the end the coach never goes anywhere but that is not the fault of the timetable. If the horse had moved things would have worked out on their own. You are skilled in logic; you would like to interrupt those who are enjoying themselves by telling them that the basic problem is that the horse hasn't moved at all for a long time. You represent the conservative sentiments of someone accustomed to earlier fashions and would like to find out the state of the stable first before you would make a move. Meanwhile, the enthusiasts of contemporary fashionable society have mounted the coach and are shaking their feet restlessly. They are using the image of a house on fire to say that they must reach their destination immediately. That seems to be the only urgent issue they have kept in view. That is why they deem it a waste of time to inquire about the condition of the horse. The only thing that they consider to be important is to mount the coach. Your book *The Tenant Farmer* is about the horse, about the issue that must be seen as most pressing.

II

But what is also worrying is the way some young people of our time are turning their attention to the question of the tenant farmer. The first thing they are doing is evolving a remedy to solve the problem. One can see that they have spotted a similar situation abroad. Just when our mind has begun to embrace the idea of doing our own thing in a big way we can see that they have adopted a grand scheme that has a "Made in Europe" stamp on it. Because of the nature and location of Europe, its people have in the course of time experimented with different ideas for transforming society such as socialism, communism, syndicalism, etc. But when we decide that we are going to do something for the welfare of our tenant farmer we can't seem to come up with a formula that is our own and that is not based on something that has evolved in Europe. This time when I went to East Bengal I saw a form of literature springing up there that is as sharp as the young shoot of the *kush* grass and as brittle too. This grass is so prickly that each of them can pierce your skin till you will bleed. The newly sprung do-gooders seem to be exhorting all to grind and trample; "Let's clear earth of landlords and money-lenders," they appear to be proclaiming. It is as if you can forcibly get rid of sin or end whatever is offensive by throwing a stick at it in the dark. It is as if daughters-in-law have ganged up to say: "Employ thugs to force our mothers-in-law to go on a pilgrimage to the Ganges, for only then will us brides be safe from them." They have forgotten that the ghost of their mothers-in-law will haunt them till they are completely overwhelmed by them. Our holy scripture tells us that when committing suicide is no option in exiting this world, you can cut yourself loose from it only by cleansing your innermost self. Europeans are instinctively aggressive. But to cleanse the evil in our innermost selves takes time; these young people, however, can't wait, they must apply desperate physic externally to get rid of the body.

Like children who play at being adults we tried to patch up the tattered clothes of politics with parliamentary methods derived from Europe. The reason that we imitated them thus is that the ideals of European politics were the ones we had in view. The stories of Europe that captured our imagination most are the ones that narrate the feats of Garibaldi and Matsini. Now a new act is being played out in their theaters. The canto of the *Ramayana* narrating the story of the destruction of Lanka was all about the royal hero's victory, the humiliation of the

King, and of the sacrifice of the queen to keep the subjects happy. In the subsequent canto we learn about the victory of the foul-mouthed, of the humiliation and the forced exile of the king so that the subjects could be appeased. The period of war revealed the king in his glory, now it is the subject's turn to look grand! Then the song that was being sung was about the victory of the land over the foreign foe; now the theme of the song is the victory of the courtyard over the edifice itself. It is not that we understand fully the nature and the workings of the new schemes emerging in the west such as Bolshevism and fascism; what we have glimpsed of them makes us realize that they are systems where brawlers will thrive. And no sooner have we viewed them from a distance than our mind, which thrives on imitation, sees the brute force of the system as the most important thing about it to emulate. The third incarnation of Vishnu when he slew the demon called Varaha was the boar which used its teeth to pry earth loose of the mud it was mired in; these people would like the world to move forward by using a stick to beat others! There seems to be no time to think or the courage to think through things to realize that mere obduracy or aggression cannot remove the disparities that exist between the upper and lower spheres. The source of the inequalities that exist in the world is in the mind of men. That is why if we at this time try to shove the lower shelf upwards today tomorrow the upper shelf will press on the one that is lower now with unbearable force. Moving from the Czarism of the past to the Bolshevism that one sees in Russia now is like turning from one side of the bed to the other while lying down. Celebrating because one has managed to transfer the abscess from the left hand to the right must surely be called madness. There are people whose blood courses through their veins so freely that it goes into their head, making them act wildly. But then there are also those people who see these wild men and begin to act crazily though their blood does not flow through their veins as freely. These are the men who suffer from what is known as hysteria. This is why when I found out a literature that advocates that the money-lender be manhandled and the landlord trampled upon I was able to see that the rude mantra it is based on is something that originates not in the blood of these men. This is evidence of the Bengali's genius for imitation, of daubing themselves in magenta hues.

Externally these actors are good at throwing their hands and feet in his-
trionic gestures but their minds are vacuous.

III

Since I am a landlord myself someone may point out that I am saying all
this because I would like to survive intact in my present position. If I re-
ally want to do so no fault should be imputed to my wanting to carry on
as I am—after all that is human nature. Just as those who would like to
snatch away my rights do so because that is what occurs to them as nec-
essary, those who would like to hold on to their positions do so because
of the same instinct of doing what is good for their existence. In other
words, there are things we do not out of a spiritual sense but because of
materialistic motives. Those who succeed in snatching away someone
else's position today will become the wildcats of tomorrow. Perhaps the
way they hunt will be different but the way they use their teeth and nails
will not be of the pacific kind characteristic of the Vaishnava mendicant.
They might talk in a high-flown manner about snatching rights away to
indicate that they have sophisticated tastes but tomorrow will prove them
to be carnivorous—and insatiable in the bargain! This is because though
they use words with sophistry they are really driven by instincts that are
voracious. Consequently, even if the landlord who sprung up in the land-
scape of the country as a thorny tree today is trampled upon till he has
been killed, there will be a second growth of such trees to take his place
which will be even more spiky. This is because there has been no change
in the nature of the soil which gives birth to such trees!

By birth I am a landlord but by nature I am given to gazing at the
heavens. This is why I have no inner inclination to hold on to the land I
have inherited. I am wanting in the respect I am supposed to have for my
profession. I know that the landlord is a leech as far as the land is con-
cerned; he is a parasite, someone surviving at the expense of others. We
render our bodies unfit and our mind lazy by not working and do not
earn; nor do we accept any sort of responsibility. Instead we depend on
the wealth that we have inherited. We are not the kind of people who

earn the right to have leisure by our prowess. Our tenants provide us with food and our functionaries spoon-feed us; there is no glory in this or heroism. We do take some kind of pride in imagining ourselves as kings according to the measurements we make with the small scales we take up in our hands. In your *About Tenant Farmers,* you have been looking into that setup and have tried to discredit the illusions we have about ourselves. You have attempted to show that we are no more than hereditary rent collectors appointed by the English crown. On the one hand our food is seasoned by the salt we are allotted by His Majesty's government and call our tenants our "subjects" and on the other hand we call ourselves "kings." We are living a massive lie. It is better to let go of such ownership of land. But who will we leave our land to? To another landlord? In the game of knaves and thieves no matter which move we make we cannot prevent another knave from taking over. Should we abdicate in favor of our subjects? Then we will see that one big landlord has been replaced by ten small ones. I do not think there is any difference between the nature of a big leech and a small one as far as their intent is concerned because both intend to suck blood. You say that the land should be owned by those who till it. But how can that be if the land is a commodity to be bought and sold and if there are no restrictions to handing it over to someone else? It can be said that those who read books should own them. It is argued in this vein that those who do not read books but like to display them deprive those who use them regularly. But if books can be bought and sold in just any shop can we stop anyone with a shelf from purchasing a book and putting it on display even though he cannot read and write? In life bookshelves are much more easily obtainable and abound compared to learning. That is why most books end up in display shelves and not in the desks of the learned. The favorite of the goddess of wealth Lakshmi ends up possessing the picture drawn by the favorite of the goddess of the arts, Saraswati. They do so not because they have the right to the picture but because they have money in the bank. Those who are irascible but have little by way of savings become hopping mad at such instances. They declare: beat up the wealthy, snatch away the picture from him. But as long as the artist has to feed himself and as long as the painting has no place to end up in except the art market, no one will be able to prevent the work from hanging on the wall of someone blessed by the goddess Lakshmi!

IV

If a piece of land is sold in the open market there is little chance that the person who actually tills it will get the opportunity to purchase it; the person who does not farm land but has money will end up buying most of the cultivable land. It is also the truth that the number of plots to be bought and sold will increase gradually. This is because land that is inherited keeps being fragmented. The land that will fall to a farmer's lot will gradually become smaller and smaller; consequently, sheer need will drive the farmer to carry out transactions involving his land. This is how small plots of land are increasingly getting entangled in the big nets being flung by the money-lenders. This is also why the tenant farmer finds himself increasingly being ground down. The few rights that the tenant farmer once had when he had only his landlord to deal with began to vanish when he has to contend with the money-lender as well. I have stepped in to prevent many of my tenants from dwindling in their fortunes further by pointing out to them where transferring the deed of their land would take them to. Although I did not deprive the money-lender in such cases, I compelled him to come to a settlement. In cases where I was unable to do anything for the tenant farmer I would hear their cry sounding all the way from my durbar to the courtyard of heaven. However, whether he will get any compensation in the afterlife for what he has had to endure in this one is not the subject of this piece.

When in the era of indigo plantations the indigo tax had got the tenant writhing in its net, it was the landlord who had to come to his rescue. If there were no laws to protect the tenant farmer from yielding his land it would have been swept away by the floodtide of the debts he had incurred in being forced to cultivate indigo. If in present-day Bengal Marwari traders decide to control the trade in agricultural produce for some reason or the other, it will become very easy for him to squeeze every ounce of juice obtainable from Bengal in the press he is using for the purpose. There is no reason for anyone to think that these traders have not been eyeing us for such an end. If the flow of profits from their current businesses are blocked the capital that the Marwaris have amassed will be looking for new outlets. The point then is what method the tenant farmer will adopt to create a channel that will allow the flood water to flow towards his plot of land for his own use. The fact is that most tenant farmers lack guile. They are not educated and are an impoverished lot. These farmers do not know how to defend themselves. However, even amongst the tenant farmers are a few exceptional individuals. These are dreadful people. I have become acquainted with the voracious appetite of such tenant farmers who are out to swallow the rest of their kind. The process through which they flourish till they become landlords smacks of the tactics that were adopted by the devil's disciples. These few rapacious tenant farmers do not hesitate to pursue any strategy that they feel will help them achieve their ends—fraud, forgery, filing lawsuits based on trumped up charges, torching homes, and destroying harvests. They become even more adept in their knavery when they are sent to jail where they pick up new strategies of appropriating land. One hears that in the United States big businesses become monstrous by swallowing up the small ones; in a similar manner the domineering tenant farmer uses every means at his disposal—guile, force, subterfuge—to take over the land of smaller tenant farmers till eventually he metamorphoses into a landlord himself. Initially he used to till his own land and load his carts himself with produce that he would sell in country markets. There was no difference between him and the other farmers at this stage of his life except for his cunning nature. But as soon as the number of his land holdings started to increase he let go of his plough and took a club in his hand. He soon sported a belly and began to recline on a dumpy bolster. He began to accumulate funds to file false cases in order to grab land. There appears to be no limits to his bullying—hectoring—yelling—abusive and brutal ways. In the big nets that are flung, big and small fish often manage to find a way to escape but the very small fish and the fries are all caught; most of the tenant farmers are like these small fish and fries.

One thing that we should keep in mind is that just as in judo where you make use of your opponent's strength to trip him in law one uses to one's advantage that piece of legislation which is supposed to put one at a disadvantage. To reverse the force that is being used against one-self is the intricate strategy used in law as well as in wrestling. There are some pretty deft wrestlers who are now using the law in this manner. Consequently, till most tenant farmers can rely on their own intelligence and finances, the law that is considered to be such an exalted thing will become a means of casting the tenant farmers into deep waters.

It does not seem right to say or hear that it is one's duty to prevent the tenant farmer from buying and selling his land freely. Looked at from another perspective, however, to give a person complete freedom may also mean giving him the right to harm himself. Only he who is not a child in his thinking should be given complete freedom. If you prevent an adult from travelling on a highway where there is constant motorized traffic you are being tyrannical; but if you fail to put some restraints in the movement of a child on such a highway you are acting irresponsibly. From what little experience I have I can say that to give the ignorant ten-ant farmers of our country the right to transfer their land freely will be tantamount to giving them the right to take their own lives. No doubt there will come a time when they must be given that right but if they are granted that right at this time will they have any rights left? What I am articulating here are my reservations about your ideas on this issue.

V

I know that the landlord is not above temptation. That is why wherever the tenant farmer is in a fix the landlord is able to get a rich haul of fish at that spot. In our country there are rigid limits imposed in marrying off girls. It is precisely these limits that become a source of income for the groom's side. Our tenant farmers share a similar predicament. But there is no reason to be happy at the loss incurred when the money-lender is appropriating the tenant farmer's land. For the farmer the fist of the money-lender is much more forceful than that of the landlord. If you don't agree with me on this point, concede at the very least that that is an additional fist he has to contend with.

It is absolutely correct to say that the land of the tenant farmer should not be subject to increased revenue collection. There is no increase in the amount of revenue the landlord has to pay the government; it is therefore unfair to impose a comma or a semicolon on the fixed amount that the tenant farmer has to pay. Besides, this arrangement is a major obstacle to the natural desire that the farmer has to cultivate his land more effectively. As a result, such an imposition would affect not only the farmer but the whole country adversely. In addition, no one can support any obstacle put up in the bid to clear trees for cultivation, build better homes, and dig more tanks.

But these are all minor points. The main thing to keep in mind is that no law can help someone to survive if he himself lacks the desire to live. This desire to live must be made part of the desire for wholeness in life and must not be located in any out-of-the-way system. It cannot be found in a special piece of legislation, in the spinning wheel, in home-spun clothes, in the limited right that enables one to vote for the Congress. It is only when rural life is completely rejuvenated that the instinct for self-preservation which one has will be activated within oneself.

How this can be achieved is something that I have been thinking about for some time. I don't know whether I will be able to come up with a satisfactory answer to the question—it takes time to come up with such an answer. But whether I am able to do so or not the answer to the question must be sought out. The answers to all the miscellaneous questions will be found in the answer to the main question. If no answer is forthcoming we will spend our days patting each other on the back, but it is to be doubted whether the person for whom we have all been trying to patch up things will survive our efforts.

1937

(From *Kalantar*)
Translated by Fakrul Alam

Crisis in Civilization

Today I complete eighty years of my life. As I look back on the vast stretch of years that lie behind me and see in clear perspective the history of my early development, I am struck by the change that has taken place both in my own attitude and in the psychology of my countrymen—a change that carries within it a cause of profound tragedy.

Our direct contact with the larger world of men was linked up with the contemporary history of the English people whom we came to know in those earlier days. It was mainly through their mighty literature that we formed our ideas with regard to these newcomers to our Indian shores. In those days the type of learning that was served out to us was neither plentiful nor diverse, nor was the spirit of scientific enquiry very much in evidence. Thus their scope being strictly limited, the educated of those days had recourse to English language and literature. Their days and nights were eloquent with the stately declamations of Burke, with Macaulay's long-rolling sentences; discussions centered upon Shakespeare's drama and Byron's poetry and above all upon the large-hearted liberalism of the nineteenth-century English politics.

At the time though tentative attempts were being made to gain our national independence, at heart we had not lost faith in the generosity of the English race. This belief was so firmly rooted in the sentiments of our leaders as to lead them to hope that the victor would of his own grace pave the path of freedom for the vanquished. This belief was based upon the fact that England at the time provided a shelter to all those who had to flee from persecution in their own country. Political martyrs who had suffered for the honor of their people were accorded unreserved welcome at the hands of the English. I was impressed by this evidence of liberal humanity in the character of the English and thus I was led to set them on the pedestal of my highest respect. This generosity in their national character had not yet been vitiated by imperialist pride. About this time, as a boy in England, I had the opportunity of listening to the speeches of John Bright, both in and outside Parliament. The large-hearted, radical liberalism of those speeches, overflowing all narrow national bounds, had made so deep an impression on my mind that something of it lingers even today, even in these days of graceless disillusionment.

Certainly that spirit of abject dependence upon the charity of our rulers was no matter for pride. What was remarkable, however, was the wholehearted way in which we gave our recognition to human greatness even when it revealed itself in the foreigner. The best and noblest gifts of humanity cannot be the monopoly of a particular race or country; its scope may not be limited nor may it be regarded as the miser's hoard buried underground. That is why English literature which nourished our minds in the past, does even now convey its deep resonance to the recesses of our heart.

It is difficult to find a suitable Bengali equivalent for the English word "civilization." That phase of civilization with which we were familiar in this country has been called by Manu *"Sadachar"* (*lit.* proper conduct), that is, the conduct prescribed by the tradition of the race. Narrow in themselves, these time-honored social conventions originated and held good in a circumscribed geographical area, in that strip of land, Brahmavarta by name, bound on either side by the rivers Saraswati and Drisadvati. That is how a pharisaic formalism gradually got the upper hand of free thought and the ideal of "proper conduct" which Manu found established in Brahmavarta steadily degenerated into socialized tyranny.

During my boyhood days the attitude of the cultured and educated section of Bengal, nurtured on English learning, was charged with a feeling of revolt against these rigid regulations of society. A perusal of what Rajnarain Bose has written describing the ways of the educated gentry of those days will amply bear out what I have said just now. In place of these set codes of conduct we accepted the ideal of "civilization" as represented by the English term.

In our own family this change of spirit was welcomed for the sake of its sheer rational and moral force and its influence was felt in every sphere of our life. Born in that atmosphere, which was moreover colored by our intuitive bias for literature, I naturally set the English on the throne of my heart. Thus passed the first chapters of my life. Then came the parting of ways accompanied with a painful feeling of disillusion when I began increasingly to discover how easily those who accepted the highest truths of civilization disowned them with impunity whenever questions of national self-interest were involved.

There came a time when perforce I had to snatch myself away from the mere appreciation of literature. As I emerged into the stark light of bare facts, the sight of the dire poverty of the Indian masses rent my heart. Rudely shaken out of my dreams, I began to realize that perhaps in no other modern state was there such hopeless dearth of the most elementary needs of existence. And yet it was this country whose resources had fed for so long the wealth and magnificence of the British people. While I was lost in the contemplation of the great world of civilization, I could never have remotely imagined that the great ideals of humanity would end in such ruthless travesty. But today a glaring example of it stares me in the face in the utter and contemptuous indifference of a so-called civilized race to the well-being of crores of Indian people.

That mastery over the machine, by which the British have consolidated their sovereignty over their vast Empire, has been kept a sealed book, to which due access has been denied to this helpless country. And all the time before our very eyes Japan has been transforming herself into a mighty and prosperous nation. I have seen with my own eyes the admirable use to which Japan has put in her own country the fruits of this progress. I have also been privileged to witness, while in Moscow, the unsparing energy with which Russia has tried to fight disease and illiteracy, and has succeeded in steadily liquidating ignorance and poverty, wiping off the humiliation from the face of a vast continent. Her civilization is free from all invidious distinction between one class and another, between one sect and another. The rapid and astounding progress achieved by her made me happy and jealous at the same time. One aspect of the Soviet administration which particularly pleased me was that it provided no scope for unseemly conflict of religious difference nor set one community against another by unbalanced distribution of political favors. That I consider a truly civilized administration which impartially serves the common interests of the people.

While other imperialist powers sacrifice the welfare of the subject races to their own national greed, in the USSR I found a genuine attempt being made to harmonize the interests of the various nationalities that are scattered over its vast area. I saw peoples and tribes, who, only the other day, were nomadic savages being encouraged and indeed trained, to avail themselves freely of the benefits of civilization. Enormous sums are being spent on their education to expedite the process.

When I see elsewhere some two hundred nationalities—which only a few years ago were at vastly different stages of development—marching ahead in peaceful progress and amity, and when I look about my own country and see a very highly evolved and intellectual people drifting into the disorder of barbarism, I cannot help contrasting the two systems of governments, one based on co-operation, the other on exploitation, which have made such contrary conditions possible.

213

I have also seen Iran, newly awakened to a sense of national self-sufficiency, attempting to fulfill her own destiny freed from the deadly grinding-stones of two European powers. During my recent visit to that country I discovered to my delight that Zoroastrians who once suffered from the fanatical hatred of the major community and whose rights had been curtailed by the ruling power were now free from this age-long repression, and that civilized life had established itself in the happy land. It is significant that Iran's good fortune dates from the day when she finally disentangled herself from the meshes of European diplomacy. With all my heart I wish Iran well.

Turning to the neighboring kingdom of Afghanistan I find that though there is much room for improvement in the field of education and social development, yet she is fortunate in that she can look forward to unending progress; for none of the European powers, boastful of their civilization, has yet succeeded in overwhelming and crushing her possibilities.

Thus while these other countries were marching ahead, India, smothered under the dead weight of British administration, lay static in her utter helplessness. Another great and ancient civilization for whose recent tragic history the British cannot disclaim responsibility, is China. To serve their own national profit the British first doped her people with opium and then appropriated a portion of her territory. As the world was about to forget the memory of this outrage, we were painfully surprised by another event. While Japan was quietly devouring North China, her act of wanton aggression was ignored as a minor incident by the veterans of British diplomacy. We have also witnessed from this distance how actively the British statesmen acquiesced in the destruction of the Spanish Republic.

214

On the other hand, we also noted with admiration how a band of valiant Englishmen laid down their lives for Spain. Even though the English had not aroused themselves sufficiently to their sense of responsibility towards China in the Far East, in their own immediate neighborhood they did not hesitate to sacrifice themselves to the cause of freedom. Such acts of heroism reminded me over again of the true English spirit to which in those early days I had given my full faith, and made me wonder how imperialist greed could bring about so ugly a transformation in the character of so great a race.

Such is the tragic tale of the gradual loss of my faith in the claims of the European nations to civilization. In India the misfortune of being governed by a foreign race is daily brought home to us not only in the callous neglect of such minimum necessities of life as adequate provision for food, clothing, educational and medical facilities for the people, but in an even unhappier form in the way the people have been divided among themselves. The pity of it is that the blame is laid at the door of our own society. So frightful a culmination of the history of our people would never have been possible, but for the encouragement it has received from secret influences emanating from high places.

One cannot believe that Indians are in any way inferior to the Japanese in intellectual capacity. The most effective difference between these two eastern peoples is that whereas India lies at the mercy of the British, Japan has been spared the shadow of alien domination. We know what we have been deprived of. That which was truly best in their own civilizations [in] the upholding of the dignity of human relationship has no place in the British administration of this country. If in its place they have established, with baton in hand, a reign of "law and order," in other words a policeman's rule, such mockery of civilization can claim no respect from us. It is the mission of civilization to bring unity among people and establish peace and harmony. But in unfortunate India the social fabric is being rent into shreds by unseemly outbursts of hooliganism daily growing in intensity, right under the very aegis of "law and order." In India, so long as no personal injury is inflicted upon any member of the ruling race, this barbarism seems to be assured of perpetuity, making us ashamed to live under such an administration.

And yet my good fortune has often brought me into close contact with really large-hearted Englishmen. Without the slightest hesitation I may say that the nobility of their character was without parallel—in no country or community have I come across such greatness of soul. Such examples would not allow me wholly to lose faith in the race which produced them. I had the rare blessing of having [Charles] Andrews—a real Englishman, a real Christian and a true man—for a very close friend. Today in the perspective of death his unselfish and courageous magnanimity shines all the brighter. The whole of India remains indebted to him for innumerable acts of love and devotion. But personally speaking, I am especially beholden to him because he helped me to retain in my old age that feeling of respect for the English race with which in the past I was inspired by their literature and which I was about to lose completely. I count such Englishmen as Andrews not only as my personal and intimate friends but as friends of the whole human race. To have known them has been to me a treasured privilege. It is my belief that such Englishmen will save British honor from shipwreck. At any rate if I had not known them, my despair at the prospect of western civilization would be unrelieved.

In the meanwhile the demon of barbarity has given up all pretence and has emerged with unconcealed fangs, ready to tear up humanity in an orgy of devastation. From one end of the world to the other the poisonous fumes of hatred darken the atmosphere. The spirit of violence which perhaps lay dormant in the psychology of the West, has at last roused itself and desecrates the spirit of Man.

The wheels of Fate will some day compel the English to give up their Indian empire. But what kind of India will they leave behind, what stark misery? When the stream of their centuries' administration runs dry at last, what a waste of mud and filth they will leave behind them! I had at one time believed that the springs of civilization would issue out of the heart of Europe. But today when I am about to quit the world that faith has gone bankrupt altogether.

As I look around I see the crumbling ruins of a proud civilization strewn like a vast heap of futility. And yet I shall not commit the grievous sin of losing faith in Man. I would rather look forward to the opening of a new chapter in his history after the cataclysm is over and the atmosphere rendered clean with the spirit of service and sacrifice. Perhaps that dawn will come from this horizon, from the East where the sun rises. A day will come when unvanquished Man will retrace his path of conquest, despite all barriers, to win back his lost human heritage.

Today we witness the perils which attend on the insolence of might; one day shall be borne out the full truth of what the sages have proclaimed:

"By unrighteousness man prospers, gains what appears desirable, conquers enemies, but perishes at the root."

1941

4

Poems

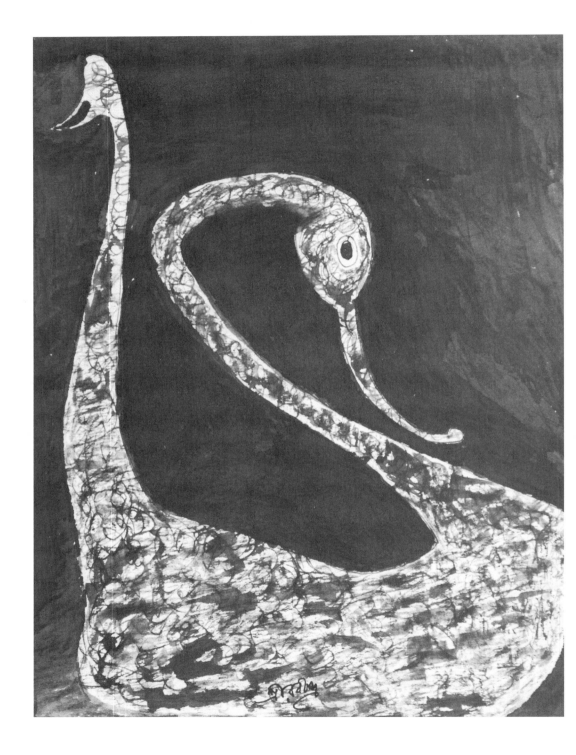

TAGORE WROTE IN ALMOST all conceivable literary forms during his lifetime, but the appellation which was stuck on him early by his readers and which has stayed with him is that of a "poet." In fact, his own people started calling him *viswa-kabi* or "the universal poet" soon after he was awarded the Nobel Prize in 1913, and surely it was primarily his reputation as a poet that took him to five continents. And, of course, it is mostly his poetry that has been translated into all the major languages of the world.

Certainly, Tagore is a poet of incredible variety and remarkable profusion. Surveying his poems, one could exclaim as Dryden did about Chaucer, "Here is God's plenty." It is said that Tagore was only a child when he began to rhyme, and biographers have recorded vividly how even as the eighty-year-old poet lay dying in 1941, poems kept coming to him. Unable to write them down, he dictated, checking even then to ensure they were perfectly formed. In all, he published over forty volumes of verse—the first collection, *Kabi-Kahini,* was printed in 1878 when he was seventeen, and the final one, *Janmadin,* in the year of his death. Not a few volumes, it may be added, were printed posthumously.

Tagore's poetry encompasses a sweeping variety of forms. Although primarily a lyric poet, Tagore also wrote dramatic, narrative, and comic verse. Innovative and given to endless formal experiments with meter, rhyme, stanza size and shape, and diction, he wrote very short as well as quite long poems, poems that were as musical as one can imagine poetry to be as well as pure prose poems. He composed historical ballads, poems for children, and plays that were essentially strung together from verse. He even wrote nonsense poems and jingles for an alphabet book to help children read and write Bengali. Mystical, meditative, and intense love poems preoccupied him throughout his life, however. Tagore kept evolving as a poet both thematically and stylistically; each book that he published departed from the previous one in form and content. True, occasionally he returned to a previous style, but as Abu Sayeed Ayub, one of the most astute critics of Tagore's poetry, has noted, "there is no arrest in movement till the last; step by step he has overreached himself; even if he has returned to a former step, that return has ascended like a winding staircase; it has not turned around in the same place" (*Modernism and Tagore,* 38). Tagore first began to write when poetry was gripped by the epic mode in Bengal and by late romantic or early pre-Raphaelite poetic styles, characterized by excessively sonorous and melancholic verse, in England. By the time he had entered his mature phase, however, modernism had changed poets everywhere. Not surprisingly, then, while his early poetry is dreamy, nostalgic, or suffused with a kind of vague romanticism, his themes as well as his technique in his mature phase reveal a poet poised on the brink of modern poetry.

This selection of translation of his verse begins with "The Fountain's Awakening," a poem from his fourth book of verse, *Prabhat Sangeet* (1883). In this volume the young poet, stirred by a quasi-mystical experience, realizes that his vocation is to articulate the wonder and variety of life. There is exuberance in his early works, and the poems from *Kori O Komal* (1886) reveal Tagore celebrating erotic love and embracing life on earth. The poems of the *Sonar Tari* volume (1894) chosen here confirm his growing apprehensions about life's burdens and are often in the symbolist mode; indeed, the poem "Voyage without End" is quite mystical in tone.

The poems that Tagore wrote as he approached middle age show his increasing awareness of the lives led by the people around him. He had no doubt come closer to them because of the experiences he had gathered in running the family estates in rural East Bengal. "My Little Plot of Land" from the volume *Chitra* (1896), a narrative poem, dramatizes the plight of the tenant farmer, driven from his land by a merciless landlord, while the lyric poem "Krishnakali" (from the collection published in 1900 titled *Kshanika*) captures the poet's delight caused by a momentary encounter with a beautiful village girl. But middle age and a series of personal tragedies made Tagore, always religious because of his upbringing but also inclined toward transcendentalism by instinct, reflect more intensely than before on the deity and afterlife. It is at this point that he evolved a very personal concept of god that finds poetic expression in "The Lord of Life."

The most celebrated of the religious verse that came from Tagore's sustained communion with God and eternity of course are the *Gitanjali* poems that he composed in the first two decades of the twentieth century. The publication of the *Gitanjali* in English in 1912, the travels to distant lands that he undertook regularly from this year, the Nobel Prize, the onset of the First World War, the display of nationalistic fervor everywhere, and the colonizer's excesses made the middle-aged Tagore increasingly restless. This sense of a world on the edge, of things changing utterly, and of the old order yielding to an uncertain one are reflected in the poems of the *Balaka* (1916) period. As even the shape of the two poems from this volume (the titular poem, "A Flight of Geese," and "The Restless One") included in this section indicate, the poet is fascinated by a world that is forever in flux. Although Tagore never stopped composing the short lyrical poems he is most often remembered by, he now started writing prose poems such as "Dawn and Dusk" (from *Lipika,* published in 1922). From this time onward, he often seems bent on muting the music that came so naturally to him.

As Tagore entered old age, his unhappiness with the lot of ordinary men and women in his country and the excesses of nationalism and colonialism everywhere was reflected in poems that even in their form and diction reveal the scars of modernity. The celebrated poem "Wind Instrument" from *Parisheshe* (1932) portrays the ugliness and pathos of urban living. Other poems written in the 1930s reflect the poet's frustration at the marginalization of women in an overwhelmingly patriarchal society ("Free!" "Woman Empowered," "Letter Writing," and "An Ordinary Woman"). "Africa," part of *Patraput* (1936), agonizes on the haplessness of the continent and its people because of the ravages of the colonizer.

The poems of the final phase reveal the poet reviewing himself, his art, and his public position. He had been in the limelight in his own country and internationally for decades by then and knew that his life and aesthetics had always been under intense scrutiny. "Panchishe Baisakh," written on the occasion of his birthday and included in *Sesh*

Saptak (1935), and poems such as "I" (from *Shyamoli,* published in 1936) and "Romantic" (from the 1940 volume *Nabajatak*) meditate on his career, ponder on the way he was being assessed, assert his aesthetics, and muse about his legacy. In his final poems, "On the Banks of Roop-Naran," "The Sun of the First Day," "The Song of the First Day," and "On the Way to Creation," all composed as he lay dying, and part of the posthumously published *Shesh Lekha* (1941), he demonstrates the amazing resilience that had carried him through the travails of a long life as he contemplates his passage out of the world.

In his admiring but balanced estimate, *Tagore: Portrait of a Poet,* the major Bengali poet-critic Buddhadeva Bose declares that "there is no single volume of Tagore's of which we can say that it is his most representative work or combines all the characteristic merits" (65). No doubt, this selection of his poems hardly does justice to Tagore. No doubt, too, the magic he wove in his Bangla poems has been largely lost in translation. Nevertheless, it is to be hoped that the English versions of the poems presented here will give a new generation of readers an impression of Tagore's infinite versatility and immense power as a poet.

A final comment needs to be made to introduce this selection of his poems. The second poem, "Enough, Enough!" is from *Pushpanjali,* a collection Tagore had put together after his beloved sister-in-law Kadambari Devi committed suicide on 19 April 1884. However, he did not publish this collection during his lifetime. "Enough, Enough!" has been translated from the manuscript version, which is in Rabindra Bhavana, Santiniketan. Also, this section includes three poems from the manuscript of the English *Gitanjali* ("On the Day Thou Breakst Through This My Name," "More Life," "Thy Rod of Justice") that are not to be found in the printed version. They have been reproduced here from the notebook in which Tagore wrote them; a copy of this notebook is part of the Houghton collection at Harvard University.

The Fountain's Awakening

O, how did the sun's first ray
Into my heart find its way?
This dawn, how could birdsongs pierce my heart's dark den?
After all this time, why does my heart suddenly stir again?
My heart stirs again,
Like a river swelling and bursting its banks
My desires overflow.
The very foundations of mountains keep shaking;
Boulders are flung time and again,
Waves foam and leap,
And roar in fury.
Like a madman whirling about
My passions run riot.
My feelings whirl but can find no way out.
Why is God forever stony-hearted?
Why does he bind on all sides with Chains?
Break heart, break all chains,
Devote yourself this day to your own desires.
Flinging wave after wave
Keep striking blow after blow.
When the heart is on fire and intoxicated
Why fear darkness or the stony-hearted?
When desire overwhelms
What in the world need one fear?

I'll stream down compassion
I'll smash this stony prison
Overflowing my banks I'll flood the world.

Spreading passionately my song of deliverance
Letting my hair flow, gathering all fallen flowers,
And spreading rainbow-colored wings,
I'll pour out my heart till the sun's rays start smiling.
I'll dart from peak to peak,
I'll throw myself on the ground willfully,
I'll laugh out loud, sing soulfully, and clap gleefully.
There's so much to say, so many songs to sing, so much life in me,
Such feelings of bliss, such desires—my heart is so full and free.
This day, what could it be that has made my heart sway?
In the distance I can hear some mighty ocean's music play.
What is the cage that would restrict me on all sides?
Break all bars, heart—strike at whatever strikes.
What is the song the bird sang this day?
The sun has finally found its way![1]

("Nirjharer Swapna-bhanga,"[2] from *Prabhat Sangeet*)
Translated by Fakrul Alam

Enough, Enough!

Enough, enough, will you please keep quiet?
My dear one is asleep;
Now, if she wakes up weeping
Seeing her tears, weep will I!

The play she loved is over,
Her heart is heavy as a stone
Today, weeping and weeping, she fell asleep
Please don't make her weep any more.

Didn't you hear her piercing wails?
With unbearable pain in her heart
Only keep staring at the moon, she would,

Enough, Enough!

Where else could she find solace?
She loved everyone,
Where else could one find such tender care?
She would cry out for all,
Did anyone cry out for her?
The tree she would water,
Its thorns would prick her feet,
And yet, would she ever complain?
Alas, who would understand the language of her eyes?

Ah, today she is asleep,
She had never slept like this before
All night her heart must have been
Restless with pain!
So many nights she must have spent thus!
In the breeze of spring,
Slowly from the eastern window
Moonlight is streaming on her.
So many nights had been spent like this
With a flute playing far away
Melody must have wept
Hovering around the bed.
So many nights must have been spent
With bakul flowers in her lap,
Playing with the flowers with eyes lowered,
Must have sighed again and again.

All those nights are over,
So is the pain of her heart,
Let her now sleep in peace.
Dear mine, sob no more, weep no more.

("Thak Thak Chup Koro," from *Pushpanjali*)
Translated by Shailesh Parekh

Life

I don't want to leave this lovely world
I want to stay in the midst of mankind.
In this sun-drenched flower-filled garden
I'd like to be at the pulsating heart of life.
Life in earth ripples on everlastingly,
Mingling unions and partings, joy and sorrow;
Out of human happiness and distress
I'd like to compose immortal songs.
But if this proves to be a vain wish
As long as I am alive, let me at least
Place myself where night and day
I can pen lyrics that blossom into songs.
Please accept my blossoms with a smile
And when they wither, cast them away!

("Pran," from *Kori O Komal*)
Translated by Fakrul Alam

Undressed

Take off all clothes; get rid of your dress
Put on only nudity's beautiful attire!
Glow in the adornment of the celestial female
Fulfilled in a perfect body—a lotus in bloom!
In the festival of life, youth and loveliness
Amidst the world's splendors be resplendent.
Let moonlight stream all over your body
Let the south wind caress all your parts
Immerse yourself under the infinite blue
Become nature undraped in a star-filled sky.
Let Cupid hide its face at you undressed

Let me view you, head bowed in bashfulness!
Let a breathtaking dawn break in this world,
Displaying you in perfect and exquisite nakedness!

("Bibasana," from *Kori O Komal*)
Translated by Fakrul Alam

Breasts

A woman's love stems from a soft heart,
Budding in youth, it's nurtured by her spring.
Coming to blossom in all its loveliness,
It maddens the soul with its heavenly scent!
The softness of her being ripples on
Seemingly spilling over her heart's banks.
What draws her bashful heart out?
Is it the flute's call or love of the world?
Suddenly it stops at the edge of light,
All draped to conceal its embarrassment.
But still the music of love plays within
Rising and falling to love's melodies.
Behold charming Lakshmi, goddess beautiful,
Behold the twin temples of a woman's heart!

("Stan," from *Kori O Komal*)
Translated by Fakrul Alam

Kissing

Only lips know the language of lips,
Know how to sip each other's hearts
The two lovers leave home for goals unknown,
Setting out eagerly on Holy Communion.

Like two waves that crest at love's pull
Lips at last melt and meld in lovers' lips,
Viewing each other with deep desire,
Both meet at the body's frontier.
Love weaves music from such refrains
Love's tale is told in quivering lips!
From flowers plucked from lips that roam
Garlands surely will be woven at home!
The sweet union of two desiring lips
Climaxes in a red bridal bed of smiles!

("Chumban," from *Kori O Komal*)
Translated by Fakrul Alam

The Golden Boat

Clouds rumble; rain pours down incessantly.
I sit all alone on the shore, uncertainly.
Heaps of paddy lie piled up—harvesting is done.
The swollen river speeds on turbulently;
While harvesting was going on, the rainy season had begun.

One tiny paddy field and I so forlorn—
Around me, the frolicking water eddies on.
On the other side, a tree-shrouded shore is in sight.
And a village cloaked in clouds in the morning light,
On this side, a tiny paddy field, and I so forlorn!

Who's singing on the boat heading for the shore?
As I look on, I feel I've seen the face before.
The boat speeds on but has no time to look around,
The helpless waves break up as they hit the ground—
As I look on, I feel I've seen the face before!

The Two Birds

Where could you be going, to which distant land?
But for once moor your boat on this strand.
Go where you will, give to anyone generously
What you would. Only, take smilingly
My golden harvest after mooring on this strand.

Load as much as you'd like to on your boat.
Do I have more? No, I've given you the full load.
All that kept me by the riverbank over the year,
I give them all up to you, layer after layer.
But pity me this once and take me away forever.

No room on that small boat—no room at all!
My golden harvest was enough to make it full.
On this rainy day, as clouds all over me swirl,
On the desolate riverbank I lie down forlorn—
All I had with that golden boat is gone!

("Sonar Tari," from *Sonar Tari*)
Translated by Fakrul Alam

The Two Birds

The captive bird in a gilded cage lay,
The free bird in the forest,
Fate decreed they would meet one day—
Was God setting up a test?
The free bird said: "Dear captive bird,
Let us to the forest fly."
"Free bird; let us peacefully to the cage,"
Was the captive bird's reply.
The free bird said emphatically,
"I'll never give up my freedom."

The captive bird said ruefully,
"How can I in the forest be at home?"

Outside the cage, the free bird sang songs
Learned from its flights in forests,
The captive bird was full of notes memorized—
The two talked in different tongues!
The free bird said, "Dear captive bird,
See if you can sing songs of the wild"
The captive bird answered,
"Learn from me songs of the caged"
The free bird said, "Never!
Will I sing songs dictated to me?"
The captive bird cried, "How can I ever
Sing the song of the free!"

The free bird said, "The sky is blue and bright,
And nowhere do I feel fettered."
The captive bird said, "The cage is proper and right,
See how I am perfectly sheltered."
The free bird said, "For once let yourself go
And become one with the sky."
The captive bird said, "To this retreat know
You can yourself firmly tie."
The free bird said, "No!
How can one there fly?"
The captive bird said, "This I know
There is no place to rest in the sky!"

This was how the birds wanted each other
Though destined to stay apart.
Through the bars of the cage one touched the other
Silently, desire stirred in each heart.
But each the other failed to understand
Failed even to give itself solace.

I Won't Let You Go!

Vainly, they their wings fluttered
And wailed, "Come closer."
The free bird said, "What if I am trapped
Inside—never!"
The captive bird said with a sigh,
"I've lost the strength to fly!"

("Dui Pakhi," from *Sonar Tari*)
Translated by Fakrul Alam

I Won't Let You Go!

The carriage is ready; it's afternoon;
The late autumnal sun blazes;
A midday breeze swirls dust
Off the deserted rural road;
In the cool shade of a peepal tree
A worn out beggar woman dozes
On a tattered cloth. As in a night
Coming after an excess of sunlight
Everything is still, silent, somnolent—
Only my house is astir,
Its inmates incapable of sleep!

Autumn's come and gone; holiday's over,
I leave for my far off workplace.
Our servants run around the house
Packing bags and baggage with ropes and strings,
Although her eyes are full of tears,
And her heart is leaden, my wife
Has not a moment to sit down and cry.
She makes sure that everything is ready
For the journey. My bags are full,
But she thinks I don't have enough!

I exclaim, "Must I take all?
Boxes, jugs, pots, pans and plates,
Bowls, bottles, and bedclothes too!
What will I do with so many things?
Let me only take some of them
And leave the rest behind."

But nobody heeds me.
"What if you need this or that?
Where will you get them then?
Here I've fine rice, excellent lentils
Betel leaves and areca nuts; in those bowls
Are date-palm molasses and ripe coconuts;
There two jugs of the best mustard oil,
Mango cakes, dried mango sticks and milk,
Here in these bottles, medicines
And in those bowls, delicious sweets—
Promise, dear, you'll eat them!"
I realize it's pointless to protest
And let bags and baggage pile up.
I look at my watch and then my dear wife,
And say softly, "Goodbye."
She glances away, turning her head,
Hiding her face in her sari's edge,
Fighting tears lest they bring bad luck.

My four-year-old daughter waits outside
Pensively. Any other day,
She would have had a bath by now
And before she had taken a bite or two,
Her eyelids would droop in sleep.
This day her mother has no time for her
And hasn't noticed that she hasn't bathed
Or had lunch. All this time she had been
Sticking close to me like my shadow,
Watching my going-away rituals in rapt silence.

I Won't Let You Go!

Tired now, thinking who knows what,
She stands outside the door silently.
When I say, "Goodbye darling,"
She declares sad-eyed and solemnly,
"I won't let you go," staying put,
Making no attempt to take me by the arm
Or blocking my way; as if proclaiming thus
The dictate of her heart. As if only saying
"I won't let you go" was enough.
And yet the time has come, alas!
She has to let me go!

Silly daughter of mine, was it you speaking?
What gave you the strength
To say so emphatically, "I won't let you go"?
What made you feel you could stop me
From leaving with only a pair of hands?
How could you think of holding me back
And blocking me with your frail little body
Stirred only by a heart full of love?
Timid and shy as we are, the most we say
Even when our heart bursts with pain is
"Don't feel like letting you go!"
And to hear your little mouth declare firmly
"I won't let you go," to hear you assert
Love's claim with such intensity!
And yet I feel the world smiling wryly
As it takes me away from my family.
I bid leave, but as in a framed picture,
I register the little one's image—defeated,
In tears, sitting in the doorway,
And I wipe my tears and leave.

As I depart I see on both sides of the road
Ripening paddy fields basking in the sun.
Towering trees border the highway,

And reflect intently on their own shades.
The autumnal Ganges is in full flow.
White cloudlets recline on a blue sky,
Like new-born calves who've had their fill
Of their mother's milk and sleep peacefully.
I sigh as I look at bright sunlight
Spreading across old, exhausted earth.

234

What immense sadness has engulfed
The entire sky and the whole world!
The farther I go the more clearly I hear
Those poignant words "Won't let you go!"
From world's end to the blue dome of the sky
Echoes the eternal cry: "Won't let you go!"
Everything cries, "I won't let you go!"
Mother Earth too cries out to the tiny grass
It hugs on its bosom, "I won't let you go!"
Someone trying to snatch from darkness
The flame of a dying lamp exclaims
A hundred times, "I won't let you go!"
It's the oldest cry resounding from earth to heaven
The solemnest lament, "I won't let you go!"
And yet, alas, we have to let go; and yet,
Of course, we must go. And this is how it has been,
From time immemorial. Since creation's currents
Began streaming relentlessly towards extinction's sea
With burning eyes and outstretched arms
We've all been crying out in vain endlessly,
"Won't let go, won't let you go!"
Filling earth's shores with laments
As everything ebbs inexorably away.
The waves up front cry out to the ones in the rear,
"Won't let go, won't let you go!"—
But no one listens. . . .

I Won't Let You Go!

Everywhere around me this day I hear
My daughter's plaintive voice; it keeps ringing
In my ears and piercing the heart of the universe.
Earth resounds with a child's unreasonable cry.
Forever it loses what it gets and yet it won't
Slacken its grip; forever it calls us
With unending love like my four-year-old daughter:
"Won't let you go!" Though sad-faced and in tears,
Its pride shattered at every step,
Love refuses to accept defeat and cries out
In desperation, "Won't let you go!"
Defeated each time it blurts out,
"Can the one I love stay away?
Can anything in the universe compare
In strength or be as boundless as my desire?"
And even as it proclaims proudly,
"Won't let you go" the one it treasures
Is blown away instantly, like dust
Wafted by the arid wayward breeze. And then
Tears stream down its eyes. Like a tree
Uprooted, it collapses headfirst, humiliated.
And yet Love insists, "God keeps his Word
I have proof in the pledge He made of a right
Given eternally." And thus emboldened,
Fragile Love stands up to Death
And boasts, "Death, you don't exist!"
Death laughs at such folly. And so Love,
Undying, though weighed down by Death,
Pervades the universe, solemn-faced,
Full of fears, forever in a flutter and tears.
A weary hopefulness covers the world
Like a gray fog. I see two inconsolable arms
Vainly trying to bind saddened, silent earth.
Under swift currents a quiet shade
—The allure of a cloud that will soon shed tears.

And thus this day the rustling trees
Induce in me yearnings. In midday heat
The lazy indifferent wind plays listlessly
With dry leaves. The slow day wanes,
Lengthening the shade under the banyan tree.
Eternity's flute plays a pastoral lament
Heard over the universe. Responding,
Listless Earth sits down in a paddy field
By the river's side, loosening her tresses,
Flinging a golden scarf across her bosom
That gleams in the golden sun. She is silent,
Her eyes still as she looks at the distant blue sky.
I take a look at her sad, sorrowful face,
As if in a doorway, silent, absorbed, sad.
Just like my four-year-old daughter!

("Jete Nahi Dibo," from *Sonar Tari*)
Translated by Fakrul Alam

Unfathomable

Do you fail to understand me?
You view me plaintively,
Straining to fathom me,
Like the moon looking steadily
At the depths of the sea.

I haven't hidden anything from you
All I have is for you to view.
Myself I have revealed;
I am all before you on show
Is that why you won't understand me?

Unfathomable

If it were merely a gem
I'd cut it into pieces.
Weaving the bits into a chain carefully
I'd place them on your neck lovingly.

If it were merely a flower,
Beautiful, and delicately shaped,
Blossoming at the break of day,
Swaying in the spring breeze—
I'd pluck it from its stalk carefully
And place it on your black tresses lovingly.

But I spread before you, dear, my heart
Can its depths from its banks be kept apart?
Too deep to fathom, too enigmatic a retreat,
How can I its past reveal or its future predict?
Nevertheless, dear, it's yours to queen over!

What would I have you believe?
About what in my innermost being,
Keeps ringing, day and night,
In silent music and wordless stillness
Spreading across the heavens,
Like tunes pervading the night.

If it were only a question of happiness,
A smile emerging on the lips
Would give rise to immense bliss
Conveying instantly the heart's tidings
Overlooking the need for speech.

If it were only a question of grieving
Of glistening eyes and tears being shed,
Of pale lips, and a sad face—

You'd see the pain in me easily,
You'd read my thoughts instantly.

But love, dear, has inundated my heart—
And there's no limiting its sorrow or delight!
It always pines away and yet always revives,
Day and night its perplexities leave me reeling.
And so I fail to tell you about it.

But what if you don't understand me?
Keep me always in sight, judge me in shifting light
Study me thoroughly day and night.
Fathom the parts of me you can—
Who could ever the whole comprehend?

("Durbodh," from *Sonar Tari*)
Translated by Fakrul Alam

Voyage without End

How much farther will you lead me, fair one?
Tell me what shore your golden boat will moor on.
    Stranger-woman, when I ask
    You only smile, sweet-smiling one:
I cannot tell what passes in your mind.
    You point a finger silently
    Towards the heaving shoreless sea,
The sun upon its western edge inclined.
What waits us there? What do we go to find?

Tell me, unknown one: there, beside the fire
Upon the evening's brink, of day's death-pyre,
    Like liquid flame the waters gleam,
    The sky dissolves in a melting stream

Or tears from the horizon-dwelling nymph—
　　Is that your home, beyond the sea
　　A voice with waves, beneath the feet
Of the cloud-kissing sunset mountain peak?
You look at me and smile, but do not speak.

The wind groans ceaselessly with driving sighs,
The waters roar in a blind agitation.
　　Across the anguished waves I scan
　　The darkening sea but find no land,
An endless wailing rocks and drowns creation.
　　Our golden boat upon it plays,
　　Upon it fall the evening rays,
And there you sit and smile your silent smile.
What fills you with such mirth? I cannot tell.

When first you asked, "Who'll go with me?" into your eyes
I only looked a moment, in that new sunrise.
　　You pointed west with hand outspread
　　Towards the endless seas ahead
Where restless light, like hope, tossed on the waters.
　　I came aboard, and questioned you
　　If I would find there life anew,
If yearning dreams there yielded golden fruit.
You looked and smiled, but even then were mute.

Then sometimes there were clouds, and waves' commotion;
Sometimes a placid sun and painted ocean.
　　The sails are full: the day wears on,
　　The golden vessel flies along—
I see the sun descending in the west.
　　And now I only ask to hear,
　　Is tender death awaiting there?
Is peace and slumber in the darkness found?
You lift your eyes and smile, without a sound.

The gloomy night with beating wings draws by,
Blotting the golden twilight from the sky.
    Only your body's scent abides,
    Only the clamor of the tides,
Only your wind-blown hair about me lies.
    With leaden limbs and weary soul
    I'll seek for you with eager call.
"O come and lay your hands on me awhile."
You will not speak; I shall not see your silent smile.

("Niruddesh Jatra" from *Sonar Tari*)
Translated by Sukanta Chaudhuri

To Civilization

Give back the wilderness; take away the city—
Embrace if you will your steel, brick and stone walls
O newfangled civilization! Cruel all-consuming one,
Return all sylvan, secluded, shaded and sacred spots
And traditions of innocence. Come back evenings
When herds returned suffused in evening light,
Serene hymns were sung, paddy accepted as alms
And bark-clothes worn. Rapt in devotion,
One meditated on eternal truths then single-mindedly.
No more stone-hearted security or food fit for kings—.
We'd rather breathe freely and discourse openly!
We'd rather get back the strength that we had,
Burst through all barriers that hem us in and feel
This boundless universe's pulsating heartbeat!

("Sabhyatar Prati," from *Chaitali*)
Translated by Fakrul Alam

My Little Plot of Land

Of my land only a little remained, the rest having been mortgaged away.
The zamindar said one day, "Know what Upen? This too should come
    my way."

I said, "O Lord, countless are the plots of land you already own,
But consider—I only have land where I can die in contentment!"
The zamindar brushed me aside saying, "Upen, I'm building a garden,
Your half-acre will allow me to design for it a lovely fountain—
You'll have to sell all you've got to me!" I replied, tears in my eyes
And hands on my heart, "Spare this poor man's land, or else he dies!
For seven generations we've tilled this plot and it's everything to me,
And selling it will be like selling my mother because of poverty!"
The zamindar reddened, kept mum for a bit, and then gave a peculiar
    smile,
In a forbidding manner, he muttered under his breath, "we'll see in a
    while!"

In six weeks I was forced out of my ancestral land and into the road
By a court decree. Falsely, it said I had defaulted on a loan and owed
The zamindar the whole lot! Alas, in this world those who have most
    want all
And even a king won't stop until he has grabbed everything—big or
    small!
I consoled myself: God has decided not to confine me to my plot of
    land;
Perhaps I am fated to roam far and wide and end up in some distant
    strand.
And so I became a mendicant's assistant and followed him everywhere
Visiting shrines that were memorable and seeing sights that were fair.
But no matter whether I climbed high peaks or reached a remote river
    bend
The thing I could never forget night or day was my little plot of land!

And so I traversed country fairs, fields, and roads for fifteen years or so
Until homesickness made me feel to my country once more I must go.

I thought as I went: lovely motherland Bengal—I bow to you lovingly!
Your exquisite riverbanks and gentle winds will surely revive me.
I'll thrill at skies kissing dust swirling up from wide open fields;
I'll seek in the sylvan shade of a tiny village an abode of perfect bliss.
I'll revel in its mango trees and cowboys playing on lush green meadows
Bengal's calm and shaded ponds will be cool and comforting to see
And surely I'll delight at sweet village belles carrying water home daily.
Such thoughts of my motherland made me sad and tears welled up in
    me.
Two days later—at noon—I entered my village—oh so eagerly!
Past the potter's shop and left of the field where festivals are held I sped
Leaving the fairground—site of all delight—and the temple ground
I hurried to my homestead—thirsty, eager and completely exhausted!

Shame, shame, oh shame on you, my shameless little plot of land!
How is it that you yielded so easily to the seducer's blandishment?
Do you remember how you once nurtured me with what little you had?
How you provided me with fruits, flowers and produce from your bed?
Who are you trying to seduce now in fancy and dazzling dresses?
Why deck yourself in alluring colors and flower-studded tresses?
It was for you I came back worn out by years of wandering
But you, wanton, are only bent on being coy and enchanting!
Riches enticed you and the landlord's wealth made all the difference
And nothing remains of what you once were—a maiden in essence!
So bountiful and giving once, so caring, sweet and pleasant,
Seduce him all you can—once a goddess, now you're a mere servant!

With a grieving heart I looked around and what then did I see?
Still erect where it always stood was my favorite mango tree!
I sat down and wept till tears doused the pain that was in me
One by one, images of childhood resurfaced in my memory.
I recollected how after summer storms I wouldn't sleep at all,

A Hundred Years from Now

Knowing I had to gather by dawn the mangoes sure to fall
I thought of still fun-filled afternoons when we played hooky
And I felt: what a pity that such days I will never again see!
Suddenly a gusting wind shook the branches of the mango tree
And two ripe mangoes fell on the spot where I happened to be.
Surely, I thought, my mother has finally seen her long lost son,
And so I gathered the mangoes she gave me on this occasion!

Suddenly, like an angel of death, an Oriya gardener was on the scene.
This man—hair all in knots—swore in a manner obscene.
I told him, "I gave up all years ago without protesting the court decree
Why fuss if I pick up two mangoes from what was my property?"
Unimpressed, the gardener seized me, directing his stick at my head.
Dragging me to his landlord, he complained to him about what I said.
The zamindar, egged on by his cronies, thundered, "You're as good as
     dead!"
But his abuse was nothing compared to what his cronies had to say.
All I could say in defense was, "my lord, those mangoes fell my way."
The zamindar said, "This scoundrel acts innocent but is a big thief!"
I smiled, though in tears, at being made the source of all mischief.
I thought: he acts the saint now but I have to play the role of the thief!

("Dui Bigha Jami," from *Chitra*)
Translated by Fakrul Alam

A Hundred Years from Now

A hundred years from now
Who could you be
Reading my poem curiously
A hundred years from now!
How can I transmit to you who are so far away
A bit of the joy I feel this day,
At this new spring dawn,

The beauty of flowers this day
Songbirds that keep chirping away
Of the crimson glow of the setting sun.
How can I lave them all with my love,
And hope you will make them your own
A hundred years from now?

However, if you keep your southern door ajar,
Sit by your window and look afar
View the horizon stretch endlessly
And imagine this possibility—
That one day a hundred years from now,
Excitement from some heaven above could flow
Could strike your inmost heart and make it glow,
That on a bright spring day
When you were feeling restless and carefree—
Suddenly,
There could blow with the southern breeze,
Impatient and eager to please,
Flying on restless wings,
Full of pollen and the scent of flowers,
And of what youth desires,
An impulse from me that could make your soul sway.
At a time a hundred years away!
A soul carried away by the tunes
Overwhelmed by the flowers on display,
Had then burst into poetry,
Lovingly,
A hundred years from now!

A hundred years from now
Who will that new poet be
Singing in your festivals merrily?
I send him my spring greetings—
Hoping he will make them his own

Let my spring song resound in your spring day
For a while let my tune stay—
In the fluttering of your soul, the humming of bees,
And murmuring in leaves,
A hundred years from now!

("Aaji Hote Shata Barsha Pare," from *Chitra*[3])
Translated by Fakrul Alam

The Lord of Life

Lord of my inmost part,
Has all your thirst been slaked at last on coming to my heart?
    I've filled your cup with all the flow
    Of a hundred thousand joys and woes
Wrung from my breast like juice of grapes with cruel torment pressed.
    From many scents and many hues,
    Many verses, many tunes,
Your marriage-bed I've woven with long care,
    And fashioned for you every day
    New figures for your passing play
By melting down the gold of my desire.

You freely chose me—who knows why? You freely sought and wooed.
    Lord of my life, do you delight
    In these my mornings, these my nights.
In all my work, in all my play, amidst your solitude?
    Did you hear from your lonely throne
    The songs that through the spring and rain,
Autumn and winter, sounded in my heart?
    Or filled your lap with flowers of thought,
    And for your neck in garlands wrought,
And wandered with a dreaming soul through the woods of my youth?

What do you see, beloved, with your eyes
Fixed on my heart? Have you forgiven all my truancies?
    How often has my prayerless day,
    My slothful night, sped on its way,
My offering-flowers drooped and died among the lonely woods.
    How often did my lyre descend
    Below the note that you had tuned:
O poet, can I ever sing the music of your verse?
    To water your garden have I gone,
    Dozed in the shade; when night came on,
With laden eyes conveyed at last the water of my tears.

Lord of my heart, is this the end of all I had to keep—
Beauty, song, life, my waking hours, the drowsy trance of sleep?
    My arms have loosened their embrace,
    My kiss does not intoxicate;
In life's grove, does the morning break upon the night of love?
    Then shatter this tryst for today,
    Give me new form and new array,
My immemorial self again within your clasp revive:
In a new marriage take me, the bonds of a new life.

("Jibandebata," from *Chitra*)
Translated by Sukanta Chaudhuri

Love Queries

Is it all true then?
My ever-fond one,
Is it true
That my lightning-bright glance
Causes your heart to blaze and thunder
Like a colliding cloud?
Is it true

Love Queries

That the sight of my sweet lips,
The reddening of my bride-shy cheeks
Spellbinds you, my ever-fond one?
Is it true
That you find the perennial mandar
Blooming in me forever?
That my ringing feet resound for you like the veena?
Is it all true?
Is it true
That the dew of night sheds at my sight?
That the dawn light makes all around me glow?
Is it true
That your head swoons at my touch?
That the very breeze seems intoxicated?
Is it all true
My ever-fond one?

Is it true
That day is eclipsed by my black tresses?
That my arms have locked yours till death?
Is it true
That the limits of your universe are my sari's border?
That the world shushes at the sound of my voice
Is it true
That I encompass heaven, earth and the netherworld
That all three are totally devoted to me
Is it all true
My ever-fond one?

Is it true
That your love has been pursuing me for eons
Whirling all over the globe to home in me?
Is it true that my speech, glance, lips and tresses
Have caught your eyes eternally?
Is it true

That on my beautiful brow is writ for you
All the truths of the infinite?
Is it all true
My ever-fond one?

("Pranayprashna," from *Kalpana*)
Translated by Fakrul Alam

Krishnakali

I call her Krishnakali,[4] my dark blossom,
Though villagers call her the dark girl.
On a cloudy day I had seen her in the field
Had seen the dark girl with doe-like eyes!
Her veil had fallen and her head was bare.
Her tresses were swinging over her neck.
Dark? No matter how dark she was to others,
I had seen her beautiful doe-like eyes!

Thick clouds had made darkness descend.
Her dappled cows had lowed in dismay.
Perplexed, this dark doe-eyed beauty
Had rushed out from her hut anxiously.
Peering intently at the sky,
She had heard the thunder rumbling.
Dark? No matter how dark she was to others
I had seen her beautiful doe-like eyes!

Suddenly, the wind swept in from the east.
The paddy fluttered playfully in the breeze.
Standing by myself in a corner of the aisle,
I saw her all alone in the middle of the field.
Whether we had exchanged glances then,

I guess no one will ever know besides us.
Dark? No matter how dark she was to others,
I had seen her beautiful doe-like eyes then!

And so always and ever moist dark clouds
Sweep in from the northeast during summer.
And so always and ever dark soft shadows
Tell of the monsoon settling in tamal woods.
And thus it is during late monsoon nights
A sudden happiness lightened up her face.
Dark? No matter how dark she was to others,
I had seen her beautiful doe-like eyes then!

I call her Krishnakali, my dark blossom.
Let others call her what they will!
I had seen her in Mainapara's field
Had seen the dark girl's doe-black eyes.
She hadn't rolled her veil over her head.
Hadn't got the time to feel embarrassed!
Dark? No matter how dark she was to others,
I had seen her beautiful doe-like eyes then.

(from *Kshanika*)
Translated by Fakrul Alam

The Poet

I am quite happy—or at least
    For sorrow's leanness none the worse;
And yet it seems a little strange
    To own to this when I write verse.
That's why I delve within my heart
    Some deep distemper to express,

And come up with some deep defect
 Of knowledge or forgetfulness.
And yet it is so very deep,
 So inaccessibly remote,
The poet doesn't really need
 To warrant if it's true or not.
He wears his smile upon his face,
 He takes his daily nourishment,
And no one ever sounds the springs
 Of his deep-rooted discontent.

You mustn't judge a poet by
 The themes he writes his verse on.
He doesn't shroud his face with blight
Or break his heart all day and night,
But bears his pangs, et cetera
 Like a wholly cheerful person.

He's fond of formal company,
 And sits with them in formal dress;
He's fond of holding merry talk
 With people, with a cheerful face.
He doesn't probe a friendly jest
 For meanings dark and recondite,
But sometimes even spots the point
 Where he should laugh with all his might.
If you set food in front of him,
 He's never torn by any doubt;
Nor does he skulk inside the room
 When cronies come to call him out.
His friends call him a witty man—
 That surely can't be quite untrue?
His foes call him a scatterbrain—
 No doubt they have their reasons too.

The Poet

> You mustn't judge a poet by
> > The things he writes his verse on.
> By river-banks he doesn't swoon
> With his eyes fixed upon the moon,
> But bears his pangs, et cetera,
> > Like a fairly happy person.

But should he write "I'm happy," why,
> He's judged a wretch of narrow spirit:
His thirst is of a mean extent,
> His hopes and dreams of feeble merit.
His readers either laugh him off
> Or else upbraid in language stern:

A bit of shallow sport, they say,
> Can cool his appetite to learn.
That's why the poet tunes his verse
> To forge a document of grief:
It may be false, dear reader, but
> You still shall weep and find relief.
With choking voice and throbbing heart
> May you then make your benedictions:
O let the poet prosper long
> To write with joy his mournful fictions!

> A poet mustn't ever be
> > Like what he writes his verse on:
> Let him not be entirely dense,
> But eat and wash with honest sense,
> And talk in simple prose, just like
> > A simple normal person.

("Kabi," from *Kshanika*)
Translated by Sukanta Chaudhuri

The Hero

Imagine, ma, we've been travelling,
   To a land far, far away
You keep looking at the way
From inside your palanquin
I'm on a crimson stallion
   Galloping steadily along.
My horse's hooves hurl dust up high,
   Reddening the evening sky.

   At sundown we reach a vast field
   Next to two ponds lying side by side.
Whichever way we care to look
Wide empty spaces meet the eye.
"Where are we?" You ask fearfully,
   And I say, reassuringly,
"Don't worry dear, we are here
   See the dead stream over there?"

   Through a weed-covered field
   The path winds its way,
No people or cattle to be seen
They are in now that it's evening.
Who knows where we are heading?
   In darkness nothing can be seen!
Suddenly, you say to me
  "Is that a light I see in the night
   Just next to the pond's edge?"

   Instantly we hear shouts, "Whoa,
   Whoa, we're here!"
Terrified, you duck inside the palanquin
Praying to God to intervene.

The Hero

The bearers to the forest flee
    Looking at each other full of fear
But I tell you confidently,
  "I'm here, ma, why worry?"

    Staff in hand, hair in disarray,
    Hibiscus in ears, thugs block our way.
I yell, "Stop—come no closer
Here's my sword, my Excalibur,
With it all of you I'll slay."
    For a moment the rogues stare
And then they cry out "Beware,
    Beware, we're here!"

    Frightened, you cry, "Don't go child."
    I say, "Ma, in a moment I'll be done."
I strike them with sword and shield
Men collapse and die in the field,
Imagine, ma, the action furious and fast
    Enough to leave one completely aghast
So many thugs run away, bewildered
    So many villains die, beheaded!

    You wonder—will my son survive?
    Will he fight such odds and live?—
I return—blood and sweat all over me—
And declare, "I've won!" triumphantly
Amazed, you alight from the palanquin
    Kiss me lovingly and take me up,
And say, "Lucky my son was there!
    Imagine what would happen without him!"
    So many fabulous things happen every day
    Why, alas, don't such events come my way?
Wouldn't it be great to narrate such a tale?
And wouldn't all listen to it breathlessly?

Surely only my older brother would demur
   "Khokon a champion? Impossible!"
Surely everyone else will declare,
   "Thank goodness, our hero was there!"

254

("Birpurush," from *Sishu*)
Translated by Fakrul Alam

Big and Small

I haven't really got to grow up yet:
   I'm just a child, and so I'm still quite small.
One day I'll be much older than Big Brother—
   As old as Father is, and just as tall.
If Dada then won't learn his lessons,
But with his pet birds keeps on messing,
I'll really scold him well and good—
"Now just you learn your lessons as you should,"
I'll tell him, and "Be quiet, you naughty boy,"
   I'll say, when I'm as big as Father is.
I'll take his bird-cage then, without more words,
And keep the very nicest baby birds.

Or in the morning, when it's half-past ten,
   I won't be in a hurry for my bath,
But slip my sandals on, take my umbrella,
   And on a round of all the neighbors start.
When Teacher came, I'd be right there,
And someone would bring out a chair,
But when he said, "Now where's your slate?
Bring out your books, it's getting rather late,"
I'd tell him, "I'm no longer just a child,
   I've come to be as big as Father is."

And he'd say, when he saw how I'd been growing,
"Well, Babu, I suppose I'd best be going!"

When Bhulu turned up in the afternoon
      To take me out into the field to play,
I'd frown at him and say, "Don't make a noise:
      I'm busy with my work, just go away."
On Chariot Day I'd even dare
To go alone to the crowded fair.
Uncle would run up in a stew
And say, "You'll get lost, let me carry you."
But I'd reply, "Uncle, why can't you see
      I've come to be as big as Father is?"
Then he would look and say, "What a surprise!
Our little Khoka's hard to recognize!"

The day I first grow up, Mother will come
      Back from the river, having had her bath.
"Why is the house so very quiet today?"
      She'd wonder, coming up the garden path.
For I'll have learnt to turn the keys
And pay the maid just what I please
Out of the safe: Mother will say,
"Why now, Khoka, what sort of game is this?"
And I'll explain, "I'm paying out the wages,
      Now that I've grown as big as Father is.
And once we've used up all we have in store,
Just tell me what you need, I'll get some more."

In Ashwin, when the Pujas are at hand,
      The big fair to the market-ground will come.
A boat sailing from far away will land
      At Babuganj, bringing my Father home.
Now Father, being a simple soul,

Will think his son is still quite small:
He'll bring some tiny shoes and clothes
In baby-colors, thinking I'll wear those.
"Let Dada wear them," I would have to say,
    "Now that I've got to be as big as you.
For can't you see," I'd say, "Just look at these!
If I should wear them, they'd be quite a squeeze."

("Chhoto Boro," from *Shishu*)
Translated by Sukanta Chaudhuri

Astronomy

I'd only said, "When the full moon you see
Caught in the branches of the kadam tree,
    Can't someone quickly go
And fetch it down below?"
But my big brother only laughed and said,
"Khoka, there's simply nothing in your head!
    The moon's up there, too far away to touch."
    "Dada," I said, "you can't be knowing much.
    When Mother from the window smiles in play,
    Would you say Mother's very far away?"
But even then, Dada just laughed and said,
"Khoka, there's simply nothing in your head."

He asked, "Where would you find a net so tall?"
"Dada," I said, "just look, the moon's quite small.
    I'd catch it as it lands
    In my two little hands."
Once again, Dada just laughed and said,
"Khoka, there's simply nothing in your head.
    If the moon were near, you'd see how big it was."

"Dada," I said, "what stuff you learn in class!
  When Mother bends her head to give a kiss,
  She doesn't suddenly grow big like this!"

But even then, Dada just laughed and said,
"Khoka, there's simply nothing in your head!"

("Jyotishshastra," from *Shishu*)
Translated by Sukanta Chaudhuri

On the Day Thou Breakst Through This My Name

On the day thou breakst through this my name, my master, I shall
be free and leave this phantasy of my own creation and take my
place in thee.

  By scribbling my name over thy writing I cover thy works.
I know not how further such a horror could be carried.

  This pride of name plucks feathers from others to decorate
its own self and to drown all other music it beats its own drum.
Oh, let it be utterly defeated in me and let the day come when
only thy name will play in my tongue and I shall be accepted by
all by my nameless recognition.

(Unpublished extract from the English *Gitanjali*)
Translated by Rabindranath Tagore

More Life, My Lord

More life, my lord, yet more, to quench my thirst and fill me.
More space, my lord, yet more, freely to unfurl my being.
  More light, my lord, yet more, to make my vision pure.
More tunes, my lord, yet more, stirring the strings of my heart.

More pain, my lord, yet more, to lead me to a deeper
consciousness.

More knocks, my lord, yet more, to break open
my prison door.

More love, my lord, yet more, to completely drown my
self. More of thee, my lord, yet more, in thy sweetness of grace
    abounding.

("Prano Bhoriye Trisha Horiye," unpublished extract from the English
Gitanjali)
Translated by Rabindranath Tagore

Thy Rod of Justice

Thy rod of justice thou hast given to every man on this earth and
thy command is to strike where it is due.

Let me take up that harsh office from thy hand with bent
head and meek heart. Where forgiveness is sickly and self-indulgent
give me the strength to be cruel.

Let truth flash out from my tongue like a keen sword at thy
signal and let me pay my best homage to thee by righting wrong
with all my power.

Let thy wrath burn him into ashes who does what is unjust
or suffers injustice to be done.

("Tomar Nyayer Danda," unpublished extract from the English *Gitanjali)*
Translated by Rabindranath Tagore

The Day I Depart

The day I depart
I'd like to declare
What I saw or got
Was beyond compare.

258

It Hasn't Rained in My Heart

Having drunk the honey
Of the lotus glowing
On the ocean of light
I feel blessed—
The day I depart
This is what I'll write.

In the play of infinite forms
I sported endlessly
And saw the formless one
With wide-open eyes.

The One beyond touch
Caressed my body,
If this is His intent
Let it then be so—
On the day of parting
I would like all to know!

("Jabar Din," from *Gitanjali*)
Translated by Fakrul Alam

It Hasn't Rained in My Heart

It hasn't rained in my heart for a while now,
Lord, I am parched. The horizon is barren,
There isn't the faintest sign of moisture
Anywhere in the sky. Nothing stirs
To herald the coming of the dark rain clouds.

Lord, if you will, summon the deadly thunder
Let it and the torrential rain create a tumult.
In flash after flash let lightning strike me,
Startle me out of my stupor, electrify me.

Singe me, Lord, with your silent, scorching heat.
With a cataclysmic, all-pervading conflagration,
Make me writhe in unbearable despair. And then,
Like a mother looking with glistening eyes
At her son being chastened by the father, pity me!

("Dirghakal Anabrishti," from *Gitanjali*)
Translated by Fakrul Alam

When Life Dries Up

When life dries up
Come in a stream of mercy.
When everything graceful is covered,
Come in a shower of songs.

When work is overwhelming,
Creating a din that hems me in,
In soundless steps, O silent one,
Come to the outskirts of my heart.

When I have made myself poor
And my cornered heart lies languishing,
Open the door, O great-hearted Lord,
And come in all your Majesty.

When dust storms of desire blind me,
And I lapse into forgetfulness,
O Holy one, O ever watchful one,
Come to me in a blaze of light!

("Jiban Jakhan," from *Gitanjali*)
Translated by Fakrul Alam

If the Day Ends

If the day ends, if birds sing no more,
If the spent wind stops blowing—
Wrap me up on all sides with a veil.
Cover me tenderly in profound darkness—
Just as you wrap the earth at night
With dreams, secretly and slowly;
Just as you shut sleepy eyelids,
Or drooping lotus petals at nightfall.

For this traveler, midway through his travels,
Losses showing, provisions all gone,
Clothes tattered, dust-covered, humbled,
Strength dissipated, ready to give up—
Relieve his pain and dress his wounds,
Keep vigil over him, and tenderly,
Remove his shame; nurse him through the night,
Letting him blossom again at a new dawn.

("Dibash Jadi," from *Gitanjali*)
Translated by Fakrul Alam

This Stormy Night

Are you on an assignation this stormy night,
My soul mate, my friend?
The sky cries out despondently,
Sleep won't come to my eyes.
Opening the door, beloved,
I keep looking for you longingly,
My soul mate, my friend!

I can't see anything outside,
I wonder which path you are taking.
Could you be on the bank of a far-off river,
At the edge of a dense forest,
Or crossing a vast expanse of darkness?
Where could you be, my soul mate, my friend?

("Aaji Jharer Raate," from *Gitanjali*)
Translated by Fakrul Alam

A Flight of Geese

At a bend, the Jhelum glimmered in the late evening glow,
Dimmed in darkness like a curved sword sheathed,
And then disappearing into its scabbard.
At ebb of day, when the evening tide was in full flow,
Flower-like stars floated in with the dark stream;
Underneath mountain slopes,
Deodar trees were lined up in rows;
It seemed that creation would speak in a dream
But failing to do so was in distress—
Unuttered syllables moaning in darkness.

Suddenly,
I heard in the evening sky,
The sound of thunder in the open expanse
Darting into the distance.
O flock of geese flying by,
Intoxicated by the storm, your wings
Flapped in gales of delight,
Arousing waves of wonder across the sky!

They flew away, wings fluttering,
Like celestial nymphs interrupting[5]

A Flight of Geese

The trance of some sage rapt in silence,
       And thrilled in passing,
  The dark mountain ranges
     And the deodar rows.

   It seemed that those wings
      Bore away tidings
       Of stillness thrilled in its innermost being
By the intensity of motion.
      The mountains yearned to be summer's wandering clouds
The deodar rows wanted to spread their wings
And follow the sound, severing all earthly ties.
   The streaks of sound appeared startled,
     As they groped for the edges of the sky.
Breaking evening's spell, a wave of pain leaped up
    To what was afar.
   O wandering wings!
Your message fluttered in the soul of the universe that day,
  "Not here, not here, but somewhere far away"

   O geese in flight,
You've lifted stillness' lid for me tonight.
  Underlying the silence,
   I heard in water, land, and the empty expanse
Indomitable wings sounding with the same restlessness.
     The grass fluttering their wings
On the earth that is their air.
  Underneath the darkness of the soil
   Millions of seeds sprouting wings.
   I see today
    The mountain range, the deodar forests
  Unfold their wings
To range over oceans and cross unknown lands.
  The stars themselves quivering their wings
As darkness is being startled by the cries of light.

I listened to the messages left behind
By those flocks of birds for mankind
As they flew over unmarked spaces,
And sped from an indistinct past to an unclear future.
I heard in my own innermost being
Flutterings
Of a homeless bird
Soaring day and night
With countless other birds

In darkness and light.
From shore to unknown shore.
Across the open spaces of the entire universe
Resounded the refrain that day—
"Not here, but somewhere else, somewhere farther away!"

("Balaka,"[6] from *Balaka*)
Translated by Fakrul Alam

The Restless One

O great river
Unseen, silent, your stream
Continuous, without cease
Flows on forever.
The void throbs to the beat of your fierce bodiless pace,
At the shock of your immaterial current's race
Masses of foamy matter arise;
The sky weeps in fire-laden clouds.
Keen shafts of light radiate in streams of color
From the speeding darkness.
Suns, moons and stars
Like bubbles dissolve
In ranks upon ranks,
Revolving and dying.

O ascetic, O anchoress,
Your melody is this undestined voyage,
    Your wordless tune.
        Does the endless afar
    Respond to you forever?
All-destroying its love, making you ever homeless.
    In that wild love-quest
        Time and again your breast
Is shaken, your necklace scatters
          Jewels of stars.
Wind-blown, your loose hair darkens the sky;
    Your lightning-earrings fly,
        Your sari's end helplessly
    Trails in the trembling grass
And restless leaf-clusters from grove to grove.
    Again and again the flowers fall—
        Jasmine, champak, bakul, parul,
          On path and way
    From your season's tray.

You race on, race on, furiously you race
        Wild, running apace,
          Never turning your face;
Whatever you have, you scatter with both hands as you go.
    You gather nothing, nothing do you keep;
        No fear have you, no grief
As you waste the journey's store in joyous speed.
In the moment of fullness, nothing is yours:
        Thus you can be
        Pure everlastingly.
Touched by your feet, the universal dust
    Forgets its dirt
        Moment to moment—
In flash upon flash, death becomes life.
        If, for an instant, you
          Wearily

Stand still
On the sudden will
Massed mountains of matter loom over the universe;
Crippled, dumb, deaf, headless, blind,
The heavy-limbed terrifying barrier,
Blocking everyone, will stand in the way;
The tiniest atom by its own mass
In an inert travesty of conservation
Will be impaled in the sky's heart
On the stake of sin's pain.
O dancer, restless sky-dancer,
Unseen beauty,
Your dance's celestial river
Ever-flowing, purifies forever
The life of the universe in death's ablution;
The sky and all creation
Blooms in infinite pure blue.

O poet, your heart is stirred today
By the music resounding in the skirts of the universe,
The ceaseless, causeless motion of unseen feet.
In your pulse-beats I hear the steps of the restless spirit;
Your heart beats in fervor.
No one knows
How the ocean's waves dance in your blood today,
How the forest trembles in yearning.
Today you recall
From age to age we have come,
Sloughing form for form,
Quietly passing
From life to life.
Night and morning,
Whatever we have gained
We have spent again
From gift to gift,
From song to song.

Look, how the stream surges into sound.
  The boat quivers.
Leave on shore what you have saved on shore:
  Do not look back any more.
  Let the call of what lies ahead
    Draw you forward
      On this vast stream
    From the clamor behind
  To unplumbed darkness, boundless light.

("Chanchala," from *Balaka*)
Translated by Supriya Chaudhuri

Dawn and Dusk

As dusk descends here, O Lord of the Sun, in which land, on which
  ocean shore, is it dawn for you?

Here the tuberose trembles in the dark, like a veiled bride at the door to
  the bridal chamber, but where has the champak blossomed to hail a
  new day?

Who is up and about? And who has put out the lamp that had been lit
  at dusk, and discarded the garland of white roses wreathed together
  by night?

Here the doors are bolted, one by one; there the windows are flung
  open. Here the ferryboat is moored at the ghat, and the boatman fast
  asleep; there the sail catches the wind.

They have left the inn and set off towards the East; the morning sun
  shines squarely on their foreheads; they haven't run out of money to
  pay the ferrymen; dark eyes filled with desire stare after them from
  windows along the way; the road ahead flourishes a colorful letter of
  invitation and declares, "All is ready for you."

Drumbeats proclaiming victory resound to the rhythm of blood
    pumped by their heartbeats.

Here everybody has taken the day's last ferryboat in grey light. They
    have spread their blankets in the courtyard of the caravanserai; some
    are alone, the companions of the others are exhausted; what lies ahead
    of them cannot be descried in the dark, what they have left behind is
    the subject of whispered conversation. Talking, they run out of words,
    fall silent. They look up from the courtyard and notice that the Great
    Bear has risen in the sky.

O Lord of the Sun, connect the dusk that lies to your left with the dawn
    to your right. Let the shadow of one hug and kiss the radiance of the
    other. Let the evening Raga Puravi bless the morning Raga Bibhasa
    and carry on.

("Sandhya O Prabhat,"[7] from *Lipika*)
Translated by Kaiser Haq

Free!

Let the physician say what he will
    Keep the windows open as I lie still
In my bed; let the breeze relieve me
    Drugs? I have had too many, you see!
    Hadn't I swallowed endlessly
      Awful tasting but supposedly potent pills
    —Hour after hour, day after day?
Life itself had become one long disease!
For me, cures or advice would never cease!
"One slip"; some cautioned, "You're dead"!
    Others said "This is good" or "That's bad"
Everyone had some advice or other to give.
    Eyes downward, veil covering my head

268

Free!

I spent twenty-two years of life this way.
            Is it any wonder that about me people say
        —She's Sati, type of the loving wife
            Sacrifice and devotion personified!

            I came to this family as a bride at nine
        Since then I've made its burdens mine
Everyone's wishes I tried to fulfill
            Till I came to where I am—land's end!
                Where was the time to think of joy or pain?
        Where was the time to think about me?
How was I to find out if life was good or bad?
        How could I see it from beginning to end?
            Weary and in a droning tone
        The wheels of work went on and on
        Dragging me with them for twenty-two years,
            Confining me within dark kitchen walls
I didn't discover myself nor understand the world
            I didn't think about the meaning of life;
        Or grasp the message that Eternity
Had for humanity. All I knew was:
    Cooking—dining—eating—cooking—
        A cycle comprising the sum total of bliss!
    It had me enchained for twenty-two years!
Now that the wheel of work is ceasing
        Why not let it? Why let drugs revive it?

        Twenty-two springs came to the forest's edge.
            The south wind spread its scent everywhere
        Pervading the innermost recesses of the heart,
                Saying to everyone, "Open wide all doors."
        But I never saw it coming and going.
                Nevertheless, secretly it must have touched me.
    All of a sudden it must have made me errant
        It could be it had stirred within me furtively

Longings for another birth. In joy or sorrow,
Causelessly perhaps, my heart would yearn
For footsteps sounding on a lovely spring day
But though from the office you'd return,
By evening you'd inevitably depart,
Eager to join in some neighborhood sport.
But be that as it may
What flutters my heart so today?

For the first time in twenty-two years
Spring has come to my house this day
Looking out at the sky through my window
I feel a spurt of delight every now and then
I feel the thrill of resurgent womanhood,
The wide awake moon has taken its cue from me
And woven me into its midnight rhapsody.
Without me this evening star will look unreal
Without me the flowers too will seem surreal.

For twenty-two years it had seemed to me,
I'd be confined in your house indefinitely.
Still, that in itself was no cause for sorrow,
In a state of stupor, I'd spend the unending day,
Knowing tomorrow too would go the same way.
My kinsmen, spreading my fame everywhere,
Proclaimed me Lakshmi, said I was such a dear!
It was as if this was my pinnacle of fame—
Though stuck at home, a household name!
But now that I'm on the brink this day,
And about to cut all ties and go away
For me life and death have become one
As I ready myself for the great unknown
Though the walls of this rented place will stay
In some infinite deep I know I'll disappear
No trace will be left of everyone's dear!

Sunday

     For the first time on this day I can hear
    Music heralding union in another sphere.
Let the trifling twenty-two years I've known
    Be consigned forever to lie in the dust.
       Eager to woo me as a suitor and not a lord,
        Death has embraced me as its prize
   I know what it is that he wants from me
       I know that he won't treat me disdainfully!
From his place in the midst of the stars
      He had beckoned to me longingly!
   Sweet is the world, sweet womanhood!
   Sweet Death, my endless supplicant
     Take me away from here forever
     Open all your doors this day for me—
Tide me past twenty-two wasted years into eternity!

("Mukti," from *Palataka*)
Translated by Fakrul Alam

Sunday

Monday, Tuesday, Wednesday
Come speeding our way;
Do they come racing
On mighty motor cars?
Why, is Sunday, mother dear,
Always in the rear?
Why does it come our way
Trailing them all the time?
Is its home far, far away,
Beyond even the stars?
Is it like you, mother dear,
From a home that is poor?

272

Monday, Tuesday, Wednesday
Seem to never go away.
As if they'll never go home,
As if they must always roam!
Why is it that only Sunday
Must be on its way forever
Departing half an hour earlier
For every hour of the day?
Does it always have to fly
To its home bordering the sky?
Is it like you, mother dear,
From a place that is poor?

Monday, Tuesday, Wednesday
Look so very severe!
As if they can never be happy
When a child is near.
But when Saturday ends
And I see the first light of day
Sunday keeps smiling away
But soon it's time for it to go
Then it looks at me in tears,
And I look at it in dismay
Is it like you, mother dear,
From a place that is poor?

("Rabibar," from *Shishu Bholanath*)
Translated by Fakrul Alam

Hymn to the Tree

Tree, first life, you heard the sun's
Summons from the blind womb
Of earth at life's first stirring.

Hymn to the Tree

Head erect, on rhythmless
Rock-breast, you voiced the first
Hymn to light, brought feeling
Into insensible cruel desert.

That day, in the midst of the sky
Your mingled spell of green and blue
Cried to heaven and the company of stars
The song of earth's greatness. The life
Which passes death's archway again and again,
Age upon age, pilgrim-bound to eternity,
Rests in new inns, in diverse new bodies—
That life's triumphal flag you raised
In fearless pride before the unknown.
At your silent clamor, dreaming earth
First awoke, in sudden delight remembering
Herself: brave daughter of the gods,
Long ago she journeyed, leaving starry heaven
In mean attire, ashy-pale and saffron-clad,
In broken space and time to savor
Fragments of heaven's joy, again and again
Shattering it with shocks of pain,
Intensely to obtain it.

O brave earth-child,
You declared battle to free earth's soil
From the desert's dread fortress. The war
Continues. Swimming through ocean waves,
On the distant island's barren shore you set
The throne of green in untiring zeal.
In the heart of impassable mountains,
On rock-tablets you wrote the tale of triumph
With leaf-letters: you charmed the dust,
Drawing your own path on traceless fields.

Water, earth and sky were speechless once,
Lacking the spell of the seasons' festival.
You wrought in your branches the primeval
Shelter of song, in which the restless wind
Learnt to know itself, coloring its viewless limbs
In melody's diverse hues, painting song's rainbow
Across its scarf. On earth's mortal canvas
You first depicted beauty's living image.
Drawing to your heart from the sun's realm
The power of form, you extolled in colors
Of light, light's secret treasure. Indra's dancers,
Clashing bracelets in the clouds, shattered
Vessels of vapor in ecstatic dance, poured
Youth's immortal nectar; with this you filled
Your leaves and flower-cups, decking the earth
In endless youth.

                O silent one, O greatly grave,
Binding bravery with patience, you showed
Power's tranquil form. Therefore to your shelter
I come to gain the sacrament of peace, to hear
The mighty utterance of the silent, to surrender
Myself, head bowed by anxiety's heavy burden,
In your gracious green shade; to receive the open,
Generous forms of life, *rasa* ever new-formed,
The all-triumphing bravery of earth, its form
As speech, into my spirit. By meditation's power
I have gone to your heart, have learnt
The sacred fire which burns as a flame
In the sun's breast at creation's rites
Takes in your inmost being, secretly,
A cool green form. O drinker of sun-rays,
The strength that you have milked from the days
Of hundreds of centuries, fills your core:
This strength have you given to man,

Making him world-victorious. Highest praise
Have you granted him, he has dared
To rival the gods: his blazing power in bursts
Of flame, creates wonders in the universe,
Breaking arduous barriers. Living by your life,
Cooled by your loving shade, strong by your strength,
Crowned by your garland is humanity; I come
This day as its messenger, O friend of man,
Bringing these holy gifts of poetry.
    I, poet, spellbound by the green god's flute,
        Salute you with these offerings.

("Brikshabandana," from *Banabani*)
Translated by Supriya Chaudhuri

Woman Empowered

Why should you not let woman empowered be
With right to conquer her own destiny,
    O Lord?
Why must I sit and watch beside the road
With lowered head, in tired patient wait
    For the day ordained by fate
To grant my hopes? Why should I gaze in space?
Why should I not by my own powers trace
      Fulfillment's path?
My questing chariot why should I not drive forth,
Checking the turbulent horses with firm rein?
    Why should I not win
    With faith invincible
From the fortress of the inaccessible
The prize of my endeavor, with my life
    Staked in the strife?

Robed as a bride, I will not make my way
To the wedding-chamber, ankle-bells at play:
Make me fearless with the valor of love.
  One day I shall receive
The wedding-garland from a hero's hand:
   Will that holy hour not extend
Beyond one solitary dim twilight?
   I will not let him once forget
   My lustrous rigor: no abject
   Submission is worthy of his respect.
    I will put by
The cloak of my weak-spirited modesty.

I shall meet him beside the raging sea:
The breakers' roar will fling the call of victory
   At our union, to the horizon's breast.
    My veil aside I'll cast
And say to him, "In heaven or on earth,
You alone are mine." The ocean birds
Will raise a roar, flailing the west wind in their flight
As they surmise their track by the Seven Sages' light.

  Leave me speechless, O Lord:
I hear a furious veena playing in my blood.
When I have scaled life's most exalted hour,
   From my voice let there shower
    Life's finest utterance
    Pouring down unrestrained.
  And what I cannot in my words impart,
Let my love apprehend within his heart.
  If then my time should cease,
In the still sea of silence let that flow find peace.

("Sabala," from *Mahua*)
Translated by Sukanta Chaudhuri

276

Wind Instrument

Kinu Goalla Lane:
ground-floor room—grilled window—
in a two-storey house
right on the road.

The walls damp—
plaster crumbling in places,
lichened patches.

Pasted on the door—
label from a bolt of long-cloth,
bearing an image of
Ganesh, fulfiller of worldly desires,

One other creature
shares the room rent free—
a gecko. We differ in this—
it never wants food.

A salary of 25 rupees—
junior clerk in a trading house.
I get my meals
at the Dattas',
tutoring their son,
go to Sealdah station
to while away evenings—
saves on fuel for the lamp—

amidst the rhythmic noise of engines,
shrill whistles,
bustle of travelers,
shouts of porters,

then at ten-thirty
get back to the dark room's lonely stillness

An aunt—father's sister—lives in a village
    On the Dhaleswari river.
A match was arranged between her brother-in-law's daughter
        and this wretch.
The time fixed was auspicious, as was presently proved—
    That's when I ran away.
        Lucky escape for the girl—
           me too.
But though she didn't come to live in my house
    she often appears in my consciousness—
        in a sari of Dhaka cotton, sindur on the forehead.
          At the monsoon's height
    spending on trams goes up,
and still there are occasional deductions from the salary.
    At the bend in the lane—
        mounting piles
of mango peel and stones
    jackfruit cores,
        waste from gutted fish,
dead kittens—
    and heaven knows what other rubbish
The umbrella is like my depleted salary—
        lots of holes.
My office wear
    is like Gopikanta Goshai's soul,
        ever steeped in rasa.
On entering the damp room
    the dark shadow of rain
        is like an animal caught in a trap—
    knocked unconscious, inert.
Day and night, it seems, I am shackled hand and foot
    to a half-dead world.

Wind Instrument

At the mouth of the lane lives Kanta Babu—
    long, neatly parted hair,
        large eyes,
            artistic bent.
    His hobby, playing the cornet.
Every now and then
        the notes float
            in the lane's horrid air—
sometimes deep at night,
        in the twilight before dawn,
      amidst the afternoon's play of light and shade.
      Suddenly one evening
the Sindhu-Barwa raga strikes up—
    the skies resound
        with the perennial lament
           of separated lovers.

    At once it's clear
        that this lane is an illusion
like the things described
        in a drunken delirium.
    Suddenly I feel it in my heart—
there is no difference
        between Badshah Akbar
           and Haripada the lowly clerk.
Borne on the plaintive notes of the wind instrument
    Tattered umbrella and royal canopy
        rise together
           towards heavenly Baikuntha.

In the eternal sunset
    where the music is true
        the Dhaleswari flows on,
its banks in the thick shade
        of tamal trees—

and in the courtyard she is waiting,

  in a sari of Dhaka cotton, sindur on the forehead.

("Banshi," from *Parisheshe*)
Translated by Kaiser Haq

Letter Writing

You gave me a gold-plated fountain pen,

  furniture and miscellaneous writing things:

    a dainty little escritoire

      made of walnut wood,

personalized stationery

    of various sizes,

a silver paper-knife, enameled,

  scissors, pen-knife, sealing-wax, red ribbon,

    glass paperweight,

  colored pencils, red, blue, green.

You'd said at parting, I must write

    Every other day.

  I sat down to write in the morning,

    after an early bath.

But I can't think of anything at all to write about!

    There's only one bit of news—

      You've gone away.

  You know that of course.

      Still, it seems

  you aren't really aware.

So I think I should let you know—

    you've gone away.

  Only, each time I start to write

it becomes obvious, this is no ordinary news.

      I'm no poet,

I can't endow words with the timbre of my voice
     Or the look in my eyes.
          The more I write, the more I tear up.

     Ten o'clock already.
     Time for your nephew's school,
          let me go and feed him:
I'll just write one last time—
     you've gone away.
     The rest is only
squiggles on blotting paper.

("Patralekha," from *Parisheshe*)
Translated by Kaiser Haq

An Ordinary Woman

     I am the woman who stays indoors
          You wouldn't know me at all.
     I've read your latest novel, Sharat Babu,
          The one titled *A Garland of Shriveled Flowers!*
               Your heroine Elokeshi[8] was doing silly things like falling
                    in love
When she was a thirty-five-year-old woman—
     And you were generous enough to let her survive such silliness!

     But let me talk about myself.
          I am young.
     The allure of my youth
     Had impressed someone.
Such power sent a thrill through my body,
     Made me forget that I was only an ordinary woman,
          There are thousands of young women like me,
               Who cast such spells through their youth.

I beg you, Sharat Babu,
Write a story of this ordinary woman.
She knows such sorrow!
If she has something extraordinary hidden within her
How will she be able to demonstrate that?
How many people could really appreciate her worth?
They are usually spellbound by youth,
They don't look out for the truth—
And we are traded for their delusions!

Let me explain how all this has come up.
Suppose there was a man called Naresh.
Suppose that he had declared that I was unique.
It was so grand a statement that I daren't believe it,
And daren't disbelieve it either!

One day he left for England.
From there he kept sending me the occasional letter.
It made me wonder: Lord! So many women in that country
They must be jostling with each other for him!
And could they all be exceptional,
Intelligent, brilliant?
And did they all discover a Naresh Sen
Who was never appreciated in his own country?

In his last letter he wrote that he went for a swim
In the sea with someone called Lizzie.
(He quoted some lines from a Bengali poet
About a nymph of mythical beauty and youth surfacing).
Then he and she sat side by side on the sand;
Fronting the blue sea's waves.
As the clear light of the sun spread all over the sky,
Lizzie whispered to him slowly—
"You came just the other day, and soon will go away;
We are like two cockleshells all open,

Let the space in between
Be filled with a solid teardrop—
Rare, priceless."
Such eloquence!
Naresh also had this to write—
"What if the words are all made up,
But how wonderful—
Like a golden flower studded with a diamond,
Not real and yet compelling!"
Can't you see,
His smile sends a message to me,
And sticks like an invisible thorn in my bosom,
Letting me know that I am a very ordinary girl.
And that I don't have the kind of riches
With which to give him his due?
And what if that is the case,
And what if I remain indebted to him all my life?

I beg you Sharat Babu, write a story about me,
A story about a very ordinary woman,
An unfortunate woman who has to compete from afar
With at least five or seven extraordinary ladies—
In other words, with seven constellations of love!
I realize that it is my fate to be frustrated
And to be defeated.
But whoever you choose to write about,
Make her win on my behalf,
So that reading about her will be inspirational,
And make one want to garland you with flowers for what
you write.

Call her Malati[9]
That is my name.
You needn't worry about being found out;

There are lots of Malatis in Bengal,
    All of them worth little,
        Ignorant of French or German,
      Capable only of crying.

How could you make her win?
Your thoughts are lofty; your pen, too, is noble!
    Perhaps you will take her to the path of sacrifice,
      To extreme suffering, as was Shakuntala's[10] destiny
        Have pity on me!
    Come down to the plains where I live.
Lying in my bed in the darkness of night
    I ask for an impossible boon[11]
      I know I will never get that boon,
    But I hope your heroine gets it!
Why don't you keep Naresh in London for seven more years.
    Let him flunk in his exams again and again,
      Have him spoiled, surround him with devotees.
        Meanwhile, let Malati graduate with a M.A.
        From the University of Calcutta.
With one stroke of your pen award her a "first" in maths.
      But if you stop at that point,
Your reputation as the greatest of novelists will be at stake.
      Let my fate be what it will be,
    But don't constrict your imagination.
After all, you aren't miserly like God.
      Send the girl to Europe.
There those who are learned, wise, or heroic,
    Those who are poets, artists, kings,
      Let them flock to see her.
Like astronomers let them discover her—
    Not only a bluestocking, but also a woman.
    Let the mystery of the world-conquering magic in her
Be discovered—not in the country of the blind—
    But in the land of wise, knowledgeable, and understanding
    people.

The land where there are English, German, and French
men and women.
Let a meeting be called to honor Malati,
A meeting of famous people with solid reputations.
Suppose that in that land amidst a torrential downpour of praise
She drifts unnoticed,
Like a sailboat riding on waves.
Looking at her eyes, they keep whispering to each other.

Everyone declares that India's moist clouds and bright sunshine
Have mingled in her bright looks.
(Here let me declare in an aside,
My eyes really have been favored by God,
Even though I say so myself,
And even though I have met no European
connoisseur till now).
Let Naresh come there
With his flock of extraordinary girls!

And then?
Then I have to wind up my tale,
And stop dreaming.
Alas, ordinary woman!
Alas, the waste of God's powers!

("Sadharan Meye," from *Punashcha*)
Translated by Fakrul Alam

Camellia

Her name's Kamala—
saw it written on her exercise book.
She was in a tram with her brother, college-bound
I was seated behind her.
I could see her exquisite profile

and the fine tendrils of loose hair on her neck,
    beneath the bun.
    Textbooks and exercise books
    occupied her lap.
    I missed my stop.

    Henceforth I'd leave home at a carefully calculated time—
    it didn't match my office hours,
but almost coincided with the time they left home
    I saw her often.
I'd say to myself, if nothing else
    we were fellow travelers.
    Her face seemed to sparkle
      with intelligence.
    Her hair was clear of her fine forehead,
      a frank expression shone in her bright eyes.
    Why didn't some danger strike, I said to myself,
      so that I could save her,
      some nuisance along the way.
      Say, an audacious goonda.
        Such things were common these days.
    Alas, my destiny was like a muddy pond,
      unable to host a grand event,
        the nondescript days sang like monotonous frogs—
neither sharks and crocs nor flights of swans could be invited there.

    One day the crush was awful.
    A half-English youth was sitting beside Kamala.
For no reason at all, I was itching to knock his hat off,
    eject him by the scruff of his neck.
I was just dying for an excuse.
    Just then he lit a fat cigar
      and began puffing away.
    I went up and said, "Get rid of it."
He pretended not to hear,

threw up a thick cloud of smoke.
    I just pulled the cigar out of his mouth
        and threw it into the street.
He made a fist and looked daggers,
    then without a word got up and jumped off.
        Maybe he recognized me.
I'm a name on the football field,

    quite a big name.
    The girl colored,
opened a book and pretended to read,
    her hands began to tremble,
        but for the hero of the hour she didn't
           even spare a sidelong glance—
though the office-bound babus said, "Good show."
    After a while the girl got off at an unfamiliar stop
        and took a taxi.

    I didn't see her the next day,
        nor the day after.
    On the third day
she set off for college on a rickshaw.
I realized I'd blundered like a bull in a china shop
    the girl could very well take care of herself,
    there was no need for me.
        Again I said to myself,
    my destiny is like a muddy pond—
the memory of my heroism kept echoing in my mind
        like a joke.
    I decided to set things aright

I found out that they went to Darjeeling for the summer holiday.
    I too badly needed a change of air that year.
        They had a holiday cottage that they had named Motia,
just off the road, in a corner, screened by trees

and facing a snow-covered mountain.
There I heard they wouldn't be coming that year.
Just as I was about to head back I met a fan of mine,
Mohanlal—
tall, skinny, bespectacled—
his weak digestion found some encouragement in the Darjeeling air.
He said, "Tanuka, my sister,
wouldn't rest until she has met you."
The girl was like a shadow,
her body had as much substance as was absolutely indispensable—

She was much interested in studies, little in food.
Hence the strange devotion to the football star—
she thought I was showing rare kindness by talking to her.
Such is the irony of fate.
Two days before I left Tanuka said,
"I want to give you something to remember us by—
a flowering plant."
This was persecution. I kept quiet.
She continued, "It's an expensive and rare plant,
takes a lot of care to grow in our soil."
"What is it called?" I asked.
She said, "Camellia."
I felt a thrill—
another name flashed through the mind's darkness.
"Camellia," I said with a laugh,
"It's hard to win its heart, I suppose."
I don't know what Tanuka made of this—she looked
suddenly embarrassed, and pleased too.

Off I went carrying the potted plant.
As a fellow traveler placed right next to you
it wasn't easy to get on with,
so I hired a double-decker vehicle
and hid it in the lower deck

Camellia

Enough of this travelogue!
    We can also leave out the trivialities
        of the next few months

The curtain rises again on this farce at the Puja holidays.
    Scene: a small place

in the Santal-Parganas. I don't want to mention the name,
    those obsessed with a change of air
haven't had wind of it yet.
Kamala's maternal uncle was the railway engineer there.
      He had taken a house
in the shade of a sal forest, in a neighborhood of squirrels.
    Blue hills lined the horizon,
        not far away a rivulet scored the sand,
silkworms abounded in the forest of palash,
    buffalos trundled beneath hartaki trees—
        naked Santal boys straddled their backs
There were no rooms or houses to let,
    so I pitched a tent by the river.
I didn't have a companion,
    except for that camellia plant.
    Kamala was there with her mother.
      Before the sun rose
and the air sweet, slightly nippy
she walked through the sal forest with a parasol,
    while meadow blossoms fell at her feet—
      not that she noticed!
    Fording the shallow stream
      she sat reading under the shishu trees on the other side.
    And I knew she had recognized me
from the fact that she didn't even throw me a glance.
    One day they were picnicking on the river's sandy bank.
      I felt like going up to ask,
  "Couldn't you use me in anything?
I could fetch water from the river,

chop and bring wood from the forest—
and besides in the nearby jungle
there might even be an unaggressive bear!"

I noticed a young man in their party—
in shorts, and a silk shirt,
sitting with splayed legs beside Kamala, puffing on a Havana.
as Kamala absentmindedly dismembered the petals of a white
lotus
A British monthly lay to one side.

In a moment it was clear that in this unpeopled corner
of the Santal-Parganas, I was utterly redundant,
with absolutely nowhere to fit in.
I'd have left at once, only there was one thing to take care of.
The camellia would blossom in a few days;
I'd have my leave after sending it off.
All day I'd roam the forest, shouldering a shotgun.

I got back before dusk,
watered the pot
and kept track of the buds.

Finally it was time.
I called the Santal girl
who brought my firewood—
she'd be the courier for my message.
I was in my tent, reading a detective story.
A sweet voice came from outside,
"Babu, why you call me?"
I stepped out and saw the camellia blossom
behind the Santal girl's ear
brightening her dark cheek.
"Why you call?" she asked again.

"Just like that," I replied.
    Then I returned to Kolkata.

(from *Punashcha*)
Translated by Kaiser Haq

The Twenty-Fifth of Baisakh

for Amiyachandra Chakravarti

The twenty-fifth of the month of Baisakh flows on—
    Another birthday coursing
        Towards the day of death.
Seated on his movable stand
At the border of minuscule births and deaths
    Who is the artist weaving
        A garland out of innumerable Rabindranaths?

Time's chariot moves on—
    The traveler treading on foot
        Lifts his drinking vessel up
And receives something to drink
    By the time he's had his fill
He's fallen behind in the dark
    While his vessel lies smashed to smithereens
Under the wheels of time.
    Pursuing him comes one
        Who has found something more to drink
    Someone who has his name
        But in reality is a different being.

I was once a boy.
    The image built up now of the man

Through the mould of a few birthdays
Doesn't resemble the boy he once was.
Those who knew him well
Have all passed away.
That boy no longer exists in his own mind
Or in anyone else's memories.
He's left forever—as has his world.
The laughter and tears he knew
Are not echoed in the wind anymore.
Even the shards of toys he played with
Have disappeared from sight.

He'd sit by the small window of life
Looking at the world outside.
His world limited
To what he could see through the opening.
His naïve eyes would open wide
Taking in everything till they reached their limits
In the coconut tree rows canopying the garden wall.
Evenings were intense because of spells
Cast by fairy tales; no fence stood
Between fact and fantasy.
The mind crossed effortlessly
From one to the other.
In the play of light and shadow in twilight
Shadows melded with substance
As if they were kin.

His birthdays were islands
Basking in sunshine for a while
And then disappearing in Time's ocean.
At memory's ebb tide from time to time
Their peaks would become visible
As would their sunset-red coral fringes.

The Twenty-Fifth of Baisakh

The twenty-fifth of Baisakh showed up next
    In another era—indistinct
        In the flush of Spring's early morning sunlight.
          The mendicant Baul singer that is youth
Strung a passionate tune on a one-stringed ektara
        Articulating some obscure pain
Seeking the invisible man in him.

Listening to those tunes in a heavenly abode
        Sometimes the muse would respond.
Sending some of her messengers
    Through shaded paths lit up by palash trees in bloom
        Seemingly drunk in a riot of colors
          On days when work didn't matter.
I'd listen to their soft accents
    Some of which I could catch.
I could see their dark eyelashes
        Glisten with tears;
I'd read on their quivering lips
          Intimations of intense agony.
I'd hear in their tinkling bangles
    The tingle of intense anticipation.
        Unknown to me
They'd leave behind
    At first light of the twenty-fifth of Baisakh
Garlands woven out of newly bloomed jasmine
        Overwhelming morning dreams with fragrance.

The world of those youthful birthdays
    Lay in the vicinity of fairy land,
        Poised between certainty and uncertainty.
Occasionally a princess would sleep there
    Her overflowing tresses all around her
Occasionally she would suddenly stir
    At the touch of a golden wand.

And so days went by
Till the ramparts of the twenty-fifth of Baisakh
Once daubed with spring colors
Came falling down.
The young man now entered paths where shadows quivered
Because of bakul leaves rustling in the breeze;
Where the wind sighed
And afternoon ached
At the plaintive note of a lovesick cuckoo
Imploring its mate to come back;
Where bee wings thrilled,
At the subtle call of fragrant flowers;
And green and grassy groves
Ended in highways built of stone.

The young man now would add
String after string to the ektara
He had strummed to play his tunes.
The twenty-fifth of Baisakh
Next brought me
Through rugged paths
To the shores of a sea of people
Whose waves swelled and roared.
I cast my net in their midst
Negotiating sound after sound.
Throughout the day
Till I was able to net some souls
Though some of them eluded me.

Sometimes the day would cloud over
And disillusionment set in
Making the mind stoop in ignominy
But when afternoons became unbearable
Images arrived from some blessed land
Through unforeseen ways,

Making the fruit of labor look beautiful,
Offering nectar to the exhausted soul.
Mocking apprehensions
With waves of ringing laughter.
They rekindled valiant flames;
From a fire almost consumed by ashes;
They retrieved heavenly messages
Giving them form.
Through sheer devotion.
They lit up again my fading lamp
Tuning strings that had slackened
Till music flowed again
Crowning the twenty-fifth of Baisakh
With garlands they had themselves
woven.

Their magic touch
Still remains in my songs and writings.
Then my life became a combat zone
Erupting in conflicts every now and then
There were thunder-like rumblings
All across the battlefield,
Forcing me to fling aside my ektara
And pick up a kettle-drum.
Even in the intense noon heat
I had to speed on
Moving through currents of success and failure.
In the process thorns pierced my feet.
My heart too bled profusely.
Relentless waves tossed my vessel
From one side to another
Aiming to drown the freight of my life
Till it was submerged in lies and libel.
My ship of life stuck to its course
Past hate and love

Envy and friendship
　　Discord and harmony.
Crossing billows of steaming emotions.
　　In the midst of travails
　　　Amidst conflicts and commotion.
　　　　Where you find me now is in an autumnal twenty-fifth
　　　　　When light is fading and age weighing me down.

Do you realize
　In what I have written
　　There is a lot that is unsaid
　　　A lot that is disjointed
　　　　A lot that has been evaded?
　　In your respect for me,
　In the love that you show
In your ability to forgive
　You've built up a complex image
Compounded out of the good and the bad
　　　The innermost me and what you see externally
　The fame I have attained and my failures.
　　　This construct is what is now on show.
　　　　He is the man you've come to garland
And the man I've become publicly
　In the winter of my life.
　　　Even as I leave behind for you all
　　　　My blessings.
As I take my leave
　Let this image remain in your thoughts.
I certainly won't be smug
　Because it is now the property of Time.

And then give me leave
　So that I can retreat
　　Beyond the black and white warp
　From which life is woven

I

        Beyond what I've become officially
     To a lonely and private existence;
         Let me mingle different tunes
     Produced from diverse instruments
              Till I reach the source of all music
            And meld with the primal melody.

("Panchishe Baisakh," from *Shesh Saptak*)
Translated by Fakrul Alam

I

My consciousness turns emerald green,
    Ruby deep red.
I turn my gaze to the sky—
    it lights up
        from east to west.
"Lovely," I say looking at the rose—
    And it grows lovely.

You'd complain it's mere theory, not a poetic utterance.
    I'd say it's the truth,
        hence this is poetry:
        such is my conceit,
    which I feel on behalf of mankind.
        It's on the canvas of human conceit
          that the Demiurge creates the universe.
The theoretician chants as he breathes in and out—
    No, no, no,
there's neither ruby, nor emerald, nor rose, nor light,
    nor me, nor you.
Meanwhile the Infinite Being himself sets to work
        within the bound of the human world—
          he's the one called "I."

Light and darkness couple in the depths of that "I,"
  Form appears, the sap of aesthetic delight rises,
"no" blossoms suddenly into "yes" through the magic of maya,
  in color and line, expressions of grief and joy.

  Don't dismiss this as theory—
 my mind's in a rapture of delight
in the cosmic-I's creative workshop,
  brush in one hand, palette of colors in the other.

  The learned pundit says—
 The old moon with a smile of heartless cunning,
  like death's harbinger advances at a crouch
   towards earth's ribcage.

One day it'll tug on mountain and ocean with all its might;
  in eternity's new ledger, a zero
   will fill the page for this mortal world,
  devouring the credit and debit columns of day and night;
human achievements will lose all pretensions to immortality,
  human history receive a wash
   of the ink of endless night.
 on the day of mankind's departure
   the eye will wring all color from the universe,
 the soul absorb all aesthetic delight.

Tremulous energy will dwindle from sky to sky,
  no light glow anywhere.
In the assembly there will be no veena, the musician's
  fingers will dance without making music.
God, deprived of poetry, will sit alone
  in a sky devoid of blue, working out
the mathematical logic of impersonal existence.
  Then in the whole of the wide universe,
to the farthest of the innumerable limitless worlds and afterworlds,

such utterances will nowhere reverberate—
   "You're lovely,"
    "I love . . ."
Will the Creator get down to work again
   for aeons together—
will he keep chanting on the eve of apocalypse
   "Speak, speak, speak,"
will he keep urging "Say, you're lovely,"
   or "Say, I love . . . ?"

("Ami," from *Shyamoli*)
Translated by Kaiser Haq

Africa

In a restless ancient age
   When the discontent Creator
Was pondering again and again the new creation
   On one such day punctuated by
    Dissatisfied shakes of His head
   The raging arms of the sea wrested you away
From the earth's eastern bosom, Africa—
Bound you behind guarding walls of opaque jungle
   Embedded in a core of miserly light
There in dark secluded leisure
   You pieced together remote mysteries
Unraveled enigmatic signs of the waters and the sky
   Learnt Nature's hidden magic
Devised in your mind spells and chants
   To taunt the monstrous terrors
    You desired to intimidate fear
Adorning majestic cloaks of horror
Turning yourself fearsome in a frenzied greatness of terror
   Amid drumbeats of destruction

O shadowy silhouette
Under your dark veil
The turbid gaze of neglect
Kept your human face obscure
They came with their iron bracelets
They whose nails were sharper than your wolves'
They came, the trappers of humanity,
They whose pride blinded them into darkness
Darker than your forest canopies
Barbaric greed of the civilized
Stripped naked brazen bestiality
Your wordless wailing condensed on jungle paths
Your tears and blood mingled to pollute dusty earth
Forever now the fetid clumps
Beneath hobnailed boots of assailant's feet
Have left their muddied imprints on your reviled history
That very moment by the shores of the sea
In every temple of every town
The church bells morning and evening rang
In the name of their most merciful God
While the children played in their mothers' laps
And their Bard devotion to beauty sang
Today, when on the western horizon
The twilight hour is breathless under raging winds
When the beasts from their hidden caves have all come to light—
To sound the ominous toll of their dusk
Come new age poet
Now in the final rays of impending night
Come stand at the doorway of the affronted woman
To say, "Forgive!"
Above the wild delirious rants
Let this be the last benediction of your civilization

(from *Samayik Patra*)
Translated by Rumana Siddique

I Saw in the Twilight

I saw—in the twilight of tired consciousness,
My body drifting down black Kalindi's stream:
With its mass of feelings, its varied sorrows,
A lifetime's memories stored in its figured shroud,
And with its flute. Farther and farther away
Drifting, its form fades, on the familiar shores
In villages embraced by tree-shade, the sounds
Of evening prayer recede, the doors of homes
Are shut, the lamp-flames doused, the ferry-boat
Is moored to the landing-stage. On either bank
Crossings cease, the night deepens, the silent
Birdsong among the forest branches offers itself
In sacrifice to immense silence. Black formlessness
Descends on the earth's diversity, on land and water.
My body, become a shadow, a point, dissolves
In endless darkness. Arrived at the stars' altar,
Standing rapt, alone, hands clasped, I look up to say,
"O sun, you have drawn up the net of your rays.
Reveal now your most auspicious form:
Let me see that Being which is one in you and me."

("Dekhilam Abosher Chetana," from *Pratik*)
Translated by Supriya Chaudhuri

Romantic

They call me romantic.
    I accept the label,
        Since I quest for existence's essence.
      Dearest, my mantle I've hued in that color!
  When I come to your door

I invoke you with a hymn
　　Based on a morning raga
Devoted to Bhairav, God of dawn.
　　　I bring to your sanctum
　　An offering of the tuberose,
Embodying the scent of spring woods,
　　　Wafted on a discreet breeze.
　　　　Tenderly, I recite poems for you,
Sentences set in placid measures,
　　　　　　The whole shaped by my art.
　　　You listen, and inebriated, smile!
　　　　　When I play an overture on my flute
　　　Based on the Raga called Multan,
In the depth of my unconscious
　　It finds out its own level.
　　　I center you in my dream world
　　Taking care to drop off
　　　All the dust coating it.
It is a world I created.
Eluding the Almighty's gaze.
　　　From his art studio I stole
　　Colors and essences,
　　　And emulated his magic of creation.
I know that most of what I do is illusive,
　　　And a lot indistinct.
When you query, "Can this be called realistic?"
I reply, "Never, I'm a Romantic!"
　　　I know the roads taken in the real world.
　　I've paid my dues to them—
　　　Knowing that you can't do so in words—
　　　I respond to their summons.
　　It's a world of affliction, ailments, and squalor!
　　　There women are scared of marauders
There I must fling my mantle and wear armor;
　　　It's a place for sacrificing, suffering and striving.

> A place where the battle-drum
Summons one to heroic action.
> Let not that be a place for playacting,
Let that be a place where the beautiful
> Walks with Bhairav, the God of Destruction!

(from *Nabajatak*)
Translated by Fakrul Alam

The Night Train

The soul is the night's train
> Setting forth—
The car is full of sleep,
> The night silent.
> In immense darkness,
The one who is ink-cloaked and naught
> Stirs on the shores of sleep,
> And the land of phantoms.
> Flickering in the faint light,
> It speeds past
> Unknowable and unfamiliar stops
> For some invisible destination.
> A pilgrim on a distant voyage,
> In the mute night—
Where it will end
> I can't comprehend.

> The driver won't reveal its name;
> Some say it's nothing but a machine.
Others say it's uncaring,
> Yet consigning itself completely to the blind
It spreads its bed.
> Some say it's indistinct,

But is sure about its motions.
 It carries forward with every breath—
Nameless unknowable spaces
 Full of invisible presences.
  Its face is cloaked, concealed.
Gaining in confidence, the train speeds on,
Not pausing for an instant under the sky,
  Moving from the hinterland of sleep, unconsciously,
  Harboring in its sleep-nurtured mind
Dreams of a distant dawn.

("Rater Gadi," from *Nabajatak*)
Translated by Fakrul Alam

Waking Up in the Morning I See

Waking up in the morning I can see
Things strewn across the room chaotically.
I fumble and find nothing where it should be.
Who knows now where I've kept my stuff?
Who knows where my manuscripts will disappear,
Dispersed without semicolons or commas?
I look at envelopes lying bereft of letters
The whole testifies to the utter insouciance
Of the male of the species! The maid appears
And in a trice the whole mess disappears!
Quickly she disposes of it all ritually
Re-ordering what I messed up shamelessly.
By responding to my embarrassed call
She covered up wounds I was exposing to all!
But one's defects can't always be concealed
And the truth about the sexes will be revealed:
Men carelessly keep piling up their bins
But women routinely forgive them their sins.

304

They Work

("Sakal Bela Uthe Dekhi Cheye . . . ," from *Rogshajyaye*)
Translated by Fakrul Alam

They Work

Adrift on time's idle current,
The mind gazes into space.
Shadow-pictures rise to my eye on the paths of that great void.
How many people, band on band,
Age upon age, have passed
Into the distant past
With furious pace, arrogant in victory.
The Pathans came, lustful of empire,
The Mughals too—
The wheels of their triumphal chariots
Blew shrouds of dust, their flags of victory fluttered.
I look at the paths of space:
No trace of them today.
Age after age, the light of sunrise and sunset,
Morning and evening, has reddened that pure blue.
Again across the void
Band on band they came
On iron-bound tracks
In fire-breathing chariots,
The fierce English
Radiating their power.
Time, I know, will flow down their paths too,
Sweep away the encircling fences of empire.

I know that their soldiers, laden with merchandise,
Will leave not the slightest trace on the constellations' paths.

When I open my eyes to this world of clay,
I see passing in constant clamor

A great rush of people
On many paths, in many bands,
From age to age, on daily human errands,
In life, in death.
They forever
Bend to the oar, hold the tiller.
In the fields
They sow and reap.
They work
In towns, in the open plains.
The royal canopy falls, the drums of war are silenced,
The pillar of victory, idiot-like, forgets its own meaning,
All those eyes of blood, those hands bearing bloody weapons
Hide their faces in children's tales.
They work
At home and abroad,
By the seas and rivers of Bengal, Bihar, Orissa,
in the Punjab, in Bombay and Gujarat.
The passage of their days resounds
In tones now deep, now soft,
Woven into night and day.
Grief and joy, day and night
Make life's great anthem ring.
On the ruins of hundreds and hundreds of empires,
They work.

("Ora Kaaj Korey," from *Arogya*)
Translated by Supriya Chaudhuri

On the Banks of Roop-Naran

I woke up on the bank
    of the Roop-Naran,
I knew for sure
    this world's no dream.

306

The Sun of the First Day

I saw spelt out in blood—
    my own self

I came to know myself
    through suffered blows,
        through anguish and pain,
    for truth is tough;
and I learnt to love this harshness—
    it never betrays.

This life is a meditation on sorrow till death—
    to realize the terrible value of truth
        and settle all debts with death.

("Roop-Naraner Kule," from *Shesh Lekha*)
Translated by Kaiser Haq

The Sun of the First Day

On the new carnival of being
    The sun of the first day asked:
Who are you?
    But there was no reply.
        Ages went by.

On the western shore,
    The last sun of the day
Asked the final question again:
    Who are you?
        But there was no reply.

("Pratham Diner Surya," from *Shesh Lekha*)
Translated by Fakrul Alam

Dark Nights of Sorrow

Dark nights of sorrow have come to my door
    Again and again.
      Its only weapons I saw—
        Pain's distorted grimace and Fear's hideousness—
          Its intention—to delude one in the darkness.

Every time I trust its fearful masked face
    I end up being defeated.
      It's a game of chance—life's sorcery—
From childhood such horrors dog us at every step,
    Mocking us even in our sorrows;
      A kaleidoscope of fears—
        Directed deftly by Death in the diffused darkness.

("Dukher Andhar Ratri," from *Shesh Lekha*)
Translated by Fakrul Alam

On the Way to Creation

You've spread out myriad nets of deception
    On Creation's path
      O Guileful One!
Shrewdly testing the naïve who succumb to false beliefs,
    You make a trial of their innocence.
Through such tests you determine greatness.
    But you haven't benighted the truly great.
      His heart is illumined with your star;
        Its passages are forever clear.
      His simple faith keeps it ever bright.
        Let him appear deviant from outside; inside he is ever
         straight.

308

That is what he takes pride in.
People say he has been deceived.
But he has embraced truth
Cleansing his innermost being by its light.
Nothing can deceive him.
He brings the ultimate prize
To his own treasure-hoard.
He who withstands deceptions effortlessly
Gathers from your own hands
The unremitting right to peace.

("Tomar Srishtir Poth,"[12] from *Shesh Lekha*)
Translated by Fakrul Alam

5

Songs

𝒻OR BENGALIS EVERYWHERE, Rabindranath Tagore is present most intensely in their lives through his songs. They are sung, hummed, or played by them in every possible situation. Lines from the songs or their tunes have possessed Bengali hearts and minds, and the unique combination of melody and words that is the essence of his music has sparked their sensibilities for generations now.

Tagore predicted on a few occasions that Bengalis would remember him most through his songs. To Edward Thompson he said that he knew their beauty would perhaps never be accessible to foreigners, since music did not travel as well as its sister arts. He was aware that a lot of his work would be "gradually lost," but he was sure that his songs had "great beauty" and would be his most valuable legacy for his people. He also knew they were his "best work" (Thompson, 125). Indeed, he told Thompson that at one point in his life he was much better known for his songs and his singing than for his poetry. In 1939, the ailing poet was sufficiently stirred by a performance of his songs to declare in an amused but confident tone to a confidante that he would certainly be unforgettable for his music: "You see, Rabi Thakur writes songs not at all badly, you have to admit they work pretty well . . . Is it a few songs I wrote? Thousands of songs, a sea of songs . . . I have flooded the land of Bengal with songs. You can forget me, but how can you forget my songs?" (quoted by Kalpana Bardhan, xii).

In all, Rabindranath composed over 2,200 songs, setting either the lyric that came to him to music or fitting the tune that came to him to words he penned for it. The genre that he created in the process is known as *Rabindrasangeet.* As Satyajit Ray, the great Bengali filmmaker, has observed, the song lyrics could be viewed as unique compositions in any context: "as a composer of songs, Tagore has no equals, not even in the West—and I know Schubert and Hugo Wolf" ("Some Reflections on

Rabindrasangeet" in *Purabi: A Miscellany in Memory of Rabindranath Tagore*, 177).

Tagore wrote his first song lyrics in his teens and continued to compose until the end of his life. Perhaps the first time he created a song was in 1875, when he contributed a piece that he thought would be perfect for a play his brother Jyotirindranath was writing. Two years later he would sing publicly for the first time in the Hindu Mela of 1877. Soon, he was creating song lyrics regularly for musical dramas and festive occasions, or to articulate purely personal emotions. He also composed devotional song lyrics steadily for Brahmo Samaj rituals; indeed, his songs, sung in his celebrated tenor voice, attracted wide attention among those who attended the sect's events and became indispensable for its congregations.

In many of his songs, Tagore expressed his sense of wonder and thankfulness at the way the song lyrics came to him. Apparently, they would often take over his life. He had not undergone formal music training, just as he had not let himself go through the rigors of formal schooling. But he knew that his songs were special and that he was blessed to have them flowing out of him.

Of course, Tagore was able to develop his innate ability to write song lyrics in part because of his upbringing; Indian classical and Bengali songs were always in the air in the Tagore house and a few of his siblings were proficient in western classical music. His English trips exposed him to English and Irish melodies while his extended stay in his family estates in East Bengal made him intimate with Bengali folk and devotional music. In later life he picked up tunes from Carnatic music and from his visits to other parts of India. Unconventional and experimental, he was always mixing *ragas* and blending melodies for the many feelings and lyric impulses he felt he had to convey musically.

Tagore published some of his song lyrics initially as poems. Although he had not mastered the skills of notation, throughout his life, members of his extended family would help him capture the melody in a form that would allow it to be sung by everyone. Later, his colleagues in Santiniketan or a gifted student would help him with the notation. Either as poems or in the form of notations, the song lyrics circulated in magazines and collections for a long time.

In 1931, Tagore compiled his song lyrics according to their dates of composition in two volumes that he called *Gitabitan*. However, this arrangement did not satisfy him, and toward the end of his life, despite failing health, he took on the massive task of classifying the lyrics into six thematic sections: *puja*, or devotional songs; *prem*, or songs of love; *swadesh*, or patriotic songs; *prakriti*, or songs of nature; *bichitra*, or miscellaneous songs; and *anushthanik*, or ceremonial songs. The anthology also included the many songs he had composed for his musical and dance dramas and on special occasions. Tagore was unable to complete the task he had undertaken of organizing all of his songs in this manner, but his reworked anthology came out as the *Gitabitan* in 1942, the year after his death.

The selections of his song lyrics included in this book, all from *Gitabitan*, follow this classification but are also arranged in the sequence he worked out for them in the revised *Gitabitan*. This section thus begins with his devotional songs; some of these are hymns or prayers while others are lyrics about his spiritual yearnings and desire to be one with god. The patriotic songs are suffused with his love of Bengal, and urge his people to unite, rely on themselves, and rekindle their lives to throw off the internal as well as external shackles constraining them. The songs of nature celebrate the beauty of the Bengal countryside and record his intense and varied response to the six seasons of the subcontinent: *grishma*, or summer; *varsha*, or the monsoonal months; *sharat*, or early autumn; *hemanta*, or late autumn; *sheet*, or winter; and *vasanta*, or spring. As will be obvious to readers, he seemed to have loved most the monsoonal months and spring for the many moods they induced in him, while late autumn and winter appeared to be too sedate to stir him into writing more than a handful of songs. But Tagore was incorrigibly romantic, and love of god and nature coexisted in him throughout his life with erotic love and devotion to the earthly beloved. It is no surprise that the second largest grouping of his song lyrics in *Gitabitan* consists of his love poems, for he responded to earthly love in myriad ways. The final part of this section of the book includes his songs composed for miscellaneous occasions or his manifold moods, for he composed song lyrics for all kinds of reasons and situations.

Many have declared that Rabindranath's song lyrics are untrans-

315

latable, and as we noted above, he himself thought his music would not travel as well as his other creations. But it was the *Gitanjali* in English, essentially a collection of his song lyrics, that made him world-famous, showing in the process that song lyrics can be appreciated in translation, even if separated from their melodic base. Two translated versions of the song *Akash bhara* have been included in this section, to demonstrate our belief in the diverse ways in which Tagore's writings can be translated today. It is this belief that has inspired our translations and justifies the space that we have given to his songs—they are, after all, most quintessentially Tagore, and no attempt to represent his work can be complete without them.

Devotional Songs

How wonderfully you sing

How wonderfully you sing, O master musician,
I listen in amazement, I am all attention!
The light from your songs spreads across the heavens
The wind that sings your songs lilts across the skies
Stones melt and in lightning speed surges
The divine stream of your music.
My heart feels like singing those tunes
But my tongue can't voice them.
I would sing them but the words just won't come—
Defeated, my soul cries out.
How you have ensnared me,
By spreading a net of music around me!

(*Tumi kemon kore gaan koro*)
Translated by Fakrul Alam

You've lighted up the fire of music

You've lighted up the fire of music in my soul.
The fire has spread all around.
It dances in dead branches
It lifts its hands to the sky to who knows whom!
All the stars of the night sky are amazed,
What crazy wind is it that sweeps past?
In the heart of darkness what pure red lotus has flowered?
Who knows what power this fire has!

(*Tumi je surer agun*)
Translated by Fakrul Alam

317

Your eyes have pleaded with me

Your eyes have pleaded with me for a song
Among flowers and stars, day and night, in the dusty light of dusk
You wonder why I do not sing
I lost my lyrics in my pain, I forget my tune
You have called to me in the fierce storm wind
From upon wild waters
In the thunder of mute clouds
In monsoon torrents, you have called me towards death
You wonder why I do not come
I cannot find my way to you across seas.

(*Tomar nayan amaye baare baare*)
Translated by Sunetra Gupta

My time flies

My time flies by every evening
In harmonizing my tunes with your tunes.
My one-stringed ektara can't keep up with your sad songs.
In vain I take part again and again in this sport
Of harmonizing my tunes with your tunes.
I have tuned my string with the music of the near
But that flute keeps playing on afar.
Can everyone join in the sport of heavenly music?
Can just anyone cross over to the shore of the Universal Soul
And cast a net of music
In harmonizing one's tunes with your tunes?

(*Amar bela je jai*)
Translated by Fakrul Alam

Beyond boundaries of life and death

Beyond boundaries of life and death
You keep waiting, my dear friend,
In my heart's lonesome sky
Your throne is covered in light
With immense hope and intense delight
I reach out to be one with you.
In the silent darkness of evening
Your footsteps cast their shadow.
What music from your veena
Spreads this night over everything?
The whole world fills with the melody
And I lose myself in the poignant tune!

(*Jibon o maraner simana chhariye*)
Translated by Fakrul Alam

Why do you call me?

Why do you all call me? My mind won't be bound.
Song after song leaves me no time at all.
People would ask me the way, but no paths please me.
I scarce know where I go, driven as I am by song after song.
Whether you would bid me go or fault me I won't be dismayed
My mind is swept away by song after song.
This day is for flowers to bloom; the sky turns into a carnival of colors,
And I am swayed in all directions by song after song.

(*Keno tomra amaye dako*)
Translated by Fakrul Alam

You stand on the other shore

You stand on the other shore of my song
My tunes find their feet, but I can't find you.
The breeze stirs miraculously, don't keep your boat tied anymore—
Cross over and come into my soul.
With you I'd frolic in song and frisk across space.
In sorrow I play my flute all day long.
When is it that you will take my flute and sing on it
In the hushed, joyous night's intimate darkness?

(*Dariye achho tumi*)
Translated by Fakrul Alam

When I see the universe

When I see the universe through a song
I find Him then, I know Him then.
Then His speech, so full of light, fills the skies with Love,

Then from every speck of dust shines His supreme message.
Then He leaves the world and comes into my heart.
Then my heart flutters in His grass.
Forms dissolve, rasas arise, one's limits are lost,
Then I find myself communing with the All!

(*Ganer bhitor diye jakhan*)
Translated by Fakrul Alam

Not your Word alone

Not your Word alone, my friend, my dear one,
From time to time caress my soul too.
I know not how else it is that I'll overcome
The fatigue of the road, the thirst from a long day—
I would like you to tell me that this darkness is fulfilling.
My soul would like to give and not take all the time,
It carries along in its movements whatever it has stored.
Extend your hand, clasp it in mine—
I'll grasp it, fill it up, and keep it with me,
It will make my lonely journey pleasing.

(*Shudhu tomar bani noi he*)
Translated by Fakrul Alam

In order to find you anew

In order to find you anew, I lose you every moment
O beloved treasure.
  Because you wish to appear you become invisible
O beloved treasure.
Dearest, you aren't mine to hide, you're mine eternally—
  absorbed in time's playful momentary current

O beloved treasure.
When I seek you, my heart trembles with fear—
    I am rocked by a wave of love.
There's no end to you—so, becoming nothing, you put an end to
      yourself—
    that smile washes away my tears of separation
O beloved treasure.

(*Tomai Notun Kore Pabo*)
Translated by Amit Chaudhuri

Where night flows

Where night flows into day's shoreline
You and I meet at that borderline
There light startles darkness into dawn
There waves dart from strand to strand.
From deep blue silence a profound call resounds
And a pure ray of golden light gleams.
I try to glimpse it; I see it now and then I don't—
Waking up from a dream, I cry out anxiously.

(*Ratri eshe*)
Translated by Fakrul Alam

Let the skies overflow with your beauty

Let the skies overflow with your beauty
How else will my heart hold some of its bounty?
All the light that courses through the sun, planets and stars
Sheds in a million directions
And fills my heart in fulfillment
The color that descends on flowers as stealthily as sleep

Touches my mind and wakes it up
The love that strikes the universal veena in mirth,
Floats upwards in an instant flash of music,
On that day my heart in total surrender will give itself up at your feet.

(*Tomar ei madhuri chhapiye akash*)
Translated by Reba Som

You dressed him as a beggar

You dressed him as a beggar in your great game
And the skies convulsed with laughter
Many roads has he traveled
Knocked on many doors
He has filled his beggar's bowl with scraps
Only so that you might steal his alms
He thought he would forever remain a beggar in this life
He thought he would be a beggar beyond death
And when at the end of his journeys
He came fearfully to your door
You received him with your own garland of flowers.

(*Ere bhikiri shajaye ki rongo tumi koriley*)
Translated by Sunetra Gupta

When the sap of life shrinks

When the sap of life shrinks, seek the showers of mercy.
When all that's lovely is hidden, come sweetly as a song.
When work overpowers and imprisons me
Within the frontiers of the heart, O Giver of life, tread softly!
When denying all pleasures and restricting itself
My mind droops, freeing it, O Bounteous One, come regally.

When dust storms of desire blind and make me forgetful,
O Holy and Vigilant One, come as a fiery, overwhelming light.

(*Jiban jakhan shukaye jai*)
Translated by Fakrul Alam

323

When will you show up?

When will you show up for our communion?
How much longer will constellations conceal you?
Your footsteps were secret envoys calling me to union,
Vibrating my heartstring every morning and evening.
O Traveler, my whole soul has been tingling this day,
Every now and then I've been feeling a stirring in me.
As if the time has come for me now to cease working,
O Lord, the very wind wafts your heady scent my way!

(*Amar milan lagi*)
Translated by Fakrul Alam

Forgive me my weariness

Forgive me my weariness O Lord
Should I ever lag behind
For this heart that this day trembles so
And for this pain, forgive me, forgive me, O Lord
For this weakness, forgive me O Lord,
If perchance I cast a look behind
And in the day's heat and under the burning sun
The garland on the platter of offering wilts,
For its dull pallor, forgive me, forgive me O Lord.

(*Klanti aamar kshama karo prabhu*)
Translated by Reba Som

In traversing the lonely road

My light has been quenched upon this dark and lonely path
For a storm is rising
A storm is rising to befriend me
Darkling disaster smiles at the edges of the sky
Catastrophe wreaks delighted havoc with my garments, with my hair
My lamp has blown out on this lonely road
Who knows where I must wander now, in this dense dark
But perhaps the thunder speaks of a new path,
One that will take me to a different dawn.

(*Jete jete ekla pathe*)
Translated by Sunetra Gupta

I will place a garland

I will place a garland conceding defeat around your neck
How much longer can I stay away deceived by my imagined strength
I know, I know hurt feelings will be washed away
And my heart will break in deep pain
The flute of my emptiness will play a song
And even the stone will melt in teardrops
The lotus will open up, petal by petal
Its honey will not remain hidden forever
Whose eyes will dominate the entire sky and gaze on?
Drawing me out of doors in silence
That day there will be nothing more to overcome
As I seek total surrender.

(*Haar mana haar parabo tomar galey*)
Translated by Reba Som

To the world's festival of delight

To the world's festival of delight
I was happily invited.
I am thankful, I am grateful
For a life thus blessed.

My eyes beheld the beauty of forms
And had their fill looking around;
My ears became enthralled
At the profound sound.

At your altar you have instructed me
To let tunes from my flute flow.
And so with music I weave a garland
Out of joy and sorrow.

Is it time now for me to depart?
Do call me to your assembly
Where I can celebrate your triumph
Through music, resoundingly.

(*Jagate anander jogey*)
Translated by Fakrul Alam

Why do I see you every now and then?

Why do I only see you every now and then and not all the time?
Why do clouds often cover up my heartscape and hide you?
When I see you in feeble light or only in the blink of an eye
I am anxious lest I lose sight of you forever.
What can I do to secure you and keep seeing you evermore?

Lord, when will my love be enough to embed you eternally in my heart?
I pledge that I won't be distracted by anyone or anything else
And if you want I'll give up all attachments and desire for your sake!

(*Majhe majhe tobo dekha pai*)
Translated by Fakrul Alam

326

Such compassion, O compassionate one

Such compassion, O compassionate one!
Touched by pure rays, my heart—like a lotus—blossomed at your feet.
Within, without, I've glimpsed you—in this world, and other worlds,
    and the ones to come—
in shadow, light, happiness, grief, seen you,
in tenderness, love,
suffusing the universe and my wakefulness.

(*Eki koruna*)
Translated by Amit Chaudhuri

O, Truly Beautiful

O, Truly Beautiful, in beatitude and munificence you reveal yourself.
Your majesty lights up the heart of the high heavens,
The universe encircles your feet with lustrous gems
Eagerly, and swiftly, the planets and stars, moon and sun,
Immerse themselves in you and partake of your immortal glow.
Your enchanting loveliness cascades onto the world in a ceaseless flow.
Flowerbud-fragrant songs and delightful colors
Convey to life in an ever-renewing flow, day and night,
Your unending blessings in life and death.
With care, kindness, love, and devotion you soften the soul,
You shower solace on the afflicted

With festivity and abundance you enrich the world.
The whole universe hymns your praise and seeks your protection.

(*Anandaloke mangalaloke*)
Translated by Fakrul Alam

I know I'll have to give you all

I know I'll have to give you all, O Lord—
All my riches; messages I've strung;
All that my eyes took in and all that I've heard;
All that I wove; all my travels—
I'll have to give you all!
Mornings and evenings stowed in my heart
Will all bloom and ascend towards you!
I string my veena for the moment
When it'll play tunes you've strung in me
I know I'll have to give you all!
My sorrows and joys will be your delight;
Just let me ascend till you can behold me!
All that I've done on my own
I'll make yours to make them truly mine—
I know I'll have to give you all, O Lord!

(*Amar je sab ditey hobey*)
Translated by Fakrul Alam

It is your company that I have earned

It is your company that I have earned, O beautiful one
My body seems blest, my spirit gratified, O beautiful one
Light awakens my adoring eyes

The breeze on my heart's horizon is heavy with fragrance, O beautiful
    one
It is the music of your touch that flushes my spirit
It is the nectar of our union that remains stored in my heart
Take me anew within yourself
And let me experience within this life span
The pangs of many births

(*Ei labhinu sanga taba sundara hey sundara*)
Translated by Reba Som

If you did not give me love

If you did not give me love
Why paint the dawn sky with such song
Why thread garlands of stars
Why make a field of flowers my bed
Why does the south wind whisper secrets in my ear?
If you did not give poetry to my soul
Why does the sky stare like that upon my face
And why do sudden fits of madness grip my heart?
I set sail upon seas whose shores I know not.

(*Jodi prem dilena praney*)
Translated by Sunetra Gupta

Beautiful One

Beautiful One! for some past piety rewarded,
A wild flower, I had nestled in your garland.
It was dawn, the first rosy rays of light
Delighted sleepy-eyed Earth.
The strains of a wordless, charming young lute

Wafted over land and water.
Now at the end of a weary day,
In extinguished light, the bird song silenced
If, fatigued, that flower should fall,
May the evening breeze blow it
Tattered and dusty
Along your footsteps

(*Ekoda ki jani*)
Translated by Ratna Prakash

It is my pleasure to keep gazing

It is my pleasure to keep gazing at the path
Sun plays with shade—the monsoon comes, as does spring
So many come and go before me bringing news
I remain happy with my thoughts, as the breeze blows softly
The whole day will I be by the door, alone
And only when the appointed hour suddenly arrives will I have a
    glimpse
Until then I happily spend my moments singing to myself
Until then in spurts there drifts along a fragrance

(*Amar ei path chaoatei ananda*)
Translated by Reba Som

I know this day will pass

I know, I know this day will pass, it will pass
At day's end, a wan sun with a sad smile
Will gaze in farewell at my face
On the wayside the flute will resound, cows will graze on river banks
The child will play in the yard and birds sing

Yet, yet this day will pass, will pass
My plea to you is this—
Before I leave, tell me why
The green earth raising its eyes to the skies had called me
Why the silence of the night had carried the message of the stars
Why the day's light had set waves in my heart
My plea to you is this—
As my tryst in this world comes to a close
May my song end at the stroke of its first beat
May I be able to fill the platter
With fruits and flowers of all six seasons
May I be able to glimpse you in the light of this life
Putting round you my garland
As my tryst in this world comes to a close

(*Jani go din jabey din jabey*)
Translated by Reba Som

Patriotic Songs

My Bengal of gold

I love you, my Bengal of gold,
Your skies and winds will play music in my soul.
O mother, in spring your mango blossoms' heady scent drives me wild
How fulfilling it is too, O mother dear
To see your fields smile delightfully in late autumn!

Such beauty and such shades, such warmth and such tenderness,
So much of your dress you've spread under bata tree canopies and
    riverbanks;
O mother, your sounds ring in my ear and comfort me

How fulfilling such sights and sounds are, O mother dear!
But when you look sad, how I drown in my tears!

In your nursery I've spent my childhood
I consider life blessed when I daub my body with your dust and clay,
And when day ends and evening descends how lovely is your light,
How pleasing it is then, O mother dear
Leaving behind all play, how I rush to climb to your lap!

In fields where cattle graze and in ferry ghats;
All day long in shaded village paths reverberating with bird songs;
And in your crop-filled fields where we spend our lives;
How fulfilling you make our lives O mother dear!
Your herd boys and farmhands all become my own then!

O mother, when I lay myself down at your feet;
Bless me with the dust that they tread, for they will bejewel me.
O mother dear, what little I have I will lay at your feet,
How fulfilling to stop adorning myself with foreign purchases,
To know that even the rope you provide for a noose can be my
    adornment!

(*Amar sonar Bangla*)
Translated by Fakrul Alam

331

O my motherland's soil

O my motherland, I touch thee with bowed head
The universal earth mother's sari-end is spread over you
You have mingled with my body
You are in the midst of my heart and soul
Your green and gentle image is etched in my mind
O Mother, I was born in your lap and will die in your bosom

I sport in sorrow and joy in your playing fields
You provide me with food
You soothe me with your cool waters
You are the all-enduring, tolerant archetypal mother
O mother, you have succored me generously,
I have taken so much from you
But I don't know how much I've been able to give in return.
My life has been wasted in futile endeavor
My days I have spent within doors;
O source of all strength, I've done nothing with your gifts!

(*O amar desher mati*)
Translated by Sanjukta Dasgupta

If no one listens to you

If no one listens to your call go your own way,
If no one talks to you, O unfortunate one,
If everyone turns his or her face the other way,
If everyone is frightened into silence—
Make sure that you open your heart
And say whatever it is that you want to say.
If people turn their back on you, O unfortunate one,
If when you've set out on a distant path,
No one looks your way,
Trampling the very thorns that make your feet bleed,
Make sure to go your own way,
If there is no one to light your path, O unfortunate one,
If on a day of storms and showers doors are bolted on you
Then in the very flashes of lightning
Kindle your ribcage and blaze your own way.

(*Jodi tor dak shuney*)
Translated by Fakrul Alam

Keep faith, day and night

Keep faith, day and night, O heart, things will work out
If you've made a pledge, it will surely be fulfilled
O my heart, such things will surely happen
That which lies like stone, will come to life
Those who are dumb now will surely speak again
It's time to act and remove your burden
If you confront your sorrow it surely will be bearable.
When the bell rings you'll see everyone join in eagerly
All travelers will traverse the same path together then!

(*Nishidin bharsha rakhish*)
Translated by Sanjukta Dasgupta

333

Confusion and irresolution lead to self-abasement

Confusion and irresolution lead to self-abasement.
Don't let imaginary fears get you down
Free yourself from fear and nurture your strength,
Conquer your own self completely
Protect the weak and strike out at the wicked
Never admit that you are poor and helpless
Free yourself from fear and dare to depend on yourself
When dharma beckons with the sound of conch-shells
Stake your life silently and obediently
Free yourself from fear
Prove through valiant action your valor!

(*Sankochero biwhalata*)
Translated by Sanjukta Dasgupta

No, don't be afraid

No, don't be afraid, you'll surely win and doors will open
I know the chains that bind you will break again and again
Often you'll lose yourself and stay awake all night
Again and again you'll regain your right to be in the world
Earth and sea will beckon you; communities will call you too
You'll always sing in happiness, sorrow, shame and fear
Flowers and leaves, rivers and waterfalls will sing along with you
The rhythm of your being will pulsate in light and darkness!

(*Nai, nai bhoy*)
Translated by Sanjukta Dasgupta

Suddenly from the heart of Bengal

Suddenly from the heart of Bengal
You have stepped out in such amazing beauty!
O Mother, I can't turn my eyes away from you
Your open doors lead today to the golden temple

While the scimitar blazes in your right hand the left assails fear
A benign smile lights up your eyes;
The third eye on your forehead is fiery
O Mother, what an awe-inspiring image of you I see today!
Your open doors lead to the golden temple
Like cloud clusters your open tresses hide the storm
O sun-clad One, your sari's end drapes the skies!
O Mother, I can't turn my eyes away from you
Your open doors lead to the golden temple

I was careless and didn't turn to you
Thinking of you as a destitute mother

Seeing you lying down and suffering endlessly in a decaying house
Where now are your poor weeds, where the sad smile?
The entire sky is dappled by the light from your gleaming feet
O mother, what an awe-inspiring image of you I see today!
Your open doors lead this day to the golden temple

Now, in this sad night, float your boat in a current of joy
Your assurance rings in my heart, O heart-conqueror,
O Mother, I can't turn my eyes away from you
Your open doors lead today to the golden temple.

(*Aji Bangladesher hriday hotey*)
Translated by Sanjukta Dasgupta

Blessed am I to have been born in this land

Blessed am I to have been born in this land
Blessed is my birth O Mother, having loved you
I don't know whether you have as many treasures as a queen
All I know is that my body is soothed by your caring shade
Can any other forest or flowers have such intense fragrance?
In which other sky does the moon rise with such a smile?
When I opened my eyes your light first enchanted me
I'll keep your light in sight till it's time to shut my eyes!

(*Sharthaka Janam Amar*)
Translated by Sanjukta Dasgupta

Delay no longer

Delay no longer, hold hand in hand; the time to act is now!
We must make way this day for the heaven of union lies ahead
Listen to the conch-shell blow; the doors of the temple are ajar

The auspicious time will soon be over; where are the prayer offerings?
Arrange whatever you have as offerings on the prayer platter now
Fill up the holy urn with the cascading spring waters of self-sacrifice
It's time to seize the day and for sacrifices; don't delay anymore;
Live if you have to live, or die if you must this very moment!

(*Ekhon aar deri noy*)
Translated by Sanjukta Dasgupta

Be resolute and stand up

Be resolute and stand up; don't sway from side to side
Don't drive away grace and fortune by worrying endlessly
Decide firmly on a course; drifting is worse than death
Don't keep playing the game of swaying from side to side
Whether you find a gem or not you'll have to keep trying—
If what you get is not what you desired, don't shed tears
Float your boat if you have to but don't keep dithering
Don't open your eyes when the light has already faded!

(*Buk bendhe tui dara*)
Translated by Sanjukta Dasgupta

To pursue auspicious action

To pursue auspiciously virtuous action
Sing fearlessly. Let weakness and fear end.
Make sure to take your fill from the fountain
Flowing from the Ever-Powerful endlessly.
Let your pure and newly aroused soul
Take the vow of sacrifice and self-denial,
Learn from obstacles and impediments,
And value trials and tribulations.

Let even sorrow be a source of inspiration!
Let's go wayfarer, let's travel day and night
And traverse the path to immortality.
Let's triumph over inertia and darkness
And break through barriers that enervate.
At day's end let's remain as steadfast
As pilgrims crossing the river of death.

(*Shubha karma pathey dharo nirbhaya gaan*)
Translated by Fakrul Alam

Love Songs

Do you hear the song?

Do you hear the song playing in my mind
As you flash past my eyes?
Sunrays suck dew from the flower's bosom;
Do you sip my soul's song in the same way?
When my listless heart strays outdoors
It yields itself up everywhere.
What tender leaves whisper to the light at dawn
Conveys my mind's innermost musings.

(*Aamar moner majhe*)
Translated by Fakrul Alam

Because I would sing

Because I would sing, you keep me awake
O sleep breaker.
You startle my soul into song

O source of sorrows.
Darkness spreads and birds nest
Boats moor on banks.
Only my soul finds no solace
O source of sorrows.
When I am in the midst of work
You won't stop the flow of tears and happiness.
Touching me and filling my soul to the brim
You steal away,
Preferring to stay beyond my pain
O source of sorrows.

338

(*Tomai gaan shonabo*)
Translated by Fakrul Alam

Last night a song came to me

Last night a song came to me unbidden
But you weren't with me then.
What I always wanted to say
In a lifetime spent silently shedding tears
Became briefly in the dark
A tune sparked from the embers of a sacrificial fire.
But you weren't with me then.
I had thought that at the break of this day
I would tell you what I then wanted to say.
The scent of flowers spreads with the wind;
Birdsong fills the sky
But what I wanted to say won't stick to my tune
No matter how hard I try
Now that you are nearby.

(*Kal rater bela*)
Translated by Fakrul Alam

Whether you'll remember me or not

Whether you'll remember me or not I won't be weighed down
And so every now and then I come to your door singing for no reason
Days fly by, but as long as I live, and I keep coming back to you,
I would like your startled face to light up with that smile again and
    again,
And that is why I keep singing without reason.
The flowers of Phalgun keep falling as this first spring month ends—
But for now time has had its fill and nothing else matters.
These days will end, the light fade, the songs cease, and the veena's
    music stop,
But as long as I am here I will keep hoping you will fill up my raft of
    delight
And because of that hope I keep singing for no reason.

(*Mone rabe ki na*)
Translated by Fakrul Alam

Keep this in mind

Keep this in mind:
In your festivals I sang my songs
As sere and withered leaves fell.
Amidst parched grass and empty woods
Forlorn forsaken
In my own mind I sang my songs
As sere and withered leaves fell.
Wayfarer of the day, keep this in mind:
Lamp in hand, I traveled all night.
Summoned from the other shore

Adrift on my broken raft I sang my songs
As sere and withered leaves fell.

(*Ei kathati*)
Translated by Fakrul Alam

340

Make me your veena

Make me your veena, take me up in your arms.
Let me vibrate at your mystical touch.
Stroke me softly, caress me gently,
Till my soul hums in your ears.
Sometime in joy, sometime in sorrow,
I'll cry out to you.
Silently, I'll lie at your feet when you slight me.
None need know what new melody will fill space,
What joyous notes infinity's shores will embrace!

(*Amare koro tomar bina*)
Translated by Fakrul Alam

Dear friend, I have felt

Dear Friend, I have felt in my mind the touch of your breath
And sensed the message you have sent through the skies
You have come, my unseen friend, with the southern breeze
Why deprive me, why tie me with invisible bonds?
Reveal, oh reveal yourself in my flower garden filling my body and mind
Reveal yourself as the champak and rangan blossoms
Reveal yourself as the kinshuk and kanchan blossoms.
Why do you lure me far away with the melody of your flute?

Surrender yourself instead at the festival of youth
Through ties that only sight can provide

(*Hey sakha, barota peyechhi mone mone*)
Translated by Reba Som

O absent-minded one

O absent-minded one,
I won't send you a garlanded message.
But if you don't find out what I have to say
How will you know the truth about me?
I'll never know your response then, O absent-minded one!
When the time is right and evening lovely and quiet
When your eyes become spellbound in the fading light,
Let me soothe you with soft tunes.
Will you listen then to the message I've strung
In languid and mild measures?
Just as a firefly flitting through sal forests,
Weaves in hushed darkness a rosary of light,
In a lonely corner of your soul's courtyard,
All alone I'll go on composing my songs for you,
Completely rapt in homage,
O absent-minded one!

(*Anmona, anmona*)
Translated by Fakrul Alam

I'll overcome you

I'll overcome you not with my beauty but with my love
I'll open doors not with my hands but with my love.
I'll deck myself neither in ornaments nor with flowers

I'll adorn your neck only with a garland made out of love
None will know about the storm swaying my soul
Invisibly, like the tide with the moon, you have me rolling!

(*Aami rupey tomai*)
Translated by Fakrul Alam

342

The moon's laughter has broken all bounds

The moon's laughter has broken all bounds and light overflows
O rajanigandha pour out, will you, the nectar of your fragrance?
The mad wind fails to understand where it has been directed;
Cherishes instead the company of all it passes by in the flower garden
The forehead of the blue skies is smeared today in sandalwood
As Saraswati's swans spread their wings today
The moon sprinkles the earth with the pollen of the flower of Paradise
Light the nuptial lamp, will you, lady in the celestial abode?

(*Chander hashir bandh bhengechhe*)
Translated by Reba Som

You may as well sit beside me

You may as well sit beside me a little longer,
    if you have something to say, say it now.
See—Sharat's sky begins to pale,
    the vaporous weather makes the horizon shine.
I know you'd longed to see something,
that's why you came to my door at dawn,
did you see it before daylight faded again?
    Tell me, traveler—

for that thing, at the most unapproachable reaches
of myself, has blossomed like a flower in my blood.

Full of doubt, you've still not entered my room,
     you made music lightly in the courtyard outside.
What will you take with you when you go abroad?
     Dear guest, this is the last hour of farewell.
In that first hour of dawn, when you left your work to one side
and set out in search of that profound
message, did you find any hint of it anywhere?
     Tell me traveler—
that message, lighting its hidden fire
in my blood, burns its lamp with the flame of my life.

(*Aro kichhu khan na hoi basiyo pashe*)
Translated by Amit Chaudhuri

May farewell's platter be replete

May farewell's platter be replete with the nectar of memories
Only to be returned at the celebration of our reunion
In tearful sadness, in depths of silence,
May life's new resolutions find secret realization
On the path you tread, you are alone,
Before your eyes you see darkness,
But in your mind's eye you see a ray of light
Through the course of the day and in secret
You will refresh your mind with the nectar of remembrances
While in the lotus garden of the heart
The farewell strains of the veena play

(*Bhora thak smriti sudhaye bidayer patrokhani*)
Translated by Reba Som

I could speak to her on a day like this

I could speak to her on a day like this,
on a day when it rains as heavily.
You can open your heart on a day like this—
when you hear the clouds as the rain pours down
in gloom unbroken by light.

344

Those words won't be heard by anyone else;
there's not a soul around.
Just us, face to face, in each other's sorrow
sorrowing, as water streams without interruption;
it's as if there's no one else in the world.

This earthly web's as untrue
as the constant noise of life.
Only our eyes drinking their own nectar
as the heart feels what's only true to the heart—
all else melts in the dark.

Surely no one in this world would come to harm
if I rid my mind of this burden?
If I said a couple of words to her
in one corner of this room in sravan's downpour
surely the world would remain unaffected?

The day passes in anxious waves
lit by flashes of lightning.
Now's the time it seems I could say
the words that, all my life, I'd kept to myself—
on such a day, when it rains heavily.

(*Emono dine tare bola jai*)
Translated by Amit Chaudhuri

The bank reverberates

This bank reverberates with the call of the peacock
Why then on that bank is the cuckoo silent?
Each laments the other's loneliness and wonders
At which blessed moment they would be united

345

The restless eastern breeze carrying the intense pain of parting sighs
   deeply
The moisture laden dark monsoon wonders in hopeless contemplation
"Why am I so bound by time that spring can never come by my side?"
For they rest on two sides of the seasons
And can never sing in chorus
A sense of deep despair fills the heart of the skies.

(*E parey mukharo holo keka oyi*)
Translated by Reba Som

What you wrote

   What you wrote has, in the dust, turned to dust.
    The letters you inscribed are lost.
Chaitra nights, I sit alone, once again, it becomes visible—
   among trees and branches, the illusion of your curved hand
in new-sprouted leaves   by some error they return   your old letters.

   The mallika blossom in tonight's forest
   is filled with fragrance—like your name.
Tender, the missive traced by your fingers brought back to mind today
   some sorrow-filled script of parting.
On madhavi branches, dancing, dancing   your old handwriting.

(*Lekhon tomar dhulai*)
Translated by Amit Chaudhuri

No, there is no time left

No, there is no time left for me, no
Will you bring this last hour to a close?
Who are they that come and go relentlessly
Drowning the strains of music in that din
Leaving momentary gaps in my song?
I have vowed to surrender myself to you
Settling all accounts today
Putting an end to all quests, all tasks,
The lonesome morning path will I tread unwavering
Immersing my awakened sight in your light

(*Nai nai nai je baki samay amar*)
Translated by Reba Som

Songs of Nature

The universal veena strums on

The people of the world are enchanted by the sound of the veena
On land, water, skylines, forests, and groves,
On mountains, caves, rivers, streams, and oceans,
Each day hums with sweet-sounding music,
Each day is full of delightful dances.

In ever-new spring ever-new joys, ever-new festive notes.
Lovely, very lovely harmonious sounds in arbors—
I hear, o hear, warbling amidst leaves and branches,
Cuckoos calling in flower gardens all by themselves,
The gentle breeze rolling over lakes,
Melodious playful sweet-sounding notes keep ringing out.
Over dense green forests the wind wanders about.

From riverbanks reed thickets rustling sounds arise.
Countless notes, innumerable voices, ever-flowing melodies everywhere!

During monsoons ever-new joys, ever-new festive notes.
Profound, very profound drum rolls rumbling through blue skies
The goddess Durga in her destructive mood dancing,
Behold clouds over rivers ceaselessly pouring,
Behold their furious frightful notes reverberating
Over secluded piyal and tamal groves.
The streaming breeze singing stirring notes in darkness,
Frenzied lightning putting on a dazzling show under the sky.
Countless notes, innumerable voices, ever-flowing melodies everywhere!

In the month of Ashwin new joys, ever-new festive notes,
On clear, very clear, very cloudless, bright days,
Earth dressing itself up in autumn's graceful guises.
The new moon glowing and sparkling, smiling brightly,
Very clearly displaying itself in the midst of the azure sky,
In its white embrace the white veena strumming on—
The overture sounding soft and sweet in the Behag mode,
Moonbeams seducing flower gardens to tunes of crickets chirping.
Countless notes, innumerable voices, ever-flowing melodies everywhere!

(*Vishwaveena rabe*)
Translated by Fakrul Alam

Stars fill the sky

Stars fill the sky, the world teems with life,
    And amidst it all I find my place!
    I wonder, and so I sing.
I feel in my veins the ebb and flow of Earth's eternal tides
        Pulling this Creation
        I wonder and so I sing

Walking along the forest's grassy paths,
I have been entranced by the sudden scent of a flower,
Around me lie strewn the gifts of joy
I wonder, and so I raise my song.
I have seen, I have heard.
I have poured my being upon the breast of Earth,
Within the known I have found the unknown.
I marvel and so I sing.

348

(*Akash bhara*)
Translated by Ratna Prakash

The sky full of the sun and stars

The sky full of the sun and stars, the world full of life,
in the midst of this, I find myself—
so, surprised, my song awakens.

Wave after wave of infinite time, to whose ebb and flow earth sways,
the blood in my veins courses to that measure—
so, surprised, my song awakens.

I've pressed upon each blade of grass on the way to the forest,
my heart's lifted in madness, dazzled by the scent of flowers,
all around me lies this gift, outspread—
so, surprised, my song awakens.

I've listened closely, opened my eyes; poured life into the earth,
looked for the unknown in the midst of the known,
so, surprised, my song awakens.

(*Akash bhara*)
Translated by Amit Chaudhuri

Songs of the Six Seasons—Summer

Come, come o month of Baisakh

Come, come o month of Baisakh
With your hot breath blow away the dying,
Let the debris of the whole year be driven far away
Let distant memories go, let dimming melodies fade,
Let teardrops into the distance dissolve.
Let weariness be wiped away, let decay be dispelled.
In a fiery shower let holiness stir.
Come and dry up the sap of desire,
Blow, blow your conch-shell of destruction.
Drive far, far away the mist of illusion.

(*Esho, esho hey baisakh*)
Translated by Fakrul Alam

I bow to you, O mendicant

I bow to you, O mendicant free from worldly desires.
Light up your flames glowing with heat,
Extinguish the self, and let the pure light of enlightenment
Arise from the soul.

(*Namo namo hey bairagi*)
Translated by Fakrul Alam

That must be a Baisakhi storm

That must be a Baisakhi storm
Engulfing the evening sky.

Why fear, who frightens you? Open all doors
Listen to that deep roar; it is your name being called.
In your tunes and in your songs
Respond to the storm's call.
Whatever shakes, shake it—whatever passes, let it pass,
Whatever breaks, let it shatter—whatever is left, let it last.

350

(*Oi bujhi kalo Baisakh*)
Translated by Fakrul Alam

Songs of the Six Seasons—the Rainy Season

Clouds pile up on clouds

Clouds pile up on clouds; darkness descends.
Why keep me sitting all alone, outside your door?
In the workaday world, I move amidst multitudes,
But this day I keep waiting, heartened by your promise.
If you do not reveal yourself, or if you choose to ignore me,
How will I spend this rain-filled day?
I let my eyes roam; I keep on gazing at the distance.
My soul cries out and wanders with the wayward wind.

(*Megher parey megh*)
Translated by Fakrul Alam

The Asadh evening sets in

The Asadh evening sets in, the day is spent.
The rampant rain pours down every now and then.
Sitting alone in a corner of the room, what is it that I keep thinking?

Blowing across the groves, what does the moisture-laden wind keep
    saying?
My heart's sap is in spate; I can't seem to find the shore—
The fragrance of wet wildflowers makes my soul cry.
What tunes will help me fill the hours and pass this dark night?
Anxiously, I wonder: what maze must I lose myself in to forget every-
    thing?

(*Asadhsandhya*)
Translated by Fakrul Alam

The rain-clouds are drum beats

The rain-clouds are drum beats rumbling across the heavens.
Their vibrant tones and reverberations flutter my heart.
Their distinctive tunes make me forget myself.
What was in the thicket of the soul as a hidden pain and a tucked away
    tune,
Spreads everywhere this day in song after song,
In the moist breeze and in the shades of cloud-colored forests.

(*Badal-meghe madal baje*)
Translated by Fakrul Alam

Asadh, from where have you been freed this day?

Asadh, from where have you been freed this day?
Wait for a while in your dark attire at the edge of the fields.
Your flag of victory stands unfurled over the heavens,
From the east to which westward route must you fly?
Rumbling like a kettle-drum, who would you arouse?
The palmyra leaves seem drunk with the spirit of dancing.
The sal forests sway with the wind as if on a high.

Who is it that darts back and forth across the sky,
Tumbling and tossing from the shades of the clouds?
Who is it that stirs the waves of the overflowing rivers?

(*Asadh, kotha hotey tumi*)
Translated by Fakrul Alam

352

Asadh, how delicately threaded are your jeweled thunderbolts!

Asadh, how delicately threaded are your jeweled thunderbolts!
Your dark beauty is set off by lightning flashes.
Your spells have the power to melt stones and sprout crops
On your winged feet you carry from sandy wastes a garland of flowers.
On withered leaves you come in torrential and triumphant showers.
Your clouds resound like tom-toms in festive abandon
In your deluge of delicious green, revive the parched earth,
But keep away your awesome, life-threatening floods.

(*Bajromanik diye gantha*)
Translated by Fakrul Alam

There—in the lap of the storm clouds—the rain comes

There—in the lap of storm clouds—the rain comes,
Its hair loosened, its sari's borders flying!
Its song beats flutter the mango, blackberry, sal and rain-trees,
And make their leaves dance and murmur in excitement.
My eyes, moving in beat to its music,
Wander in the falling rain and lose themselves amidst the sylvan shades.
Time and again, whose familiar voice calls me in the wet wind,
Stirring a storm of anguish in my soul on this lonely day?

(*Oi je jharer meghe*)
Translated by Fakrul Alam

Tear-filled emotions stir everywhere

Tear-filled emotions stir everywhere.
Whose desire resounds in the dark clouds this day?
The turbulent wind speeds across tempestuously,
Whose lament can be heard in its song?
Who has devoted himself to such lonely and futile worship?

(*Ashrubhara bedona*)
Translated by Fakrul Alam

353

Beloved, stay

Beloved; stay, stay with me,
This dense cloud-covered dawn.
Were you in my dreams through the lonely night?
Beloved, time flies fruitlessly.
In this rain-soaked, restless wind
Speak to my heart, keep your hand in my hand.

(*Bandhu. raho, raho sathey*)
Translated by Fakrul Alam

In the dense obsession of this deep dark rain

In the dense obsession of this deep dark rain
You tread secret, silent, like the night, past all eyes.
The heavy eyelids of dawn are lowered to the futile wall of the winds
Clotted clouds shroud the impenitent sky
Birdless fields
Barred doors upon your desolate path.

Oh beloved wanderer, I have flung open my doors to the storm
Do not pass me by like the shadow of a dream.

(*Aaj sravan ghana gahan mohey*)
Translated by Sunetra Gupta

354

Are you out for a tryst this stormy night?

Are you out for a tryst this stormy night,
My soul mate, my friend?
The sky cries out despondently,
Sleep won't come to my eyes.
Opening the door, beloved,
I keep looking for you longingly,
My soul mate, my friend!

I can't see anything outside,
I wonder which path you are taking.
Could you be on the bank of a far-off river,
At the edge of a dense forest,
Or crossing a vast expanse of darkness?
Where could you be, my soul mate, my friend?

(*Aaji jharer raate*)
Translated by Fakrul Alam

It has arrived again

It has arrived yet again—Asadh with overcast skies
With the breeze, bearing the fragrance of rain on parched earth
This ancient heart of mine sways and resounds in delight today
Gazing at the newly formed rain-cloud formation
From time to time, across the vast meadowlands

Rain clouds cast shadows across patches of fresh grass
"It has arrived!" says my heart
"It has arrived!" proclaims my song
It has entered my vision—it has raced through my heart!

(*Abar eshechhey asadh*)
Translated by Reba Som

An Asadh day

Thick new clouds fill the Asadh sky this day;
Children, outside the house don't stray!
The rain keeps pouring endlessly
Aush-rice fields fill with water steadily
Behold ink-black clouds darken the other shore.
Children, don't go outdoors anymore!

Listen to the boatman being called on the other shore,
His boat will not be ferrying people anymore!
The east wind blows; no one seems to be on the shore;
Waves roll over banks as rivers overflow,
The pouring rain splashes into the ground.
The boatman won't be ferrying other people around!

Bring in the white cow—don't you hear it mooing?
Soon daylight will fade and night will be falling.
From the doorway see if you can tell
If from fields all have returned.
What impulse has set the cowboy roaming?
Soon daylight will fade and night will be falling!

Children outside the house don't stray!
The sky darkens, and there is little left of the day.
Thick showers will drench your clothes

And you'll spill in the slippery paths to the ghats.
Behold the wind making reed-forests sway,
Children don't go outdoors today!

(*Neel naboghaney*)
Translated by Fakrul Alam

356

Like a peacock dancing

Like a peacock dancing, my heart dances this day.
Like a peacock fanning its tail rapturously,
Shimmering with joyous thoughts and emotions,
Eagerly peering at the sky for some visitation.
Like a peacock dancing, my heart dances this day!

Rain-laden clouds roll across the sky, reverberating,
Rainwater cascades down time and again
Tender rice-plants bend and sway,
Frogs croak on while spent doves shiver in their nests,
Rain-laden clouds roll across the sky, reverberating!

Moist-dark-blue clouds tint eyes, making them sky-blue!
The newly sprouting grass of the shaded forest
Becomes the place where I would love to rest.
Aroused Kadamba trees kindle my heart.
Lovely moist-dark blue clouds tint my eyes!

Who unravels her hair in the turret of the sky today,
Covering her bosom languorously
With her newly woven sky-blue dress?
Who frisks amidst sudden spurts of lightning?
Who unravels her hair in the turrets of the sky today?

Who sits amidst riverbank reeds, dressed all in green?
Who could it be, tearing off the tender jasmine,

While gazing for someone absent-mindedly,
Even as her pitcher floats away from the quay?
Who sits amidst riverbank reeds, dressed all in green?

Who swings on secluded bakul branches swaying away?
Who scatters bakul flowers in quick showers?
Hem of her sari quivering against the sky,
Tresses flying in her eyes and then unraveling,
Who sways on secluded bakul branches swaying away?

Whose boat moors amidst blooming ketakis with maidenly ease?
Bunches of moss and cotton-plants
Loosely drape her sari's hem.
She stirs my soul with her tear-filled rhapsody of the rain.
Amidst blooming ketakis she moors her boat with maidenly ease!

Like a peacock dancing, my heart dances this day.
Showers stream down on newly sprouted branches,
Cricket songs stir forests,
The rampaging river roars over banks and floods villages,
Like a peacock dancing, my heart dances this day!

(*Hriday amar*)
Translated by Fakrul Alam

Songs of the Six Seasons—Early Autumn

Over paddy fields this day

Over paddy fields this day sunlight and shadows play hide-and-seek
Who floats a raft of white clouds—playing hide-and-seek?
This day bees hum about, heedless of honey, drunk with light.
This day ducks and drakes flock to sand-banks.
For sure, this day I won't stay, won't stay indoors.

For sure, this day I'll raid the sky and rob what's outdoors.
Like a wave foaming in the tide, the wind breaks into a smile.
All day long I'll play my flute, and the hours beguile.

(*Aaj dhaner khete*)
Translated by Fakrul Alam

358

Who waits outside my soul's gate

Who waits outside my soul's gate this autumnal day?
Heart, sing out in joy, and strike a welcome note.
Let silent thoughts of blue skies and dew-daubed yearning
Resound from every string of your lyre.
Tune into songs singing of golden harvests.
Float a raft full of melodies into serene seas.
Gaze in deep contentment at the guest who waits outside.
Then open the gate and roam with him outdoors.

(*Sharate aaj kon atithi*)
Translated by Fakrul Alam

You were wide-awake in my heart

You were wide-awake in my heart,
But now you are part of the autumn sky.
How did you depart this morning,
Wetting your dress's border in the dew?
What song should I sing now?
I can't find the right words.
Song, you scatter over groves with shiuli flowers,
You stream into air with the gusting wind

(*Hridaye chhiley jegey*)
Translated by Fakrul Alam

I know not your name

I know not your name, I know only your tune
You are the message of light heralding the autumnal dawn
Drowned in my thoughts I remain the whole day
In the forest of shiuli blossoms
By what mistake did you leave behind in my heart a flute of pain?
What I had to say is spoken by tear-drenched dewdrops
What I sought to see remains within, in image omnipresent,
In shade and light, woven through my fabric,
Holding the veena of my unexplained pain

(*Tomar nam jani ne shur jani*)
Translated by Reba Som

Night gives way to an autumnal morning

Night gives way to an autumnal morning.
My flute, who will I hand you over to now?
On many a Phalgun or Sravan morning
You had cried out soulfully,
Weaving welcoming notes out of parting tunes.
In song after song you stole away
Thoughts hidden in the depth of the soul
Like the stars at the break of day
Your time is now at an end—
Bring it to a close with the shedding of shiuli flowers.

(*Amar raat pohalo*)
Translated by Fakrul Alam

On this cool late autumnal night

In the dewy night sky the starry lamps
Remain hidden by the cloak of autumn
Word spreads from door to door
"Light the lamps, kindle them in their own glow
Decorate the earth in this radiance"
The garden of flowers is now empty
The doyel and koyel sing no more
The bulrushes weep into the riverbanks
Banish the darkness of weariness and despair
Light the lamps, kindle them in their own glow
Speak of light's triumphal message
As the gods look on, arise children of the world
To awaken the night with light
Darkness comes, daylight will be over soon
Light the lamps, kindle them in their own glow
And conquer this pervading gloom.

(*Heemer rater*)
Translated by Reba Som

Songs of the Six Seasons—Late Autumn

The full moon has brought this autumn

The full moon has brought this autumn a glimpse of spring.
On bakul treetops moonlight has spun a fantasy of flowers.
What secret whispers has the full moon brought tonight?
The woods are entranced by the white oleander's untimely awakening.

Some sleepless nameless bird sings every now and then.
Whose sweet memories has the full moon brought tonight?

(*Hemantey kon bansanteri*)
Translated by Ratna Prakash

You had your say that day

You had your say that day,
But I had no time, and so you turned away.
It was time for play then; fields filled with jasmine flowers,
And leaves kept fluttering in the wayward wind forever.
Now Hemanta days are here,
Fields are mist-filled and bare,
The day ends; is it time to go away?
Sitting by the door, I keep looking at the way.

(*Shedin amai bole chiley*)
Translated by Fakrul Alam

Songs of the Six Seasons—Winter

The winter wind

The winter wind quivers amlaki branches.
Leaves shiver and drop off one by one
Till trees look barren and forsaken
And amlaki fruits no longer can stay hidden.
All day long I wait for Him
Whose whim it is to empty and fill up again.

Every now and then winter seems to be calling:
At what dawn will I know it's time to give up everything?

(*Sheeter hawar*)
Translated by Fakrul Alam

362

Winter days are here

Winter days are here and the year is ending.
Get set for reaping and gathering crops in.
Hurry up, hurry up, field loads of work remain
And even as we tarry, twilight sets in.
The work of harvesting must end,
When the evening star lights up heaven.
Prepare a place lovingly in your courtyard then
For one who will be your night's companion.

(*Elo Je Sheeter Bela*)
Translated by Fakrul Alam

Poush calls you all

Poush calls you all to its festival—come, come away.
Miraculously, its baskets fill with ripe harvests this day!
Village wives in paddy fields are stirred by the wind.
Wondrously, golden sunlight spreads all over the world.
The sound of flutes playing in fields delights the heavens.
Open all doors—who would not thrill at such a sight!
Rice sheaves bathe in the dew and light breaks into a smile
Earth's joy overflows and the wonders of life beguile.

(*Poush toder*)
Translated by Fakrul Alam

What maya made you hide yourself

What maya made you hide yourself in decrepit winter?
My soul can't bear the scene, can't endure the sight at all,
O Supreme One, will you be so miserly with yourself
In the midst of your own teeming creation?
Not knowing whether you will take its offerings or not,
The wintry wind moans in forests like a mournful veena
Why lavish yourself on some desert landscape?
Where have you concealed your cornucopias?
How can cuckoos sing in withered leaves and barren branches?
Timorously, we muse on your mute message and empty assembly.

(*Eki maya*)
Translated by Fakrul Alam

Songs of the Six Seasons—Spring

This day spring stirs

This day spring stirs at doorsteps.
Don't keep it away from your cloistered life.
This day open the petals of your heart;
Distinguish no more between near or far ones.
In skies resounding with music
Let your essence surge like waves.
Spread what is sweet in you everywhere
And let yourself blend with space.
This day what deep pain spreads across forests
And sounds through leaves?
This day all dressed up and expectant,
Who does earth look for in far-off skies?

The south wind has grazed my soul,
Who is it seeking by knocking at doors?
On this fragrance-filled night
Whose footfalls can be heard?
O beautiful, beloved, and radiant one,
Whom do you call so profoundly?

(*Aaji basanta jagrata dwarey*)
Translated by Fakrul Alam

A slight caress, a few overheard words

A slight caress, a few overheard words—
With these I weave in my mind my spring songs.
Intoxicated by palash in bloom, by champak flowers too,
I spin my webs of tunes, colors, and desires.
Aroused by what comes my way in fleeting moments,
I paint images in a corner of my mind.
With whatever drifts away, I wander about in tunes,
Thus I let time fly, counting the beat of ankle bells.

(*Ektuku chhowan laage*)
Translated by Fakrul Alam

Is spring solely a festival of flowers in full bloom?

Is spring solely a festival of flowers in full bloom?
Isn't spring a play of dried leaves and fallen flowers too?
Waves leaping up to its tunes sound across oceans
Waves lapsing to its tunes break up all day long
See how spring is a play of fallen flowers too!
Who says only jewels keep glowing at my Lord's feet?
At his feet lie strewn thousands of chunks of earth too!
How many of the men by his side are meek and mild?

He became my guru when He took me in though I was wild!
The King of Festivals beholds the play of fallen flowers too!

(*Basante ki*)
Translated by Fakrul Alam

Spring, you enchant earth

Spring, you enchant earth.
Your boundless beauty
Pervades everything.
In forest outskirts, green fields,
Shaded mango groves,
Lakesides and in river waters,
Blue skies and the south breeze,
You are immanent.
In cities, villages, and gardens,
Daylong or at nighttime,
Cuckoo calls, dances, and songs
Enthrall the world.
Houses and palaces hum with music,
Hearts fill with delight,
Life upsurges today,
The mind stirs, becomes restless,
Rings out like bells on dancing feet.

(*Basanti he bhubanmohini*)
Translated by Fakrul Alam

Alas, how quickly spring days fly by!

Alas, how quickly spring days fly by!
On far-off branches cuckoos call away,
The restless breeze sheds bakul flowers;

Whose fragrance the mind overpowers.
Phalgun's heat warms up mango groves,
Humming bees quiver tree shades
All day long, absent-mindedly,
Who strums the veena on my soul, needlessly?

366

(*Choley jai mori hai*)
Translated by Fakrul Alam

Fallen leaves

Fallen leaves, I belong to your lot.
With many a smile, many a teardrop,
Phalgun sends my soul on its way.
Fallen leaves—have you put on spring's light orange colors
For your last show?
Have you been rolling over grass and dust
Ritually, to herald spring's ultimate outburst?
Let me be like you in my final passage,
With the color of fire set me ablaze.
Let the setting sun stir my soul
And prop it up as it moves towards its goal.

(*Jhora pata*)
Translated by Fakrul Alam

Miscellaneous Songs

When my footprints no longer mark this road

When my footprints no longer mark this road,
I'll stop rowing my boat to this ghat,

I'll cease all transactions,
I'll settle my accounts and clear all dues.
All business will stop in this mart—
It won't matter if you stop thinking of me then,
Or cease calling me while looking at the stars.

When the strings of my tanpura gather dust,
When prickly shrubs sprout in my doorsteps,
When the garden flowers put on a mantle of weeds,
When moss spreads all over the pond's banks,
It won't matter if you stop thinking of me then,
Or cease calling me while looking at the stars.

Then the flute will play on in this music hall,
Then Time will flow on,
Then days will pass just as they do now.
Then ghats will fill with boats as they do now—
Cattle will graze while cowboys play in that field.
It won't matter if you stop thinking of me then,
Or cease calling me while looking at the stars.

Who can say I won't be there that morning?
I'll be in all your fun and games then—this very me!
You'll name me anew, embracing me as never before,
It won't matter if you stop thinking of me then,
Or cease calling me while looking at the stars.

(*Jakhan porbe na, Bichitra*/Miscellaneous)
Translated by Fakrul Alam

Light of mine, O Light

Light of mine, O Light, Light that fills this world!
Light that washes my eyes, Light that steals my heart.

Light that dances, O friend, near my being
Light that plays, O friend, on the veena within me
The sky awakens, the wind races and the entire earth smiles
In the stream of light, a thousand butterflies raise their sails
In the waves of light, dance mallika and malati
In the clouds that you have touched with gold,
O friend, the gems cannot be counted
In every leaf that smiles, O friend,
There is a pile of merriment
The river of music has submerged its banks
And there is the endless shower of nectar!

(*Aalo amar aalo ogo aaloye bhubon bhora, Bichitra*/Miscellaneous)
Translated by Reba Som

Only coming and going

Only coming and going
Only drifting with the tide.
Only tears and laughter in the twilight.
Only stolen glimpses and fleeting touches
And looking back with grief while walking away
Driven on by false aspirations,
Leaving behind belied hopes.
Endless desires possessed of only broken resolve
Endless striving with imperfect results.
Adrift on the river, clutching a broken craft
Deep thoughts find meager expression.
A half relationship, an unfinished conversation,
In shame, fear, anxiety and doubt,
Only a half-love.

(*Shudhu jaoa aasha, Bichitra*/Miscellaneous)
Translated by Ratna Prakash

Has he come? Or hasn't he?

Has he come? Or hasn't he?
Hard to say!
Is he a dream image? An illusion?
Or is he merely a delusion?
Can he be caught in beauty's drapes?
Can I catch him in the notes of a song?
He is the always-elusive object of my devotion!
His flute plays a sad tune
A raga blending motifs of union and separation.
Whether in joy or sorrow he can be found,
The restless breeze blowing through my heart
Tells me: he's the true end of all my devotion.

(*O ki elo, O ki elona, Bichitra*/Miscellaneous)
Translated by Fakrul Alam

The clouds drift away

The clouds drift away, saying to the moon, "Come, come."
Overcome with sleep, the moon says, "where—oh where?"
Who knows where they go? Who knows what they will see?
In the midst of the night sky the moon looks everywhere.
Far, far away, in some realm of music that is their home
The stars surround them and play flute-like music soulfully.
No wonder the clouds drift in the sky, smiling away,
No wonder the moon, hiding its smile, looks their way!

(*Meghera chole chole jai, Bichitra*/Miscellaneous)
Translated by Fakrul Alam

369

Nothing has worked out

Nothing has worked out;
Overwhelming grief—loud lamentations;
Flowing tears—a pained heart!
Nothing gives peace;
Nothing whets desire!
I'd looked for love; I'd found it too;
I still love—yet what is it that's lacking?

(*Kichhu to holo na, Natyagiti*/Songs from Plays)
Translated by Fakrul Alam

370

O herald of the new

O herald of the new,
Let the auspicious hour of birth come around once again.
Reveal yourself from the midst of a mist-filled sky
Like the sun.
Burst through the heart of the void and unveil yourself.
Let life be revealed as triumphant
Let the infinite's endless marvels be revealed in you.
The conch sounds in the east;
My mind responds to the call for renewal
Sent out this day every year
On the twenty-fifth of Baisakh.

(*Hey nutan, Anushthanik*/Songs for Ceremonious Occasions)
Translated by Fakrul Alam

Plays

Tagore grew up in a family of theater enthusiasts. His older brother Jyotirindranath had a passion for the theater and all things literary; the Jorasanko house where the Tagore children grew up was the location for numerous theatrical productions and eventually the poet became part of them. When Jyotirindranath was discussing a line from his play *Sarojini* with his publisher one day in November 1875, the fourteen-year-old Tagore intervened, suggesting that the dramatic moment required a song that he had ready. Two years later Tagore made his debut as an actor by playing the lead role in his brother's production of Molière's *Le Bourgeois Gentilhomme*. When Jyotirindranath and the eldest brother Dwijendranath started editing a literary monthly called *Bharati* that year, among the precocious Tagore's many contributions to it was *Rudra Chandra,* a historical play in blank verse. But Tagore's first notable work as a dramatist was *Valmiki Pratibha* (1881), a musical, in which he also played the part of the protagonist Valmiki, the author of the *Ramayana*. Throughout his life, Tagore continued to be attracted to the theater in manifold ways. He would not merely write, produce, and direct plays; he would also perform in them enthusiastically. Initially, his passion was that of an amateur dramatist, but toward the end of his life he even tried touring India with his troupe to raise money for Visva-Bharati.

Tagore wrote well over forty plays. A few of them were essentially strung together from songs. Others were verse dramas, and he even composed dance dramas when in his seventies. He first composed fairly conventional comedies and tragedies in blank verse. As he matured as a dramatist, he began to experiment with plays written in the symbolist and lyrical mode. He composed several poetic plays to commemorate the seasons but also wrote farces and satirical skits. Occasionally, he adapted his own work in another genre for the stage or went back to a play he had written earlier to recast it drastically. Almost all his plays bore the mark of the poet and the master-lyricist.

374

Tagore moved Bengali drama away from the realist mode and incorporated indigenous theatrical traditions. He turned to Indian epics and legends for his plots and also used songs and dances to give his dramatic compositions the flavor of Indian theatrical traditions such as jatra, or popular folk theater. He also eschewed plain speech, often preferring poetic or elevated styles of dialogue. Significantly, his theatrical innovations and experiments paralleled techniques adopted by contemporary European dramatists like Belgium's Maurice Maeterlinck, Ireland's W. B. Yeats, Germany's Gerhart Hauptmann, and the Russian Leonid Andreyev. All of them, like Tagore, had experimented with approaches that would transform theater in the twentieth century—using the symbolist mode, or deploying myths and legends to move away from naturalism. Quite often, Tagore composed plays that explored a mood or an idea that had seized him. He seemed to care little about creating a tightly woven plot or complex characters or constructing scenes full of dramatic action.

Among his most successful plays are *Chitrangada* (1891), written when he was thirty but recast when he turned seventy-five. It celebrates the nature of love as well as man-woman relationships. A play that is of enduring popularity in Bengal is the light comedy *Chirakumar-Sabha* (1896). His most performed theatrical work outside Bengal is *Dak Ghar* (in English, *The Post Office*), an allegory about death as a way out of a constricting world and as a step toward spiritual freedom. It was staged by the Irish players in London in 1912 and performed in Sweden in 1921 when he went there to receive the Nobel Prize. Another play widely available in English and performed abroad is *The King of the Dark Chamber* (1914); based on his Bengali play *Raja* (1910), it is written in the allegorical vein of *The Post Office*. It depicts a king, alienated from his people, who must break out of the shackles imposed by seclusion. A play that has great contemporary relevance is *Muktadhara* (1922). It is about a tyrant who builds a huge dam to control the flow of a mountain spring on which his people depend until his son, the crown prince, resists his father at the cost of his own life. In *Varsha-Mangal* (1922), Tagore expresses his love for the seasons of Bengal through a fusion of music, poetry, drama, and dance. Outstanding among the plays of the final years of his life is

Chandalika (1932). The plot, based on a Buddhist legend, explores selfishness and vanity, and juxtaposes solipsism with selfless love. In his biography of Tagore, Krishna Kripalani suggests that it was inspired by Mahatma Gandhi's long fast against the British government's decision to separate the "untouchables" of the country from the rest of the electorate through the Communal Award (Kripalani, 391–392).

The two plays chosen in this section are *Roktokorobi* (1926; in a previous English translation, *Red Oleanders*) and *The Kingdom of Cards* (1933; in Bengali, *Tasher Desh*). They embody the combination of symbolism with realism and dialogue with music that is characteristic of Tagore's dramaturgy. They also show that he could range easily from the tragic to the comic and indicate that his plays embody his humanism and instinctive dislike of totalitarianism.

Roktokorobi is set in the mythical land of Jokkhopuri where the main source of wealth is a mine. Its reclusive and avaricious king oppresses his citizens with the help of zealous henchmen titled Sardars who exploit the excavators of the mine. They, in turn, are assisted by a priest called Gosain-ji. Suddenly, in this carceral society enters a girl called Nandini, who has the strength of mind to upset the state's repressive and ideological apparatuses. The play can be related to ideas that Tagore held dear such as his critique of the nexus between imperialism and technology.

The Kingdom of Cards is much more explicitly satiric in intent. The play uses exuberant dance and songs as well as comic dialogue to narrate the lively tale of a prince and his companion. They find themselves shipwrecked in a land inhabited by playing cards. Like *Roktokorobi* the play seems to have been inspired by Tagore's resentment of imperialism and the mechanical impositions of state apparatuses on the individual. That the play was meant to be inspirational for Indians and anti-Raj in tone is clear from the fact that Tagore dedicated the expanded version of the play in 1939 to Subhas Chandra Bose, the radical leader of the Indian National Army, with the words: "You have taken up the holy mission of instilling new life into this nation; keeping this in mind I dedicate the play *Tasher Desh* in your name."

Tagore's plays are performed regularly in India and Bangladesh;

they are a part of the repertoire of many theatrical companies in these countries. This is not surprising because their themes and the dramaturgy are rooted in the theatrical traditions of the region. But they also deal with universal themes and display Tagore's humanism dramatically.

Roktokorobi

INTRODUCTION

This play is rooted in truth. But readers will be deprived of its substance if the onus of gathering the evidence of the events depicted here is placed on historians. It will be enough to state that in accordance with the poet's wisdom and conviction the play is fundamentally true.

Regarding the original name of the location concerned, geographers may have individual opinions. But everyone is aware about its local name being Jokkhopuri. Pundits believe that there existed in this Puranic land the throne of Kubera, the divinity of wealth. But this play is not at all derived from those antique settings; it cannot even be classified as a fable. The landscape being dealt with possesses a buried Yaksha treasure trove. Awareness about that trove has induced an ongoing project of tunneling in the lower earth; and for this alone the folk have endearingly dubbed the place Jokkhopuri. In short, while on this stage, we shall be acquainted with the excavators of this region.

The natural name of the Raja of Jokkhopuri does not pose a problem for historians. We will know that he has a pet name, "Makar Raja." The meaning of the name will be understood through the tongues of the folk in due course of time. On the outer walls of the royal palace there is a latticed window. From the cover of this window the Makar Raja, in accordance with his own fancy, interacts with the people. What could be the reason for such mysterious behavior? It is difficult to say, for nothing more is known besides what the protagonists discuss in their limited conversations.

The Sardars of the state are laudable people and proficient. They constitute the Raja's personal confidants. Because of their meticulous organization the excavators cannot take advantage of anything even for a moment and Jokkhopuri's everlasting progress goes on unabated. The local Headmen here were once excavators who have been promoted in accordance with their own virtues. On several counts of daily endeavour they surpass even the Sardars. If Jokkhopuri's legislation can be reckoned, in the poet's language, the full moon in radiance, then the responsibility for its dark facade can be attributed to the Headmen.

Besides these, there is one Gosain-ji—he acknowledges the name of God but accepts his daily bread from the Sardars. Jokkhopuri gains a lot through his efforts.

At times, in the fisherman's net, by sheer chance, totally unpalatable creatures of the water get caught. Through them not only is one's appetite not satisfied nor the pocket replenished, but they also escape after tearing apart the net. Into this play's net of action a girl by the name of Nandini appears suddenly. The screen-window behind whose cover the Makar Raja withdraws is not to be withstood, it seems, by this girl.

At the play's very start this girl will make her appearance on the open veranda of the Raja's latticed window. To describe lucidly the nature of this window would be quite an impossible task. Only those who have given it shape will fathom its artful ingenuity.

Whatever dramatic action we are to witness here will take place on the latticed veranda of the royal palace. What takes place inside is something we come to know very little about.

Introduction translated by Rupendra Guha Majumdar[1]

Characters

NANDINI	a fearless young woman
RANJAN	a young rebel, beloved of Nandini
RAJA	supreme lord of Jokkhopuri

BISHU	folk-singer, ex-spy, close friend of Nandini
PROFESSOR	an intellectual with a flair for the Physical Sciences
CLASSICIST	a scholar in the Indian Puranic context, rather than Greek or Latin ones
KISHORE	a young excavator
GOKUL, PHAGULAL	rustic excavators
CHANDRA	wife of Phagulal
GOSAIN	a local Vaishnava
FIRST SARDAR	
SECOND SARDAR	
THIRD SARDAR	
WRESTLER	
SENTRY	
DOCTOR	
GROUPS OF VILLAGE FOLK	

378

The setting of the play is the city of Jokkhopuri. Its people work daily in its gold mines. The king of the land remains ensconced behind a latticed screen wall—on the left of centre of the stage—throughout the play—until the end, only his voice indicating his presence. Lower down the wall there is a single, large window. It is shut. Before it is a strip of open veranda adjoining a flat, rocky centre stage. On the right corner is the jagged entrance to the gold-mine, like the open mouth of a beast of prey.
(Enter NANDINI *and* KISHORE, *a young miner)*

KISHORE: Nandini! Nandini! Nandini!

NANDINI: Why do you call me so loudly, Kishore? Am I stone deaf?

KISHORE: I know very well you can hear me. But it's just that I like calling you. Do you need more flowers? Then I can fetch some.

NANDINI: Be off; Go back to your work at once. Don't delay!

KISHORE: Ah! All day long I keep digging for gold from the core of the earth. It's only in the little time that I can steal away in-between shifts to gather flowers for you that I feel totally alive!

NANDINI: My dear Kishore! If they come to know this, they will surely flog you.

KISHORE: But didn't you tell me you had to have Roktokorobi flowers? What makes me really happy is that these flowers are so rarely found in this region. After searching all over I have come upon one in a solitary place where a lone bush stands hidden behind a rubbish dump.

NANDINI: Do show me the place. I will go there and pluck some flowers myself.

KISHORE: Oh, please don't say such things! Nandini, you need not be so cruel. Let this tree remain hidden . . . as my one and only secret. Bishu regales you with his own exclusive songs. From now only I will fetch flowers for you, flowers which are *entirely* mine.

NANDINI: But these monsters will work you to death . . . and my heart will be shattered at the sight!

KISHORE: It is that very pain that makes me feel that the flowers that blossom, do so entirely for me—they become the priceless jewels of my sorrow!

NANDINI: But how do you expect me to bear the sight of the suffering you all have to endure?

KISHORE: What suffering are you talking about? One of these days I will lay down my life for you, Nandini! This very thought revolves continuously within my mind.

NANDINI: You who have given me so much—what can I possibly give you in return, tell me Kishore?

KISHORE: Well you can give me the promise Nandini that it is from my hand that you will receive flowers every morning.

NANDINI: Fine! So be it! But do be a little careful.

KISHORE: No, I'd rather not be careful! In the face of their constant violence I am going to fetch you flowers every day.

(Exit KISHORE*)*
(Enter TEACHER*)*

PROFESSOR: Hey, Nandini! Don't leave as yet! Look back at me!

NANDINI: What is it Professor?

PROFESSOR: Why do you ignite a spark in me every once in a while and then disappear? Since you stir up the mind, before leaving you could perhaps afford to give a response. Please wait a minute. I'd like to talk to you for a while.

NANDINI: Why, what could you need me for?

PROFESSOR: Now that you raise the question of need, look that way! Our gang of miners has ripped open the earth to extract the needful which they bear on their heads as ants do in tunnels when they climb to the surface. In Jokkhopuri, all our wealth comes from the dusty entrails of the earth—gold! But, you know, beautiful one, the gold nugget that you are, you were not born of dust but of light! And who will include *that* gold in the fine circle of our needs?

NANDINI: You keep on repeating to me the same words, the same thoughts. Why are you so astonished, anyway, at seeing me, Professor?

PROFESSOR: When the morning sunlight descends on the flower-glades it is not astonishing at all. But when light enters through a crack in a massive wall—then it is another matter. Inside Jokkhopuri you are that pristine, sudden radiance! Share with us your thoughts about this place. Come, speak up, do!

NANDINI: I am amazed at what I see! The entire city has thrust its head under the soil, and is groping around in the dark with outstretched hands. You are all tunneling into the underworld, digging out the treasures of Yakshas, excavating the extinct wealth of millennia that Earth had chosen to bury a long time ago.

PROFESSOR: But it is precisely that extinct treasure that we worship. We would tame its daemonic spirit. If we can harness that daemon the entire planet will be in our grip.

NANDINI: Moreover, you have stowed away your king behind this outrageous screen-wall, wary about exposing his human limitations. This gloomy, subterranean labyrinth of yours—how I'd like to pry it open and flood it with a gust of light. I'd like to pull apart that disgusting net and salvage the man trapped within it!

PROFESSOR: But our human king is no less powerful than the daemonic, supremely energized guardian of our treasure house.

NANDINI: Oh, come on! This is a myth spun from your local fantasy!

PROFESSOR: Fictional it is. The naked need no introduction. It is only when one is dressed that one is introduced as a lord or a beggar. Come home with me. I feel delighted to explain to you these theories of knowledge.

NANDINI: Just as your miner disappears into earth as he keeps digging away you too have been burrowing deep into your books. Why would you waste your time with the likes of me?

PROFESSOR: We are ineffectual insects of the nether world preoccupied in a complex task. And you . . . you are the evening star in the sky of empty time! On sighting you our wings tend to become restless. Come with me to my home. Allow me to squander some time in your company!

NANDINI: No, no! Please, not now! I have come here to meet your king in his palace.

PROFESSOR: He dwells behind a latticed wall. He won't let you in.

NANDINI: I hardly care for the obstacle created by latticed walls. I have come here to see him in his chamber.

PROFESSOR: Do you know Nandini, I too am walled in? The pundit in me prevails at the expense of the mortal man. Our own king may be awe-inspiring but as pundit I am no less . . . awe-inspiring!

NANDINI: You must be joking! You don't look that terrible. Let me ask you something. I was brought here by them. But why didn't they bring Ranjan along as well?

382

PROFESSOR: They tend to fetch things bit by bit. But I can't help asking . . . Still I say—why do you want to place your heart's precious jewel in the midst of this treasure pit?

NANDINI: If my Ranjan is brought here even their fossilized ribs will start to dance!

PROFESSOR: Even by herself Nandini befuddles the minds of the sardars of Jokkhopuri. Imagine what Ranjan's arrival would do to them!

NANDINI: They have no idea how weird they are. If only the almighty would break out into a peal of laughter in their midst would they come out of their reverie. Ranjan is that peal of the almighty's laughter.

PROFESSOR: God's laughter is like the sun's rays under which though glaciers can melt rocks won't. To unsettle our Sardars force will be required.

NANDINI: My Ranjan's power is like your Sankhini River. Like that river he will laugh as well as demolish! Professor, let me reveal the latest secret—today I shall be united with Ranjan.

PROFESSOR: How can you be so sure?

NANDINI: It will happen, it will! Our meeting will come to be! The message has already reached me.

PROFESSOR: By what route could the message infiltrate, evading the Sardar's eyes?

NANDINI: The route down which the message of spring arrives—that route colored with the hues of the sky and the stirring of the breeze.

PROFESSOR: Which means the rumour has been wafted by the sky's colours and the wind's passion.

NANDINI: When Ranjan arrives I will show you clearly how a stray rumour lands on earth.

PROFESSOR: Whenever Ranjan's name comes up, Nandini's tongue is not inclined to stop. Anyway, I have my study of natural science to preoccupy me and into its mysteries let me quietly withdraw—I cannot dare further *(He takes a few steps and then returns)*. Nandini, let me ask you something—aren't you scared of Jokkhopuri?

NANDINI: Why should I be?

PROFESSOR: The beasts of the jungle fear the eclipsed sun, but never the sun in its entire glory. Jokkhopuri is caught in the grip of an eclipse— the demonic Rahu of the quarry of gold has devoured it ravenously. He is no longer whole and does not relish the wholeness of any being. Let me urge you—do not loiter here. If you go away, those chasms in the earth will open their jaws even more menacingly before us. Nevertheless, I must insist, flee from here! Go live in contentment with Ranjan in a land where people do not shred the garment of Vasundhara, the earth-mother, into little pieces *(He goes out for a while and returns)*. Nandini, will you take out for me one of the Roktokorobi flowers from that bracelet in your right hand?

NANDINI: Why, what are you going to do with it?

PROFESSOR: How often have I wondered why you wear the Roktoko-robi ornaments on your person?

NANDINI: I have no clue about their significance.

PROFESSOR: Perhaps your governing deity does! In this blood-red hue there must be some secret fear, not merely sweetness.

NANDINI: Do you mean a fear within me?

PROFESSOR: The good Lord has placed a bloody paint-brush in the hands of beauty. Who knows what story you have come to narrate with your crimson pigment! The Malati, the Mallika and Chameli flowers were ready at hand. What made you choose this one flower after discarding the rest? Is this the way that a man unwittingly sifts out his destiny?

NANDINI: Well, every now and then, Ranjan affectionately calls me Roktokorobi! It seems to me, the color of Ranjan's love is crimson too. I have worn that color around my neck, upon my breast and here on my wrists.

PROFESSOR: Give me one of his flowers—if only a suspended gift of course! Let me try to understand the philosophy that led him to its blood-red colour.

NANDINI: Here, take this one! Ranjan will be here with us in a while. The joy I feel in the thought that he is coming makes me present you this flower!

(Exit PROFESSOR*)*
(Enter GOKUL, *a miner)*

GOKUL: Could you once turn your face this way—I want to see you! Somehow I can't really figure you out. Who could you be?

NANDINI: I am nothing else than what you see. Why do you need to *understand* me?

GOKUL: I feel quite disoriented when I can't figure out something. Why has the king summoned you here?

NANDINI: For a project that is . . . worthless.

GOKUL: You wield some kind of spell. You have snared everyone. Those who will be enticed by your pretty face will surely die. Hey! Let's see what's that . . . dangling in the parting of your hair!

NANDINI: Only a tuft of Roktokorobi flowers.

GOKUL: What does it signify?

NANDINI: Oh, nothing whatsoever!

GOKUL: But I can hardly believe you. You must be surely into some intrigue! Before this day is over some disaster is bound to take place! No wonder you have put on this fancy make-up! She-devil! O you she-devil!

NANDINI: Why do I appear so terrible in your eyes?

GOKUL: Seeing you, it seems, you are a blazing red firebrand! Let me go and warn the uninitiated: Beware ye all! Beware, beware!

   (*Exit* GOKUL)

NANDINI: *(Banging on the screen door)* Hey! Can you hear me?

RAJA'S VOICE *from within:* Nanda, I do hear you. But stop calling me! I have no time to spare, no time at all!

NANDINI: Today my mind is brimming with joy! Bearing that joyous feeling I want to enter the threshold of your house.

RAJA'S VOICE: No, you can't visit me there. Whatever you have to say you can tell me from outside.

NANDINI: The garland of Jasmine flowers that I wove—I have wrapped it in lotus leaves.

RAJA'S VOICE: Wear it yourself!

NANDINI: It doesn't suit me. My garland is made of Roktokorobi flowers.

RAJA'S VOICE: I am like the crest of a mountain. In isolation is my splendor!

NANDINI: But down that mountain's chest rivulets flow. On your neck too garlands will sway. Throw open the screen. I'd like to go in.

RAJA'S VOICE: I will not let you in. What you have to tell me—do so quickly! Time is running out.

NANDINI: Can you hear the strains of a distant song?

RAJA'S VOICE: What sort of song?

NANDINI: It is the song of Spring's arrival! The crop is ripe and it's harvest time . . . and the song is summoning us all to join in the harvest.

(The song can be heard from the distance):

Spring is beckoning you all!
Come running! Come, come, O come!
Her basket's brimming with the ripe harvest!
O what unbounded joy!

NANDINI: Can't you see the spring sunlight spreading the aura of the harvest across the sky!

In the wake of the wind's intoxication
Dryads come dancing into the paddy fields;
The sun's golden rays are spread across Earth's mantle—
O what immense joy!

NANDINI: You too must come Raja! We'll lead you to the fields!

The music of the flute coming from the fields
Makes the whole sky rejoice!
Who would stay indoors on such a glorious day!
Open wide all doors!

RAJA'S VOICE: I go to the fields? What do you think I will do there?

NANDINI: The labors of the field are a lot easier than what you have to do in Jokkhopuri.

RAJA'S VOICE: What is considered easy is difficult for me. Can the lake's expanse dance like a waterfall wearing tinkling anklets of foam? Be gone! Stop talking—time is running out.

NANDINI: Amazing is your strength! When you let me into your treasury the other day I wasn't in the least surprised to discover your hoard of gold. But what fascinated me was the ease with which you shaped them into a mound. But I wonder if piles of gold nuggets can respond to the astounding rhythm of your hands the way those rice fields can? All right, tell me Raja! Does it not scare you to tinker with the phantom treasures of the earth?

RAJA'S VOICE: Why? What is there to fear?

NANDINI: The earth on her own delivers its heart's wealth to us joyfully. But when you tear open her breast and snatch out the dead bones that you call "treasure," then out of the gloom you evoke the curses of a blinded demon. Can't you see the discontent on people's faces, the suspicion, the fear all around you?

RAJA'S VOICE: Curses?

NANDINI: Yes, curses arising from murder and violent conflicts.

RAJA'S VOICE: I don't know about curses. I only know that we are born with a certain degree of strength. Are you happy about the strength I possess, Nandini?

NANDINI: Yes, it makes me immensely happy! That's why I say to you: come out into the light, plant your bare feet on the soil, let earth awaken with joy!

(Song in the background)

> The joy of light awakens
> Sensing the dew-laced rice-stalks;
> Dear ones, our joy has no bounds!
> It truly spills over,
> O what joy!

RAJA'S VOICE: Nandini, are you aware that the Lord has preserved your beauty by veiling it in the folds of illusion? I'd like to snatch you away and possess you completely, but I . . . just cannot get at you! I would like to toss you up and down to view you from every possible angle . . . and if that proves futile then I would like to dismantle you completely!

NANDINI: What are you saying!

RAJA'S VOICE: Why can't I extract the dark essence of your Roktoko-robi flower and wear it as a kohl-lining around my eyes? Only a few layers of cloth cover you. The same kind of veil shrouds your self—it is so difficult to take off precisely because it is so delicate. Well, Nandini, what do you think of me? Tell me quite frankly!

NANDINI: That I shall divulge to you another day. After all, you don't have the time to spare now, right? Today I have to go.

RAJA'S VOICE: No, no, do not leave! Tell me before you go. What you think of me—do tell me!

NANDINI: How often have I told you that—I think you are simply amazing! In those massive arms of yours great strength has been mounting like clouds ushering a storm. My mind dances at the sight!

RAJA'S VOICE: The way your spirit dances when you see Ranjan? Is that also . . . ?

NANDINI: Never mind that. After all, you *have* no time to spare!

RAJA'S VOICE: I *do* have time. Just tell me *this* one thing before you depart.

NANDINI: The pulse of that dance is something else . . . you will not understand.

RAJA'S VOICE: I will! I want to understand!

NANDINI: I won't be able to explain everything to you adequately. I must be off.

RAJA'S VOICE: Don't go. Tell me—do you like me or not?

NANDINI: Yes, I do like you.

RAJA'S VOICE: Just as you like Ranjan?

NANDINI: Oh dear—back to square one! These things you don't seem to understand.

RAJA'S VOICE: Bits and pieces of it I do understand. I know how I differ from Ranjan. I merely contain the strength. Ranjan possesses magic within himself.

NANDINI: What do you mean by "magic"?

RAJA'S VOICE: Shall I elaborate? In the earth's subterranean realms are rock and iron and gold, there lie the iconic images of power. In the upper regions on freshly laid out soil, grass sprouts, flowers blossom—that is all magical! I extract diamonds and rubies from such forbidding depths but I fail to snatch away the soul's magic from domains of easy access!

NANDINI: You who possess so much—why do you constantly talk with such greedy intent?

RAJA'S VOICE: Whatever I possess is a sheer burden. The act of hoarding gold will not lead one to the philosopher's stone. The mounting strength that I amass does not lead to the threshold of youth. So I would like to tie you up while I have you in my sight here. If only I had Ranjan's youth I could have "tied" you up in a state of freedom! It is in tightening the ropes of attachment that time goes by. Alas! All other obstacles crumble, only joyousness cannot be confined.

NANDINI: After all, you have enmeshed yourself in the net. Why, then, are you thrashing around so restlessly, I just can't understand you!

RAJA'S VOICE: You never will! I am an awesome desert—I reach out with my hand to an insignificant blade of grass like you and say—I am a conflagration, I am emptiness, I am enervation. The blazing thirst of this desert has colonized immeasurable stretches of fertile soil to extend its domain. And yet it has failed to draw into itself the life of that minuscule, helpless blade of grass.

NANDINI: It does not really appear that you are so weary. I can only see your gigantic strength.

RAJA'S VOICE: Nandini, once in a distant land I came upon a fatigued mountain just like myself. From outside I could not understand that its rocky entrails had become inflamed from within. Late one night I heard a terrible roar. It was as if a demon's protracted nightmare had been shattered abruptly. In the morning I discovered that the mountain had been completely sucked under by the earthquake. I could only wonder then how titanic strength under its own weight can crumble into pieces—this I realized on seeing that mountain. And in you I see . . . its opposite!

NANDINI: What do you see in me?

RAJA'S VOICE: The flute of the cosmos playing upon the pulse of dancing feet—that rhythm!

NANDINI: I could not quite follow you.

RAJA'S VOICE: In that rhythm the great weight of material things is dispersed into the air. In that rhythm the constellations, like poor mendicant boys, dance across the expanse of the sky. In that rhythm, Nandini, you appear so simple, so lovely. Compared to me you are so diminutive and yet . . . I cannot help envying you.

NANDINI: By segregating yourself from everyone you have been unduly depriving yourself . . . Why don't you make yourself easily accessible?

RAJA'S VOICE: By concealing myself I wait for the opportunity to steal the world's weighty possessions. But all my bodily strength cannot access the gift hidden in the clenched fist of the Almighty as much as your finger, so like a champa flower-bud, can. That tightly clenched fist of the Lord I must surely undo!

NANDINI: I cannot follow these thoughts of yours. I better be leaving.

RAJA'S VOICE: All right, go! But, here, I am extending my hand through the window—do place your hand, just this once, on my palm.

NANDINI: No, no! The sudden extension of your hand detached, as if from the rest of your body—is too scary for me!

RAJA'S VOICE: Because I want to touch others with only one hand—they all run away from me. But if I wish to touch you with my entire being—will you oblige me, Nandini?

NANDINI: It is you who did not allow me to enter your house—then why say such things now?

RAJA'S VOICE: I have never wanted to usher you into my bleak existence, pushing against the current. Only on the day when you will come to me with the incoming breeze of the sail, will the auspicious moment of your arrival be solemnized. If that wind happens to be the wind of a rising storm, it will be welcome! The time has not come as yet.

NANDINI: I am telling you Raja—that sail's wind will be ushered in by Ranjan. Wherever he ventures he brings freedom along with him!

RAJA'S VOICE: The freedom that your Ranjan carries with him in his wanderings—do I not know who fills him with the honey of the Roktokorobi flower? Nandini, you have given me news of a hollow freedom. Where do you think I will find the honey that I seek?

NANDINI: For the moment let me take your leave.

RAJA'S VOICE: You must answer me before you depart though.

NANDINI: How can liberty be filled with honey—is a question you will be able to answer when you see Ranjan yourself. He is awfully beautiful!

RAJA'S VOICE: Beauty answers Beauty itself. When Beauty's opposite tries to force an answer, the strings of the veena refuse to play—indeed they tear. That is enough, now go, you must leave! Or else there surely will be trouble.

NANDINI: I'll leave. But let me tell you before I go—today my Ranjan will arrive. He will! He surely will! By no means can you stop him!

(Sound of wind, dhak and conch shells fills the air auspiciously)
(Enter PHAGULAL *the excavator and his wife* CHANDRA*)*

PHAGU: Where the hell have you hidden my bottle of wine, Chandra? Out with it!

CHANDRA: What do you mean by this? Drinking bouts from the morning itself?

PHAGU: Today's a holiday. Yesterday they observed their Maran-Chandi ritual fast. Today's the Dhaja Puja as well as the Astra Puja.

CHANDRA: What are you saying? Do they believe at all in gods and goddesses?

PHAGU: Haven't you seen their stock of wine, their armory and temple—all set up side by side.

CHANDRA: So just because you are on leave do you have to go for the bottle? In the village on a festive day you would . . .

PHAGU: Within a forest a bird can fly away in its freedom. Freed from a cage all of a sudden it will smash its head and die! In Jokkhopuri a holiday is more of a misfortune than hard labor can be.

CHANDRA: Why don't you leave work? Hey! Why don't we return home?

PHAGU: The homebound path is closed for us—don't you really know?

CHANDRA: Why is it closed?

PHAGU: They have nothing to gain from our houses anymore.

CHANDRA: Are we going to remain stuck to the body of their needs . . . like husks on grains of rice?

PHAGU: Our Bishu, crazy man that he is, declares, that to remain whole is the prerogative of the billy-goat. Those who eat his flesh, do so after removing his bones, ribs, hooves, and tail. So much so that even the bleating before the chopping block—"Baaaa!"—is objected to as redundant! There comes crazy Bishu singing merrily!

CHANDRA: For the last few days he has been singing with full-throated gusto.

PHAGU: That's what I can see!

CHANDRA: He is, I must say, Nandini-smitten! She has drawn his heart-strings and drawn out his songs as well.

PHAGU: What's so surprising about that?

CHANDRA: Nothing really! Take care dear. One of these days, she might prompt you to sing too! Can you imagine the fate of our neighbors then? I can! The enchantress knows her charms well! She is going to cause havoc!

PHAGU: Bishu's fate wasn't sealed this day. He came to know Nandini long before coming here.

CHANDRA: Bishu, listen to me! Hear me out! Where are you off to? If you are looking for an audience for your singing—you may find a few stragglers here as well. It will not be a terrible loss!

(BISHU *enters and sings*)

Who are you, steering my dream-boat?
The drunken wind blows the sails,
The wayward soul advances singing!
Blot out all memory
In your rocking,
Row me to remote shores.

CHANDRA: Then there can be no hope, we are too close!

BISHU: My anxieties are in vain!

All I have has been left behind!
Discard your veil!
Look upwards,
Engulf my soul in your smile!

CHANDRA: I know *who* the pilot is that is steering *your* dream-boat!

BISHU: How will you know him from the outside? You haven't seen her from the centre of the boat.

CHANDRA: I warn you one of these days your admirable Nandini will sink your boat.

(Enter GOKUL, *the miner, flustered)*

GOKUL: Look here Bishu! I have my doubts about that Nandini of yours.

BISHU: Why, what has she done?

GOKUL: Nothing at all! And that's what's so worrisome! What made the king bring her here so needlessly in the first place? I can't figure out what she is up to at all!

CHANDRA: This is our abode of sorrow. How can we stand the sight of her pruning her beautiful feathers all day long?

GOKUL: We believe in plain and solid-looking people.

BISHU: In Jokkhopuri the weather is such that the beautiful is soured—this is the problem! Hell too has its charms, but no one can appreciate them. That is the supreme punishment of the denizens of hell.

CHANDRA: That's enough! As if we are the only foolish ones! But do you know that even the Sardar of this place can't stand her sight?

BISHU: Look here Chandra! Let not the contagion of the Sardar's two eyes alight on you, or your eyes too may become blood-shot at our sight! Well, what do you have to say to that, Phagulal?

PHAGULAL: To tell you the truth—whenever I see Nandini, I feel ashamed to look at what I am. I can't bring myself to speak in her presence.

GOKUL: Bishu, because the sight of that girl is so overwhelming you are not able to detect the curse she has brought with her. Let me tell you, it won't be long before you find out what's going on.

PHAGULAL: Bishu, your sister wants to know why we booze!

BISHU: By the immense mercy of the Lord, the allotted share of wine is available abundantly all across the globe; even your arched feminine glances are intoxicating! Our arms enable us to work, just as you, by the amorous manner in which you entwine your arms, intoxicate us; in this mortal world we must work hard but we must also become insensible at times. Without wine how can we forget how hard our work is?

CHANDRA: You don't say! Because of born drunkards like you, the good Lord's mercy must be endless. For you he has positioned the wine vessel in such a way that it will always seem to be flowing out!

BISHU: On one side hunger lashes its whip; thirst too punishes us—inflicting pain, they say, get to work! On the other side, the green hue of the forest spreads out its charm, the golden rays of the sun dazzles, intoxicating us, crying out, we are free, free!

CHANDRA: Do you attribute all of this . . . to the effect of wine?

BISHU: The soul's wine, marginally inebriating, but its effect lingers day and night. See the proof for yourself! I came to this kingdom, but when I joined the despicable occupation of mining, the easy supply of liquor was cut off. That is why we are all so entranced with the locally brewed stuff. Only when regular breathing is blocked does a man gasp for breath!

(Song)

> Your soul's juice is drying up—
> Then fill your cup with death's own juice
> Squeezed out from the flaming pyre,
> Brightening the bleak void
> With its tumultuous laughter!

CHANDRA: Why don't you join me, brother, let's run away!

BISHU: Below that great blue firmament is an open-air boozing joint! That road is closed. That's why we are so drawn to this prison's contraband liquor. We neither possess the sky above, nor do we have the leisure;

so all the laughter and songs and sunshine of these twelve hours we have distilled into one draught of mellow fire. The sense of liberty is as strong as the bondage it springs from.

(Song)

Your sun is stuck in impervious clouds,
Your day ends in pointless chores;
Then let grim night approach,
Prime companion of drunken sleep
Perfect to shade weary eyes
In goal-obscuring darkness!

CHANDRA: Whatever you say, Bishu, it is you men who got carried away on arriving at Jokkhopuri. For us women nothing has really changed.

BISHU: Of course it has! All your flowers have withered and now your soul craves more and more gold.

CHANDRA: Not in the least!

BISHU: And I say, "Yes!" Look at that wretched Phagu! He adds four hours to the regular twelve he spends in deathly labor—whatever for? He doesn't know. Neither do you! The Almighty is aware, of course. Your dreams for gold whip his insides more brutally than the lashes of the Sardar.

CHANDRA: That's fine with me! Then why don't we go? From here let us return to our own land.

BISHU: It's not that the Sardar has only blocked our exit points. He has clogged the very desire in us to return. Even if you reach home today you won't rest in peace there. You will be rushing back here tomorrow since your blood is intoxicated by gold, just as a bird fed on opium will always prefer its cage to freedom.

PHAGU: By the way, Bishu, wasn't there a time when your habit of reading one book after another almost forfeited your eyesight? Why did they lump you with numbskulls like us in handling spades?

CHANDRA: In all the time we have spent here, we could not induce him to answer this question!

PHAGU: Yet everyone knows why!

BISHU: Well, what do they say?

PHAGU: That they kept you here to spy on our lot.

BISHU: If you all have been in the know why did you spare my life?

PHAGU: We also know that you made a mess of it!

CHANDRA: What? Couldn't you survive even with such a cushy job?

BISHU: A cushy job? To have it fester like a sore on the back of a robust body? I had remarked, "I will return to my country. My health is terrible!" Retorted the Sardar, "How do you intend to journey with such bad health? Still you must surely try." I made the attempt. At the end I realized that the jaws of Jokkhopuri are bound to close upon you once you enter its mouth. Now the only path left for me is towards its belly. Today I am drifting within that bleak domain of darkness. Now between the two of us the Sardar seems to be more indifferent about me. The shredded plantain leaf draws less neglect than the cracked clay pot.

PHAGU: Why lament, Bishu? We have been holding you high above our heads.

BISHU: When the truth is out I'll be killed. The object of your affections also draws the Sardar's eye. The welcoming croak of the golden frog, meant for the toad, reaches the ears of the viper as well.

CHANDRA: When will your project end?

BISHU: The schedule, alas, does not mention an ending. After the first day, the second; after the second the third. I keep burrowing along the tunnel—one arm's length followed by two, two arm's length followed by three. I shovel and throw up heaps and heaps of gold. One heap followed by a second, two heaps followed by a third. In Jokkhopuri numbers follow numbers in strident columns without reaching the sum total. So in their eyes we are not human, merely digits. Phagu, what's your number?

PHAGU: It's stitched on the back of my shirt. I am 47-F.

BISHU: I am 69-U. Back home in the village I was a man. Here I am a fraction of 10 by 25. I am the object of continuous gambling.

CHANDRA: After their amassing of so much gold, is there need for any more?

BISHU: Because necessity thrives there must also be an end to consumption. Because we need to eat does not mean that the stomach can be filled forever with food. Intoxication has no real need but no end either. The gold down there is the stored wine, the petrified wine of the king. Can't you see that?

CHANDRA: No!

BISHU: With a glass of wine in hand we tend to forget that we can only operate within the limitations set for us by fate. We fancy that our freedom is limitless. The master of this place is under the same illusion because he has the plate of gold in his hand. He imagines that the earth's gravity, directed as it is on the commoner, doesn't affect him at all. He feels himself soaring in an extraordinary sky.

CHANDRA: Because it is harvest time, in village after village preparations for it are going on. Hear my plea, let's go home! If we approach the Sardar once . . .

BISHU: Haven't you yet fathomed out the Sardar with your woman's intuition?

CHANDRA: Why, seeing him I was quite . . .

BISHU: Well, quite . . . dazzled? The crocodile's jagged white teeth bites with sure firmness. Even if the Crocodile King in person wanted to he could not loosen the jaws.

CHANDRA: Here comes the Sardar!

BISHU: That does it! I'm quite sure he's overheard us.

CHANDRA: So what? We have not said anything that would . . .

BISHU: Sister, all we can do is to speak—it is they who provide the meaning! So, who knows what cinder of a word will set ablaze what thatched roof—none is any wiser!

(Enter SARDAR)

CHANDRA: Grandpa Sardar!

SARDAR: Hullo, granddaughter, is all well with you?

CHANDRA: You must give me leave to go home this once.

SARDAR: Why? I've given you such a superb place to live in, one much better by far than your own home. I've even kept a guard there at government expense. What is it, 69-U? Your presence here reminds me of a Sarus crane appointed to teach dancing to a gaggle of herons.

BISHU: Sardar, I am not in the least amused by your wisecrack. If my legs had the strength to teach anyone dancing I would have definitely used it to flee from this place. I have found plenty of evidence to prove how hazardous this whole business of making others dance in your area can be. Subsequently it's happened that the feet tremble in taking even regular steps.

SARDAR: Granddaughter, I have a piece of good news! I have appointed Kenaram Gosain to preach the holy word to them. The costs will be covered by the daily contributions of the devotees. Every evening from the Gosain's own mouth they will . . .

PHAGU: No, no, Sardarji that can never be! Till now the worst we do in the evenings is to act drunk after some drinks. If he comes to deliver sermons . . . I tell you, we will witness murders.

BISHU AND PHAGULAL: Shhhh . . . !

(Enter GOSAIN)

SARDAR: Well, we were speaking of the devil and . . . he's here! Prabhu, my *pranam!* Our feeble-minded artisans now and then become unduly agitated. Kindly pour a few mantras of peace into their ears . . . they need it so much.

GOSAIN: Are you talking about these people? Aha! They are the very tortoise-incarnation of Vishnu! They have taken the world's burden on their backs—that's why it's still upright! The very thought gives me goose pimples! Dear 47-F, for a moment, consider carefully—my very mouth that chants kirtans, will be the recipient of the rice grains you offer in obeisance. The sacred cloth I wear to purify my body has been woven by the sweat of all your labors. Is that a small matter? May my blessing forever keep you unshaken; only then will the good Lord's grace flow without interruption. Son, cry out once full-throatedly. The name of "Hari." May your entire burden be lightened! Let Hari's name mark the beginning, middle and the end!

CHANDRA: Ah! How exquisite! I have not heard such words of wisdom for ages! O do . . . do bless me . . . with a small portion of the sacred dust of your feet!

PHAGU: I have been keeping quiet till now but I cannot stand it any more. Sardar, such colossal wastage—whatever for? I am willing to offer you the money you intend to collect for the prayer rituals, but I won't tolerate any fraud.

BISHU: Once Phagulal goes on the warpath there will be no respite! Be quiet I say! Quiet!

CHANDRA: Have you decided to mess up both this life as well as the next one? What will be the outcome? Never before did you strike such a pose. I can see quite clearly Nandini's influence wafting across all of you.

GOSAIN: All said and done, Sardar—such innocence! What will we teach those who say exactly what they feel? It's more likely that they will teach us! Do you understand?

SARDAR: Certainly I do! I also understood what the source of the trouble is. I shall have to take charge. It's better that you proceed with your sermons over there where the woodcutters seem to have begun to mutter under their breath.

GOSAIN: Where Sardar?

SARDAR: Over there in the "T" and "Th" pockets. The chief there is 71-T. To the left of where 65-N lives is where the section ends.

GOSAIN: My son, though the D/N–sector is still somewhat unstable, the M/N–sector seems to be under the sway of a sweet tune at present. Their ears must be attuned to their mantras. Nonetheless, it is better to retain the soldiers in the block for a few more months since, as they say, "pride is the greatest adversary." The forces will contain the excess of pride, following which . . . we shall prevail. So, let me leave . . .

CHANDRA: Prabhu, give your blessings so that good sense prevails in them. Don't take any offence.

GOSAIN: Don't fear Mahalakshmi! They will become completely at ease!

  (Exit GOSAIN*)*

SARDAR: Now then, 69-U, I sense an uneasy mood in your neighborhood.

BISHU: Perhaps so. Gosain-ji sees them as the Tortoise Incarnation of Vishnu, but the *shastras* have foreseen that incarnations vary. The Tortoise suddenly emerges as the Boar. In place of armor flashes out teeth; in place of patience, pig-headedness.

CHANDRA: Bishu, pause for a while! Sardar, please don't forget what I told you!

SARDAR: Not a chance—whatever I've heard I'll remember.

  (Exit SARDAR*)*

CHANDRA: Well, did you see? The Sardar is such a sport! He is so genial with everyone.

BISHU: The crocodile's teeth first break out into a smile but then bite!

401

CHANDRA: Where does "bite" come into this?

BISHU: Aren't you aware they have decided that from now on artisans can't be accompanied by their wives.

CHANDRA: Why?

BISHU: In terms of numbers it's true we make it to their account books. But the units of women here don't tally with numerical digits in their mathematical set up.

CHANDRA: How come? Don't they have wives in their own homes? What do *they* have to say?

BISHU: They too have become intoxicated by gold platters! Indeed, they surpass their husbands where intoxication is concerned. They won't even look at us!

CHANDRA: Bishu, you too had a wife under your roof—what has happened to her? I haven't heard of her in a long while.

BISHU: As long as I held the exalted position of a spy she would be invited to play with the wives of the sardars. But once I had aligned with Phagu's group, her invitations from that quarter ceased abruptly. She left me and departed after such humiliation.

CHANDRA: For shame! To commit such sins!

BISHU: To expiate that sin she will be reborn as a sardar's wife!

CHANDRA: Bishu, look, look . . . look at those people over there, moving with such ceremony! Columns of peacock-gilded palanquins, taffetas on the elephants' howdahs! What fabulous horsemen! As if they have skewered single beads of sunlight on the tips of their lances!

BISHU: There go the chieftain's wives to feast at the Festival of Banners.

CHANDRA: Ah! What a celebration of fashion! What looks! Bishu if you had not left their service you too would have been a part of this rollicking ceremony! And that wife of yours—

BISHU: Yes, we too would have shared the same fate!

CHANDRA: Now is there no going back, none at all?

BISHU: Of course . . . through the passage of the gutters!

Offstage, resonant voice of NANDINI: O crazy brother of mine!

BISHU: What *is* it, my crazy sister?

PHAGU: There comes your Nandini calling for you. Well that's the end of Bishu's company for today!

CHANDRA: Don't hope for Bishu to be with us anymore. Do tell me; into what blissful realm has she enchanted you?

BISHU: She has enchanted me with her sorrow.

CHANDRA: Why do you talk so cryptically?

BISHU: You folks will never understand. There are sorrows which no charm can undo.

PHAGU: Bishu, talk straight, otherwise I'll lose my cool.

BISHU: Listen to me carefully! Animals bear the sorrow of nearby desires; man yearns in sorrow for desires far away. Nandini expresses the far-off, eternally flickering flame of my sorrow.

CHANDRA: I really can't understand any of this talk. All I know is that the girl you men least understand proves to be the one most attractive to you. We are simple folk, our worth is meager; yet we lead you down the straight path, whatever happens. But today let me state quite clearly— this girl will drag you down the path of doom with her garland-noose of Roktokorobi flowers!

(*Enter* NANDINI)

NANDINI: My crazy brother, when they were going along the distant highway to the fields today, they were singing the songs of spring. Did you hear them?

BISHU: Is my morning like yours? I hardly have the time to listen to songs! They are nothing but the discarded remains of a weary night!

NANDINI: Today in my mind's delight I thought I wanted to climb the rampart walls to join in their singing. I could not find a path anywhere. So I have come to be with you.

BISHU: I am hardly . . . a rampart!

NANDINI: You *are* my rampart! When I come to you I can lift myself and see the world outside!

BISHU: It amazes me to hear such things from your lips.

NANDINI: Why?

BISHU: All this time after I had entered Jokkhopuri I used to feel that I had lost sight of the horizon. It seemed that I had become part of chopped-up humanity, flung into a common pot and set to be cooked into gruel! There was no way out. Just then you appeared and peered at my face so intently. I realized that a light was still visible within me!

NANDINI: Crazy brother of mine, within the confinement of this fortress only a singular strip of sky survives between the two of us. Everything else has been blotted out completely.

BISHU: Because that strip of sky still survives I can still sing my songs to you.

(Song)

You keep me awake only to sing to you
O wrecker of sleep!
You beckon me, stirring my soul.
O arouser of sorrows!
Birds return to their nests
With twilight approaching;
Boats reach the shore,
Only my heart finds no respite
O awakener of sorrows!

NANDINI: Bishu, are you calling me "Awakener of Sorrows"?

BISHU: You are the herald from my ocean's farthest shore. The day you arrived in Jokkhopuri you were the breeze across the salt waves stirring my heart.

(Song)

> In the midst of my daily chores
> You didn't let the grief cease;
> After your touch,
> When my soul was with your nectar brimming
> You chose to depart;
> You stand in the shadow of my pain,
> O awakener of sorrows!

405

NANDINI: Let me tell you, mad one! The song of sorrow that you sing—I have never heard it before!

BISHU: Why, not even from Ranjan?

NANDINI: No. With his two hands gripping the two oars of the boat he ferries me across the turbid river; clasping the mane of the wild stallion, he speeds me through the jungle! Scattering my fears, he shoots his arrow between the eyebrows of the pouncing tiger, laughing aloud all the while. Just as he thrashes the waves after plunging into the Nagai River, he tosses me about the same way! He stakes his whole life in the game of profit and loss. In that very game he had won me. One day you too were a part of that game; but for some reason of your own you quit that group of gamblers and went your way. When you left you kept looking at me in that strange manner . . . I could not understand what you were seeking. Then for a very long time I got no news of you. Tell me—where have you been?

BISHU: *(Sings)*

(Song)

> O Moon, a tidal wave of tears has moved the sea of sorrow,
> Whispers have spread to the outer shores on every side;

My boat tied to a familiar bank has lost its mooring;
Onrushing winds have taken it to some unknown frontier

NANDINI: From the edge of that great unknown who dragged you back and made you dig tunnels in Jokkhopuri?

BISHU: A girl. Just as a bird in flight is brought down to earth by a sudden arrow, she has flung me to this dust. I had lost sight of myself.

NANDINI: How was she able to touch you?

BISHU: When one who is thirsty is denied the hope of water, mirages deceive easily. Then the trackless self loses all bearings. One day I was viewing a golden city of clouds through the western casement. She was looking at the Sardar's golden spires then. As if to rebuke me, she said sharply, "Take me down to that place; let me see how potent you are!" I replied defiantly, "You can be sure I will." Thus I brought her to the base of the golden spires. And then my illusion was scattered.

NANDINI: I have come to take you away from this place. I will smash these manacles of gold!

BISHU: Since you have been able to sway the king of this region, what can possibly stop you! By the way, aren't you scared of him?

NANDINI: Fear is what you feel when you stand outside the screen but I have been inside and I have seen with my own eyes.

BISHU: What did you see?

NANDINI: I saw a man. But he looked awesome. His forehead was like the lion-crested-gate of a seven-storied palace, his two arms the iron bolts of an impregnable fortress. It seemed that someone from the *Ramayana* or *Mahabharata* had descended to our human level.

BISHU: And on entering his room what did you see?

NANDINI: A falcon was perched on his left arm. He placed it on a stand and kept looking at me intently. Then in the same manner in which he had been ruffling the feathers of the falcon he took hold of my hand and stroked it ever so softly. After a while, he asked me abruptly, "Aren't you scared of me?" I replied, "Not in the least!" Then, sinking his two hands into my flowing hair, he sat for some time with his eyes shut.

BISHU: How did you feel?

NANDINI: I enjoyed it! How can I put it? He was like a thousand year-old banyan tree, I a tiny bird. Surely if I perched for even a moment on the tips of his branches it would send a thrill right down to his marrow. I felt like giving that bit of happiness to the lonely soul.

BISHU: And what did he say next?

NANDINI: At one stage he arose with a jerk, and casting a sharp glance upon my face, blurted out, "I want to know you!" A strange shudder ran through my body. I asked, "What is there to know? Am I your manuscript?" He replied: "All that is written in the manuscript—all that I know; but I have no knowledge of you." Then somewhat anxiously he said to me: "Tell me about Ranjan! In what way do you love him?" I said, "Like the rudder under water loves the sail in the upper sky—the sail that is wafted by the song of the breeze and the rudder that is aroused by the dancing waves." Like a massive glutton of a boy he stared at me with a fixed gaze and listened to what I had to say silently. Suddenly, he startled me by exclaiming, "Would you lay down your life for him?" I said, "At once!" He seemed quite furious as he roared: "Never!" I replied, "Yes, I can!" "What would you gain by doing so?" he demanded. I said, "I have no idea at all." Then he spoke with a flustered voice: "Go away! You can leave my room now, go! Don't spoil my work." I could not understand what exactly he meant.

BISHU: He wants to understand the full significance of every word. That which he cannot fathom makes him sink in despair before he rises in fury.

NANDINI: O crazy brother of mine, don't you have any pity for him at all?

BISHU: The day the good Lord will take pity on his soul will be the day of his death!

NANDINI: No, no, you have no idea how wretched he is in his desire to live.

BISHU: You will find out later today what he means by "surviving"—I do not know whether you will be able to bear it.

NANDINI: Look there my crazy brother; look at that looming shadow. Certainly the Sardar must have been listening to us secretly.

BISHU: Here on all sides falls the Shadow of the Sardar, how can you avoid it? What do you make of the Sardar?

NANDINI: I have never seen such a piece of deadwood; he is like a bunch of canes cut from the cane groves. No leaves, no roots, no marrow within, starkly dry and spent!

BISHU: To rule over life he has forsaken his own, the pathetic man!

NANDINI: Shhh! Be silent, I say! He'll overhear you!

BISHU: But if he hears me shushing you it will make matters worse! He gets to hear this silencing as well, that's what worsens the calamity. When I am with the gold diggers I am very careful about what I say in the Sardar's presence. That is why they call me a fool and yet let me go on. They are averse to touching me, even with their rod. But my dear mad girl, before you my mind is emboldened; you make me feel that to be cautious is hateful!

NANDINI: No, no! You must not usher in danger here. There he is! The Sardar has arrived . . .

(Enter the SARDAR*)*

SARDAR: Hullo there, 69-U! You seem to be in love with everyone at large! Shouldn't you be a little more discreet?

BISHU: It began with you too. My discrimination brought things to a halt.

SARDAR: What are you chatting about?

BISHU: We are plotting how best to escape from your fortress?

SARDAR: You don't say! What daring! Aren't you scared to admit this?

BISHU: Sardar, in your mind, you have figured out everything haven't you? The caged bird always pecks at the bars with its beak—it doesn't display any fondness for them. It hardly matters whether this question is acknowledged or not.

409

SARDAR: We all know that there is no love lost between us! But it is obvious over the last few days that he isn't afraid to own it.

NANDINI: Sardarji, you had promised that you would recall Ranjan today. Aren't you going to keep your word?

SARDAR: You'll get to see him today.

NANDINI: I knew that. Still, since you give me hope may you prosper, Sardar! Here, take this garland of jasmine flowers.

BISHU: Oh no! You've ruined the garland! Why couldn't you keep it for Ranjan?

NANDINI: His garland is kept aside.

SARDAR: No doubt it is! Is it the one swaying on your neck? This garland of jasmine, a gift you bestowed on him with your hands, the welcome garland of red Roktokorobi blossoms, a gift of the heart. Good, very good! The gift of the hands should be dispatched immediately or it will wither; but for the heart's gift—the value increases the more you linger.

(Exit SARDAR*)*

NANDINI: *(Next to the window)* Can you hear me?

RAJA'S VOICE: Speak! What would you like to tell me?

NANDINI: Just this once, Raja, stand near the window!

RAJA'S VOICE: Here I am.

NANDINI: Let me come inside, I have much to talk about.

RAJA'S VOICE: Why do you keep making these vain requests? The time is not yet ripe. Who is there by your side? Is it Ranjan's twin by any chance?

BISHU: No, Raja! I happen to be Ranjan's other side, the side where light never descends. I am the pitch dark night of the moulting moon!

RAJA'S VOICE: Why does Nandini need you? Nandini, tell me—How is this man related to you?

NANDINI: He is my companion, he teaches me to sing. He is the one who has taught me to sing—

(Song)

"I love you!"
The flute plays this tune, close by and far away
Lilting the waves, the shore . . .

RAJA'S VOICE: This is your companion? If I take him away from your side now what will happen?

NANDINI: What has happened to the pitch of your voice? Stop! Have you no one to keep you company?

RAJA'S VOICE: Company? Can the afternoon sun have a companion?

NANDINI: Never mind! Well, let that be! O Mother! Goodness gracious! What's that in your palm?

RAJA'S VOICE: A dead frog!

NANDINI: What will you do with it?

RAJA'S VOICE: This very frog one day entered a crevice in a boulder. He remained sheltered within it mutely for three thousand years. I learnt from him the inner secret of surviving for so long a span of time. But he himself had no clue about the art of living. Today I thought I have had enough. I could not bear it any longer. So I destroyed the shelter of the rock—and rescued it from its predicament of unending mortality. Is that not cheerful news?

NANDINI: Today, your rock-hewn fortress will open up for me from all sides completely. I know I'll get to see Ranjan today!

RAJA'S VOICE: I'd like to see that reunion for myself!

NANDINI: You will get to see nothing through your glasses, from behind the screen.

RAJA'S VOICE: I will plant you both within my room and then take a look at you.

NANDINI: What good will come of that?

RAJA'S VOICE: That is what I want to find out!

NANDINI: I get scared when you talk of "knowing."

RAJA'S VOICE: Why is that?

NANDINI: It seems then you have no sympathy for that which can't be known by the mind or understood by the heart.

RAJA'S VOICE: Yes, I'm too scared to trust such a one lest I be cheated. You better go now; don't waste time. No, no, wait! Give me the bunch of Roktokorobi flowers dangling from your hair onto your cheeks.

NANDINI: What will you do with them?

RAJA'S VOICE: I see these flowers and meditate: these are my blood-illumined Saturnian flowers. At times I have the urge to snatch them from you and tear them apart! Then again I think, if Nandini crowns me with the red blossoms one day with her own hands, then . . .

NANDINI: What will happen then?

RAJA'S VOICE: Perhaps, then I will die more easily.

NANDINI: I know a man who loves Roktokorobi flowers. Keeping him in mind I have made ear-rings with them.

RAJA'S VOICE: In that case let me declare that they will be my Saturn, and will be his Saturn too.

NANDINI: What a thing to say! I better go.

RAJA'S VOICE: Where will you go?

NANDINI: I will go and sit before your fortress gate.

RAJA'S VOICE: Why?

NANDINI: When Ranjan comes by he will see that it is only for him that I have been waiting.

RAJA'S VOICE: But suppose I ground him into the dust so that he can't be recognized at all?

NANDINI: What is the matter with you today? Why are you scaring me needlessly?

RAJA'S VOICE: Scaring you needlessly! Don't you know that I can be terrifying?

NANDINI: Why this sudden outburst? That people fear you—is this only what you love to discover? In our village jatras, Srikantha plays the role of a demon. When he comes on to the stage he is very amused when kids tremble in fear of him. You too seem to be like him. Shall I tell you what I actually think? You won't be angry?

RAJA'S VOICE: Let me hear you.

NANDINI: The people here thrive by intimidating others. That is why they have been displaying you inside a screen enclosure in such a manner. Aren't you ashamed to be decked up as a macabre toy?

RAJA'S VOICE: What do you mean Nandini?

NANDINI: Those you have intimidated till now will be ashamed to be afraid one of these days. If my Ranjan was around he would have defied you openly before dying willfully . . . without the least fear!

RAJA'S VOICE: Your insolence is too much! I'd like to make you stand on the peak of a mountain and view for yourself all that I have completely destroyed so far. Afterwards . . .

NANDINI: Afterwards what . . . ?

RAJA'S VOICE: Afterwards will feature my final act of destruction. The way they crush pomegranate seeds between ten splayed fingers to extract the juice—thus will I take you between my two hands and . . . Go! Go . . . run away right now . . . at once!

413

NANDINI: I'd rather stand right here! Do what you can! Why do you roar in this beastly manner?

RAJA'S VOICE: I feel like showing you as clearly as I can how very cruel I am. Haven't you ever heard piercing tremors of pain issuing from my room?

NANDINI: Indeed I have. What were those screams about?

RAJA'S VOICE: I destroy the wiliness of the Lord of Creation. I intend to snatch away the world's treasures hidden underground! You hear the screams of those dispossessed souls! To steal the fire of a tree, the tree itself must be burnt down! Nandini, you too have fire inside you, glowing, crimson fire! One day I shall take it out of you through cremation by fire! Till then there is no deliverance!

NANDINI: Why are you cruel?

RAJA'S VOICE: I either acquire things for myself or annihilate them! Whatever I cannot possess I cannot pity. Even in destroying him there is an acute sense of possession!

NANDINI: What are you doing? Why do you extend your clenched fist?

RAJA'S VOICE: All right, I am withdrawing my hands. Now run, like the pigeon flies when the eagle's shadow looms circling overhead.

NANDINI: All right, I'll take my leave. I'll anger you no further.

RAJA'S VOICE: Hear me! Listen! Come back to me! Nandini, Nandini!

NANDINI: Well, tell me.

RAJA'S VOICE: On one side of your face and in your eyes are life's Passion-Play! Beyond, cascades your black hair, death's tranquil waterfall. The other day came the bliss of death by drowning, when I plunged these, my pair of hands, into that jet-black stream. I never imagined death would be so sweet. I still yearn to sleep with my face buried under those abundant black tresses. You have no idea how weary I am.

NANDINI: Don't you ever fall asleep?

RAJA'S VOICE: Sleep is fearful.

NANDINI: Let me sing for you the rest of my song—

(Song)

I love, I love
With this tune wafting near, afar, in water, on land
The flute plays on,
The sky sounds in the midst of someone's heart
A note of pain;
The horizon overflows with tears
Of her kohl dark eyes!

RAJA'S VOICE: That's enough! Enough! Stop! Sing no more!

NANDINI: *(Continues singing)*

By the seashore that tune,
Unshackles bonds,
A loud lamentation ascends;
That tune plays on the mind
Unaccountably,
Words from long forgotten songs,

Tears and laughter
From days gone by.

NANDINI: Look, my mad brother, he dropped that dead frog and stole away! He seems too scared to listen to songs.

BISHU: The aged frog in his heart, surviving because it has come into contact with myriad melodies, wishes for death on hearing music. That is the cause of his fear. My crazy sister, today I see a glow on your face. Won't you tell me what idea has dawned in your mind?

NANDINI: What has struck me is that this very day Ranjan will surely arrive!

BISHU: Surely that news must have come from some source?

NANDINI: Well, listen! I'll tell you how! Every day a blue jay bird perches on the branch of the pomegranate tree next to my window sill. At dusk I bow to the North Star and pray for a single feather from that bird to blow into my room as an omen of my Ranjan's arrival.

BISHU: I see! And I also see the saffron dot you have put on your forehead today.

NANDINI: When I meet him I will place this feather on his crown.

BISHU: Folks say the Blue Jay's feather is an omen of victorious journeys!

NANDINI: Ranjan's victorious march is through the core of my soul!

BISHU: My crazy girl! Let me proceed on my rounds!

NANDINI: No, today I won't allow you to work!

BISHU: Then tell me: what should I do!

NANDINI: Just keep singing!

BISHU: What song should I sing?

NANDINI: The song of the road-watch!

(Song)

For ages he must have desired me.
Is he waiting for me by the wayside?
Today why do I recall the time when I had a glimpse of him
In dusk's opacity.
It must be him there, sitting on my way.
Today the moon will be welcomed by the melody of light,
The shadow on Night's face will dissolve at once
In the glow of the blanched night!
We'll see each other in a flash
When every veil will drop away!
And I'll see him waiting by my pathway.

NANDINI: O crazy one! Whenever you break into song, I feel an immense indebtedness to you; I feel I've given you nothing at all!

BISHU: The "nothing" that you have given me I'll cherish and wear on my forehead and depart. I will not sell my songs for a pittance! Now where will you go?

NANDINI: To the roadside where Ranjan will show up. Sitting there, waiting, I'll listen to your songs once again.

(Exit together)
(Enter FIRST SARDAR *and the* MOROL*)*[2]

FIRST SARDAR: No way, we can't afford to allow Ranjan to come to this neighborhood.

MOROL: It was to keep him at a distance that I sent him to dig the tunnels of Vajragar.

FIRST SARDAR: So what happened finally?

MOROL: We couldn't achieve anything. He said, "I am not in the habit of working under compulsion!"

FIRST SARDAR: What's wrong with trying to do so?

MOROL: We did try. We did. The chief headman came with the police. The man is utterly without any fear. No sooner do our voices ring with stern authority then he bursts out into peals of laughter! Whenever we question him he replies: "High seriousness is the mask of the fool! So I have come to get rid of it!"

FIRST SARDAR: Why didn't you release him amidst the crowd in the tunnel?

MOROL: I did. I thought he would surely conform under pressure. But the opposite happened! The excavators too felt that the pressure on them had been lifted. He worked them into a frenzy, declaring, "Today we shall do the excavation-dance!"

FIRST SARDAR: The Excavation Dance? Whatever on earth is that?

MOROL: Ranjan began to sing. They cried out: "Where can we find a drum?" He replied: "If we don't have drums we can use our spades!" The spades, I tell you, marked every beat! What a game of throwing and catching we had with the golden balls! The Chief Inspector himself remarked aloud: "What kind of work is that?" Ranjan replied: "I have undone the knots of work; we no longer have to drag the ropes ourselves; they will dance along on their own!"

FIRST SARDAR: The man is nuts, for sure!

MOROL: Raving mad! I gave the order, "Grip your spade!" He replied, "There will be much more work done if you fetch me a sarangi!"

FIRST SARDAR: You all took him to Vajragar. How did he come down to Kubergar?

MOROL: How do I know, your lordship! He was in chains! A few moments later I saw that he had slipped out somehow and come away!

Somehow his body cannot be fastened to anything! And in the twinkling of an eye he can put on a new costume. Fantastic are his powers! If he remains here for a few more days, even the excavators won't have their shackles on.

FIRST SARDAR: Hey! Isn't that Ranjan singing down the road? He has got himself a broken sarangi! Imagine his audacity!—not even bothering to hide!

MOROL: You said it! When could he have broken through his prison walls to escape? He's into magic!

FIRST SARDAR: Now go! Catch him right away! In no way should he be able to meet Nandini in this neighborhood.

MOROL: So rapidly has his following grown! Soon we all will be dancing to his tune!

(Enter THIRD SARDAR*)*

FIRST SARDAR: Where are you going?

THIRD SARDAR: I am going to tie up Ranjan!

FIRST SARDAR: Why you? Where is the Second Sardar?

THIRD SARDAR: On meeting Ranjan, he was so amused he was reluctant even to touch him. Says he, his very smile reveals how strange us Sardars are turning out to be.

FIRST SARDAR: Listen! You need not tie him up. Just have him sent to the Raja's chamber.

THIRD SARDAR: But he pays little heed to the Raja's summons.

FIRST SARDAR: Go inform him that the Raja has made his Nandini his serving woman.

THIRD SARDAR: But if the Raja . . .

FIRST SARDAR: You needn't worry in the least. Let's go! I myself will come along.

(All exit)
(Enter PROFESSOR *and* CLASSICIST*)*

CLASSICIST: Can you tell me what is that cyclonic storm going on within that is creating such commotion?

PROFESSOR: The Raja, it appears, is mad at himself. So he is smashing up some of his own handiwork.

CLASSICIST: It seems that gigantic pillars are crashing down noisily there.

PROFESSOR: Spread across the entire base of that mountain there was a lake into which the waters from the Sankhini River used to collect. One day the rocky promontory on its left flank tilted to one side. The dammed up water, like a madman's exuberant laughter, gushed out in a rush. For quite some time it seems, from the Raja's appearance, that the barricade wall around his treasured reservoir has been damaged, the base appears to be crumbling . . .

CLASSICIST: Physicist, what place have you brought me to? And what do you really want me to do, now that you made me come here?

PROFESSOR: He wants to possess all the knowledge the world has to offer! He has almost drawn out all I know of the physical sciences. At times he bursts out in anger to exclaim: "Your kind of knowledge merely breaks down one wall with a bungling tool to expose another one behind it! But where is the sanctum sanctorum of the spirits' Central Man?" It struck me, I said to myself: let's distract him for some days with discourses concerning antiquity. My own satchel has been emptied out of its contents. Now let the pick-pocketing of antique resources follow! Hello! Can you see who goes there?

CLASSICIST: A mere girl clothed in the color of paddy grain!

PROFESSOR: That's our Nandini who has drawn into her being all that is delightful in the world! In Jokkhopuri are sardars, headmen, excavators, and pundits like me; there are constables, executioners, and cremators—all living quite amicably with each other. But she doesn't quite meld with them though the market's clamor seeps in from every side. She is like a tuned tambura. On some days the breeze in the wake of her passage blows away my speculations on physics! My attention then takes wing through the gaps she has created with a—whoosh!—like a bird taking off in the wilds!

CLASSICIST: What are you saying, man! Do your tempered bones get rattled by such casual knocks?

PROFESSOR: When the desire to survive overtakes the desire for knowledge the inclination to escape from school cannot be contained.

CLASSICIST: Now tell me please—where shall I get to see your Raja?

PROFESSOR: Seeing him is out of the question! You may get to know each other through the screen there.

CLASSICIST: Really! Through that screen?

PROFESSOR: What else do you expect? You aren't going to be in the kind of spicy tête-à-tête that features mysterious veiled ladies! It is going to be a more down-to-earth conversation. It is quite likely that the cows in his shed produce butter directly instead of milk!

CLASSICIST: To stop talking rubbish and to extract the truth—that is the pundit's business.

PROFESSOR: But not the Lord's! He has created the real thing to prop up bogus ones! He pays his respects to the fruit's kernel; he offers his love to the flesh of the fruit.

CLASSICIST: Nowadays I can see your physics sparked off by the sight of something the color of a paddy sheaf! But tell me Professor, how can you stand that Raja of yours?

PROFESSOR: Shall I tell the truth? I actually love him a lot!

CLASSICIST: What are you saying, man!

PROFESSOR: You have no idea—he is so awesome that even his faults can't spoil him!

(Enter FIRST SARDAR*)*

FIRST SARDAR: Hey, Physicist! So you have chosen your man carefully, have you? Listening to the details of his expertise has sent the Raja into a tizzy!

PROFESSOR: In what way?

FIRST SARDAR: The Raja says there's nothing that is old. It is the present that keeps moving ever forward.

CLASSICIST: But if the past doesn't exist, does anything else? If the rear is missing can the front prevail?

FIRST SARDAR: The Raja believes that eternity proceeds by placing the new in the forefront. Suppressing that idea, the pundit claims that eternity bears the past on its shoulders.

PROFESSOR: The Raja seems to measure in the silhouette of Nandini's vivacity the fleeting mirage of the New which he sees in flashes but cannot grasp. And he takes out his frustration . . . on my Physics!

*(*NANDINI *enters)*

NANDINI: Sardar! Sardar! What's going on! Who are these people?

FIRST SARDAR: What is it Nandini? I will wear your Jasmine garland in the witching hour of the night. Perhaps the garland will become me as well when two-thirds of my body mingles with the darkness.

NANDINI: Just look! What a fearsome spectacle! Have the gates of the underworld been flung wide open? Who are those marching ahead with the sentries? See, they are rushing out from the private exit door of the Raja's palace!

FIRST SARDAR: We call them the Raja's leftover dishes!

NANDINI: What do you mean?

FIRST SARDAR: You too will understand everything one of these days. But let that be for now.

NANDINI: But what are these visages? Are they human? Are they of flesh and marrow, mind and soul?

FIRST SARDAR: Perhaps not.

NANDINI: Did those things ever exist?

FIRST SARDAR: Perhaps they did.

NANDINI: Where has it all vanished?

FIRST SARDAR: Hey, Physicist! Try explaining it all; I must go now!

(*Exit* SARDAR)

NANDINI: What's going on? I can see familiar faces amidst those shadows. There, I am sure, is our Anup and Upamanyu. Professor, they belong to our neighboring village. Both brothers are as tall as they are strong. They are known by all as the "Tal and Tamal," the tall tree duo. On the fourteenth day of the month they would take part in the long-boat race. O God! Let me perish! Who has brought them to this miserable state? There, I can see Shoklu—he used to be the first to be awarded the garland for fencing. (*Calling out plaintively*) Anuuuuup! Shokluuuu! Turn your eyes this way! This is me, your own Nandini! Nandini from Ishanipara! Why don't you look up? Your heads have been bowed forever! What! Isn't that Kanku! Alas! Alas! Even a boy like him has been chewed up like a frond of sugar-cane and flung aside! He was too shy a person. He used to sit by himself on the shallow banks of the river where I used to go to fetch water. He used to pretend that he had come there to pluck reed stalks for the arrows he was making. My girlish teasing caused him so much pain then. O Kanku please look at me for once! Alas, he whose blood would be dancing at my slightest whisper does not even respond to my call! It's all gone! The lamps of our village are blotted out! Professor, the iron is worn out and black rust is all that remains. O has all this come to be?

PROFESSOR: Nandini, your eyes move only in the directions of ash heaps this day. For once, look at the flame. You'll see its flickering tongue!

423

NANDINI: I can't follow you?

PROFESSOR: You have seen the Raja, haven't you? I believe you were mesmerized by him.

NANDINI: That's quite true. He looks awesome.

PROFESSOR: The "awesomeness" being to his credit, the "grotesque" is his debit. The inferior part continues to become ash; and that eminent one . . . the burning flame! This is the crux of greatness!

NANDINI: Ah! But that is the principle of the demonic.

PROFESSOR: To be furious about any principle would be wrong. A principle by itself is neither good nor bad—whatever will be will be. If you oppose that view you are opposing being itself.

NANDINI: If this happens to be the road towards the evolution of man then I certainly don't want to evolve at all! I will depart with these shadows, please show me the path.

PROFESSOR: When the time comes for showing the path, these people will do the needful. No point in bothering about paths before then. Look, the classicist has slipped away a long time back believing that survival depends on flight. He will see as he goes a little distance, that the wire-mesh fencing starting from here is linked from post to post for miles. Nandini; you are angry; the bunch of red Roktokorobi flowers upon your cheeks are like the sunset clouds of apocalypse!

NANDINI: *(Pushing aside the window)* Listen, O listen!

PROFESSOR: Who are you calling?

NANDINI: Your king . . . who is hidden behind the haze of the screen.

PROFESSOR: The door of the inner chamber has already closed. He won't hear your cries.

NANDINI: O crazy Bishu! My dear mad brother!

PROFESSOR: Why are you calling him?

NANDINI: He has not got back still! I can't help being afraid for him!

PROFESSOR: I saw you with him only a while ago.

NANDINI: The Sardar explained that he had been summoned to identify Ranjan. I was keen on accompanying him. They didn't approve— hush! What is that soul-rending cry?

PROFESSOR: It is likely that of the wrestler.

NANDINI: Who's he?

PROFESSOR: He is the world renowned Gajju whose brother Bhajan chose to dare the Raja to a wrestling bout. Later we couldn't even trace a torn thread of his loin-cloth anywhere. The infuriated Gajju got back to the arena with his challenge. I had advised him at the outset: "If you care to dig tunnels in this kingdom you will barely survive for a few days. But if you intend to display heroic stuff he won't tolerate you for a single moment. This is a very cruel land!"

NANDINI: Can they at all remain good, if day and night they contrive to capture men with their traps?

PROFESSOR: The question of "goodness" is irrelevant here; the only question here is that of staying put! The idea of "staying" on has been inflated so fearfully that if they don't pressurize lakhs of people who else would bear their burden? Thus the net goes on widening, because they are *compelled* to remain.

NANDINI: Compelled? If death is the condition needed to retain human dignity, then what is the problem in that?

PROFESSOR: Once more that furious response? The crescendo of bright Roktokorobi flowers! How charming is your indignation! But the truth will always remain the truth! If declaring that "death is the condition for existence" gives you solace, then do say it by all means! But only they will remain who are able to assert that to *remain* one has to kill! You all protest that this leads to the death of humanism. But you forget in your indignation that this precisely is what constitutes humanism! Tigers do not grow up by devouring their own kind! It is only humans who gorge on fellow humans and become bloated that way.

(Enter the WRESTLER*)*

NANDINI: Oh, no! Look there, see how he approaches, reeling. O wrestler, come here and lie down. Professor, why don't you examine where he has been hurt?

PROFESSOR: You cannot possibly see his scars from outside.

WRESTLER: O merciful Lord, may I be strong once in my life, just for a single more day!

PROFESSOR: What for, man?

WRESTLER: Just to wrench that Sardar's neck!

PROFESSOR: What has he done to you?

WRESTLER: It is he who has caused the whole mess. I've never wanted to fight. Now he is telling everyone that I am the one to blame.

PROFESSOR: Why, what is his stake in all this?

WRESTLER: Only when they will render the world impotent will they rest in peace! O Hari! Merciful One! If only one day . . . I could pluck out his eyes and rip out his tongue!

NANDINI: How do you feel now, O wrestler!

WRESTLER: I feel . . . my insides have turned hollow. What monsters are these people, knowing magic . . . sucking out not merely one's strength but the very substance of one's hopes! If ever I get the chance, O Hari! Ah! If only once . . . with your mercy . . . what is there that cannot be achieved! If only once I could sink my teeth into the Sardar's chest!

NANDINI: Professor! Please hold on to him! Let us take him to your house.

PROFESSOR: I cannot dare to do that Nandini! It would be seen as an offence against the laws of the land!

NANDINI: And letting the man die wouldn't be considered an offence?

PROFESSOR: When there is no one to punish an offence, the act can be a sinful one and still not be seen as an offence. Nandini, you mustn't get involved in all these things. Where the tree spreads its roots under the earth to absorb moisture, there it does not induce its flowers to bloom. Flowers only blossom on the branches above, under the open sky! O Roktokorobi! Do not try to enquire into the state of affairs of our world below the nether earth! We, of course, keep eagerly gazing to see you swaying in the breeze above—Ah! There's the Sardar! Let me depart! He cannot bear the sight of me talking to you!

NANDINI: Why is he that angry with me?

PROFESSOR: I can merely guess. You have inwardly plucked his mind's strings somehow! The more you fail to match the scales, the discord in equal measure screams its fury.

(Exit TEACHER*)*
(Enter FIRST SARDAR*)*

NANDINI: Sardar!

FIRST SARDAR: Nandini, seeing the garland of jasmine flowers that you gave me in my room, Gosain-ji's eyes nearly popped out! Ah! Here he is in person! Receive my homage! O Lord! That garland over there was given to me by Nandini herself!

(Enter GOSAIN*)*

GOSAIN: Oh, yes! The pure heart's offerings, God's own pure jasmine flower! It has not lost its purity even after falling into the hands of such a worldly man. This gives hope in the strength of purity and makes one look out for the redemption of the sinner!

NANDINI: Gosain-ji, do something about this man. What little does he have left of his life?

GOSAIN: Taking all things into account the extent to which he needs to live . . . I am sure our Sardar will go on living for just that long. But, my student, this discussion appears somewhat improper on your lips and we don't quite appreciate it.

NANDINI: In this kingdom is there a question of the degree to which someone is kept alive?

GOSAIN: But of course! The worldly life is, after all, bound within limits. Therefore only after understanding the *pros* and *cons,* can it be apportioned. God has bestowed a tremendous responsibility on the people of our class; and if we are to discharge it we must be given the right to ascertain life's value. They can afford to live minimally because we have the burden of keeping them alive. Is that compensation for them anything less?

NANDINI: Gosain-ji, what heavy burden has God made you bear for the welfare of those people?

GOSAIN: He, whose soul is not bound by limits, does not need to quarrel about his share with anybody. We Gosains have come to show them that path of salvation. Their contentment in this regard will sustain our friendship toward them.

NANDINI: In that case, will this man remain sprawled here half-dead, trying to hold on to his limited life?

GOSAIN: Why should he remain in this sprawled condition? What do you say Sardar?

FIRST SARDAR: You are quite right! Why should we allow him to lie down in this manner! From now on he won't need to move on his own! Our strength will suffice to move him about! Hoy! Gajju!

WRESTLER: What master?

GOSAIN: O Blessed Hari! Hari! Within this while, already the voice appears to have somewhat mellowed down. It seems that he can be drawn into our band of kirtan singers.

SARDAR: You can proceed to your quarters in the Haw-Khaw section of the headman's building.

NANDINI: What kind of an idea is that? How could he possibly move?

FIRST SARDAR: Look here Nandini! Our *business* is to make people move. We know very well that whenever a man stumbles and falls clumsily on his face to bite the dust, with a shove he can be made to go a little further on! Now, proceed, Gajju!

WRESTLER: Sir, as you command!

NANDINI: Wrestler, I too am off to the Headman's house. There will be nobody there to take care of you.

WRESTLER: No, no! Let things be, the Sardar will be furious!

NANDINI: I am not scared of the Sardar's temper!

WRESTLER: But I am. By your leave, please don't add to my troubles!

(Exit WRESTLER*)*

NANDINI: Sardar! Do not leave before telling me where you have taken our mad Bishu!

FIRST SARDAR: Who am I to take anyone away? The wind drives away the clouds. If you consider that a fault, find out who has driven the wind forward!

NANDINI: Oh, what a wretched country is this? You all are not human, and those you drive away are also not human? You are the wind, they are the clouds. Gosain, surely you know where my mad Bishu is!

GOSAIN: Of course I do, I know, that wherever he may be, everything is for the good!

NANDINI: For whose good do you mean?

GOSAIN: That is something you won't be able to figure out—Ah! Let it be! Let it be! That is my prayer-bead. Oh, no! Now it's torn! Listen Sardar, this girl you have . . .

SARDAR: Who knows how she was able to find a crevice within our laws and managed to settle there . . . Our king himself . . .

GOSAIN: Oh my goodness! Now she will tear my holy body-wrap as well! I'm doomed! I must take your leave . . .

(Exit GOSAIN*)*

NANDINI: Sardar, you'll have to tell us where you have taken away mad Bishu!

FIRST SARDAR: He has been summoned to a Court of Law. That's all that I can tell you. Let me be, I have nothing more to say.

NANDINI: Aren't you afraid of me because of my sex? Lord Indra hurls his thunderbolts through the glistening arms of lightning! The lightning that I have brought along will smash to the dust your authority's golden spires!

FIRST SARDAR: Well, in that case let me tell you the truth before I go: you are the cause of Bishu's troubles.

NANDINI: I!

FIRST SARDAR: Yes, you! Till now he was burrowing noiselessly under the earth like a worm. It was you who taught him to spread out his wings of death, O fiery thunderbolt of Lord Indra! You will entice many and only then will the final squaring off take place between the two of us! That time is not far away.

NANDINI: So be it. But one word before you go. Will you allow Ranjan to see me?

FIRST SARDAR: Absolutely not!

NANDINI: Absolutely not! I'll see how you can stop me! My union with him will take place for sure, will certainly happen this very day! Let me *assure* you of that!

(*Exit* SARDAR)

NANDINI: (*Knocking fiercely on the window*) Listen to me! Listen, O Raja! Where is your Court of Law? I am going to smash the exclusive haven of your screen. Oh! Who is that? It appears to be Kishore! Do tell me . . . do you know where our Bishu is?

(*Enter* KISHORE)

KISHORE: Yes, Nandini! You'll meet him right here; just keep a hold over yourself! I have no idea why the head guard took pity on me after scrutinizing my face—he agreed to take Bishu down this path at my request.

NANDINI: Head guard? In that case is it . . . ?

KISHORE: Yes, that's right! Here they come!

NANDINI: What is this? Your fists in handcuffs! My mad brother, where are they taking you in this manner?

(*Enter guards, escorting* BISHU)

BISHU: There's no fear! Nothing to fear at all! My crazy girl, I am free at last!

NANDINI: I don't understand; what do you mean?

BISHU: When I used to tread step by step in fear, measuring pitfalls ahead with bated breath, I was free in a way. But such shackled freedom no longer exits.

NANDINI: What wrong have you done that they should lead you away chained like this?

BISHU: After a long time I spoke the truth today.

NANDINI: What is wrong with that?

BISHU: Nothing at all.

NANDINI: Then why have they bound you like this!

BISHU: So what is the harm in that? I have gained freedom through the truth. This manacle bears true witness.

NANDINI: They are dragging you down the road, tethered like a beast—don't they feel any shame on their part? It's disgusting! They are supposed to be human after all!

BISHU: The point is, there lives a huge monster within them! Their heads are not bowed by the insult inflicted. The tail of the beast inside wags as it swells!

NANDINI: Alas, my mad brother! Have they so cruelly whipped you? What scars are these on your body?

BISHU: They thrashed me with the whip they use to beat their dogs! The rope with which their whip is made also provides the strings for the holy prayer beads of Gosain-ji! He quite forgets that when he chants the name of the Lord. But only the Lord knows what's happening around here lately!

NANDINI: Let them tie me up in the same way as you and take me away as well, my dearest brother! If I too do not receive the same whipping that you have known, from this day, may my mouth forfeit the taste of food!

KISHORE: Bishu, if I try they will surely let me replace you. Please get the consent for that.

BISHU: This idea of yours is quite insane!

KISHORE: Their flogging won't bother me, I am young, I will be able to bear it cheerfully!

NANDINI: Ah, no Kishore! Do not say such things!

KISHORE: Nandini, I have skipped my work—they have sensed that. Their bloodhounds are on my trail. This punishment will save me from their insults.

BISHU: No Kishore! You cannot afford to be caught now! A risky mission yet remains! Ranjan has just arrived here. You must help him to get out any which way you can. But it won't be easy.

KISHORE: Nandini, in that case, I shall say goodbye. If I happen to meet Ranjan—shall I convey any message of yours to him?

NANDINI: No, nothing at all! If you hand him this bunch of Roktokorobi flowers, all that I have to say will be conveyed to him!

(*Exit* KISHORE)

BISHU: May your union with Ranjan take place on this occasion!

NANDINI: That union will not make me content. I shall never be able to forget the fact that I let you depart empty-handed. And that lad there, Kishore, whatever did he get from me?

BISHU: The fire that you have ignited in his mind has illumined the entire treasure within his heart! What else can one expect? Do remember—you have to stick that blue jay's feather in Ranjan's crown?

NANDINI: Here it is in the folds of my sari.

BISHU: My crazy sister! Do you hear that distant song of harvesting?

NANDINI: Yes I can hear . . . and my very heart cries out!

432

BISHU: The passion-play of the fields is now done with! The plantation's owner bears his harvest home. Let's go, sentry, we have no more time at hand . . .

(Song)

Reap this final harvest, bind it in sheaves,
What need not be borne away, let it replenish earth!

433

(Enter DOCTOR *and* FIRST SARDAR*)*

DOCTOR: I had a look. The king is out of sorts. This disease is not outside but in the mind.

FIRST SARDAR: What is the means of healing?

DOCTOR: A massive jolt! Either an encounter with another kingdom or from an uprising incited by his own subjects!

FIRST SARDAR: In other words he will afflict himself if he is obstructed from afflicting others?

DOCTOR: They are of the elite, grown up babies playing games. When they have had enough of one game they will smash their toys if another game is not provided them at once. But be prepared Sardar. Not much time is left!

FIRST SARDAR: Having seen the signs I have already set things at readiness. But alas! What grief! The way our golden city had prospered is unprecedented. And just at this point . . . All right—go ahead while I think matters over.

(Exit DOCTOR*)*
(Enter MOROL*)*

MOROL: Sardar, my Lord, did you summon me? I am the Morol and I am in charge of sector Y.

FIRST SARDAR: Aren't you 321?

MOROL: The Master has such a superb memory! He has not forgotten a miserable fellow like me!

FIRST SARDAR: My wife is coming from the village. The post will be changed when it crosses your neighborhood. You must fetch her promptly here.

MOROL: An epidemic among cows is ravaging our neighborhood. Bullocks for pulling carts have become scarce. It hardly matters though! We can recruit the excavators for the purpose.

FIRST SARDAR: You know your destination don't you—the garden-estates, venue of the feast of the Sardars?

MOROL: I am going there, but I'd like to say something before I go. Please listen. Here is 69-U who is better known as Bishu, the crazy one. The time has come to cure him of his madness!

FIRST SARDAR: Why? Does he disturb your peace?

MOROL: No, not so much in his speech as in his gestures and expressions!

FIRST SARDAR: No need to worry any more. Do you understand?

MOROL: Really? That's great! One more thing—here is 47-F who shacks up a bit too much with 69-U.

FIRST SARDAR: That has, indeed, come to my notice.

MOROL: Sir, your aim is right on the dot! Still, one has to keep an eye in every direction! One or two may even give us the slip! Take for instance our 95—in terms of village kinship ties we are in-laws from the father's side. He is even ready to make clogs from his own ribs for the sweeper of the Sardar maharaja. Seeing such devotion makes his better half hang her head in shame. Yet till today . . .

FIRST SARDAR: His name has featured in the Grand Register.

MOROL: Anyway, his long and loyal service has been vindicated at last. The news must be conveyed to him gently for he is epileptic. Who knows if suddenly—

FIRST SARDAR: All right, we'll see about that. You must now go at once!

MOROL: I must tell you about one more person—though he is my own brother-in-law. When his mother passed away, my wife reared him with her own hands . . . still when loyalty to his lord—

FIRST SARDAR: We'll talk about him tomorrow. You better scamper off now!

MOROL: Here arrives the Second Sardar! Please tell him a couple of things on my behalf. He does not see me very positively. I suspect that when 69-U used to frequent the homes of our bosses, it was then that he took my name to . . .

FIRST SARDAR: No, no I've never heard him mentioning your name in any instance. . . .

MOROL: That's his very cleverness! To destroy an eminent man you only have to stifle his name. It is not proper to negotiate in devious whispers. That is what our 33 tends to do. I can see he has no other business. Whenever he feels like it he moves in and out of the officer's quarters. I fear the calumnies he may be spreading about us. However, if the truth about his own household . . .

FIRST SARDAR: There's no more time today, go at once!

MOROL: Then, I bow to you. One more point—that neighborhood's number 88 entered service at a salary of 30 tanka only. Though merely two years have passed he earns no less than a thousand or fifteen hundred a month now. The Masters have innocent minds; like gods they are overcome by empty invocations. On seeing those in full prostration before them—

FIRST SARDAR: Yes, yes, we'll talk about that tomorrow . . .

MOROL: I too possess the quality of mercy; I am not devising ways of cutting his earnings. But do think about whether placing him in the treasury is a wise thing or not! Our Bishu-da knows him inside out. He can recall him—

FIRST SARDAR: I will have him summoned today. You may go now!

MOROL: Master, my third son has come of age. He was here to pay his respects. For three days he walked up and down hoping to meet you, but not obtaining an audience, he has gone back. His mind is deeply disturbed. My daughter-in-law has prepared an offering of mashed pumpkin for the master with her own hands . . .

FIRST SARDAR: All right, ask him to come day after tomorrow—he will have the desired audience.

(*Exit* MOROL)
(*Enter* SECOND SARDAR)

SECOND SARDAR: I have bid goodbye to the nautch girls and the musical accompanists at the garden itself.

FIRST SARDAR: And how far . . . is that thing about Ranjan?

SECOND SARDAR: I can't really tackle this job! The Third Sardar has himself volunteered for this chore. By now he must have . . .

FIRST SARDAR: Has the Raja . . . ?

SECOND SARDAR: The Raja could not have done it. Ten people were made to mix with him . . . But I do not think it is right to cheat him this way.

FIRST SARDAR: It is out of that very sense of duty towards him that we must deceive the Raja and stall him too. That is my lookout. But this time that girl must be immediately . . .

SECOND SARDAR: No, no! Don't raise these issues with me! The Morol in charge is a responsible person and can't be intimidated.

FIRST SARDAR: Does Kenaram Gosain know about Ranjan's case?

SECOND SARDAR: He has an inkling of the whole thing, but has no desire for the details.

FIRST SARDAR: Why?

SECOND SARDAR: Later, the phrase "I don't know!" may not be a closed option of speech!

FIRST SARDAR: And even if it is?

SECOND SARDAR: Don't you understand? We have only one face—that of the sardars! But he is presented on one side as the Gosain, and on the other as the Sardar. If the holy cloth gets twisted a little it turns into a noose! So the ways of the Sardar have to be nurtured stealthily to enable one to chant the holy mantra undisturbed.

FIRST SARDAR: Could he have dispensed with the chanting!

SECOND SARDAR: But the point is, his mind is God fearing, whatever his passions! That is why chanting lucidly and bossing around obscurely keeps him very happy. Because he is around, our God is comfortable, his blemish has been concealed; otherwise he wouldn't have appeared so presentable at all.

FIRST SARDAR: Second Sardar, I have noticed that your blood too does not quite match with that of the Sardars!

SECOND SARDAR: When the blood dries up no worries will remain—still, that hope exists. But till this day I cannot bear the presence of your # 321. When you have to embrace in the midst of a gathering the very person whom you would be disgusted to touch with a kitchen-pincer at arms length, then even bathing in the holy waters of pilgrimage won't give one a sense of purity. Ah, there comes Nandini!

FIRST SARDAR: Come along, Second Sardar!

SECOND SARDAR: Why? What are you so anxious about?

FIRST SARDAR: I cannot trust you! I am aware that your eyes have been smitten by Nandini!

SECOND SARDAR: But you don't realize that even in your eyes the blood of duty seems to have blended with the blood-red Roktokorobi flower—in that, an awesome redness has thus emerged!

438

FIRST SARDAR: Perhaps that is the case. The mind does not know itself. Now come along with me!

(They exit)

Scene Seven

(Enter NANDINI*)*

NANDINI: Today's twilight takes on the hue of the vermilion clouds! Is that the color of our reunion? It appears the vermilion in my hair's parting has become splayed across the sky. *(Banging on the window.)* Hear me! O hear me! I will lie here night and day as long as you do not listen to me!

(Enter GOSAIN*)*

GOSAIN: Whom are you waking up?

NANDINI: That python of yours that swallows men on the sly!

GOSAIN: Good grief! When God destroys us puny beings he does so by making our small mouths flaunt big words! Look Nandini, I am sure you know I think about your blessedness constantly.

NANDINI: But that will hardly ensure my blessedness!

GOSAIN: Come to my temple sanctorum, let me chant for you the holy name.

NANDINI: What will I do with just the name?

GOSAIN: Your mind will gain peace.

NANDINI: If I achieve such peace, let shame, utter shame be my lot! I will go on waiting beside this doorway.

GOSAIN: Does your belief in man exceed your belief in God?

NANDINI: That flagpole God of yours will never mellow down! But will the man beyond the screen be forever bound by the wire-mesh? Be gone! Be gone! Go! Be gone! It is your trade to mystify with names those unfortunate souls you have torn asunder.

439

    (Exit GOSAIN*)*
    (Enter PHAGULAL *and* CHANDRA*)*

PHAGU: Bishu accompanied you here, didn't he? Where is he now?

NANDINI: He has been arrested by them and taken away.

CHANDRA: Wretched demoness! It is you who have snared him for them! You are their spy!

NANDINI: How could you even say such a thing?

CHANDRA: What is your business here then? All you do is flit around, enticing the minds of one and all.

PHAGU: Here everyone suspects each other! Yet I have always kept my belief in you. In my mind's eye you have . . . But let that be! Today . . . something is happening that is disturbingly against the grain!

NANDINI: Perhaps. It was his accompanying me that got him into trouble. With you all he was safe. He said so himself.

CHANDRA: Then why did you have to entice him here, you wretched woman?

NANDINI: Because he called out—because it was freedom he wanted!

CHANDRA: Ah! Wonderful indeed is the freedom you have presented him!

NANDINI: I could not follow all that he wanted to say, Chandra. What-ever made him cry out that liberty only comes after descending into deepest calamity? Phagulal, how do you expect me to save the man who wants to be free from the stern measures of security?

CHANDRA: I cannot understand all this talk! If you cannot get him back right here you will die, you will! I have not lost my bearings gazing upon that "beautiful" face of yours!

PHAGU: Chandra, what's the point of bickering? Let us get together a group from the artisans of the neighborhood. We shall smash the prisons into rubble!

NANDINI: I'd like to accompany you all.

PHAGU: Whatever for?

NANDINI: I want to destroy as well!

CHANDRA: Oh, my, my! Much destruction have you accomplished al-ready, sultry siren! There's nothing more to be done!

(Enter GOKUL*)*

GOKUL: Before anybody else, that witch there must be burnt to death!

CHANDRA: Mere death? That'll hardly be punishment enough for her! You must squash the beauty that she wields in her rounds of destruction! Weed it out as grass is weeded with a spade!

GOKUL: I can do just that! Once you see this Hammer Dance that I can do . . .

PHAGU: Don't you dare! If any one even touches her then . . .

NANDINI: Phagulal, stop—desist! He is a coward! He fears me! So he wants to put me to death! I am not afraid of his blows! Let the coward do his worst!

GOKUL: Phagulal, you have not attained enlightenment yet. You know the Sardar as your chief antagonist. Be that as it may, I bow to the plain enemy who identifies himself. But that honey-tongued, exquisite beauty of yours . . .

NANDINI: It's like the soil under one's soles paying homage to the shoe!

PHAGULAL: Gokul, the time has now arrived when you can display your virility. But not in front of a girl. You can come with me.

441

   (Exit PHAGULAL, CHANDRA *and* GOKUL*)*
   (Enter a band of people)

NANDINI: O Listen, you all there! Where are you heading?

1ST PERSON: We bear offerings for the flag-ritual ceremony.

NANDINI: Have you met Ranjan?

2ND PERSON: Five days ago I did get a glimpse of him, once. But that was all. You could ask those people there. They may be able to say something.

NANDINI: Who are they?

3RD PERSON: They are carrying wine for the Sardar's party.

   (Exit)
   (Enter another group)

NANDINI: O you folks with red turbans—have you seen Ranjan?

1ST PERSON: I saw him the other night in Sambhu Morol's house.

NANDINI: Where is he now?

2ND PERSON: Do you see those people there going with gifts for the feast of the Sardar's spouses? Ask them. They have come to know all sorts of things that never reach our ears.

(The group enters)

NANDINI: O hear me! Do you know where they have kept Ranjan?

1ST PERSON: Shhh!

NANDINI: You must surely know! You have got to tell me!

2ND PERSON: Whatever enters through our ears does not exit through our mouths only—thus do we survive! Why don't you ask those men carrying the weapons—try them if you will!

(Exit)
(Enter another group)

NANDINI: O comrades! Pause a while! Tell me what you know of Ranjan's whereabouts.

1ST PERSON: Listen, I will tell you. The auspicious moment is almost here. During the Flag Puja the Raja will have to make an appearance. It is him you should ask. We only know the prologue; about the epilogue we have no clue!

NANDINI: *(Banging on the window)* The time has arrived, unbar the door!

VOICE OF RAJA: *(within)* Once more you come at an inopportune moment! Depart at once, go—you!

NANDINI: There's no time to wait. You'll *have* to listen to what I say!

RAJA'S VOICE: Whatever you have to say—say it from outside and then depart!

NANDINI: From outside my voice will not reach your ears!

RAJA'S VOICE: Today is the Flag Puja. Do not make me mad! The prayer ceremony will be disrupted! Go, go away! Go at once!

NANDINI: All my fears have disappeared! You cannot drive me away in this way! Death would be preferable. I will not budge without having the door unbarred!

RAJA'S VOICE: Is it Ranjan you want? I have instructed the Sardar, he'll fetch him shortly. Don't stand at the door when I go for my prayers. Then there will be disaster!

NANDINI: God has no scarcity of time! To receive the worship of devotees he can wait for millennia! But men's sorrows cry out for the proximity of men. There is little time remaining for that.

RAJA'S VOICE: I am exhausted, extremely exhausted! I shall dispense with my fatigue at the Flag Puja and return. Do not tire me out. If you come in my way now you will surely be broken into little pieces under my chariot's wheels.

NANDINI: Let the wheels roll over my body but I shall not budge!

RAJA'S VOICE: Nandini, because you were close to me, you have gained a certain license—so you do not fear me. Today fear is what you must have though!

NANDINI: I want you to frighten me the same way that you go about intimidating everyone. I despise your so-called "license"!

RAJA'S VOICE: *You* despise me? I will smash your impudence to bits! The time has come to reveal my true self to you!

NANDINI: I am eagerly waiting for that moment. Open the door!

(The door slowly opens)

What is that I see! Who's that lying on the floor? It appears to be someone very much like Ranjan!

RAJA: What did you say? Ranjan? It cannot possibly be Ranjan!

NANDINI: Yes it is! Here is my very own Ranjan!

RAJA: Why did he not utter his name? Why did he approach with such defiance?

NANDINI: Wake up Ranjan! I have come, your companion! Raja, why does he not stir?

444

RAJA: Cheated! They have cheated me! It's disastrous! My own engines are not obeying me! Call everyone! Summon the Sardar before me! Bind him and drag him here!

NANDINI: Raja, please wake up my Ranjan! Everyone tells me you know magic. O please wake him up!

RAJA: I have learnt magic from Yama Raja himself. I cannot raise anyone to life. I can only destroy the act of awakening!

NANDINI: Then you must lull me into sleep! I can't bear this anymore. Why did you create such a disaster?

RAJA: I've destroyed youth—all this time, with the sum of all my powers I only succeeded in destroying youth. The curse of decimated youth has blighted me.

NANDINI: Has he not pronounced my name?

RAJA: The manner in which he pronounced it . . . I could not tolerate it! Fire seemed to blaze through every single vein in my body!

NANDINI: *(Facing Ranjan)* My brave one, the feather of the blue jay I here place on your crown! Your victory march has begun today. I will be your journey's vehicle. Ah! Here it is—he holds in his hand my bunch of Roktokorobi flowers! In that case Kishore must have met him. Where has he disappeared? Raja, where is that boy?

RAJA: Which boy?

NANDINI: The boy who handed Ranjan this bunch of flowers.

RAJA: He was an amazing lad, girl-like, with soft features; but amazing was his speech. But he even dared to attack me.

NANDINI: After that what happened to him? Tell me! What happened? You have to answer me! You can't be silent!

RAJA: Like a bubble he disappeared into the air!

(Silence)

NANDINI: Raja, now has the time come!

RAJA: Time for what?

NANDINI: To confront you in battle with all the power that I have!

RAJA: *You* confront me in battle! I can snuff out your life this very instant!

NANDINI: But from that point onwards, second by second, my phantom self will slaughter you! I have no weapons to speak of, my weapon is death itself!

RAJA: Then come closer. Do you possess the courage to trust me? Let us journey onward together! This day, make me your companion, Nandini!

NANDINI: Where shall we go?

RAJA: To wage a war against *me*—but while placing your hand in my own! Don't you understand—the battle has already begun? This here is my flag! I will break the rod and you can shred the banner! Let my hand become *your* hand to slay me . . . kill, completely annihilate me! That itself will ensure my salvation!

A MAN: My Lord! What is this? What madness have you committed? You've broken the flag . . . our revered god's flag whose unconquerable staff penetrated the earth with one end and looked up to the heavens with the other, that immaculate flagstaff of our pride! What a sacrilege on this auspicious day! Come, let us go and inform the sardars!

(The MAN Exits)

RAJA: Much remains to be broken up! And I expect you too will be going with me, Nandini, my guiding flame, down the storm's cyclonic path!

NANDINI: Yes, I will go!

446

(Enter PHAGULAL*)*

PHAGU: They will definitely not release Bishu! Who's this? Huh? Could this be the Raja? You witch! So are you being cozy with him? You wretched traitor!

RAJA: What is the matter with you all? What have you come out for?

PHAGU: To break open the prison doors! Even death cannot make us retreat!

RAJA: Why should you retreat? I too am going to follow the path to destruction! There, that is the prime symbol—my shattered flag, my final handiwork!

PHAGU: Nandini, I can't keep up with what is going on. We are simple folks; have mercy; do not befuddle us! You are our kin, our own girl!

NANDINI: But Phagu, you have all made a wager with death itself! You have left nothing for deceit!

PHAGU: Nandini, then you too must come along, step by step, with us!

NANDINI: That is precisely why I am still alive! Phagulal, I had wanted to bring Ranjan here amongst you all. Just see! How my brave-heart has arrived, scorning death itself!

PHAGULAL: What disaster! Is that Ranjan? Is he the one lying there in absolute silence!

NANDINI: Not absolute silence! I can hear clearly within death itself . . . the undaunted voice resounding! Ranjan will surely rise up, he will be found alive . . . he can never die!

PHAGU: Alas, Nandini, my dear, my beautiful one! Was it for this that you had waited so long in the depths of our blinded hell?

NANDINI: I waited knowing he would come. And he *has* arrived! I will now await his second coming! He *will* come again! Where is Chandra, Phagulal?

PHAGU: She's gone with Gokul to appeal to the Sardar with tears in her eyes. They have such unbounded faith in him! But Maharaja, you have not misunderstood us, have you . . . ? We have ventured here to pull down your prison-house!

447

RAJA: Yes, my own prison house. We have to work together, hand in hand. This is not your work alone.

PHAGU: The sardars will come down to oppose us as soon as they get the news.

RAJA: My fight is with them.

PHAGU: The soldiers are not going to acknowledge loyalty to you.

RAJA: I shall fight alone . . . accompanied, I expect, by you all.

PHAGU: Can you win?

RAJA: At least I can face death! At last I have come to see the meaning of death—I now live!

PHAGU: Raja, do you hear the distant thunder?

RAJA: There—I can see the Sardar leading his troops! How was it all possible so soon? They must have been ready, though I was the only one to be ignorant of their plans. They've made a fool of me! They've trussed me up with my own resources!

PHAGU: My motley band of followers has not yet shown up!

RAJA: The Sardar must have held them at bay. They will never reach this place!

NANDINI: Remember—they were supposed to bring my crazy Bishu to my side. Will that not come to be?

RAJA: No such chance! I have not met anyone with the Sardar's unique talent of blocking paths!

PHAGU: In that case, let us go Nandini! After leaving you in a safe area we shall see what fate has in store for us! If the Sardar sees you he will not spare you!

NANDINI: Will you send me alone into the security of that exile all by myself? Phagulal, the Sardar is far better than you—he has opened up the path of my victory passage! Sardar! Sardar! Look! He has hung on the tip of his spear my garland of Jasmine! With the blood of my breast I will redden that garland in the colour of the Roktokorobi flower! Sardar! He has seen me now! Hail Ranjan! Victory to you!

(Rapid exit)

RAJA: Nandini!

(Exit RAJA*)*
(Enter PROFESSOR*)*

PHAGU: Where are you dashing off, Teacher?

PROFESSOR: Someone noted that the Raja has emerged after a long time, having found evidence of the primal soul—I dumped my books and papers to join his company!

PHAGU: But the Raja has gone out there to die! He has responded to Nandini's summons.

PROFESSOR: She has torn down his screen! Where is Nandini?

PHAGU: She has gone ahead of all others. She can't be overtaken any more.

PROFESSOR: This time I think I can. She won't be able to elude me further, I will catch her!

(*Enter* BISHU)

BISHU: Phagulal, where is Nandini?

(*A moment's stunned silence*)

PHAGU: How did you reach here?

BISHU: Our artisans have broken down the prisons! There they rush to join the battle! I am searching for Nandini! Where is she?

PHAGU: She has gone ahead of everyone!

BISHU: Where?

PHAGU: Towards the final redemption! Bishu, who, do you think, is lying there?

BISHU: Ranjan himself!

PHAGU: Have you seen that streak of blood in the dust?

BISHU: I now understand! That is the bloody talisman of their supreme union! Now the time has come for me to embark on the great journey, alone! After all, she may want to hear me sing! My dearest witless girl! Come my brothers! Now onward to the battlefront!

PHAGU: Victory to Nandini!

BISHU: Victory to Nandini!

PHAGU: And, look there! Her armbands of Roktokorobi flowers are trailing in the dust. Who knows when they slipped from her right hand? She has emptied her hands today before departing forever.

BISHU: I had said to her, I would take nothing from her hand! But I am bound to receive this, her last offering.

(Exit BISHU*)*
(Distant song)

Spring has summoned you all
Come, come, O come!
In one corner of the earth's dusty sari
The golden harvest has gathered, O what joy!
O come, come, come away!

The End

1924/1926
Translated by Rupendra Guha Majumdar

The Kingdom of Cards

Scene 1

(The PRINCE *and the* MERCHANT[3]*)*

PRINCE: This can't go on any longer.

MERCHANT: Prince, what is it that is stirring you so?

PRINCE: How can I say? Tell me, what is it that stirs those flocks of geese that fly in spring towards the Himalayas?

MERCHANT: But that is where their home is!

PRINCE: If that is their home, then why do they come away? No, no, it is the pleasure of flight, an inexplicable pleasure!

MERCHANT: Would you like to fly away too?

PRINCE: Certainly!

MERCHANT: I can't figure you out at all. I'd say it is better to stay in a cage for a reason than to fly away for no reason at all.

PRINCE: Reason? What reason?

MERCHANT: We stay confined in a golden cage, chained, for the love of food.

PRINCE: O you wouldn't understand, you just wouldn't understand!

MERCHANT: Yes, I have this problem: I simply am incapable of under-   451
standing that which cannot be understood. Why don't you explain a little more clearly what is it that you can't understand?

PRINCE: The monotony of living in this palace.

MERCHANT: Monotony? There are so many different ways of engaging oneself here, of amusing oneself!

PRINCE: I feel like a stone idol in a golden temple. The conch-shells and the bells sound the same notes to one's ears. The same offerings of food are repeated monotonously but I don't feel like eating them at all. How long can this go on?

MERCHANT: People like us are quite content with what we get! Thank heaven that the offerings are so regularly repeated, for otherwise we would feel starved. We are happy with what is on offer; yet your mind craves for that which is unattainable.

PRINCE: To have to listen to the hymns sung in my praise every day, and in the same unvarying notes!

MERCHANT: I think the more one listens to hymns sung in one's praise, the more one gets to like them; they hardly grow old!

PRINCE: The same songs wake me from my sleep each dawn. Each morning, the same priest comes to offer me his blessings. The same old sentinel stands watch at the door. The moment I venture out, guards rush in from every direction to ask where I would want to go. All of these people seem to be conspiring to keep my spirits in chains.

MERCHANT: Why, when you go on hunts every now and then, there is nothing to threaten you except the wild animals!

PRINCE: You call them wild animals! I fear the royal hunter has drugged the tigers with opium! It seems even they have been tutored in the ways of nonviolence; not one have I seen capable of a proper leap.

MERCHANT: Contrary to what you say, I don't consider that a sign of discourtesy on the part of the tiger. It is in keeping with the pageantry of the hunt and yet it is a way of ensuring that the heart won't have to beat faster during the encounter with the beast!

PRINCE: The other day when I shot the bear from afar, I was showered with praise; everyone acclaimed the accuracy of the prince's aim. Later, I came to know that the bear was a stuffed animal. That was too humiliating and I ordered that the royal hunter be sentenced to prison.

MERCHANT: That of course has been a boon for him. His cell is adjacent to the Queen's chambers, so he is living in comfort there. The other day, three maunds of ghee and thirty-three lambs were sent for his consumption from our estate.

PRINCE: Whatever for?

MERCHANT: It was the Queen who ordered the stuffed bear to be put up there.

PRINCE: That's just it. We are all caught up in a mesh of untruths. Our wings have become idle from staying cooped in cages. It's all mere playacting! I have been cast in the role of the princely mummer. How I long to tear away my princely outfit! When I see those farmers toiling in the fields over there, I envy their lot.

MERCHANT: And would you care to find out what they think of your lot? Prince, you are talking nonsense. You seem to be hiding your real thoughts. Patralekha,[4] perhaps only you will be able to gauge the depths of our prince's secret thoughts; do ask him what he is really thinking.

(PATRALEKHA *enters*)
(*Song*)

PATRALEKHA: Secret thoughts will no longer remain secret.
They have blossomed in the silent gaze of the eye.

PRINCE: No, no, it seems they can no longer be hid.

PATRALEKHA: In the winning smile or the flute's music,
In the corners of the lips or in the depth of sleep–

PRINCE: No, no, they can no longer be hid!

PATRALEKHA: The bee hums, the asoka blooms in sweet agony in quest
of light.
The lotus-shaped heart sways in the early morning sun—

453

PRINCE: No, no, they can no longer be hid!

PRINCE: Yes, I do have my secrets; they lie hidden in the distant sky. I
sit by the seaside, gazing far out towards the west. I'll go there in quest of
what my fate has stowed away from me as Yaksha, the follower of the god
of wealth and custodian of his treasures, once did!

(Song)

For trade I'll venture forth;
Even if Lakshmi, goddess of wealth,
Is nowhere to be found,
Alaksmi, her rival, is sure to be around!

MERCHANT: What do you mean? Trade? You spout the mantra of the
merchant!

PRINCE: Decking my ship with a thousand oars
What palace I'll reach and land on what shores!
Which lode-star shall I set my sight on?
Forgetful of what shores,
In which direction shall I navigate?
In what black waters seek my fate?
And not die, pursuing failed hopes
Only to be dashed on golden sand shores!

MERCHANT: To lose one's way by sailing aimlessly is not any way to do
business. Have you found something to go by?

PRINCE: Yes, certainly.

(Song)

I have found it in hints and dreams.
In the midst of the vast blue is an emerald isle
Surrounded by red corals.
High on mountain peaks nest sea-birds.
Coconut palms sway in the gale
And a mountain stream winds its way
Through deep green forests into a vale.
There if I descend I'll surely find
All those ancient kings' treasure mine.

MERCHANT: Your song makes it clear that this heirloom is not what we merchants trade in. What is its name?

PRINCE: Navina! Navina![5]

MERCHANT: Navina? Now it all seems to make sense.

PRINCE: It still needs some time to take shape.

(Song)

Navina, O Navina.
In the dust of much-treaded paths you can't be known.
Your messages waft in the spring breeze,
And appear in the golden sun of dawn.

MERCHANT: It will be tough finding the treasure you saw in your dream.

PRINCE: You surface in my dreams to tease me.
    What flowers of Aloka were woven into the garland you are
        wearing?
    What is the tune you play on your veena all alone?

(Enter the QUEEN-MOTHER[6])

MERCHANT: Your Highness, our prince wants to capture a mirage; he would like to find out where fairyland is.

QUEEN-MOTHER: What? Do you wish to be a child again?

PRINCE: Yes, mother. I am weary of the wise all-knowing world of adults.

QUEEN-MOTHER: Oh I see! Son, what you think you lack is not lacking anything! What you have disgusts you. You haven't had the opportunity to want anything, and that is what is bothering you.

PRINCE: *(Song)*

> My soul keeps saying, "I long for the unattainable."
> In the midst of all that I possess, my heart aches for the
>   unattainable.
> It will come to me only when I am able to lose it.
> The evening star fades only to reappear again as the morning
>   star;
> It therefore keeps saying, "I go, I go, I go."

QUEEN-MOTHER: My child, I know if I try holding on to you, I will lose you. You will find it tedious to be burdened with creature comforts, and will find it impossible to stand the attention of those who are eager to serve you. I won't stand in your way. Rather, I'll anoint your forehead with the mark of the white chandan, and wreathe your turban with a bunch of white oleanders. Let me go and get the offerings for the household deity. In the evening, I'll daub your eyes with the propitious kajal, so that all obstacles can be overcome.

(Exit)

PRINCE: *(Song)*

> See how the ocean waves swell, and the wind blows.
> The sun sinks in the west and clouds reflect its glimmer.
> Whether south or north, all one sees are the waves rolling

Even if no land in sight, I will surely hit the bottom always
there.
Certainly I won't remain confined to the house corner,
despairing.
I've ventured out into mid-sea in search of the unknown,
I'm the sole navigator in my solitary bark.
With new winds in my sails, I'll reach new lands,
Fill my ships with priceless merchandize,
And my pauper soul will return a king!

Scene 2

(The PRINCE *and the* MERCHANT*)*

PRINCE: We started from one shore and were shipwrecked in mid-sea; now we have been washed ashore in an alien land. After all these years, it seems that a new chapter in my life is about to begin.

MERCHANT: O Prince, you are constantly hankering for the "new." It is this "new" that I fear; I think the "old" is always more pleasing.

PRINCE: Yes, indeed; the toad is at home only in the well! Can't you see that we have risen afresh from death itself? It was Yama who anointed our foreheads with the stamp of a new life.

MERCHANT: But you were born with the mark of royalty stamped on your forehead.

PRINCE: But that legacy has been my misfortune. Yama has washed away that birth-mark from my forehead in the waters of the deep and ordered us to test ourselves with new zeal in this new-found land.

(Song)

We've come to a new-found land
The ship sank to the bottom of the sea,
And we came floating ashore.

The message from a stranger's heart
Will convey new hopes,
And weave new threads of pain and pleasure,
Resonating with new tunes in the soul,
New griefs will move me to laughter and tears
A secret lover will offer garlands of unknown flowers
Even as she merges her heart with mine.
In springtime, passionate youth
Will sound the nupur on the green grass,
The intoxicating south wind will carry
The fragrance of the blooming clove-plant
Into her long flowing tresses.

MERCHANT: Prince, the words sound fine when you sing them so. But, where did you find youth looking completely "new" in this land? I did look around. What I saw was a wooden bower made by a carpenter. I saw people flat in shape, walking in stiff geometrical gait, making clicking noises with their feet as though they had put on wooden ankle bells, no doubt made out of tamarind timber.[7] You call this wasteland the land of the "new!"

PRINCE: That should make you realize that none of this is real. This is all made-up, imposed from above, a shell fabricated by the pundits of this country. What are we here for? We'll shatter the shell. Then, you'll be amazed to see the fresh uninhibited spirit that will emerge, resplendent in all its natural splendor.

MERCHANT: We merchants only estimate the worth of that which is clearly visible to the eye. Yet you seem to wager all your faith on that which remains unseen. Well, let's see, if the ashes can rekindle a flame. I fear we shall end up merely wasting our breath in trying to fan a dead fire. See, here they come. This is like a ghost dancing!

PRINCE: Let us stand apart and watch the sight!

(Enter the CARDS, *marching)*
(Song)

Up and down,
In the front, to the rear,
To the left, to the right,
Neither looking, nor glancing,
Squatting, rising,
Disbanding, assembling,
Topsy turvy,
Whirling around—
Enough, enough, enough!

MERCHANT: Do you see? Red tunic, black tunic: Moving up and down, reclining, squatting, all to no purpose whatever—how bizarre! Ha, ha, ha!

CHHAKKA: What do you think you are doing? Laughing at us?

PANJA: Aren't you ashamed? Laughing at us?

CHHAKKA: Don't you follow the rules? Laughing at us?

PRINCE: One laughs because of a reason. But the things that you are doing make no sense at all.

CHHAKKA: Sense? Who needs sense? All that's required is discipline. Don't you understand? Are you mad?

PRINCE: It is difficult to recognize the truly mad man. How did you manage to think of us so?

CHHAKKA: From your behavior.

PRINCE: And what did you see in us?

CHHAKKA: We noticed that you have only motion and no real style.

MERCHANT: And I guess you have only style and no motion?

PANJA: Don't you know that style is traditional, movement modern— imbecile, idiotic, and immature card that you are![8]

CHHAKKA: Have you not been taught by proper school-masters? Have you not been told that paths are strewn with hurdles—swamps and marshes, thorns and thistles, and that any attempt to move is fraught with risks?

PRINCE: Since this is the land of school-masters, we will seek their help.

CHHAKKA: Now, tell us—who are you?

PRINCE: We are from another country.

PANJA: That explains it all. And that means you have no race, no caste, no clan, no pedigree, no social standing.

PRINCE: Nothing, nothing at all. Forget all those things and just see us as we are now; could we have your identity, please?

CHHAKKA: We are the world-renowned dynasty of Cards. I am Chhakka Sharman.

PANJA: And I am Panja Barman.[9]

PRINCE: And those others, standing apart so meekly?

CHHAKKA: The one in black is Tiri Ghosh.

PANJA: And the other, in red, is Duri Das.[10]

PRINCE: And where are you all from?

CHHAKKA: Brahma grew tired after the hard work he put into Creation. Then, at sundown, he yawned. And from that first sacred yawn we were created.

PANJA: Therefore in certain alien tongues we are referred to not as the card-dynasty, but the yawn/high-dynasty.[11]

MERCHANT: That's amazing!

CHHAKKA: At the auspicious hour of dusk, Brahma's four heads yawned simultaneously.

MERCHANT: My goodness! And what was the outcome?

CHHAKKA: Out came Iskaban, Ruhitan, Haratan, Chiretan.[12] All of them worth worshipping! He bows down to them.

PRINCE: And are they all of high social ranking?[13]

CHHAKKA: Yes, certainly. They are of prime social status,[14] having emerged from the very mouths of Brahma.

PANJA: The foremost poet of the Card-dynasty Lord Tashranganidhi,[15] having slept through the hours of the day,[16] built up a remarkable beat in his dreams; marking time with that beat our thirty-seven-and-a-half codes of behavior have been devised.

PRINCE: Perhaps we should learn at least one of them.

PANJA: Okay. Then turn your faces around.

PRINCE: Why?

PANJA: That is the rule. Brother Chhakka, chant the thung[17] mantra and blow into their ears.

PRINCE: But why?

PANJA: Because those are the rules!

(Song of the cards)

Ya—a—a—a—wn
Nothing to be done.
The day passes slowly.
Come, come, come, come.
Nothing to be done.

PRINCE: Impossible! I have to look the other way.

PANJA: Ah! You've broken the spell! You've profaned everything.

PRINCE: Profaned?

PANJA: Yes, profaned. The spell has been broken by a stranger's glance.

PRINCE: So, what is the way out?

CHHAKKA: The seed of the gab, nibbled by the bat, will have to be blackened in fire and the soot applied to the eyes. Only then will our peeved forefathers who art in heaven break their fast.[18]

PRINCE: We seem to have caused a lot of trouble. In future we will have to be careful in moving around in your country.

CHHAKKA: It would help if you don't move around at all; you'd manage to stay pure that way.

PRINCE: And what if one manages to remain pure?

PANJA: If you stay pure, you stay pure, that's all. Don't you understand?

PRINCE: It's tough for us to understand. May I ask you something? What were you doing on that ridge in battle formation?

CHHAKKA: Getting ready for battle!

PRINCE: You call that a battle?

PANJA: Of course. All in strict adherence to the codes of the Card-dynasty.

(Song)

We are painted, we are strange,
Most untainted, most chaste.

MERCHANT: Even then, a battle needs some conflict, some degree of rage.

CHHAKKA: Our rage is depicted in our colors. In our battles, no one is ever rattled.
See our Golam,[19]
most gentle and warm.

MERCHANT: Even so; cannons and firearms go well with warfare.

PANJA: Neither weapons, nor military uniforms,
   Neither greed, nor rancor
   Neither leaps, nor dives.

PRINCE: But there must be some allegation, some complaint. That is what a fight is all about.

CHHAKKA: We go by the code; we obey the law
   Be it foe, be it friend,
   Be it a rival, be it anybody.

PANJA: O Stranger, surely there must be a story of your genesis scripted in some ancient text?

MERCHANT: Certainly. When Grandfather[20] Brahma, in the early stages of creation, mounted the sun on the anvil, a ball of fire entered his nostrils and he sneezed aloud like a cannon discharging; it was out of that earth-shaking sneeze that we were created.

CHHAKKA: That explains why you are so restless.

PRINCE: Yes, we wander all over the place, and can hardly stand still.

PANJA: That's awful!

MERCHANT: Who said it's any good? The effects of that primordial sneeze still keep us on the move.

CHHAKKA: One good effect is obvious. That sneeze will soon drive you away from our island, and won't have you lingering here for long.

MERCHANT: Yes, it may be difficult to stay on.

PANJA: What kind of battle do you fight?

MERCHANT: One fought on two sides, to the measure of four pairs of sneezes on each side.

CHHAKKA: To the measure of sneezes? That can surely end in heads banging against each other.

MERCHANT: You bet!

CHHAKKA: Did your ancient bard chant any mantra?

MERCHANT: Yes, of course he did.

(Song)

Aitchooo!
Do you think you can scare me?
I'll take you by the scruff of your neck,
And boxes will land on your face,
And then ask: how do you feel after that!

CHHAKKA: Brother Panja, these are pariahs for sure! What race do you belong to?

MERCHANT: Nasakas,[21] born from nostrils.

PANJA: We know of no high-born race by that name.

MERCHANT: The vapor of the yawn took you high above, to the shores of afterlife; the tremor created by a sneeze pushed us down to earth.

CHHAKKA: The unseemly consequences of Brahma's sneezing have made you people so odd.

PRINCE: Right you are, we are odd indeed.

(Song)

We are messengers of youth,
We are frolicsome and odd.
We break down barriers,
We get high on the red asoka,
We shatter the fetters of the storm,
We are lightning bolts.
We make our share of mistakes,
We dive deep and strive to reach the shore.

We are ever ready, ever at the beck and call
Of life—death—tempest—all!

CHHAKKA-PANJA: (looking at each other): This won't do. This won't do at all.

PRINCE: We move what seems immovable.

CHHAKKA: But what about rules?

PRINCE: When you cross barriers the rules regulating highways reveal themselves. Otherwise, how would one ever advance?

PANJA: Goodness me, has anyone ever heard of such things? Move on! Without even batting an eyelid, he talks of advancing!

PRINCE: But why else would one go on?

CHHAKKA: "Go on?" Why think of going at all? What goes on are the rules.

(Song)

Move in pace with the rules.
Don't look afar, don't bend your head,
Move along the even path.

PRINCE: Look at the forests over there,
Where are the shackles of rules?
The waterfall cascades down the mountainside
In reckless free delight.

CARDS: Don't even look that way
Don't even go that way
Move along the even path.

PANJA: Enough! There come the King and the Queen. They will hold court here today. Hold these shoots of pumpkin in your hands.

PRINCE: Shoots of pumpkin! Ha, ha,—why?

PANJA: Silence! Don't laugh! That's the rule. Keep your faces turned to the north-west, be careful not to look towards the north-east end.

PRINCE: Why?

CHHAKKA: That's the rule!

(*Enter the* KING, *the* QUEEN, TEKKA, GOLAM,[22] *and others*)

PRINCE: My friend, let us please the king by singing paeans to him. You keep swaying the pumpkin shoot.

(*Song*)

Victory be yours,[23] O Heir of the Card-dynasty
O denizen of the world of sleep
And destroyer of all rest

CARDS: Enough! Enough! Enough! The proceedings have been interrupted! Barbarians!

KING: Peace! Who are these people?

CHHAKKA: Foreigners.

KING: Foreigners! Then the rule will not apply to them. Just change positions, and you will be absolved of all blame. First of all, let's have the national anthem of the great court of Cards.

(ALL: *Song*)

Chiretan, Haratan, Iskaban
Dance in traditional rhythm.
Some rise, and some fall,
Some make no motion at all,
Some lie flat on the ground biding time.
Not speaking nor smiling,
Blindly following the one in front
Constrained by age-old traditions

Neither veering nor altering
Nor opting for change!

KING: O Stranger!

PRINCE: Yes, O Great King?

KING: Who are you?

PRINCE: I am a messenger from a distant shore.

GOLAM: What offerings have you brought?

PRINCE: That which is most rare in this kingdom.

GOLAM: And what is that?

PRINCE: Trouble.

CHHAKKA: Just listen to him speak, O Mighty King; has anyone heard anything like it? He wants to move forward. You wouldn't believe it, he laughs. He will make us all light and frivolous in no time at all!

GOLAM: The air of this land is incomparably still and heavy. The thunder of Indra cannot move it, let alone the efforts of others!

ALL: Let alone the efforts of others.

GOLAM: What if this frivolous stranger dares to lighten this atmosphere?

KING: That is worth serious consideration. That is worth thinking about!

ALL: That is worth serious consideration. That is worth thinking about indeed!

GOLAM: A light breeze ushers in a storm. And in such a storm all norms are blown away. Perhaps, even our priest, Nahala Goswami,[24] then would begin to chant; we desire to move on.

PANJA: God forbid, then laughter may become infectious here.

KING: O Golam of Iskaban.

GOLAM: Yes, my King.

KING: You are the Editor, aren't you?

GOLAM: Yes, I am the Editor of the *Lamp of Card-Island*.[25] I am the preserver of culture in this Island of Cards.

KING: What is this "culture" thing? Doesn't sound that good!

GOLAM: No, Your Majesty. It is neither pleasant, nor lucid. But it is the newest innovation. It is the sort of culture that is under threat today.

ALL: Culture! Culture! Culture!

KING: Do you have columns in your editorial?

GOLAM: Two large ones.

KING: Everybody must be deafened by the roar of those columns. Such lightening of our air won't be tolerated.

GOLAM: We need mandatory laws.

KING: Whatever is that? Mandatory laws?

GOLAM: This is an euphemism for boxing the ears. This is also a recent addition.

KING: Never mind. Stranger, do you have anything to declare?

PRINCE: Yes, but not to you.

KING: Then to whom?

PRINCE: To these princesses here.

KING: Very well, go on.

PRINCE: *(Song)*

Fair maids seemingly carved in stone,
Enshrine in hearts the frolicsome one.

Come all alone to the forest-bower
Tears glistening in your eyes,
In the soft hue of the rising sun
Let the flower of pain blossom.

QUEEN: How irregular! How improper!

PANJA: Mighty King, he should be banished instantly.

KING: Banished! Queen, what have you to say to that? Don't remain silent. Did you hear what I just said? What is your response? Should it be banishment?

QUEEN: No, not banishment.

(FEMALE CARDS[26] *one by one):* No, not banishment.

KING: My Queen, you are acting strangely.

QUEEN: I am feeling strange.

GOLAM: Tekkakumari, Bibisundari,[27] remember I handle the editorial columns.

OTHERS: Culture! Culture! Card-Island's-culture! Protect our culture!

GOLAM: Enforce the law.

KING: Meaning . . . ?

GOLAM: Box the ear of offenders!

KING: Yes, yes, I get it. Queen, what do you say? Should we enforce the Rule of Law?

QUEEN: We can try enforcing it in our private chambers too. Then we shall see who banishes whom.

(FEMALE CARDS—in chorus): We shall enforce Misrule and Indiscipline.

GOLAM: What! Alas, culture! O culture!

KING: The court is hereby dissolved. Leave this place at once. It is no longer safe to stay here.

(Exit the CARDS*)*

MERCHANT: Friend, it is impossible to put up with this situation any longer. They all travesty creation. If we remain with them any longer, we will ruin ourselves.

PRINCE: Haven't you noticed the undercurrents? Haven't you felt the first signs of life throbbing in these dolls? I shan't leave till I've seen the end of this.

MERCHANT: But this is death-in-life; their minds are transfixed by rules.

PRINCE: Look that way.

MERCHANT: So I see, my friend. The spell of alien shores has been cast on this place. The Nine of Spades is sitting idly under the tree, looking at distant skies. It seems that all their laws are about to dissolve into thin air!

PRINCE: He is listening for the sound of Chiretani's footfalls, echoing in the skies. Perhaps he won't appreciate our company at this time; come away, let us make ourselves scarce.

(Exit)

Scene 3

(Iskabani busy dressing up. Tekkani enters[28]*)*

TEKKANI: *(Song)*

O my friend, whisper his name quietly in my ears,
The name ringing out in the melody of your *veena.*
The name murmuring in the zephyr through forest-bowers,

Even as the companionless bird sings in pain
That name makes us heady with the scent of the bakul,
Perhaps it will resonate through the maidenly chatter.
On the night of the full moon, when the heart is heavy,
That very name will I chant in song after song

470

ISKABANI: Friend, what do you think has happened to our kingdom of cards? What kind of crazy wind has these foreigners brought along with them? Those strangers have blown in what wind of frenzy? My heart is so wobbly.

TEKKANI: You are right, Iskabani. Who would have thought even a few days back that those cards would try to shed off our identities and imitate humans? How shameful!

ISKABANI: To behave like humans—that's crazy! Haratani started all this. Haven't you noticed, she can hardly control herself? She keeps imitating those humans. She isn't bothered by protocol anymore. The whole realm is buzzing with rumors. This is bringing our kingdom of cards to disrepute.

(CHIRETANI *enters*)

CHIRETANI: O here you are Mistress Tekkani! I believe that you have been defaming us, saying that we have sacrificed all norms, sitting when we should rise, and rising when we should sit?

TEKKANI: Yes, but I only said what is true and so what's wrong with that? What color, my sweet one, makes your cheeks glow so red? And what has made your painted eyebrow take on the hue of the kajal of moonless nights of alien shores? This is hardly in tune with the sacred codes of our kingdom of cards. Do you think all these things pass unnoticed?

CHIRETANI: My word! And what sacred codes sanctify your whisperings with your companion under the bakul-tree? Whereas look at the poor poor Golam wandering aimlessly in search of his mate.

ISKABANI: That's enough, mistress, you needn't advise us. The colored ribbon in your hair will perhaps serve as a halter to hang the codes and rituals of our kingdom of cards. Such impudence in a card!

CHIRETANI: So what! I'm not scared of anybody. I don't play hide and seek like you. The other day Dahalani came to mock me and called me a "woman." I told her clearly that I would rather be a live woman than a dead card.

ISKABANI: O don't be so arrogant. Do you know, everyone is saying that you may be declared an outcast?

CHIRETANI: Cast out of the card family? I have discarded myself already. And so I am hardly scared.

ISKABANI: My goodness! Never heard such impertinence in a card! She is brazen enough to openly declare herself a "woman." Come away, Tekkani, if we are seen talking to her, perhaps we too will be in danger.

(Exit)

Scene 4

(Enter Srimati Tekka HARATANI[29]*)*

HARATANI: *(Song)*

> I came to pluck flowers from the garden
> Unaware of what was in my heart.
> This is no mere plucking of flowers,
> I can hardly understand myself,
> And tears keep welling up in my eyes.

(Enter the Sahib of RUHITAN[30]*)*

RUHITAN: Haratani, what are you doing here? I've been searching for you the whole day long.

HARATANI: Why? Whatever for?

RUHITAN: You have been asked to report to the royal court.[31]

HARATANI: Go and tell them: "I am lost!"

RUHITAN: You are?

HARATANI: Yes, I am totally lost. You'll no longer find her whom you have been seeking for so long.

RUHITAN: How strange! How brazen! How dare you come to this forest? Don't you know it is out of bounds for you?

HARATANI: Yes, out of bounds indeed. But could you tell me why thick clouds cover the skies of our rainless kingdom this day? Waking up in the morning, I noticed the sky filling up with these dark clouds. Till now, your peacocks trod mindfully and danced cautiously; why have they suddenly flung all caution to the winds and why do they dance merrily now; holding their outspread tails so outrageously?

RUHITAN: So has the one who considered one's portals alien come to the forest today to pluck flowers? How could you think of doing such a crazy thing?

HARATANI: It occurred to me all of a sudden that I must have been a flower-girl, in another life. The east wind has wafted in the fragrance of those gardens from my earlier life. The humming bee has found its way from there into my very heart.

(Song)

The bee came humming into my chamber.
Whose message did it carry to my ears?
What light reflected in the skies
Encouraged the madhavi to blossom in the forest,
Bringing that news to me?
That is what it has been chanting in my ear all day long.

How can I then remain confined to my room?
My heart flutters
And time passes painfully
What magic has overpowered me, making me forget my chores?
And why do I spend my days weaving a net of tunes?

RUHITAN: I have been looking for the other card-maidens so that I can summon them to the palace-court. Are they here?

HARATANI: Yes, they are also here—on the river bank and under the trees.

RUHITAN: Doing what?

HARATANI: Dressing up. Much like me. How do I look?

RUHITAN: It seems that the veil has been torn away, the clouds have moved away from the face of the moon, and a new being has emerged!

HARATANI: Go and see what has happened to Chhakka and Panja.

RUHITAN: Why? What has happened to them?

HARATANI: They are moving around like crazy, sighing away; and at times even singing to themselves.

RUHITAN: Singing? Chhakka-Panja singing?

HARATANI: Yes, singing; even if not always in tune. I was doing my hair then, but found it impossible to continue.

RUHITAN: Doing your hair? Who taught you that skill?

HARATANI: No one. Look how the dried-up stream has filled up with water; see how the waves criss-cross in plaits. Who taught them? Come with me and, I'll take you to where you can hear Chhakka-Panja singing.

(Exit[32]*)*
(CARD-MAIDENS *enter*)

CARD-MAIDENS: *(Song and dance)*

> Who sings to my ears the unknown tune
> Making my mind wander on the wings of melody?
> In the shadowy world of the forgotten past
> A vagrant ragini wanders weeping
> Mourning for the loss of the veena.
> In a spring night, when the time of union has come
> My songs waft my thoughts to the stars.

(RUHITAN and HARATANI re-enter)

RUHITAN: Who could I blame when my own heart longs to sing?

HARATANI: Mind you, make sure that the editor doesn't overhear. He will then mention you in his columns. I saw him roaming around trying to gather information about this forest.

RUHITAN: Look here Haratani, I have stopped being afraid. I can hardly explain this, but I am craving to do something desperate for your sake.

HARATANI: Whatever you do, please don't try to sing. The hibiscus is in bloom in the forest; please fetch some for me, so I can redden my feet with them.

RUHITAN: My dear, it dawned on me after I woke up this morning that this card-life of ours is a hollow dream, which has crumbled to pieces this day. A new life is wafting in the winds towards us, reaching out to us through the words we now speak, through the songs we now hear. Listen; can you hear how from the skies floats down the song I had composed for you once upon a time?

(Song)

> Let the soles of your feet redden
> With the crimson flowers budding in my soul.
> The tuneful notes of my song

474

Bedeck you like ear-rings,
And let me weave the blood-red beaded necklace
With my heart's desire.

HARATANI: Was it you who composed this song for me one day? How
did you manage to do so then?

RUHITANI: Like you managed to do your hair.

HARATANI: Do you remember that I had danced to the rhythm of your
tune once upon a time?

RUHITAN: Yes, those memories are coming back to me. How could we
have forgotten them all this time?

(Song)

The wild wind has filled the sails of my song's boat.
Swaying it in the swirl of your dance.
If the ropes snap, if the rudder breaks free,
If the waves billow,
If Death looms large,
We shan't lose heart,
But press forward resolutely
Till we've snatched victory!

RUHITAN: Look Haratani, my spirits are up since I must tussle with
Yamaraj. I can visualize clearly you anointing my forehead with the mark
of victory; I setting out to rescue a damsel in distress; reaching the bolted
gates of the fortress and sounding my horn. I even seem to hear the song
you sang to bid me farewell.

(Song)

Bring the garland of victory to me,
I'll stay up all night for you.
When you tread the realm of death
Your footsteps will resound in my heart,
If all is lost, at least I'll share your fate.

HARATANI: Come, my hero, let us venture forth, risking death. The black boulders scowl menacingly before us; we have to smash them to smithereens even if they break upon our heads. We have to even split open rocky mountains, carving our way through them. Why have we come here? Why do we linger here? O shame! What meaningless days, what lifeless nights have we been spending? What futile moments have entangled us!

RUHITAN: Would you dare, o beautiful one?

HARATANI: Yes, for sure!

RUHITAN: Won't you be intimidated by the unknown?

HARATANI: Certainly not.

RUHITAN: Your feet will be gashed and the path will seem endless.

HARATANI: In some distant past, we had set out together on a perilous journey. I had held the torch before you at night, carried your banner in front of you by day. Let's rise up once again this day; we have to break down this fence of idleness, this bondage of inertia, we have to cast aside this rubbish that has accumulated.

RUHITAN: Tear away this shroud, shred it to pieces. Be free, be pure, and be whole.

(Exit)
(Enter CHHAKKA *and* PANJA*)*

CHHAKKA: O Panja, what do you think has been happening?

PANJA: I'm ashamed to look at myself. Fool! Fool! What have I been doing all this while?

CHHAKKA: After all these years why have we started to question the meaning of it all?

PANJA: There comes Dahala Pundit,[33] let's ask him.

(Enter DAHALA*)*

CHHAKKA: What is the meaning of the daily rituals of rising-and-falling, squatting-and-lying-down that we have been following for ages?

DAHALA: Shut up!

CHHAKKA-PANJA *(together):* We won't shut up.

DAHALA: Aren't you afraid?

CHHAKKA-PANJA *(together):* No, we aren't. You'll have to tell us what the meaning is.

DAHALA: There is no meaning, there is only the law.

CHHAKKA: And if we refuse to follow the law?

DAHALA: You'll go to hell.

CHHAKKA: Then we will.

DAHALA: But why?

PANJA: To fight against any abomination that we may find there.

DAHALA: What mule-headed talk is this in this peaceful land of ours!

PANJA: We have resolved to disrupt that peace.

(Enter HARATANI*)*

DAHALA: Do you hear, Mistress Haratani? They want to disrupt the peace of this island of ours, washed though it is by the waters of the Pacific Ocean.

HARATANI: The peace here is like an old gnarled tree, lifeless and worm-infested; it needs to be hewn down.

DAHALA: For shame! How can you say such things? You are of the fairer sex, whose aim should be to maintain peace, while we men are to uphold the traditions of our land.

HARATANI: Pundit, you have deceived us for far too long, but enough is enough. Your talk of peace has congealed in our blood; we won't be hoodwinked any longer!

DAHALA: Damnation! Who has been giving you such ideas?

HARATANI: From him, who we are invoking with all our hearts, absorbed as we are in the melody of his songs wafting in the skies.

DAHALA: Good lord! Songs in the skies! This is the end of the Kingdom of Cards! No, I won't be able to tarry here any longer.

(Exit)

CHHAKKA: Haratani, please show us the way.

PANJA: Now that you have been initiated in the mantra of disharmony, won't you share that mantra with us?

HARATANI: We live under the curse of God's slight. Come, let's away.

CHHAKKA: But they cry out "Sacrilege" at the slightest movement that we make.

HARATANI: Let them. There is nothing more sacrilegious than to remain dead.

(Exit)
(Enter ISKABANI *and* TEKKANI *plucking flowers)*

TEKKANI: Goodness! Here comes Dahalani. We are in for it!

*(*DAHALANI *enters)*

DAHALANI: Trying to hide, are you? You can hardly be recognized. Why, this is our very own Tekkani, and that's our Iskabani! Goodness! How you have dolled yourself up! Trying to pass yourselves as humans, I suppose? How shameful!

TEKKANI: We haven't tried to dress ourselves in any way; on the contrary, the dresses we had on came off all by themselves.

DAHALANI: The laws of this land are fixed, tied up as they are in many knots. How could anything come loose of its own?

ISKABANI: A fresh breeze has started to blow!

DAHALANI: Just listen to her! The wind of this land blowing away all knots! How can you accuse our Pavandev[34] of such misconduct! What makes you think that this is a land inhabited by strange creatures, where even the slightest breeze causes trees to shed their leaves?

ISKABANI: See for yourself, sister, what change Pavandev has wrought.

DAHALANI: Look, it doesn't become one to spout maxims if one is a nobody! Our Pavandev has the weight of tradition. But the scriptures, of course, say that he has a son who is heroic,[35] someone who leaps from place to place. Perhaps it is this son who has possessed you.

TEKKANI: Why single us out for blame? Haven't you noticed? He has been leaping all over the island of the Cards. He has kindled a new flame in the hearts of the card-maidens.

ISKABANI: Those people from the strange shores are claiming that he was their ancestor.

DAHALANI: That is possible. They have perhaps descended from the Leaping-dynasty.[36]

TEKKANI: But do tell us the truth sister—don't you feel something stirring deep in your heart? No, it won't do to remain silent, please answer my question.

DAHALANI: You sure you won't tell anyone else? Promise?

TEKKANI: We promise that we won't.

DAHALANI: Last night I dreamt that I had suddenly become human, and was moving around just like a human being. I felt so ashamed of myself upon waking up. But . . .

TEKKANI: But what?

DAHALANI: Never mind!

ISKABANI: Yes, yes, we understand perfectly. The bird that is chained during the day is set free in dreams!

DAHALANI: Hush! Quiet! If Nahala Pundit gets to know of this, he will prescribe penance even for dreams. But what a sense of delight in that wonderful dream!

TEKKANI: You'll have to agree that a strong gust of wind from alien shores is now raging through the land of cards. Everything is being blown away; we can hardly keep anything under control.

DAHALANI: Though some things have been blown away, yet other things remain. The veil perhaps has slipped off, but the anklets that chain your feet are yet to be straightened.

ISKABANI: Right you are. The mind oscillates between one shore of the ocean and the other. See, Chiretani's urge to become a human being has led her to wear the mask of a woman because she can't become one. And yet that mask is crafted in the workshop of card-land. How funny she looks!

DAHALANI: I wonder whether we realize what we are doing to ourselves. The other day, I heard the Prince's friend say that we were mimicking humans.

TEKKANI: How embarrassing! And what did the Prince say?

DAHALANI: The Prince wasn't amused; he declared that the way we are dressing up at least indicated a maturing of taste. And that in any case it was better than the attempts made by some humans to mimic the cards.

ISKABANI: Is that possible? Humans mimicking cards? How is that possible?

DAHALANI: The Prince was recalling how they redden their lips and paint their eyebrows, and so on, much like us painted cards. The funniest part of it all is they cover their feet with heeled-goatskins.

480

TEKKANI: But why would they do such a thing?

DAHALANI: It gives them status; then they don't have to come into contact with the soil then. All painted, all embellished—just like the cards.

ISKABANI: Pavandev seems to be encouraging them to indulge in such a crazy sport: Imagine! Cards wishing to discard their make-up to become humans, and humans wishing to become like cards. I have of course made up my mind to ask the Prince for a charm so that I can be transformed into a human being.

TEKKANI: So have I.

DAHALANI: I too long for the same thing to happen to me, but dread the consequences. I have heard that there is no end to human sorrow; cards don't have to bother with such a thing.

ISKABANI: Sorrow, sister? Don't you feel sorrow dancing in your heart already?

TEKKANI: Yet, this sorrow is so intoxicating that I don't even wish to let it go. I don't even know why these tears stream down my cheeks so.

(Song)

> Why do the eyes rain such tears?
> Why does the heart ache so?
> As if it's trying to recall that which can't be recalled?
> To revive a pain caused by something someone said?
> As if someone has left feeling slighted
> A slight that has left its twinge on my heart.
> As if all of a sudden one recalls some event
> And yet it slides back into the mind and remains
> unremembered.

ISKABANI: Let's flee! Here comes the Editor! If he gets you into his newspaper even once you won't ever be able to show your face.

DAHALANI: The entire assembly is headed in this direction. The court will be held under the old neem tree. Let's depart.

(Exit)
(Enter THE KING *and company)*

KING: There is something strange about this place. What smell is that?

PANJA: The kadamba flower.

482

KING: Kadamba! Funny name. What bird is that cooing?

PANJA: We've been told that it is called the dove.

KING: Dove! No, no, give it a name that suits the lexicon of cards; name it binti.[37] It has been particularly difficult to concentrate on work today. Whispers can be heard in the skies, while the breeze seems to be full of melodies. I've had to force myself to concentrate. We've had a tough time keeping the Queen indoors; she is prancing around like one possessed. Members of the Court, you don't look yourselves today—you haven't followed the dress-code, you look most uncivilized.

ALL: We are not to blame. The clothes we had suddenly felt loose and came off on their own; they now lie strewn all along the way.

KING: Editor, you seem to have lost your sting too.

GOLAM: I've been moving through the forests since early morning, gathering information about truants. The breeze had affected me as well. In trying to fill the editorial columns, I found rhymes flowing freely from my pen. I understand doctors have a name for this sort of infection—it's called "influenza."

KING: Give us a sample.

GOLAM: In the land where the wind refuses to comply

With mandatory laws,
How will the scholar, Dahala Tattwanidhi,
Hope to preserve its traditions?
For sure in such a land,
Anarchy will thrive.

KING: Enough! No more! Include this in the syllabus for the fourth grade so that the young pupils of card families may memorize it.

CHHAKKA: Master King, we are not your pupils studying in the fourth grade. Today we seem to have matured. That rhythmic measure no longer attracts us.

PANJA: Strangers from a distant land, can you teach us the rhymes of your country?

PRINCE: Yes, of course. Listen.

(Song)

> The clouds thunder overhead
> Speaking the language of lightning,
> Inspiring in the branches of trees
> The desire for motion.
> The bird flies, drunk in reaching dizzy heights,
> Propelled by the speed of its wings.
> The heart stirs, moving to varying rhythms—
> Playing off the black against white,
> Good against evil, the straight against the narrow.
> Rhythms dance in the flames of the sacrificial fire,
> Play on the arched brow of the warrior,
> And roll on the rim of Rudra's chariot-wheels
> As he hurtles along the path of destruction.

KING: What sense did you make of that?

CARDS: None whatever.

KING: Then?

CARDS: But our hearts danced to the tune.

KING: That's not good. Pay heed to this traditional measure of ours—

> To the meek one comes Death;
> It pushes him around,

Saying, "This fellow has no use for me"
And so away goes he!
Listen to me, Stranger.

PRINCE: Yes, Mighty King?

KING: Why do you cavort all over this card-island so impetuously—diving in its waters, climbing its mountain-tops; hacking your way through its forests? Why this restless behavior?

PRINCE: And why do you merely stand, sit, turn round, or roll on the ground?

KING: That is our Law.

PRINCE: And that is our will.

KING: "Will"? My goodness! "Will" in this land of ours? What say you, friends?

CHHAKKA-PANJA: We have schooled ourselves in the "Power of the Will" under his tutelage.

KING: Schooled yourselves in what?

CHHAKKA-PANJA: *(Song)*

Will, Will, the power of the Will,
That which creates and dissipates,
That which knocks at bolted locks,
That which breaks free from all bonds,
And yet turns around to bind oneself.

KING: Go away, leave this place at once. Haratani, don't you hear me? Chiretani, note how she behaves? How did all this get to happen?

HARATANI: By the power of the Will.

OTHERS: Will, Will, the power of the Will.

KING: Queen, what's up? Why do you rise?

QUEEN: Because I can't sit down anymore.

KING: My Queen, I fear there is a fluttering in your heart as well.

QUEEN: You bet! My heart is fluttering in excitement.

KING: Don't you know excitement is the gravest crime in card-land?

QUEEN: Yes, I do. But I also know that it is what is relished most.

KING: Is a crime a thing to be relished? Have you forgotten the language of card-land?

QUEEN: In our card-land, chains are called ornaments; it's time to forget such words.

RUHITAN: Yes, O Queen. They refer to prison as the house where one's in-laws reside!

KING: Silence!

HARATANI: Whimsy they call "holy scriptures"!

KING: Silence!

HARATANI: They call the "dumb" "honest."

KING: Silence!

HARATANI: And the "idiot" to them is a "scholar."

KING: Silence!

PANJA: They call "death" life!

KING: Silence!

QUEEN: And aiming for paradise is to them a "crime." Come let's all chant, "Hail, Power of the Will."

KING: Queen, you are hereby banished to the forest!

QUEEN: What a relief!

KING: You are exiled!—Where are you going?

QUEEN: To live in exile.

KING: Leaving me here all by myself?

QUEEN: Why would I leave you here?

KING: Then, what do you propose to do?

486

QUEEN: Take you along!

KING: Where?

QUEEN: To live in exile.

KING: And my subjects?

ALL: We shall all live in exile.

KING: Dahala Pundit, what do you think of this plan of exile?

DAHALA: I think that will be for their good.

KING: But your scriptures?

DAHALA: I'll immerse them in the waters.

KING: And the Mandatory Laws?

DAHALA: They will no longer do!

ALL: They will no longer do!

QUEEN: Where are those foreigners?

PRINCE: Here we are.

QUEEN: Do you think we can become human beings?

PRINCE: Yes, of course you can.

KING: O Stranger, do you think even I could do so?

PRINCE: I've my doubts but that the Queen is on your side is to your advantage. Glory be to the Queen!

(Song in Chorus)

Smash all dams; smash them all!
Free the imprisoned spirit,
Let life's endless joys flood the dry river-bed,
Sing the victory-song of the spirit of destruction.
Let everything tattered and traditional be washed away.
We have heard the clarion call of the nameless new.
No fear of the unknown can impede our march
Let's ram down the bolted gates of an unexplored world.

487

1933
Translated by Abhijit Sen

Stories

"*It is one of the joys of story-writing*," declares Tagore in *Chhinnapatra* (27 June 1894), "that the people I write about can fill my spare time, night and day, become the companions of my solitary spirit, dispel the narrowness of my closed chamber on a rainy day, and in my mind's eye, traverse the radiant landscape of the Padma shore when the sun shines." Tagore's delight in writing stories never deserted him. He published his first story, "Bhikharini" ("The Beggar Woman"), in 1877, when he was only sixteen. His last story, dictated from his deathbed, was published posthumously. In all, he wrote almost a hundred stories, published in diverse periodicals and anthologies, and collected in the four volumes of *Galpaguchchha*. He wrote some of the earliest short stories in Bengali and left a lasting influence on the history of the genre in his country.

More than half of Tagore's stories were composed during the immensely productive period between 1891 and 1895. This is sometimes called the *Sadhana* phase, after the periodical edited by Tagore. Most of his stories from this period were published in that journal. During this phase, Tagore was deeply influenced by his experience as a landowner in East Bengal, where he saw rural life firsthand. For the first time in Bengali fiction, ordinary people were treated as protagonists. Six stories from this period are included in this volume. "The Return of Khoka Babu" (published in the first issue of *Sadhana*, November–December 1891) and "The Legacy" (December–January 1891–1892) are haunting tales about blind faith and superstition. "Subha" (1893) presents a poignant picture of the silencing of women in a conservative society. The terse, cryptic narrative of "Mahamaya" (1893) tracks the forbidden relationship of Mahamaya and Rajiblochan, through which social malpractices such as sati (the widow's ritual self-immolation on her husband's funeral pyre) and kulinism (polygamy practiced by high-caste Brahmins) are critiqued. "The In-Between Woman" (1893) presents the tensions of a triangular relationship between a man and his two wives. The eerie, ghostly atmosphere of "Hungry Stone" (July–August 1895) has led some critics to draw comparisons with "A Tale of the Ragged Mountains" by Edgar Allan Poe, but the story was actually inspired by Tagore's recollections of his 1878 visit to the Shahi Bagh palace in Ahmedabad, built in the seventeenth century by Prince Khurram, who would later become the Mughal Emperor Shah Jahan.

"A Broken Nest" (1901), a "long story" sometimes described as a novella, is probably based on Tagore's memory of his complex relationship with his brother Jyotirindranath and his sister-in-law Kadambari Devi. As in his contemporaneous novel *Chokher Bali* (1903), the attention is centered upon the inner life of the protagonist—the lonely wife Charu who falls in love with her husband's cousin Amal—rather than on external events that further the plot.

Tagore's second major creative phase is sometimes called the *Shabuj Patra* period after the journal of the same name, in which several of his stories appeared between 1914 and 1917. These stories focus on middle-class life, especially the position of women within the household. "The Wife's Letter" is a bold narrative about a wife's rebellion. It caused considerable controversy in its time. Critics point out real-life parallels to some aspects of the story: Bindu's suicide, for instance, recalls the contemporary case of Snehalata, a young woman who killed herself to relieve her father of the task of arranging her dowry, and Mrinal's fondness for Bindu resembles Kadambari Devi's caring attitude toward Tagore's child bride Mrinalini Devi.

Tagore wrote three major stories shortly before he died: "Robibar" ("Sunday"), "Laboratory," and "Shesh Katha" ("The Final Word"). Published in a collection called *Tin Sangi* (*The Three Companions*, 1940–1941), these narratives emphasize the ennobling effect of separation at the end of a man-woman relationship. In "The Final Word," it is the woman, Achira, who liberates Nabinmadhav, leaving him free to pursue his scientific mission. The story first appeared in *Shanibarer Chithi* in 1939; a revised version was published in the journal *Desh* later the same year.

"The Tale of a Muslim Woman" is a draft, dictated by an ailing Tagore in June 1941 and published posthumously in 1955. Probably inspired by the story of Jodhabai, the Rajput woman who joined the household of Mughal emperor Akbar, this story about a Hindu woman converted to Islam reveals Tagore's secular attitude in the face of the rising tide of communal feeling that swept India in the years leading up to Partition.

Tagore insists that his stories are written in a realist vein: "I wrote from what I saw, what I felt in my heart—my direct experience . . . Those who say that my stories are fanciful are wrong" ("Granthaparichay," *Galpaguchchha,* vol. 4, 1005). Yet he also wants readers to understand that "a story is not a photograph. What I have seen, what I have heard, cannot find a place within a story until it dies, disintegrates and mingles with the five elements to reach an organic state" (Letter to Hemantabala Devi, 24 September 1931, *Chithipatra,* vol. 9, 45).

Tagore's experiments with the short story evince a constant concern for form and language. "I was compelled to create a language for Bengali prose," he claims. "There was no language available. At every stage, and every level, I had to create it myself . . . Along with the flow of the story, I had to construct a prose style" ("Granthaparichay," *Galpaguchchha,* vol. 4, 1005). The transition from the traditional *sadhubhasha* or classical Bengali to *chaltibhasha* or colloquial Bengali was one of Tagore's significant contributions to the modernization of Bengali prose.

Several of Tagore's stories have been successfully adapted for the screen: for instance, *Kshudhita Pashan* ("Hungry Stone"), directed by Tapan Sinha in 1961, "A Broken Nest," made into the cinema classic *Charulata* (1964) by Satyajit Ray, *Subha,* directed by Parthapratim Chaudhuri in 1964, and *Strir Patra* ("The Wife's Letter"), directed by Purnendu Patri in 1973. Also memorable are Ray's film *Teen Kanya* (1961), based on the three stories "Postmaster," "Manihara," and "Samapti," and Tapan Sinha's screen version of *Kabuliwala* (1957). Many of Tagore's stories, such as "The Return of Khoka Babu" and "Hungry Stone," have also been dramatized.

Describing Tagore as a short-story writer of world stature, the Bengali writer and critic Buddhadeva Bose compares him to masters of the genre, such as Maupassant and Chekhov. Like them, Tagore immerses the reader directly in the natural flow of his stories, without preamble or preaching; yet, as Bose points out, he avoids the breathless pace of Maupassant's stories, sometimes creating narratives that cover several years (Bose, *Rabindranath: Kathasahitya,* 1955, 50). In Tagore's development as a short-story writer, multiple influences were at work: the creative atmosphere in his family home; his exposure to literature from diverse traditions such as folktales, myth, classical models, and history; landscape; and personal experience. Yet he assimilated these diverse elements and transformed them into a creative practice entirely his own.

The Return of Khoka Babu

I

When Raicharan first came to work at the home of his master, the Babu, he was only twelve years of age. He belonged to Jessore District. Long hair, big eyes, a dark glossy-skinned slim-built boy. By caste he was a Kayastha, as were the Babus he worked for. His main job was to help them in the care and protection of their one-year-old baby.

With the passage of time, the child progressed beyond the ambit of Raicharan's care. He went to school, from school to college, and finally after college he entered the legal profession at the office of a Munsif. Raicharan was now his personal servant.

The number of his masters had, however, increased by one: a lady bride had arrived in the house. Consequently, most of Raicharan's previous claims over Anukul Babu had naturally been appropriated by the new mistress.

However, just as the mistress had curtailed some of Raicharan's earlier authority, she had also restored most of it by giving him a new responsibility. Just a while ago, Anukul had been blessed with a baby boy —and Raicharan by sheer effort and perseverance had taken full charge of the little one and brought him completely under his wing.

He would enthusiastically swing the baby back and forth. He would expertly lift him up with his two hands and toss him up towards the sky. He constantly came close to his face and wagged his head making loud noises. Without expecting any response he would even start asking the baby, in a sing-song manner, such completely meaningless and irrelevant questions that this tiny image of Anukul just had to see Raicharan to look absolutely delighted.

Eventually, the boy began to crawl and ultimately also learnt to climb carefully over the threshold. Peals of laughter would accompany his rapid escape into a safe hiding place, whenever anyone tried to catch him. Raicharan was absolutely fascinated by the child's extraordinary intelligence and sense of judgment. Going up to the boy's mother, he would declare, with great pride and wonder, "Ma, when your son grows up he will surely become a judge and even earn five thousand rupees!"

Raicharan was unable to comprehend that other human offspring, at this early age, could also possibly show evidence of such outstanding skills. Specially, the kind that enabled them to violate the barriers created by thresholds and other such physical obstructions. He was sure that nothing was really impossible, where a future judge was concerned.

Ultimately, when the baby began to walk with unsteady steps, that was to him another wondrous event. When he began to address his mother as Ma, his father's sister as Pichi and also Raicharan as Channa, Raicharan at once announced this unbelievable news to all and sundry.

The most astonishing thing is that he addresses "Ma as Ma, Pishi as Pishi but me he calls Channa." How this idea came to a baby's mind was really difficult to explain. Surely, even an adult could never have displayed such a rare sense of proportion? Even if he had, his chances of becoming a judge would still have been considered doubtful by most ordinary people.

After some time, Raicharan was obliged to suspend a rope from his mouth and act like a horse. He even had to pretend to be a wrestler, and fight with the little boy. In fact, if he did not fall down on the ground defeated, there were rebellious reactions from the little fellow.

At this time, Anukul was transferred to one of the coastal Zilas along the shores of the river Padma. Anukul had purchased a perambulator from Kolkata for his son. Dressing the baby in a satin suit, a cap embroidered with gold threads, gold bangles around his wrists and two pairs of anklets on his feet, Raicharan took the baby prince out in his pram twice a day to enjoy the fresh air.

The monsoons arrived. The mouth of the hungry Padma began to devour, one by one, the gardens and corn fields of the village. The tall grass and wild tamarisk trees on the sandy beaches sank under the waters. Waves relentlessly crashing against the river banks echoed loudly all around. The rushing heaps of froth and foam made the senses visibly perceive that the river was in spate.

One afternoon, clouds had gathered but there seemed no possibility of rain. Raicharan's moody little lord and master just refused to stay indoors. He climbed into his pram. Slowly pushing the perambulator, Raicharan arrived at the paddy fields bordering the river. There was not a single boat on the river, not a single person in the fields. Through a slight opening in the clouds, the deserted sandy banks on the other side could be seen. Over them, silently, grand preparations were being made for the sun to set. In that silence the baby suddenly called "Channa, phoo!" and pointed his finger in one direction.

Not too far away on some marshy land, a few flowers had bloomed on the highest branches of a tall kadamba tree, and the baby's covetous gaze had been attracted by them. It was only a few days ago that Raicharan had fashioned a cart for the baby made of kadamba flowers pierced together with bamboo sticks. The boy had been so delighted to pull the cart around with a string that Raicharan had not been required to don a bridle at all the whole day. He had obviously been directly elevated from the position of a horse to the post of a groom.

Channa definitely had no inclination to wade through all that slush to pluck the flowers. Therefore, quickly pointing his fingers in the opposite direction he said, "Look, look—look at that bird, there it's flying away. Come bird, come here, come here." In this manner, incessantly making a variety of loud noises with his mouth, he began to push the pram away at great speed.

However, to hope that a child who in the future had the possibility of becoming a judge would be distracted by these ineffectual means, was an exercise in futility. More so, as nowhere around was there even a single thing worthy of attracting the eye and one could not after all persist for too long with an imaginary bird.

Raicharan finally said, "Okay, you sit in the pram and I will quickly go and pluck the flowers. Don't you dare go anywhere near the water." Saying which, he lifted his dhoti above his knees and went towards the kadamba tree.

However, his departure following the warning given against going near the water, only served to instantly bring back the baby's attention from the kadamba flower and make it fly towards the water. He saw the fast-flowing river, gurgling and splashing on its way; as though a stream of one lakh mischievous little babies, in their attempt to avoid being caught by some gigantic Raicharan, were collectively escaping to the forbidden land amidst a chorus of laughter and hilarity.

Their wicked example excited the mind of the child. He climbed down slowly from the pram and went towards the edge of the water. Picking up a long straw and imagining it to be a fishing rod, he bent over, pretending to catch fish. The restless river in her obscure choral language seemed to repeatedly invite the baby to come and play with her.

Once there was the sound of a loud splash. However, along the banks of the River Padma, during the monsoons, such sounds could be heard very often. Raicharan filled the entire aanchal-border of his dhoti with kadamba flowers. After climbing down from the tree, he came back to the pram with a smiling face and found no one there. He looked all around, but saw no trace of anyone anywhere.

Within seconds the blood in Raicharan's body ran cold. The entire world began to turn into a pale colorless haze. From the depths of his broken heart he cried out once, desperately, "Babu—Khoka Babu—my dear little Dada Babu!"

However, no one answered back saying "Channa"; no child's voice erupted laughing mischievously; all that could be heard was the gurgling and splashing sound of the Padma flowing swiftly by as before. It was as though she knew nothing, and was too busy to spare even a moment's attention on this extremely insignificant everyday earthly event.

As soon as dusk fell, the anxious mother sent people out in different directions. Carrying lanterns in their hands, the people who reached the river banks found Raicharan running helter-skelter like a stormy night wind, crying out in a broken voice "Babu—my Khoka Babu." Finally, Raicharan returned home and fell down with a thud at the feet of his mistress. To whatever questions were asked of him, he only wept, "I don't know, Ma."

498

Although everyone had mentally accepted that this was the doing of the river Padma, still the suspicion did not go that a group of gypsies who had assembled in the village may have also been responsible. In fact the mistress became so suspicious that she even thought Raicharan could have stolen the child. To the extent that she actually called him and said, "Just bring my baby back—and I will give you any amount of money you want." Hearing this, all Raicharan did was to keep striking his forehead with his hands. The mistress finally turned him rudely out of the house.

Anukul Babu had sincerely tried to remove this unjust suspicion regarding Raicharan from his wife's mind. He had asked her how it would benefit Raicharan to have perpetrated such a heinous crime. His wife had replied, "Why not? After all, the child was wearing gold ornaments."

II

Raicharan returned to his village. In all these years he had had no children and there did not seem much hope of having any either. Yet, by some divine miracle, before a year could pass, his wife, at an advanced age, gave birth to a male child and unfortunately passed away.

In Raicharan was born an extreme animosity towards this new child. He thought this baby had somehow tricked his way into taking Khoka Babu's place.

He even felt that having allowed his Lord and Master's only child to drown, to now savor the joy of having a son himself was like committing a deadly sin. If Raicharan's widowed sister had not been present, this infant would not have enjoyed the atmosphere of this earth for very long.

What was surprising to him was that, like Khoka Babu, this baby too in time began to climb over the thresholds and to flout every forbidden rule with as much curiosity and cleverness. In fact, even the sounds of his voice, his laughter and tears were very much like that of the other child. On some days when he heard the baby crying, Raicharan's heart would suddenly begin to throb. It felt as though Dada Babu, having lost sight of Raicharan, was crying out for him somewhere.

Phelna—Raicharan's sister had named him Phelna or cast away— in due course, called his aunt Pishi. Hearing that familiar mode of address, one day Raicharan suddenly thought, "That means Khoka Babu has not been able to sever the ties of his affection for me. He has actually come back and been reborn in my house."

There were certain irrefutable arguments that favored his belief. First, his birth so shortly after Khoka Babu's passing away. Second, that his wife should have after so many years suddenly given birth to a child, was not an achievement that could be credited entirely to her own virtues. Third, this child also crawled, waddled about unsteadily and called his aunt Pishi. Moreover, of all the several traits which could ensure a child's future as a judge, many were present in this baby boy.

He then suddenly remembered his Mathakrun's terrible suspicion. Surprised, he told himself mentally "Aha, so the mother's mind had instinctively known that it was I who had stolen her son." He then began to regret having neglected the baby for so long. Finally, he became involved with the child once again.

Since that day, Raicharan began bringing up Phelna as though he was the son of a very rich man. He brought satin garments for him. He brought a cap made of gold thread. By melting his dead wife's gold ornaments, a variety of bangles were made for the boy. He did not allow him to play with any of the boys of the locality. Whether night or day, he became his son's one and only playmate. Whenever they got the opportunity, the local boys laughed at Phelna, calling him a Nawabputra or son of a Nawab. The people of Raicharan's village were equally astounded at his almost insane behavior.

When Phelna needed to go to school, Raicharan sold all his lands and took the boy to Kolkata. There, with great difficulty he procured a job and started sending Phelna to a school. Living in a haphazard manner himself, he did not compromise on good food, good clothes or good education for the boy. Mentally he told himself "Dear boy, even though you have come to my home out of love for me, do not think you will be neglected in any way, you will not."

In this way twelve years passed by. The boy was well-educated and even looked and sounded very impressive. He was well-built with a glossy light-brown skin. He was extremely particular about his hairstyle and his clothes. He had a somewhat happy disposition and was partial to the niceties of life. He was unable to really think of his father as his own. This was because Raicharan showered the love of a father on him, but cared for him more like a servant. His other fault, that he had kept a secret from everyone, was that he was Phelna's father. In the student hostel where Phelna resided, his fellow mates were always very curious about Raicharan, who spoke in the distinctive East Bengal dialect. They poked fun at him, in fact, in the absence of his father. One could not confidently say that Phelna did not contribute in some ways also to this amused curiosity of his fellow-mates. Yet the gentle and affectionate Raicharan was dearly loved by all the students. Phelna too loved him, but as I have already mentioned, not really like a father. There was a slight mixture of condescension in it.

As time passed, old age caught up with Raicharan. His Lord and Master was constantly finding fault with him. Actually his body had grown slack and he was unable to concentrate much on his work and kept forgetting things. But a man who pays a full salary was not likely to accept the excuses of old age. In fact, the money Raicharan had brought with him after selling all his property had almost dried up. Nowadays, even Phelna had begun to express his constant irritation with shortcomings in his attire.

III

One day Raicharan suddenly quit his job and giving Phelna some money said, "It has become necessary, so I am going back to the village for a few days," saying which he went back to Barasat. Anukul Babu had been appointed the Munsif there.

Anukul had never had a second child. His wife, deep within her heart, was still nursing her grief at losing her son.

One evening, Anukul Babu was resting after returning from the courts and his wife was in the process of buying an invaluable plant root and blessings from a mendicant in the hope of having a child. Just then there was a sound in the courtyard, "May you prosper, Mother."

The Munsif asked, "Who is it?"

Raicharan came forward and after paying obeisance to him, said, "It's me, Raicharan."

Seeing the old man, Anukul's heart melted with affection. Asking him innumerable questions about his present condition, he also proposed that he reinstate him in his service once again.

Smiling cheerlessly, Raicharan said "I would like to pay my respects to Mother."

Anukul personally escorted him to the inner courtyard reserved for the women of the household. The Mathakrun, however, did not receive him with equal warmth and joy. Carefully ignoring this, Raicharan spoke up with folded hands in a supplicatory manner, "Babu—Ma, I am the one who stole your son. It was not the Padma, nor anyone else but I, who have shown such despicable ingratitude to my benefactor—"

Anukul exclaimed "What are you saying! Where is he?"

"Begging your pardon, he has been with me all along. I will bring him to you the day after tomorrow."

That day was a Sunday and so the courts were closed. From early morning, both husband and wife sat anxiously waiting, looking out for him. Accompanied by Phelna, Raicharan finally arrived at around ten o'clock.

Anukul's wife, without asking any questions or making any judgments, took Phelna on to her lap. She touched and smelt him all over. With insatiable eyes she examined his face and laughed and cried, all at the same time. Actually the boy was rather handsome. There was no trace of poverty either in his clothes and appearance or bearing. He had an extremely pleasing, polite and modest air about him. Looking at him, a sudden rush of affection welled up in Anukul's heart as well.

In spite of this, he assumed an impassive air and questioned Raicharan, "What proof do you have?"

Raicharan said, "How can there be proof of such a deed? That I stole your son, only God Almighty knows, no one else on earth does."

After much thought Anukul took a decision. Since his wife had enthusiastically taken the boy to her heart as soon as she received him, it would not be advisable now to try and collect proof. Whatever happened, it was best to believe him. Moreover, from where could Raicharan have possibly got such a boy? Also, why should an old servant want to deceive him for no reason at all?

While conversing with the boy, he also came to learn that since babyhood he had lived with Raicharan and had considered him to be his father. Raicharan however, never treated him as a father should. His behavior actually resembled that of a servant.

Removing all doubts from his own mind, Anukul finally said, "However, Raicharan, you do realize that you can never ever reenter this house again."

With folded hands, Raicharan spoke in a voice choked with emotion, "My Lord, where will I go now in my old age?"

Mathakrun said, "Aah, let it be. My son should prosper. I forgive him."

A man of integrity, Anukul, remained firm. "The deed he has done is unpardonable."

Raicharan clasped Anukul's feet and implored, "I did not do anything, it was the hand of God."

On seeing his attempt to shift the burden of his own sins onto the shoulders of the Almighty, in even greater irritation Anukul said, "It is no more a duty to trust someone who has committed such a treacherous deed."

Releasing his Babu's feet, Raicharan said, "That person is not me, my Lord."

"Then, who is it?"

"My destiny."

However, this kind of an explanation would never satisfy any educated person.

Raicharan again beseeched his master, "I have no one else in the whole world."

When Phelna realized that he was actually the son of a Munsif, and that Raicharan had stolen him and insulted him for so long, by claiming he was his own son, he had initially felt some anger. Subsequently, however, he generously told his father, "Baba, please forgive him. Even if you don't allow him to stay in your house, at least fix some monthly remuneration for him."

Finally, without saying a word, Raicharan examined his son's face just once, and paid his respects to everyone. He then went out through the door and was absorbed into the teeming millions who inhabit this earth. At the end of the month, however, when Anukul sent some remuneration to his village address, the money was returned. No one lived there anymore . . .

1892

("Khokababur Pratyabartan," from *Galpaguchchha*)

Translated by Nandini Guha

The Legacy

I

"I am leaving this very minute!" announced Brindavan Kundu to his father in a fit of rage.

"Ungrateful wretch!" cried his father Jagyanath Kundu. "Not a word about repaying me for all I have spent on your upbringing since you were a child! How arrogant you are now!"

Not that too much had been spent, considering the lifestyle in Jagyanath's home. In ancient times, the sages lived incredibly frugal lives, spending very little on food and apparel. It was clear from Jagyanath's conduct that he shared these lofty ideals, but had not attained them completely. For this, the fault lay partly in modern society, and partly in nature's unjust laws of survival.

His son tolerated his parsimony as long as he remained a bachelor, but after he was married, differences developed between the father's extremely pure ideals and those of his son. It became evident that the son's goals were gradually shifting from the spiritual to the material. Corresponding to the needs of a physical world subject to heat-cold-hunger-thirst, there was a steady increase in the yardage of fabric and quantity of food that he consumed.

This gave rise to frequent arguments between father and son. Ultimately, when their naturopath, the kobiraj, arranged for some very costly medication for Brindavan's wife who was seriously ill, Jagyanath took this for a sign of the medicine-man's lack of experience and immediately dismissed him. At first Brindavan begged and pleaded, then he flew into a rage, but to no avail. When his wife died, he cursed his father for having murdered her.

"Why, does no one die after taking medicine?" argued his father. "If expensive medicines were sufficient to ensure survival, why would kings and emperors die at all? Should your wife die with more fanfare than your mother or your grandmother?"

Truly, if Brindavan had considered the matter calmly instead of being blinded by grief, he would have found much solace in these words. Neither his mother nor his grandmother had received any medication before death. That was the sacred tradition of their family. But modern people don't even want to die in old-fashioned ways. At the time we speak of, the British had newly arrived in this land, but even in those days, the old-fashioned people would inhale deeper puffs of tobacco as they marveled at the behavior of the modern generation.

Anyway, Brindavan, a modernist of those times, quarreled with the old-time traditionalist Jagyanath, and declared, "I am leaving."

Promptly granting him permission to leave, the father announced in public that if he ever gave Brindavan a single paisa, it would be no less a sin than shedding the blood of a holy cow. Brindavan also acknowledged in public that to accept Jagyanath's wealth would be no less a sin

than shedding the blood of one's own mother. Father and son were es-
tranged, ever since.

The people of the village were delighted at this minor rebellion,
after a long spell of peace. After Jagyanath's son was disinherited, all of
them did their best to assuage Jagyanath's unbearable grief at parting
from his son. All of them agreed that only in modern times could a son
quarrel with his father merely for the sake of a wife.

They put forth a very strong argument: if a wife dies, another can
be acquired without any delay, but when a father dies, no amount of
head-banging can procure a replacement for him. It was a powerful argu-
ment, no doubt; but I believe that a young man like Brindavan would
feel reassured rather than remorseful if he heard it.

Brindavan's departure did not appear to have caused his father
much distress at the time. For one thing, Brindavan's absence reduced his
household expenses. Moreover, Jagyanath was freed of a great anxiety. He
had always been afraid that Brindavan might poison him. The fear of
poison that constantly haunted his extremely frugal meals had abated
a little after his daughter-in-law's death, and once his son left, he felt
greatly relieved.

Only one thing pained him. Brindavan had left with Jagyanath's
four-year-old grandson Gokulchandra. As the cost of feeding and cloth-
ing Gokul was exceedingly low, Jagyanath's affection for him was more or
less free of anxiety. All the same, when Brindavan actually took the boy
away, a financial calculation flashed through Jagyanath's mind, even in
the midst of his unfeigned grief: how far his monthly expenditure would
decrease after the two of them had left, the yearly savings he would make,
and how far these would cover the interest he owed on borrowed money.

But still, without Gokulchandra's pranks, it became hard to live
in that empty house anymore. Now Jagyanath found things very diffi-
cult, for there was nobody to disrupt his prayers, snatch away his food
at mealtimes, or run off with the inkpot when he was scribbling away at
his accounts. He bathed and ate undisturbed, but it made him feel des-
perate.

Only after death do people achieve such untroubled emptiness,
he felt. The sight of the holes his grandson had pierced in the embroi-

dered kantha bedspread, and the ink stains created on his reed floor mat by the same artist, agitated him even more. That outrageous youngster had been sternly reprimanded by his grandfather for having completely ruined his dhoti and for rendering it unusable within just two years; but now, seeing that tattered, faded, discarded piece of cloth in the boy's bedroom, tears welled up in Jagyanath's eyes. Instead of using the fabric for lamp-wicks or some other domestic purpose, he carefully folded it away in his iron safe, and vowed that if Gokul came back, he would not scold the boy even if he ruined one dhoti every year.

But Gokul did not return. Jagyanath seemed to age much faster than before, and the empty home seemed emptier by the day.

Jagyanath could not remain quietly at home anymore. Even at noon, when all respectable folks enjoyed a nap after their meal, Jagyanath would roam, hookah in hand, from one locality to another. During his silent afternoon wanderings, the boys in the street would abandon their games and escape to a safe place, from where they would loudly and audibly recite rhymes about his miserliness, composed by local poets. Nobody dared pronounce his proper name, lest they choke on their food; so they all gave him new names as they pleased. The elderly would call him "Jagyanash," destroyer of holy ceremonies, but why the boys named him "Chamchike" the tiny bat, was not clear. Perhaps there was some physical resemblance between his thin, bloodless skin and that of the flying creature.

2

At noon one day, wandering down the village path in the cool shade of mango trees, Jagyanath saw that an unknown boy had assumed the leader's role in the gang of village boys, intending to teach them a new prank. Overwhelmed by his strong personality and innovative skills, the other boys had surrendered to his authority, body and soul.

The other boys abandoned play when they saw the old man, but this boy darted up close to Jagyanath and shook out the chador he wore as a wrap. Out sprang a chameleon, released from the folds of the chador. It slithered down Jagyanath's body to escape towards the forest. The sudden fright gave the old man goose pimples. The boys erupted in mirth.

Jagyanath had not gone much further when his gamchha vanished from his shoulder, to reappear as a turban on the unknown boy's head.

Jagyanath derived great satisfaction from this unconventional form of civility from the strange little fellow. It was a long time since any boy had approached him with such unconstrained familiarity. After much calling and coaxing, Jagyanath managed to get the boy to draw a little closer.

507

"What is your name?" he asked.

"Nitai Pal."

"Where do you live?"

"I won't tell you."

"What is your father's name?"

"I won't tell you."

"Why not?"

"I've run away from home, that's why."

"Why?"

"My father wants to send me to the pathshala."

It immediately struck Jagyanath that sending such a boy to the village school was a waste of money, a sign of the father's lack of financial judgment.

"Do you want to stay with me?" Jagyanath offered.

Without any protest, the boy unhesitatingly took refuge in Jagyanath's house, as if merely sheltering under the shade of some roadside tree.

Not only that, he began to make shameless demands for food and clothing, as if he had paid for them in advance. He would sometimes quarrel openly with the master of the house about these matters. It had been easy to vanquish his own son, but Jagyanath was defeated by this boy, a stranger's son.

3

The people of the village were amazed at the unprecedented hospitality enjoyed by Nitai Pal in Jagyanath's house. They realized that the old man did not have long to live, and that he would bequeath all his property to this alien boy from nowhere.

Growing very jealous of the boy, they all resolved to harm him. But the old man went about guarding him closely like a bone from his own ribcage.

Sometimes when the boy threatened to leave, Jagyanath would tempt him: "Bhai, I'll leave all my property and assets to you." The boy was young but he fully understood the value of this assurance.

Now the villagers set out in search of the boy's father.

"Ah, how his poor parents must suffer!" they all declared. "What a sinful boy!"

So saying, they would hurl unutterable abuse at the boy. So bitter was their condemnation, it smacked of selfish jealousy rather than moral outrage.

One day, the old man heard from a traveler that a man called Damodar Pal was heading towards their own village to search for his missing son. Nitai grew extremely agitated at this news. Abandoning all his would-be assets, he was ready to abscond.

"I'll hide you in a place where nobody can find you, not even the villagers," Jagyanath assured Nitai repeatedly.

The boy grew very curious. "Show me where it is, won't you?" he urged.

"If I show you now, people will get to know. I'll take you there tonight," Jagyanath promised.

Nitai was elated at the prospect of a new, mysterious revelation. He resolved that as soon as his father departed after his failed mission, he must lay a wager with the other boys for a game of hide-and-seek. Nobody would find him. What fun! His father would come there, search the whole area, and still find no trace of him. That would be a great joke, too.

At noon, Jagyanath locked the boy into the house and went away somewhere. When he returned, Nitai pestered him with questions.

"Let's go," he insisted, as soon as dusk descended.

"It's not yet night," Jayanath objected.

"It's night now, Dada, let's go," Nitai pleaded once more.

"Our neighbors aren't asleep yet."

"They're sleeping now, let's go," urged Nitai, a mere second later.

It grew late. Nitai began to nod off, despite a desperate struggle to control his drowsiness. At midnight, Jagyanath took Nitai's hand and stepped out into the dark street of the sleeping village. There was no sound save the occasional barking of a dog, and all the dogs, near and far, joined in. Every now and then, a night bird, disturbed by their footsteps, would flap its wings and fly into the forest. Frightened, Nitai clutched Jayanath's hand tightly.

Having crossed many fields, they arrived at a dilapidated shrine without an idol, in the middle of a forest.

"Is this the place?" asked Nitai, sounding rather disappointed.

It was not at all as he had imagined. There was nothing mysterious about the place. After leaving his father's house, he had been obliged to spend the occasional night in such ruined temples. The spot was not unsuitable for a game of hide-and-seek, but it would not be impossible to find someone hiding there.

Jagyanath lifted a slab of stone from the centre of the temple floor. Below, the boy saw a small chamber-like space, with a lamp burning within. The sight aroused his wonder and curiosity, but he also started feeling frightened. Jagyanath climbed down a ladder, with Nitai following timidly behind.

In the area down below, he saw large brass pots arranged around a reed mat. Placed before the mat were sindoor, chandan, flower garlands and ritual items of worship. Peering inside curiously, the boy found the pots full of silver rupees and gold coins.

"I promised you, Nitai, that I would give you all my wealth," said Jagyanath. "I don't have much; all I possess is in these few pitchers. Tonight, I shall leave all this in your hands."

"All this?" cried the boy, jumping in delight. "You won't take a single rupee-coin?"

"May leprosy strike my hands if I do. But there is one condition. If ever my missing grandson Gokulchandra should return, or his son or grandson or great-grandson or any descendant of their family should come here, all this money must be counted and handed over to him."

The boy thought Jagyanath had lost his mind. "Sure," he agreed at once. "Then come and sit on this asana," Jagyanath invited, indicating the mat.

"Why?"

"Prayers must be offered to you."

"Why?"

"Those are the rules."

The boy took his place on the asana. Jagyanath applied chandan on his brow, marked his forehead with a sindoor tika, placed a garland around his neck. He sat facing Nitai, and began to mutter some mantras.

Enshrined as a deity, Nitai began to feel apprehensive at the chanting of mantras.

"Dada!" he called.

Jagyanath did not reply. He continued chanting mantras.

Finally, with great effort, he dragged each pitcher close to the boy and dedicated it to him. Each time, he made Nitai repeat: "I shall count out all this money and hand it over to Gokulchandra Kunda, son of Brindavan Kunda, son of Jagyanath Kunda, son of Paramananda Kunda, son of Prankrishna Kunda, son of Gadadhar Kunda, son of Judhishtir Kunda, or to his son or grandson or great-grandson or to the rightful heir of this family."

Reciting these words again and again, the boy seemed to lose his wits. Slowly his speech grew slurred. As the ceremony drew to a close, the tiny cavern became saturated with the vapor from their breath and the lamp-smoke. The boy felt the roof of his mouth go dry, his hands and feet seemed to be on fire, and he was close to suffocation.

The lamp grew dim and suddenly went out. In the darkness, the boy sensed that Jagyanath was climbing up the ladder.

"Dada, where are you going?" he asked in terror.

"I'll be off. You stay here. Nobody will ever find you. But remember: Gokulchandra, son of Brindavan, son of Jagyanath."

With these words, he ascended and pulled up the ladder.

"Dada, I want to go to Baba, I want my father," pleaded the boy, speaking with difficulty in a choking voice.

Jagyanath replaced the stone slab on the mouth of the cavity. Placing his ear against it, he heard Nitai call out again in a strangled voice: "Baba!"

Then there was a thud, and after that, no sound at all.

Having thus surrendered his wealth to the yaksha, guardian spirit of underworld treasures, Jagyanath began to cover the stone slab with earth. Above that, he piled bricks and sand from the ruined temple. On top, he arranged patches of turf, and planted forest vines. The night was almost over, but he could not tear himself away from that spot. Every now and then, he would put his ear to the ground and listen. He began to feel as if he could hear a remote cry, rising up from far, far away, from the bottomless depths of the earth. He felt as if the night sky was filled with that single sound, as if all the sleeping people of this earth had awakened to this sound and were straining to listen.

The old man was desperately piling up layer upon layer of soil. It was as if he wanted somehow to suppress the voice of the earth in this way. There was that cry! He could hear someone calling:

"Baba!"

"Quiet!" cried the old man, striking the ground. "Everyone will hear."

"Baba!" that voice called out, once again.

He saw that the sun was up. Afraid, he left the temple and came out into the fields. There, too, someone called out:

"Baba!"

Jagyanath turned around with a start and saw that it was Brindavan.

"Baba, I was told my son has been hiding in your house," said Brindavan. "Hand him over to me."

His face contorted, the old man leaned towards Brindavan. "Your son?" he asked.

"Yes, Gokul . . . now his name is Nitai Pal, and I am called Damodar. You are well known everywhere in the vicinity, so we had to change our names, out of shame. Otherwise, nobody would want to call us by name."

The old man clawed at the sky with his fingers, as if trying to clutch at the air. He fell to the ground.

When he regained consciousness, Jagyanath dragged Brindavan to the temple.

"Can you hear the sound of weeping?" he demanded.

"No."

"Listen carefully now, is anyone crying out for 'Baba'?"

"No."

The old man now seemed very relieved.

Ever since, he would go about asking everyone: "Can you hear the sound of weeping?" Everyone laughed at his crazy words.

He died four years later. As his vision grew dim and his breath became choked, he suddenly sat up in a delirium. The dying man groped in the air and asked: "Nitai, who has removed my ladder?"

Unable to find the ladder that would lead him out of that vast, airless, lightless abyss, he collapsed back onto his bed. In life's game of hide-and-seek, he disappeared into the place where no-one can be found.

1891–1892

("Sampatti Samarpan," from *Galpaguchchha*)

Translated by Radha Chakravarty

Shubha

I

When the girl was named Shubhashini[1] no one knew she would be dumb. Her two elder sisters were named Shukeshini and Shuhashini,[2] so for the sake of rhyme her father named her Shubhashini. Now everyone calls her Shubha for short.

After a long search and much expense the two elder daughters were married. Now the youngest remained, as a silent pressure on her parents' hearts.

That she cannot speak does not mean she cannot feel: this is something most people forget. That is why everyone expresses disquiet about her future in her presence. From childhood she has understood that she has come as a divine curse on her home. That is why she always tries to keep herself hidden. If only everyone could forget I exist, she moans. But can anyone forget pain? Her mother, in particular, looks upon her as some sort of personal flaw. Mothers often regard their daughters, not their sons, as part of themselves. Any lack or incompleteness in the child is seen as something acutely shameful. The girl's father, Banikontho, seems to love Shubha just a little more than his other daughters, but her mother looks upon her as the one who shamed her womb, and is continually vexed with her.

Shubha cannot speak, but she has two large black eyes fringed with long lashes. Her lips tremble like tender young leaves at the very hint of emotion.

The feelings we express in words we construct ourselves, almost like a translation. The approximation is not always exact; mistakes do occur. But eyes don't have to translate. The mind immediately casts its shadow over them; feelings ebb and flow at ease. Sometimes the eyes sparkle, sometimes they look faded and listless. At times, like the setting moon, they gaze on all impassively. At other times their glance bounces off objects like swift, glittering lightning. The language of the eyes of the one who cannot speak is limitless, benevolent and profound—somewhat like the clear sky, the site for an endless battle between dawn and dusk. In these mute individuals lies a certain grandeur, a grandeur as great as that of nature itself. That is why the other children are a little afraid of Shubha. They do not play with her. Like the deserted summer afternoon, she is silent and without companions.

2

The village is called Chondipur. The river is a minor stream of Bengal, like a domesticated young girl. It doesn't flow very far. The slender river flows, remaining within its banks as it goes about its business. It has relations of some sort or the other with all the villagers. On either side are huts, and the high banks are dense with trees. The river, like the village's Lakshmi, performs its innumerable good deeds silently, on swift feet and with a light heart, completely oblivious of itself.

Banikontho's home is right on the river. His bamboo fences, his many-roofed house, his cowsheds, his threshing room, his haystacks, his kitchen garden, his orchards of mango, banana and jackfruit attract the attention of all who sail by on boats. In the midst of all this rustic opulence I don't know if anyone notices the mute girl. Whenever she has any leisure from her chores, she comes and sits by the river.

Nature seems to complete her lack of words. It seems to speak for her. The river's murmur, the people's bustle, the fisherman's song, the birds' chirps, the rustle of the leaves—everything mixes together and breaks like a mighty wave on the girl's silent heart. Nature's many sounds and many rhythms are also the mute, long-lashed, black-eyed girl's language. From the grassroots to the stars there are only hints, songs, sobs and sighs.

In the heat of the afternoon the fisherman goes home to eat, the householder takes a siesta, the birds stop chirping, the boats stop plying and the workaday world comes to a halt. Then, under the stern sky, only mute nature and one mute girl sit face to face, the one in the glare of the sun, the other in the shade of a slender tree.

It's not as if Shubha does not have a few close friends. There are two cows named Shorborshi and Panguli. They never hear the girl call out their names but they recognize her footsteps. They understand that sad, wordless melody more easily than words. They understand better than humans when Shubha is fondling them, when she is chiding them and when she is pleading with them.

When Shubha enters the cowshed she puts her arms around Shorborshi while Panguli, with a warmly moist gaze, gives her a lick. Every day Shubha visits the cowshed three times on an official basis. There are, besides, numerous unofficial visits. Whenever she has to face harsh words at home she runs to her mute friends. They sense her sorrow from her patient, sad gaze. They rub themselves against her time and time again in an effort to comfort her.

There are, besides, goats and a kitten. They are not such close friends although they are very fond of her. The kitten climbs unhesitatingly into Shubha's warm lap any time of the day or night and curls up for a nap, hinting that her soft touch on its throat and back would help it fall asleep.

3

Shubha has another friend from a higher species. But it is difficult to gauge the exact nature of the relationship because one of them can speak. They have no language in common.

The youngest son of the Goshais is called Protap. He is an idler and a good-for-nothing. After many an attempt, his parents have given up all hope that he will ever be a useful member of society. However, good-for-nothings have one advantage—their relatives are always annoyed with them but they are the favorites of strangers. Since they are not gainfully employed, the good-for-nothings become the property of the state. Just as every town must have a few state-owned public parks that don't belong to any household, similarly every village must have a few good-for-nothing individuals who serve the state. Whenever there are a few people short, be it in work or play, these good-for-nothings can be put to use.

Protap's chief hobby is fishing. Much time can be spent at ease in such an occupation. In the afternoons he is often to be seen on the river bank. This is how he frequently runs into Shubha. Protap likes company—and a silent companion is ideal for fishing. Protap appreciates Shubha's worth. So while everyone calls Shubha "Shubha," Protap affectionately abbreviates her name further to "Shu."

Shubha sits in the shade of the tamarind tree and, not very far off, Protap, fish rod in hand, gazes reflectively into the water. Protap likes eating paan; Shubha prepares one with her own hands. And I think sitting there she yearns to come to his aid in some way, yearns to prove to him that yes, she too is of some use in the world. But there is nothing for her to do. She prays to God miraculously to fabricate some startling event which will lead the astonished Protap to exclaim, "Really, I never knew our Shubha had it in her!"

Imagine that Shubha is a mermaid. She takes a precious gem from a snake's head and places it on the river bank. Protap sees the gem, abandons his frivolous fishing, and jumps into the river, grasping the jewel in his hand. And who does he see in the depths of the river, seated on a golden four-poster bed in a silver palace? That mute daughter of Banikontho, Shu. Shu is the sole princess of that vast, silent, gem-encrusted land beneath the sea. Could such a thing not happen? Is it all that improbable? Actually, nothing is improbable. But still, Shu is not born in the royal family of the citizen-less land beneath the sea, but to Banikontho. And there is no way in which she can astonish the Goshai boy, Protap.

516

4

Shubha is gradually growing up. She begins to discover herself. It is as if on some full moon night an ocean wave comes and floods her soul with a new, indescribable consciousness. She can see herself, think, and pose questions—but she cannot find the answers.

On a dense, full moon night, Shubha slowly opens her bedroom door and peeps out. The moonlit night presides, alone and wakeful, over the silent and sleeping world much like Shubha herself. The mysteries of youth, its delights and conflicts, lie spread across the limitless, lonely expanse up to the horizon and even beyond. Silent, throbbing, unable to utter a syllable. A speechless, anguished young girl faces speechless, anguished nature.

Her parents are getting worried: an unwed daughter is a heavy burden to bear. Tongues are wagging. There is even talk of breaking all ties with the family. Banikontho is well-off. He eats fish and rice twice a day, hence he has enemies.

Husband and wife confer together. Bani leaves the village for a while. Eventually he returns and says, "Come, let's go to Kolkata."

Preparations are made for the journey. Like a foggy dawn, Shubha's heart is suffused with the mist of tears. She begins to tail her parents like a dumb animal, her heart full of an unknown, indistinct anxiety, her large eyes trying to read their faces. But they do not explain anything to her.

In the meantime, flinging his fishing line out on a lazy afternoon, Protap laughingly says, "Hey, Shu, seems like they've found a husband for you, and you're off to be married. Mind you don't forget us now." And he returns to his fishing.

Just as a trapped doe stares at the trap and silently asks, "What harm have I ever done you?" so Shubha stares at Protap. She doesn't sit in the tree's shade that day. Banikontho is enjoying a chew of tobacco after his siesta. Shubha comes and sits at his feet and begins to weep. In the end, after trying to comfort her, a few tears roll down Bani's withered cheeks.

They are to leave for Kolkata the following day. Shubha goes to the cowshed to bid her childhood friends goodbye. She feeds them with her own hands, puts her arms around them, and looks at them with eyes brimful of all the words they can hold. The tears fall silently, one by one.

It is three nights before the full moon. Shubha comes out of her house and flings herself on the young grass by the river bed. It is as if she is embracing a mammoth and mute Mother Earth and pleading, "Please don't let me go, Ma. Hold me just as I am holding you, and don't let me go."

In a lodging-house in Kolkata, Shubha's mother dresses her up. She ties her hair in a bun, threads it with a zari ribbon, covers her with jewelry so that her natural grace is completely obscured. Shubha is weeping. Lest her eyes grow puffy and spoil her appearance, her mother gives her a fierce scolding. But the tears refuse to listen and keep falling.

The groom comes in person to inspect the bride, accompanied by some friends. The girl's parents are anxious, eager to see to everything at once. It is as if the god himself has come down to choose the animal for the sacrifice. The mother takes Shubha aside and increases her tears a thousandfold by many imprecations. When the candidate is presented for inspection, the examiner stares at her for a long time before saying, "Not bad."

Seeing the girl's tears he understands that she has a heart. And he calculates that the heart that is so pained at the prospect of leaving her parents can be put to good use in future for his own benefit. Like the pearl in the oyster, the girl's tears only increase her worth: they do not speak on her behalf.

After consulting the almanac and choosing an auspicious date, the marriage is conducted. Handing their daughter over to strangers, the parents leave for the village. Their caste and their life beyond death remain safe.

The groom works in the west. After some time he takes his bride with him. Within a week everyone knows that the new bride is mute. But no one understands that this is not her fault. She has not duped anybody. Her eyes revealed everything freely, but no one understood their language.

She gazes at everyone—she can't find the words—she can't locate those known faces that would comprehend a mute's language. Inside the girl's ever-silent heart a huge, wordless cry begins to boom—but no one save the Almighty can hear it.

This time her husband, after checking both speech and hearing, marries a girl who can speak.

1893
(From *Galpaguchchha*)
Translated by Shormishtha Panja

Mahamaya

I

Mahamaya and Rajiblochan met in a ruined temple by the riverbank.

Without a word, Mahamaya, with her characteristic gravity, glanced reprovingly at Rajib. Meaning, "How dare you summon me here today, at this odd hour? Is it because I've complied with all your wishes up until now, that you have grown so audacious?"

Rajib, always somewhat afraid of Mahamaya, was extremely perturbed by this look. He had prepared a set speech, but had to abandon those plans at once. And yet, it was essential to offer some reason for this meeting immediately. So he quickly blurted out:

"I propose that we run away and get married."

Rajib did manage to utter what he had in mind, but without any of the preliminaries that he had thought up for the occasion. His proposal sounded utterly dry and stark, even bizarre. Dumbfounded at his own words, he no longer had the power to soften the statement with a few embellishments. Having summoned Mahamaya to the ruined temple by the riverside at this noontime hour, all the foolish man could say was: "Come, let's get married!"

Mahamaya was an unwed woman from an exclusive, high-caste kulin family. She was forty, and as developed in her beauty as she was mature in her years. An image of pure gold she was, like the early autumn sunlight of the Sharat season, radiant and silent as that sunshine, her gaze open and fearless as the daylight itself.

Her father was dead but she had an elder brother named Bhabanicharan Chattopadhyay. Brother and sister were alike in temperament. They spoke little, but had a silently scorching spirit, as fiery as the midday sun. People were unaccountably afraid of Bhabanicharan.

Rajib was from a distant land. The manager of the silk factory here had brought him along. Rajib's father had served this saheb; when he died, the saheb assumed the guardianship of his employee's son, and brought the child to this factory at Bamonhati. The boy was accompanied only by his loving paternal aunt, his pishi. They lived close to Bhabanicharan's house. Mahamaya was Rajib's childhood playmate, and Rajib's pishi was very fond of her.

By and by, Rajib grew up to be sixteen, seventeen, eighteen, and even nineteen. But despite his pishi's insistence, he was reluctant to marry. The saheb was delighted at this evidence of rare wisdom in a Bengali boy, imagining himself to be the model that this lad had adopted. For the saheb was unmarried. In time, the pishi also passed away.

Without spending beyond their means, it was also not possible to find a suitably well-born match for Mahamaya. She too was growing older, and was getting to be confirmed as a spinster.

It is needless to tell my readers that although Prajapati, the god of marriage, displayed such indifference towards this couple, Kandarpa, the god of love, had not been wasting his time. While old Prajapati was nodding, the youthful Kandarpa was wide awake.

Different people feel the influence of Lord Kandarpa differently. Instigated by him, Rajib constantly sought an opportunity to say what was on his mind, but Mahamaya would not give him a chance. Her silent, somber gaze filled Rajib's yearning heart with apprehension.

Today, Rajib had succeeded at last in getting Mahamaya to this ruined temple by a hundred solemn oaths and entreaties. He had resolved on this day to lay his heart bare, and then it would be either lifelong happiness or a living death for him. But on this crucial day in his life, all Rajib said was, "Come, let's get married." And then, like a student who had forgotten his lesson, he had lapsed into a confused silence. Apparently, Mahamaya had not expected such a proposal from Rajib, for she was speechless for a long time.

In the midst of this silence, the numerous vague, plaintive sounds of that noontime hour began to make themselves heard. From time to time, the half-closed door of the temple began to slowly swing open and shut in the breeze, with a low, excruciating groan. The pigeon called at the temple window, the woodpecker knocked away monotonously on the branch of the shimul tree outside, the chameleon rustled through the heaps of dry leaves, a sudden gust of warm wind blew in from the field and hissed through the foliage of all the trees, and suddenly aroused, the river waters sloshed against the steps of the broken ghaat. Amidst all these idle sounds, from the shade of a faraway tree, the rustic strains of a cowherd's flute drifted to their ears. Not daring to glance at Mahamaya's face, Rajib leant against the temple plinth and gazed at the river in a weary, dreamlike daze.

After a while, he turned his head and looked beseechingly at Mahamaya's face once more.

"No, it is not possible," she declared, shaking her head.

With that shake of Mahamaya's head, Rajib's hopes were reduced to dust. For he knew perfectly well that Mahamaya's head followed her own dictates; it was beyond anyone else's power to move it at their will. With the fierce caste pride that flowed through the veins of Mahamaya's family though so many generations, could she ever agree to marry a non-kulin, non-high-caste Brahmin like Rajib? Love was one thing, but marriage was quite another. Anyway, Mahamaya realized that it was her own indiscretion that had encouraged Rajib to become so audacious. At once, she prepared to leave the temple.

"I'm off tomorrow, moving away from this place," announced Rajib hastily, sizing up the situation.

"How does that piece of information matter to me?" Mahamaya's first impulse was to signal this reaction, but she couldn't. When she tried to leave, her feet failed her.

"Why?" she asked, quietly.

"My saheb has been transferred to the kuthi, the factory at Sonapur," Rajib told her. "He is taking me with him."

Again, Mahamaya lapsed into a long silence. Their two lives were moving in contrary directions, she thought. One could not keep a person under one's eye forever. So, she unclenched her pursed lips slightly, to say:

"Achchha." Her utterance sounded rather like a deep sigh. "Very well."

With this bare statement, Mahamaya was again about to leave, when Rajib gave a start.

"Chatujje mohashai!" he exclaimed.

Mahamaya spotted Bhabanicharan approaching the temple. She realized he had spotted them. Sensing that Mahamaya was likely to face a precarious situation, Rajib tried to escape by jumping out through the broken wall of the temple, but Mahamaya gripped his hand, holding him back by force. Bhabanicharan entered the temple. Just once, silent and still, he glanced at the two of them.

Unperturbed, Mahamaya looked at Rajib. "Rajib, it is to your house that I will go. Wait for me," she said.

Without a word, Bhabanicharan left the temple, and without a word, Mahamaya followed. As for Rajib, he stood there dazed, like one condemned to the gallows.

2

That very night, Bhabanicharan brought Mahamaya a red cheli.

"Go put this on," he instructed her. Mahamaya came back to him, dressed in the bridal sari.

"Come with me," he now commanded.

Nobody had ever disobeyed a command, or even a signal, from Bhabanicharan. Not even Mahamaya.

That night, the two of them headed for the cremation ground. The place was not far from where they lived. There, in the hut reserved for dying men brought to the holy shore of the Ganga, lay an old Brahmin awaiting his death. The two went and stood beside his bed. A Brahmin priest was present there, in a corner of the room. Bhabanicharan signaled to him. Without delay, the priest made arrangements for an auspicious ceremony, and waited in readiness. Mahamaya realized that she was to be married off to this dying man. She evinced no sign of protest. In the light from a couple of burning pyres nearby, inside the almost pitch-dark hut, to the mingled sound of agonized death-cries and indistinct mantra-chanting, Mahamaya's wedding ceremony was conducted.

The very morning after she was wed, Mahamaya became a widow. But the widow felt not the slightest grief at her bereavement. And Rajib, too, was not as thunderstruck at the news of Mahamaya's widowhood as he had been at the tidings of her sudden marriage. In fact, he actually began to feel rather cheerful. But that mood did not last long, for a second thunderbolt struck him down into the dust. He received news of a grand ceremony at the cremation ground that day. Mahamaya was to die on her husband's funeral pyre.

His first thought was to inform the saheb, and with his help, to forcibly stop this horrific event. Then he remembered that the saheb had been transferred and had left for Sonapur that very day. He had wanted to take Rajib with him, but the latter had stayed back on a month's leave.

"Wait for me!" Mahamaya had said to him. He could never go against that injunction. For the moment, he had taken a month's leave, but if required, he would take two months, then three, and ultimately, give up his job with the saheb and go about begging from door to door. But still, all his life, he would not give up waiting.

Like a madman, Rajib was about to commit suicide or some other drastic act. Just then, as dusk descended with torrential rain, a great storm broke. So violent was the tempest that Rajib felt as if the roof of his dwelling would collapse on his head. Seeing even the external world of nature convulsed by a terrible upheaval, just like his inner self, he felt somewhat pacified. It seemed to him that the entire natural world, on his behalf, had begun some sort of counter-process. From the heavens to the netherworld, nature was at work, using all the force that Rajib himself might have wanted in vain to deploy.

Just then, someone gave the door a violent push from outside.

Rajib quickly opened the door. A woman entered the room, her clothing drenched, her head covered to hide her entire face. Rajib recognized Mahamaya at once.

"Have you risen from the pyre to come here, Mahamaya?" he asked eagerly.

"Yes," replied Mahamaya. "I had promised that I would come to your house. I have come here to keep my vow. But Rajib, I'm not quite the same person anymore. I'm a different person altogether. Only in my heart, I remain the same Mahamaya as before. Speak even now, and I can still return to the funeral pyre. But if you give me your word that you will never remove the covering on my head, never look upon my face, then I can live with you in your home."

Enough that she had returned to him from the clutches of death; at that moment, all else seemed insignificant.

"Stay just as you wish," Rajib hastened to assure her. "If you abandon me, I shall die."

"Let's leave at once then," said Mahamaya. "Let's go where your boss has been transferred."

Leaving behind all his possessions in that house, Rajib ventured forth into the storm, along with Mahamaya. So fierce was the tempest that it was hard for them to remain erect. Like a spray of buckshot, the gravel, stirred up by the force of the gale, flew up and pierced their bodies. Fearing that falling tree trunks might smash their heads, the two left the path and began to walk through the open fields. Gusts of wind assailed them from behind, as if the storm had torn the two of them away from human habitation, and was blowing them towards an apocalypse.

3

My readers should not consider this story utterly baseless or supernatural. In the days when it was customary for wives to die on their husbands' funeral pyres, such incidents were not unheard of.

Bound hand and foot, Mahamaya had been offered up to the pyre, which had been set aflame in due course. The fire had just caught, the flames flaring upwards, when a tremendous storm broke, along with

523

a torrential downpour. Those who had come for the cremation had quickly taken shelter in the hut meant for dying men, and had closed the door. Before long, the rain doused the flames of the pyre. Meanwhile, the bonds on Mahamaya's wrists had burnt to ashes, freeing her hands. In terrible, burning agony, Mahamaya had sat up without a word and unbound her feet. Then, wrapping her body closely in her partially burnt garment, the near-naked Mahamaya had arisen from the pyre and first returned to her own dwelling. There was no one at home; they had all gone to the cremation ground. Lighting an oil lamp, Mahamaya had dressed, and glanced once at the mirror. Flinging the mirror to the ground, she had paused for a moment to think. Then, drawing her ghomta low over her face, she had gone to Rajib's house, not far away. What happened subsequently is not unknown to the reader.

Now Mahamaya lived in Rajib's house, but his life was bereft of joy. Separating the two of them was just her head-covering, no more. But that mere veil was as permanent as death, yet more agonizing than death itself. For despair gradually numbs the pain of bereavement; but in the minor separation wrought by the veil lurked a living hope that was a source of torment, everyday, every moment.

Mahamaya had always been silent and motionless in her demeanor. Now the stillness within the head covering made things twice as intolerable. She seemed to be living within a wrapping of death. This silent death embraced Rajib, wearing him down day by day. He had lost the Mahamaya he used to know, and this veiled figure, forever by his side, also began to silently prevent him from enshrining in his home the beautiful memory of her that he had cherished since childhood. Rajib used to believe that there was already a sufficient natural distance between separate human beings. Mahamaya, especially, was like Karna as the scriptures described him in the Puranas, protected naturally by an amulet, true self concealed by a screen from birth. And then, it was as if she had been reborn, this time with an additional veil to conceal her. Though she was by Rajib's side day and night, she had grown so remote that she seemed to be beyond his reach. From outside a magic boundary, with an unsatiated, thirsting heart, he was constantly trying to unravel this subtle yet impenetrable mystery—as a star spends every night sleepless and unblinking, with downcast gaze, trying in vain to penetrate the darkness of the night.

In this way, these two companionless, solitary beings spent a long time together.

Then during the rains, on the tenth night of the new moon, the clouds parted and the moon appeared for the first time. The unwavering moonlit night kept its vigil by the side of the sleeping world. That night, throwing sleep to the winds, Rajib too was sitting at this window. The scent of the heat-oppressed forest drifted into his room, along with the tired chirping of crickets. Rajib was gazing at the tranquil lake that glittered like a sheet of polished silver beyond the dark line of trees. It is hard to say whether a human being can think clearly at such a moment. But his whole inner being flows in one particular direction, giving off a smell like the forest, making vibrations like the chirping of crickets. What Rajib thought I do not know, but he felt as if all former rules had broken down that night. Now the rainy night had cast off its cloud cover and made itself visible, silent, beautiful and grave, just like the Mahamaya of yore. His whole being surged impetuously towards that image of Mahamaya.

Like a sleepwalker, Rajib arose and went into Mahamaya's bedchamber. She was asleep.

Rajib went up close to her. Bending his head to look, he saw that the moonlight was streaming down upon Mahamaya's face. But alas, what was this! Where was that well-known face! The flames of the funeral pyre, with their cruel, greedy tongue, had licked off an entire portion of Mahamaya's left cheek, leaving only a mark of their hunger.

I think Rajib must have started; an inarticulate sound must have escaped his lips. For Mahamaya awakened with a start. She saw Rajib standing before her. At once, drawing her veil over her face, she left her bed and stood bolt upright. Realizing that the thunderbolt was about to strike, Rajib collapsed on the ground.

"Forgive me!" he beseeched, clutching at her feet.

Without saying a word and without looking back for a single instant, Mahamaya left the house. She would never come back to Rajib's abode. No trace of her could be found again after that. The silent, angry fire of that unforgiving, eternal goodbye branded Rajib's entire life with a very long scar.

1893
(From *Galpaguchchha*)
Translated by Radha Chakravarty

The In-Between Woman

Nibaran's domestic set-up was extremely run-of-the-mill; nothing in it smacked of poetry. It had never occurred to him that there might be any need for such a flavor in life. Just as one slides one's feet securely into one's slippers automatically everyday, he would claim his place in the world that he knew without thinking about it, every day of the week. He would never engage in any reflection, debate or philosophical analysis about his place in the world, even inadvertently.

Nibaran would get up every morning, sit bare-bodied by the front door of his street-side house, and smoke his hookah in an extremely un-perturbed fashion. On the road people would come and go, carriages and horses would pass, beggars and mendicants would sing out, and rag-pickers would call out loud for old bottles. This mobile scenario would occupy his mind in a superficial way. On days on which a hawker selling green mangoes or topshi fish came around, there would be much hag-gling. Afterwards his household would gear up for a somewhat special kind of cooking. Then, at the appointed time, he would massage oil on his body and take a bath. At the end of his meal, he would wear a loose-fitting chapkan from the washing line, chew up an entire paan with a pinch of tobacco in it and then stuff another paan into his mouth as he left for his office. On his return from office, he would spend the evening, relaxed and pensive at his neighbor Ramlochan Ghosh's house. After din-ner at night he would meet his wife Harasundari in their bedroom.

The brief exchanges that took place there were about sending food to the Mitras' house for the aaiburo bhaat, the customary bachelor's last supper prior to their son's wedding, the insolence of the newly ap-

pointed maid and the appropriateness of specific condiments and partic-
ular stir-fried vegetable preparations. These are not subjects that any poet
has set to rhyme and meter to date, and Nibaran felt no regret on that
account.

However, in the month of Phalgun, Harasundari contracted a
critical illness. Her fever just wouldn't abate. No matter how much qui-
nine the doctor gave her, the fever intensified like a strong current that
rushes forth with greater force the more it is obstructed. For twenty days,
twenty-two days, forty days, the ailment continued.

Nibaran had now stopped going to his office; he hadn't been at-
tending the evening gathering at Ramlochan's place for ages, and he was
at a loss about what could be done. He would once peep into the bed-
room to ascertain the patient's condition; at another time he would sit in
the verandah, puffing at his hookah anxiously. He would change doctors
morning and evening, and try out whatever medicines anybody recom-
mended.

Despite the disorganized nursing that was the result of such con-
cern, Harasundari recovered from her illness on the fortieth day. But she
became so skinny and frail that it seemed as if her corporeal being could
merely say, "I'm here!" from far, far away to feebly affirm its existence.

It was spring, and the southern breeze had started wafting in. And
the moonlight on those warm nights tiptoed into the wide-open doors of
married women's bedchambers.

Just below Harasundari's room was the back garden of the neigh-
bors. I can't say that it was a specially beautiful or romantic place. Once
upon a time, somebody had consciously sown some croton seeds there
but had not given it much attention thereafter or bothered to cast a
glance that way. A pumpkin vine had grown over a scaffolding of dry
boughs; there was a lot of undergrowth below the ageing berry tree. The
wall next to the kitchen was broken, and some fallen bricks lay in a pile
of debris. And alongside, the burnt out remains of coals as well as ashes
were heaping up day after day.

But in her uneventful life, Harasundari had never experienced the
sense of joy that she now had all the time lying next to the window and
gazing at that patch of land. When a country stream's current weakens in

summer and it lies shrunken on its bed of sand, it becomes very transparent. Dawn's first light then pulsates through the deepest recesses of its body. The caress of a breeze delights its entire being. The stars in the firmament get reflected clearly like joyful memories on its crystal mirror. In a similar way, all of joyous nature's fingers caressed the slender strand of Harasundari's life though she couldn't fathom the tenor of the melody that seemed to awaken within her.

528

At that time, when her husband would sit next to her and ask, "How are you?" tears seemed to well up in her eyes. On her face that was emaciated by her disease, her eyes would look extremely large. She would raise those large, grateful eyes, immersed in his love, towards his face, hold his hand in her own frail one and just sit there motionless. From somewhere deep within, a new, unfamiliar sensation of pleasure would gain access into his being as well.

Some days passed like this. One night, a large full moon shone through the quivering branches of the dwarfish banyan tree above the broken wall. Penetrating the sultry ambience of the late evening, a nocturnal breeze had suddenly started blowing. At this juncture, stroking Nibaran's hair, Harasundari said, "We could not have any children—please, please marry again!"

This thought had been with her for sometime now. When intense happiness and love overflow one's heart, the person imagines that she/he could do anything for its sake. At such moments, a desire for self-sacrifice wells up within. Just as the raging sea spreads itself on the shore with great force, an outburst of love and excessive happiness wants to surrender and pledge itself to noble self-denial or immense sorrow.

In such a state of mind, brimming with excessive elation, one day Harasundari decided, "I will do something very magnanimous for my husband. But alas! Do noble desires ever match the ability to do good? Is there anything within my reach that I can gift him? I have no riches, no intelligence, no talent—all I have is a soul. I would renounce that just now for something to which it could be dedicated, but would that be of any value?

"Also, if only I could gift my husband a cute baby, a baby as fair as the froth of milk, soft as butter, and beautiful like the infant god of love! But even if I were to die of that heartfelt desire, that is not going to happen." Then it crossed her mind that she must get her husband married again. She could not understand why wives felt so distressed by this—this was not such a difficult thing to do! It is nowhere near impossible for somebody who loves her husband to also love her co-wife. As she reflected on this, the thought made her heart swell with pride.

The first time Nibaran heard the proposal, he laughed it off. On the second and third occasions, too, he turned a deaf ear. Noting her husband's disapproval and reluctance, Harasundari's sense of conviction and gratification grew all the more and the more determined she became to fulfill her resolve.

On the other side, hearing this request many times made Nibaran dismiss the unfeasibility of it from his mind. And sitting at his doorstep chewing his tobacco, the blissful image of a home alive with children shone more brightly in his heart.

One day, he introduced the subject himself and said, "If I marry a girl child at my age, I won't be able to bring her up."

"You don't have to worry about that," Harasundari replied. "The responsibility of raising her properly rests with me." As she announced this, the outline of a young, gentle, bashful, newly wedded bride, lately separated from her mother's bosom, formed in the mind of this childless woman and her heart melted.

Nibaran added, "I have to work for a living; moreover, I have you to look after, so I won't have time to pander to the whims of an immature girl."

Harasundari repeated that he would not have to waste any time on that. And in the end, she said jocularly, "Alright, I will see when the time comes how much work you will end up doing, where I will stand in relation to you and where you direct your attention."

Nibaran didn't think these words even merited a reply, and in a gesture of chastisement, he playfully tapped Harasundari's cheek with his forefinger.

This, then, was the prologue.

2

Nibaran got married to a petite young girl wearing a nose ring, whose eyes brimmed with tears. Her name was Shailabala.

Nibaran mused to himself that the name was very sweet, and her face quite lovely. He felt like observing her expression, her appearance and her movements with some special attention, but he just could not manage to do so. On the contrary, he had to pretend as if she was just a slip of a girl, that he had invited trouble by marrying her, and that he could get some respite only if he could somehow avoid her and attend to the sphere of duty that suited his age.

Observing Nibaran's greatly distressed state, Harasundari felt very amused. On some occasions, she would press his hand and say, "Ah, where are you running away? She's such a little girl, she's not going to eat you up."

Nibaran would assume a doubly busy manner and say, "Oh wait, wait—I have a rather important chore to attend." But he would not find an escape route. Harasundari would smile, bar his exit from the door and say, "You won't be able to shirk today." Eventually, finding no way out, Nibaran would sit down helplessly.

"After bringing a strange girl home, you shouldn't treat her with such contempt," Harasundari would whisper in his ear.

Saying this, she would hold Shailabala and seat her to the left of Nibaran, and forcibly remove her veil. Holding her by the chin, she would raise Shaila's bowed face and say to Nibaran, "Ah, see what a lovely face she has—just like a moon!"

On some days, she would seat both of them in the room and get up and go away on the pretext of some work. She would slam the door shut from outside. Of course, Nibaran knew that a pair of curious eyes would fix themselves to watch through some gap in the door. With an air of extreme indifference, he would try to sleep. Shailabala would pull down her veil, curl up, turn away from him and retreat into a corner.

Ultimately, Harasundari gave up her mission as hopeless, but she was not terribly disappointed.

When Harasundari let go, Nibaran took charge himself. This was indeed very intriguing, a profound mystery! If one found a diamond, one felt like turning it around to view it from all angles. And here was the mind of a beautiful young person, like nothing he had seen before. One had to experience her in many ways—with touch, with affection, secretly, face-to-face, from the sides and from within. One would at times rock her earrings to and fro and at others lift her veil slightly to uncover new levels of beauty in her; sometimes suddenly and startlingly, like a flash of lightning, and at other times lingeringly, like gazing at a star.

In the fortune of Srijukta Nibaran Chandra, the head clerk of the MacMoran company, such an experience had never occurred before. When he had married for the first time, he was just a boy; when he entered his youth, his wife had become ever familiar to him, as if he had always been habituated to married life. Of course he loved Harasundari, but love had never gradually and consciously welled up in his heart.

Let an insect born inside a ripe mango, never having needed to explore and discover the fruit's succulence or slowly relish the taste of its juices, be once set free in a flowering springtime meadow in full bloom. How eagerly it would then hover around the half-opened buds of the roses that are on the verge of blossoming! How infatuated it would become by imbibing their delicate fragrance and their subtle, sweet taste!

Nibaran would now and then buy a porcelain doll in western attire, a bottle of perfume or some sweetmeats and secretly come and give it to Shailabala. A little intimacy was initiated between the two in this manner. Ultimately, one fine day, in between household chores, Harasundari came and spied through the hole in the door and saw Nibaran and Shailabala playing "ten twenty-five" with cowry shells.

An adult game indeed! Nibaran would eat his morning meal and pretend to go to his office, but instead of going to work, he would enter the inner rooms. Was this deceit necessary? Suddenly, somebody seemed to awaken Harasundari with a blazing thunderbolt. Its intense heat made her tears evaporate.

Harasundari said to herself, "It was I who brought her home, I who united the two—then why do they treat me like this? As if I am a thorn in their flesh . . ."

Harasundari used to train Shailabala in housework. One day, Nibaran proclaimed outspokenly, "She is just a child—you are driving her too hard. Her constitution is not that strong."

A stinging reply formed in Harasundari's mouth, but she did not utter anything, and lapsed into silence instead.

Ever since then, Harasundari did not let her co-wife touch any housework. She did all the cooking, serving and overseeing herself. It came to such a pass that Shailabala became almost immobile. Harasundari served her like a maid and her husband entertained her like a jester in a play. She never learnt that the duties of one's life include contributing to housework or being considerate of others.

There was an immense pride in the way Harasundari started working silently like a maid. There was no feeling of pettiness or wretchedness in her demeanor. "Go on—play like babies, both of you," she seemed to say, "for I have taken upon myself the entire responsibility of the household."

3

Alas, where was that strength today which had shored up Harasundari's assurance that she could unreservedly give up half her claim to her husband's love forever? Suddenly, on a moonlit night, as the high tide floods one's life, overflowing its shores, one thinks of oneself as limitless. At that time, one commits oneself to a stupendous vow. During the protracted ebb tide of one's life, it stretches one's entire spirit to keep that vow. During a life of eternal poverty, we have to reclaim bit by bit, moment by moment, whatever we write off in one scratch of the pen during a sudden windfall. Then we realize that man is very poor, his heart extremely weak, and his ability extremely insignificant.

Emaciated, anemic and sallow-complexioned after her prolonged convalescence, Harasundari was at that time like a thin sliver of the ascendant moon on the second day of its cycle. She floated very lightly through her household. She felt she hardly needed anything. As her body gradually acquired strength, and her blood regained its spirit, a group of cohorts appeared in her mind. "You may have written a letter of resignation," they seemed to announce stridently, "but we will not give up our claim."

The day Harasundari understood her own situation clearly, she gave up her bedroom to Nibaran and Shailabala and slept alone in a separate room.

She vacated after twenty-seven years the bed in which she had first slept on her wedding night, at the age of eight. Putting out the lamp, this young woman whose husband was still living landed on her widow's bed with an intolerably heavy heart. On the other side of the street, at that moment, a youth with a musical flair was singing in the raga Behaag of a woman who tended her garden. Another was accompanying him on the bayan-tabla, and at the end of each cycle of beats, his audience cheered appreciatively.

In the room next to Harasundari's, that song of his sounded rather melodious on that silent, moonlit night. At that time, young Shailabala's eyes were drooping with sleep, and moving his face close to hers, Nibaran cooed "Oh my beloved!" softly in her ear. He had already read Bankim Chandra's *Chandrashekhar* and also recited the compositions of a few modern poets to Shailabala.

Thus jolted, the fountain of youth always suppressed in the lower registers of Nibaran's being suddenly gushed forth at a very inappropriate moment. Nobody was prepared for this. Consequently, not only his common sense but all the arrangements of the household also turned topsy-turvy unexpectedly. That poor man had never known that there are such disturbing elements and such unruly, untamable passions inside man that upset all calculations and reckonings, all order and propriety.

Not just Nibaran but even Harasundari experienced something newly poignant. What yearning, what unbearable agony was this! Her heart had neither desired what she longed for now nor had she ever got it. When Nibaran used to go to work regularly and respectably, when they would discuss for some time the milkman's accounts, the rising prices of things and their social obligations before going to sleep, there had been no trace of this upheaval within her. They undoubtedly loved each other, but there was no sparkle or intensity in it. That love was merely like fuel that remained unignited.

Today, she felt that somebody had always been depriving her of fulfillment in life. It seemed as if her heart had always been starved. Her woman's life had been spent in dire poverty. She had spent these precious twenty-seven years just slaving away, shopping, procuring betel leaves, spices and vegetables. And midway through her life, she saw today that in the room very next to her own bedroom, unfastening the lid of a treasure chest of resplendent wealth, a wisp of a girl occupied the throne of a queen goddess. Women are slaves by nature, but they are also queenly. But when the roles are divided so that one woman becomes a queen while the other remains a slave, it destroys the pride of the female slave, yet cannot sustain the happiness of the queen.

For even Shailabala did not get the happiness due to a woman's life. She received such relentless affection that it did not spare a moment for her to express *her* love. Flowing towards the sea and immersing itself in the sea, I believe that the river finds a great sense of fulfillment. But pulled by the tide, if the sea constantly confronts the river, the river swells up within itself. The world perpetually advanced towards Shailabala with all the affection and connubial love it could proffer. It raised Shailabala's self-esteem excessively, and yet it prevented her from showering her love on the world. She learnt that everything was meant for her, yet she was never meant to do anything for anybody. This was a source of great conceit, but no gratification at all.

4

One day, the sky became overcast. It grew too dark to do any work inside the house. It was raining pitter patter outside. Under the berry tree, the bushy undergrowth of vines and weeds was virtually submerged in water, and through the drain adjacent to the wall, a current of muddy water flowed by with a murmuring sound. Harasundari sat silently at the dark, desolate window of her new bedroom.

Around this time, Nibaran appeared near her door like a thief, unable to decide whether to advance or return. Harasundari noticed it but did not say a word.

Swift as an arrow, Nibaran rushed up to Harasundari and in one breath, blurted out, "A few ornaments are required. You know there are some outstanding loans—the creditors are really insulting me. Some will have to be pawned, but I'll be able to redeem them soon."

Harasundari said nothing in reply, and Nibaran lingered there guiltily like a thief. Ultimately he reiterated, "One can't have them today, I suppose?"

"No," replied Harasundari.

Just as it is difficult to enter a room, it is also hard to get out of it without any delay. Nibaran looked here and there, hesitating. "Then let me go and try elsewhere," he said, and left.

Harasundari fully understood who Nibaran owed money to and where the ornaments had to be pawned. She realized that on the previous night, the new bride had inquired vehemently of the man she had tamed, the man who was now so nonplussed, "Didi has a trunk full of ornaments, but can't I wear even one of them?"

After Nibaran left, Harasundari opened the iron safe and took out all the ornaments one by one. She then summoned Shailabala and adorned her in her own wedding sari. One by one, she covered her from head to toe in all her jewels. She plaited her hair nicely and lit a lamp to observe that the young maiden's face was very sweet. It was flawless and luscious like a freshly ripened, sweet-smelling fruit. When Shailabala departed, her ornaments tinkling at every step, the sound chilled the blood in Harasundari's veins for a long time. "There can hardly be any comparison between you and me today," she mused to herself. "But at one time I was also of your age, and my youth had blossomed to its fullest. Yet why had nobody ever communicated that to me? I never even got to know when the time came and when it was over." Yet with what pride and arrogance Shailabala moved, creating ripples as she sauntered along!

When Harasundari only knew domestic work, how precious these ornaments had seemed to her. At that time, could she have let them slip out of her hands so stupidly, in a single instant? Now, housework apart, she had uncovered the identity of something else that was vital; the price of jewelry and accounting for the future had all become trivial for her now.

And Shailabala strutted away towards her bedroom in her sparkling gold and rubies without pausing a moment to think how much Harasundari had given up for her. She knew that from every direction—

all service, all riches, all fortune—would naturally come to her; because she was Shailabala, because she was the beloved.

5

Some people intrepidly traverse a very dangerous path in their dreams, without a moment's anxiety. Many people are affected by such a perpetually dream-like state even when awake. Oblivious of all, they advance through the narrow path of disaster without a care. Eventually, they awaken after landing in the middle of a terrible catastrophe.

Such was the condition of the Head Babu of the MacMoran Company. Shailabala spun like a relentless whirlpool at the center of his life, while many precious things from far, far away, drawn in by her attraction, were sucked into her vortex. Not just Nibaran's humanity and monthly salary, Harasundari's comfort and well-being or her dress and ornaments but even the MacMoran Company's cash box felt this furtive pull. A few bundles of cash began to vanish from there as well. "I will repay it slowly, starting with next month's salary," Nibaran would resolve. But no sooner would he get the next month's salary in hand than the whirlpool would pull at it, and the very last coin of his earnings would glisten tremulously and vanish with the speed of lightning.

Eventually, he got caught one day. This was a job that Nibaran had inherited from his forebears. The saheb boss was very fond of him— he gave him just two days to replenish the treasury.

Nibaran could not fathom how he had gradually depleted the treasury of two thousand rupees. Like a madman, he rushed to Harasundari and declared, "There's been a disaster!"

Upon hearing the whole story, Harasundari turned pale.

"Take out your jewelry immediately," he implored.

"But I have given them to the young bride," she protested.

"Why did you give them to the younger wife? Why? Who asked you to give them to her?" Nibaran began to rant impatiently, just like a child.

Without giving a direct answer, Harasundari replied, "What is the harm in that? It's not as if they have sunk."

The cowardly Nibaran pleaded helplessly, "Then see if you can get the ornaments from her on some pretext. But swear by me you won't tell her I am asking for them or why."

With acute exasperation and disdain, Harasundari asked, "Is this any time for false pretences or a great display of conjugal love? Come on." So saying, she dragged her husband into the younger wife's bedroom.

The younger wife could not comprehend anything. To all they said, she only responded: "What do I know of that?"

Was there ever any contract with her that she might sometime have to worry about some domestic crisis? Everybody must fend for themselves, and collectively care about Shailabala's comforts. It seemed to her a grave injustice that there should suddenly be an exception to this rule.

Nibaran now clutched at her feet and broke down. "I care nothing for all this. Why should I give what belongs to me?" Shailabala repeated again and again.

Nibaran realized that this frail, tiny, lovely, charming young woman was tougher than an iron safe. Observing her husband's weakness at such a critical juncture, Harasundari felt devastated by her contempt for him. She tried to forcibly snatch Shailabala's keys from her. Immediately, Shailabala threw the bunch of keys over the wall, into the pond.

"Why don't you break the lock?" Harasundari suggested to her dumbfounded husband.

"Then I will hang myself," Shailabala announced with a calm exterior.

"Let me try something else," Nibaran mumbled, and without more ado, rushed out in a disheveled state.

Within two hours, Nibaran returned, having sold his ancestral house for two thousand and five hundred rupees.

With great difficulty, he escaped arrest, but lost his job. His movable and immovable property now comprised two wives. Of them, the younger wife, who was terrified of any kind of distress, became pregnant, and immovable indeed. This small family now took shelter in a small, damp house inside a narrow alley.

6

There was no end to Chhoto Bou's frustration and displeasure. She refused to understand that her husband had no resources. If he had no means, why did he marry her?

They had just two rooms on the upper floor. One was the bedchamber where Nibaran and Shailabala slept. Harasundari lived in the other one. "I cannot spend my entire day and night in the bedroom," Shailabala would grumble.

"I am on the lookout for a better house; we will move soon," Nibaran would reassure her dishonestly.

"Why, there is another room next to this!" Shailabala would point out.

Shailabala had never spared a glance for her former women neighbors. Pained by Nibaran's current adversity, they came to pay a visit one day. Shailabala locked herself inside her room, refusing to open the door. After they left, Shailabala's raving and ranting, weeping, fasting and hysterics raised hell in the neighborhood. This kind of menace became a regular occurrence.

In her delicate condition, she was ultimately afflicted by a serious ailment—in fact, almost threatened by a miscarriage.

Clutching Harasundari's hands, Nibaran pleaded with her to save Shailabala.

Harasundari began to tend to Shailabala, day and night. At the slightest lapse, Shaila would abuse her, but she would never answer back.

Shaila would object strongly to eating a concoction of sago, tossing the bowlful away. In her feverish state, she wanted to eat her rice with green mango ambal. If she did not get it, she would rant, weep and raise hell. Harasundari would cajole her as if she was an infant, coaxing. "Come on, my dear," "Oh please, my sister," "Now, now, my little Didi!"

But Shailabala did not survive. With all the affection and marital love in the world, the young woman's petty, unfulfilled, worthless life was snuffed out prematurely by extreme illness and discontent.

7

At first, Nibaran received a dreadful blow. Thereafter, he realized that an enormous bond had been severed. Even in the midst of his grief, he felt the joy of a sudden release. He felt all of a sudden as if a nightmare had been pressing down on his chest all these days. The awareness instantly made his life seem utterly burden-free. Was this tender life-string that snapped like a madhabilata creeper his beloved Shailabala? Sighing, he realized suddenly that on the contrary, she was the hangman's noose.

539

And what about Harasundari, his eternal life-companion? He perceived that she alone occupied the memorial shrine of all the joys and sorrows of his life. Yet there was a breach. It was as if a tiny, beautiful, gleaming but pitiless knife had carved a line dissecting the left and the right portions of his heart.

Late one night, when the city was fast asleep, Nibaran slowly entered Harasundari's solitary bedroom. Silently, as before, he lay down, on the right side of his former bed. But this time, he intruded like a thief into what had always been rightfully his.

Harasundari did not say a word. Neither did Nibaran. As before, they slept next to each other. But between them, right in the middle, lay a dead young woman—neither of them could overstep her presence.

1893
("Madhyabartini," from *Galpaguchchha*)
Translated by Nivedita Sen

Hungry Stone

We met him on the train, my cousin and I, on our way back to Calcutta after a trip around the country during the Puja holidays. At first we took him for a north Indian Muslim, because of the way he was dressed. As for his conversation, it left us utterly baffled. He held forth on every conceivable subject, and with such confidence that you would think the Creator himself never moved a finger except on his advice. We'd had no idea that there were so many unheard-of goings-on in the world: that the Russians had advanced so far, that the British had so many hidden designs, that there was so much trouble brewing amongst our own rajas and maharajas—we had been entirely at peace with the world till then, not having known anything about all this. But then, as our new-found friend said with a tight little smile, *"There happen more things in heaven and earth, Horatio, than are reported in your newspapers."* We were real innocents: this was the first time we had been away from home. He held us spellbound: on the slightest of pretexts, he would switch from lecturing us on science to expounding the Vedas or reciting Persian poetry—and since we knew nothing about science or the Vedas or Persian poetry, our awe of him increased with every word he uttered. My cousin, who was a theosophist, was even convinced that he had some sort of supernatural power—some magnetism or divine force, or an astral body, or something of the kind. He hung upon the lightest word from this unusual man with the rapt attention of a devotee, even jotting down notes in secret. I felt the great man too knew what was going on and, although he didn't let on, he was not in the least bit displeased.

When we got to the station where we were to change trains, we went off to the waiting-room together. It was half past ten. We learnt there was a long wait ahead: our train had been delayed for some reason or the other. I made up a bed for myself on one of the tables, hoping to catch some sleep. But just then the great man launched upon a story.

There was not to be any sleep for me that night.

When I went to work for the Nizam's government in Hyderabad, having quit my job in Junagadh State because of certain disagreements over administrative matters, my new employers chose to send me, because of my youth and good health, to the outlying town of Barich to handle the collection of cotton revenues.

Barich stands upon a very romantic site. Beneath a range of lonely mountains, the fast-flowing river Shusta (from the Sanskrit *svachchhatoa,* limpid) runs like a nimble dancer through towering forests along its winding, rippling course. Right on its banks, looming in solitude at the foot of the mountains, at the top of a flight of one hundred and fifty stone steps, rises a palace built of white marble. There is no habitation anywhere near by. The village and the cotton market of Barich are a good distance away.

Some two hundred and fifty years ago, Shah Mahmud II had built this palace here, upon this remote and lonely site, as his house of pleasure. At that time, secluded deep within the mansion's cool moist interior, rosewater flowed from fountains in the bathing-chambers; and young Persian women, their hair loosened before their bath, sat on smooth wet stone seats with their bare feet in the clear water of the pool, strumming sitars and singing ghazals of the vineyard.

The fountains are silent now; there are no songs, and no fair footsteps resound on the white marble. Today the palace serves as an enormous empty residence for lonely womanless revenue-collectors like myself. An elderly clerk in my office, Karim Khan, warned me repeatedly against living in that palace. "Go there during the day if you must," he said, "but don't on any account spend the night there." I laughed. My servants said they would work there during the day but would not spend the night. I agreed. The palace's reputation was such that even thieves would not go there at night.

At first the emptiness of that abandoned marble mansion bore down on me like a crushing weight. I spent as much time away as I could, working through the day without a pause; and when I went back at night, I would fall asleep at once in exhaustion.

But before a week had passed, the house began to assail me like a strange addiction. It is hard to describe the state I was in, and just as hard to make it sound credible. The palace was like a living thing, slowly ingesting me in its entrails.

Perhaps the process had started the moment I set foot in the place; but I still remember, perfectly clearly, the day when I first became aware of the way it was working on me.

The hot weather was just beginning to set in, so the market was slow and I didn't have much to do. It was a little before sunset; I was sitting by the river, at the bottom of the great flight of steps, relaxing in a long-armed chair. The river was running low then: a broad stretch of sand had appeared on the far shore and was glowing with the colors of the sunset sky; on this side, close at hand, pebbles glistened on the steps that lay beneath the clear shallow water. It was very still that day. The air was heavy with the thick scent of wild herbs and jungle foliage wafting down from the nearby mountains.

The moment the sun slipped below the mountain-tops, a low dark curtain descended upon the stage of the day. Because the hilly terrain shut out the last light of the sun, twilight was of short duration here. Toying with the idea of going for a ride, I had half-risen from my chair when I heard a footstep on the steps behind me. I turned to look: there was no one there.

My hearing had played a trick on me, I decided; but no sooner had I sat down than I heard a sound again, a number of footsteps this time, running quickly down the stairs. I was transfixed, seized by an excited delight not unmixed with a tinge of fear. There was nothing in front of me, no discernible form; yet I knew, as well as if I could see them, that a group of high-spirited young women had just stepped into the river to bathe at the end of the hot summer's day. Even though there was not so much as a whisper anywhere that evening, neither in the mountains, the river nor the house, I still heard the bathers perfectly clearly as they swept past me one after another, laughing and chattering like a playful mountain stream. They did not notice me: I seemed to be just as invisible to them as they were to me. The river was as calm as ever, but I still felt clearly that the waters were being stirred by many brace-leted arms, as the women laughed and splashed water on each other, and their feet sent the water-drops arcing through the air like fistfuls of pearls.

A great ferment of excitement was stirring within me now: whether it grew out of fear or joy or curiosity I cannot say. I began to wish I could see everything properly, but there was nothing to see; I thought, if only I listened carefully, I would be able to hear everything they were saying—but no matter how intently I listened, all I could hear was crickets chirping in the forest around me. I thought: swinging in front of me is a dark curtain, two and a half centuries old. Let me pick up a corner of it and cast an apprehensive glance inside: I would see a great gathering of people. But there was nothing visible in that inky darkness.

Suddenly the pall of stillness was swept aside by a gust of wind. The Shusta's surface was quickly teased into wavelets, like the braids of a heavenly nymph, and the shadowy evening forest gave a deep sigh, as if waking from a bad dream. Dream or reality, the unseen mirage from two hundred and fifty years ago that had presented itself before me vanished in the twinkling of an eye. The magical creatures that had brushed past me with swift disembodied steps and shrill silent laughter to plunge into the Shusta did not make their way back, wringing the water from their dripping clothes. They vanished in that single breath of spring, as a whiff of perfume is lost upon the breeze.

Then, all of a sudden, I had a fright. I began to wonder whether the muse of poetry had chosen to descend on me, finding me off my guard in that desolate place—perhaps I, who had to sweat for my living by collecting cotton-revenues, had suddenly been doomed to the curse of poesy. I thought to myself, I must make sure to eat properly: it's when your stomach's empty that obstinate sicknesses of all kinds crowd in on you. I called my cook and ordered a truly Mughal dinner, rich and spicy.

Next morning the episode began to seem ridiculous. I clapped a sola-topee on my head like an Englishman, and went rattling off to work in the best of spirits, driving the trap myself. I expected to be home late that day, as I had my quarterly report to write. But no sooner did evening come than I began to feel that the house was summoning me back. Who summoned me, I cannot say; but I kept thinking, it won't do to stay any longer, everybody will be waiting. I left my report unfinished, put on my sola-topee, and drove back to that great silent palace below the mountains, startling the lonely twilit tree-lined path with the rumbling of my wheels.

At the top of the palace's main stairway was an enormous room. Three rows of monumental columns held up the ceiling on intricately carved arches. The very emptiness of that vast room sent its echoes resounding through the house all day and all night. It was still early in the evening, so no lamps had been lit yet. The moment I pushed the door open and entered the great room, I had the distinct feeling that I had caused an uproar—that a large gathering had suddenly broken up, and people were tumbling through the windows and out of the doors, fleeing where they could in every direction, down the terraces and corridors. In my astonishment, seeing nothing anywhere, I stayed exactly where I was. A rapture stole over my body; the mild scent of vanished perfumes and pomades, relics from another epoch, wafted past my nostrils. Standing there in that great dark empty room, amongst those long rows of ancient columns, I heard the gurgling of fountains upon the marble floor and the sound of sitars playing an unknown tune. Somewhere, a copper gong was striking the hour; from somewhere else came the ringing sound of anklets and gold jewelry; musical instruments were playing far away; crystal chandeliers tinkled in the breeze; bulbuls sang in cages on the terrace, and the palace cranes called in the garden, the whole weaving a ghostly music around me.

I was in such a trance that I began to imagine that this ineffable, unattainable, unreal setting was the only reality on earth, that everything else was a mirage. That I was the person I was—So-and-so, eldest son of the late So-and-so, who earned a salary of four hundred and fifty rupees collecting cotton-revenues, who went to his office every morning in a trap wearing a sola-topee and a short jacket—all this seemed such an absurd, unfounded lie that I began to shout with laughter, standing in the middle of that great silent room.

At that moment, my Muslim servant entered the room with a lighted kerosene lamp. Whether he thought me mad or not I do not know, but as for myself I recalled at once who I was, that I was indeed the worthy Mr. So-and-so, son and heir of the late So-and-so. I also bethought myself that only seers and poets can tell whether, in this world or beyond it, water can really spout endlessly from invisible fountains, and unending melodies sound on illusory sitars; but it was certain that I earned four hundred and fifty rupees a month collecting taxes in the cotton markets of Barich. The thought of my recent trance began to seem ridiculous; sitting down at my lamplit camp-table, with a newspaper in my hands, I soon succumbed to laughter.

After a meal of rich Mughlai food, having read my newspaper, I took myself off to the small corner room that served as my chamber, put

544

out the lamp and lay down on my bed. A brilliant star shone through an open window: perched high above the dark forested Aravalli mountains, from its exalted place in the sky millions of leagues away, it fixed its gaze upon the humble Mr. Tax-Collector on his humble camp-cot. Diverted by this odd conceit, I soon drifted off to sleep: for how long I cannot say, but suddenly I felt myself shiver, and I was awake again. It was not as though there had been any sound in the room, or that anyone had entered it. But by that time, the dim glow of the waning moon was creeping in diffidently through the open window, while the star that had gazed so fixedly upon me had dipped beneath the gloomy mountains.

I could not see anybody in the room. But I had a clear sense that someone was nudging me, ever so gently. The moment I sat up, five beringed fingers beckoned and, without a word being said, gestured to me to follow cautiously behind.

I rose stealthily to my feet. I knew there was no living soul but me in that immense hundred-chambered palace, filled with a great emptiness, with sleeping sounds and waking echoes; yet with every step I took along those deserted, echoing corridors, I was stricken with fear, terrified that somebody would awaken suddenly. Most of the rooms in the palace were kept shut, and I had never ventured to enter any of them. I cannot clearly tell where I went that night, following that invisible, beckoning figure with silent step and hushed breath. I could not begin to count the dark narrow passages, the broad corridors, the still somber council-hall and small hidden airless chambers through which we made our way.

Even though I had not set eyes on my guide, my mind was not entirely ignorant of her appearance. She was from Arabia: her firm rounded arm, looking as if it were carved from marble, showed below her broad sleeve, a fine veil hung down from her cap across her face, and a curved dagger glinted in her waistband.

It seemed to me that a night from the *Thousand and One Nights* had transported itself here from the realms of fiction; that I was stealing through the narrow unlit alleyways of the sleeping city of Baghdad on a dark night, on my way to some perilous assignation.

All of sudden, my guide came to a halt and gestured towards the bottom of an indigo curtain. There was nothing there, but the blood froze in my veins. I sensed that at the foot of the curtain, swathed in a robe of silk brocade, lay the drowsing form of a gigantic Kafir eunuch, his legs outstretched, a drawn sword resting on his lap. My guide stepped lightly over his legs and lifted up a corner of the curtain.

A part of room was visible inside, its floor covered with a Persian rug. There was a seated figure too, but all that could be seen of her was the lower part of a pair of loose saffron-colored leggings and two beautifully-shaped feet in gold-worked slippers, resting on a cushion of pink velvet. On a table beside her, arranged on a blue crystal platter, were apples, pears, oranges and bunches of grapes; and beside them, as though in expectation of a visitor, two wine-glasses and a gold-encrusted decanter. An intoxicating scent of incense drifted from the room and overcame me.

Heart pounding, I raised a foot to climb over the eunuch's outstretched legs when he suddenly awoke, his naked sword falling to the floor with a clatter.

I started at the sound of a piercing shout, and found myself sitting on my camp-cot, drenched in sweat. The waning moon had turned pale in the first light of dawn, like a sick man after a sleepless night; and crazy old Meher Ali was marching down the empty road as was his custom, shouting, "Stay away, stay away."

Thus untimely ended the first of my Arabian nights—with a thousand left, yet remaining.

A strange feud now arose between my days and my nights. By day, I would take my weary body off to work, heaping curses upon my beguiling nights full of empty dreams. But once evening had set in, it was my workaday daytime existence that seemed trivial, false and absurd.

Once evening came, I would feel myself caught in a web of rapture. I would become a different being, a character in an unrecorded history of centuries ago. My short English jacket and my tight pantaloons would begin to seem oddly incongruous; with the greatest care, I would put on a red velvet fez, loose leggings, a flowered shirt and a long silk achkan, with a colored attar-scented handkerchief. Then, putting away my cigarettes, I would light a great hubble-bubble filled with rosewater, and sink into a high upholstered sofa. And thus I would sit, as though I were waiting in the most eager suspense for some extraordinary night-time tryst.

As the darkness gathered around me, strange things would happen that are impossible to describe. It was as though the pages of some extravagant romance were blowing through the strange rooms of that vast palace on sudden gusts of summer breeze—episodes that could be followed only to a certain point and no further. Setting out in pursuit of those swirling fragments, I would wander from room to room all through the night.

Whirling through those disjointed dreams—gusts of wind moist with scented waters, whiffs of henna and snatches of sitar music—I would sometimes catch fleeting glimpses of a woman, like flashes of lightning. Hers were the saffron leggings, the soft pink feet shod in up-turned gold-worked sandals. Her breasts were tightly bound in a flowered bodice with gold braid, and a fringe of gold hung from her red cap to veil her forehead and cheeks.

I was besotted with her: it was to meet her that I would roam every night among the alleyways of that labyrinthine dream world, in the subterranean realm of sleep.

Sometimes, standing before my wide candle-flanked mirror, changing into my princely night-time attire, I would catch sight of her, that Persian woman, reflected back at me beside my own mirror-image, bending her neck, glancing passionately, painfully, sensually out of her great dark eyes, hinting with full red lips at some unspoken utterance, pirouetting with her slim youthful figure in a light graceful dance—and then, in a trice, melting into the glass in a shower of incandescence from her pain and desire and rapture, laughter and sidelong glances and shimmering jewelry. Then a strong wind, redolent of all the scents of the forest, would blow out my candles; I would abandon my elaborate costume, close my eyes, and stretch out my ecstatic body on the bed in the corner of my dressing-room. In the breezes that blew over me, in all the mingled scents borne from the Aravalli hills, I would discover many kisses, many caresses, many a touch of a soft hand floating in that solitary darkness. I would hear murmuring voices, feel the warmth of perfumed breath upon my forehead and the gentle scented touch of a woman's kerchief blown across my cheek, again and again. It was as though a bewitching she-serpent was binding me in her intoxicating coils: with deep sighs, my benumbed body would sink into a heavy sleep.

One evening, I thought of going out for a ride. I have no idea who it was that kept dissuading me, but I paid no heed. My sola-topee and short jacket were hanging from a wooden rack. Just as I was about to change into them, a sudden whirlwind swept down, carrying the sand of the Shusta and dead leaves from the Aravallis like a pennant, and bore away my jacket and my hat. They went cartwheeling through the air: a sweet chorus of laughter swirled along with them, rising through several octaves, sounding every note on the scale of derision, until finally it dissolved into the sunset.

I did not go riding that day; and never again did I wear my absurd little English jacket and sola-topee.

That very midnight, sitting up suddenly on my bed, I heard the sound of weeping—racking, broken-hearted sobs. It was as though beneath my bed, beneath the floor, among the foundations of this vast mass of stone, a voice was calling out from a dark and musty grave, crying: "Take me away, give me my deliverance; break down the doors of this rooted illusion, this deep sleep, this futile dream. Put me on your horse, take me in your embrace—carry me away through the forest, over the mountains, across the river into your own sunlit room. Give me my deliverance!"

I! But who was I? How could I save her? What lovely creature of desire was I to draw out of the flowing, whirling torrent of dreams in which she was immersed? Where did you live and when, you otherworldly beauty? Where were you born, in which palm-fringed oasis, by which desert stream? What desert dwelling nomad woman brought you into this world? What Bedouin raider plucked you from your mother's arms like a tender flower from its parent creeper, and carried you off on his lightning-swift horse across the searing sands to the slave market before some royal palace? What servant of the emperor counted out his gold upon seeing your first bashful bloom of youth, transported you across the seas, and then carried you on a litter of gold as a gift for his master's harem? And what then was your history? The sound of the sarangi, the tinkling of ankle-bells, the golden wine of Shiraz—and interspersed among them, the glint of a dagger, the sting of poison, a wounding glance. Limitless wealth, perpetual imprisonment.

Diamonds glitter on the bracelets of slave-girls as they wave their fans on either side; the Shah-en-shah Badshah lies beneath those gleaming feet, beside those pearl-embroidered slippers; a gigantic Ethiopian stands at the door, drawn sword in hand, like a messenger of death in angel's dress. And then that rich, envy-spuming, blood-soaked, intrigue-ridden torrent sweeps over you, fearsomely bright—to what abyss of cruel death, my fragile sprig of the desert, or still more cruel shore of noble living?

Then Meher Ali began to shout: "Stay away, stay away. It's a lie, all of it's a lie." Opening my eyes, I saw that it was morning: a messenger from my office handed me the day's mail, and the cook came to ask what meals he should prepare that day.

I told myself, "It won't do to live here any longer." That very day I packed my things and moved into my office. The old clerk, Karim Khan, smiled wryly upon seeing me. His smile annoyed me. Without responding, I began on the day's work.

As the day wore on, my mind began to wander. It was as though I had an appointment to keep. The cotton-revenue accounts lost their urgency, indeed the affairs of the Nizam's entire estate dwindled into insignificance. Everything that was actual and current, everything happening around me—people coming and going, eating and working—seemed utterly mean, trivial, devoid of sense.

Flinging my pen aside, I shut my enormous account-book and leapt into my trap. It seemed to halt of its own accord at the gates of that great marble palace at the very point of dusk. I raced up the staircase to the vast room at the top.

Everything was quiet today, as though the chamber had taken offence and was sulking. I was stricken with remorse—but to whom could I express it, of whom could I ask pardon? I wandered vacantly from room to room, wishing that I had an instrument in my hands so that I could sing to one absent: "O flame, the moth that tried to fly away from you has come back to die. Give it its absolution, set its wings alight and turn it to ashes."

Then, suddenly, I felt a couple of teardrops falling on my cheek. The sky above the Aravallis had been heavy with rain-filled clouds that day. The darkness-shrouded forest and the Shusta's inky waters were still with fearful expectation. Suddenly, the water, the earth and the sky quivered, all at once; and a howling storm burst forth out of the distant forest like a madman that had burst his chains, baring its teeth in lightning-flashes. The palace's empty cavernous rooms began to shriek in torment, beating their doors wildly in the wind.

All my servants were at the office that day, and there was nobody at hand to light the lamps. Thus it happened that there, in the impenetrable darkness of that room, on that overclouded, moonless night, I sensed, with perfect clarity—a woman, lying face down on a rug beside the bed, tugging at her unbound hair with clenched fists, blood pouring from her ivory forehead: sometimes bursting into fierce arid laughter, sometimes into heart-rending sobs, tearing away her dress and beating upon her bared breasts with both hands—and all the while, driven by the roaring wind, sheets of rain poured in through an open window, drenching her entire body.

Neither the storm nor the weeping stopped that night. I spent those hours wandering in the dark from room to room, grieving helplessly. There was no one anywhere; no one to whom I could offer solace. Whose was this dreadful sorrow? What was it that lay behind such a perturbation?

Then there came the lunatic's cry: "Stay away! Stay away! It's a lie, all of it's a lie."

I saw that it was dawn. Meher Ali was making his rounds and shouting out his cry as usual, even on this unpropitious morning. It occurred to me then that perhaps Meher Ali too had once lived like me in this palace. Emerging deranged by the experience, he returned each morning even now to wander around the palace, still held in thrall by the great stone monster.

Right then, in the pouring rain, I ran up to the crazy old fellow and asked: "Meher Ali, what is it that's a lie?"

He thrust me aside without an answer and went on his way, circling around and around in a mesmeric trance, like a bird caught in the hypnotic spell of a python's gaze. But over and over again, as though his life depended on it, he kept warning himself: "Stay away! Stay away! It's a lie, all of it's a lie."

I left for my office at once, careering like a madman through the storm. I summoned Karim Khan and demanded: "Tell me clearly, what does all this mean?"

The gist of what the old man said is this. There was a time once when many flames of unfulfilled desire and demented lust had teemed and flared inside that palace. Every block of stone within it is still hungry, still athirst, from the curse of that anguished and frustrated longing. Whenever they find a living human being within their grasp, they seek to devour him like ravening demons. Of all the people who had spent three nights in that place, Meher Ali was the only one who had emerged alive, although he too had lost his reason. No one else has ever been able to elude its grasp.

I asked: "Is there no way to save me?"

The old man said: "Only one, and a very difficult way it is too. I'll tell you what it is—but to do that I must first tell you the old story of the Persian slave-girl in that rose-garden. In all the world there has never been another tale so strange or so affecting . . ."

Just then the porters came to inform us that our train was pulling into the station. So soon? By the time we had repacked our bedrolls, the train had arrived. An Englishman, just up from sleep, thrust his head out of a first-class compartment to read the name of the station. Spotting our fellow-traveler, he cried out "Hullo" and invited him into his compartment. Ours on the other hand was a second-class carriage. So we never learnt who the gentleman was, nor did we get to hear the end of his story.

ize I

said, "The man took us for fools and had a good laugh at our expense. The story was all made up from beginning to end."

The argument that followed led to a lifelong rupture between me and my theosophist cousin.

1895

("Kshudhita Pashan," from *Galpaguchchha*)
Translated by Amitav Ghosh

552

A Broken Nest

I

Bhupati had no need to work. He had enough money to live on and the country was warm. But, born under the influence of certain planets that drive a man to action, he took to running a newspaper. In consequence time took to running too and he had no reason to bewail the length of the hours.

From childhood onward Bhupati had a fancy for writing and discoursing in English. Hence he sent scores of letters to newspapers without any provocation whatsoever and couldn't restrain himself from holding forth at meetings and conferences even when he had nothing substantial to say. His opinion of his penmanship and oratorical skills in English had matured and ripened in the warmth of the eulogies showered on him by political leaders keen on getting a wealthy man like him on their side. And so, when his wife's brother Umapati, after the failure of his own legal practice, incited him with the words, "Start a newspaper, Bhupati. Your extraordinary command over the language" etcetera . . . etcetera, Bhupati was instantly enthused. "Nothing is to be gained," he thought, "from sending letters to other peoples' newspapers. The thing to do is to start one of my own and let my pen race freely without impediment." Appointing his brother-in-law as his assistant, he took on the honorable position of Editor. Being fairly young, at an age when politics and editing are equally intoxicating prospects, Bhupati came under the grip of the latter soon enough. Needless to say, many of his friends and acquaintances stood ready and willing to encourage him.

During the time that Bhupati remained immersed in his newspaper, something happened of which he was totally unaware. Preoccupied with Britain's policy of expansion of her empire—to the extent that threatened to cross the limits of endurance—the newspaper editor failed to notice that his bride Charu had left her childhood behind and entered her youth. With nothing to do in her husband's wealthy home and no one to take note of her growth, physical or spiritual, the flower whiled the hours away suffused in its own scent. Another woman in her circumstances would have made a great fuss of her husband, cosseted and coquetted him making conjugal dalliance stretch the bounds of decency. But for Charu there was no such scope. It was impossible for her to pierce through the armor of paper in which her husband had wrapped himself and claim his attention. If at times a female relative drew Bhupati's notice to his negligence of his young wife his conscience was instantly stirred. "True," he thought ruefully. "Charu is lonely in this house. She has no one of her age to talk to." He decided to take up the matter with his brother-in-law. "Send for your wife," he told Umapati. "Charu needs a companion." The editor's reasoning told him that his wife was pining for the company of another female and he had to do something about it. So, with the arrival of Mandakini, Bhupati was able to heave a sigh of relief and get back to his paper.

There is a time in the life of a couple when first love dawns; when each perceives the other in ever new, ever changing, forms and colors; when the whole world seems wrapped in golden light . . . Such a time came and went but neither Charu nor Bhupati heard its footfalls.

Being fond of reading and writing Charu's days did not seem too burdensome to her. A lot of her time and effort went into educating herself and she roped in Bhupati's cousin, Amal, to take her up on her lessons. Amal was in third-year college and took his tutoring duties so seriously that he demanded return for the slightest service rendered. At times this took the form of hard cash with which he bought English books and dined at hotels with his friends. Sometimes he brought them home and Charu had to organize a gargantuan meal. Bhupati wanted nothing from Charu but there was no end to Amal's demands. Charu, though expressing a mock anger at times, loved to indulge her young brother-in-law's absurd expectations. The thought that somebody needed her and claimed her attention warmed the cockles of her heart.

"Bouthan," Amal said to her one day. "A boy in our college is son-in-law to a Raja. He wears carpet slippers woven by a pair of fair hands hidden in the royal zenana. I must have some like his or my prestige will roll in the dust."

"Of course!" Charu exclaimed mockingly. "As if I have nothing better to do than sit making slippers for you. I'll give you the money. Go buy them from the market."

"Un hunh!" Amal shook his head. "That won't do. It won't do at all."

Charu had no idea of how carpet slippers were made. But she had no intention of admitting the fact. No one in this house asked anything of her. Only Amal. How could she refuse him? She started spending the hours that Amal was away from home in learning to weave carpet slippers. Then, one summer evening, when Amal had forgotten all about the slippers, she invited him to the terrace where his meal was laid out. Having just returned from college Amal washed his hands and feet, changed into his home attire and came and sat on the asan that faced a thala covered with a brass dome to keep out dust and flies. Lifting it he was startled. A pair of colorful slippers nestled coyly on the thala. Behind him Charu's laughter rang out like a peal of bells.

After receiving the slippers Amal's expectations reached a crescendo. Now he wanted a handkerchief with embroidered borders; now a coat with a Chinese collar; now a crocheted throw for his bedroom sofa. Charu objected to his demands, every time, but could not find it in her heart to refuse them. She worked painstakingly, with infinite love, and gave him what he wanted. But she couldn't resist teasing him a little. Amal was not one to wait patiently. "So Bouthan," he would prod her from time to time. "How far have you got?" Charu would pull a long face and shake her head. "I've just begun," she would lie. Or—"O Ma! I'd completely forgotten." But Amal wouldn't let her off so easily. Reminders from him came thick and fast—almost every day. Charu, enjoying the squabbles that followed, went on playing her game till, suddenly one day when Amal was least prepared to receive it, she proudly presented her handiwork.

Behind Bhupati's house was a stretch of land which, even with the grossest exaggeration, could not be called a garden. For hardly anything grew in it except a solitary hog plum tree. One day Charu and Amal took it into their heads to turn it into the most exotic park ever seen. Forming a two-member committee they made plans and drew sketches pouring the entire wealth of their combined imaginations on the project:

AMAL: "You must water the plants each morning, with your own hands Bouthan. Like the princesses of yore."

CHARU: "Yes. And we'll build a little hut in that corner for the doe."

AMAL: "We must have a small lake with swans."

CHARU: "And blue lotus floating on the lake. I've always wanted to see blue lotus."

AMAL: "There'll be a bridge across it. And a small dingy tied to the ghat."

CHARU: "The ghat will have steps cut out of white marble."

At this point Amal brought out his sketch book, pencils and compass and proceeded to make a drawing of the ghat. Every day they had something new to add and the pile of discarded drawings swelled by the hour.

The next thing to consider was the finance involved. It was decided that Charu would pay for the garden from her monthly allowance and it would take shape little by little. Then, when all was done, Bhupati would be invited to see it. How startled and delighted he would be! He, who noticed nothing of what went on in the house would think the garden had been transported from Japan overnight with the help of Aladdin's magic lamp. So far so good. But the estimate, though ridiculously low for the project they had conceived, went far beyond Charu's means.

"Let's cut out the lake," Amal suggested—ready to draw a fresh map.

"No. No! We can't cut out the lake. I must have my blue lotus."

"Do we really need a tiled roof for your doe's hut? We could have ordinary thatch."

The suggestion angered Charu. "Cut out the hut then," she snapped. "I don't want it."

Amal's next proposal, which was that instead of importing saplings—clove from Mauritius, sandal from Karnataka, and cinnamon from Sri Lanka—they buy whatever was available in Maniktala Market, was received with a curt refusal. "Let's forget it all," Charu said, her face glum and swollen. "I don't want a garden."

This, of course was no way of curbing expenses. Charu wouldn't compromise, even the tiniest bit, with the garden of their dreams. And, if truth were to be told, neither would Amal. "Then Bouthan," Amal said at last, "There's only one thing to be done. Ask Dada to give you the money."

"Absolutely not," Charu objected vehemently. "We'll do it ourselves or all the fun will be lost. Your Dada can place an order with the sahebs and turn the place into an Eden Garden. But what will become of our plan?" The two sat for a long time under the hog plum tree trying to achieve the unachievable, to create a garden fit for kings on a young housewife's pocket money.

"What are you two doing out there?" Umapati's wife, Manda, called out leaning from the balcony.

"Looking for ripe plums." Charu called back.

"Pick some for me."

Charu and Amal exchanged a conspiratorial smile. Their greatest pride and delight lay in keeping their plans to themselves and hiding them from Manda. Manda might have many good qualities but imagination wasn't one of them. What could she contribute? Thus they artfully dodged her efforts to join them and kept her out of their secrets.

The hog plum committee carried on its work, in this manner, for some weeks. Unable to expand their finances or rein in their imaginations, Amal and Charu spent their time marking the areas where the lake, the doe's hut and the marble pavilion would stand. One day as Amal, spade in hand, was digging a ring around the hog plum tree to demarcate the exact shape of the stone platform that would be built around it, Charu, sitting in its shade said suddenly, "It would be nice if you could write stories."

"Why would it be nice?"

"Then you could write one about our garden. Only you and I would recognize the descriptions. That would be fun—wouldn't it? Why don't you try? I'm sure you'll succeed."

"What will you give me if I write the story?"

"What do you want?"

"An embroidered top for my mosquito net. I'll draw the design myself and you must embroider it with silk thread."

"You're the limit!" Charu cried out exasperated. "Has anyone ever heard of an embroidered mosquito net?"

Now Amal took pains to point out that a mosquito net need not be an ugly prison in which one confined oneself, night after night, and the fact that everyone did so was proof that a quest for the beautiful in everyday existence was a rare occurrence. Charu accepted the explanation with alacrity. He was right of course. Most people were content to live drab, dull lives. How many of them sought the beautiful? Only she and Amal . . .

"Alright," she said agreeably, "I'll do the embroidery. You start writing."

"You think I can't write?" Amal looked at her out of the corners of his eyes.

"That means you've written already." Charu cried out in excitement. "Show me your notebook."

"Not today Bouthan."

"Why not? I want to see it today. This minute."

Amal had been wanting to show his notebook to Charu for quite some time now. His only fear, that which had made him hesitate, was that she might not understand what he had written, that she may not like it.

Blushing a little, coughing a little, Amal brought out his notebook and started reading from it. Charu leaned against the hog plum tree and listened with rapt attention. The title of the essay was "Khata."

Oh my notebook! My unblemished khata! Amal read with feeling. *My flights of fancy have not yet touched your pages. You're as pure, as filled with mystery, as the brow of a newborn infant in the birthing chamber. The day I write my conclusion on your last page is far off. Your tender, white leaves have no notion of what the ink-blemished last leaf . . .* etcetera, etcetera.

Amal's reading came to an end. He looked up hopefully. Charu was silent for a few moments, then she sighed and said, "And all this time I thought you couldn't write." This was Amal's first draught of the vintage of literary appreciation. The evening shadows were lengthening. His *saki* was young and innocent . . .

"We'll have to pick a few plums," Charu's voice broke the spell. "How else will we satisfy Manda?"

2

The days passed. Amal and Charu's grandiose plans, like many of their earlier ones, died a natural death. But, wrapped up in each other, they scarcely noticed the fact. Their chief preoccupation, now, was Amal's penmanship. Their interaction went somewhat like this . . .

"Bouthan," Amal says, "I've got a wonderful idea." Charu is instantly enthused. "Let's go to the south veranda. Manda will be here any minute with her paan box." Hastening to the Kashmiri veranda Charu sinks into a battered cane sofa while Amal, perched precariously on the narrow slab below the railing, commences outlining his idea. But the idea is, as yet, unformed and Amal's powers of expression—limited. He goes round and round in circles stopping, from time to time, with a crestfallen, "I don't think I'm explaining myself very well."

"Oh no!" Charu is quick to reassure him. "I've understood quite a lot. Start writing it at once." The truth is that Charu understands little of Amal's ideas. But, fired by his enthusiasm, and the manner of his telling, she fills the gaps with her own imagination and works herself up into a fever of excitement.

"How much have you written?" she asks the same evening.

"Writing takes time." Amal replies ponderously.

"You haven't even begun?" She rails at him first thing the next morning.

"Give me time. I must think about it a bit more." Amal replies. Charu, her patience exhausted, exclaims angrily. "You don't have to write a word."

By evening, when Charu hasn't talked to him for several hours, a wad of paper nestles shyly in Amal's pocket. He pulls it out, as if by mistake, along with his handkerchief. Charu breaks her silence with an excited, "You were just pretending! Show me what you've written this minute."

"I need to write some more," Amal replies. "I'll read it out to you when it's completed."

"I want to hear it now."

Amal, more than willing to show it to her, makes her beg and plead some more. Then, with a great show of reluctance, he takes out the wad, opens it, shuffles the sheets a bit and makes some marks with a pencil, Charu leaning over him all the while, her heart as full of emotion as an overladen cloud. The few paragraphs Amal writes have to be read out to Charu as and when they are written. The unwritten part is discussed and imagined by both . . .

All these days the two were engaged in building castles in the air. Now they had shifted their activity and brought it to the realm of literature.

One afternoon Amal came home with a bulge in the pocket of his coat. Charu, looking out of the window, noticed it as soon as he entered the house. She waited for him to come and tell her what it was but the hours passed and Amal didn't come. Charu went to the door that led to the outer rooms and clapped her hands several times but got no response. A miffed Charu then picked up Manmatha Datta's *Kalakantha* and, sitting in a chair on the veranda, attempted to read it. Manmatha Datta was a new writer with a style not unlike Amal's. Hence Charu's fascination for his work and Amal's disdain. Whenever he saw her reading one of the author's books Amal would snatch it from her and, declaiming some of the lines in an unnaturally loud and caustic tone, fling it away. That day, as soon as she heard his approaching footsteps, Charu leaned possessively over the book and kept her eyes glued to its pages.

"What are you reading Bouthan?"

Charu didn't bother to reply.

"Manmatha Datta's *Galaganda*?"

"Aah!" Charu exclaimed in pretended annoyance. "Let me read my book in peace."

Standing behind her Amal peered into the pages. *"I'm grass. A mere blade of grass."* He read in a loud, mocking voice. *"And you Asoka tree are clad in royal garments of crimson. I bear no flowers. I give no shade. My head , unlike yours, is not raised to heaven. The cuckoo does not call from my branches in Spring. Yet, do not look down on me from your high, blossom-covered branches, brother Asoka. I'm a wretched blade of grass lying at your feet. Yet do not despise me."*

Reading this much from the book Amal added some lines of his own, his face twisted with mockery—*I'm bananas! A bunch of raw bananas. Brother pumpkin! You who hang high from the thatch of the house do not look down on me. I'm only a wretched bunch of bananas. Yet*—Charu forgot her anger and started laughing. Flinging the book away she cried, "You're jealous! You don't like anyone's writing but your own!"

"And you're the world's best reader. The flimsiest blade of grass is good enough for you."

"You win," Charu said, appeased. "And now, Moshai, stop teasing me and take out what you have in your pocket."

"What do you think it is?" Amal made Charu guess a number of times then, when her patience was nearly at an end, drew out a copy of *Suroruho*. *Suroruho* was a popular journal and Amal's article "Khata" was printed in it.

Charu's mood changed. She sat, silent, a far away expression in her eyes. Amal was puzzled. He had expected her to be overjoyed but saw no signs of it. "Only the best writing is published in *Suroruho*," he muttered defensively. "The editors are very particular. They choose one out of every hundred articles they get." Which, of course, was a gross exaggeration. Anything and everything was published in *Suroruho*. Charu tried to be happy but couldn't. She wondered why. She sought in her mind for some answer but could come up with none.

All this time Charu had considered Amal's work their private property. He was the author—she the reader. The secrecy with which the writing was shrouded was its chief merit. Now everyone would read his work and many would appreciate it. But why that should hurt her so much—she couldn't imagine. Writers are, as a rule, not content with one reader for long. Neither was Amal. He started publishing freely and was rewarded with a fair measure of praise. Fan letters started arriving and Amal loved showing them to Charu. Charu was happy and dejected at the same time. The realization that she was no longer indispensable to Amal; that her pushing, prodding and encouraging had become redundant in his life, saddened and bemused her. And, when Amal presented her with anonymous letters in a female hand, Charu made a great show of teasing and tormenting him but pain gnawed at her heart.

One day Bhupati said to her. "I must say, Charu, I had no idea that our Amal was such a good writer." Charu was pleased. Amal lived under their protection like so many others. But he was far superior; far above the rest. The thought brought a little glow in her heart. She felt as though Amal, by proving his worth to Bhupati, had justified her interest in him; her care and nurture of him. "You've realized his value only now," she said to herself. "I've known he was someone special for a long time."

"Have you read Amal's work?" Charu asked her husband.

"Y-yes . . . no . . . not really. Where's the time? But our Nishikanta was praising him a lot the other day. Nishikanta understands Bangla writing much better than I do."

Charu sighed in satisfaction. Bhupati had learned to value Amal. It was what she had wanted for a long time.

3

Bhupati and his brother-in-law were in confabulation. There was a slump in the sales of the paper and heavy losses were being reported. Umapati's advice was that they distribute some gifts along with the newspaper but how spending some more money would help to cut costs and bring in profits, Bhupati could not, for the life of him, comprehend. The talk went round and round in circles . . .

Charu entered the room but seeing her brother turned and left. She came back again, several times, but the meeting was still in session. After some time Umapati realized that his sister wanted to be alone with her husband, and making some excuse, rose and left the room. Bhupati continued studying the papers in front of him.

"You're still at it!" Charu cried out in exasperation. "How you can spend hour after hour with those dry sheets I can't imagine. Can't you think of anything else to do?"

Pushing the papers aside Bhupati smiled at his wife. *Poor Charu!* he thought, *She must be so bored and lonely. Really! I neglect her exceedingly. It is very wrong of me.* "Why aren't you at your lessons?" he asked affectionately, "Has the master run away? Everything goes contrary in your school Charu. The pupil waits patiently with her books and the master plays truant. Doesn't Amal help you with your lessons anymore?"

"Is it fair to expect him to spend all his time teaching me? Is he a private tutor?"

Bhupati put his hands on Charu's waist and drew her to him. "Is this an ordinary pupil? If I had a Bouthan like you I'd . . ."

"I-i-i-sh!" Charu's voice cut into his mockingly. "Having you as a husband is enough for me. Don't wish to be anything else."

Her words hurt Bhupati—just a little. "Alright," he said peaceably, "I'll start teaching you from tomorrow. Bring your books. Let me see how far you've got."

"Hunh!" Charu tossed her head in dismissal. "You've done s-o-o-o much for me already. You don't need to do anything more. Now— what I've come to say is this—Will you put away your papers and pay some attention?"

"Of course I will. I'll turn my head in whichever direction you wish to take it."

Pushing a magazine towards Bhupati Charu said, "Now read this and see how good it is. The editorial says that, according to Nabagopal Babu, Amal is Bengal's Ruskin."

Bhupati put out a diffident hand and took the magazine from

Charu. The title of Amal's article was "Asadh Moon." Bhupati had been wrestling, for the past two weeks, with highly complicated sums in government budgets and thoughts related to them were still wriggling in his head. He was in no condition, really, to read an essay in Bengali called "Asadh Moon." It seemed quite a long one too . . . Still, pulling himself together, he began reading:

563

Why does the moon of Asadh hide itself behind the clouds tonight? Guiltily—as though it has stolen a rare gem from Heaven and must cover itself in shame. In Phalgun, when the sky had not a shred of cloud in any corner, it had shone unblushingly all over the earth. But tonight . . . where has her lovely laughter gone? Like the dreams of infants, memories of a beloved; like the strings of pearls that trail from the tresses of Sureswari Sachi . . .

"Good . . . good!" Bhupati scratched his head. "But why me? What do I understand of such poetic stuff?"

Charu snatched the paper from Bhupati's hand. "What do you understand then?" she asked testily.

"I'm a man of the world. I understand human beings."

"Don't writers write about human beings?"

"They do. But the pictures they present are false. Besides, when I can see human beings all around me, why do I have to look for them in books?" Caressing Charu's chin playfully he added, "I understand you so well. But I didn't need to read *Meghnadbadh Kavya* or *Kabikankanchandi* for that."

Bhupati prided himself on the fact that he was a practical man and didn't understand "poetic stuff." Yet, there was a core of admiration, in his heart, for Amal whose work he hadn't even read. "How Amal writes reams and reams with nothing at all to back it beats me," he thought with reverence. "I couldn't do it if I knocked my head against the wall! Who knew Amal had so much in him?"

Though Bhupati had no pretensions to even the slightest knowledge of literary matters he was generous to litterateurs. He had paid for the publication of many a book—on one condition alone. That it was not to be dedicated to him. He bought large quantities of books and subscribed to many journals. *I don't read any,* he thought ruefully, *and if I don't even buy them there'll be no washing away of my sins.* He had no objection to mediocre and less than mediocre writing simply because he didn't have to go through it. In consequence the shelves of his library groaned under the weight of inferior stuff.

Amal, who used to help Bhupati correct his proofs, now came into the room with a sheaf of papers in his hand. "Amal," Bhupati smiled at his young cousin. "I have no problem with your writing pages and pages on moons in Asadh or ripe palm fruits in Bhadra. I give you full freedom to do so. But why is *my* freedom to be curtailed? Your Bouthan is hell bent on making me read them. What have I done to deserve such punishment?"

"Really Bouthan!" Amal turned towards Charu. "It's very wrong of you. If you torture Dada like this I'll give up writing altogether." Amal, not a little piqued at this slight to his "Asadh Moon," on which he had spent so many hours of loving labor, felt very cross with Charu. Charu sensed his anger and was hurt by it. In an effort to change the subject she said to her husband. "Find your brother a wife. She'll cure him of his malady."

"Today's young men are not as foolish as we were." Bhupati replied. "All their romance is on paper. In the real affairs of life they keep their wits about them. You've tried hard enough to marry off your brother-in-law. But could you get him to agree?"

After Charu's departure Bhupati said to Amal. "The paper keeps me so busy—I can't give Charu any time. She peeps into this room and goes away, disappointed, half a dozen times a day. She needs something to do. Why don't you keep her busy? Translate extracts from English into Bangla and read them out to her. They will do her good. She has quite a feel for literature."

"That's true," Amal agreed instantly, "Bouthan is very intelligent. She could become a good writer herself if she works a bit harder."

"My expectations don't go that high," Bhupati said. "But Charu's understanding of literature is far superior to mine."

"She has a good imagination. Rare in a woman."

"Not that all men are equally endowed. Look at me." Smiling at his cousin he added, "Fall to the task Amal. If you can mould your Bouthan into a literary figure you'll get a reward from me."

"What is it to be?"

564

"I'll scour heaven and earth and find a prototype of your Bouthan for you."

"Hai re! Then I'll have to mold her too. Is there no end to the tasks you are setting for me?" The brothers were modern men. They spoke their thoughts freely without constraint.

4

With his increasing popularity among his readers Amal's maturing took on a quick tempo. He, who was a mere college boy, now became a full-fledged adult; an important member of society. Invitations to read from his work started coming his way from clubs and societies. He was dined and feted and even invited to preside at literary gatherings. His prestige rose so high in Bhupati's household—it almost touched the sky.

Mandakini hadn't thought much of Amal till now. Looking upon his animated discussions and whispered conversations with Charu as the height of childishness, she kept herself busy with her paan box and other domestic work. She felt herself to be a cut above the two. Maturer. Indispensable to the household. She had been assigned the task of making up all the paan the family required and she took it very seriously. Amal ate enormous quantities, raiding her box with Charu's help every now and then. This playful pilfering annoyed Manda. She looked upon it as a waste of the household's resources seeing that Amal was only a poor relative who lived on Bhupati's charity. The fact that she and her husband were exactly in the same position escaped her. Whatever little extra work she had to do for Amal irked her. She felt resentful; humiliated. Aware of Charu's preference for him she dared not complain. That did not prevent her, however, from ignoring his presence or taking sly digs at him. Or even gossiping about his shortcomings with the servants in which, needless to say, they joined in with gusto.

But with Amal's rise to prominence her feelings changed. Amal was not the same Amal now. The boyish diffidence; the shy humility of old was gone. He was a man who knew his own worth and didn't hesitate to proclaim it before the world. The privilege of ignoring others had now passed into his hands. Such a man is bound to attract a woman's attention and so it happened with Manda. Like many others in Bhupati's household, she started looking up to him and the glow of pride and confidence she saw in the youth's handsome eyes filled her own with enchantment. There was no need, now, for Amal to steal paan from her box. Quantities of it came to him unasked.

566

This was another of Charu's losses. The sweet conspiracy that they had shared; the joy of keeping Mandakini out of their company was gone. Manda, bent upon making amends for her past behavior, made an appearance whenever she saw them together sending a chill through Charu's heart. It was impossible to keep her away; impossible to have a few minutes alone with Amal! She felt the light of her life being eclipsed by Manda's shadow.

Needless to say, Amal didn't mind the intrusion as much as Charu did. Winning over a hostile woman is a heady experience for a man and Amal wasn't proof against it. He felt flattered by Manda's attention and looked forward to it. Yet whenever Charu, seeing Manda approach them, exclaimed disdainfully, "There she comes," Amal was quick to reply, "Honestly. What a pain!" Then, when Manda joined them, he turned to her as though with forced civility and said, "So Manda Bouthan! What news of your paan box? Have you checked for losses this morning?"

"You only have to ask bhai," Manda smiled sweetly at him. "You'll get as much as you want. Why do you have to steal?"

"Stealing is more fun than begging."

"Go on with your reading. What makes you stop? Me? But I love to hear you read."

In all the time that Manda had spent in this house she had never shown any interest in hearing what Amal read out to Charu. But such is the power of fame! Charu, totally averse to including Manda in their reading session, said curtly, "Amal has written a review of *Kamalakanta'r Daptar.* You might not be interested—"

"Of course I will," Manda cut in quickly, then continued humbly, "I may not be well-educated. But, maybe, I'll understand some of it." Amal was reminded of the day he had walked into Charu's room to find the two women playing *binti*. He had brought an article with him which he wanted to show Charu. But the game went on and on and finally, his patience at an end, he said, "Carry on with your game then. I'll read out what I've written to Akhil Babu." Charu put out her hand and clutched his shawl. "Sit quietly," she commanded. Then ending the game by deliberately making wrong moves and losing it, she asked Amal to begin his reading. "I'd better leave then," Manda rose hastily to her feet. "Why don't you stay and listen too?" Charu invited her politely. "No bhai," Manda replied, "I don't understand your literary nonsense. It makes me fall asleep." Annoyed at the premature conclusion of her beloved game Manda had left the room in a huff. The same Manda was expressing a desire to listen to a critical analysis of *Kamalakanta'r Daptar*. The change in her pleased Amal.

"Of course," he cried heartily, "It's my great good fortune, Manda Bouthan, that you—" Turning back the pages he began reading from the beginning. "Thakurpo," Charu interrupted suddenly, "You promised to bring me the back numbers of some journals from Jahnavi Library."

"That wasn't today."

"Of course it was. You've forgotten."

"Why should I forget? You said—"

"Very well then. You needn't trouble yourself. I'll send Paresh." And with those words Charu swept out of the room. Amal looked on her departing form with trepidation. He understood the reason for Charu's annoyance but was neither moved nor flattered by it. His heart filled with negative feelings against her. He sat biting his lips, wondering what to do. Should he carry on with his reading or go after Charu? Manda helped him make up his mind. "Go Amal," she said with a little smirk, "Cool her down. You'll be in deep trouble if you sit here any longer."

After this it was impossible for Amal to leave the room. "Why should I be in trouble?" he cried and went on with his reading. "No bhai," Manda put out her hands on the paper and stopped him. Then, rising abruptly as though trying hard to fight back her tears, she ran towards the door.

5

"Bouthan!" Amal came into Charu's room to find Manda sitting on the bed plaiting thread into a tape for her hair. Charu had gone out to attend an invitation and Manda was alone. "Poor Amal Babu," she gave him an arch smile, "To look for one person and find another in her place. What bad luck!"

"The haystack to the left is no different from the one to the right. A donkey is equally pleased with both." Amal said. Then, sitting down beside her, he continued, "Talk to me Manda Bouthan. Tell me about your life before you came here."

Amal used to collect material for his writing, in this manner, from everyone he knew. Why not Manda? He asked her question after question probing curiously into her past. Her infancy and childhood; her parents and siblings; the village in which she had lived before she was wed; her early years as a bride in her husband's home; her thoughts and feelings on the subject. This was the first time someone was taking an interest in Manda's life. That too a renowned writer like Amal. Flushed with triumph Manda prattled on happily, stopping from time to time with a "Ma go! I'm talking too much." But Amal was quick to assure her that she wasn't. And so she went on and on. In the middle of an account about her father's steward—a one-eyed fellow who had quarreled with his wife and pretended to be on a hunger strike and was subsequently caught by the same wife eating a huge meal in the master's house—Charu walked in. An uneasy silence followed. But only for a few seconds. Amal pulled himself together quite quickly and exclaimed, "Why Bouthan! You're home early."

"Yes I see that. A little too early." Charu turned to leave the room.

"I'm so glad you're back," Amal said hastily. "I was torturing myself with the thought that you'd be really late. I've brought Manmatha Datta's *Evening Bird* to read out to you. Shall I—?"

"Not now. I have some work."

"Command me. I'll do your work for you."

Charu knew that Amal was buying the book today and was looking forward to the reading session that would follow. She would tease him with loads of praise for the author and he would retaliate by distorting the language and sentiments with his reading. In a fever of anticipation she had feigned illness and come away home—only to find him chatting happily with Manda. "I should have stayed where I was," she thought, her heart swelling with pain and envy, "I was a fool to come rushing back."

What a shameless creature Manda was . . . Charu thought indignantly. Sitting with Amal alone in the bedroom! Simpering and giggling! What would people think? She dared not broach the subject with Manda or upbraid her. What if Manda turned around and cited her own example? The two, of course, were totally different. She, Charu, was Amal's muse. She was there to give him encouragement and inspiration. And she didn't hesitate to criticize him where criticism was due. But Manda had no such intentions. She was out to trap an innocent youth with her feminine wiles. What a dangerous situation for poor Amal Thakurpo! She had to save him. But how? Suppose he laughed her fears away? Suppose—oh! horror of horrors—he thought she was jealous?

Her thoughts turned to her brother. Poor Dada! Working day and night for her husband's newspaper without a thought for himself. Without an inkling of what was going on behind his back. He loved Manda so much! He had such great faith in her. And Manda! She, Charu, could not let this go on. Not after seeing it with her own eyes. She had to stop it. But how? Amal was not the same Amal. Would he be guided by her? It was all her fault. She was the one who had pushed and prodded him into writing. Fame followed as she should have known it would. He didn't think of her as an equal anymore. He was a famous author; she a mere reader. Now that he was the apple of so many eyes he could afford to ignore her.

It was clear to Charu that Amal had passed from her hands into the hands of many others. *Dangers lurked for him at every step. Poor, innocent, unprotected Amal! Clever, seductive siren Manda! Loving, trusting Dada!*

6

That afternoon, the sky was overcast with Asadh clouds. It was so dark in the room that Charu was leaning out of the window to catch the faint light that still clung to the earth. She was writing something in a little notebook. Amal came and stood behind her but she didn't sense his presence. Seeing some of his articles spread out on a table beside her Amal realized that she was writing one herself—using his work as a model. Looking over her shoulder he read some lines.

"Why do you pretend you can't write?" Amal's voice broke into the silence. Charu looked up startled. Covering the notebook with her sari she tried to hide it. "It's very wrong of you," she said severely.

"Why? What have I done?"

"Why were you hiding behind me?"

"Because I won't get to read what you've written otherwise."

Charu was about to tear the pages out but Amal snatched the notebook from her hands. "Don't read," she cried, her face flushed, "If you do I'll never talk to you again."

"If you stop me from reading *I'll* never talk to you again."

"Please Amal Thakurpo, I beg of you—"

The battle went on and finally Charu had to concede defeat. That was, not in a small measure, owing to her intense desire to show Amal what she had written. That desire was mixed with acute embarrassment. She sat, as though frozen, watching Amal's eyes run over the first page. Then, rising hastily she said, "I'll fetch some paan," and ran to the next room where she busied herself in dressing paan leaves and twisting them into cones. Amal finished his reading and came to her. "Excellent!" he exclaimed heartily, "It's very well-written."

"Go on!" Charu forgot to smear her paan leaves with catechu. "You don't have to tease me. Give me my notebook."

"Not now," Amal replied. "I'll copy the article out, first, and send it to some journal."

"Send it to some journal indeed!" Charu tried to pluck the notebook out of his hands. "You can't do that. I won't let you."

Some more pulling and snatching followed. Finally, when Amal was able to convince her that the article was, indeed, good enough to be published Charu sighed and said, as though in utter despair, "There's no getting around you Amal Thakurpo. You always do as you please."

"I'd like to show it to Dada"—

"No. Never," Charu left her paan and sprang to her feet. "If you do that I won't write another line."

"You're making a mistake Bouthan," Amal tried to pacify her. "Dada may not show it but he's very proud of you. He'll take pleasure in reading what you've written."

"I don't care for his pleasure."

Charu had begun her writing with a goal in view. She wanted to please and surprise Amal. To make him understand that there was a world of difference between her and Manda. She had written quite a lot prior to this article but, dissatisfied with it, had torn it all up and thrown it into the pond. Whenever she thought something was good it turned out to be identical to something Amal had written. And when it wasn't —the style, it seemed to her, was raw and awkward; the ideas unformed. She had thought her first composition "Clouds of Sravan" to be a new kind of writing—full of pathos and fine sentiments till she realized, in a moment of clarity, that it was an exact copy of Amal's "Asadh Moon." *Dear Moon,* Amal had written, *Why do you hide behind the clouds like a thief? Dear Cloud,* Charu had written, *Why do you hide the stolen moon beneath your blue veil and try to escape?* And so on . . .

Unable to get out of Amal's orbit Charu decided to change the whole direction of her writing. Out went all the moons, clouds, shiuli flowers and song birds. She fell back, instead, on her recollections of a small Kali temple that stood by the pond in her ancestral village—a shadowy silhouette buried in trees. "Kali tala" she named her composition and into it she poured all she remembered of her rural past. The legends and fables associated with the deity that she had heard in her childhood; the awe and reverence she had felt on seeing the collective faith of the villagers; her fear of the goddess and her fascination. The opening lines were reminiscent of Amal's ornate labored style but after a while it had acquired a flow, a simplicity and spontaneity of language and thought that was entirely her own. This was the composition that Amal had snatched from her hands and read. His considered opinion was that, though the beginning was promising, somewhere down the line it had fallen short of the reader's expectations. The aesthetic quality had not been sustained. Still, for a first attempt, the work was commendable.

"Why don't we start a journal of our own Thakurpo?" Charu put out a feeler.

"A number of silver discs are required to keep a journal going."

"We won't need a single one. Our journal will be hand-written—not printed. There'll be only two readers and two writers. You and I. No one else will be allowed to catch even a glimpse of it."

A short while ago Amal would have been excited by the proposal. Now he thought writing was a waste of time if it didn't reach a good number of readers. Still, for old times sake, he said enthusiastically. "That will be fun."

"But before we start," Charu went on, "you must take a vow. That you'll write for only our journal and no other."

"The editors will kill me."

"Don't I have weapons to kill?"

Amal took the vow and a two member committee was formed to chalk out the details. "What shall we name our journal?" Amal said, "Let's call it *Charupath*."

"Oh no!" Charu exclaimed. "I've decided on the name already. It's to be *Amala*."

Putting their plan into action Charu became a changed person. Her discontents vanished. Her heart felt light and free. There was no way Manda could enter this world—a world in which she and Amal were the sole inhabitants. Everyone else would be kept away too. What bliss! What utter bliss!

7

Bhupati said to his wife one day. "You've become a famous writer Charu! That's good. Very good. But why was I kept in the dark?"

"I? A writer?" Charu blushed a fiery red. "What nonsense! Who told you that?"

"You've been caught red-handed." Bhupati laughed at his wife's panic-stricken look. "You can't escape." Pulling out the latest issue of *Suroruho,* he held it out to her. Charu saw that all the compositions she and Amal had written for their personal journal, all that she had considered their secret treasure, had found a place in *Suroruho.* She felt as though someone had opened the door of her secret cage and sent her beloved birds flying across the sky . . . to be buffeted by storm, wind and rain.

Charu forgot her embarrassment at being caught by Bhupati. Her heart hardened with anger at Amal's betrayal.

"Take a look at this," Bhupati opened the sheets of the morning paper, *Bishwabandhu,* and held it out to her. A column bearing the title "Writing Styles in Present-Day Bangla" met her eyes. "Why should I read it?" Charu pushed the paper away. "What do I have to do with all this?"

"Arre take a look. You'll find it interesting."

Charu took the paper from her husband's hand and ran her eyes over the column. It was a critical evaluation, a fairly long one, of the style writers of Bangla favored these days. Hitting out at the florid, over-embellished prose churned out by Amal and Manmatha Datta and making considerable mockery of it, the writer went on to discuss the work of Srimati Charulata Debi which, in his opinion, was far superior. Commending the clarity of her images and the unpretentious lucidity of her style he went on to say that Amal and his ilk would do well to follow her example. Else their writing would soon be relegated to the annals of history.

"This is what I call beating the guru at his own game," Bhupati smiled indulgently at his wife. But Charu's pleasure was not unmixed with pain. She tried to be happy at the new status accorded to her but couldn't. She felt as if she had been offered a pot of nectar; she wanted to drink from it but was forced to thrust it aside.

She knew why Amal had sent her compositions, in secret, to *Suroruho.* It was to surprise and please her. He had intended, she also knew, to show them to her, when they appeared in print together with some favorable comments, and share her triumph. Why hadn't Amal brought them to her then? Why had he kept them hidden? Was he hurt at the comparisons drawn by the critic? The tiny nest of comfort she had built deep within her heart; that which she had nurtured with hours of patient labor, was being battered by a hail storm of acclaim. Charu didn't like it. She didn't like it at all.

Bhupati left the room. Charu sat on the bed staring at the wall with vacant eyes. Sneaking up quietly behind her, note book in hand, Amal saw her sitting, sunk deep in thought, with the open sheets of *Suroruho* and *Bishwabandhu* spread out before her. Bitterness welled up in his heart and he went away as silently as he had come. Bouthan, he thought, was so ecstatic at her elevation and his downgrading that she was lost to the world. She should have realized that the critic was a fool and that his was not the last word on the subject. She should have torn the paper into pieces and thrown them into the fire. But she hadn't. She sat preening herself, convinced that she was the better writer.

574

"Manda Bouthan!" Amal's disappointment with Charu brought him to Manda's door. "Come, bhai, come." Manda gave him a warm welcome. "To see you without looking for you. What luck!"

"Would you like to hear some extracts from my latest work? Shall I read them out?"

"You keep promising to read to me. And I sit patiently waiting and hoping. But . . . but . . . it is better, perhaps, if you don't. Someone may see us together and get angry. Then you're the one who'll be in the dock. Not I."

"Why should anyone get angry? And why should I be in the dock? Anyway—all that can be thought later. Now sit quietly and listen."

Manda settled herself comfortably on the bed. Her face took on an eager expression. Amal began—his voice loud and dramatic; his manner pompous. Manda, of course, could make neither head nor tail of what Amal was reading. But the less she understood; the more abstruse the subject got—the happier she looked. Amal stole sly glances at her face now and then and, enthused by what he saw, read on with renewed vigor. His voice rose higher and higher, reaching a point where it threatened to burst Manda's ear drums. Amal was reading . . .

Just as Abhimanyu had learned the intricate art of penetrating a line of battle while still a fetus in his mother's womb, but not that of leaving it— so the river, gushing out of the stone walls of a mountain cave, had learned the art of flowing on but that of turning back she had not learned. Thus it is with all things! Alas River! Alas Youth! Alas Time! Alas World! You have only learned to move forward. The path that you have traversed, that which is strewn with golden nuggets of memory—you can never retrace. Only the human mind can find its way into the past. Nothing else in this infinite universe gives it a backward glance . . .

At this point a shadow appeared at Manda's door. She saw it but, choosing to ignore it, she continued to gaze wide-eyed at Amal's face. The shadow moved swiftly away.

Charu had been waiting for Amal to come to her. She had decided to pull the carping critic to pieces in his presence; tear the paper to bits and also scold him heartily for breaking his vow. She also had her newest composition, all ready, to show him when he came. But the hours passed. There was no sign of Amal. Suddenly she heard his voice. It seemed to come from Manda's room. Charu rose from the bed and tip-toed her way to Manda's door. She stood there for a few seconds. *Only the human mind* she heard Amal's voice declaiming, *can find its way into the past. Nothing else in this infinite Universe gives it a backward glance.* Charu felt something sharp pierce her heart. Amal was reading out his latest article to Manda and not to her . . .

Charu could not go back as silently as she had come. She had received several blows that morning, one after another, and her endurance was at an end. Amal knew very well that Manda didn't understand a line of what he had written. Yet, like a fool, he was taking pleasure in her pretended absorption. Charu felt like screaming this out before the two of them. But she didn't utter a word. She ran to her room and slammed the door so hard that Amal looked up startled. Manda smirked and pointed in Charu's direction. "This is too much!" Amal thought angrily. "Does Bouthan think I'm her slave? Why must I read out my work only to her and to no other person? This is an outrage!" Raising his voice another octave he continued reading out to Manda.

Passing Charu's door, half an hour later, he didn't falter even for a second. Charu heard his footfalls and her breast heaved with mortification. Her eyes burned but she didn't weep. Picking up her notebook she tore every page she had written into shreds and heaped them on the floor. Hai! Hai! Why had she and Amal started this writing business? It was killing her.

8

It was the hour of dusk. The juin flowers, growing in pots on the veranda, were dispersing their cool sweet scents. The stars winked and sparkled between shreds of cloud in a soft, black sky. Charu hadn't braided her hair that evening or changed her sari. She sat by the window, her hair blowing gently in the wind; tears streaming down her face. She didn't put up a hand to wipe them away and they fell thicker and faster.

Bhupati entered the room. His face was pale and his heart sick with worry. He usually sat in the outer rooms all evening checking proofs and came to the women's wing fairly late at night. What was he doing in his wife's room at this hour? And why did his eyes have that lost bewildered look? As though, floundering in a sea of troubles, he had come to Charu for solace and support.

The lamp had not been lit and the room was dark. In the faint light that came from the stars Bhupati saw a dim figure huddled by the window. It was his wife. He came and stood behind her. Charu heard him but did not turn her head. She sat like a stone figure—rigid and silent. "Charu!" Bhupati called out in surprise. At the sound of his voice Charu stirred in her chair but still didn't turn around. "Why Charu!" Bhupati ran his fingers tenderly through her hair. "Why are you sitting here all alone in the dark? Where is Manda?"

Everything had gone wrong for Charu that day. Nothing had happened the way she had hoped it would. She had waited for Amal to come and make up with her; to say he was sorry. She was waiting even now. But he hadn't come. Bhupati had come instead. At the sound of her husband's voice, full of compassion and concern, something snapped within her and she burst into a storm of loud weeping.

"Why Charu!" Bhupati exclaimed, alarmed. "What's wrong?"

How could Charu tell him what was wrong? What, in any case, was her complaint? That Amal had read out his latest article first to Manda and not to her? Wouldn't Bhupati laugh at her foolishness? Yet she was suffering. Suffering horribly. But why—she couldn't tell. The lack of rationale behind the emotions that were driving her mad, frightened her and her anguish multiplied a hundred fold.

"Tell me Charu," Bhupati pleaded. "Is it something that I have done? You know how tied up I am with this wretched paper. But if I have upset you in any way it was without intention. I'm truly sorry."

Unable to give any answers to her husband's questions Charu felt disturbed and restless. Resentment stirred within her. She wished he would go away and leave her in peace. "I know I can't come to you as often as you wish," Bhupati continued humbly, "I am guilty and deserve your censure. But things will change from now on. I've decided to give up slaving day and night for the paper. You'll have me by your side whenever you want me."

"It isn't that," Charu said quickly; too quickly.

"What is it then?" Bhupati lowered himself on the bed. "Tell me."

"Not now," Charu didn't bother to keep the exasperation out of her voice. "I'll tell you later." Something in her manner hurt and puzzled Bhupati. He had come to her in the hope of laying down his own burden and finding comfort and consolation. But the time, it seemed, was inappropriate. "So be it," he murmured. Then, rising to his feet, he walked slowly to the door. Charu realized that she had wounded his feelings and the thought saddened her. She half-rose from the chair to call him back then sat down again. What was the use? She had nothing to say to him.

Filled with a remorse she had no way of alleviating, Charu sat helplessly staring at the sky. Night fell. She rose from the window and, going to the kitchen, laid out Bhupati's meal with special care. Then, palm leaf in hand, she waited for him to come. "Braja! Braja!" Suddenly Manda's voice came to her ears, loud and imposing, calling out to the servant. "Has Amal Babu had his dinner?"

"Yes," Braja's reply—soft; submissive.

"Then why haven't you taken paan for him?" Manda was still scolding the old retainer when Bhupati came and sat on his plank next to Charu.

Charu had made up her mind to be easy and pleasant with her husband. She had thought of several things to say to him but after hearing Manda's voice all her plans crumbled to dust. She waved her palm leaf, listlessly, unable to utter a word. Bhupati was silent and preoccupied and ate little. "You've eaten nothing," Charu said at last, her voice strained with the effort.

"No," Bhupati answered gravely. "I've eaten quite a lot."

Later at night, when husband and wife were together in their bedroom, Bhupati reminded Charu, "You had something to say to me. What is it?"

"I've been meaning to talk to you for some time now," Charu replied. "I'm not happy with the way Manda conducts herself. I'm afraid to keep her in this house any longer."

"Why? What has she done?"

"Her behavior with Amal is unseemly. Brazen and shameless. And—"

"Are you crazy?" Bhupati laughed at her fears. "Amal is only a child."

"You know nothing of what goes on in the house. All you do is collect news from outside. Poor Dada! Manda doesn't bother her head one bit about his comforts. All her concern is for Amal. The slightest delay in serving him and she scolds the servants mercilessly. You heard her yourself."—

"I must say you women are very suspicious of one another," Bhupati began but Charu cut him short. "Alright—we are suspicious. But I cannot allow this kind of thing in my house."

Bhupati smiled. He did not take Charu's accusations seriously but he was charmed by her concern for the sanctity of marriage and the purity of the household. Women were the custodians of all that was good, he thought. Hence their excessive fear of immorality, however slight or even imagined it might be. His heart was filled with love for Charu and something like reverence. He bent forward and kissed her brow tenderly. "There's no need to worry anymore," he said. "Umapati is leaving for Mymensingh in a few days. He's to take up his legal practice once again. And Manda is going with him."

9

He still hadn't shared his troubles with Charu or sought comfort from her. "Later," he thought, "at a more opportune time." Instead he picked up her notebook from the table and said. "Read something to me Charu."

Charu snatched it from his hands and said, "You won't like what I've written. You'll make fun of me."

Bhupati was pained by her attitude but didn't show it. "No I won't make fun of you," he said smiling. "I'll listen so quietly you'll think I've gone to sleep." But Bhupati's assurances were in vain. Charu wouldn't read to him and gradually, other, more painful thoughts, came crowding into his mind.

579

What Bhupati had come to tell Charu, but didn't get a chance, was that his newspaper had run into trouble. He had made Umapati his manager and put him in charge of all matters relating to finance. Collecting money from vendors, paying salaries and reimbursing the bills of the printing press and suppliers were his responsibility. Some days ago Bhupati had received a lawyer's notice from a paper dealer claiming an amount of two thousand seven hundred rupees. Bhupati was shocked. Sending for his brother-in-law he asked, "What does this mean? I gave you the money long ago. Have you not made the payment?"

"There must be some mistake," Umapati muttered. But there was no mistake. Within a few days everything came to light. Not only this amount—many others like it had not been paid. Worse—Umapati had borrowed large sums in Bhupati's name from various dealers. He was building a double-storeyed house in his ancestral village and most of the bills had been made out in Bhupati's name. When confronted, Umapati was loud and brazen in his defense. "I haven't run off with your money, have I?" he exclaimed. "I'll stay here and pay it all back with interest. If I keep even a paisa of yours I forfeit the name of Umapati."

Needless to say, Umapati's promise of forfeiting his name was no help to his brother-in-law. It wasn't the financial loss that distressed Bhupati so much. It was the loss of faith. He felt as though the ground had been pulled away under his feet and he was left dangling in the air. He needed something to hold on to. And so, like a homing bird, he had flown straight to Charu. For here, surely, was a heart that beat for him alone. A citadel of faith in which his place was totally without question. He had found Charu sitting by the window in a dark, unlit room wrapped in her own unhappiness.

Umapati, for all his brave words, was ready to leave for My-
mensingh the very next day. It was a matter of expediency. He wanted to
see the last of Kolkata before more of his misdeeds came to light. Shocked
and repulsed by his attitude Bhupati didn't exchange a word with him
before he left. Umapati took it as a blessing.

"Manda Bouthan!" Amal came into Manda's room to find her
busy with boxes and bundles. "What is all this?"

"We're leaving, Amal." Manda said sadly, "We didn't come here to
stay forever."

"But where are you going?"

"Back to the village."

"Why? Is there a problem?"

"There's no problem from my side. I was very happy here with all
of you. But others have difficulties—" She glanced towards Charu's door.
Not knowing how to react Amal fell silent. "Chhi! Chhi!" Manda clicked
her tongue. "I've never been more ashamed in my life. What Bhupati
Babu must be thinking of me!" Amal did not ask any more questions. He
knew what had happened. Charu had said something to Bhupati. Some-
thing so terrible about himself and Manda that Manda couldn't even
pronounce the words.

His breast heaving with indignation he walked about in the streets
for hours. "If Dada believes what Bouthan has told him I must leave the
house too," he thought. "They haven't asked me to, as yet, but driving
Manda out is, perhaps, the first step. My duty lies clearly before me. I
must start fending for myself. But I can't leave under a cloud of suspicion
and doubt. Dada has kept me with him for so many years. He has loved
me and trusted me. I can't allow him to think unworthy thoughts of me.
I shall speak with him. I shall convince him that I have done nothing
wrong; nothing that could shame him or anyone else."

Bhupati, swindled by his own brother-in-law, harassed by credi-
tors, struggling with falsified accounts and vastly depleted funds was all
alone in his misery. There was no one to whom he could turn. At such a
time Amal stormed into his cousin's presence. Bhupati looked up startled
"Why Amal!" his voice was fearful; as though he thought Amal had

brought worse tidings than those that were oppressing him already. "Is anything the matter?"

"Dada," Amal asked gravely. "Do you have any suspicions about me?"

"Suspicions about you?" Bhupati echoed in a dazed voice. Inwardly he thought, *The way things are going—it might well be true. I'll be suspecting Amal of breach of trust, next.* "Has Bouthan accused me of any misbehavior?" Amal went on agitatedly. "Has she cast aspersions on my character?"

So that was it. Bhupati sighed in relief. A silly misunderstanding. Bhupati, pressured by his own troubles, was in no mood to sort out the quarrels of two foolish children. But the world is hard and demanding. The bridge may be rocking dangerously but one is constrained to cross it. Only a few days ago Amal's agitation would have afforded Bhupati considerable amusement. But not today.

"Are you out of your mind?" he asked quietly.

"Has Bouthan said anything about me?"

"She loves you and is concerned about you. If she has said anything it is for your own good."

"It's time I started looking for a job. I shall be leaving this house shortly."

"Don't talk like a child Amal," Bhupati's voice was stern. "You're a student. Pay attention to your studies. We can think of jobs later."

Amal left the room, his face pale and preoccupied. Bhupati sighed and went back to his work of tallying this year's bills and receipts with those of the last three years.

10

Amal decided to confront Charu and wrest the truth out of her with forceful arguments. And, with that end in view, he began rehearsing all the strong arguments he would make; all the harsh words he would use. Charu, on the other hand, was waiting for Manda's departure after which she would send for Amal and soothe his anger with her many winsome ways. But she had to have a pretext. Charu knew that Amal didn't care for her independent style of writing. He was happiest when she was emulating him. So she sat down and wrote a composition entitled "The light of the new moon" in which she berated the full moon heartily for shamelessly shedding her beams. *The abysmal, unfathomable dark of a new moon night,* she wrote, *keeps hidden within it every one of its sixteen lunar digits. Not a trace is lost. In consequence, the black shroud of a moonless night is vastly superior to the radiance . . .* etc. etc. Amal's talent was like the radiance of a full moon night. Visible to all. Charu's light she preferred to keep hidden. Was Charu's comparison conveying a hint of this?

While all this was going on Bhupati, reeling from the blow of Umapati's treachery and his own impending insolvency, went to his friend Motilal to ask for repayment of a loan of several thousand rupees which the latter had taken some years ago. Motilal had just had a bath and was sitting, bare-torsoed, under the punkah writing Goddess Durga's name a thousand times on a sheet of paper propped on a wooden platform. He looked up on Bhupati's entrance and welcomed him warmly. "Ah! Come, come," he smiled. "One hardly gets to see you these days." But the moment Bhupati mentioned the loan his brows came together in deep thought. "What loan are you talking about?" he asked in a perplexed voice, "Have I taken anything from you recently?" When Bhupati told him the date he shrugged the matter off unceremoniously. "Oh! That!" he exclaimed, "That has lapsed long ago."

The world grew dark before Bhupati's eyes. His limbs grew numb with fear. The mask had fallen from a part of the world he thought he knew well and the reality staggered him. Just as a man, swept off his feet by a mighty tidal wave, seeks the highest spot in his view for refuge, so Bhupati rushed to the women's wing. "Let the worst happen," he said to himself over and over again. "I have Charu by my side. She will never, never deceive me."

He found Charu sitting on the bed with a pillow on her lap on which her notebook rested. She was bent over it writing furiously. So absorbed was she in her task that she didn't hear her husband enter. Only when he came and stood be her side did she look up with a start. Then, with a swift movement, she slipped the book under her thigh. Bhupati had suffered intense anguish for a number of days and his spirit had become weak and vulnerable. Charu's act of hiding her book from him hurt him unbearably. Why was Charu being so secretive with him? Where was the need? He sat beside her on the bed but Charu, flurried by his entrance, had nothing to say to him.

Bhupati had come to her that day with empty hands. Not to give but to receive. A few words of love, an anxious enquiry, would have soothed his tormented soul. But Charu had lost the key to her trove of love and tenderness. She sat still, her face flushed, and the silence of the room became unbearable in the cloud of their combined silence.

After a few minutes Bhupati sighed and, rising from the bed, walked slowly away. At the door he collided with Amal. "What's wrong Dada?" Amal took in Bhupati's pale face and trembling lips at a glance and asked anxiously, "Are you unwell?" Bhupati's heart swelled at Amal's concern and rose to his eyes in a rush of stinging tears. Curbing them with difficulty he gave a pained smile. "No Amal. I'm quite well. How's your writing coming along? Anything new in the papers?"

Amal forgot all the harsh words he had planned to say to Charu. Entering her room he exclaimed, "What has happened to Dada?"

"I . . . d . . . don't know," Charu replied in a faltering voice. "I didn't notice . . . Someone may have criticized his paper."

"Un hunh," Amal shook his head. The fact that Amal had come to her on his own, and was conversing with her in his everyday voice soothed and comforted Charu. She decided to come to the point without wasting time. "I've written a composition," she said shyly. "It's called 'The light of the new moon.' Your Dada very nearly saw it." She had expected Amal to be pleased; to insist on reading it at once. She even flipped the pages of her notebook once or twice. But Amal said nothing. His eyes looked into hers with an intense, penetrating glance. What he saw in them; what he understood wasn't clear—even to him. Like a traveler walking a mountainous path, on a sudden lifting of the fog, sees himself within a few inches of a vast abyss so Amal, hit by something he couldn't put into words, rose to his feet with a jerk and rushed out of the room. Charu stared after him. She didn't know what to make of his strange behavior.

II

The next day Bhupati came to his wife's room, again, at an unusual hour. "Charu," he said, "A proposal of marriage has come for Amal." Charu seemed lost in her own thoughts. "A proposal of what?" she muttered absentmindedly.

"Of marriage."

"Why? Am I not good enough?"

"I haven't asked Amal that." Bhupati burst out laughing. "But even if he says you are I'm not going to give you up that easily. After all I have the prior claim."

"What nonsense you talk!" Charu exclaimed, her face red with embarrassment. "Didn't you say a proposal of marriage had come for you?"

"If that was the case would I come running to give you the news? I couldn't have expected a tip from you—surely."

"A proposal has come for Amal. That's good news. What are you waiting for?"

"Raghunath Babu, a wealthy lawyer of Bardhaman, wishes to marry his daughter to Amal and send him to England for higher studies."

"To England!"

"Yes."

"Amal is to go to England? What fun! Have you told him about it?"

"Isn't it better that you do so?"

"I've begged and begged him to marry. I've asked him at least three thousand times. But he doesn't listen to me. I don't want to ask him again."

"You think he'll refuse?"

"He has refused all the offers that have come so far. We've tried so many times—"

"But this is an extraordinarily good proposal. He shouldn't reject it. I've lost a lot of money and am deeply in debt. I can't pay for Amal's needs the way I could earlier."

Sending for Amal, Bhupati told him about the offer, adding,

"Raghunath Babu wishes to send you to England for further studies. What do you say?"

"If you have no objection," Amal answered promptly, "I have none either."

Charu and Bhupati exchanged surprised glances. They hadn't expected him to agree so readily. *"If you have no objection!"* Charu echoed mockingly, "Where was your brotherly reverence all these years Thakurpo?" Amal tried to smile. He had no answer to her question. "What an obedient brother!" Charu continued. There was a sharp edge to her voice. "Why can't you admit the truth? That you're dying to get married! Why all this hypocrisy?"

"He was afraid of hurting your feelings," Bhupati teased Charu. "He thought you might be jealous of your sister-in-law."

"Jealous!" Charu's cheeks flamed. "Me? I'm not jealous of anyone. It's very wrong of you to make such allegations!" Charu nearly burst into tears.

"Arre! Arre! I was only joking. Can't I pull my wife's leg just a little?"

"No. I don't like such jokes."

"Well, well," Bhupati hastened to soothe Charu. "I've made a mistake. Pray forgive me." Then, turning to Amal, he said. "Do I take it then that the matter is settled?"

"Yes." Pat came Amal's reply.

"Don't you even want to see the girl?" Charu cried. "To find out if she's pretty or ugly? Who ever thought you were in such a state! You didn't let out a hint—"

"If you wish to see the girl," Bhupati told Amal, "I can arrange a viewing. But I've made enquiries. The girl is beautiful."

"There's no need to arrange a viewing." Amal said quietly.

"Don't listen to him." Charu cried out to her husband. "How can we have a wedding without a viewing of the bride? We'll go and see her even if he doesn't."

"No Dada," Amal said firmly. "There's no need to delay the matter."

"No need indeed." Charu said sarcastically. "You'd better don the bridegroom's crown and set off at once." Then, turning to her husband, she cried, "Your brother is afraid to waste another moment. He thinks someone will snatch his priceless treasure of seven kingdoms right from under his nose."

But Charu's taunts fell on deaf ears. Amal stood steadfast in his resolve.

"He's dying, simply dying to run off to England," Charu tried again, "To wear a hat and coat and become a saheb. Really, the young men of today! Will you recognize us after your return Thakurpo? Or will you turn your eyes away from black natives like us?"

"Why else do you think I'm going to England?"

"He's crossing the seven seas to avoid us blacks!" Bhupati laughed. "Don't worry Charu. We'll stay right here and show Amal that black natives have no dearth of admirers."

Delighted with the success of his mission Bhupati sent a letter to Bardhaman that very night fixing the date of the wedding.

12

In the situation that Bhupati had found himself he had no option but to wind up the newspaper. To build the edifice had taken him twelve years of hard labor. To demolish it took only a few hours. His life was suddenly at a standstill. It stretched out before him like a great sheet of stagnant water. A totally unprepared Bhupati didn't know how to deal with the change. What would he do with his unbounded energy and limitless zeal? In what course could he channel them? Like starving, bereft orphans they looked up to him for direction. Where could he take them but to his own private sanctuary? Where a woman, her heart brimming over with love and truth, waited for his coming?

The same woman was, at that time, rapt in thoughts that had nothing to do with her husband. "That Amal is to be wed is good news," she said to herself, "But how strange that he has no qualms about leaving us and going off to England! We've loved him and nurtured him all these years but it seems as though he was only biding his time. Waiting for an opportunity. The instant it came he was ready to slip away. Not a tinge of regret. Not a moment's hesitation. So sweet-tongued yet so self-centered!

Really, how little one knows of another! Whoever thought that Amal, who wrote so well, didn't have a heart?" Comparing her own heart with Amal's non-existing one, Charu tried hard to drive him away from her thoughts. But she couldn't. Sharp spasms of pain rose from deep within her and wouldn't let her rest. "Amal will go away any day now," she thought bitterly, "yet he stays away from me. He hasn't even bothered to clear the misunderstanding between us."

Over the next few days Charu waited patiently for Amal to come and assure her that the parting was transitory. That the bond between them was as strong as ever. But Amal did not come.

The day before his departure Charu sent for him. "I'll come in a while," Amal sent back a message. Charu came and sat on the old sofa in the southern veranda, prepared to wait. It was a hot, close morning and the sky was packed with clouds. Lifting the dense mass of her hair she wound it into a knot on top of her head. Then, picking up a palm leaf fan she waved it gently over her sweating limbs. Time passed. Her hand grew heavy and listless. The fan moved slower and slower even as her heart filled with sorrow and anger. "He won't come," she thought resentfully, "But why should I care? Let him suit himself." Yet she waited, all her senses alert, for the sound of footsteps.

The ringing of church bells in the distance brought her back to her duties. It was eleven o'clock. Bhupati must have had his bath by now and would come in for his meal in half an hour. It was time for her to go into the kitchen and supervise the serving. But still she sat and waited for Amal to come. "If I see him for even a few minutes we'll make up our quarrel," she murmured to herself. "I can't bear this war of silence anymore. He can't go away from me like this." The companionship that brother-in-law and sister-in-law had shared all these years, the time they had spent together talking, laughing, reading each other's compositions, fighting and making up, swam before Charu's eyes. It was like a shadowy, secluded garden which was exclusively theirs, in which no one else had the right of entry. Was it to wither, overnight, and turn into a stretch of desert sand? Could it not be saved? Would she never get a chance to sprinkle upon it a few drops of life saving water? Her tears?

Half an hour passed. Charu released her hair from its knot and started twisting the strands around her fingers with sharp agitated motions. Tears stung her eyes and threatened to roll down her cheeks. "Ma Thakrun!" Lost in her thoughts she didn't see the servant standing before her. "It's time to give Babu his green coconut water. Will you—" Charu untied the bunch of keys from the end of her sari and flung it at his feet. The servant picked it up with a puzzled expression. They were the keys to the store room where all the household groceries were kept. A hard knot formed in Charu's throat and her eyes glittered with unshed tears.

588

A little later a smiling Bhupati came in for his mid-day meal. Amal came with him. But Charu didn't favor him with even a glance. She kept her eyes on Bhupati's thala and waved her palm leaf fan to ward off the flies.

"You sent for me Bouthan," Amal said. "What is it?"

"Nothing. It doesn't matter anymore."

"Then I'd better go and finish my packing. There's a lot left to be done."

Now Charu lifted her eyes and flashed them at Amal. "Go," she said imperiously. Amal stared at her for a few seconds then, lowering his head, walked slowly away.

It was Bhupati's custom to retire to his bedroom, after the mid-day meal, and spend some time with Charu. That afternoon, deluged with piles of bills and vouchers, he said ruefully, "I can't sit with you for long, Charu. I have a lot to sort out."

"Why don't you go then?"

Bhupati thought that Charu's reaction proceeded from resentment at his inability to spend time with her. "That doesn't mean I'm going this instant," he said peaceably. "I'll rest for a while." He glanced at his wife's face and saw that it was morose and melancholy. *Poor Charu*, he thought tenderly, his heart full of concern. He sat for a long time, chatting of this and that, trying to cheer her up. But nothing he could say seemed to make any difference. "Amal is to leave tomorrow," he said at last. "You'll miss him a lot—the first few days." There was no reply. Then, as if she had just remembered something, Charu got up and went to the next room. Bhupati waited a long time for her to come back. Then, rising to his feet, he went about his business.

In the brief moment that Charu had looked into Amal's face she noticed that it had gone pale and thin and the youthful vivacity that had marked it had disappeared. The fact gladdened and saddened her heart at the same time. She realized that he, too, was suffering the pain of imminent parting. But, if that was so, why was he behaving so strangely? Why was he avoiding her and filling their last moments together with bitterness and discord? Suddenly an idea struck her and she sat up on the bed with the impact. Was Amal in love with Manda? Was it because Manda had gone away—? No, no—that couldn't be true. Amal would never stoop so low. Coveting a married woman! Could his character be so flawed? His heart so impure? She tried to drive the thought away but it kept coming back to torture her.

The moment of Amal's departure came but the cloud of suspicion and doubt was not blown away. "I'm going Bouthan," Amal said in a trembling voice. "Look after Dada. He is beset with many troubles. Only you can soothe and comfort him."

Amal's eyes, unlike Charu's, had clearly seen Bhupati's wan and preoccupied looks. He had made enquiries and found out the truth. He knew that Bhupati was fighting against immense odds and he was fighting alone. He had sought no help, no comfort from the members of his family. He hadn't allowed a breath of his troubles to touch them. Amal thought of himself. He thought of Charu and his ears flamed with pain and shame. "To hell with Asadh moons and moonless nights," he muttered to himself, "I'll succeed as a barrister and help Dada pay up his debts. If I can't do that I'm no man."

Charu had stayed awake the whole of last night thinking about the moment of farewell. What should she say to Amal? What was her demeanor to be? Cheerful indifference or tender empathy? She had rehearsed painstakingly; structuring and restructuring the sentences; honing the words. But when the time came they spread their wings and flew away. "Will you write to us Amal?" was all that she could say. Amal prostrated himself on the floor, in answer, and touched his head to her feet. Recoiling from him Charu ran to her bedroom and shut the door.

13

Bhupati accompanied Amal to Bardhaman and, after the rites of marriage were concluded, set him off on his journey to England. But he returned to Kolkata a changed man. An intense apathy for the outside world took hold of him. He stopped meeting friends and acquaintances; gave up his clubs and parties. "I've wasted the best years of my life in this tomfoolery," he thought regretfully. "I've turned my face away from true peace and happiness. The burden of the newspaper is off my back at last. Good riddance! I'm a free man now." Just as the bird, at the first sign of dusk, turns wing and flies towards its nest so Bhupati turned to Charu. "This is where I belong and where I'll stay," he said to himself. "The paper boat with which I played all day has sunk. It's time for me to go home."

It is possible that Bhupati, like all other men, had been conditioned into a belief that one didn't need to earn a wife's love and devotion. It was there for the taking. A wife was like the northern star, constant and steadfast, illumined in her own light. A light that needed no fuel; that wouldn't be blown away by a gust of stormy wind. Even when his outer world collapsed before him it didn't occur to Bhupati to check if his inner world stood firm. If even one of the columns on which the edifice rested had developed a crack . . .

It was late evening by the time Bhupati returned from Bardhaman. Washing his hands and feet he had an early meal and, retiring to his bedroom, prepared to regale Charu with news of the wedding and Amal's departure. Charu, he knew, was waiting eagerly to hear his account. She wouldn't allow him to skip any part of it. She would insist on details. And he would indulge her. In that frame of mind he stretched himself out on the bed, puffed at his albola and waited for her coming. Hours passed. The tobacco in the albola burned to ashes. His eyes grew heavy with sleep and his head nodded on his breast. But Charu did not come.

Waking up with a jerk Bhupati wondered what was keeping Charu. Unable to bear the suspense he sent for her and, on her appearing before him, asked anxiously, "Is anything the matter, Charu? You're so late—"

"Yes," Charu addressed herself to the latter part of his question and answered coolly, "I got delayed." Bhupati had anticipated a flood of eager questions but, not one forthcoming, he felt perplexed and somewhat disturbed. Did it mean that Charu didn't really care for Amal? Had she just been whiling away her leisure hours in his company? And the moment he left she was ready to forget him? Was Charu's spirit shallow and inconstant? Incapable of deep and strong attachments? The possibility saddened and bewildered him. A woman who is incapable of love, he thought, was not a true woman.

Bhupati had always looked on Charu and Amal as a fond elder looks on a pair of lovable children. Their games and secrets, squabbles and agreements amused and entertained him. He had also noticed Charu's pampering of Amal and that pleased him. Was all that a pretence? Or was it light and fluffy like an autumn cloud liable to be blown away by a gust of unruly wind? Was Charu without a heart? His own turned to ice as he thought, "If Charu has no heart where can *I* find shelter?"

"How were you Charu?" Bhupati began tentatively. "Were you well?"

"Yes. Quite well."

"Amal's wedding went off very smoothly." Bhupati paused a few seconds giving Charu a chance to speak. Charu tried hard to respond; to say something fitting to the subject, but couldn't. She sat stiff and still in tongue-tied silence.

Bhupati was not an observant man as a rule but the pain of Amal's departure opened his eyes to Charu's lack of it. Her indifference struck a hard blow at his heart. He had wanted, had looked forward, to pouring out his grief before Charu and sharing hers. Then, with unburdened hearts, they could comfort and console each other.

"The girl is very pretty," Bhupati tried again. "Are you asleep Charu?"

"No."

"Poor Amal! He had to leave all by himself. When I put him on the train he burst into tears. And I, old fool that I am, started crying too. There were a couple of Englishmen on the train. Their lips curled in amusement at the sight of two grown men weeping so unashamedly."

The lamp had been extinguished and the room was dark. Charu sat up with a quick movement and rushed out of the door. "Do you feel unwell Charu?" A startled Bhupati called out anxiously. There was no reply but he could hear the sound of muffled sobs. Bhupati came to the veranda and found his wife lying on the floor the end of her sari stuffed into her mouth, her body shaking uncontrollably.

The sight of this overwhelming grief confused Bhupati. Had he misunderstood her? Was her nature so restrained; so reticent that she couldn't share her sorrow even with her own husband? People like her had profound and powerful feelings and their suffering was intense. Charu did not express her devotion the way other wives did. She kept it deeply embedded in her soul where it swelled in silence, in secret, in an ever-widening pool. It was the same with Bhupati. The thought brought a glow to Bhupati's heart and he was at peace once more.

Dropping down to the floor by Charu's side, Bhupati ran his fingers over her head and limbs. Her anguish was so overwhelming that he had no words with which to alleviate even a part of it. Bhupati, with his deficient understanding of women, did not realize that, at that moment, Charu wished to be left alone. When a woman is struggling against her feelings so hard that she is constrained to choke and smother them with all her might, she would prefer to do so unobserved.

14

Around the time that Bhupati gave up the newspaper he had taken a vow not to be drawn again into any business that might rob him of the simple joys of life and the companionship of his wife. He had formed certain ideas of how to pass his days. They would be quiet and leisurely, the hours rolling by, slow and graceful, in a steady rhythm. He would read books with Charu and discuss their finer points with her. He would laugh and play games; tease and pamper her. He would become her friend and share her concerns about the trivial matters of the household. *These were the true joys of life,* he thought, *the true compensations.*

But, getting down to the task, he found that these simple joys were hard to come by. They couldn't be bought with money. They had to come on their own. And, if they didn't, there was no place on the earth in which one could find them. Bhupati despite all his efforts, found himself orbiting around Charu's world. He could not enter it. And true to his nature, he blamed himself for this. "I've spent twelve years collecting trash and printing it," he thought. "I've lost the ability to entertain my wife."

Each day at dusk, after the lamps were lit, Bhupati hastened to his bedroom looking forward to a pleasant evening with Charu. But, invariably, his hopes were dashed. He would make a few observations. Charu would reply briefly. After that—silence. Bhupati would rack his brains for something interesting to say but could think of nothing. This inability confused him; filled him with guilt. He felt diminished somehow. "Who would have thought chatting with one's wife was such a difficult task?" he muttered to himself. "Making a speech from a public podium is easier."

Bhupati's evenings with Charu became fraught with problems. He struggled to strike up a conversation but, failing, didn't know what to do next. Should he get up and leave? But what would Charu think? The hours went by in a strained silence. "Would you like to play cards Charu?" Bhupati would fall back on his last resort. The choice for Charu being limited, cards or silence, she would settle for the lesser of the two evils. Fetching the pack she would play the game, but so negligently, with such a marked lack of interest, that she lost in a few minutes. Where was the pleasure in such a game? Bhupati thought and thought then, one evening, he said to her. "Shall we send for Manda? You're left alone for hours—"

"Never!" Charu's eyes blazed with anger. "I don't want her in this house."

Bhupati smiled and was pleased. A true sati, he thought, never compromises on a moral issue—however slight. But after her initial sharp reaction, Charu reconsidered the suggestion. It might not be such a bad idea, she thought, to bring Manda back. It would be good for Bhupati. He needed company; someone he could open his heart to. He had given up all his other interests and was reaching out to Charu. But she, his wife, was unable to respond. The fact saddened her and she was filled with fear. How long could such a situation go on? Why, oh! why didn't Bhupati find something else to occupy him? Why didn't he start another newspaper? She had never been called upon to entertain her husband; she

593

hadn't a notion of how to do it. Bhupati had never made any demands on her; never expected any service of her. In consequence Charu hadn't learned the art of making herself indispensable to him. Now, out of the blue, he was looking to her for all his needs. And she, who didn't quite understand them or, even if she did, found no way of fulfilling them— had nothing to give him. If Bhupati's dependence on her had come slowly; by degrees, it might have been easier for Charu. But Bhupati had been robbed of all he had in a single night and had come to her with an empty bowl in his hands. The situation flustered Charu. She couldn't cope with it.

"Alright," she said. "Send for Manda. She can look after you."

"Look after me!" Bhupati laughed. "There's no need for that." Inwardly he thought. "I'm such a dullard. I'm incapable of making my wife happy."

The thought pushed him in a new direction. He embarked on a bull-headed chase of literature. His friends, on visiting him, were amazed to find him reading the works of Byron and Tennyson and the novels of Bankimchandra. Teased about this strange development Bhupati was quick to retort, "The bamboo clump flowers too, brother! Only, one is never sure when."

One evening Bhupati, sitting by the brightest lamp in the room with a book in his hands, asked shyly, "Shall I read to you Charu?"

"Why not?"

"What shall I read?"

"Whatever you like."

Bhupati, though somewhat quelled by Charu's lack of enthusiasm, picked up courage and asked, "Shall I translate some verses from Tennyson?"

"Yes. Do."

It was a dismal failure. Bhupati's inherent reticence and irresolution, grown double-fold under Charu's clearly visible apathy, made him stutter and stumble over the lines. The right words and phrases eluded him. It was obvious from Charu's far-away gaze that she wasn't even listening. Bhupati tried a couple of times more then gave up the attempt.

15

When one receives a rude shock the nerves get deadened and pain is felt but slightly. It was so with Charu. As time went on the agony of Amal's loss grew in intensity. Her world became dark and empty. Frightened by this she didn't know where to turn. What was happening to her? She had been thrown from a flowery bower into an arid desert whose margins were increasing every moment. She hadn't even known that such a desert existed.

She woke, each dawn, her heart thumping out the message that Amal had gone away. Every morning, sitting on the veranda making up paan cones, she found herself waiting for his footsteps. Absentmindedly, she prepared large quantities till she remembered that most of it would go uneaten. Going to the storeroom, in the late afternoons, she realized, with a start, that Amal would not come back from college clamoring for food. There was no need to watch out for a new book; write a new composition; garner interesting news. There was nobody to wait for; embroider for. No one for whom to buy pretty things.

The extent of her agitation and misery shocked and frightened Charu. "Why is this happening to me?" she kept asking herself. "Why do I feel such unbearable anguish? What is Amal to me that I must suffer so? What is to become of me, oh God! After all these years what is to become of me?"

The unprecedented vehemence of her own feelings filled her with wonder and she kept plying herself with questions. But her agony would not ease even a minuscule. Thoughts of Amal obsessed and tortured her day and night. She wanted to flee from them. But where was she to go? Her husband was no help to her. Instead of protecting her from the assaults of Amal's memory, he tried to place the burden of his own pain at the parting from a beloved brother on his wife's frail shoulders. The gentle, self-effacing, suffering fool was constantly reminding her of Amal.

Worn out by the battle raging within her Charu surrendered. Admitting defeat she faced and accepted the truth. She couldn't fight Amal's memory anymore. She wouldn't. On the contrary she would keep it enshrined in her heart. She started spending hours thinking of Amal and, gradually, these thoughts became her fondest, her most prized possessions. She culled some time from her day-to-day activities and set it apart for her secret occupation. Shutting herself in her bedroom she let her mind wander at will reliving all her moments with Amal. "Amal, Amal, Amal," she whispered, laying her cheek against the cool satin of her pillow. And her ears caught the faint sounds coming in answer to her call, across the vast expanse of seven seas . . . "Bouthan! What is it, Bouthan?" Wiping her wet cheeks Charu closed her eyes and murmured softly, "Why did you leave me Amal? What had I done? And, even if you had to leave, why did you do it in anger? Had we parted as friends I could have borne it better. I try to forget you but I can't. Not a single moment passes but you are in my thoughts. I was a lump of clay before you came. You were the one who fanned my soul into life. You'll be the object of my worship for all time to come."

Thus Charu dredged through the deepest layers of her being and created a space for herself. Hiding it beneath her numerous duties and obligations, she installed in it a shrine of sorrow hung with garlands of tears. This shrine, deep, secret and beloved—was hers alone. No one, least of all her husband, was allowed to enter it. Here her heart found sanctuary. Here she came, everyday, discarding the mask of her outer self and, offering her worship, went back again.

16

Having resolved the conflict that was tearing her apart Charu was enabled, at last, to turn her attention on her husband. Making up for her negligence of the past she lavished upon him all the care and devotion she was capable of. His needs and desires came first in everything she did. Charu slaved from dawn till dusk in his service. Aware of his concern for the well-being of the numerous relatives who lived with them, she spent hours working for their comfort. Each morning, on waking, she touched her head to her sleeping husband's feet. And, at the end of the day, her chores done, she ate the leavings from his thala and felt her soul being flooded with peace.

A broken Bhupati grew whole again. His youth returned—rejuvenated by Charu's tender care. He felt as if he was tasting the joys of the marital state for the first time. As if he hadn't been married for years and years. Just as a man recovering from a long illness feels his appetite return with gusto, so Bhupati, thrusting his worries aside, reached out for his pleasures with both hands. He started enjoying his food; took pains with his appearance and spent long hours reading poetry. "The loss of the paper and the suffering it brought has done this for me," he thought humbly, "I'm discovering my wife for the first time."

"Charu," Bhupati asked her one day. "Why have you given up your writing?"

"I was hardly a writer," Charu replied dismissively.

"To tell you the truth," Bhupati said, "I think your Bangla is far superior to that of the writers of today. I agree with the critic of *Bishwabandhu*—"

"Stop it," Charu cried, her face flaming.

"Look at this," Bhupati opened an issue of *Suroruho* and started reading out a comparison of Charu's work with that of Amal's. Charu snatched the journal from his hands and covered it with her sari. "One needs a companion," Bhupati thought, "in order to keep up one's interest in writing. Just you wait Charu. I'll need to hone my skills a bit more—then we'll write together."

After this Bhupati started writing in real earnest. He labored secretly but diligently, consulting books and dictionaries, writing and rewriting; making fair copies; and the hours flew by on wings. The throes of creation were so painful that he couldn't find it in his heart to abandon any of it. Every word he wrote was like the child he had never begotten and his heart was filled with compassion for it.

Finally the day came when he sent for Charu and put his notebook in her hands. "A friend of mine has just turned writer," he said shyly. "He has sent me some of his work and asked for my opinion. But, as you know, I don't understand much of all this. Do go through it and tell me what you think." Before giving Charu the notebook Bhupati had taken the precaution of having the work copied in another hand. But Charu was not fooled by the subterfuge.

Charu read Bhupati's compositions. Noting the style and choice of subjects her lips curled in disdain. "Hai! Hai!" she thought. "This husband I'm straining every nerve to honor and obey is such a child! Such a foolish dim-witted child! It would have been so much better if, instead of craving for my attention, he had ignored and slighted me. I could have respected him then." Snapping the notebook shut she leaned against the pillow and started thinking of Amal.

That evening Bhupati tiptoed into Charu's room and, going straight to the veranda, proceeded to examine the plants as though they were the sole reason for his presence there. He longed to ask Charu if she had read what he had given her but couldn't get up the courage.

"Is this your friend's first attempt at writing?" Charu decided to help him out.

"Yes."

"It's excellent! Very mature."

Charu's reaction thrilled Bhupati. And now he started thinking of ways and means of erasing the friend's name from the notebook and affixing his own. After this it only a matter of time. Bhupati's literary legs started running at an alarming pace and, needless to say, the writer's identity did not remain hidden any longer.

17

Charu used to keep a sharp lookout for letters from Amal. The first one came from Aden. It was addressed to Bhupati and contained pranams for Charu. The second came from Suez. Again Charu was honored with pranams. The third came from Malta. This time the pranams were an afterthought. They came in the form of a postscript. Charu didn't receive a single letter of her own. She took the ones Amal wrote to Bhupati and scanned them eagerly. There was no mention of her. Not a single word. Only pranams.

The peace that Charu had wrested for herself in the interim was torn to shreds by Amal's deliberate neglect. The old symptoms returned. Her heart, as if under the impact of a massive earthquake, pounded violently. Her working routine got muddled and she could not sleep for nights at a stretch. Bhupati found her several times sitting by the window, at dead of night, staring at the sky. "The room was so warm—I couldn't sleep," Charu explained, "That's why I'm sitting here." A worried Bhupati arranged for a punkah to be fixed in the bedroom. And, fearing for her health, he took to hovering around her. "There's nothing wrong with me," Charu smiled at him, "Why do you worry so much?"

Now Charu made some mental adjustments. The journey to England was long and arduous, she decided. Naturally Amal was finding it difficult to write to her. Once he reached England he would write a long letter full of news. Amal reached England but no letter came for Charu.

Mail days came and went. She woke up each morning, in a fever of excitement, her heart thumping with hope. She longed to ask Bhupati if a letter had come for her but didn't. She dreaded the reply. One mail day Bhupati came to her and said. "I have something for you. Would you care to take a look?"

"Of course!" Charu rose agitatedly to her feet. "Give it."

"Patience, patience." A slow smile creased Bhupati's face. "All in good time."

But Charu couldn't wait. Flinging herself on her husband she groped under his shawl and tried to wrest her much awaited, long anticipated, treasure from him. *I knew it would come today,* she thought, *I've been getting the vibes since morning.* Bhupati decided to tease Charu some more. Wriggling out of her grasp he ran around the room—Charu in hot but fruitless pursuit. Finally, when a defeated Charu sank down on the bed with tears in her eyes, Bhupati took out his notebook from under his shawl and threw it in her lap. "Don't be angry with me," he said smiling. "Here. Take it."

18

Although Amal had warned Bhupati that he would be too busy with his studies to write often, Charu felt she was sleeping on a bed of thorns if a single mail day went without a letter from him. She took care, however, to conceal her uneasiness from the rest of the household. "O go!" she said to her husband one evening, "Why don't you send a telegram and find out how Amal is?" She said this carelessly. As though it was just a passing thought; as though it didn't matter to her much—one way or another.

"Why?" Bhupati was surprised. "Amal wrote only two weeks ago. He was perfectly well. He's working hard at his studies. That's why—"

"Leave it then," Charu replied. "I just thought . . . you know . . . he's in a foreign country . . . if he's ill or something. One never can tell."

"Don't worry. We would have had news if he was sick or in trouble. Besides sending a telegram is an expensive business."

"How expensive? A rupee or two at the most?"

"What are you saying?" Bhupati laughed. "A telegram to England will cost at least a hundred rupees."

"Ore baba! Then, of course, there is no question of it."

A couple of days later Charu said to her husband. "Will you do something for me? Will you go to Chinsura, today, and find out how my sister is?"

"Why? Has she been ill?"

"No, of course not. But you know how happy she is to see you always."

Bhupati, always ready to oblige Charu, set off for Howrah Station. But a row of bullock carts came in the way and stopped his carriage from moving. While he was waiting for the road to clear the postman poked his head at the window and handed him a telegram. It was from England. Bhupati's face turned pale. "Amal is ill," he thought, his heart beating painfully. Opening it with shaking fingers he read the message. *I am well.* That was all. Turning the telegram over he saw that it was sent in response to a prepaid one from India. Abandoning the journey to Chinsura Bhupati came home and put the missive in Charu's hands. "What does this mean Charu?" he asked, "I don't understand—" Charu's lips went white. She had no answer.

In a few days the truth came to light. It was Charu who had sent the prepaid telegram. She had pawned some of her jewelry to obtain the money. But why? A puzzled Bhupati couldn't figure out the reason. If she was that worried all she had to do was to tell him. He would have sent the telegram himself. Pawning her jewelry! And doing it all so secretively! It didn't sound good. Un hunh . . . It didn't sound good at all. The more

Bhupati thought about it the less sense he could make of Charu's action. Gradually a faint cloud of suspicion started forming in his head. *Was all as it should be between him and Charu?* He tried hard to convince himself that it was. But the cloud grew heavier and more oppressive with the passing days—threatening to choke his life breath. He tried, desperately, to shrug it off but couldn't.

19

Charu couldn't evade the truth any longer. Amal was perfectly well. Yet he wasn't writing to her. She wanted to ask him why. She wanted to face him, fairly and squarely, and demand an answer. But a vast sea separated them. Physical as well as spiritual. There was no way in which she could bridge the divide.

Charu couldn't support herself any longer. Crumbling under the weight of her humiliation she lost her grip. She started neglecting her household tasks; she made mistakes. Her servants stole from right under her nose. Relatives sniggered and passed snide comments. But she heard nothing. Cared nothing. She passed her days as though in a trance. She would sit for hours by the window then, starting up, run to a secluded corner and burst into tears. And with any mention of Amal the blood drained away from her cheeks.

Eventually even Bhupati had to admit the truth. What he had thought impossible; what he hadn't expected in his wildest dreams had come to pass. The knowledge aged him in one go. His world turned dark and dreary. Robbed of meaning. Remembering the few days of bliss he had enjoyed he was overwhelmed with shame. How blind he had been!

How foolish! Like a grinning, gibbering monkey he had held a pebble in his hand and thought it the rarest of gems.

Thinking of the hours he had spent struggling with pen and paper to please Charu, he wished the earth would open up and swallow him. "Fool! Fool! Fool!" he lashed himself with abuse. Then, driven by a passion he hadn't known existed, he stormed into Charu's presence. "Where is the notebook I gave you?" he demanded.

"It is with me." Charu replied.

"Give it."

Charu was sitting in the bedroom before a bucket of burning coal frying egg kochuries for Bhupati. "Do you want it now?" she asked timidly. "Yes. I want it now." Charu placed the smoking wok on the floor and went to the cupboard. Drawing the notebook from the shelf she held it out to her husband. Bhupati snatched it out of her hand and dropped it in the fire. "What have you done?" Charu cried and tried to retrieve it. But Bhupati held her hand in an iron grip. "Leave it," he roared. Charu stood like a figure of stone and watched her husband's labor of love burn to ashes. Then, abandoning her kochuries, she walked slowly out of the room.

Bhupati hadn't meant to burn the notebook in Charu's presence. But his blood was boiling and the fire was right there. He couldn't resist the temptation. She he had loved so tenderly had taken advantage of his innocence and deceived him. Let the beguiler watch the destruction she had wrought with her own eyes.

Every word Bhupati had written burned to ashes. And, with the death of all his hopes, the passions that had flared up within him died too. He watched Charu leave the room, her face white and expressionless—her head bowed under a weight of guilt. Suddenly he remembered that Charu had sat before a hot fire all afternoon cooking his favorite snack . . .

Bhupati came out of the room and leaned against the railings of the veranda. "All the efforts Charu makes to please me," he thought, "is part of a gigantic web of deceit. Can anything in the world be more cruel? Yet, I can't look on it as base and contemptible. She's suffering too—perhaps more than I am. The strain of hiding her agony is increasing it four-fold. Her heart is wrenching out drops of blood. Poor woman! Poor, pathetic, helpless woman! Why did she take so much trouble for me? I have lived without her love for so long—I didn't even know it wasn't there. I could have gone on as I've done all these years, collecting news and checking proofs. There was no need to suffer so much pain for my sake."

Distancing himself from Charu, the way a doctor distances himself before examining a serious patient, Bhupati started analyzing her.

"She's only a soft, weak-willed woman," he thought. "From where would she find the power to resist the pulls and temptations of a ruthless world? She has no one to turn to. No one to whom she can disclose her sufferings. No one before whom she can weep till her heart is drained of its sorrow. She goes about her household tasks carrying her burden of guilt and shame and pretends that nothing is wrong; that all is as it had been."

Bhupati went back to the bedroom. Charu was standing by the window. Her eyes were stark and dry. Her hands clutched the bars as though they were her only support. Bhupati came and stood by her. Without a word he placed a hand on her head.

20

"What news Bhupati?" his friends asked him. "What keeps you so busy?"

"The newspaper—"

"Another newspaper? Are you determined to sink your entire patrimony in the Ganga?"

"This isn't my own paper."

"Then—?"

"This one is published from Mysore. They've made me Chief Editor."

"You're moving to Mysore then? Are you taking Charu with you?"

"No. My uncle is bringing his family over. They'll look after her."

"The bug of editing hasn't left you—it seems."

"A man has to have some bug to keep him going."

As Bhupati was getting ready to depart Charu came to him. "When will you return?" she asked. Bhupati moved away from her. "If you get lonely," he said from the door, "just write a letter. I'll come—" Charu gazed at him, stony-eyed, for a few seconds. Then, rushing to him she clutched his hand. "Take me with you," she begged, "Don't leave me here alone." Bhupati turned and looked at her. There was something in his eyes that made her recoil from him. Her hand slackened and fell to her side. Bhupati knew why Charu wanted to go with him. There were too many memories of Amal in this house. They were burning in her brain; stalking her. Like a hunted doe she wanted to flee from them. "But where am *I* to go," Bhupati murmured to himself, "Has Charu thought of that? How can I go on living with a wife who has made another man the object of her worship? Her presence will bring back the most bitter memories—no matter how far I run. Exiled in a foreign land; lonely and friendless, I'll be constrained to forget my own sorrow and be a mute witness to hers. Days of back-breaking work. Long, solitary evenings spent in the company of a silent, broken-hearted woman. What a terrifying prospect! How long can I sustain and comfort a woman who bears a dead weight in her heart! Is that what life has ordained for me? Year after year of fumbling with the broken stones of my shattered sanctuary. Year after year of carrying the ruins on my back. Can I do it?"

"No," Bhupati said aloud. "I can't do it."

Charu's face turned the color of ashes. She sank on the bed and gripped the post till the knuckles of her hand stood out—white as paper. Bhupati saw it and changed his mind in a flash. "Come Charu," he said gently. "Come to Mysore with me."

"No," Charu shook her head. "There's no need."

1901–1902
("Nashta Neer," from *Galpaguchchha*)
Translated by Aruna Chakravarti

The Wife's Letter

My submission at your lotus feet—

We have been married for fifteen years, but to this day I have never written you a letter. I have always been at hand—you have heard so many words from my lips, and I too have listened to you—but there has never been an interval in which a letter might have been written.

Today I have come on pilgrimage to the seat of Lord Jagannath in Puri, while you remain tied to your work in office. Your bond with Calcutta is like that of a snail with its shell; the city has grown into your body and soul. That is why you did not apply for leave from the office. Such was the wish of the Almighty; he granted *my* application for leave.

I am the second daughter-in-law of your father's house. Today, after fifteen years, standing by the ocean's shore, I have learnt that I have a different relation as well with the world and the Lord of the world. That is why I have taken courage to write this letter; it is not a letter from the second daughter-in-law of your family.

In infancy—when no one but God, who had fated my relation with your family, knew of its possibility—my brother and I were struck down together by typhoid. My brother died; I survived. The women of the neighborhood began to say, "Mrinal lived because she's a girl; if she'd been a boy would she have been spared?" The god of death is skilled in the art of theft; he covets what is precious.

Death will not come for me. It is to explain this properly that I have sat down to write this letter.

When a distant uncle of yours came with your friend Nirad to our house to inspect the prospective bride, I was twelve years old. We lived in an inaccessible village, where you could hear the jackals howl by day. To reach it you had to take a carriage from the railway station for fourteen miles, and cover the last three miles of dirt road in a palanquin. How sorely were they harassed that day! And on top of that, our East Bengal cooking—your uncle has still not forgotten the farce of that meal.

Your mother was determined that her second daughter-in-law's looks should make good the elder one's deficiency in beauty. Otherwise why should you take so much trouble to visit our village? In Bengal, no one has to hunt out diseases of the spleen, the liver, or the stomach, nor need you search for a bride; they come and fasten on you themselves, they will not let you go.

My father's heart began to quake, my mother called on the goddess Durga. How was a rustic worshipper to appease the gods of the city? Their hope lay solely in the beauty of their daughter. But their daughter took no pride in that beauty—it was priced at whatever the buyer offered. It is for this reason that women never lose their diffidence, whatever their beauty or virtues.

The anxiety of the entire household, indeed of the entire neighborhood, lay on my heart like a stone. That day it seemed as though all the light in the sky and all the powers of the universe were joint bailiffs firmly holding up a twelve-year-old country girl for the scrutiny of her two examiners' two pairs of eyes. I had nowhere to hide.

The whole sky wept to the strains of flute-music as I entered your house. Even after a minute scrutiny of my imperfections, the crowd of housewives acknowledged that on the whole I was indeed beautiful. This verdict made my elder sister-in-law grave. But I wonder what use my beauty was! If some ancient pedant had created beauty out of holy Ganga silt, then you would have valued it; but as it is, it was created by God for His own pleasure, and so it has no value in your righteous household.

It did not take long for you to forget that I had beauty—but you were forced to remember at each step that I had brains. This intelligence is so much a part of my nature that it has survived even fifteen years in your household. My mother feared for this cleverness of mine; for a woman it was an impediment. If one who must follow the limits laid down by rule seeks to follow her intelligence, she will stumble repeatedly and come to grief. But what was I to do? God had carelessly given me much more intelligence than I needed to be a wife in your household; to whom was I now to return it? Your family have abused me daily as an over-clever female. Harsh words are the consolation of the weak—so I forgive them.

I had one possession beyond your household, which none of you knew about. I used to write poems in secret. Whatever rubbish they were, the walls of your women's quarrels had not grown round them. In them lay my freedom—I was myself in them. You and your family never liked, never even recognized, whatever in me exceeded the "second daughter-in-law" of your household. In fifteen years, you never discovered that I am a poet.

The most vivid of my first memories of your house is of the cattle-shed. The cattle were housed in a shed just next to the stairs leading to the women's quarters; they had no room to move in except for the court-yard in front. In a corner of that courtyard stood the wooden trough for their fodder. The servant had much to do in the mornings; meanwhile the starving cows would lick and chew the sides of the trough to a pulp. My heart wept for them. I was a country girl—when I first entered your house, those two cows and three calves seemed to me as my only familiar relatives in the whole city. When I was a new bride, I would feed them secretly out of my own food. When I grew up, my evident fondness for the cows led those of my in-laws on jesting terms with me to express doubts about my lineage.

My daughter died almost immediately after she was born. She called to me, too, to go with her. If she had lived, she would have brought to my life whatever is great and true: from being the second daughter-in-law, I would then have become a mother. A mother, even within the confines of her own family, belongs to the family of the world. I suffered only the pain of motherhood; I never experienced its freedom.

I remember that the English doctor was astonished at the sight of our women's quarters, and scolded us angrily about the state of the lying-in room. There is a garden to the front of your house; your outer rooms lack nothing by way of furniture and ornaments. The inner rooms are like the reverse of a piece of work in wool; they have neither decorum, nor grace, nor ornament. There lights burn dimly; the air enters by stealth, like a thief; the courtyard is immovably choked with rubbish; the stains on the walls and floors reign undisturbed. But the doctor made a mistake: he thought that this caused us constant suffering. In fact the reverse was true. Neglect is like the ashes which cover a fire: perhaps keeping it alive, but preventing its heat from being outwardly felt. When self-respect dwindles, neglect does not seem unjust; for this reason, it causes no suffering. That is also why women are ashamed to feel pain. I say, therefore, if it is your decree that women must suffer, then it is best to keep them in as neglected a state as possible; in comfort, the pain of suffering becomes greater.

Whatever the condition in which you kept me, it never occurred to me that there was any suffering involved. In the lying-in room, death came and stood at my head, yet I felt no fear at all. What is life to us, that we should fear death? Death is unwelcome only to those whose hold on life has been strengthened by love and care. If death, that day, had pulled me by the hand, I would have come away roots and all, like a clump of grass from loose earth. A Bengali woman speaks of dying in every second utterance. But where is the glory in such death? I am ashamed to die, so easy is death for the likes of me.

My daughter was like the evening star, appearing briefly only to fade away. I became occupied again with my daily chores and the cows and their calves. Life would have rolled on in this way to the very end, and there would have been no need, today, to write you this letter. But a tiny seed is blown by the wind to take root as a peepal shoot in a mortared house; in the end its ribs of brick and timber are cracked apart by that tiny seed. From somewhere a little speck of life blew into the firmly mortared arrangements of my household existence, and from that day the cracks began to appear.

After the death of their widowed mother, my elder sister-in-law's young sister Bindu was driven by her cousins' ill-treatment to seek refuge in her elder sister's house. All of you thought: what a nuisance! So vexatious is my nature that there was no helping it, the moment I saw all of you growing irritated and angry, my whole heart ranged itself to do battle by the side of the helpless girl. To have to take shelter with strangers against their wishes—how immense a humiliation! Is it possible to push aside one who has been forced to submit even to this?

I then became aware of my sister-in-law's situation. The claim of affection alone had prompted her to give shelter to her sister. But when she realized her husband's unwillingness, she began to pretend that the whole matter was a great nuisance—that she would do anything to be rid of this burden. She lacked the courage to show her love openly, from the heart, to her orphaned sister. She is an obedient wife.

Her dilemma grieved me still further. I saw that she made a point of demonstrating to everyone the coarseness of the clothes and food she provided for Bindu, as well as the fact that Bindu was put to work at the most menial of household chores. At this I felt not only pain but shame. My sister-in-law was anxious to prove to everyone that our household, by some fluke, had secured Bindu at a bargain price. She yielded much labor but cost very little.

My elder sister-in-law's family had little to boast of beyond its lineage: they possessed neither wealth nor good looks. You know how they pleaded with and importuned your father to agree to the marriage. My sister-in-law had always thought of her marriage as a great offence to your family. For this reason she tried, in every way, so to restrict herself as to take up very little space in your house.

But her wise example makes life difficult for us women. It is impossible for me to so limit myself in every point. When I decide that something is right, it is not my nature to be persuaded for someone else's sake that it is wrong. You too have had many proofs of this.

I drew Bindu to my rooms. Sister-in-law said: "Meja Bou is simply spoiling a poor man's daughter." She went around complaining to everyone as though I had brought about some terrible disaster. But I know that in her heart, she was relieved. Now the burden of blame would fall on me alone. Her heart was at peace in the knowledge that I was providing her sister with the love she herself could not show her.

My sister-in-law had tried to strike a few years off her sister's age. But it would not have been wrong to say, if only in secret, that she was no younger than fourteen. You know that the girl was so ill-favored that if she fell and hurt her head, people would be worried that the floor had suffered some damage. As a result, in the absence of her parents, there was no one to arrange a marriage for her, and who would be so hardy as to want to marry such a girl?

Bindu came to me in great trepidation of heart, as if she thought that I would not survive the contagion of her touch: as though there was no need for her to have been born at all in this world, as though she must pass by unobtrusively, avoiding people's eyes. In her father's house, her cousins had been unwilling to give up to her even a corner where some unwanted thing might lie forgotten. Inessential rubbish can easily find a place around our houses, because people forget it, but an inessential girl is in the first place unwanted, and moreover impossible to overlook; hence she does not find a place even in the rubbish-heap. One cannot say that Bindu's cousins are utterly necessary to this world either; but they do well enough.

So when I called Bindu to my rooms, there was a trembling in her heart. Her fear filled me with sadness. I conveyed to her in many loving ways that there was a little place for her in my household.

But my household, after all, was not mine alone, and so my task was not easy. After a few days with me she developed a red rash on her skin: perhaps a heat rash, perhaps something else. All of you said it was smallpox—because it was Bindu. An inexperienced doctor from the neighborhood came and said that he could not tell what it was until a day or two had passed. But who was prepared to wait that day or two? Bindu herself was ready to die of shame at her illness. I said, "Never mind if she has smallpox, I'll stay with her in the lying-in room. No one else need be troubled." When all of you were in a fury at me over this, and even Bindu's sister was putting on a show of extreme irritation and proposing to send the poor girl to hospital, suddenly the rash disappeared completely. At this you became even more concerned. You said that undoubtedly the smallpox had settled deep into her. For she was Bindu.

One great virtue of being reared in neglect is that one's constitution becomes virtually indestructible. Ailments refuse to visit you—the highways to death are wholly shut off. So illness mocked at Bindu and passed on—nothing happened to her. But it grew abundantly clear that the most insignificant person in the world was the one that was hardest to give shelter to. One who has most need of shelter finds the greatest obstacles to it.

When Bindu lost her fear of me, she tied herself in yet another knot. She developed so great a love for me that it made me afraid. I had never seen such an image of love in my household. I had read of such love in books, but that was love between men and women. For a long time, there had been no occasion for me to recall that I was beautiful—now, after so many years, this ugly girl became obsessed with my beauty. It was as if her eyes could never have enough of gazing on my face. She would say, "Didi, no one but me has ever seen this face of yours." On the days when I braided my hair myself, she would be hurt and offended. She loved to handle the weight of my hair. I did not need to dress up unless we were invited out; but Bindu would plague me to dress up every day. The girl was infatuated with me.

There is not even the smallest patch of earth in the women's quarters in your house. A gab tree has somehow taken root by the north wall near the gutter. When I saw the leaves of that tree flush red, I would realize that spring had come to the earth. In the midst of my household cares, when I saw this unloved girl's heart one day glow with color, I realized that in the heart's world too, there is a breeze of spring-time—a breeze which comes from some far-off heaven, not from the end of the lane.

The unbearable force of Bindu's love made me restless and uneasy. I confess that sometimes I felt angry with her. Yet that love made me glimpse a true image of myself, one that I had never seen before. This was the image of my free self.

Meanwhile, all of you thought it excessive that I should lavish such care on a girl like Bindu. As a result, there were endless complaints and objections. When my armlets were stolen from my room, you were not ashamed to suggest that Bindu was somehow involved in the theft. When the police started searching people's houses during the Swadeshi Movement, you began to suspect that Bindu was a female informer in the pay of the police. There was no other proof of this than that she was Bindu.

The maids in your house refused to do any work for her. Bindu herself would grow rigid with embarrassment if I asked any of them to do something for her. As a result, my expenditure on her behalf went up. I had to keep a maid especially for her. You did not like this. When you saw the clothes I gave her, you became so angry that you stopped my allowance. From the very next day, I began to wear the coarsest mill-produced dhotis at twenty annas a pair. I also forbade Mati's mother to take out the dishes after my meal; I would myself feed the leftover rice to the calves and scrub the dishes at the pump in the courtyard. You were not very pleased by the sight when you saw me at these tasks one day. Yet I never learned this wisdom: whether I was pleased or not did not matter, but you had to be pleased at all costs.

Meanwhile, as your anger increased, so did Bindu's age. This natural event made you unnaturally concerned. I am still amazed at one thing: why did you not send Bindu away from your house by force? I know very well that you are secretly afraid of me. Inwardly, you cannot but respect the intelligence that God gave me.

In the end, unable to get rid of Bindu by your own means, you

had recourse to Prajapati, the god of marriage. A bridegroom was ar-
ranged for Bindu. My sister-in-law said, "Thank heavens, Mother Kali
has saved the reputation of our family."

I did not know what the groom was like; I heard from you that
he was eligible in every respect. Bindu clasped my feet and wept, saying
"Didi, why need I get married?"

I tried to persuade her, telling her, "Bindu, don't be afraid, I've
heard he's a good groom."

Bindu answered, "If he's so eligible, what have I got that might
please him?"

The groom's family did not even come to see Bindu. My sister-in-
law was greatly relieved at this.

But Bindu's tears continued incessantly, day and night. I know
what she suffered. I had fought many battles for Bindu in my household,
but I did not have the courage to say that her marriage must be stopped.
How should I say this? What would happen to her if I died?

In the first place she was a girl, and on top of that she was dark-
complexioned. It was better not to think of where she was going or what
might happen to her. The thought sent shudders through my heart.

Bindu said, "Didi, there are still five days to the wedding. Mightn't
I die in this time?"

I scolded her severely, but God knows that I would have been re-
lieved if there had been an easy means of death for Bindu.

The day before the wedding, Bindu went to her sister and asked
her, "Didi, I'll live in your cattle-shed, I'll do whatever you ask of me. I
beg of you, don't throw me away like this."

Her sister had been shedding tears in secret for the past few days;
she wept then as well. But we do not have hearts only, we have the scrip-
tures too; she said, "Bindi, you know that a husband is the sole end of a
woman's life. If you are fated to suffer, no one can avert it."

The truth was that there was no escape anywhere. Bindu must
marry, whatever befell her.

I had wanted the wedding to take place in our house. But you an-
nounced that it must be held in the groom's house—this was the custom
in their family.

I realized that your household deity would never endure it if your family were forced to spend on Bindu's wedding. So I had to fall silent. But there is one thing you did not know. I had wanted to tell my sister-in-law, but I did not, because she would have died of fear. I adorned Bindu with some of my jewelry. Perhaps my sister-in-law saw this but pretended not to notice. I beg you in the name of righteousness, forgive her for this.

Before leaving, Bindu embraced me, asking, "Didi, are you all abandoning me?"

I answered "No, Bindi, whatever happens to you, I'll never abandon you."

Three days passed. In one corner of the coal-shed on the ground floor of your house, I had reared a lamb which one of your tenants had sent as a gift for your table, and which I had rescued from the flames of your appetite. Every morning I would feed it gram with my own hands; for a few days I had tried relying on your servants, but found that they were more interested in eating it than in feeding it.

That morning, when I entered the coal-shed, I found Bindu crouched in a corner. On seeing me she collapsed on the floor, clasped my feet and began to weep silently.

Bindu's husband was mad.

"Are you telling the truth, Bindi?"

"Could I tell you such a big lie, Didi? He is mad. My father-in-law did not want this marriage; but he is mortally afraid of my mother-in-law. He left for Varanasi before the wedding. My mother-in-law had set her heart on marrying her son off; she went ahead with it."

I sat down, overcome, on the heap of coal. Women have no pity for women. They say, "She's only a woman. So what if the groom's mad, he's a man, isn't he?"

One could not tell at first sight that Bindu's husband was insane; but he would sometimes grow so violent that he had to be locked up in a room. He had seemed normal on the night of the wedding, but staying up at night and all the excitement had brought on an attack the next day. In the afternoon, Bindu had sat down to her meal of rice, served on a brass platter, when suddenly her husband snatched the platter and threw it, rice and all, into the courtyard. He had got it into his head that Bindu was Rani Rasmani; the servant must have stolen her golden plate and served her on his own brass platter. This was the reason for his anger.

Bindu was terrified. On the third night, when Bindu's mother-in-law commanded her to sleep in her husband's room, she shriveled up in fear. Her mother-in-law had a vicious temper; in a rage, she lost control of her senses. She too was insane, though not so completely as her son, and therefore she was more terrible. Bindu was forced to enter her husband's room. That night he was quiet, but Bindu's entire body grew stiff with fear. Very late at night, when he had fallen asleep, Bindu found a means to flee the house and come here. I need not describe in detail how she managed this.

My whole body burned with anger and disgust. I said, "Such a fraudulent marriage isn't a marriage at all. Bindu, stay with me as you used to. Let me see who dares take you away."

You said, "Bindu is lying."

I answered, "Bindu has never lied."

You asked, "How do you know?"

I answered, "I'm certain of this."

You tried to frighten me by saying that if Bindu's in-laws lodged a case with the police, we would be in trouble.

I answered, "They deceived us by marrying her to a madman. Will the court not listen to us?"

You said, "Must we go to court, then? What obligation is it of ours?"

I replied, "I'll sell my jewelry and do what needs to be done."

You asked, "So are *you* going to go to the lawyer's chambers?"

There was no answer to this. I could beat my forehead in despair, but what more could I do?

Meanwhile, Bindu's brother-in-law had arrived and was kicking up a great row in the outer rooms. He was threatening to go to the police.

I do not know where I got the strength; but I could not bring myself to send back to the slaughter-house the calf that had run away from there to take shelter with me. I said defiantly, "Let him go to the police, then!"

Saying this, I decided to take Bindu to my bedroom, lock the door, and stay there with her. But when I looked for her, Bindu was gone. While I had been exchanging words with you, she had gone out of her own accord and turned herself over to her brother-in-law. She had realized that if she stayed in this house, I would be in great trouble.

By running away Bindu had simply added to her suffering. Her mother-in-law's argument was that her son had not after all tried to eat Bindu up. The world had many instances of bad husbands; compared to them her son was pure gold.

My sister-in-law said, "She's an ill-fated girl. What's the point of being sorry for her? He might be a madman or a stupid goat, but he's her husband all the same."

You recalled the supreme instance of wifely devotion: how a wife carried her leprosy-stricken husband herself to his whore's house. You never felt the least embarrassment about proclaiming this tale of the greatest cowardice in the world. Hence being born a human being never prevented you from being angry at Bindu's behavior: you felt no shame. My heart burst with pity for Bindu, but I could not contain my shame for you. I was a village girl, and cast moreover into your household: through what crack had God filled me with such sense? I could not bear this righteous talk of yours.

I knew for certain that Bindu would die rather than come back to our house. Yet had I not given her my word, the day before she was married, that I would never abandon her? My younger brother Sharat was at college in Calcutta. You know that he was so enthusiastic a volunteer for every kind of social mission, from killing rats in the plague quarter to relief work in the Damodar floods, that even two successive failures in the First Arts Examination had not curbed his zeal. I called him and said, "You must arrange to bring me news of Bindu, Sharat. Bindu will not dare write to me—and even if she does, the letter would never reach me."

Rather than this, if I had told him to abduct Bindu from her

615

house and bring her to me, or to beat her mad husband's head, Sharat would have been better pleased.

As I was talking to Sharat, you came into the room and asked, "What trouble are you starting now?" I said, "It's the same trouble that I began when I entered your household—but that was your doing."

You asked, "Have you brought Bindu here again and hidden her somewhere?"

I answered, "If Bindu came, I would certainly hide her here. But she won't come: you need have no fear."

Your suspicion grew at seeing Sharat with me. I knew that you had never liked Sharat's visits to our house. You were afraid that the police were watching him; some day he would get involved in a political case, and drag the lot of you into it as well. For this reason I was even forced to send him my blessings through a messenger on Brothers' Day; I did not invite him to the house.

I heard from you that Bindu had run away again, and so her brother-in-law had come to enquire at your house. It was as though I had been pierced to the heart. I realized how terrible was the unfortunate girl's suffering, yet there was nothing I could do about it.

Sharat hurried off to bring news. He returned in the evening and told me, "Bindu had gone to her cousins' house, but they flew into a terrible rage and took her back immediately to her in-laws. They still haven't got over the sting of the expense and carriage-hire she cost them."

Your aunt was staying in your house on her way to Puri on pilgrimage. I said to you, "I'll go with her."

You were so delighted by this sudden evidence of piety in me, that you made not the least objection. The thought was also in your mind that if I remained in Calcutta, I would again create a problem over Bindu some day. I was myself a terrible problem.

We were to leave on the Wednesday; by Sunday it had all been decided. I called Sharat and told him, "By whatever means, you must put Bindu on the train to Puri on Wednesday."

Sharat's face lit up; he said, "Never fear, Didi, I'll put her on the train and go to Puri myself as well. I'll get to see Lord Jagannath into the bargain."

That evening Sharat came again. The look on his face stopped my heart. I asked, "What is it, Sharat? Couldn't you manage it?"

He said, "No."

I asked, "Weren't you able to persuade her?"

He said, "There's no need any longer. Yesterday night she set her clothes on fire and killed herself. I got word from one of the nephews of the house, with whom I'd struck up a friendship, that she'd left a letter for you, but they've destroyed it."

Peace at last!

Everyone in the land was annoyed. They began to say, "It's now the fashion for girls to set their saris on fire and kill themselves."

You said, "This is all play-acting." That may be so. But one should reflect why this play-acting takes its toll only of the saris of Bengali women, not of the dhotis of brave Bengali gentlemen.

Bindi was always unlucky! So long as she was alive, she was never known for beauty or talent; even in dying, it never occurred to her to work out some novel means of dying which all the men in the land could applaud! In death, too, she made people angry.

My sister-in-law hid herself in her room and wept. But there was some consolation in her tears. Whatever befell, the family was saved; Bindu had only died. If she had lived, who knows what might have happened!

I have come on pilgrimage. Bindu did not need come after all, but for me there was need.

I did not suffer in your household, as suffering is commonly understood. In your house there is no lack of food or clothes. Whatever be your elder brother's character, you have no vices of which I can complain to the Almighty. Even if your nature had been like your brother's, I might have passed my days somehow or other, and like that devoted wife my sister-in-law, might have tried to blame not my lord and husband but only the Lord of the Universe. And so I have no complaint to make against you—that is not the purpose of my letter.

But I will never again return to your house at number 27, Makhan Baral Lane. I have seen Bindu. I have learnt what it means to be a woman in this domestic world. I need no more of it.

618

And I have also seen that though she was a woman, God did not abandon her. Whatever the powers you exercised over her, there was a limit to them. She was greater than her wretched human birth. Your feet were not long enough to tread her life underfoot for ever, at your wish and by your custom. Death is more powerful than you. In that death, she has attained greatness. There, she is no longer simply the daughter of a Bengali household, the young "sister" of her tyrannical cousins, the deceived wife of an unknown, mad husband. There she is infinite.

When the flute-call of that death sounded through the broken heart of a young girl to the Yamuna-bank of my own life, it seemed at first as though I had been struck by an arrow. I asked God, "Why should the most petty things in life prove the most difficult? Why should the fragile bubble of a joyless life, immured in this little lane, be so terrible an obstacle? When Your whole earth beckons me, holding out the nectar-bowl of the six seasons, why can I not, even for a moment, cross the tiny threshold of these women's quarters? In this universe You have created, with this life I have been given, why must I die inch by inch in this petty shelter of brick and wood? How trivial is this daily commerce of my life, how trivial are its set rules, set habits, set phrases, set blows—yet in the end, must the stranglehold of this pettiness triumph, and your creation, this universe of joy, be defeated?"

But death sounded its flute-call: "What are these wails of masonry, these thorny hedges of your domestic laws? By what suffering or humiliation can they still imprison human beings? See, the triumphal flag of life waves in the hands of death! O second daughter-in-law, you need have no fear! It takes not even a second to cast off your wifely slough."

I am no longer afraid of your lane. The blue ocean is before me today, and the rain-clouds of Asadh are gathered overhead.

You had shrouded me over in the darkness of your habits and customs. For a short space, Bindu came and stole a glimpse of me through the rents in that shroud. And it was this very girl who, through her death, tore my shroud to tatters. Today, having come out, I find no vessel to contain my glory. He who found my slighted beauty pleasing, that Beauteous One is gazing at me through the whole sky. The second daughter-in-law is dead at last.

Do you think I am going to kill myself? Have no fear, I shan't indulge in such a stale jest with you. Mirabai too was a woman like me. Her fetters were not light either, but she did not need to die in order to live. Mirabai said in her song, "Let father, mother, everyone abandon her, O Lord, but Mira will never let you go, whatever befalls her!" It is this holding on which is life.

I too shall live. At last, I live.

Bereft of the shelter of your family's feet,
Mrinal.

1914
("Streer Patra," from *Galpaguchchha*)
Translated by Supriya Chaudhuri

The Final Word

Heroes and heroines of stories trace their origins from their genealogical history, long before the plot suddenly appears to acquire its real shape in the muddled flow of life's turbid waters. On hindsight therefore, I am compelled to adopt a style of story-telling that begins with its pre-history. And so I will take some time to explain who I am, although I will have to assume a false name else I will not be able to cope with the thousand and one explanations which the circle of my friends and acquaintances will demand. I am pondering what name to assume. I don't want a romantic sounding one that would hitch my tale to the pancham note of the Vasanta raga, a springtime melody. Nabinmadhab may sound passable. Nabarun Sengupta could have more successfully washed off any suggestions of a dark-complexion, but that would not sound authentic as people do not place faith in a story that parades attractive names. They would presume that decked in borrowed garb, it is trying to pass itself off as "high" literature.

I belonged to the band of Bengali revolutionaries who had been almost hauled to the shores of the Andamans by the magnetic pull of British imperialism. I had travelled as far as Afghanistan, taking several tortuous routes, in order to evade the noose of the CID. I finally reached America, working as a shipmate. The obduracy peculiar to the people of East Bengal is in my blood. And I could not even for a day forget that as long as I was alive I would have to chafe against the shackles fastening India's hands and feet. However, brief sojourn in a foreign country made me realize that the means we, Indians, had adopted to start a revolution amounted to hurling fire crackers at our poor selves and left no blotch on the British royal seat. It was like a moth's blind attraction to the flame. I did not understand then that while arrogantly plunging into the fray, I was lighting small funeral pyres for our own annihilation and not igniting the sacrificial fire of History. In the meantime the ravaging image of an arsenal-stacked World War had manifested itself on the horizons of my vision and almost immediately my dreams of installing that epoch-transforming Power in the shrine of goddess Chandi in the courtyard of my humble abode, evaporated into thin air. I knew I was ill equipped to stage an elaborate act of suicide and decided to fortify the edifice of nationalism instead. I could clearly comprehend that in order to stay alive, I needed more than the primitive strength of my bare hands. I would have to wage a modern war, armed with modern weapons. It is easy enough to die but to emerge as Viswakarma, an apostle of industrialism, less so. I realized that there was no point in losing patience; the path was long and the effort required, arduous. I had to begin at the beginning.

Finding a place for myself somehow in Ford's car plant in Detroit I enrolled as a mechanical engineer. I was involved in acquiring the necessary skills, all the time aware I was not making much progress. Then suddenly I had a brainwave. Rather foolishly, I thought that if I gave Ford a hint that I was not aiming at self-gain rather striving to rescue my own country, then the freedom-loving financial wizard would be so pleased with me that he would help me make my work worthwhile. Ford gave me a suppressed smile and said, "My name is Henry Ford. It's an old English name; to make my useless English cousins efficient is my sole resolve." I presumed he would be equally enthusiastic about instilling proficiency amongst us Indians. But the rich favor the rich is a bitter truth I learnt. I became aware that chances of my progress in learning the complex processes of the production of car tires were indeed slim. At the same time another truth dawned on me, namely that I would have to dig deep into the very foundation of mechanical engineering; I would have to learn how to procure raw materials for the manufacture of mechanical goods. Our mother earth has stored hard substances in her inaccessible bowels for those who are strong, and using them, such people have conquered the world. But she has left crops growing on her surface for the poor with their protruding ribs and shrunken stomachs. With this understanding, I immersed myself in the science of mineralogy.

621

Ford proclaimed that the English were good for nothing—was not India a proof enough of this truth? In India the English have tried indigo plant cultivation and then grown tea. They have implemented a liveried "law and order" regime in civil administration, but they have failed to uncover India's immense internal resources: its environmental treasures and the nature of its human beings. And yet they have remained entrenched there, wringing the last drop of blood out of the hapless jute workers. Coming to the conclusion that my job was not to play with fire crackers but to breach the stone walls of that formidable fortress of the country's underworld, I saluted Sri Jamshedji Tata from across the seven seas. I resolved not to sing paeans to our Mother Country along with those who refuse to grow up, and instead to acknowledge the poor of this country for what they really were: hungry, illiterate and incompetent. Nor did I want to continue to chant celebratory mantras sanctifying poverty. I had in my youth, time and again, entertained myself by building edifices of words, had shed tears at the feet of tinsel images glorifying the nation, formed in the potter's den of poetry—but no more! Arriving at this country of Reason and Enlightenment, I have come to accept the reality for what it is. I have learnt to gird myself to work with eyes shorn of illusions. Now—the scientist from Bengal is about to emerge, spade in hand, armed with axe and hammer, in search of the country's hidden treasures. Will those emotional disciples of the poet recognize such an act as a form of patriotism or as another way of worshipping the motherland?

Resigning from Ford's car plant I spent nine years educating myself in mining and mineralogy, traveling all over Europe, laboring at the desks of several centers, even inventing a couple of mechanical devices.

In this, I was a great deal encouraged by my professors who helped instill confidence in myself, and I derided my former slavish, ungrateful persona.

These big words have little to do with my slender story and it would have been appropriate, even better, if I had left them out. But the situation demands I say something and that is, I had been completely impervious, even hostile, to female charms during the early days of my youth, a time when it is natural for one to be held captive by the magnetism of women, who appear as colorful aurora on life's deserted landscapes. I regarded myself as an ascetic, a person totally dedicated to work, my mind strictly contained by the import of those high-sounding words. And so when approached by those burdened with daughters of marriageable age, I made it clear to them that unless their offspring were fated to become untimely widows they should not think of me as a prospective groom.

In the countries of the West, nothing came in the way of the companionship of women and it was there that I had felt very apprehensive. I had not been aware that I was good-looking because while in my own country, the only indication I had received about this was through the silent language of women's eyes. Otherwise, the fact had remained outside my consciousness. Coming to the West I discovered that I was not only more intelligent than average but handsome to look at as well. And to tell the truth there were indications that momentous events were about to happen in my life which could have roused the envy of my Indian readers but I did not allow them to cast a magic spell on me, numbing my thoughts. Perhaps I am made of sterner stuff than those over-emotional, refined gentlemen from West Bengal. I had packed my resolve into an iron chest of inflexible will. By nature averse to the idea of playing around with girls and then abandoning them at will, I knew, for certain, that if I slipped even once from my avowed determination, I would be crushed under the weight of broken promises. For me evasion had no place between these two fates. Besides, I come from the countryside and thus far, I have not been able to shed my traditional inhibitions regarding women. That is why I have contempt for people who boast about the love of the female species.

I had acquired a good educational degree in the West but knowing I would not be able to put it to use in any governmental work in India I took up a job at the court of the ruler—let us say Chandrabir Singh —of a princely state in Chotanagpur. Fortunately for me, his son, Debikaprasad, had spent some time as a student at Cambridge, and I had come across him by chance in Zurich. He was already cognizant of my reputation. I explained my project to him and he enthusiastically put me in the service of the department of geological survey in his state, ignoring many English candidates and incurring the wrath of the authorities. Debikaprasad was unbending in his convictions and I lasted out even the old king's vacillations about me.

Ma said, before I came away to join work, "Son, you have a good job now, take a bride and fulfill my life's dreams."

"And ruin my job as a result? Marriage and work do not follow the same rhythm." I rejoined.

I was unrelenting in my decision; my mother's entreaties fell on deaf ears. Packing my instruments I came away to this forest land. Then all of a sudden a story blossomed on the horizons of my impending country-wide fame which had the countenance of a Will-o-Wisp as also the Venus star. I was traversing wooded landscapes, one after the other, scrutinizing the earth buried below the hard rocks. The sky was overpowered by the mad riot of red palash flowers. The sal trees had budded and the bees were hovering above them in swarms. The traders were going about their business of collecting wax, or skimming the leaves of kul trees for the tusser silk-worms, the santals gathering mature mahua flowers shed by the trees. A slim stream danced its way past the woods, spreading its soft lyrical music about the place. I had given the name Tanika to the little rivulet, thinking to myself this place was not a factory, a manufacturing plant or a university classroom—it was a dark twilight country where the unguarded mind becomes somnolent and Nature, the sorceress, piles colors on it just as it does on the sunset scene.

My mind had become somewhat mesmerized; the pace of my work turned sluggish. I was annoyed with myself and drove myself from within, thinking that I had got entrapped in the silken web of the tropical climate. The demonic Tropics have from time immemorial injected

623

the formula of defeat into our bloodstream, in tandem with the breeze of hand fans. I knew that I would have to steer clear of the moisture-soaked magic of the Tropics.

The day advanced. The river flowed on dividing itself into two, leaving behind a strip of sandy land, more like an island in the middle, where a flock of cranes sat still. At the end of each day such a scene signaled the need for a new turn in the rhythm of my work. That day, returning to my bungalow home, my shoulder bag filled with samples of stones gathered on the way for laboratory inspection, I felt that the interval between the afternoon and evening lay stretched in vain, like a piece of scorched earth, hard for a lonely youth to navigate, especially when staying in a deserted forest land. I had reserved that part of the day for laboratory experiments. Wringing electricity from the dynamo I had often sat with chemicals, the microscope and the weighing machine. At times I worked past midnight. That day I was walking with added enthusiasm as I had come to know that deposits of manganese lay in a certain place in the woods. The crows were flying to their nests; the orange sky resonated with their cawing. Just about then something happened to interrupt my return home to resume work.

The sal trees had formed a row on the top of a hillock along the wooded path. A person who sat in its closure could be glimpsed only from a gap at a particular angle. An unusual radiance had burst through the clouds on that day, throwing its rainbow-colored effulgence into the opening, like an unleashed fistful of gold. A girl sat in the illuminated landscape, pushing her folded knees up to her chest, resting her back against a tree trunk, and scribbling intensely in her diary. In a flash, something wondrous, a rare occurrence in one's life, revealed itself to me. Like the tidal waves of the sea during the full-moon, emotions surged within me and beat against my heart. Hiding myself behind the tree trunk and fixing my gaze at her, I stood without moving. And a remarkable picture began to etch itself in my mind's memory bank.

In the long span of my experience many captivating and unexpected occasions had risen which I had left unexplored but today I felt I had become connected with life's supreme moment. I am not in the habit of either thinking or talking in this manner. How was it that the one blow by which man's secret, wonderful self comes out into the open could strike me in this way? I had always thought I was like some rocky mountain, hard and dry, devoid of emotions. And yet a waterfall seemed to be gushing out from within.

I wanted to say something but could not decide what ought to be the opening gambit of my life's most important communication. Should it be something like the first words of Creation, according to the Christian text: Let there be Light or let whatever is inarticulate become articulate! At one time I thought the girl—I came to know her real name much later and so I will not call her by that name but will refer to her as Achira. What does the name signify? It means something like an instant revelation, a flash of lightning. I allowed the name to stick to her, feeling she was aware that someone had been standing concealed from her view. Perhaps human presence sends out a silent message. She stopped writing but made no effort to leave the place, not wanting perhaps, to be caught in the act of making an escape. I felt like saying, excuse me—but reasoned, why would I want to do that? What rules had I broken that I had to be exonerated? I moved some steps away and pretended to dig the earth with my stumpy foreign spade and dropped some rubbish into my shoulder bag. Then bending my body low and fixing my gaze on the earth like some scientist, I slowly left the place. But I knew for certain I had not succeeded in pulling the wool over the eyes of someone who just would not be deceived. I had no doubt that she had, time and again, made note of the several symptoms discernible in besotted men and I hoped that she was secretly enjoying seeing me in a similar state. I wondered what would have happened had I deigned to leap over the moral boundary wall separating us—ever so little. Who knew what would have transpired! Would she have become angry or would she have only pretended to? I walked towards my bungalow nursing a restless mind. When all of a sudden an envelope torn into two came to my sight. I picked it up although it was not a geological specimen! The writing was feminine, the name the envelope carried was of one Bhabatosh Mazumdar ICS, the address: Chhapra. Although stamped there was no sign it had been posted, as if indicating the inhibitions of a virgin. My scientific mind became at once active. I clearly comprehended that the torn envelope carried the scars of a tragic event. Was it not my job as a scientist to retrieve the history of our universe from that stratum of the earth which had been ripped open? Subsequently, my researching mind spread its antennae, and resolved to explore that particular mystery.

My inner life was a terra incognita, I told myself. I was taken aback by this recognition, especially when I saw what a novel shape my internal life had assumed in the context of this out-of-the-ordinary situation. All this time, I had thought I knew my own mental disposition, striving for life's supreme goal by sheer hard work, in place after place, thought that it was my mind's true make-up, the truth of which I was ready to vouch for. I little knew then that ignorance, external to the rule of reason though hidden among its folds, had made its first appearance. Thus the primitive self, who did not believe in reason but in illusions, was caught red-handed. There is magic in the forest in the silent conspiracy of the trees, and the call of the wilds. Its measured, deep baritone music continually hums in one's ears, both in the mid-day heat of the sun and in the middle of the night, rousing one's self-awareness. And reason is consumed by an unfathomable longing for the primal moment.

Thus, the primal urge was active in me even in the most rational and scientific moments of my geological research. I was hunting for a granule of radium among the crevices of unyielding rocks when I came across Achira embraced by the shadows of flowering sal trees. I had seen Bengali women earlier, but not in such an intimate way, distinctly apart from the rest of the world. Here it seemed that the soft hue of her skin had taken on shades of the tender foliage of the woods and had become one with them. In my life, I had come across many foreign beauties, had found them attractive too, but this was the first time I had seen a Bengali girl in an environment where she could be her complete self. And yet she did not blend into the realities, both known and unknown, of the secluded forest region and I could easily identify her as someone who had attended the Diocesan school, swinging her hair plaits, or held a degree from Bethune college, or laughingly offered tea to guests at a Ballygunge tea-party. Years ago, in my childhood I would hear the songs of Haru Thakur or Ram Bosu. I had forgotten that those songs were no longer

626

played on the radio or relayed through the gramophone records, resounding in the neighborhood. I did not know why I had the idea that the melody of those ragas would act as an introduction to the beauty of the girl—*my heartache, dear friend, resides in the depths of my heart*—the pathos the particular song carried seemed to clearly materialize in her female form, or so it seemed to me at that moment! I had read in my studies of the geological science how the incendiary matter lying hidden inside the bowels of the earth are thrown above the ground during a violent earthquake. Likewise, I too suddenly discovered, in the clear light of day, that part of my self which had lain ravaged in the dark recesses of my being. I had never imagined such an upheaval in the unshakable inner world of the stern scientist Nabinmadav.

I realized she had seen me many times taking this path returning home in the evening about which, absent-minded, I was not even aware. I had begun to take pride in my looks after traveling abroad and was getting used to people exclaiming, "O how handsome!" in admiration. However, I was given to understand by my England-returned friends that the taste of Bengali girls was different and that they looked out for men who were good-looking in an effeminate way. In common parlance—someone who resembled the Kartik idol! Whatever you may think we can in no way assume the Bengali Kartik to be the leader of an army of the gods. A girlfriend in Paris told me that the Europeans were too pale and that their skin lacked color. The hue that the sky etched on the physical form of an oriental was true color and she adored it! I did not think that such a notion would find acceptability among those residing on this side of the Bay of Bengal.

All this time I had not given a minute to such thoughts! But now they had me enthralled. I was sun-burnt in skin-tone, tall in my physical frame and lacking in vitality; my elbows were coarse, my walking pace quick. And I had heard that my eyes were keen, and that several features of my face—ears, forehead and nose—were distinguished. Epstein had wanted to make a stone statue of me in stone, but I could not spare him the time. I knew all along that the Bengali men were their mother's darlings and that their mothers loved to see their sons, resembling wax dolls nestled in their laps. Such thoughts stirred within me and made me angry. I started fighting with Achira in my imagination. I said to her, "The men you regard as handsome are lost cases, they will not last even if you were to worship them. And how is it that you take no notice of someone like me who has brushed aside the appeal of so many women in important cities?" Then I laughed at the childishness of my imaginary angry exchanges, and my scientific mind became ready to come up with reasonable arguments. So I cogitated that if Achira had actually desired solitude she would have moved away from the place where she sat, a path I passed by returning home each day. In the beginning I glanced at her from out of the corner of an eye, pretending I had not seen her at all. But of late our eyes had met—more than once—and as far as I could gather she had not taken this as an unfortunate accident!

There was still a more severe yardstick to validate my assumptions. Heretofore, I had passed by the sal-tree-shadowed road only once during the day—returning home in the evening after digging stones and the earth. Recently the number of my journeys along the route had increased manifold and I passed her by with additional frequency. Achira was old enough to guess that the reason I went past her so often was certainly not a geological one. When I discovered that I could not dislodge Achira from her habitual resting place I became even bolder, and turned back several times to look at her and found her staring straight in my direction, quickly taking her eyes away and poring over her diary when I turned to face her. I suspected her diary jottings were beginning to lose some of their intensity. And thus my scientific mind was sufficiently roused to tackle head on the mysteries of human psychology. I understood that the person the girl had declared her devotion to was called Bhabatosh. He had taken up the post of the district magistrate at Chhapra, after returning from England. They had been deeply in love before he left for the foreign shores and some untoward incident had occurred on the eve of his taking up his job—a matter serious enough for me to investigate. This was easy as my Cambridge colleague Bankim now worked at the University of Patna.

I posted him a letter.

Bhabatosh has joined the Bihar Civil Service. He is reputed to be a coveted groom among people with eligible daughters. A friend of mine has requested me to help fix the marriage of his daughter with him. I will be grateful if you let me know whether that can be arranged smoothly. I will be glad to have some idea of the kind of person he is as well.

The answer arrived.

The road sports a no-exit sign. But you wanted to know more about the kind of person he is? Then here it is: When at college, I studied under Doctor Anil Kumar Sarkar, a person with several degrees appended to his name. He was both extremely learned and extremely childlike at the same time. The joy of his life was his only grandchild, a girl, who looked as if the goddess Saraswati had bequeathed her not only her intelligence but also her beauty. The devil Bhabatosh made an entry into this paradise. He had a sharp mind and a loquacious tongue. He won over first the professor and then his granddaughter. My palms would itch with envy witnessing their growing intimacy but there was no way I could intervene. The engagement was announced and they only had to await Bhabatosh's return from England, after passing the civil service exam. The professor had even provided for his travel and other expenses. The devil was prone to catching chill. I had begged God twice a day that he die of pneumonia before the wedding took place but that was not to be. Bhabatosh passed his exam and married the daughter of a high-ranking government officer with a lot of clout. Heartbroken, the professor gave up his job and along with his granddaughter disappeared lord knows where in anger and shame. I have had no news of them since.

I read the letter several times over and made up my mind that I would rescue the girl from the depths of such ignominy and despair.

In the meantime I grew impatient wanting to somehow start a conversation with Achira. I am sure that had I been an aficionado of literature and not a scientist, a West Bengal modern rather than a Bangal, a natural from East Bengal, words would have simply flowed from my lips. I was generally diffident vis-à-vis Bengali girls, perhaps because I did not know them at all. Besides, I had the idea that Indian girls were totally inaccessible to men other than their husbands and that they would be offended if one were to begin a frivolous conversation with them. Such is blind prejudice! Before joining work I had spent a few days in Kolkata, and had, in the company of my friends and acquaintances, come across heavily made-up Bengali women—the eternal female companions, crowding the acting profession—but I would rather not talk about them. Achira seemed to belong to another world I concluded, not having a clue about her true nature. She seemed to belong to a different age, with her spotless dignity and her fear of being touched. I kept racking my brains for a suitable opening sentence to our conversation.

630

A couple of robberies had taken place in the neighborhood. I thought it the right moment to tell Achira, "I'll request the ruler of the state to arrange for proper security for you." Had she been an English-woman she would have taken this gesture as a sign of a daring, unwarranted familiarity and would have looked the other way and said, "That's my business." I had little experience as to how a Bengali girl would react. My long stay abroad had made me accustomed to European mores.

The daylight had begun to dim and time arrived for Achira to prepare to go home or her grandfather to come and join her for a walk. Just then a northern Indian devil-may-care sort of fellow suddenly appeared on the scene and tried to snatch her bag and diary. I immediately made my appearance from my hiding place behind the trees and said, "Don't you have any fear?" and jumped on the fellow, who ran away abandoning the bag and the diary. I came and handed Achira the looted goods.

"Thank heaven for your . . ." Achira said.

"Do not say anything more . . . how lucky I am that fellow turned up," I responded.

"What do you mean?"

"I mean I could talk to you because of him. All this time I was racking my brains what to say."

"But he was a robber!"

"Not at all, he is not a thief but my footman."

Achira burst into peals of laughter covering her mouth with the end of her maroon sari-anchal. Such lilting melody, as if emanating from the sound of a waterfall resonating against a sea of pebbles! Laughter subsiding, she said,

"But it would have been such fun if it were true . . ."

"Fun for whom?" I asked.

"For the target of the robbery, I have read something like that in books."

"And then what would have been the fate of the rescuer?"

"I would have brought him home and given him tea."

"Then what is to happen to this fake rescuer?"

"He wanted to know how to begin a conversation and in the bargain has had the opportunity to exchange so many words. He would not want anything more!"

"And would that bring an end to all the reckoning?"

"Why would it?"

"Okay . . . what would you have said had you started the conversation?"

"I would have asked him, 'What childish games are you playing picking pebbles along the way? Are you not a grown man?'"

"Why didn't you?"

"I was nervous."

"Nervous? Because of me?"

"Why, you are such an important person. My grandfather has told me everything about you, he has read all the articles you have written in foreign scientific journals. He always tries to explain to me whatever he reads."

"So he has done that too?"

"O yes, daunted by the display of a mountain of Latin terms I had pleaded, 'Please Grandfather, let us forgo this and allow me to fetch your book on quantum theory.'"

"And you can follow quantum theory?"

"Not one bit—but grandfather has a firm belief that there is nothing beyond human comprehension, and I would not want to destroy that. He has an even more strange idea that women, driven by common sense, possess sharper wit than men. That is why I wait with trepidation in my heart for him to begin discoursing on the confluence of time and space. In actual fact his compassion for women knows no bounds. When grandmother was alive she would stop him from approaching a difficult subject. He could not derive any notion of how far woman's reasoning could take her from my grandmother, and I do not want to disappoint him. I have heard much that I do not understand and will hear more that will remain incomprehensible to me."

Achira's two eyes glistened with affection and amusement, and I wished that her soft-voiced utterances would not come to an end. But daylight was fast losing its brightness and the evening star was already making its appearance in the sky beyond the sal treetops. One could hear the santal girls singing as they gathered firewood to take home. Just then a voice interrupted my meditation.

"Didi, where are you? It is getting dark and the times are bad."

"I know we are living in bad times, that is why I have employed a bodyguard," she said.

I bent forward to take the dust off the professor's feet as soon as he appeared on the scene. He was suddenly alert and I introduced myself, "My name is Nabinmadhab Sengupta."

The old man's eyes became bright. "What are you saying—you are the famed Doctor Sengupta? But you are so young!"

"Really young," I rejoined, "just about thirty-six years old."

Again the sound of Achira's sweet laughing voice, like the slow melodious strokes of the sitar. She said, "Everyone is youthful in Dadu's eyes and Dadu is ahead of all the youths of the world—he is an agarwala!"

The professor exclaimed, "Agarwala? A new word has been imported into the Bengali tongue for sure. Where did you find this?"

"Do you remember your favorite Marwari pupil Kundanlall Agarwala? He used to supply me with jars of mango chutney. One day I asked him what his name meant and he said Agarwala means pioneer!"

The professor said, "Doctor Sengupta, now that we know you—you will have to come home."

"Say no more, Dadu, he is dying to come with us. He has heard that you are about to expound an important time-space theory taking off from Einstein," Achira interposed.

"How naughty!" I said to myself.

"Are you interested in time-space . . . ?" the professor began, greatly enthused.

I became very anxious. "I do not understand a thing about it, you will be only wasting your time explaining the theory to me."

"Time!" the Professor ejaculated. "We have all the time in the world in this place. But let us decide on this one thing. Why not have a meal with us to-night?"

I jumped up, about to ask, "Right now?"

Achira intervened. "It is not for nothing I call you childish, Dadu. You invite people home at the drop of a hat and put me in a spot! Where in this jungle will I find Firpo's tearoom? He is used to all kinds of European food. Why must you wreck my reputation in this way? We must at least arrange for mutton and bhekti fish, no?"

"Okay then, when will it be convenient for you to come?" the old man asked.

"I can come tomorrow," I said, "but I do not want to inconvenience Achira Debi. You see, I have to travel through dense forests, visit caves and pits, and that is why I always carry a packet full of flattened rice, a bunch of bananas, tomatoes, sprouted beans, even peanuts at times. If I could just bring along my vegetarian meal and allow Achira Debi to serve it to me mixed with curd, then there would not be any problem."

"Dadu, for Heaven's sake do not believe in such people! He has read in the journals what you have written about the lack of vitamins in Bengali food and is now trying to impress you with his list of vitamin-rich natural food."

I thought, what a bother! I am not inclined to read what doctors have written in the Bengali papers about the theory of vitamin intake, but how was I to prove that? Especially, when a greatly encouraged professor asks me, "So you have read about it?"

"It does not matter whether I have read the article or not, actually . . ." I broke off.

"Actually," Achira rejoined, "he knows too well that if he came tomorrow he would be given a non-vegetarian feast, not a bird or beast spared. That is why he is so confidently singing paeans to the virtues of tomatoes. Just regard his physique—would anyone mistake it for one which has been nourished by only vegetables? Dadu you are so gullible!

You believe in all I say too. That is why I dare not say anything to you in jest."

We were conversing while walking towards their house when all of a sudden Achira exclaimed, "Now go back to your place."

"Why—I thought of walking you to your doorstep."

"The place is in a mess—you will say Bengali girls are untidy. I will arrange things nicely so that when you come tomorrow you will be reminded of your English girl friends."

"Please do not mind all this talk Doctor Sengupta, although it is not in Achira's nature to say so much. It is very lonely out here so she keeps me happy babbling away, and it appears to have become a habit with her. But when she is silent the place becomes eerie and my soul turns morbid. And she knows that. My only worry is that people might misunderstand her."

Achira flung her arms around her aged grandfather and said, "Let them, Dadu. I do not wish to appear all that good. It sounds dull—uninteresting."

"Do you know Sengupta, my didi has a way with words. I have not seen any one quite like her."

"You have not seen anyone quite like me, neither have I seen anyone quite like you!" Achira quipped.

"You have to give me your word about something before I leave, Acharyadeb," I requested.

"Most certainly."

"If you addressed me informally, discarding the formal 'thou,' I would feel that I have truly gained your affection. I bite my tongue in shame every time you address me as 'thou.' I am sure your granddaughter will aid you in placing me in the category of those who you consider close enough to address as 'tumi.'"

"What a calamity! I am an ordinary being, I cannot aim so high and you are such an important person! I would say, let a few days pass, let me forget you are a person with so many academic degrees, then it may come naturally. But in grandfather's case it is different. Why not start right now Dadu? Say, 'Come for a meal tomorrow.' If Didi by mistake adds more salt to the fish then put up with that good-naturedly and ex-claim, 'It is wonderfully tasty! Can I have some more?'"

Resting his arm on my shoulder affectionately, the professor said, "Brother if you had only known her but a few days ago you would have realized how shy she really is. Quite tongue-tied! That is why she talks so much when obliged to carry on a conversation."

"Can you see how sweetly Dadu rebukes me! As if with a whip made of sugar cane! He could have easily reprimanded me by saying 'You are too talkative. Your sauciness is intolerable!' You will have to defend me though . . . what will you say, tell me please."

"I will not declare that in front of you."

"Something harsh then?"

"You know what is in my mind?"

"Then let it be, go home!"

"There is something that remains to be said. The occasion for my invitation to your place tomorrow is my new naming! From tomorrow the title Dr. Sengupta will disappear from my name and I will be known simply as Nabinmadhab. It is the same as what happens to a comet when it nears the sun. It loses its tail and what remains is merely its head."

"In which case it will be akin to namkirtan, or singing the deity's name in praise, rather than namkaran, bestowing a new name—so why call it that?"

"Okay, okay, I concede."

And that is how it ended—the first big day in my life. Old age possesses such calm beauty and peace, such dignity of presence! Even the eyes appear to rain benediction! A polished cane stick in hand, a milky-white carefully pleated scarf around his neck, the dhoti neatly folded, clad in a tussar shirt, his thinning snowy white hair neatly combed down —there was no mistaking the granddaughter's expert hands had been at it day and night. And he had put up with all the sweet tyranny only to keep the girl happy.

My interest in their news superseded my interest in scientific events. It is time I gave the professor a name. I will call him Anil Kumar Sarkar. One among those in the previous generation who had earned a

Ph.D. degree from Cambridge. He had resigned from his position of principal of a provincial college a few months ago and relocated himself in an abandoned Dak Bungalow of this state, making it habitable with his own money. These in sum are the skeletal historical details—the rest has already been provided in my friend Bankim's letter.

636

I have come to the end of the introductory chapter of my story. There is hardly an interval between the beginning and the end of the short story and I will not violate its nature by unnecessary elaboration. Very soon a time arrived when I could talk freely with Achira. A picnic was arranged on the banks of the Tanika river. The professor suddenly asked me with child-like candor, "Nabin, are you married?" There was no way I could evade answering a question whose intention was so clearly articulated. So I said, "Not yet." There was nothing that escaped Achira's ears. She said, "Those words are meant to put the minds of anxious parents of marriageable daughters at rest. There is hardly any truth in them."

"How can you be so certain there is not an iota of truth in my words?"

"It is a matter of calculation—not high mathematics, mind you! We have heard you are a thirty-six-years-old child. I calculated that your mother must have entreated you at least five times saying, 'Son, I want to welcome a daughter-in-law into the household!' And your replying, 'After I stuff the iron chest with money.' Mother must have wiped her tears in silence. After that you underwent every possible experience, except for facing the gallows! Finally when you managed to be employed by the state government on a coveted salary, your mother again entreated, 'You will have to marry now, son, how many days will I last?' You said, 'Science is my life; I will dedicate my scientific findings to my country and remain a bachelor for ever.' Mother must have given up all hope and resigned herself unhappily to her misfortune. Now tell me have I wrongly calculated your thirty-six-year-old life? Tell me truly."

I realized it was dangerous to converse unthinkingly with this girl. The other day something had happened—Achira had said, in the course of our conversation, "The women of our country are fit to be companions for life but those who are not wont to settle down to domesticity

have no need for such women. On the other hand men who are dedi-
cated to the pursuit of science in the west do find someone to share their
passion with, like Professor Curie's wife Madame Curie. Didn't you find
some one like her in that country?" I immediately thought of Catherine.
We had researched together while I lived in London, and had even writ-
ten a book together. I had to agree with Achira's remark.

"Why did you not marry her?" she asked, "Was she not willing?"

I had to admit that it was she who had proposed.

"So?" Achira demanded.

"But I am dedicated to my country India, and not only to abstract
science."

"You mean the desire for success in love is not for the likes of a
votary of science as you are. The supreme goal for women is personal but
for you it is impersonal."

I could not find anything to say in response to this at that mo-
ment. Seeing me silent, Achira continued, "Perhaps you are not familiar
with Bangla literature—there is a long poem titled 'Kach and Debjani,'
which is about how women are determined to enslave men and how men
build their road to immortality breaking free of such bondage. Kach was
able to come out of the confinement imposed by women, disregarding
Debjani's pleas, as you have by overcoming your mother's entreaties. It is
an identical situation. You have won the eternal battle between men and
women. And so hurrah for the victory of the male! Let the women weep,
and you gather their sorrow as an offering. Because though offerings are
made to them, the gods themselves remain unaffected."

The professor could not understand where the argument was
leading. He proudly declared, "See how the deep truth finds a natural
expression in Didi's lips. If some one were to hear her now he would have
. . ." he broke off. The professor was forever apprehensive his grand-
daughter might be misunderstood.

Achira piped up, "Outsiders can not tolerate clever women. You
do not have to worry on that score Dadu, everything will be alright if
you understand me."

She appeared very thoughtful today although she was prone to
make fun of herself even when discoursing seriously. I wondered if Bha-

batosh had explained to her that he had plucked a wife from the highest echelons of the government of India because he was aiming at something both high and impersonal. But it could not have been easy for him to deceive Achira—the torn envelope was proof enough of her mental attitude.

Achira repeated, "Know how Debjani cursed Kach?"

"I do not."

"'You can not use the knowledge you have gathered for your own good, nor can you bestow it on others,' she had told Kach. I find such admonition strange indeed. If someone had flung such a curse on Europe today, he would have offered them a blessing in disguise, as then Europe would have been spared the destruction they are experiencing coveting the goods of the whole world. Is not that the truth, Dadu?"

"Absolutely, but it is incredible how you have thought all this up!" Dadu responded.

"Not on my own, surely, I have heard you say the very same thing so often. You are Bholanath, you have the gift of forgetting when and what you say. You remain undaunted even when passing off someone else's wisdom as your own."

"Plagiarism is a great art, indeed," I added, "whether in learning or in governance one borrows ideas from others. The great rulers of this world are the greatest thieves. Actually it is the small fry or the petty thieves who get caught in the act because of their ineptitude."

Achira said, "So many students of Dadu have taken down ideas he has uttered in class and have produced books and become famous. He reads their work with wonderment and praises them sky high, not realizing he is indulging in self-praise! I have had the good fortune to have had a share of that. I am sure, if asked, Nabinbabu would vouch he is making notes about the various aspects of my originality in an exercise book full of information about India's mineral resources during the copper age. Remember Dadu, many years ago when I was at college you had recited to me the Kach and Debjani poem? I have believed in the superiority of the male species from that day onwards, although I have never admitted to it."

"But Didi, I have never denied women their glory, have I?"

You—How could you—a blind admirer of the female species! I am amused listening to you singing paeans to womenfolk. How unashamedly women lap up such adulation. They have got used to taking in all this easily available praise.

The conversation that took place that day was no simple banter, it presaged a full-fledged war. Achira's nature had two sides to it as she also had two places to seek refuge—her own house and the woody grove. I had decided that when our relationship began to take on the contours of an easy familiarity I would apprise her of my life's most recent predicament and somehow steer ourselves towards a solution to all that amidst laughter and amusement in the secluded grove. But that way was forever closed to me. Just as I did not know how to start a conversation on the first day of our meeting, so now too Achira did not provoke any utterance from me and I could not discover the means by which I could negotiate with her mind or carry any message to its depths. Her laughter-filled garrulity at the threshold of her home stopped me from proceeding one step further, and the secluded shady forest land rendered all my inner turmoil into a soundless silence. On days when enjoying their company over a cup of tea I felt I had arrived at a breach in the defensive wall separating us, Achira, apprehending the danger of our becoming too close, indulged in such ceaseless chatter that I was not given a chance to put in a word edgewise—so inhospitable the environment had become.

My mind turned extremely restive. I felt ashamed that my work was suffering. A report from me to be submitted to the research department at its official budget meeting, asking for sanction of further funds, lay half done. In the meantime for some days now, I had been subjected to elaborate discussions on Croce's aesthetics, a subject repugnant to my taste and well beyond the reach of my understanding. Achira was only too aware of this. She egged on her grandfather while herself enjoying a secret laughter. Now the argument turned on the innumerable explanations countering the theory of Behaviourism. The difficulty in all this theorizing was that Achira would take leave precisely at such moments in order to attend to her garden. She would say she had had her fill of such arguments. I would stay back like a fool, glancing at the door from time to time. It was good that the professor did not question me about whether I could follow the knotty arguments or not. He assumed that things were crystal clear to me. But I knew that I could not let things be, and that I had to find an opportunity to introduce the pressing topic.

One day, taking time off from a picnic, as we sat among the stunted ebony shrubs while the professor, settled on the steps of the ruins of a temple, was perusing a newly published book on chemistry, Achira suddenly said to me, "The power of blind nature lies in these eternal woods. It gradually overwhelms me with fear."

"How surprising! This is exactly what I had written down in my diary the other day."

"It is like the shoots of an oak tree that at times sprout hidden among the cracks of ancient pillars," Achira continued, "and then entangle those in their roots destroying them completely. This is what I had discussed with Dadu and he had told me that human character becomes weak under the influence of Nature and if one were to stay far away from society in solitary splendor, one would find that one's primitive instincts have gained the upper hand. I had asked him what one could do in that case and he replied, 'We can carry humans along with us—in these books. We get to know human beings better in solitude through reading their books.' All this suits Dadu, it can not apply to every one. What do you feel about it?"

"I will say what I think and you must try to correctly understand what I say, okay? It is my opinion that in a place like the one we are in, one must develop a complete understanding of another human being, in both internal and external senses, something that would bestow completeness to one's existence, and unless that is achieved one is prone to be perpetually overcome by some blind force or the other. I would have hesitated to utter my true thoughts to you had you been an ordinary woman."

"Say what you think, and do not dither."

I said, "I am a scientist and must speak like one, in an impersonal manner. You had loved Bhabatosh once. Do you love him still?"

"Consider that I do not."

"I have, perhaps been responsible for the change?"

"Possibly, but it is not you alone. These woods have a fierce blinding power, that is why I do not regard my moving away from him with any sense of pride, rather I feel embarrassed."

"And why is that?"

"It is because my love for you is some kind of a blind attraction. Human beings shape their thoughts according to some ideal, through persistent effort, whereas their blind primal instincts continually disrupt that."

"You are casting abuse on love although you are a woman!"

"I do so because I am a woman. Love is an ideal to be worshipped by women. It is but another name for the eternal virtue of fidelity, an ideal to be striven for by women. It is not some primary instinct. I had dedicated myself to this ideal in this solitude despite all distractions and innumerable deceptions. I cannot safeguard my probity if I do not remain true to that ideal."

"Can you respect Bhabatosh?"

"No."

"Can you go to him?"

"No. And he is not the first love of my life either. Love to me today is impersonal. It does not have to assume form."

"I fail to understand you."

"And you never will. Your gifts are of the intellect and at the highest level it involves a knowledge that is impersonal. Women are gifted with sense perceptions of the external world—what can be seen, touched and enjoyed. Even so, something else remains and that is the idea of true love. It is beyond sense gratification; it is abstract and impersonal."

I said, "Look, there is no time left for us to wallow in argumentation. You have, perhaps, come to know through the local bulletin that my work here has come to an end. The assistant geologist has suggested that I look for places to dig at some distance from here, but . . ."

"Why not take it up?"

"I cannot till I know from you . . ."

"Know what is my last word, or the final decision? Is that it? You have already wrested from me what had been my initial response, no?"

"Yes, exactly."

"Then let me make a few things clear . . . I have been watching you without your knowing, sitting inside this woody grove for some time now. I have seen you at work through the day, braving the sun's immense heat and not looking out for human company. Sometimes, I have felt that you were filled with disappointment for not having found what you had been, with some certainty, looking for. But you never gave up and went back to digging without respite. As if a powerful mind hoisted on an equally Herculean body was on a victory march. I must confess I had never come across such devotion to science as yours, and had worshipped you from afar!"

"And now you . . ."

"It is not that . . . do let me continue. Your devotion to work weakened at the same ratio as my acquaintance with you gathered strength; you put aside your work for such trivial reasons. I became frightened about myself, about my female identity. And I castigated myself for disseminating the seeds of defeat in you. But this is looking at the situation from your point of view. Let me now tell you my side of the story. I also had a goal in life to cherish, an ideal to pursue. I knew for certain that devotion to the abstract would purify me, ennoble my existence. But I found myself continually backtracking. The agitation that overtook me had its roots in the primal urge that pervades this shaded forest land. At times, surrounded by all-embracing night, I have felt that there reigned in the woods some primary instinctual power that could easily snatch me away from Dadu, and that it was reaching out to me with its innumerable arms. I would jump out of bed and rush towards the waterfall and bathe myself gloriously in the streaming water at such moments . . ." and Achira called out, "Dadu," before she finished her sentence.

The Professor dropped what he was reading and came and stood in front of her. "What is it Didi?" he asked her affectionately.

"The other day, did you not say that the truth of man is expressed by his ability to embrace severe self-discipline, to adopt an ascetic way of life? It is not manifest in his physicality or in biology."

"Yes, that is what I say. On this earth the barbarian or the primitive man exists on the animal plane; it is only through self-abnegation, through the denial of everything material, that man becomes like a god.

The gods in the epics belong to the realm of imagination. They did not actually exist in the past although they will in the future. They will come into their own during the final stages of human history."

"Let us resolve our little quarrel, Dadu, it has been agitating my mind for some days now."

"Then I will take my leave," said I, getting ready to go.

"Not at all. You must stay . . . Dadu, the post of the principal which you had occupied in the college has become vacant. The secretary had written a letter begging you to take it up again. You show me all your letters but you hid this one from me. That is why, suspecting the worst, I stole the letter and read it."

"It is all my fault."

"You are not to blame. I have dragged you down from your exalted place. The likes of us only know how to do that!"

"What are you saying, Didi?"

"I am saying the truth. The Supreme One would become defunct if there were no universe, similarly you will be jobless without your students. Am I not right?"

"I have been a schoolteacher all my life, that is why . . ."

"You a schoolteacher—you are a born teacher, a guru. Your learning is not for self-gratification but for the edification of others. Have you not noticed that Nabinbabu? As soon as an idea comes to Dadu's mind he takes hold of me. He is without pity. I do not follow three-fourths of what he says. Then he sits with you and the situation turns even more intolerable for he cannot for the life of him comprehend the direction of your thinking. He presumes you are inclined towards pure science. Dadu—I know you need pupils but you must also learn how to discriminate."

The professor said, "But it is the student who chooses the teacher. It is his interest that guides the choice."

"That will do for now. It has occurred to me that I am reducing the pedagogue to his pedagogy, collapsing the differences for my reckless amusement. You must return to your calling; leave this place now."

The professor looked up at Achira, stunned. She continued, "Oh, I know, you are worried about my future no? You are my future—dear absent-minded professor! If you do not like me then you will have to acquire a second wife. I will sell off the library, deck her with jewels and disappear. Unless you think no end of yourself, you have to concede that you can not do without me for a second. If I am not around, you take 15 Ashwin for 15 October, and you shut yourself up in your library room and immerse yourself in solving a difficult problem just on the day you invite your junior colleague to your house for dinner! Getting inside the car you direct your driver to an address which simply does not exist. But Nabinbabu must think that I exaggerate?"

"Absolutely not. I have been observing him for some days now and I have no doubt that what you say about him is the unadulterated truth."

"Why are you uttering such unpleasant truths today, Achira? Do you know, Nabin—she has developed a tendency to indulge in such irrelevancies nowadays!"

"Everything will fall back into its proper place. Come, let's go back to your natural work routine. I will regain my normal heart beat, and stop all this rant."

"What would you advise?" The professor asked, looking up at me.

I was quiet for a while. I understood that he had such faith in the intelligence of a geologist because he was a man of learning. Then I said, "I do not think anyone else can advise you as truly as Achira Debi."

Achira got up and came and touched my feet. I moved back a few steps, extremely disconcerted. "Do not feel distressed," Achira said, "compared to you I do not count and in time this fact will come to be known and accepted. I am taking my final leave of you at this hour, in this very place. We will not meet again."

The professor was truly taken aback. "What are you saying, Didi?"

"Dadu, you know so much but have the humility to accept that in certain matters I am wiser than you," Achira answered.

I bowed to touch the professor's feet. He held me in his arms.

"I know that the path to fame is wide open to you," he said.

My little story ends here. The sequel belongs to the geologist. Returning home, I unlocked my research notes and the records of my findings. I felt suddenly very light-hearted, and realized that what I had experienced was perhaps the ultimate freedom. In the evening, after completing my days work, I came out into the verandah only to become aware that although the little bird had come out of its cage, a piece of shackle was still tied to its feet. It clinks with every movement.

1939

("Shesh Katha," from *Galpaguchchha*)
Translated by Rani Ray

The Tale of a Muslim Woman

It was a time when the rule of law in the land was threatened by the agents of anarchy. Every moment of night and day people trembled under unprecedented blows of tyranny. A nightmarish web seemed to tangle the most normal rituals of living. People put all their faith in God, living in imagined terror of false gods. It was impossible to trust anyone, be it god or man. Tears were their only recourse. It was difficult to distinguish between the consequences of good actions and bad ones, so faint had the borderline become. At every step people stumbled into calamities.

Under such circumstances, the birth of a beauteous daughter in someone's home seemed like a curse from the almighty. Relatives greeted the arrival of such a girl with curses, wishing that the wretched child would die. It was a nuisance of this kind that had arrived in the home of Bansibadan Talukdar of Tin Mohalla. Beautiful Kamala had lost her parents. The family would have breathed a sigh of relief if she had also perished with them. Instead, her uncle Bansibadan had so far brought her up with infinite love and great care.

Her aunt often complained to the neighbors, "Look at the unfairness of it all, my dears. Her parents left her behind to bring doom upon us. Anything can happen at a moment's notice. I have a house full of children. In the midst of it all she is like a burning brand. Evil-intentioned people lurk around eyeing her constantly. One of these days she alone will cause my complete ruin. This terror keeps me awake at night."

Somehow days passed in this manner. Then came a marriage proposal. How could one keep her safe amidst all the pomp and show of a wedding? Her uncle used to say: "That is why I am looking for a match for her from a family that would be able to protect her." The groom was the second son of Parmanand Seth of Mochakhali. He was heir to a huge treasury of cash, which was destined to disappear as soon as the father expired. The young man had decidedly luxurious tastes. He had no compunctions in practicing ways to make money vanish, such as hawking, gambling, staging bird fights with bulbuls. He was very proud of his wealth, of which he had a great deal. He deployed stout wrestlers from Bhojpur, each one a redoubtable wielder of bamboo clubs. He used to go around boasting that there was no one in the whole countryside who could lay a finger on him. The young man was quite a ladies' man. He already had a wife and was on the lookout for another nubile maiden. The news of Kamala's beauty reached his ears. Tremendously powerful and rich were the Seths. They were determined to acquire Kamala for their family.

Kamala wept before her uncle, "Kakamoni, why are you abandoning me?"

"My dear, you know that if I had the resources to keep you safe I would have cherished you for ever," replied the uncle.

The match having been finalized, the young man arrived with much aplomb to the wedding venue. There was no lack of pomp and show, of music and fanfare. Kamala's uncle folded his hands and urged, "Son, it is not wise to make such a display. Times are bad." In answer the young man swore arrogantly: "Let me see how anyone dares to confront me!"

Kaka pleaded, "Till the wedding ceremony is over, the girl is our responsibility. Then she belongs to you. You must take charge of seeing her home safely. We do not have the power to assume that responsibility."

"Have no fear," said the groom boastfully. The guards from

646

Bhojpur tugged at their moustaches and lined up, holding forth their bamboo clubs.

Accompanying his bride, the groom proceeded to cross the notorious expanse of Taltorir Math.

Modhumolla was the leader of a gang of dacoits. It was midnight, when with loud yells and flaming torches his gang rushed down upon the marriage party. Soon there were not many Bhojpuris to be seen. Modhumolla was a notorious dacoit; no mercy was to be expected if you fell into his hands.

Terrified, Kamala left her litter and was about to hide behind a bush, when behind her Habir Khan, feared by all like the Prophet himself, stood tall and called out, "Lads, keep your distance. Habir Khan is here." The dacoits protested, "Khan Sahib, we cannot disobey you. But why do you have to disrupt our trade?" Even so, they had to give up and leave the field. Habir approached Kamala and spoke, "Daughter, don't be afraid. Come home with me away from this ominous place." Kamala became extremely diffident. Habir said, "I understand. Daughter of a Hindu Brahmin family, you are hesitant about entering a Muslim home. But there is one thing you must realize. A true Mussalman will also respect a devout Brahmin. In my home you will be able to live the life of a Hindu woman. My name is Habir Khan. My house is nearby. Come with me. You will be completely safe."

Still, Kamala, a Brahmin woman, could not overcome her diffidence. Seeing this, Habir said, "Look, while I am alive, no one in this countryside will dare to touch your faith. Come with me. Don't be afraid."

Habir Khan took Kamala to his house. Surprisingly, amongst the eight levels of this Muslim estate, there was one part which housed a temple to Shiva and all the paraphernalia for Hindu rituals. An old Hindu Brahmin approached. He said, "Daughter, consider this place as pure as the home of a Hindu. There is no danger to your faith here."

Kamala burst into tears and said, "Have mercy. Please inform my Kaka. He will fetch me back."

Habir replied, "Child, you are mistaken. Now no one in your

family will accept you. They will throw you out into the street. Put it to test, if you will."

Habir Khan accompanied Kamala right up to the entrance of her uncle's home, and said, "I will wait for you here."

Entering the house, Kamala embraced her uncle and pleaded, "Kakamoni, don't abandon me." Tears fell from Kaka's eyes. Kaki saw her and shouted, "Get rid of her. Throw out this ill-omened girl. Wretch, have you no shame, to return from the abode of people of a different caste?" Kaka said, "There is no way out, my dear. This is a Hindu household. No one will accept you back. We will be thrown out of the community as well." Kamala sat for a while hanging her head. Then she slowly stepped out of the backdoor and left with Habir. Her uncle's door closed behind her forever.

In Habir Khan's home arrangements had been made for her to perform all her religious ceremonies. Habir Khan assured her, "None of my sons are going to enter your quarters. You will be able to carry out all your religious observances with the help of this old Brahmin."

This house had a certain history attached to it. People used to call this palace "Rajputani's Mahal." In the past a Nawab had brought a Rajput woman here.

But he had allowed her to keep her religion intact by letting her live separately.

She used to worship Shiva, and even travel on pilgrimages occasionally. Elite Muslims of those days respected staunch Hindus. In this mahal, all the Hindu begums who were given shelter by the Rajputani were able to preserve their beliefs and customs. It was said that Habir Khan was the son of that Rajput lady. Though he didn't follow his mother's religion, he worshipped her in his heart of hearts. His mother was no more. But in her memory he had adopted a mission to give succor to oppressed Hindu women who were exiled from their community.

From her own family Kamala had never received the love she was shown in this house. There her Kaki used to curse her. Constantly she had to hear that she was an ill-omened one, liable to cause total ruin, that she had brought misfortune with her, that only at her death would the family gain deliverance. Secretly her Kaka used to buy her a few clothes, but it had to be kept hidden from her Kaki. After arriving in Rajputani's Mahal, Kamala was treated like a queen. Here there was no end to the love and care she received. She was surrounded by many servants, all from Hindu families.

Eventually the bloom of youth filled her body. Secretly a son of the house began visiting Kamala's mahal. The two of them fell in love.

She said to Habir Khan, "Baba, I have no religion. My faith lies in the one whom I love. I could never find the face of God in a religion which denied me all kinds of love that life offers and flung me in the garbage heap of neglect and indifference. I cannot forget that their God humiliated me every day. Bapjan, it was in your home that I experienced love for the first time. I realized that even an unfortunate girl has some worth. The God who sheltered me, and gave me recognition and love, he alone is my God. I worship him. He is neither a Hindu nor a Muslim. I have given my heart to your second son Karim. My faith and worship inheres in him. Baptize me as a Muslim. I have no objections. Let me belong to both faiths."

Heretofore their life followed a new course. Any contact with her family was now out of the question. In an attempt to make Kamala forget that she was different from his family, Habir Khan named her Meherjan.

Then it was time for the marriage of her uncle's second daughter. Arrangements were made as before. Once again the same danger befell them. On the way, creating a great uproar, the same dacoits attacked. They had felt thwarted at having been cheated of their prey once. Now they were determined to avenge that.

But closely following their shout was heard another roar, "Beware!"

"Oh ho! Here come the followers of Habir Khan to spoil everything."

The bride's party looked for ways to escape, leaving the bride behind in her litter. Then from their midst arose the tip of a spear with the flag of Habir Khan bearing its emblem of the crescent moon. Fearlessly stood a woman holding that spear.

She addressed Sarala, "Sister, you have nothing to be afraid of. For you I have promise of shelter from one who protects everyone, he never discriminates on the basis of faith or caste . . . Kaka, I greet you. Have no fear, I will not touch your feet. Now take her home with you. No one has touched or defiled her. Tell Kaki, for many years I have been nourished on food and clothing provided by her so grudgingly, but I never imagined that I would be able to pay off that debt so fittingly. Here is a red wedding garment and a brocade cushion. Let my sister remember, if she ever faces any trouble, her Muslim sister will be ready to protect her."

1955, posthumously; the draft story was composed in June 1941
("Musalmanir Galpa," from *Galpaguchchha*)
Translated by Kalyani Dutta

8

Novels

TAGORE IS KNOWN TO THE WORLD primarily as a poet, mystic, and nature-lover, but it is important not to underestimate his novels, which represent another significant dimension of his creative genius. He wrote his first novel when he was barely seventeen. *Karuna (Pity)* was serialized in the periodical *Bharati* from 1877–1878 but not published as a book. The novel form had already been introduced into Bengali literature by Bankimchandra Chatterjee. Bankim's influence is evident in Tagore's early historical romances, *Bouthakuranir Haat* (1883) and *Rajarshi* (1887, later dramatized as *Visarjan*). Tagore's novel *Chirakumar Sabha* (a comic romance later converted into a successful play), serialized in *Bharati* from April 1900 to May 1901, was renamed *Prajapatir Nirbandha* when it appeared as a book in 1907–1908.

It was with *Chokher Bali* (*Binodini,* 1903) that Tagore made a conscious break with Bankim's plot-driven and history-centered narratives, announcing in his preface the advent of the modern, psychological novel: "The literature of the new age seeks not to narrate a sequence of events, but to reveal the secrets of the heart." In his bold depiction of the forbidden desires aroused when an attractive young widow Binodini enters the lives of a newly married couple and their friend Bihari, Tagore tries to steer clear of sensationalism and narrow moralizing to probe the inner impulses of his characters.

With *Gora* (1910), a monumental novel about a group of characters caught up in the turmoil of rising nationalist sentiment in Bengal, Tagore began experimenting with the novel of ideas. He was deeply affected by the Swadeshi movement that gathered momentum after the first Partition of Bengal by the British in 1905, but soon became disenchanted with the militant version of Hindu nationalism. He was also disturbed by the conflict between orthodox Hindus and reformist Brahmos, and by the spectacle of a society divided by inequalities of class, caste, religion, and gender. *Gora* was serialized in the journal *Prabasi* from 1907 to 1910, and appeared as a book in 1910. Through the character of its eponymous hero, who thinks himself to be a Brahmin until he discovers that he is Irish, the novel critiques the idea of a "pure" identity. Though set in the late nineteenth century, *Gora,* often read as a postcolonial rewriting of Kipling's *Kim,* resonates with ideas, debates, and controversies more in tune with the historical moment of its composition.

Ghare Baire (*The Home and the World,* 1916), Tagore's best-known novel, is set during the Swadeshi Movement of 1905, when Indian women stepped out of seclusion to participate in the nationalist struggle. Through the intertwined lives of the visionary but politically ineffective landowner Nikhil, the flamboyant, militant nationalist Sandip, and Nikhil's wife Bimala, torn by her divided loyalties, the sophisticated, multivoiced narrative lays bare the troubled interface between the confines of home and the turbulent world outside. Georg Lukacs criticized the novel for presenting "a contemptible caricature of Gandhi," forgetting that the narrative is set in a period that precedes Gandhi's rise. But Bertolt Brecht recognized this as a "wonderful book, strong and gentle," about the limitations of nationalism (26 September 1920, *Diaries 1920–1922,* 55). *Chaturanga (Quartet),* published in the same year, traces the complex undercurrents of desire that develop between Sachish, a former atheist who becomes an ascetic, his friend Sribilash (also the narrator), and Damini, a passionate woman who destabilizes Sachish's holy pursuits.

In 1929, *Jogajog (Connections)* and *Shesher Kabita (Farewell Song)* were published. These two major novels contrast starkly with each other in tone, technique, and narrative content. Extracts from both are included here. *Jogajog,* a dark, brooding tale about the young woman Kumudini, trapped in a family feud between her husband Madhusudan and her beloved brother Bipradas, presents a society in transition, where declining aristocratic order gives way to the cruder but more robust ways of an emergent mercantile class. Serialized in the journal *Bichitra* from 1928–1929, it appeared in book form in 1929. The first two installments of the serial bore the title *Teen Purush (Three Generations).* In the third installment, the text was renamed *Jogajog.* Tagore explains this change of title in the defense *(Kaifiat)* published in the October 1927 issue of *Bichi-*

tra. Teen Purush, he claims, was an exploratory working title, which he discarded when it threatened to impose preconditions upon his narrative. Instead, he chose a title so general that it would leave the writer's creative imagination unfettered. *Jogajog* is remarkable for its use of marital discord, especially sexual hostility, as a way of exploring class antagonisms.

Shesher Kabita, an effervescent blend of sharp satire and tender romance, is Tagore's answer to his detractors, who claimed that he had lost his capacity for innovation. Serialized in *Prabasi* from 1928–1929, it was published as a book in 1929. The Amit-Labanya love story occupies an almost legendary place in the Bengali imagination because of its representation of romantic bliss without the mundane constraints of marriage. The narrative is interspersed with poetic exchanges and allusions to love poetry through the ages, generating a lively debate about modernity and literary value. Tagore's style, ranging between epigrammatic wit and exquisite lyricism, demonstrates his capacity to cross the dividing lines between different genres, combining prose with poetry, and satire with romance. Tagore at this time had begun his experiments with painting. In its evocative descriptions of landscape and vivid "portraits" of various characters, this text reveals a strong connection with the visual arts.

In his last novel *Char Adhyay (Four Chapters,* 1934), Tagore resumes his exploration of the impact of political issues on personal lives. The protagonist Atindra is probably modeled on Brahmabandhab Upadhyay, a man of ascetic temperament who became a fiery nationalist in reaction to Lord Curzon's attempt to divide Bengal. Upadhyay, Tagore suggests, eventually began to feel trapped by the duties he had imposed on himself. The novel sparked a sharp controversy about Tagore's politics, but in self-defense, he insisted that the representation of political revolution in the text is important only insofar as it impinges on the relationship between Atindra and the female protagonist Ela. This novel is significant for Tagore's ability to distance himself from topical issues, to take a broader view of history.

In his later texts, Tagore's preoccupation with language is intensified into a kind of self-reflexivity, a meditation on language itself. His novels tend to be episodic in structure, probably because they were usually serialized in periodicals before they appeared as books. He found this method of composition congenial, as he explained to John Graham Drummond in a letter (21 January 1920): "I need, for keeping up my own interest in writing, fresh shocks of surprises in the growth of my story—and therefore I never think of a plot but only a central situation which has psychological possibilities."

Several of Tagore's novels have been adapted for the stage and screen, in various languages. Tagore himself wrote a dramatized version of *Jogajog,* for instance, and Shambhu Mitra attempted a memorable stage adaptation of *Char Adhyay* in 1951. Well-known cinematic renderings include Satyajit Ray's film *Ghare Baire* (1984), Kumar Shahani's *Char Adhyay* (1997), and Rituparno Ghosh's *Chokher Bali* (Hindi, 2003).

Tagore's evolution as a novelist reveals his lifelong interest in the relationship between individual and society. The narrative voice that emerges in many of his novels is wry, witty, and often self-critical. His protagonists are subjected to penetrating, unsparing psychological scrutiny, and placed in relationships and situations that reveal Tagore's sympathetic, yet always critical, understanding of the broad social processes that shape human character. In dealing with fractured realities, Tagore favors the dialogic form, which permits the exploration of diverse, often contradictory ideas. As Amartya Sen says: "It is in the sovereignty of reasoning—fearless reasoning in freedom—that we can find Rabindranath Tagore's lasting voice" (*Argumentative Indian,* 120).

From *Gora*

27

At sunset, Magistrate Brownlow was walking along the riverside path. With him was Haranbabu. Not far away, his wife, the mem, was savoring the air in the motor car, along with Poreshbabu's daughters.

From time to time, Brownlow saheb would invite the Bengali *bhadralok* to garden parties at his house. It was he who acted as chief guest at prize distribution ceremonies at the district entrance school. If invited to wedding rituals at some well-to-do person's house, he would accept the householder's hospitality. In fact, when invited to a jatragaan performance of songs from indigenous popular theatre, he would recline on a large armchair and, for a while, patiently try to listen to the music. During the last puja, he had particularly appreciated the performance of the two lads who had played the bhisti or water-carrier and the methrani or scavenger-woman, in the jatra enacted at the house of the government pleader at his court. At his request, their scene had been replayed for his benefit more than once.

His wife was a missionary's daughter. Sometimes, they hosted a tea for missionary women at their house. He had established a girls' school in the district, and tried very hard to ensure that it had no shortage of students. He always encouraged the educational discussions he had witnessed among the female members of Poreshbabu's house. He would drop them a line every now and then, even when he was far away, and send them religious books for Christmas.

The mela was on. Borodasundari and the girls, accompanied by Haranbabu, Sudhir and Binoy, were present at the occasion, all of them. They had been offered accommodation at the Inspection Bungalow. Poreshbabu had no patience for such noisy events; he had stayed behind in Kolkata, by himself. Sucharita had tried very hard to remain with him, to give him company, but advising her strongly that it was her duty to respect the magistrate's invitation, Poresh sent her away. It had been decided that on the next day but one, in the presence of the Commissioner Saheb and the Lieutenant Governor and his wife, during the after-dinner party at the magistrate's house, Poreshbabu's daughters would perform and recite. Many of the magistrate's British friends from the district as well as from Kolkata had been invited to the event. A few select Bengali bhadraloks were also to attend. There would even be snacks prepared for them by Brahman cooks in a garden tent, or so it was rumored.

In a very short time, Haranbabu had succeeded in winning the heart of the magistrate saheb by virtue of his lofty conversation. The saheb had been amazed at Haranbabu's extraordinary knowledge of Christian theology, and he had even asked Haranbabu why he had the slightest hesitation in embracing the Christian faith. This afternoon, pacing the riverside path, he was deeply engaged in discussion with Haranbabu about Brahmo and Hindu practices. At this juncture, Gora appeared before him.

"Good evening, sir," he said.

Trying to meet the magistrate the previous day, he had realized that he must grease the sentry's palm to cross the saheb's threshold. Unwilling to tolerate such subjugation and insult, he had come to meet the saheb during his outing today. During this interchange, Haranbabu and Gora showed no sign of mutual recognition.

The saheb was rather perplexed when he saw this man. He could not recall having encountered such a person in Bengal, more than six feet tall, heavy-boned, sturdy. Even his complexion was unlike that of the ordinary Bengali. Khaki shirt, coarse, faded dhoti, bamboo stave in hand, chador wound around his head like a turban.

"I've just come from Ghoshpur Chor," Gora told the magistrate.

The magistrate gave a surprised whistle. He had received news, the previous day, that an outsider was obstructing the investigations at Ghoshpur. So this was the man!

"What is your caste?" he asked Gora, surveying him once from top to toe.

"I am a Bengali Brahman."

"Oh! Do you have any connections with the press?"

"No."

"Then what are you doing at Ghoshpur Chor?"

"I took shelter there during my wanderings. Having witnessed the predicament of the village under police torture, and realizing the likelihood of further trouble, I have come to you to ask for redress."

"Are you aware that the people at Ghoshpur Chor are utter scoundrels?"

"They're no scoundrels. They're bold and independent, unable to endure unjust oppression in silence."

The magistrate was incensed. He concluded privately that this new Bengali had learned to parrot some words gleaned from history books. This was insufferable!

"You understand nothing of the present situation!" roared the magistrate.

"You know much less than me about the situation here," thundered Gora in reply.

"I warn you," declared the magistrate, "if you interfere in the Ghoshpur matter in any way, you will not get off easily."

"Since you have decided not to counter the injustice that is taking place, and since your attitude towards the villagers is predetermined and unshakable, I have no choice but to incite the villagers against the police, by my own efforts."

"What!" The magistrate stopped suddenly in his tracks. "How dare you!" he roared, wheeling about to face Gora.

Gora stalked away slowly, without uttering another word.

"Haranbabu," said the magistrate, "what does the behavior of your countrymen signify?"

"It's due to lack of in-depth study, especially due to the total absence of spiritual and ethical education in our country that all this is happening," Haranbabu asserted. "They have not yet earned the right to receive the best of English education. If these ungrateful people are reluctant even now to acknowledge British rule in India as God's decree, it's only because they have merely learned by rote. Their religious sense is extremely underdeveloped."

"Without embracing Christianity, people's religious sense will never develop to maturity in India," the magistrate declared.

"In a sense, that is true," Haranbabu assented. He had then engaged the magistrate in a discussion of his possible conversion to Christianity, making fine distinctions between where his opinions coincided with or differed from a Christian's. So deeply had he kept the magistrate engrossed that when the memsaheb, returning in the carriage after dropping Poreshbabu's daughters at the dak bungalow, called to her husband: "Harry, we must go home," the magistrate gave a start, took out his watch and exclaimed: "By Jove, it's eight twenty!"

Before stepping into the car, he wrung Haranbabu's hand. "Our discussion has made this evening very enjoyable," he said, by way of fare-well.

Back at the dak bungalow, Haranbabu recounted his interchange with the magistrate in detail. But he made no mention of his encounter with Gora.

28

Forty-seven accused persons had been condemned to prison without be-ing tried for any crime, just to keep the village under control. After his meeting with the magistrate, Gora set out in search of a lawyer. Someone told him that Satkori Haldar was a good lawyer.

"Wah, it's Gora, isn't it?" exclaimed Satkori, as soon as Gora ar-rived at his house. "What brings you here?" It was as Gora had thought: Satkori was his classmate.

"The accused at Ghoshpur must be released on bail and their cases fought in court," Gora declared.

"Who will stand security for bail?" Satkori asked.

"I will."

"What resources do you possess, to stand guarantor for forty-seven persons on bail?"

"If all the mukhtars, the legal representatives, collectively offer se-curity, I shall pay their fees."

"It won't be a small amount."

The next day, they applied for bail at the magistrate's court. Look-ing askance at the previous day's hero dressed in his faded garments and turban, the magistrate ignored the request. From a fourteen-year-old boy to an old man of eighty, all the accused were condemned to rot in jail.

Gora requested Satkori to defend their case.

"Where will you find witnesses?" Satkori asked him. "All potential witnesses are among the accused. Moreover, the people of this area are overwrought due to the investigation into the case of those murdered sa-hebs. The magistrate is convinced there is a secret bhadralok hand in this whole affair. Who knows, perhaps he even suspects me! The English pa-pers keep saying that if the local people are incited to such daring, the unprotected, helpless British can't survive in the provincial areas anymore. Meanwhile, things have reached a stage where our countrymen can't survive in their own land. I know there is oppression, but there's nothing we can do."

"Why not?" thundered Gora.

"You're exactly as you were in school, I see," smiled Satkori. "When I say there's nothing we can do, I mean we have wives and children at home. If we don't earn our daily bread, many will go hungry. There aren't many in this world willing to give up their lives shouldering other people's burdens, especially in a country where the family is not taken lightly. Those with many dependents have no time for the problems of all and sundry."

"So you'll do nothing for these people?" said Gora. "If, by a motion in the high court, we . . ."

"Arre, they've killed Englishmen, don't you see!" cried Satkori impatiently. "Every Englishman is a raja, after all. To murder even an ordinary Englishman amounts to a minor act of treason. I can't let myself fall into the magistrate's bad books in a false bid to achieve something futile."

Gora set out the next morning, planning to catch the ten-thirty train to Kolkata, to see if some lawyer there could help him with the case, when he encountered an obstacle. To coincide with the local mela, a cricket tournament had been scheduled, between students from Kolkata and the local students' team. The Kolkata boys were playing amongst themselves to hone their skills. One of the boys was severely hurt when the cricket ball hit him on the leg. There was a large pond at the end of the field. Carrying the injured boy to the pond's edge, a couple of students shredded a chador, soaked the strips and began to bandage his leg with them. Suddenly, a watchman appeared from nowhere, and shoved a student by the shoulder, abusing him in obscene language. The Kolkata students did not know that it was forbidden to enter this pond because it was reserved for drinking water. Even had they known, they were not used to accepting such sudden humiliation from a watchman. Being physically strong as well, they began to suitably avenge the insult. Witnessing this spectacle, four or five constables rushed to the spot. At that very moment, Gora arrived on the scene. The students recognized Gora, for he had often played cricket with them.

"Don't hit them! I warn you!" cried Gora, unable to bear the sight of the students being beaten and dragged away.

When the watchman's party swore abominably at Gora as well, he created such a commotion, hitting and kicking them, that a crowd collected on the street. Meanwhile, the students quickly formed a cluster. As soon as they attacked the police, at Gora's urging and command, the watchman's party beat a hasty retreat. Onlookers in the street found this highly amusing. But needless to say, this spectacle did not remain a mere piece of entertainment for Gora.

At around three or four in the afternoon, when Binoy, Haranbabu and the girls were busy rehearsing at the dak bungalow, a couple of students known to Binoy came and reported that Gora and a few students had been arrested by the police and put in the lockup. The following day, the case would come up at the magistrate's very first session in court. Gora in the lockup! Everyone but Haranbabu was dumbfounded. Binoy immediately rushed to their classmate Satkori Haldar and having first told him the whole story, took him along to the lockup. Satkori offered to defend Gora in court, and to try getting him out on bail at once.

"No," said Gora. "I won't engage a lawyer, and there's no need to try and get me out on bail either."

How could he say that!

"Look at this!" expostulated Satkori, turning to Binoy. "Who would think Gora was out of school! His mindset remains exactly the same."

"I don't want to be free of lockup and handcuffs simply because I'm fortunate enough to have money and friends," declared Gora. "According to our nation's religious law, we know it is the ruler's responsibility to ensure justice; it's the ruler who must be blamed if his subjects suffer injustice. But in this kingdom, if subjects must rot in the lockup and die in jail because they can't afford the lawyer's fee, if even under a king's rule one must go bankrupt trying to buy a fair verdict with money, I wouldn't spend a paisa on such justice."

"But in the days of the kazis, one had to sell one's soul to afford the bribes," Satkori pointed out.

"But bribery was not the ruler's decree," Gora insisted. "Corrupt kazis would demand bribes, and that continues even in the present regime. But now, to seek justice at the ruler's door, the subject must suffer, be he plaintiff or defendant, guilty or innocent. For the destitute, both victory and defeat spell disaster in their fight for justice. And where the ruler is the plaintiff and the defendant is a man like me, lawyers and barristers would all take his side. And as for me, I'd be lucky to find someone, or else I'm at the mercy of my fate! If a court case doesn't need a lawyer's assistance, why have government lawyers at all? If legal help is necessary, why must the party opposing the government have to find his own lawyer? Does this make the government an enemy of the nation's subjects? What sort of political ideology is this?"

"Bhai, my brother, why are you so angry?" asked Satkori. "Civilization is no cheap affair. For fine judgment, fine laws must be formulated, and to create fine laws, one must become a trader in law. To run a business you must buy and sell, hence the court of justice called civilization automatically becomes a market where judgments can be bought and sold. And it will remain likely that a person without money will have a raw deal. Tell me, what would you do if you were king?"

"If I created laws impenetrable even for a judge on a salary of a thousand rupees or a thousand-and-a-half, I would employ government-paid lawyers for both unfortunate parties, plaintiff and defendant alike. I wouldn't insult the Pathans and Mughals, vaunting the fairness of my own judgment while forcing my subjects to bear the costs of a well-conducted trial."

"Good idea," said Satkori, "but since that auspicious day has not yet arrived, since you have not become king, since at present you are the defendant of a civilized monarch's court, you must either spend from your own pocket or seek the help of a lawyer friend. Or the third option would not be pleasant for you."

"Let my fate be that which comes of making no effort," said Gora obstinately. "Let me share the fate of those who are utterly helpless in this kingdom."

Binoy tried very hard to persuade him, but Gora paid no heed to his pleas.

"How did you suddenly turn up here?" he asked Binoy.

Binoy flushed slightly. Had Gora not been confined in the lockup,

Binoy might have explained his presence in defiant terms. But now he could not offer an outspoken reply.

"We'll talk about my affairs later . . ." he demurred. "Now as for you . . ."

"Today, I am a royal guest," declared Gora. "Today, the king himself is concerned about me, so none of you need have any concern."

Knowing it was impossible to sway Gora, Binoy had to relinquish his efforts to engage a lawyer.

"I know you can't swallow the food here," he said. "I'll arrange to have some food sent to you from outside."

"Binoy, why do you struggle in vain?" cried Gora, losing his patience. "I don't want anything from outside. I want nothing more than what's meted out to everyone in the lockup."

Binoy went back to the dak bungalow with a heavy heart. In a bedroom facing the street, Sucharita was awaiting his return, with her door shut and window open. She could not bear the company and conversation of others. Seeing Binoy approach the dak bungalow looking worried and dejected, her heart lurched in fear. Forcing herself to remain calm, she picked up a book and made her way to the drawing room. Lalita did not enjoy needlework, but today she was sewing silently in a corner. Labanya was playing a spelling game with Sudhir, with Leela as her audience. Haranbabu was discussing the next day's festivities with Borodasundari.

Binoy gave them a detailed account of Gora's confrontation with the police early that morning. Sucharita sat frozen still. The sewing fell from Lalita's lap and her face grew flushed.

"Have no fear, Binoybabu," Borodasundari assured him. "This evening, I shall personally petition the magistrate saheb and his mem on Gora's behalf."

"No," said Binoy, "please don't do that. If Gora hears of it, he will never forgive me all his life."

"But we must make some arrangements for his defense," Sudhir insisted.

Binoy told them all about Gora's objections to seeking bail or engaging a lawyer.

"This is too much!" exclaimed Haranbabu impatiently.

Whatever Lalita's opinion of Haranbabu, she had shown him deference up until now, and had never argued with him. But now she burst out, shaking her head violently:

"It's not too much at all! Gourbabu has done the right thing. If magistrates entrap us, are we supposed to defend ourselves? Must we provide taxes for them to receive a fat salary, and then pay a lawyer from our own pockets to escape their clutches! Better go to jail than receive such justice."

Haranbabu had known Lalita since she was very tiny; he had never dreamt that she had opinions of her own. He was amazed to hear such sharp words from her lips.

"What do you understand of such things?" he admonished her reprovingly. "You are carried away by the irresponsible, frenzied delirium of those who have just cleared college by learning a few books by rote, those who have no religion, no considered opinions."

He proceeded to recount Gora's meeting with the magistrate the previous evening, and his own discussion about it with the magistrate. Binoy was unaware of the incident at the Ghoshpur Chor. Hearing about it, he was filled with apprehension, realizing that the magistrate would not easily forgive Gora. Haran's purpose in telling this story was completely thwarted. Sucharita was wounded by the secret pettiness of his having kept his meeting with Gora a total secret until now. Haranbabu's personal envy of Gora, evident in every word he uttered, elicited the disrespect of all present, at this time when Gora was in trouble. Sucharita had remained silent, but now she felt the urge to say something. Controlling herself, she opened her book and began to turn the pages with trembling hands.

"However closely Haranbabu's views might match the magistrate's, the Ghoshpur affair has demonstrated the greatness of Gourmohanbabu!" declared Lalita with pride.

29

Because the lieutenant governor was expected that day, the magistrate arrived at the courthouse punctually at half past ten, and tried to dispense with the day's legal business as early as possible.

Satkoribabu tried to save his friend by defending the schoolboys. Given the circumstances, he had realized that pleading guilty was the best strategy here. He pleaded for mercy, arguing that boys were naturally mischievous, that they had acted immaturely and foolishly, and so on. The magistrate ordered that the boys be taken to jail, and caned five to twenty times, according to their age and the gravity of their offense. Gora had no lawyer to defend him. In his own defense, he tried to say something about police torture. The magistrate at once silenced him with a sharp reprimand, sentenced him to a month's rigorous imprisonment for obstructing police activities, and acclaimed this "light" sentence as extremely lenient.

Sudhir and Binoy were present in the courtroom. Binoy could not bear to meet Gora's eyes. Feeling suffocated, he rushed from the courtroom. Sudhir begged him to return to the dak bungalow for his bath and breakfast, but he would not listen. He walked some distance down the path that skirted the field, and collapsed under a tree.

"Go back to the bungalow," he told Sudhir. "I'll come after a while."

Sudhir went away. How long he remained in this state, Binoy had no idea. When the sun that had been directly overhead was declining westwards, a carriage stopped just in front of him. Raising his head, Binoy saw Sudhir and Sucharita dismount and approach him. Quickly, he rose to his feet.

"Come, Binoybabu," pleaded Sucharita tenderly, coming up close.

Binoy suddenly realized that people on the street were highly entertained at this spectacle. He quickly stepped into the carriage. Nobody said a word, all the way. Arriving at the dak bungalow, Binoy found that a fight had broken out there. Lalita had stubbornly refused to participate in the magistrate's program that evening, under any circumstances. Borodasundari was in a grave dilemma. Haranbabu was outraged at such inappropriate rebelliousness in a girl so young. "How perverted today's youngsters have become!" he kept exclaiming. "They won't observe any discipline! This is the outcome of discussing all sorts of ideas in the company of all sorts of people."

"Forgive me Binoybabu," Lalita blurted out as soon as Binoy arrived. "I have wronged you greatly. I had not understood any of your words before this. It's due to our total ignorance about the outside world that our notions are so mistaken. Panubabu says it's by God's decree that magistrates rule Bharatvarsha. In that case, it's by the same God's decree that one feels a heartfelt desire to curse this rule."

"Lalita, you . . ." began Haranbabu angrily.

"Please be quiet!" Lalita interrupted, turning her back on Haranbabu. "I am not speaking to you. Binoybabu, please ignore all requests. The show cannot be allowed to take place today."

"Lalita, you are quite amazing, I must say!" Borodasundari hastily intervened, to silence Lalita's outburst. "Won't you give Binoybabu a chance to bathe and eat today? It's one-thirty already, do you realize? See how drained he looks!"

"Here we are guests of the magistrate," declared Binoy. "I can't bathe or dine in this house."

Borodasundari pleaded with Binoy, trying hard to persuade him. Observing the girls' silence, she scolded them angrily:

"What's the matter with all of you? Shuchi, why don't you try to explain to Binoybabu? We have given them our word. People have been invited. We must somehow manage this occasion, or what will they think, tell me! We could never face them again."

Sucharita bowed her head in silence.

Binoy left by steamer from the riverside not far away. The steamer with its passengers would depart for Kolkata in a couple of hours, to arrive there at approximately eight o'clock the next day.

Haranbabu began to agitatedly criticize Gora and Binoy. Quickly rising from her chowki, Sucharita went into the adjacent room and slammed the door. Soon afterwards, Lalita pushed the door open and came in. She saw Sucharita lying on the bed, both hands covering her face. Locking the door from within, Lalita gently sat down beside her, and began to run her fingers through Sucharita's hair. After a long while, when Sucharita had calmed down, Lalita prised away the arms shielding her face, and bent close to whisper in Sucharita's ear:

"Didi, let's go back to Kolkata. After all, we can't go to the magistrate's tonight."

For a long time, Sucharita offered no answer. When Lalita persisted, she sat up in bed.

"How is that possible my dear?" she said. "I had no wish to come here. But since Baba has sent me here, I can't leave without completing my undertaking."

"But Baba knows nothing of what has transpired. Had he known, he would never have asked us to stay on."

"That I couldn't say, bhai!"

"Didi, can you really bring yourself to do it?" asked Lalita. "Tell me, how can you go there? And then, we must don our costumes to recite poems on stage! Even if I bit my tongue till it bled, I couldn't utter a word!"

"I know that bon, sister of mine! But even hell must be endured. There's no way out now. I'll never forget this day, all my life!"

Incensed at Sucharita's compliance, Lalita left her room.

"Aren't all of you going, Ma?" she asked.

"Have you lost your mind?" said Borodasundari. "We're supposed to go there after nine."

"I'm talking about going to Kolkata."

"Listen, just listen to this girl!"

"Sudhirda, will you remain here as well?" Lalita demanded.

Sudhir's heart was broken at the sentence passed on Gora, but he lacked the capacity to resist the temptation of displaying his learning before all those powerful sahebs. He uttered something inarticulate, signifying that although he was hesitant, he would stay back, after all.

"With all this confusion, it's already very late," Borodasundari interrupted. "We can't delay any longer. Now nobody must arise from bed before five-thirty—you have to rest. Otherwise you'll get tired and look haggard in the evening, and what an ugly sight that would be!"

She firmly propelled everyone to their rooms and to bed. They all went to sleep. Only Sucharita could not sleep, and in another room Lalita remained sitting upright in bed.

The steamer horn sounded, again and again.

As the steamer was preparing to leave and the sailors were about to draw up the gangway, from the upper deck Binoy saw a woman, seemingly from a respectable bhadra family, rushing towards the vessel. From her attire and appearance she looked like Lalita, but Binoy could not immediately believe it. Ultimately, when she came closer, he was left in no doubt. For a moment he thought she had come to take him back, but it was Lalita after all who had opposed their participation in the magistrate's program. She boarded the steamer. The sailors pulled up the gangway. Full of foreboding, Binoy descended from the upper deck to face Lalita.

"Take me to the upper deck," she said.

"But the steamer is about to leave," protested Binoy.

"I know."

Without waiting for Binoy she ascended to the upper deck. Sounding its horn, the steamer set out.

Having offered Lalita an armchair on the first-class deck, Binoy looked at her questioningly without saying a word.

"I'm going to Kolkata," she said. "I found it impossible to stay on."

"What about all of them?"

"They don't know as yet, any of them. I've left a letter; as soon as they read it, they will know."

Binoy was astounded at Lalita's daring.

"But . . ." he faltered.

"The steamer has left, so there's no room for ifs and buts!" she quickly interrupted. "I don't understand why I must bear everything in silence just because I'm born a woman. Even women are capable of distinguishing between just and unjust, possible and impossible. I'd rather commit suicide than perform at tonight's event."

Binoy realized that now the deed was done, it was no use brooding over the pros and cons of having taken such a step.

"Look," Lalita resumed after a short silence, "privately, I had gravely misjudged your friend Gourmohanbabu. I don't know why, from the moment I saw him and heard him speak, my heart grew averse to him. He spoke too forcefully, and all of you seemed to comply. This used to make me angry. Such is my nature—if I see anyone use force in their speech and behavior, I just can't tolerate it. Gourmohanbabu exerts force not only on others, though, but also on himself. That is real power. I have never seen such a person."

Lalita prattled on in this fashion. Not that she was saying all this only from remorse about Gora. Actually, embarrassment at her impulsive act was constantly threatening to make itself felt. She was beginning to doubt whether she had acted wisely. Until now, she had never imagined how awkward it might be to confront Binoy alone on the steamer. But because the slightest expression of shame would at once make the whole affair utterly shameful, she desperately babbled on. Binoy found himself at a loss for words. For one thing there was Gora's misery and humiliation, then the shame of having come here to entertain himself at the magistrate's house, and to top it all, this sudden predicament created by Lalita. All this, taken together, had rendered Binoy speechless.

On earlier occasions, such daring on Lalita's part would have evoked Binoy's disapproval, but today, that did not happen at all. In fact, the amazement aroused in him was mingled with respect. There was the added satisfaction that, out of their entire group, only Binoy and Lalita had made the slightest attempt to oppose Gora's humiliation. For this, Binoy would not have to suffer too much, but Lalita's act would cause her great torment, for a long time to come. Yet Binoy had always regarded the same Lalita as hostile to Gora. The more he thought about it, the more he began to respect Lalita's courage, so heedless of her actions' outcome, and her extreme contempt for injustice. He could not think of a way to demonstrate or articulate this respect. Binoy was haunted by the feeling that Lalita's disdain for him as a spineless person constantly relying on others' views was entirely justified. He could never have forcefully disregarded the approval and disapproval of all relatives and friends, to express his own views on any subject through courageous action in this fashion. Today, secretly acknowledging that he had often avoided following his own instincts for fear of hurting Gora's feelings or appearing weak in Gora's eyes, and that he had often used a web of subtle arguments to delude himself that Gora's ideas were his own, he admitted that Lalita was vastly his superior in her capacity for independent thought. He was ashamed to remember that he had often privately censured Lalita. Indeed, he wanted to apologize to her, but could not think of a way. Binoy saw Lalita's graceful feminine figure illumined by such inner glory, that he felt that this revelation of woman's uniqueness had made his own life worthwhile. Today he surrendered all his pride, all his pettiness, to this shakti, this power infused with sweetness.

1910
(From *Gora*)
Translated by Radha Chakravarty

671

From *Connections*

56

Two days later Nabin brought Motirma and Hablu on a visit. Hablu got into his aunt's arms and wept with his head on her chest. It was hard to say why he wept—whether it was a demand for affection that he had long missed or the expression of apprehension for the future.

Kumu hugged him and said, "It's a tough world, Gopal, there's no end to tears here. What do I have that will assuage the tears of our children?"

"We'll go away to our ancestral home in Rajabpur," Nabin said. "The episode here is over."

"All because of this poor wretch," Kumu said sadly.

"It's the other way round," said Nabin. "I'd been thinking of leaving for a long time. I was getting ready for the move when you came. I'd had enough of that household, but the Lord had other ideas!"

It was clear that Madhusudan had kicked up quite a fuss when he got home that day.

Nabin's words notwithstanding, Motirma had no doubts it was Kumu who had turned the household topsy-turvy, and this was a crime she could not readily forgive. She thought Kumu ought to return to her husband with bowed head and accept whatever persecution was to follow. "Will you never go back to your husband?" she asked sternly.

"No, I won't," said Kumu firmly.

"Where will you go then?" Motirma asked.

"I'll be able to find a place for myself in this vast world," said Kumu. "Even when one has lost everything in life, something still remains."

Kumu realized that Motirma had little sympathy for her. She turned to Nabin and asked, "What will you do now?"

"I own some land by the river. That will bring us coarse rice, and there's clean air to breathe."

"No, sir," said Motirma with some heat. "We have some rights on the Mirzapur Palace that none can take away. We are not so proud that we'll leave for good at the slightest rebuke from the master of the household. He'll call us back again, and when he does we'll come back. Meanwhile we'll wait patiently."

"I know that," said Nabin. "But that's not something to be proud of. If there is rebirth I'd like to be born with some pride, even if it meant being hard up!"

Nabin had in fact often thought of abandoning the protection of his elder brother and taking up farming. Motirma had voiced her discontent with her situation, but when it came to the crunch she refused to budge and held Nabin back. She believed she had a claim on her brother-in-law. A husband's elder brother after all deserved the respect due to a father-in-law. In her view the wrong he did her was not a humiliation. As for Kumu, no matter how her husband behaved towards her, Motirma found it absurd that she should abandon his home.

Word came that the doctor had called. "Excuse me," said Kumu. "Let me see what the doctor has to say."

The doctor told Kumu that the patient's pulse was erratic, he was sleeping badly and was probably not getting enough rest.

Kumu was going back to her guests when Kalu stopped her. "I have to say something unpleasant," he said. "The net is tightening. If you don't go back to your husband now, the threat of ruin will become imminent. I can't think of a way out."

Kumu stood in silence. "Your husband has asked that you should be sent back," Kalu said. "Do we have the strength to ignore his request? We are helpless in his grip."

Kumu gripped the railing of the verandah. "I don't understand anything, Kalu-da," she said. "My soul is exhausted. It seems death is the only path open." Then she hurried away.

During Kumu's absence Khema Auntie had a few words with Motirma. They agreed that Kumu showed signs of pregnancy. Motirma was pleased. She prayed inwardly to the goddess Kali to make it really true. This would take care of Kumu! The proud woman might disdain her husband, but this would be a knot in the guts, not the ritual knot of her sari and his scarf. There was no escape.

Motirma took Kumu aside and told her about her suspicions. Kumu turned pale. She tightened her fists and exclaimed, "No, no, it can't be. Never!"

"Why not?" Motirma said in some annoyance. "No matter what your lineage, the laws of the world can't be turned upside down just for you. You have married into the Ghosal family. Will their household god let you off so easily? He will block your escape."

Kumu's brief intimacy with her husband had left an impression that became increasingly grotesque; the apprehension of pregnancy made this very clear. Insurmountable barriers between people are often made up of subtle components. The signs of alienation are scattered in nuances of language and gesture, hints in one's behavior, tone of voice, taste in things, existential values. There was something in Madhusudan that not only hurt Kumu; it made her feel deep shame. It seemed obscene. Madhusudan had experienced intolerable poverty in his early years, and so his boasts of wealth expressed the meanness of his inherited poverty. Kumu was repulsed, physically and mentally, by Madhusudan's characteristic meanness, his coarseness of language, his arrogance and lack of generosity, and the vulgarity of his personality. The more she tried not to think about them, the more they accumulated all around like garbage. Kumu had been struggling desperately to quell her disgust. There had been no end to her efforts to maintain the purity of wifely devotion, but her failure had never before been so obvious. The thought that her fleshly bond with Madhusudan had become inescapable tormented her in all its hideousness. "How can you be sure?" she asked Motirma anxiously.

Motirma felt greatly annoyed, but controlled herself. "I am a mother, so who should know better than I? Still, it's too early to be sure. Better get a good midwife to have a look at you."

It was time for Nabin, Motirma and Hablu to leave. But Kumu could only think of the injustice of fate and bade her friends a perfunctory farewell. Before leaving Nabin said, "Everything in this world has an end. But I could never imagine this. But we shall meet again." He saluted her in a pranam, Hablu began sobbing noiselessly, but Motirma just hardened her face and said nothing.

57

The news reached Bipradas. The midwife came and had a look; there was no doubt that Kumu was pregnant. The news reached Madhusudan as well. He had wanted wealth and had acquired as much as anybody could ask for, together with a commensurate title. All that remained to complete his worldly duties was to pass on his glory to future generations. The more pleased he became at the news the more he tended to transfer all blame to Bipradas. He wrote Bipradas a second letter, starting with a "Whereas" and signing it "Your obedient servant Madhusudan Ghosal." "I shall have the painful necessity, etc. etc." lay in between. This sort of threatening letter generally had the opposite to the desired effect on the Chatterjees, especially when there was a risk of suffering loss. Bipradas showed the letter to Kalu. Kalu grew red in the face. "Even in an ordinary man like me such a letter makes the blood boil in a royal rage," he said. "I feel like shouting an order to an imaginary officer to go get the fellow's head."

Bipradas had some paperwork to attend to during the day. He finished these in the evening and asked to see Kumu. She had been skulking all day.

Bipradas left his bed and sat down on a couch, for lying in bed like an invalid made one feel mentally weak. Facing him was a small stool, set for Kumu. The lamp was placed in a corner of the room, out of the direct line of vision. A large punkah waving overhead made a whistling noise. The heat still shimmered in the summer sky. A southerly breeze blew intermittently, tiring after a few puffs. The leaves on trees were still, like eavesdroppers. The dying light of laggard twilight mingled with the darkness. It was like the blue sea at the estuary, where the water from rivers cuts pale swathes. The pond in the garden would have become invisible as it fell in the shade, were it not for the still reflection of a bright star, like a finger pointing it out in the sky. Servants carrying lanterns moved to and fro under the trees, and an owl screeched occasionally.

Kumu took her time to come. "Dada," she said as soon as she had sat down. "I feel totally out of sorts. I feel like going off somewhere."

"You're wrong, Kumu," Bipradas replied. "You'll be all right. In a few days your soul will fill with delight, you will feel complete."

"But then," Kumu began, but stopped.

"I know—but who can free you from your bond now?"

"Do I have to go back, then?"

"I don't have the right to say you shouldn't. How can I deprive your child of his or her rightful home?"

For a long time both Kumu and Bipradas sat in silence. At last, in hushed tones, Kumu asked, "Then when do I have to go?"

"Tomorrow. Putting it off will only add to the pain!"

"Perhaps you realize that if I go back now they won't ever let me visit you again."

"I know that very well."

"So be it, then. But I must ask you not to go to their place under any circumstances. I know I'll become desperate to see you, but I don't want to meet you there. It'd be too painful for me."

"You needn't worry about that."

"They'll try to make trouble for you."

"When they finish doing all they can to me, they'll also lose their power on me. Then I'll be free. Why call it trouble then?"

"Dada, make me free too, when that day comes. By then I'll be able to hand over their son to them. There are some things one can't give up even for one's son."

"Very well, but let the son come first."

"You may not believe me, but mother willed her own death. She no longer felt at home in the family, so she could easily leave her children behind. When a person wants escape, there's nothing stopping her. Dada, I want to be free. One day, when I break free, mother's spirit will bless me, I can assure you."

The two of them remained silent for a long time. Suddenly a strong wind sprang up, turning the pages of the book that lay on Bipradas's tea table. The scent of jasmine filled the room.

"Don't think they have willfully made me unhappy," Kumu said. "I'm made in such a way that it's beyond them to make me happy, and I can never make them happy either. Those who readily make them happy will only have trouble visited upon them. Then why this harassment? Why should I accept the guilt that society heaps on me, while they remain untouched by scandal? One day I'll break loose. I'll come back, just wait and see. I can't make a lie of myself amidst a world of lies. I am the senior housewife in their household, but does that have any meaning if I cease to be Kumu? Dada, you don't believe in any god, but I do. I believe even more strongly than I did three months ago. All day I've been wondering how much chaos there is all around, and yet it hasn't overwhelmed the whole world. Beyond lie the sun and the moon, who preside over the human world, and beyond them is the realm where my god dwells. It's embarrassing to say all this to you, but I might as well say it since there won't be another opportunity. If I don't say it you might worry unnecessarily for me. I have understood that after all is lost something yet remains. And that is the inexhaustible divinity of my god. If I didn't know this I'd have killed myself knocking my head at your feet rather than go back to that prison. Dada, I have understood this because you were here in this world to teach me."

When she finished speaking Kumu prostrated herself in a pranam at her brother's feet. The night deepened. Bipradas stared out of the window, lost in thought.

58

The next morning Bipradas asked to see Kumu. She found him sitting up in bed, an esraj on his lap, and another one lying beside him. "Come, let us play a duet," he said. It was still a little dark, the breeze—cooled by the night—rustled amidst the peepal leaves, and crows began cawing. The two began to play an alap in the calm and somber bhairo raga. It was like Siva's morning meditation, when he had overcome his restlessness at being separated from his consort. As they played, the light brightened through the flowering krishnachura, and the sun appeared above the garden wall. Servants came to the door and turned back; the furniture remained undusted. Sunlight flooded into the room, the darwan softly entered and left the morning paper on the teapoy.

677

When they stopped playing, Bipradas said, "Kumu, you may think I have no faith. I don't talk about my faith because it escapes if I try to put it into words. I can see its form in music, in which deep sorrow and profound joy commingle, but I can't give it a name. You are leaving us today, and we may never meet again. Try to imagine that in playing the duet I've walked with you to a point beyond all the dissonance and all the discords. You've read *Shakuntala*—Kanwa walked some way with Shakuntala when she set off for Dushyanta's home. Where she was being sent lay sorrow and humiliation. But that wasn't the end, for Shakuntala went beyond that and found unruffled peace. This morning's bhairo raga contains that note of peace, and may all the blessings of my inner soul take you towards untainted fulfillment; and may that fulfillment flood your inner being and outer life and drown out all your sorrow and humiliation."

From *Jogajog* (1929)
Translated by Kaiser Haq

From *Farewell Song*

13   Apprehensions

Next morning, Labanya found it difficult to concentrate on her work. She had even missed her morning walk. Both she and Amit were responsible for ensuring that he kept his vow not to visit her before leaving Shillong. That morning, Amit would have to take the route along which she usually took her daily walk. So, she was sorely tempted, and had to curb her eagerness with great difficulty. Yogamaya would customarily pluck some flowers for her prayers, after an early bath. Before she emerged outdoors, Labanya left that part of the garden to seek out the shade of the eucalyptus tree. She carried a couple of books, perhaps to delude herself as well as others. A book lay open, but the hours passed, and the page was not turned. In her heart was the persistent feeling that her days of celebration were over. From time to time this morning, she felt the harbinger of separation flash his message across the sky, in the gaps between cloud and sunshine. She felt a deep conviction that Amit was an eternal fugitive, never to be found once he had slipped away. During their journey together, he would begin a narrative. Then, night would descend, and the next morning, it would be discovered that the wayfarer had vanished, leaving his story incomplete, full of loose ends. So Labanya was sure that his narrative would forever remain unfinished. Today, the gloom of that incompleteness could be felt in the morning light, and the mournful breeze was laden with the weariness of an untimely decline.

Meanwhile, at nine in the morning, Amit burst noisily into the house, calling out, "Mashima! Mashima!" Morning prayers over, Yogamaya was busy sorting daily provisions. Today, she, too, felt troubled. All these days, Amit had filled her loving heart and home with his garrulity, good humor and liveliness. Weighed down by the sorrow of his departure, her morning drooped like a flower cast down by the weight of falling raindrops. Today, in this household racked with the pain of separation, she had not summoned Labanya to assist her with daily chores, realizing that she needed to be alone, away from the public eye.

Labanya jumped to her feet, the book slipping from her lap without her noticing it. Meanwhile, Yogamaya came rushing out of the store-room.

"What's this, Amit, my boy, is there an earthquake?" she cried.

"An earthquake, indeed. My baggage was dispatched, the car arranged, when I went to the post-office to check for mail. There, I found a telegram."

"All is well, I hope?" enquired Yogamaya anxiously, watching his expression.

Labanya joined them in the room.

"My sister Sissy is arriving this very evening, along with her friend Katy Mitter, and Katy's elder brother Naren," Amit informed her, with great agitation.

"So what's there to worry about, my son? There's a vacant house beside the racing track, I'm told. If that's unavailable, can't we offer them accommodation of sorts at my place?"

"I have no worry on that score, Mashi. They have booked themselves into a hotel on their own."

"Under no circumstances can we let your sisters come here to find you living in that godforsaken cottage, son. They will blame us for the madness of their own kinfolk."

"No, Mashi, mine is a case of paradise lost. I must bid goodbye to that paradise of bare essentials. My dreams of happiness must fly from their nesting place in that rope-strung cot. I, too, must seek refuge in some ultra-civilized room of that ultra-clean hotel."

The words were not particularly significant, yet Labanya's face grew pale. It had not occurred to her, all these days, that Amit's social world was a thousand leagues removed from her own. In an instant, this realization dawned on her. Amit's imminent departure for Kolkata had not borne the harsh semblance of separation. But from his compulsion to move into a hotel today, Labanya understood that the home which the two of them had until now been building in their imagination, with various invisible ingredients, would perhaps never materialize.

"Whether I move to a hotel or to hell, this house remains my real home," declared Amit to Yogamaya, after a brief glance at Labanya.

Amit had realized that the arrival of visitors from the city did not bode well. He was mentally conjuring up many plans, to prevent Sissy and her group from visiting this house. But of late, his mail had been directed to Yogamaya's address, for he had not anticipated then that this could one day become a source of trouble. Amit's inner feelings were not readily repressed; rather, he tended to overstate them. His extreme anxiety about his sister's visit had struck Yogamaya as excessive. Labanya, too, felt herself a source of embarrassment for Amit where his sisters were concerned. She found this a distasteful, humiliating thought.

"Do you have time to spare?" Amit asked Labanya. "Would you care to go out with me?"

"No, I have no time," was Labanya's rather harsh reply.

"Why, my child, why not go out for a while?" Yogamaya urged her, anxiously.

"Korta Ma, I have really neglected Suroma's studies of late. It was remiss of me. I had decided last night that I must not show any slackness today." With these words, Labanya pursed her lips, her face grim.

Yogamaya was familiar with Labanya's stubbornness. She did not dare pester her.

"I, too, must set out to do my duty," said Amit, in a listless tone. "I must see that things are in order for their arrival."

Before taking his leave, he paused for a moment in the veranda. "Look, Banya," he urged. "Beyond the trees, you can catch a brief glimpse of the thatched roof of my cottage. I haven't told you yet, but I have bought that cottage. The owner is surprised. She probably thinks I've discovered a secret goldmine there. She has substantially raised the price of the property. I had indeed discovered a goldmine there, something known only to me. The wealth of my shabby hovel will remain hidden from everyone's eyes."

Labanya's face was shadowed with a deep sadness. "Why do you think so much about what everyone would say?" she demanded. "So what if everyone got to know? Indeed, they ought to know the truth about us, so nobody would dare to show any disrespect."

"Banya, I've decided we must spend a few days in that very cottage, after we are married," Amit informed her, without answering her directly. "My garden-estate on the shores of the Ganga, that ghat of ours, that banyan tree, they have all merged into that cottage. Mitali, the name of your choice, suits that cottage alone."

"You have left that cottage today, Mita. If you try to re-enter it on some other occasion, you will find it too small to accommodate you. In today's home, there is no room for tomorrow. You had said, the other day, that in life, a person's first struggle is with poverty, the second with wealth. But you didn't speak of the third phase of the sacred endeavor, which has to do with renunciation."

From *Farewell Song*

"Banya, that's your Robi Thakur's idea. He writes: 'today, Shah Jahan has even renounced his Taj Mahal.' It doesn't occur to your poet that we create only to transcend the created object. In the created world, that's what is known as evolution. A strange demon possesses one, commanding one to create. With the act of creation, the demon is exorcised, and the created item also becomes redundant. But this doesn't imply that moving on, leaving things behind, is the ultimate goal. In the world, the immortal saga of Shah Jahan-Mumtaz Mahal continues unabated. They are not mere individuals, after all. That's why the Taj Mahal could never be rendered vacant. As a concise postcard-reply to your celebrated poet's *Taj Mahal*, Nibaran Chakrabarti has written a poem about the bridal chamber:

> When the night grows restless
> > At the sound of dawn's chariot-wheels,
> I must leave you, O bridal chamber!
> > In the world outside, alas,
> Separation lurks like a fiendish robber.
> > Yet, though he may smash and destroy,
> And rip apart our wedding-garlands,
> > You remain untouched,
> > Always;
> Your festive celebrations
> > Never silenced or disrupted.
> Who says the newlyweds have abandoned you,
> > Leaving your bed desolate?
> > They have not gone away.
> At your call, they return
> As new sojourners, knocking
> > At your welcoming door.
> > Love is undying, O bridal chamber!
> > And you, too, are immortal.

Robi Thakur only speaks of parting, he can't sing of lovers remaining together. Banya, does the poet say that when we, too, knock on that door, it will not open for us?"

"Please Mita, I request you not to invoke the war of the poets today. Do you imagine that I have not realized, from the very first day, that you, yourself, are Nibaran Chakrabarti? But don't immediately begin constructing a poetic monument to our love: at least wait for our love to die."

Labanya realized that Amit today was trying to suppress some inner turmoil by saying all sorts of nonsensical things.

Amit, too, sensed that the battle of the poets, though it had not seemed inappropriate yesterday, had struck a discordant note this morning. All the same, he did not like the idea that Labanya saw this clearly, as well.

"Let me go, then," he proposed, rather dully. "I, too, have work to do; at the moment, my task is to conduct a survey of hotels. Meanwhile, it seems that for the unfortunate Nibaran Chakrabarti, the honeymoon is over."

"Look, Mita," pleaded Labanya, clasping Amit's hand, "I hope you will always be able to forgive me. If ever the moment of our parting arrives, I beseech you not to abandon me in anger." She rushed to the adjoining room, to hide her tears.

For a while, Amit stood stock-still. Then, slowly and absently, he went to stand beneath the eucalyptus tree. There, he saw some scattered walnut-shells. His heart was seized with pain at the sight. The scattered traces we leave behind us in the course of our lives are pathetic in their very triviality. Then he saw a book lying on the grass: it was Robi Thakur's *Balaka*. The back of the book was damp. He thought once of returning the book, but placed it in his pocket instead. He almost left for the hotel, but again, thought the better of it; instead, he reclined beneath the tree. The damp clouds of night had polished the sky sparkling clean. In the breeze, washed free of dust, the picturesque surroundings were clearly visible. The silhouettes of mountains and trees seemed etched against the deep blue sky. The world, seen up close, seemed to directly touch the heart. The day was declining slowly, to the strains of the ragini Bhairavi.

Labanya had vowed she would immediately set about her household chores in real earnest, but espying Amit under the tree, she could restrain herself no longer. Her heart heaved, her eyes swam with tears.

"What are you thinking, Mita?" she asked, coming up to him.

"The very opposite of what I had thought all these days."

"It's essential for your well-being to turn your mind upside-down and scrutinize it from time to time. So, let's hear what upside-down thoughts are in your mind."

"All these days, I kept constructing houses for you in my heart, sometimes beside the Ganga, sometimes atop a mountain. Today, in the morning light, my mind casts up the inviting image of a path, stretching across those mountains, shaded by forests. I walk, clutching a long stick topped by a sharp metal blade; strapped to my back is a square bag. You will accompany me. May your name prove true, Banya! Your tide, it seems, has swept me from my enclosed chamber, out onto the open path. In the chamber are all kinds of people, but on the path, only the two of us."

"The garden-estate at Diamond Harbor was already lost, and now the poor seventy-five-rupee room is gone, as well. Never mind! Let them go. But on our journey, how will you ensure our separation? At the end of the day, will you enter one travelers' inn, and I another?"

"There is no need for that, Banya. The journey makes us new, at every step; there is no time for staleness. Aging occurs when we remain static."

"How did this suddenly occur to you, Mita?"

"Very well, let me tell you. I have suddenly received a letter from Shobhanlal. You may have heard of him: he's an expert on the Raichands and Premchands of this world. For some time, he has been out on a journey to discover the ancient travel-routes of Indian history. He wants to retrieve the lost pathways of the past. I want to create pathways for the future."

Labanya's heart gave a sudden, violent lurch. "I took the M.A. examination with Shobhanlal, in the same year," she interrupted. "I would like to hear all his news."

"He had once been excited at the prospect of rediscovering the old route through the ancient Afghan city of Kapish. That was the route of Huen Tsang's pilgrimage to India, and before that, of Alexander's military invasion. He earnestly studied Pushto, and practiced Pathan customs. With his handsome appearance, dressed in loose-fitting clothes, he didn't look quite like a Pathan, more like a Persian. He came and begged me for a letter of introduction addressed to the French experts who were working in the same field. Some of them had tutored me when I was in France. I gave him the letter, but he was denied permission by the Indian government. Ever since then, he wanders in search of old routes in the Himalayas, sometimes in Kashmir, sometimes in Kumaon. Now, he feels the urge to explore the eastern sector of the Himalayas as well. He wants to discover the routes through which Buddhism spread in this region. The thought of that compulsive wanderer makes me melancholy, too. Our sight grows dim scanning the books to find our direction in life, but that lunatic has set out to scan the book of the road, written in the Lord's very own script. Do you know what I think?"

"Tell me."

"In the first flush of youth, Shobhanlal must have received a blow from some bangle-adorned hand, which flung him from his home onto the streets. I am not clearly acquainted with his whole story, but once when the two of us were alone together, we stayed up chatting till the wee hours. Suddenly, from our window, we saw the moon appear behind a flowering jarul tree; at that moment, he tried to tell me about someone. He took no names, nor did he describe her at all; he had barely given me the slightest hint when his voice choked, and he quickly left the room. I could tell that, lodged somewhere in his heart, remains the sting of some extremely cruel experience. That's what he probably tries to erode, step by step, as he travels on his journey."

Labanya suddenly developed a fascination for botany. She bent low, gazing at a wild flower, yellow-and-white, blossoming in the grass. She felt a sudden, urgent need to count the petals of the flower, with single-minded concentration.

"Do you know, Banya, you have flung me out into the road, to-day?" Amit asked her.

"How?"

"I had constructed a house. This morning, your words made me feel that you were hesitant to step inside. I have spent two months men-tally decorating that house. I called out to you, saying, 'Come, my bride, enter my home!' Today, you discarded your bridal finery, and said, 'There is no room for us here, my friend. We shall spend our lives walking round the fire.'"

The botanical study of wild flowers would not do anymore. Rising to her feet, Labanya pleaded, in anguish, "Mita! Please say no more! Time is up."

14   Comet

It took a long time for Amit to realize that his relationship with Labanya was known to all the Bengalis of Shillong. Discussion among clerks in government offices usually centered upon the determination of their own career prospects by the position of ruling planets on their professional horizon. Then, in the astral sphere of human life, they saw a pair of twin stars appear, emitting light of the first magnitude. The star-gazers, as is their wont, propounded many theories about the fiery drama behind the birth of these two new stars.

Having come to Shillong to savor the mountain air, Kumar Mukherjee, the attorney, had found himself drawn into these theoretical speculations. Some called him Kumar Mukho for short, while others nicknamed him Mar Mukho, the One on the Warpath! Though not a member of Sissy's private circle, he could be described as her acquaintance, for he belonged to the group of people she knew. Amit had named him Comet Mukho. For though he did not belong to the coterie, Mukho would occasionally sweep his tail across their orbit. It was everybody's guess that he was especially attracted by the planet named Lissy. This was a source of general amusement, but Lissy herself was annoyed and embarrassed about it. Hence, she would often vigorously wrench his tail in passing, but clearly, this made no difference to the comet, for his head and tail remained intact.

Amit had caught an occasional distant glimpse of Kumar Mukho on the streets of Shillong. It would be hard not to spot him. Because he had not yet been to England, Mukho's English style was flagrantly visible. Between his lips would be a thick, heavy cigar, the main reason for the nickname Comet. Amit tried to avoid him by keeping a safe distance, deluding himself that the Comet had not sensed this. But to see without taking any notice takes immense skill, just like the art of burglary. The proof of its success lies in evading detection. It requires expertise in fixing one's gaze somewhere far beyond the scene before one's eyes.

From the Bengali social circles of Shillong, Kumar Mukho had culled many facts which could be broadly classified under the head: "The Excesses of Amit Raye." The persons most vocal in their criticism had secretly derived the greatest relish from the situation. Kumar had planned to spend some time in Shillong to mend a disorder in his liver, but his acute urge for rumor-mongering made him hasten back to Kolkata within five days. Once there, by means of his cigar-smoke-filled exaggerations about Amit, he generated a crisis in the Sissy-Lissy circle, arousing a mixture of mockery and inquisitiveness.

The seasoned reader would have guessed by now that Katy Mitter's elder brother Naren was the vahana or sacred beast devoted to the service of goddess Sissy. There was a rumor that his prolonged devotion would now culminate in marriage. In her heart of hearts, Sissy was amenable to the idea. But by pretending indifference, she had created a haze of uncertainty. Naren had decided to overcome this obstacle by obtaining Amit's consent, but Amit, the humbug, would neither return to Kolkata, nor answer his letters. Like arrows piercing the sound-barrier, he had already dispatched in Amit's direction all the English expletives at his command, both in public and in private speech. In fact, he had not balked at sending an extremely rude telegram to Shillong; but like a firework missile aimed at an indifferent planet, it vanished without leaving any burn-marks. Ultimately, by general consensus, it was decided that the situation demanded a spot-investigation. In the flood-tide of disaster, if they could but catch the slightest glimpse of Amit's floating head, it was their urgent duty to grab him by the forelock and drag him to the safety of the shore. In this respect, the enthusiasm of Amit's own sister Sissy was far exceeded by that of Katy, sister to someone else. Katy Mitter's attitude closely resembled our own political heartburn at the loss of Indian riches to foreign powers.

Naren Mitter had spent a long time in Europe. Son of a zamindar, he did not have to worry about earning or spending; his urge for learning was proportionately muted. While abroad, he had concentrated mainly on wasting both time and money. One can simultaneously attain freedom from responsibility and undeserved self-esteem by calling oneself an artist. Therefore, he had inhabited the bohemian quarters of various big cities of Europe, in pursuit of the goddess of art. After some initial attempts, he was forced to give up painting upon the insistence of his plain-spoken well-wishers. Now, he introduced himself as an art critic, for that required no credentials. He could not make art blossom, but was able to mangle it with gusto. In the Parisian mode, he had lovingly sharpened the pointed ends of his moustache, while remaining carefully careless about his unruly head of hair. His appearance was quite pleasant; but in the holy endeavor to improve it further, his dressing table was weighed down with various Parisian forms of self-indulgence. The paraphernalia arranged beside his wash-basin would be excessive even for the ten-headed Ravana's toilet. There was no doubting his noble birth, from the easy nonchalance with which he discarded his expensive Havana cigar after a couple of puffs, and his regular practice of sending his garments by parcel-post to Parisian laundry houses. The best European tailoring-houses kept a record of his measurements in their registers, where one might encounter the aristocratic names of Patiala and Karpurtala. His slang-ridden enunciation of the English tongue was slurred, drawling, and understated, accompanied by the lazy glance of his half-shut eyes; those in the know opined that such inarticulate intensity was to be found in the voices of many rich, blue-blooded Englishmen. In addition, Naren was a role model among his peers for his command of obscenities in the form of racecourse swear-words and English oaths.

Katy Mitter's real name was Ketaki. Her deportment was refined, thrice-distilled in her own elder brother's etiquette factory; it contained the pungent essence of British aristocracy. She had arrogantly scissored the ordinary Bengali woman's pride in her long tresses, shedding her hair-knot like a tadpole's tail, with the new convert's eagerness to imitate. The natural fairness of her countenance was enameled with layers of paint. In the early stages of her life, Katy's dark eyes bore a gentle expression; now, it appeared, she couldn't even see ordinary people. If she did see them, she failed to notice them, and if she did notice them, her glance had the edge of a knife half-unsheathed. In childhood, her lips had a simple sweetness, but now, from frequent sneering, they had developed a permanent resemblance to a hooked elephant-goad. I am inexperienced at describing women's dress. I don't have the vocabulary. To put it simply, one noticed her wearing a flimsy outer layer, like cast-off snakeskin, through which was visible a hint of inner garments of some other hue. Much of her bosom was exposed; and she made a careful attempt to arrange her bare arms carelessly, now on the table, now on the arms of a chair, now entwined with each other. And when she smoked a cigarette, holding it between two fingers embellished with well-polished nails, it was more for decorative effect than from a desire to inhale the smoke. Most disturbing of all were the intricate postures of her high-heeled shoes. When the Creator forgot that the human foot should be modeled on the goat-hoof, this evolutionary flaw was rectified by the cobbler's gift, the high-heeled shoe, that bizarre device for tormenting the earth with the distorted gait of artificially elevated feet.

Sissy was still at an in-between stage. She had not yet attained the highest degree, but was steadily earning double promotions. In her peals of laughter, excessive cheerfulness and nonstop chatter, there was a constant, bubbling vivacity, highly prized by her admirers. In literary accounts of the adolescent Radha, her manner seems sometimes mature, sometimes naïve; the same was true of Sissy, as well. Her high-heeled shoes were the victory-gate signaling entry into the new era, but in her knot of uncut hair remained traces of the old order. The lower edge of her sari was draped a few inches too high, but in their extent of exposure, her upper garments still conformed to the bounds of modesty. She wore gloves habitually, for no particular reason, yet she still sported balas—thick bangles—on both wrists instead of one. Smoking a cigarette no longer made her dizzy, but she still had a strong addiction to chewing paan, betel leaf. She didn't mind having pickles and mango papad sent to her, camouflaged in biscuit tins; given the choice between Christmas plum-pudding and the pitha served at the Poush-festival, she had a slight preference for the latter. Though trained by a white dancer, she demurred at ballroom dancing.

They had rushed to Shillong, all of them, because the wild rumors about Amit had made them anxious. The point of contention was that, according to their definition of class difference, Labanya was a governess, specially created to destroy the caste purity of the men of their own class. They were convinced that it was out of greed for money and prestige that she had clung to Amit so tenaciously. To rescue him from her clutches, it was necessary for the ladies to intervene, with their purifying touch. Brahma, the four-faced deity, must have simultaneously glanced at and sided with women with his four pairs of eyes; hence, he had created men to be complete idiots where women were concerned. That explained why, unless assisted by women of their own social group, untouched by class ambitions, men found it so hard to escape the webs of enchantment woven by women of a different class.

At present, the two women had agreed upon the procedure to be adopted for this rescue operation. It was decided that Amit must be kept in the dark at first. The enemy and the battle-terrain must first be inspected. Then, they could challenge the powers of the sorceress.

The first thing they noticed upon arrival was that Amit had acquired a strong vein of provincialism. Formerly, too, Amit's attitude had not matched that of his coterie. But still, he was then a keen urbanite, scrubbed, polished, shining. Now, it wasn't as if his complexion had darkened from exposure to the open air; rather, it was as if trees and vines had cast their shade upon him. He seemed to have become raw, and in their opinion, somewhat stupid. His deportment was almost like that of ordinary folk. Formerly, he would treat all subjects with an element of humor, but now, he had virtually lost that urge. They took this for the ultimate danger-signal.

"We had imagined from afar that you were descending into a tribal lifestyle," Sissy told him bluntly, on one occasion. "But now we realize that you are ascending into a state of greenness, like the pine trees of this region: healthier, perhaps, than before, but not as interesting."

Borrowing Wordsworth's idea, Amit retorted that living in close proximity to nature, one's body, mind and soul acquire the stamp of "mute insensate things."

We have no complaint against mute, insensate things, thought Sissy to herself; we are concerned about those ultra-sensate beings who specialize in fluent sweet-talk.

They had hoped that Amit himself would bring up the subject

690

of Labanya. A day passed, two days, then three, but he was utterly silent on the subject. Only one thing seemed certain: like a wave-tossed boat, Amit's desires were in turmoil. Even before they were up and dressed, Amit would be back from an outing somewhere; his face then would seem ravaged, like banana leaves shredded by the stormy breeze. Even more disturbing was the fact that some people had spotted a copy of Robi Thakur's works on Amit's bed. On the inside leaf, the first syllable of Labanya's name had been crossed out in red ink. Her name was the touchstone that had probably raised the book's value.

Amit would go out every now and then. "I'm going to appease my hunger," he would say. The others were not unaware of the source of the hunger, or of the fact that his hunger was acute. But they would feign ignorance, as if it was impossible to imagine that Shillong could offer anything beyond its air, which increased the appetite. Sissy would smile to herself, while Katy would nurse the burning jealousy in her heart. Amit's own problems loomed so large, that he lacked the power to notice any outward signs of trouble. Hence, he would unabashedly say to his female companions: "I'm setting out in search of a waterfall." But he failed to realize that others may have some doubts about the nature of the waterfall and the direction of its flow. This morning, he departed, claiming he was going to trade orange honey. Meekly, in very simple language, the two ladies expressed a desire to accompany him, as they felt an irrepressible curiosity about this exquisite honey. The route was difficult, Amit informed them, and could not be negotiated by car. Nipping the discussion in the bud, he rushed away. Noting the restlessness of this bee, the two friends decided to delay no further. It had become imperative to make an expedition to the orchard where the oranges grew. Meanwhile, Naren was at the races. He had been very keen to take Sissy with him, but she did not join him. Who but a sympathetic soul would understand how much self-control such abstinence had entailed!

1929
(From *Shesher Kabita*)
Translated by Radha Chakravarty

From *Four Chapters*

The Third

Nestling jostling foliage of pale green and dark, yellow-green and brown-green vegetation in entangled embrace; the sludge of rotting bamboo leaves rising in layers to a pond's surface; and twisting past the pond, a lane which cartwheels have scarred deep. Overrun with scrub and bulbous tubers of ole, kotchu, wild flowers of ghetu and thorny mansa, and occasionally a straggling fence of ashsheora. Through the gaps, a sudden glimpse of water standing in the fields of young paddy cut across by demarcating strips of embankments. The lane ends at the steps of a ghat on the Ganga. Built of small bricks from an earlier age, the cracked ruins of the ghat list to one side: the Ganga has silted and moved some distance away from the bank. A little further away from the ghat, in the accursed shadow of an ancient ruined home in the jungle, the ghost of one who had committed matricide some century and a half ago has taken refuge—so it is believed. Against that insubstantial being, for long there has not been the slightest effort on the part of a living proprietor to come forth and assert his claim. The scene is of a deserted puja space, once the site of annual ritual celebrations, opening out into a vast courtyard irregular with mounds of moss-grown rubbish. A little further away by the river, a temple in ruins, the fragments of a performance space—a raasmanch, and the few remaining signs of an ancient wall crumbled. In the darkness where a banyan tree has gathered into itself its descending roots, a shored up broken boat bares its ribs.

Here in the last hour of the day, in the veranda heavy with shadows, into Atin's present living quarters entered Kanai Gupta. Atin started. Even Kanai was not supposed to know of Atin's present whereabouts.

"It's you!"

"I've come on detective work," said Kanai.

"Explain the joke, please."

"It's no joke. I'm just one of those ordinary people who organizes things for your group. The tea shop was raided by Saturn; I walked out. Saturn's evil eye followed me wherever I went. I finally had my own name put down on their list of "agents." For those who have no other path left excepting the one leading to the cremation grounds, this is the Grand Trunk Road—the highway that cuts straight and long from east to west, across the country's breast."

"You've left off making tea and begun to brew information?"

"You don't run this business on made-up stuff. You've got to provide hundred per cent genuine information. All I do is to tighten the noose on game that's already been snared. They had ninety-five percent of the data on Haren from your group; I merely provided the frills. These days he's relaxing in the government guesthouse at Jalpaiguri."

"So it's my turn now?"

"It's imminent. Botu has done much of the groundwork already. The little that has been left for me will give you some time. You recall the sudden loss of your diary in your former home?"

"I remember very well."

"It would definitely have gone to the police; therefore, I was obliged to steal it."

"You?"

"Yes, the one with a pure motive finds an ally in the heavens. You were engrossed in writing that day when you had to leave the room for five minutes—an exit I had arranged for. That's when I slipped it out."

"You've read it," Atin said in despair.

"I have indeed. It was half past one at night by the time I was done with my reading. I had not known the Bengali language to possess such vigor, such passion. Of course, the diary had many secrets as well, though not quite pertaining to the British Empire."

"Was it right to have done this?"

"Can't tell you how right! You are a litterateur: there are no details—you have not even mentioned anyone by name, but every letter breathes your contempt, the extent of your disillusionment. Had the words come from any government employee with ministerial ambitions, he would have ensured his salvation at the royal court. If Botu were not working against you, the notebook alone would have altered the planetary positions in your favor."

"What do you mean? You've read all of it!"

"Of course, I have. My dear boy, if I had a daughter and if she was capable of inspiring such writing, it would have thoroughly gratified my paternal feelings. Frankly, Indranath-bhai has inflicted a loss on the country by involving you in his group."

"Do the others in the group know of this business of yours?"

"Not one."

"Master-moshai?"

"He is intelligent. He guesses, but he has not asked me about it, nor have I spoken of it to him."

"But you've told me."

"That is the strange part. It's my job to be suspicious; if I cannot trust at least one person, I will suffocate to death. I'm not a dreamer, nor am I an idiot, so I don't keep a diary but if I did, I'd have felt the lighter by handing it to you."

"Master-moshai—don't you confide in him . . ."

"One may pass on information to the Master, but not bare one's self to him. I am Indranath's chief counsel, but do not ever think that I know everything about him. There are things about him I wouldn't dare imagine. I believe that Indranath sweeps into the hands of the police those of our group who drop off naturally, as I do too. Reprehensible, but not sinful. Let me tell you right away: one day, it will be with his help or with mine that you are going to be finally handcuffed—you must not hold it against me when that happens. It's Botu who has just let on to the Gossip Department at the police station about your move to this house. Consequently, I had to trump his move: I've taken a photograph and handed it to them. Back to business. I'm giving you notice of twenty-four hours; if you persist in staying on, I shall have to push you to the police station myself. I've written down the details of the route you are to take to get to your destination once you've quit this place. The ciphers you already know; nevertheless, memorize the note and tear it up. Here's a map: your quarters are on this side of the road, the corner room in the schoolhouse. Directly facing the house is the police station. There's a man there who is distantly related to me, a grandson of sorts. He is a writer-constable I call Raghab Boal, the Monster Extortionist. They've been settled for three generations now in the western region of the country. You've been given the job of teaching him Bangla. Once you're there, Raghab alias Raghubir will ransack your trunk, whisk your pockets and probably give you a couple of blows in the bargain. Accept it all as a generous gift from the gods. Raghab's Hindi fairly bristles with references to his firm belief that every Bengali is a son of something or the other. Don't even try to resist him in any way, and don't ever come back to these parts for as long as you live. You will find a bicycle outside. As soon as you get a sign, jump on it and get away. Come, a final embrace."

After they had embraced, Kanai left.

Atin sat in silence, looking inwards into his life. The last act of his life had come before it was time. . . . In the soft unsullied light of dawn, a journey had once begun; he had moved far away since then. Nothing was left of the resources with which he had set foot on the path; he had survived the last stretch only by feeding on self-deception. Now it seemed miraculous that one day, suddenly at a bend in the path, the goddess of fortune had appeared before him with an extraordinary gift of beauty; he had never thought it possible that such divine splendor would come his way; he had only visions of it in poetry, in history. How often he had felt that Dante and Beatrice had been reborn in the two of them. It was an inspiration from history that spoke to his inner self: like Dante, Atin too had leapt into the vortex of a political revolt, but for him where was truth? courage? glory? He had been sucked inexorably into the mire, into an infernal darkness of masked banditry and murder from which no pillars of light would ever rise radiant in history. At the cost of annihilating his soul he had found no worthy realization in this path, only an unequivocal submission. There is virtue in submission, but not in the submission of spirit that is dragged out from furtive secret terrors, that has no meaning and no end.

The light of day faded. In the courtyard the crickets began their shrill cry, and from somewhere far, came the tortuous groans of a bullock-cart on its way.

Suddenly Ela rushed into the room, disheveled and in blind haste, like one about to plunge into the waters and end all. As Atin sprang up, she flung herself on his breast. "Atin, Atin, I could not keep away," she was saying, the tears choking her.

Atin slowly loosened himself from her embrace and held her before him, looking on all the while at her tear-stained face. "Eli, what madness is this?" he said.

"I know nothing of what I have done."

"How did you come to know of this address?"

"You did not let me know your whereabouts," said Ela in grave reproach.

"Whoever has given it to you is no friend of yours."

"Yes, I know that too, but when I do not know where you are my mind is lost wandering in the emptiness like a restless creature. It is intolerable. I'm in no state to judge friend from foe. Tell me, how long is it since I've met you!"

"You are remarkable!"

"It is you who are remarkable, Antu! You obeyed the order—as soon as you were forbidden to come to my home."

"That was my natural arrogance. Desire, intense, coiled around me like a python, day and night, but I could not yield to it. They say that I'm sentimental; they'd made up their minds that when danger came it would be proved that I was made of clay. They could not dream that in that very sentiment lies my strength."

"Master-moshai knows this."

"Ever since the days of the British Empire, Eli, when this haunted locale came into being, no Bengali bhadramahila has shown herself here."

"That is only because there is no lady in all of Bengal who has ever had a need, so urgent and so unbearable."

"But Eli, what you've done today is prohibited."

"Yes, I know. I shall acknowledge my weakness, but I shall break all rules—not only on my behalf but yours as well. Every day my heart has been telling me that you are calling out to me. I feel stifled because I cannot answer your call. Tell me you are happy that I have come."

"So happy that I'm ready to accept any danger only to prove it."

"No, no, why should you be in danger! Whatever happens should happen to me. Let me go away then, Antu."

"Never. You've come here breaking all the rules: I shall keep you here breaking all rules. Let us share the blame even-handedly. I had seen you once in the fresh wonder of the colors of spring, a vision that has

since slipped away into another millennium. Let us invoke that day to-
gether inside this ancient room. Come, come closer still."

"Wait, let me try and tidy up."

"Alas, that would be like running a comb on a bald head."

Ela was walking around, examining the room. On the floor lay a
blanket and over that a woven mat. An old canvas bag stuffed with books
did for a pillow, and a packing case for writing. In the corner, a jar with a
little earthen cover for storing water. A bunch of bananas in an old bam-
boo basket. A mug with the enamel chipped off, for that rare cup of tea.
On a sturdy chest in the far corner of the room stood an image of Ga-
nesh, making it clear that Atin's habitat had another occupant besides
him. A rope had been strung between one pillar and another: dirty cot-
ton towels with many hued splotches of color hung on the line. The
damp room held the humid odors of the still air outside, threatening to
suffocate its inmates.

Ela had often witnessed a similar, if not exactly the same sort of
scene. It had never particularly saddened her; rather, she had inwardly
applauded these brave boys, renouncers of hearth and home. Once, on
the edges of the jungle, she had come upon the remains of a fire that
had been made with bits of old thatch and bamboo splints—the work of
hands obviously inexpert at the task. Etched in those glowing embers she
thought, was the very picture of revolutionary romance. But now she was
unable to speak for the pain. Ela had only scorn for the wealthy young
men who had grown up in the lap of luxury; but she was unable to fit
Atin with the mean squalor of these surroundings.

Atin laughed loudly at the strained expression on Ela's face. He
said, "You are astounded by my wealth; but you do not see most of it,
and that is what surprises you. We have to keep our feet unfettered.
When it's time to run, not a person, not a thing, can hold us back. There
are workers of a jute mill who live nearby—they call me 'Master-babu.'
They get me to read and address their letters, check out receipts for loans
and the like. Some of them dream of doing something for their children,
hoping that some day, their sons might move on from the working class
to the mastering classes. They ask me for help. They bring me fruits;
those that keep cows get me some milk."

"That chest in the corner—whose property is it, Antu?"

"One begins to stick out if one lives alone in such places. A Marwari, thrice-bankrupt, swept off the road by misfortune has also landed up in this room. I begin to suspect that his primary business is in going bankrupt. The haunted veranda out there is a training academy of sorts for his two nephews. They come to work here every morning after an early breakfast of chhatu—they dye cheap clothes for the women of the laborer quarters, pay back interest with their earnings, and something of the capital too I would imagine. These earthen vats that you see here —they're not vessels for my sacrificial cooking; they're for dyeing stuff. They stow away the dyed clothes in the chest; it also contains an assortment of finery to be sold to the young girls of the slum—Bellary glass bangles, small mirrors, combs, brass arm-clasps and the like. The onus of protecting the chest has been vested on me and on the spirit of the house. They set off at three in the afternoon on their business and don't get back until the following morning. I don't quite know the nature of the brokering the Marwari does in Calcutta. They'd wanted to make me a shareholder—born of a desire to learn English; I haven't agreed, out of compassion for living creatures. There were also attempts to probe into my financial affairs. I've let them know that about eighty percent of whatever my ancestors possessed has been reborn as their ancestral holdings."

"How long will you be staying here?"

"Twenty-four hours, I would think. This veranda will continue to witness an endless repertoire of colorful pageants, spectacles of divine play. Atindra will dissolve into the pale colorless horizon. The Marwari who has been infected by my presence should not be struck by the plague—of handcuffs and the rest. He may yet end up as a shareholder in my business, without his having invested anything in it."

"Your address in future?"

"I'm not allowed to say it."

"Does that mean I shall not even be able to imagine where you might be?"

"There's no harm in imagining, is there? The bank of the heavenly lake, Manasarovar, is not such a bad place; it will do."

Meanwhile Ela had been looking at the books she had taken out from the pillow-bag—books of poetry, some English and a couple in Bangla.

"I've been lugging them around with me all this time, lest I forget my caste," said Atin. "In their world of words was my original home staked. You will find the penciled signs of those tracks if you leaf through the pages. Behold me now where I have come. . . ."

Ela sank to the floor and clasped Atin's feet as she said, "Forgive me, Antu. Forgive me."

"What have I to forgive you for, Eli? If there be a god and if he be boundless compassion, then it is he who will forgive me."

"When I brought you to this path I had not learnt to know you."

"So, you will not even grant me the privilege of my own madness which has brought me full-steam to this hideout?" Atin said with a laugh. "I tell you, I shall not tolerate it if you cast me in the role of a minor and play the mentor yourself. Far better that you climb down the stage and look directly at me while you say, 'Come my beloved, come and sit by me on my sari spread for you.'"

"I might have said so, but what makes you frantic today?"

"Why should I not be frantic? Do you still say that the magic of your lotus arms led me to this path?"

"Why should you be angry if I speak the truth?"

"Is that the truth? I've been hurtled on to this path by my own volition—you were a mere pretext. If it had been a bhadramahila of some other class, I would have been playing bridge in the mixed clubs where the blacks and the whites fraternize; or, I would have been at the races contemplating the Governor's box as the next step to paradise. If it has to be proved that I am an idiot, I shall announce with a flourish that the responsibility was mine alone—part of what you might call a god-given talent."

"Please, Antu, don't talk any more rubbish. I shall never cease to regret that it is I who have destroyed your livelihood. The very roots of your life have been severed."

"Finally that woman, the woman who is real. How apparent it is that you are a romantic on stage—in the cause of the nation. You are in the very heart of that world of nurture—a plate heaped with milk, rice and fish . . . a fan in your hand. When you brandish the political bludgeon you appear with wild forbidding eyes, your hair disheveled, in the very impulse that is unnatural, not emerging from a compassionate understanding."

"How you can speak, Antu! When it comes to words, you surpass women."

"Do you think women can speak! They only babble. Storm clouds had once amassed in my mind and I had believed that I would smash the ignorance of deadweight tradition with a tornado of words. You are out to plant your victory pennant on that very ignorance, armed only with the right of force."

"Tell me, tell me please, why did you make a mistake only because I did? Why did you take upon yourself the sorrows of an abandoned calling?"

"That is my vyanjana in my language of extremity, what you call gesture in English. If I hadn't accepted sorrow you would have gone, turned your face away and never known how much I love you. Do not erase this and say it was love for the nation."

"Is the country not a part of this love, Antu?"

"Love for the country and my love for you became one and, therefore the country is also a part of it. There was a time when a man had to win a woman through a test of bravery. I've now a chance to put myself through that test—a mortal one. This you forget, my bountiful goddess; you are hurt only because I lack a means of livelihood!"

"We women are of the everyday material world. We cannot endure any want in that world. You must make me a promise: I have inherited a house and have some money saved up; I beg you, listen to my request and don't be shy about accepting the money from me. I know how badly you need it."

"If it comes to that, the possibilities are many—from churning out guidebooks for matriculating students to becoming a load-bearing coolie."

"Antu, I admit that I should have spent all this money that I have saved up in the cause of my country. But we women have such limited means of earning that we save blindly whatever little we have. We are cowards."

"That is the counsel given by your natural intelligence. Women

lose their essential beauty and nobility—their sree, when they are with-
out any resources."

"Ours is a small nest and into it go all the odds and ends we have
salvaged. But it is not simply a survival instinct, it is to sustain love. If
only I can make you understand that whatever I have is all for you!"

"That I shall never agree to. Thus far, women have provided ser-
vice and men subsistence. It is shameful if the opposite were to happen.
You've pushed away the desire with which I may have come to you un-
abashedly and put up in its stead the barrier of your vow. That day you
were busy checking the accounts of Narayoni High School . . . I dropped
down next to you—like an eagle bruised in a storm laid low in the dust.
I had come to you with a defeated mind. It's impossible to tear a woman
away from her unshakable dedication to any odd nonsense that she con-
siders her duty: you did not look up. I sat gazing, thirsting for a touch
of those beautiful fingers to rain their sweetness on my body and soul.
You remained unmoved, untouched. Miser! You couldn't give me even a
trifle! I told myself that I would have to pay a heavier price. I would fall
one day to the ground with a smashed head, a lacerated body—only then
would you enfold my shattered self into your embrace!"

Ela's eyes brimmed over. She said, "Ah, Antu, I can never keep up
with you! Could you not have taken this trifle from me without having
to ask me? Why didn't you snatch away the notebook? Don't you under-
stand? It is your diffidence that makes me diffident. Antu, you are like a
woman in this respect; your desire might be intense but it goes against
your grain, your inherent refinement, to demand forcefully."

"It is an inherited belief, in my very bones since childhood. I've
always felt that it is an inherited tradition to defend with diffidence the
purity of a woman's mind and body. If ever your heart is softened to-
wards my diffident self or feels the slightest desire to be encouraging,
then do not wait for me to beg anything of you. It is a boundless hunger
I have but that won't make me a glutton; it is not in my nature. I cannot
destroy the integrity of my desire."

Ela came and sat pressed against Atin. She drew his head to her
breast and rested her own head against him. Gently, she ran her fin-
gers through his hair. A little later Atin sat up. Gripping her hand, he

said, "I didn't realize when I took the ferry at the Mokamma crossing that my ancestral goddess of fortune had smartly tweaked my ears with her invisible fingers. Ever since, I have been culling unreal flowers from the boundless sky of my memories. Do you find it wearisome? Is it faded in your mind now, that day?"

"Not one bit."

"Listen then: my Bihari servant had already taken my heavy luggage from the deck to the train. I had only a small leather case and I was looking around, waiting for a coolie." "Want a coolie?" you asked innocently enough, as you suddenly appeared by my side. Then added, "There's no need, really; I'll take it." "Wait!" I cried out, "What are you doing!" You had already picked up the case. You saw my plight and remarked, as though making a request, "Here's something you can do, if it embarrasses you: that's my trunk, you may carry it, and then we shall be even." I had to carry your trunk, four times as heavy as my suitcase. I kept changing hands and lurched towards the train where I placed it in the third-class carriage. By then, the silk kurta was quite drenched with sweat and I was panting. Silent laughter played on your face. Perhaps there was sympathy lurking somewhere, but it was well hidden; it was your duty not to express it. After all, the great responsibility of making a man of me rested that day in your hands."

"For shame, Antu, don't say more. Stop. I'm ashamed to think of it. How stupid, how peculiar I was then. My arrogance was unchecked because you did not laugh out loud at me. Oh, how could you ever bear it!"

"It doesn't matter. When you appeared before me it was not a matter of higher mathematics or logic. It is what one may call moh, an illusive attraction—even that super champion, Shankaracharya, failed to make a dent in it. It was late afternoon: the clouds had taken on that irresistible golden red light by which would-be brides have traditionally been shown. The radiant waters of the Ganga brimmed full. This slender swift moving form of yours bathed red in the light is dyed into my very being. What was it that happened next? I heard your call. But where have I come? How distant from you! Do you even know how far?"

"Why don't you tell me, Antu?"

"There are orders I have to follow. It's not just that. What is the use of telling you all? The light is almost gone . . . come, come closer still. My eyes have come to seek you out like a court of reprieve. In you alone is my release. How infinitesimally small are its boundaries, like that of a glided frame. Why not fix the image within it? These unruly strands of your hair that have strayed over your eyes, that you keep pushing away with quick fingers, your tussar silk sari, black bordered, no brooch to pin the sari against your shoulders, the end pinned into your hair, tired shadows beneath your eyes, in your lips the shades of an appeal, and around us daylight dissolving into its final intangibility. This, what I now see, is an astonishing truth. I will not be able to explain to anyone what it means. In its unspoken sweetness lie hidden such depths of sorrow because no master poet has given words to it. This little drop of exquisite fulfillment is ringed on all sides by something that is monstrous, huge, grotesque and shadowed."

"What do you mean!"

"A lot of it is lies. I remember that you had asked me to rent a room in a working-class slum. You had a certain objective—of destroying my pride in my lineage. I was amused at your noble attempt. Stepped in to take part in that democratic picnic. I made the rounds of the carters' quarters. Became a nephew to numerous uncles as I wended my way past cattle and cattle-sheds. But as to the tenuous and transient nature of those professions of kinship, neither they, nor I was deceived for an instant; we both knew it would not stand the test of time. There must be a few noble individuals who can pluck a tune on any instrument, including the single-stringed one used to card cotton; but when we try to imitate them, we fail to make music, or even to bring out a note. You've seen the disciple of Christ on his beat in your neighborhood; it is part of his institutional program to embrace all and sundry as his 'brother.' He only mocks Christ when he does so."

"What has come over you, Antu? What bitter regret makes you say such things? Are you trying to say that one cannot overcome all that is distasteful and accept duty as duty?"

"It is not of taste we are speaking, Eli; it is of one's own nature, innate disposition—swabhava. Sri Krishna had asked Arjuna to carry out the ordained duty of a brave warrior, utterly distasteful although it might be; he did not ask him to engage with the discipline of agricultural economics with a view to cultivating land in Kurukshetra."

"What would Sri Krishna have told you, Antu?"

"He has already told me many days ago—he whispered into my ears. I am commanded to speak out those very words. When the guru says: 'Everyone, without exception, has exactly the same duty to perform' —it is already false. I will tell you to your face that even you have no place in those quarters where you go to bestow your kindness with so much pride. Goddess! You are goddesses, all of you! But the ornaments and attire of a false goddess, like all other pieces of a woman's attire, are manufactured in the shops of male tailors."

"Look, Antu, I've not understood to this moment why you did not forcibly move away from a path that you recognized not to be your own?"

"Let me tell you then. There was much that I had not known, much that I did not even imagine until I had stepped on to this path. One by one, I came close to such boys before whom I would have bowed, touched their feet in respect, if I was not older than they. No one will ever come to know of those boys, what they have witnessed and what they have endured, how they have been humiliated and insulted—a story untold. It has been intolerable, that pain; it spurred me on. I have sworn to myself so often that I will let neither fear nor suffering overwhelm me: I would die beating my head against the stone wall, yet care naught for that heartless wall."

"What made you change your mind?"

"Listen to what I have to say. He who fights against the strong even if he be without any means, stands as an equal before the other—his honor is safe in such a confrontation. I had imagined the right to such an honor. As the days went by, it became all too clear that the very boys who were the most outstanding and had the highest ideals, were gradually losing their humanity. There is no greater loss that this. I knew with certainty that they would laugh away my words or mock me in their anger; yet, I have told them that the wrong may perhaps be the same as the wrongdoers themselves, but in the face of defeat and before death, we have to prove that we are greater than they are, in humanity. Why else would we be playing a terrific losing game against such might as they possess? Only to destroy our foolishness? A few alone understood what I said."

"Why did you still not leave them?"

"Was it possible to have left then? They were hemmed in by the snares of cruel punishment. I saw for myself their history, felt their mortal agony, and so, however angry or disgusted I was, I could not abandon those in peril. But from this experience one thing became fully clear to me: to use physical force against those with whom we are totally unequal, to engage fist upon fist with them using brute force can only end in brutalizing our very beings."

"For some time now, Antu, I too have seen the outline of a horrific tragedy taking shape before my eyes. It was in response to a glorious call that I had come; but with each passing day it is my shame that grows. What can we do now, tell me?"

"Before every person comes the dharmayuddha of the *Mahabharata* . . . in that battle of truth, to die is to earn the highest heaven. But for us, at least for some of us, that path is closed in this life. We have to repay to the last paisa the fruits of our karma here and now."

"I understand it all. Yet Antu, it hurts me deeply that you've been saying such harsh things about the work one does for one's country."

"There's no point speaking of the reason now; the time is past."

"Tell me still."

"I shall acknowledge to you today—I am not a patriot as you conceive of one. There is something bigger than patriotism. There are those who will not accept this but will climb on to its back as they would a crocodile, deeming it a boat to ferry them across. Deception, pettiness, mutual suspicion, conspiracies for power and spying will one day pull them down into cesspools. I see this clearly. In the ugly world inside the pit, the poisonous air engulfs us by day and night. I shall never be able to defend the paurush in myself, without which no great work is ever achieved in this world."

"Tell me Antu, what you call self-destructive and annihilating—is it only to be found in our country?"

"I do not say so. All over the world there are nationalists who have begun howling out the terrible lie that you can give life to your country after you've killed its very spirit. I protest this in my mind, racked by an unbearable pain. I might have enunciated my protest with integrity: it would have lived on as a universal truth—far greater than playing hide and seek inside tunnels and trying to save the nation. But there will be no time to say so in this life. That is why my agony has turned so cruel today."

Ela's sigh was wrung from the depths of her being. "Come back, Antu," she said.

"There is no path of return, not any more."

"Why not?"

"Even if I find myself at an unworthy end here, one is still bound by its duties."

Ela put her arms around Atin's neck and said, "Come back, Antu. You have destroyed the very foundations of the belief I had inhabited for all these years, I am adrift, clinging on to a boat, rudderless and broken. Take me and save me as well. Antu, don't sit there so silently. Speak. Say something, Antu. You can order me this very minute and I shall break my vow. I have made a mistake, forgive me."

"There is no way."

"Why is there not a way? There must be one."

"The arrow may not find its mark but it cannot return to its quiver."

"I am a swayamvara, I have chosen my groom like the princesses of old—marry me, Antu. I can't waste any more time. Let us be our own witnesses; make me your wedded companion and take me on your path."

"Had it been a path of danger I would have. But where dharma itself has been destroyed, I cannot make you a companion! Why bring it up! Let's not speak of such things. There might still be some truth worth salvaging before the boat finally sinks. Let me hear it from your lips."

"What shall I say?"

"Tell me you have loved."

"Yes, I have loved."

"Tell me that when I cease to be, you will remember even then that I have loved you."

Ela sat silently. She did not reply. The tears fell. After a long time she said, her voice choking, "I'm asking you again. Take something from me, Atin . . . take this necklace." She took it off and laid it across his feet.

"Never."

"Why, are you hurt?"

"Yes. There was a time when I'd have worn it around my neck, had you given it to me then. It's meant for my pocket today, into a hole of want. I'll take no alms from you."

Ela flung herself on the ground near Atin. "Take me with you as your companion," she said.

"Don't tempt me, Ela. I've told you several times that my path is not yours."

"Then it's not yours either. Turn back, come back."

"It is not a path of my making, I am of the path. No one would call a noose a necklace."

"Know for certain, Antu, if you go, I would not live a second longer. I have no one but you. If you doubt this now, I pray with all my being that there might be some way of quenching that doubt after my death."

Atin sprang up suddenly. The sound of a far-off whistle had cut through the air like a sharp arrow. Startled, he said, "I'm off."

Ela held him tight. She said, "Stay. Stay a little longer. . . ."

"No."

"Where are you going?"

"I know nothing."

Ela fell at his feet, "I'm your servitor at your feet. Don't leave me behind, don't."

Atin stopped short and for a while he did not move. The whistle sounded a second time. "Let go of me," he thundered. He tore himself away as he said the words and was gone.

The evening light thickened. Ela lay face down on the floor. Her heart seemed to have completely shriveled up, her eyes dry.

"Ela!" Suddenly she heard a deep voice call out her name. She started up. She saw it was Indranath, with a flashlight in his hands. She was up immediately. "Bring back Atin," she said to him.

"Nothing of that now. Why have you come here?"

"I came here knowing that it was dangerous."

"Who cares about the danger to you!" said Indranath in fierce rebuke. "Who gave you information about this place?"

"Botu did."

"And you still did not realize his intent?"

"I did not have the intelligence to understand. I was longing, suffocating."

"I would have killed you this very moment, if I could. Get home. There's a taxi outside!"

1934
(From *Char Adhyay*)
Translated by Rimli Bhattacharya

9

Humor

CAFTER READING THE ENGLISH *Gitanjali* or looking at portraits of the bearded, saintly looking poet in his prime, readers may end up with the impression that Tagore is entirely a "mystic" writer, always serious and completely given to writing intensely spiritual lyric poems. In fact, he often regaled everyone around him with laughter and displayed a strong inclination toward whimsy in his writings. Remembering her uncle, Indira Devi Chaudhurani writes about how he would entertain the family "with his comic style of singing" and how he and his eldest brother Dwijendranath would regularly enliven everyone's spirit with "childish fun and frolic" (*Rabindranath Tagore: A Centenary Volume 1861–1961,* 5). Leonard Elmhirst, Tagore's close friend and adviser, says that his "most vivid memories [of the poet] are of his abundant good spirit, of the overflowing of his laughter, of the kindly way in which he could 'pull one's leg'" as well as the "depth and breadth of his knowledge and interest" (ibid., 16). When writing Tagore would often resort to doodling. In certain moods he would transform his doodles into comic or grotesque faces and shapes, revealing in the process his love of the fantastic. When he had children around him—whether his own or from the extended family or from his school—he would end up composing nonsense verse or comic skits for them.

It is not surprising, therefore, that Tagore's oeuvre includes works where his wit and humor blend or alternate with his serious side. Every now and then he would compose light-hearted poems—often aimed at children—such as "The Hero," "Big and Small," and "Astronomy" (see Part 4, Poems, here; also published in *Sishu* [The Child]). Sometimes he would insert a hilarious poem such as "The Invention of Shoes" in an essentially serious collection of poems such as *Kalpana* (1900). He could display his sharp wit and humor in a novel that ends on an almost tragic note, *Shesher Kabita (Farewell Song,* 1929) and present his ironic side in a short story like "The Editor." He indulged his love of fantasy in the short work "Ekta Ashader Galpa" ("A Fanciful Story," 1892), which he later transformed into the exuberant comedy *Tasher Desh* (*The Kingdom of Cards,* 1933—see Part 6 here, "Plays"). His travel and autobiographical writings are also enlivened by his sharp eye for human foibles and his wit.

What is more, Tagore composed some sparkling nonsense verse and produced a number of delightful comedies and farces. He also wrote a number of purely satirical works. He was quite young when he wrote light comedies like *Goday Galad* (*Flawed at the Outset,* 1892) and *Baikunther Khata* (*Baikuntha's Manuscript,* 1897), but even after he had become the grand old man of Bengali letters he composed the rollicking comedy *Chirakumar Sabha* (*The Bachelor's Club,* 1926). In 1907, the year that saw him deeply disturbed by the excesses of the movement for self-rule and the death of his beloved son Samindranath, he published the collection of farces *Hasya Kautuk,* as well as the anthology of comic-satiric prose pieces and humorous plays *Vyanagakautuk.* Toward the end of his life, he brought out in quick succession his collection of nonsense rhymes, *Khapchhara* (*Out of Sync,* 1937), the whimsical *Chharar Chhabi* (*Pictures in Rhymes,* 1937), a work in the fantastic mode, *She* (*He,* 1937), and a book of comic-playful poems, *Prahasini* (*The Smiling One,* 1939).

Our selections of Tagore's humorous works begin with Tagore's satiric prose piece "Denge, the Black Ant's Observations," taken from *Vyanagakautuk.* Although the black ant of the piece claims altruistic motives (its goals are "to preach progress and reform") in consuming the sugar of the red ants, its scorn for the smaller insects is obvious, as are its parasitic instincts. Contemporary readers must have read the story of black and red ants as an allegory of the colonizer and the colonized, but the narrative is surely timeless in its indictment of greed masquerading as philanthropy.

This section also includes four short comic and irreverent plays by Tagore that he published in *Hasya Koutuk.* The first of these, "Aryans and Non-Aryans," mocks the snobbery and pretensions of upper-class Hindus who exalted themselves because of their Aryan heritage. "The Funeral" makes fun of the hypocrisy and sycophancy of well-off Indians bent on attracting the patronage of the British at any cost. Perhaps the best known of the four skits and the one that has been performed most often, "Ordeal" ridicules insatiable donation-seekers who would cook up any excuse to extort money, hounding their targets to distraction. The farce "Testing the Student" derides teachers who resort to physical abuse to make up for their pedagogic inadequacies. All four skits are obviously topical and aimed at exposing abusive behavior and mocking greedy, self-seeking, and opportunistic people in contemporary Indian society.

Tagore's ability to spin purely comic verse is displayed here through the poem "The Invention of Shoes." Written in rollicking rhymes and a galloping rhythm, it amounts to an ingenious and flippant take on the unforeseen consequences of imperial desire. The four short poems from *Khapchhara* that conclude this section indicate that Tagore relished nonsense verse in the tradition of Edmund Lear and Lewis Carroll. Tagore's humorous prose and verse is endlessly inventive and always full of surprises. With his imagination and art, Tagore can take us any-where—even to the realm of the absurd.

Denge the Black Ant's Observations

Look, Look! Look at the ants! Tiny, red, thin—all those are ants, what they call Pipilika in Sanskrit. I am a Denge, hailing from the exalted dynasty of the dains. Whenever I see these ants, I feel like laughing.

Ha, Ha, Ha. Look at their style! Look how they move! Indistin-guishable from the dust.

When I stand, my head touches the sky! If the sun had been a piece of sugar candy, I think I would have stretched out my feeler and broken off pieces to pile up in my nest. Ouf, I dragged a large piece of straw down such a long stretch of road, but look at what they are up to— three of them tugging at one dead grasshopper! The difference between us is staggering! Really, it is such fun watching them.

Compare my legs to their legs! My legs are so very long! You can't expect legs that give one a greater standing or dignity! But the ants are fully contented with their tiny legs. It is so strange. Well, after all they are ants.

To begin with they are so small, and moreover we view them from an enormous height. Hard to see them in their entirety. But by looking out of the corners of my eyes and down from the height of my six long legs, I have managed to understand them completely. Because the ants are so tiny, it does not take much time to view them. I am going to lecture and write a book on the ant species in the Dain language.

I have extensive experience based on my conjectures regarding the social system of the ants. The Denges love their children; therefore it follows that ants never do. The reason being that they are ants, mere ants, and nothing else but ants. It is said that ants can make their nests on the ground. It is clear that they learned architecture from the Denges. After all they are ants, ordinary ants, called Pipilika in Sanskrit.

I feel a great compassion for the ants. My urge to help them has grown so strong that I feel like giving up the civilized society of the Denges for a short time and with bands of my Denge brothers, establish homes among the nests of the ants and initiate a mission to reform them. I am ready to sacrifice so much. We are willing to spend our days, swallowing their grains of sugar and spreading ourselves out somehow in their holes, if even at this cost they are improved somewhat.

They don't want progress. They want to eat their own sugar themselves and live in their own holes. That is because they are ants, mere ants. But since we are Denges, we are going to bring progress to them, and eat their sugar, live in their nests—we, our nephews and nieces and our brothers-in-law.

If you ask why we should eat their sugar and live in their holes, then let me point out that the primary reason is that they are ants and we are Denges. Secondly, we have selflessly dedicated ourselves to improving the lives of the ants, so we will eat their sugar and live in their nests. Thirdly, to make us forget the sorrow of leaving our beloved Dainland, it will be necessary for us to eat substantial amounts of sugar. Fourthly, in an alien land, moving amongst a different race, so many diseases could afflict us. In that eventuality we might not live long. Alas! What a lamentable plight! So sugar we must have and whatever space is available in the holes, we and our brothers-in-law will share out amongst ourselves.

If the ants protest, we will call them ungrateful. If they want to eat sugar and ask for space in the holes, we will tell them frankly, "You are ants. You are small. You are Pipilika!" Could there be a stronger rationale than that?

What will the ants eat? Well, I don't know. Perhaps, there may be insufficient food and living space. But they should calmly consider that by continued long prostration at our feet there is an opportunity of their rise in stature. There will be no lack of order and security. Peace and order can only be maintained if an arrangement can be arrived at whereby we continuously keep consuming their sugar as they are gradually reformed. What else can prevent a huge clash? You have to move with utmost consideration, when heavy responsibility lands on your shoulders.

What if the race of ants dies for lack of sugar to eat and under the weight of peace and order? Then we shall proceed elsewhere to preach progress and reform—for we are the Denges, extremely advanced on account of our lofty positions!

Translated by Kalyani Dutta

Aryans and Non-Aryans

(ADWAITA CHARAN CHATTOPADHYAY *and* CHINTAMANI KUNDU)

ADWAITA: Who are you?

CHINTAMANI: I'm an Aryan, a Hindu.

ADWAITA: What is your name?

CHINTAMANI: Sri Chintamani Kundu.

ADWAITA: What is your intention?

CHINTAMANI: I want to contribute to your paper.

ADWAITA: What would you like to contribute?

CHINTAMANI: I'm an Aryan. I would like to write about the Aryan religion.

ADWAITA: Sir, what is this thing that you call Aryan?

CHINTAMANI: *(surprised)* Sir, you don't know who an Aryan is? I'm an Aryan, my father Sri Nakur Kundu is an Aryan, his father, Late Nafar Kundu is an Aryan, his father—

ADWAITA: I see! What is your religion?

CHINTAMANI: That is a tough question! If I can put it in a nutshell, the religion of the non-Aryans is not that of the Aryans.

ADWAITA: Now, who are the non-Aryans?

CHINTAMANI: Those who are not Aryans are non-Aryans. I'm not a non-Aryan, my father Sri Nakur Kundu isn't a non-Aryan, his father Late Nafar Kundu wasn't a non-Aryan, his father—

ADWAITA: Say no more! So, since Sri Nakur Kundu isn't my father and since I have no relationship with Nafar Kundu, I'm a non-Aryan.

CHINTAMANI: I can't say that for sure.

ADWAITA: *(annoyed)* What kind of talk is that? What do you mean that you can't say for certain? Can't you say for certain that Nakur isn't my father? What caste are you? What could I have to do with the likes of you?

CHINTAMANI: I'm not talking about caste, I'm talking about dynasty. You too have been born in the world-famous Aryan dynasty—

ADWAITA: I born in the same dynasty in which your father Nakur Kundu was born? How dare you—the son of a peasant—even imagine such a thing?

CHINTAMANI: Yes, sir. You might not be an Aryan, but my respected father and I are Aryans. Alas! Where could my glorious ancestors be? Where are Kashyap, Bharadwaj, Bhrigu? What kind of talk is that?

ADWAITA: What rot this man speaks! Kashyap happens to be my ancestor. We are all part of the Kashyap clan—how can Kashyap, Bharadwaj, Bhrigu be your ancestors?

CHINTAMANI: Since you know nothing about these issues there is no point in discussing these things with you. I'm afraid this is all the tragic consequence of English education.

ADWAITA: Hasn't English education affected you?

CHINTAMANI: Sir, you can't blame me for such a thing. Because of the Aryan blood coursing through my veins, I ran away from school at quite an early age.

(*Enter* HARIHAR BABU *and several other writers*)

ADWAITA: Please come in. Have you got it all in writing?

HARIHAR: Yes. Here it is.

CHINTAMANI: Sir, what have you been writing about?

HARIHAR: Lots of things.

CHINTAMANI: Have you written anything about the Aryans?

HARIHAR: No.

CHINTAMANI: About the science of the Aryans?

HARIHAR: The Europeans are Aryans and their science—

CHINTAMANI: The Europeans are a very inferior race and compared to the knowledge that our Aryan forefathers had, they are really illiterate. I can prove this. Even now all descendants of Aryans invoke Aswathama before massaging oil over their bodies and then pour oil thrice on the earth. Do you know why they do so?

HARIHAR: No.

CHINTAMANI: Do you?

ADWAITA: No.

CHINTAMANI: Do you?

FIRST WRITER: No.

CHINTAMANI: If you don't, then why talk about science? Do you know why Aryans click their fingers when they yawn?

ALL: *(in unison)* No, none of us do.

CHINTAMANI: Really? Do you know the reason why our Aryan women beat the hand-fan on the floor if the fan touches the body of the person they are fanning?

ALL: No, not at all.

CHINTAMANI: See, you know nothing. Without discussing these issues at all, without any sort of enquiry into such matters, you persist in saying that European science is the best. And yet you don't even know why Aryans sneeze, yawn or massage oil.

HARIHAR: All right, sir. You tell us. Why must oil be poured on the ground before it is poured over the body?

CHINTAMANI: Magnetism! Nothing else. This is what is known in English as magnetism.

HARIHAR: *(surprised)* Have you read anything about magnetism in English science?

CHINTAMANI: Nothing. No need for that. There is no need to study English to learn science or anything else. What do our Aryans say? There are three forces in nature—life force, causality and positivism. Just before taking a bath, the slippery force of oil being added to these forces creates physical negativity within our body. This is nothing but magnetism. Just think—the practice of wiping the body with a towel prevalent among Englishmen since the nineteenth century has been practiced by our Aryans for thousands of years for they have been using the gamchha for the same purpose since then.

THE WRITERS: *(with surprise)* Wow! How commendable! What scientific skill the Aryans have! What great research our Aryan Kundu Sir has undertaken!

HARIHAR: We have fallen into the hands of a real idiot today! But there is no point in annoying him. He writes for several newspapers. I have heard that this Aryan Kundu is quite adept at cursing gentlemen a lot. That is why he is famous.

719

CHINTAMANI: Look over there. That Aryan Brahmin is plucking flowers early in the morning. Why do you think is he doing such a thing?

ADWAITA: To give them to the god during prayers.

CHINTAMANI: Shame, shame. You don't bother to get to the bottom of things. When the sages permitted the plucking of flowers at dawn it became obvious that they were aware of the presence of oxygen in the air. Since they knew of this, there is no doubt that they also knew of the presence of other gases too. In this manner we can clearly prove by moving from point to point that they were aware of all that was subsequently discovered by modern European chemistry. Why do we click our fingers when we yawn? That is also magnetism. When the rising gases combine with positivism, then the negative force conducted by the physical force exceeds the life force, causality and the positive force by its own power. Then the three qualities of *sattwa, rajah* and *tama* achieve exceptional attributes. During this phase, the heat caused in the air as a result of the friction between the middle finger and the thumb combines with the heat of the nervous system and solar heat to prevent the ultimate destruction of physical heat. If this can't be called science, what can it be called? Isn't it curious that none of our Aryan sages ever read any book by Darwin?

THE WRITERS: Amazing! Blessed be the achievements of the Aryans. All this time we couldn't understand such theories.

HARIHAR: *(to himself)* But even today I don't understand anything.

CHINTAMANI: If you are wondering about the hitting of the hand fan on the floor, then that too is magnetism. Expansion, expulsion, repulsion and attraction—these physical acts add up to—

ADWAITA: Spare us, spare us Sir. My head is reeling. You can write about the hitting of the hand fan in my newspaper. You have said enough already. Let me get you a paan so that you can chew on it.

CHINTAMANI: No, sir. I haven't come here to have a paan. You aren't following Aryan customs and actions. The spiritual force flowing in our Aryan veins for generations, that force—

ADWAITA: Enough, enough! I won't give you a paan; you need not have one. If you permit me I will get you some tobacco instead.

CHINTAMANI: Tobacco! What horrors! What a thought! It is even worse. Do you know why high caste people don't smoke the hookah used by lower caste people? Why doesn't one caste consume food touched by another caste? Why did the Aryan in earlier times not even tread over the shadow of a non-Aryan? Don't you think there is a science behind it? Of course, there is. Let me explain it all to you. That too is magnetism. The three kinds of bodily radiance—excellent, mediocre and base—

ADWAITA: Stop, stop. I won't give you tobacco. You need not smoke the hookah. No need for paan or for tobacco—do what is convenient for you, something that will retain your bodily radiance.

THE WRITERS: Shame on you, Adwaita babu. You did not allow us to listen to the learned words of Sri Kundu, the best of the Aryans.

FIRST WRITER: (to the second writer) Sri Kundu has such exceptional reasoning skills and knowledge. But, did you understand anything?

SECOND WRITER: No, nothing. Let us ask him properly once again. Sir, you spoke of causality, reason, and many other forces, what are they?

CHINTAMANI: They are nothing more than what is known in English as force and magnetism.

THE WRITERS: (in unison) Oh, we've understood.

HARIHAR: Sir, I am none the wiser!

THE WRITERS: (disgusted) You still can't understand anything? Magnetism, force,—these are easy concepts. You know what magnetism is. You know what force is. This is also the same thing. We know all of this because of the exceptional scientific enquiry pursued by the Aryans.

FIRST WRITER: If you have to understand these things clearly then you need to know all sorts of scriptures. Haven't you read the scriptures?

CHINTAMANI: No, I haven't. My father and I, and Nafar Kundu, are Aryans—that's why I don't consider it necessary to study the scriptures.

SECOND WRITER: That's true. But you've certainly read science very well.

CHINTAMANI: Not at all. I've acquired the theories of sneezing, coughing, breaking the knuckles of the fingers and other specific scientific theories from my imagination. It wasn't necessary for me to study science. You will probably not believe it, but swearing on the Aryan holy books I can say that I have studied neither Aryan scriptures nor scientific discourse. Everything that I know is the product of my imagination.

HARIHAR: Yes, but you certainly don't need not swear by it. No one will ever accuse you of studying!

(From *Hasyakoutuk*)
Translated by Somdatta Mandal

The Funeral

Scene One

Ray Krishnakishore Bahadur is lying on his deathbed. His three sons Chandrakishore, Nandakishore and Indrakishore are busy consulting each other. A doctor is present. The women are close to tears.

CHANDRA: Who are the people we should write to?

INDRA: Write to Sir Reynolds.

KRISHNA: *(with great difficulty)* What will you write, son?

NANDA: The news of your death.

KRISHNA: But I am not yet dead, son.

INDRA: You might not die right now, but we have to fix a time for the event and write that down . . .

CHANDRA: We should collect the condolence letters from all the Englishmen here and get them published in newspapers. No point in publishing them when all the excitement is gone!

KRISHNA: Patience boys; let me die first.

NANDA: We can't wait, father. Let's make a list of the letters to be sent to the people in Shimla and Darjeeling. Come on, let's get all the names down.

CHANDRA: The Governor, Sir Ilbert, Sir Wilson, Beresford, Macaulay, Peacock—

KRISHNA: Boys, what names are you chanting so close to my ears? Chant God's name instead. When the time comes He is the only one who can save us! Hari—

INDRA: Yes, good thing that you reminded us, we forgot to include Sir Harrison.

KRISHNA: My sons, say Rama, Rama—

NANDA: Really, I had forgotten about Sir Ramsey.

KRISHNA: Narayan, Narayan!

CHANDRA: Nanda, write down the name of Sir Noran also.

(Enter SKANDAKISHORE*)*

SKANDA: So, you people seem so relaxed! You still haven't done the real thing!

CHANDRA: And what is that?

SKANDA: We have to inform in advance all the people who will be part of the procession going to the funeral ghat.

KRISHNA: Sons, which one do you consider the real thing? First I'll have to die, only then—

CHANDRA: No worries on that account. Doctor!

DOCTOR: Yes sir!

CHANDRA: How much time is left for father to go? When do the public have to be here?

DOCTOR: Perhaps—

(The women start wailing)

SKANDA: *(disgusted)* Ma, will you stop it? You're creating quite a scene! It's better to sort out everything in advance. When doctor will—

DOCTOR: Most likely this night at—

(The women start wailing again)

NANDA: This is a huge problem! You shouldn't disturb us during work. What do you think your crying will accomplish? We are planning to publish condolence letters sent by important Englishmen in newspapers.

(The women are sent out)

SKANDA: Doctor, what do you think?

DOCTOR: From what I can see I think he will expire around four a.m.

CHANDRA: Then there is no time—Nanda, go quickly, get the slips printed at once right in front of your eyes.

DOCTOR: But first mustn't the medicine—

SKANDA: Look here! Your medicine shop will not run away. On the other hand, we'll be in trouble if the printing shop shuts down.

DOCTOR: Sir, the patient might not—

CHANDRA: That is why you must hurry. For who knows what might happen if the slips are printed before the patient—

NANDA: Here I go.

SKANDA: Write down that the procession will begin at eight tomorrow.

Scene Two

SKANDA: What, doctor? It's already seven now instead of four.

DOCTOR: *(apologetically)* Yes, yes, amazing the pulse is still strong.

CHANDRA: You are a fine one doctor to have got us into this mess!

NANDA: Everything went wrong when I was late in bringing the medicine. In fact, Baba began to recover as soon as the doctor's medicine was stopped.

KRISHNA: All this time you were so very cheerful; why is everyone looking so glum all of a sudden? I am feeling fine now.

SKANDA: We aren't feeling that great. We had already finalized all preparations to go to the funeral pyre.

KRISHNA: Is that so? I guess I should have died.

DOCTOR: *(feeling irritated)* Do one thing and that will solve all problems.

INDRA: What?

SKANDA: What?

CHANDRA: What?

NANDA: What?

DOCTOR: Why doesn't one of you die instead of him when the time is ripe?

Scene Three

(A lot of people have assembled in the outer house)

KANAI: Hello, It's already eight thirty. Why are you all late?

CHANDRA: Please sit down. Have some tobacco.

KANAI: I've been chewing tobacco from the morning.

BOLAI: Where is everybody? I can't see signs of any arrangements being made.

CHANDRA: Everything is ready—it's not our fault—now only—

RAMTARAN: Hey, Chandra, we shouldn't waste any more time.

CHANDRA: Don't I understand that—but—

HARIHAR: What is causing the delay? We'll be late for office; what's the matter?

(INDRAKISHORE enters)

INDRA: Don't be impatient. We are almost ready. In the meantime why don't you read the condolence letters?

(He distributes them)

This is from Lambert, this from Harrison, this is Sir James's—

(SKANDAKISHORE enters)

SKANDA: Here take them. In the meantime read the obituary notices on father in the newspapers. Here is *The Statesman,* here *The Englishman.*

MADHUSUDAN: *(to Yadav)* Isn't this typical? Bengalis won't ever learn what punctuality is all about.

INDRA: You're absolutely right. They will die and yet never learn to be punctual.

(The guests shed tears reading the newspapers and the condolence messages)

RADHAMOHAN: *(in tears)* Oh God, the poor man's friend!

NAYANCHAND: Alas! To think that even such a good man has his share of troubles.

NABADWIPCHANDRA: *(in a deep breath)* Lord! Everything is your will!

RASIK: "The lotus that blooms in the heart"—I'm forgetting what comes after that—

> The lotus that blooms in the heart
> Has been plucked untimely
> The lotus heart sinks in the sea of sorrow!

This is exactly the case here. The lotus heart in the sea of sorrow. How sad! Add esquire. O tempora! O mores!

TARKABAGISH: *Challachittam, challabittam, challajiwan*—The mind is inconsistent, wealth is transitory and one's life is perishable. Oh how sad!

NYAYABAGISH: *Yadupathe kri gata mathurapuri, raghupate*—Where is the city of Mathura that belonged to the Lord of the Yadavas (i.e. Krishna), to the Lord of the Raghus (i.e. Rama Chandra)? . . . *(chokes)*

DUKHIRAM: Oh Krishnakishore Bahadur, Where have you gone!

A faint voice can be heard from within: I am here. Please, don't shout.

Translated by Somdatta Mandal

Ordeal

Scene One

The lawyer DUKORI DUTTA *is sitting on a chair.*
KANGALICHARAN *enters nervously, ledgers in hand.*

DUKORI: What do you want?

KANGALI: Sir, you are a well-wisher of the nation—

DUKORI: Everyone knows that. But what do you actually want?

KANGALI: You have devoted your life for the welfare of the ordinary man—

DUKORI: And I do so while I am carrying on my legal business, but what is your point?

KANGALI: Sir, actually I don't have much to say.

DUKORI: Then why don't you finish soon?

KANGALI: Think for a while and you'll have to admit *ganat paratram nahi,* that is to say, nothing is better than music—

DUKORI: Look here, man. Before I admit anything I need to know the meaning of what you just said. Say it in Bangla.

KANGALI: Sir, I don't know the exact Bangla meaning. But the main idea is that one loves to listen to songs a lot.

DUKORI: Everyone doesn't like them.

KANGALI: Anyone who doesn't like songs must be—

DUKORI: Lawyer Dukori Dutta.

KANGALI: Sir, don't say such things.

DUKORI: Then should I lie?

KANGALI: The sage Bharata is the first Aryan to have—

DUKORI: If you have any law suits to file against the Sage Bharata then tell me. Otherwise stop giving a speech on him.

KANGALI: I had a lot of things to say.

DUKORI: But I don't have the time to listen to a lot of things.

KANGALI: Then let me state the case in brief. In this city we've established a society called Ganonnati Bidhayini, that is to say, The Society for the Betterment of Music. Sir, we want you—

DUKORI: To deliver a lecture?

KANGALI: No, Sir.

DUKORI: To be the chairman?

KANGALI: No, Sir.

DUKORI: Then tell me what it is that I have to do. Let me tell you beforehand, as far as singing songs and listening to songs is concerned, I have done neither previously, and will not do either of these things in the future.

KANGALI: Sir, you won't have to do either. *(advancing a receipt book)* Just a small donation—

DUKORI: *(startled, gets up)* Donation! Good grief! You aren't an easy man to please. When you came in you appeared to be a good-natured man and entered with an embarrassed face—I thought then that you were in legal trouble. Take your donation booklet immediately or I will file a police case against you for trespassing.

KANGALI: Wanted a donation but got a beating! *(to himself)* But I'll teach you a lesson.

Scene Two

DUKORI BABU, *some newspapers in his hand.*

DUKORI: This is great fun. Someone called Kangali Charan has informed all English and Bengali newspapers that I have donated five thousand rupees to their Gannonati Bidhayini Society. What donation? The only thing I didn't do is throw him out by the collar. In the meantime I've gained a reputation that will be very good for my business. They will also benefit from this. People will think that since they have got five thousand rupees as donation, it will turn out to be a huge meeting. No doubt they will get greater donations from elsewhere. Nevertheless, fortune will surely favor me.

(The CLERK *enters)*

CLERK: Sir, have you donated five thousand rupees to Gannonati Sabha?

DUKORI: *(scratching his head and smiling)* Well, it is just a story someone has made up. Why do you listen to it? Who told you that I have donated anything? Suppose I did, so what? Why make a fuss about it?

CLERK: Oh, what humility! Paying five thousand rupees in cash and then trying to conceal the deed is no feat for an ordinary man.

(Enter SERVANT*)*

SERVANT: Plenty of people have assembled downstairs.

DUKORI: *(to self)* See! In one day my income has increased. *(gladly)* Bring them upstairs one by one—and bring paan leaves and betel nut as well as some tobacco.

(The first supplicant enters)

DUKORI: *(shifting a seat)* Come—be seated. Sir, have some tobacco. Who is it? Hey—could we have some paan?

FIRST SUPPLICANT: *(to himself)* Really, what an amiable person! If he doesn't fulfill one's desires, who will?

DUKORI: And what could have brought you here?

FIRST SUPPLICANT: Your generosity is famous all over the country.

DUKORI: Why listen to such gossip?

FIRST SUPPLICANT: What humility! I had heard about you earlier, but today the difference between sight and sound has been eliminated.

DUKORI: *(to self)* I hope he will come to the point now. Plenty of men are waiting downstairs. *(openly)* So, what do you need?

FIRST SUPPLICANT: For the development of the nation, from the heart—

DUKORI: Yes, it is good of you to mention the heart.

FIRST SUPPLICANT: That's right. Great honorable persons like you are India's—

DUKORI: I am agreeing to all that you are saying so why don't you concede this part to me? And so—

FIRST SUPPLICANT: It's the habit of people who are full of humility that when it comes to their own virtues—

DUKORI: Spare me sir. Come to the point!

FIRST SUPPLICANT: You know, the fact is that day by day our country is regressing—

DUKORI: That is because people don't know how to say things concisely.

FIRST SUPPLICANT: Our once rich and glorious motherland is now mired in poverty.

DUKORI: *(like a long-suffering person, covering his head with his hand)* Go on.

FIRST SUPPLICANT: Day by day sinking in the well of poverty—

DUKORI: *(in a pleading tone)* Sir, what is the point?

FIRST SUPPLICANT: Then let me tell you the real thing—

DUKORI: *(enthusiastically)* That's better.

FIRST SUPPLICANT: The English have been looting us.

DUKORI: This is something worth pursuing. Collect proof and I will appeal to the magistrate's court.

FIRST SUPPLICANT: The magistrates too are sharing the spoils.

DUKORI: Then I will lodge an appeal in the court of the District Judge—

FIRST SUPPLICANT: The District Judge is a dacoit.

DUKORI: *(surprised)* I can't figure you out.

FIRST SUPPLICANT: Let me tell you, all the money from the country is being sent abroad.

DUKORI: That is terrible!

FIRST SUPPLICANT: So a meeting—

DUKORI: *(alarmed)* A meeting?

FIRST SUPPLICANT: Yes, see this is the booklet.

DUKORI: *(wide-eyed)* Booklet?

FIRST SUPPLICANT: Some donation would be—

DUKORI: *(jumping up from the bench)* Donation! Get out—out—out!

(Quickly the table is overturned, ink spilled, the first supplicant tries to exit hurriedly, falls down, gets up, chaos ensues)
(The SECOND SUPPLICANT *enters)*

DUKORI: What do you want?

SECOND SUPPLICANT: Your country-wide munificence—

DUKORI: I've gone through it all once before. Tell me if you have anything new to say.

SECOND SUPPLICANT: Your patriotism—

DUKORI: Good lord! He seems to be saying exactly the same things!

SECOND SUPPLICANT: Your virtuous acts for the motherland—

DUKORI: This is too much! Come straight to the point!

SECOND SUPPLICANT: A meeting—

DUKORI: What? Another meeting?

SECOND SUPPLICANT: Here, see this booklet.

DUKORI: Booklet? What booklet?

SECOND SUPPLICANT: To collect donations.

DUKORI: Donations! *(pulls his hand)* Get up, get out, out—if you love your life—

(*The man leaves without saying anything else.*)
(*Enter* THIRD SUPPLICANT)

DUKORI: Look, here. Appeals to my patriotism, generosity, politeness —all these have been exhausted. Try something else.

THIRD SUPPLICANT: Your openness, philanthropy, and liberal views—

DUKORI: That's somewhat better. At least he's saying something new. But sir, leave all those things and start our discourse.

THIRD SUPPLICANT: We have a library—

DUKORI: Library? Not a society?

THIRD SUPPLICANT: No sir, no society.

DUKORI: Oh! I'm relieved. Library! Excellent. Go on.

THIRD SUPPLICANT: Here, see the prospectus.

DUKORI: Sure this isn't a subscription booklet?

THIRD SUPPLICANT: No sir, not at all. Merely printed leaflets.

DUKORI: Oh! What next?

THIRD SUPPLICANT: A small donation.

DUKORI: *(jumping up)* Donation! Who's there? There's a dacoit in my house today. Policeman! Policeman!

(The THIRD SUPPLICANT *escapes as fast he can. Enter* HARASHANKAR BABU*)*

DUKORI: Come in, come in, Harashankar. I remember our college days. But we haven't met since then. You don't know how happy I am feeling after seeing you.

HARASHANKAR: I too have a lot of pleasant and unpleasant things to share with you. But I will do those things later. First let us finish a piece of business.

DUKORI: *(excited)* I haven't heard anyone talk to me about business for a while now, brother. Tell me, tell me so that I can fill my ears with business talk. *(Harashankar takes out a booklet from under his shawl.)* Oh, what is that? I see a booklet coming out!

HARASHANKAR: The boys in my locality have decided to hold a meeting—

DUKORI: *(startled)* Meeting?

HARASHANKAR: Yes, sort of. So for a small donation—

DUKORI: Donation! See I have loved you for a long time now but if you utter that word in my presence we will become enemies for ever.

HARASHANKAR: Is that so! You can donate five thousand rupees to some Ganonnati Sabha of Khargachhia but cannot sign a cheque of five rupees at the request of your friend? One must be a heartless person to step in here to seek your company!

(Exits with great speed)
(A MAN *enters, notebook in hand)*

DUKORI: Notebook? Bringing a notebook to me yet again? Get lost, will you?

THE MAN: *(scared)* I've come from Nandalal Babu—

DUKORI: I don't care for Nandalal or anyone else. Leave immediately.

734

THE MAN: Sir, what about giving some money—

DUKORI: I won't pay you any money. Get lost.

(*The* MAN *runs away.*)

CLERK: Sir, what have you done? He was trying to return the money Nandalal Babu owed you. We need to get the money back today. We can't do without it.

DUKORI: Good grief! Go and call him back.

(*The* CLERK *goes out and comes back a little later.*)

CLERK: He's gone. I couldn't find him anywhere.

DUKORI: This is a problem indeed.

(*A* MAN *enters with a mandolin in hand.*)

DUKORI: What do you want?

THE MAN: We need connoisseurs of music like you. What haven't you done for the advancement of music! I will sing a song for you.

(*He starts playing his mandolin immediately and sings a song set to the tune of Raga Iman Kalyan.*)

Glory be to Dukori Dutta
In the world his munificence . . . etc. etc.

DUKORI: What nonsense! Stop, stop.

Ordeal

(Enter a SECOND MAN *with a mandolin in hand.)*

SECOND MAN: Sir, what does he know of music? Listen to my song:

Dukori Dutta you're a blessed man
Whoever knows your greatness can . . .

FIRST MAN: Glory—g—l—o—r—y

SECOND MAN: D—u—u—u—u—kori—i—i

FIRST MAN: Duk—o—o—o—

DUKORI: *(with fingers in his ears)* Oh my god! I can't take it anymore!

(A man enters, tabla in hand)

PLAYER: Sir, a song without musical accompaniment? How can that be?

(He begins playing. A second player enters.)

2ND PLAYER: What does he know of accompaniment? He cannot even hold the tabla correctly.

1ST SINGER: Stop.

2ND SINGER: Why don't you stop!

1ST SINGER: What do you know about singing?

2ND SINGER: What do *you* know?

> *The two start arguing about the scales and rhythm of music. Then they fight with their mandolins.*
> *The two players start bandying the beats used in tablas such as "dhekete didhey ghene gedhe ghene." The contest climaxes with a tabla duel.*
> *(Enter a group of singers and some more men with donation booklets in hand.)*

1ST PERSON: Sir, song—

2ND PERSON: Sir, donation—

3RD PERSON: Sir, meeting—

4TH PERSON: Your benevolence—

5TH PERSON: A Khayal in Raga Iman Kalyan—

6TH PERSON: For the welfare of the country—

7TH PERSON: A tappa song by Sari Miyan

8TH PERSON: Shut up, shut up!

9TH PERSON: Please stop, brother. Let me finish my words.

Everyone starts pulling Dukori's shawl and shouts of "Sir, listen to me, Sir, listen to my words" can be heard, etc.

DUKORI: *(in a voice admitting defeat)* I am going to my uncle's place. I will stay there for a while. Don't give my address to anybody.

(Exit)
The brawl between the singers and the musicians continues in the house for the whole day. In the evening the clerk tries to stop the quarrel, gets injured, and collapses.

Translated by Somdatta Mandal

Testing the Student

The student is called SRI MADHUSUDAN *and* SRI KALACHAND MAS-TER *is his tutor.*
(Enter the GUARDIAN)

GUARDIAN: Kalachand babu, how is Madhusudan faring in his studies?

KALACHAND: Sir, Madhusudan is a very naughty boy but good in his studies. I never have to repeat anything twice to him. He never forgets what I have taught him once.

GUARDIAN: Really! So let me put him to a test today.

KALACHAND: Sure, go ahead.

MADHUSUDAN: *(to himself)* Yesterday Mastermoshai beat me so badly that my back is still hurting. I will have my revenge today. I am going to have him thrown out.

GUARDIAN: So now Modho, do you remember all that you've been taught till now?

MADHUSUDAN: I remember whatever Mastermoshai has taught me.

GUARDIAN: OK. Tell me then—what is a plant?

MADHUSUDAN: Something that comes out of the earth.

GUARDIAN: Give me an example.

MADHUSUDAN: An earthworm!

KALACHAND: *(with eyes flashing)* What did you just say?

GUARDIAN: Shhh Sir . . . , don't tell him anything now.

(To MADHUSUDAN*)*

You have studied poetry; so, tell me, what blooms in the garden?

MADHUSUDAN: Thorns.

*(*KALACHAND *takes out a cane)*

Why sir, why are you caning me? Am I lying?

GUARDIAN: All right. Who destroyed Siraj-a-daullah? What does history teach us?

MADHUSUDAN: Insects.

(He is caned again.)

Sir, I am being caned for no reason at all! Not only Siraj-a-daullah, but my entire history book has been eaten up by insects. Have a look.

(He shows the book. Kalachand Master scratches his head.)

GUARDIAN: Do you remember any of the grammar you've been taught?

MADHUSUDAN: Yes.

GUARDIAN: What is a "subject"? Explain it with the help of examples.

MADHUSUDAN: OK. The subject is Joy Munshi who lives in the other village.

GUARDIAN: Can you tell me why?

MADHUSUDAN: He is a doer, busy with many virtuous rituals and activities.

KALACHAND: *(angrily)* You must be off your head!

(He canes him on his back.)

MADHUSUDAN: *(startled)* Sir, it's not the head I am talking about, it's my back.

GUARDIAN: Tell me, what is the best way of compounding words?

MADHUSUDAN: I don't know.

(KALACHAND BABU canes him again.)

I know the answer to this one very well. It's the grammar of the cane.

(The guardian laughs. KALACHAND BABU is not amused at all.)

GUARDIAN: Have you learned your maths lesson?

MADHUSUDAN: Yes, I have.

GUARDIAN: All right. Suppose you are given six and a half pieces of sweets and told to eat as many as you can in five minutes. Whatever remains will have to be given to your younger brother. If you need two minutes to eat one sweet, how many will you end up giving to your brother?

MADHUSUDAN: Not a single piece.

KALACHAND: How come?

MADHUSUDAN: I'll eat all of them. I wouldn't want to give the sweets to anybody!

GUARDIAN: All right. Suppose a banyan tree grows a quarter of an inch each day. If the tree was ten inches tall on the first of the month of Baisakh, how tall will it be on the first of Baisakh the next year?

MADHUSUDAN: If the tree grows crooked then I won't be able to say; but if it grows straight then we'll be able to measure it and find out its exact height; but in the meantime if it dries up then there is nothing to be done.

KALACHAND: Your brain won't function at all till you get a good beating. Rascal, it's only when I'll beat you black and blue that you'll straighten up.

MADHUSUDAN: Sir, even very straight things will bend if you keep beating them.

GUARDIAN: Kalachand babu, you're mistaken. Physical abuse won't get you far. There is a saying that you cannot flog a donkey and turn it into a horse, but sometimes a flogged horse can turn into a donkey. Most students are capable of learning, but most teachers aren't capable of teaching. But it's the pupil who gets the beating. Please take yourself and your cane away and let Madhusudan's back rest for a few days, and then I myself will start teaching him.

MADHUSUDAN: *(to himself)* Oh, I am so relieved!

KALACHAND: Sir, I am so thankful. Only a laborer will enjoy teaching this boy—all it amounts to is manual labor. After working on him for thirty days all I get is only five rupees, while the same labor in tilling the earth would fetch me at least ten rupees per day!

Translated by Somdatta Mandal

The Invention of Shoes

"O Minister Gobu!" King Hobu declared,
    "Do you hear? I stayed up all night,
Wondering why my feet should be smeared
    With dust when I walk? It's not right!
The money you earn is your sole concern;
    As for serving the king, no one cares.
For my feet to be soiled by the land I govern—
    What a terrible state of affairs!
        You must do something about it fast,
        Or this very day shall be your last!"

Worried to death, Gobu started to sweat,
    For the king's words had given him a fright.
All the pundits paled at this royal threat,
    And the courtiers were sleepless all night.
No stoves were lit, no food prepared
    In their homes, for they wept instead.
With tears flowing down his greying beard,
    Gobu fell at Hobu's feet, and said:
        "If we get rid of dust, what blessings sweet
        Shall we obtain, when we bow at your feet?"

At this, King Hobu rocked to and fro
    In thought, then said: "That's spoken truly.

But first the wretched dirt must go,
    Then think about my blessings, duly.
If blessings are lost for lack of dust,
    You are not worthy of your wages.
Why then should I place my trust
    In all these scientists, all these sages?
        First things first; once that is done,
        All other battles will be won."

Reeling at the king's commands,
    The minister hunted everywhere
For learned men and expert hands
    From every land, both far and near.
They donned their glasses, all those men,
    Took nineteen kegs of snuff in vain,
And having pondered, said, "But then
    No soil means we can grow no grain!"
        "If that is so," the king enquired,
        "Why have all these men been hired?"

A million brooms were now purchased,
    In a plan to make the world dirt-free.
Such clouds of dust their sweeping raised,
    It choked the king, this cleaning spree.
For dust, they couldn't see clearly enough;
    The sun was lost in a dusty cloud;
The dust made people sneeze and cough;
    The town was wrapped in a dusty shroud.
        Said Hobu, "In trying to end the curse
        Of dust, you've made things even worse."

With water bags, the bhishtis rush
    In hordes, to make the dust subside.
With lakes and rivers turned to slush,
    No boat could float in the muddy tide.

For water, water-creatures pined,
    While land-beasts tried to swim, in vain
In depths of slime all trade declined,
    And fever plagued the whole terrain.
        Fumed the king, "What foolishness!
        To make my land a sodden mess!"

Again came the wise men from far and wide,
    To talk about what could be done.
They grew dizzy-brained and bleary-eyed,
    But the war against dust could not be won.
"Let's cover the earth with mats," they said,
    "We'll smother the soil with carpeting."
Some said, "An airtight room, instead,
    Is a good place to lock up the king.
        If he treads not on the filthy floor,
        His feet will grow dusty no more."

Said Hobu, "The plan would work, I trust,
    But there might be a price to pay:
This land will be ruined for fear of dust,
    If I stay locked up night and, day."
"Then send for a leather-smith!" everyone cried,
    Let's wrap the earth in a leather pall,
In a bag the filthy world we'll hide.
        Let the great king's feat be known to all!"
        "That's easily done," they all agreed,
        "A suitable leather-smith is all we need."

Here and there the king's men raced,
    To their other tasks they paid no heed.
But no capable leather-smith could be traced,
    Nor hides enough to match their need.
The aged master leather-smith now
    Came forth, and smiling, said, "O Sire,

If you kindly allow, I can tell you how
    To easily gain your heart's desire.
        Just cover your feet, and it will be found
        That there is no need to cover the ground."

"How simple!" said Hobu. "But this is absurd,
    When the entire country has tried and failed!"
Cried Gobu, "This man's a wretch, by my word!
    Let him be speared! Then let him be jailed!"
The leather-smith knelt at the feet of the king,
    And wrapped them in hide from heel to toe.
Said Gobu, "I'd already thought of this thing!
    I wonder how this man got to know?"
        So that is how footwear had its birth:
        Gobu was spared, and so was the earth!

743

Translated by Radha Chakravarty

From *Out of Sync*

Bird-seller says, "This is a black-colored chanda."

Bird-seller says, "This is a black-colored chanda."
Panulal Haldar says, "I'm not blind—
It is definitely a crow—no God's name on his beak."
Bird-seller says, "Words haven't yet blossomed—
So how can it utter 'father' 'uncle' in the invocation?"

In Kanchrapara

In Kanchrapara
    there was a prince
[wrote but] no reply
    from the princess.
With all the stamp expenses

will you sell off your kingdom?
Angry, disgusted
    he shouts: *"Dut-toor"*
shoving the postman
    onto a bulldog's face.

744

Two Ears Pierced

Two ears pierced
   by crab's claws.
Groom says: "Move them slowly,
   the two ears."

Bride sees in the mirror—
in Japan, in China—
thousands living
   in fisher-folks colony.
Nowhere has it happened—in the ears,
   such a big mishap.

In School, Yawns

In school, yawns
Motilal Nandi—
says, lesson doesn't progress
in spite of concentration.
Finally one day on a horse-cart he goes—
tearing page by page, dispersing them in the Ganga.
Word-compounds move
float away like words-conjoined.
To proceed further with lessons—
these are his tactics.

1937
(From *Khapchhara*)
Translated by Sudeep Sen

10

Travel Writing

In BOYHOOD DAYS, TAGORE vividly recounts the solitary hours he spent as a child, hidden inside an abandoned palanquin in the courtyard of his family home, fantasizing about journeys to exotic faraway places where extraordinary adventures awaited him. In *My Reminiscences,* he recalls how as a young boy, he traveled with his father via Bolpur and Amritsar to Dalhousie (near Kashmir), where he was left to wander across the Himalayan mountain peaks on his own. At seventeen, he was sent to England to study; though he returned to India without a formal degree, this first journey to a foreign land awakened his curiosity about cultures other than his own. These early experiences infused in the young Tagore's mind an intense wanderlust that was to remain a constant feature of his psyche. In his adult life, Tagore toured the world several times, and also traveled to different parts of the Indian subcontinent. The essays, letters, poems, and lectures in which he reflects upon these experiences offer a panorama of the outer world viewed through Tagore's eyes and also some invaluable glimpses of the poet's inner world, for they are replete with thoughts and emotions about life, art, history, philosophy, and literature.

In 1912, during Tagore's visit to England, Yeats read the *Gitanjali* poems at William Rothenstein's home in Hampstead Heath. Later, Tagore spent some time in Staffordshire at the home of a clergyman, a friend of C. F. Andrews. Tagore's essays and letters, written at this time, appeared in various journals such as *Tattwabodhini, Prabasi,* and *Bharati,* and were published as the collection titled *Pather Sanchay (Glimpses of the Road)* in 1939. An expanded version appeared about 1948. Several pieces in this section are from this important collection, in which Tagore reflects upon cultural practices at home and abroad, and the idea of travel itself.

On his way to the United States in 1916, Tagore traveled to Japan on a Japanese vessel, *S.S. Tosha Maru.* He spent four months in Japan.

His impressions of this visit, in *Journey to Japan* and *In Japan,* were serialized in *Sabuj Patra,* edited by Pramatha Chaudhuri, and appeared as a book, *Japanjatri (A Traveler in Japan),* in 1919. Chaudhuri's wife Indira Devi translated many of the pieces for volume three of the *Visva-Bharati Quarterly.*

748

After his trip to Holland in 1920 and his exposure to Dutch scholars of Hindu and Buddhist culture, Tagore longed to trace India's civilizational links with neighboring regions. In 1927, he set out on a journey to Southeast Asia, stopping in Java, Bali, Siam, Singapore, and Malaya. Many of his experiences on this trip are recounted in *Java Jatrir Patra (Letters from Java),* serialized in *Bichitra* and published in book form as *Jatri* in 1929. This tour had a major impact on Tagore's creative practice. Along with his daughter-in-law Pratima Devi, for instance, he pioneered the art of batik in India on his return. Tagore also incorporated Balinese elements into Rabindra *nritya,* the dance form he had created. In a letter to Jawaharlal Nehru, Tagore speaks of the need to revive "the historic forces of Asiatic unity": "India's great awakening had crossed deserts and mountains, the overflow of her glorious epoch of culture touched far continents and left permanent deposits in distant shores of Asia. In my visits to China and Japan, and to Siam, Java, and Bali, I felt profoundly moved to find how the communion of our culture had persisted even up to our own days" (Santiniketan, 17 August 1939).

In 1930, Tagore traveled to Russia and spent two weeks in the country, observing the Soviet system and the position of its peasants. In *Russiar Chithi (Letters from Russia,* 1931) he praises Soviet policies concerning education and economic development, but critiques the lack of freedom in Russian society. The British Raj banned the English translation of *Russiar Chithi,* primarily because Tagore seemed to feel that British policy in India compared unfavorably with Russian educational practices.

In April 1932, Tagore traveled by air to Iran as a guest of the ruler Reza Shah Pahlavi. Here, he was moved by the people's hospitality and by their artistic achievements. He then moved on to Iraq, where he spent a day in a Bedouin camp in the desert, fulfilling a long-cherished dream.

Tagore's vivid responses to his experience in this part of the world are recorded in *Parasye* (*In Persia,* 1932).

Tagore also traveled to China, Sri Lanka, Europe, the United States, and Latin America. Some of his experiences in these places are represented in other parts of this volume. He never adopted the superficial approach of the average tourist. Always he probed beneath the surface and critically examined his own culture in light of the practices he had observed abroad. His journeys were undertaken with a variety of motives, including education, fundraising for Visva-Bharati, literary activities, and personal invitations. In the course of his travels, he forged personal and emotional bonds as well as professional ones. Once his reputation as a writer was established, the boundaries between public and private tours became blurred.

His journeys to different parts of India were as significant as his foreign tours. His visit to Shahi Bagh in Ahmedabad as a teenager inspired one of his best-known stories, "Hungry Stone." His sojourn in East Bengal had a profound effect on his social vision. For the first time, he encountered rural life, and as a zamindar or landowner, witnessed the plight of the poor. He was also deeply moved by the landscape. The impact of this experience is apparent in some of the writings included elsewhere in this volume, especially in the extracts from *Chhinnapatra* and *Chhinnapatrabali.*

Tagore's travel writings vary in style and mood according to occasion and audience. In his letters, the tone is often intensely personal and not always guarded; for instance, some of his early comments on life in England, published as *Europe Prabasir Patra* (1881), proved embarrassing for him in later life, and he felt compelled to revise them. Some travel essays are episodic and in the style of a journal or diary. In public speeches, the language is more formal, and it concerns Tagore's impressions of a place as much as his own self-image. Sometimes he recorded his impressions in verse, as in his two poems on Thailand, "To Siam" and "Farewell to Siam" (1927), and on Bali, "Sagarika" (1927).

Travel made Tagore aware of the relativity of things; it broadened his horizons and contributed to his complex, nuanced understanding of the relationship between the civilizations of the East and West. His travel writings demonstrate his eclecticism, his curiosity about the world, his passion for life, and his openness to new ideas and influences.

The City of Bombay

Yesterday afternoon I went out to get a glimpse of the city of Bombay. My first impression was that the city of Bombay has a distinctive feature; Calcutta has no such special feature, as if it has somehow been haphazardly patched together. The fact is that the sea has given a particular shape to the city of Bombay. It has hung on to this shape through its semicircular beaches. The pull of the sea seems to be at work in all the streets and lanes of Bombay. I feel that the sea functions like a gigantic heart; it courses through the veins and arteries of the city and sustains them. The sea has made this city look out to the vast beyond forever.

The River Ganges once was one of Calcutta's ties with nature. Its flow was the open path that carried with it news from distant lands and what took it towards unknown mysteries. It was the one window of the city from where you could look out and realize that the world was not confined to this settlement. But the once natural strength of the Ganges has been dissipated—it has been dressed up in such tight clothes on both its banks and its waist band has been tightened so that the Ganges seems to be the image of an undertaker of the city. One cannot figure out now how once upon a time it could have had functions apart from transporting huge bales of jute on barges. Haven't the feelers of dolphins hid themselves in shame within the spiky masts of the ships?

The special glory of the sea is that it serves man but does so without wearing the yoke of slavery on its neck. The business of shipping jute cannot hide from view the blue jewel in its mighty heart. That is why the image of an ocean flowing next to this city is of something that is indefatigable. On the one hand, it spreads the fruit of man's work around the world; on the other, it keeps out of sight man's feeling of exhaustion, dispersing the sense of leisure before the possibility of endless work.

So when I saw hundreds of decked up men and women sitting on the beach, I liked the sight very much. They could not ignore the call of the ocean that relaxing afternoon. They do their work close to the lap of the sea and they also enjoy themselves in her lap. In our Calcutta we have the Eden Gardens, but she is the daughter of a miser—there is no lure in her voice. In that garden created by the men of the Raj, there is much disciplining and many things that are forbidden. But the ocean was not created by someone and so there is no way that one can fence it in. This is why there are regular festivities and such merriment taking place on the beaches of Bombay regularly. Calcutta has no such place for such uninhibited enjoyment.

What delighted me most of all is the sight of the men and women who had assembled there all around. The poverty of the Calcutta scene, bereft as it is of womenfolk strikes one here. We see only half of mankind there, and that is why we do not see it in its joyous elements. Surely, not being able to delight in the sight is a sort of punishment. Also, the lack of such sights constrains the minds of people and has prevented them from blossoming. How unfortunate are those human beings who cannot savor the very natural beauty of the view of men, women and children all gathered on the beach in an afternoon to partake of the same happiness. We have become used to a sadness that has kept us in a state of stupor but there is no doubt that the losses we suffer in the process keep piling up everyday. Men and women meet all the time within the four walls of a room, but can only such meetings suffice? There is a wide open world out there that exists for men to meet one another—cannot we enjoy the simple delight of meeting in such a natural ambience?

Our car came and parked in front of a garden in the hills of Matheran. The small garden was encircled with benches on all sides. Here also I saw housewives sitting with their relatives and enjoying the natural breeze. Apart from some Parsi ladies, there were also Marathi women with *sindur* on their foreheads, a sort of loveliness writ large on their faces. That one's existence is imperiled, that one has to protect oneself from the gaze of anyone around them—this idea is least in their

752

minds. I kept thinking to myself how the burden of constraint had come off the head of the whole country and how compared to us, the lifestyle here has become easy and beautiful in many ways. If the simple right to spread the natural air and light of the earth is prevented, mankind erects an unnatural barrier for itself—this truth can be perceived by anyone observing the always hesitant and helpless state of the women of our country. The long history of cruelty against the women of our country becomes evident when we view our women in railway stations. Strolling in this garden at Matheran, I tried to remember our own Beadon Park and Goldighi—how wretched they appeared now to be.

When butterflies go to look for honey in the garden of flowers, they are not inclined to show off; as a matter of fact, they are then too rapt up in their work. But this does not mean that they don black over-coats for going to office then. When I see the assorted colors of the clothes that people wear here, this is the thought that occurs to me. I do not believe that there is a dire necessity for making our working atmo-sphere deliberately drab. The colors in the turbans, sari borders and saris of the people of Bombay express and encourage happiness in their lives. No sooner had I left Bengal, I began observing this phenomenon. The farmer who is working in the field has a turban on his head and a coat frock on his body. Needless to say, the women are as colorfully appareled. This external difference between us and the people here does not seem insignificant to me. It is this external difference from us that has led me to respect them. They do not neglect themselves; they make themselves remarkable through appearing neat. This is an obligation men owe to other men; if this penchant for dressing up is absent then man's bareness expresses itself in a very ugly manner. If each person does not try and protect his own society from the squalor associated with the failure to dress up because of habitual insensitivity, our slackness will lower the es-teem of our country in the eyes of the world.

I noticed one other thing in the city of Bombay. This was the wealth of the locals. How many Parsi, Muslim and Gujarati traders' names I saw emblazoned on the walls of mansions! So many names in-scribed so prominently cannot be seen anywhere in Calcutta. There the wealth stems from salaried service and the zamindari system, hence it is very drably displayed. The wealth of the zamindars is like stagnant water; it shrinks with use and gets polluted through profligacy. We do not find the expression of human strength there; there is no new flow of revenue either. It is for this reason that the people in Bengal feel so timid despite whatever wealth they possess. I see that the Marwaris, Parsis, Gujaratis and Punjabis are more liberal in their donations, but Bengalis are the least charitable of people. The donation books in our region are like local cows—they are hardly found grazing in the fields. The people of our region have not been able to experience wealth hence their miserliness is ugly, while their notion of extravagance is even more horrifying. It makes me happy to see that while the lifestyle of the rich people here is simple, they are liberal with their wealth.

1939
(From *Pather Sanchay*)
Translated by Somdatta Mandal

Crossing the Ocean

Arabian Sea,
17 Jaisthya, 1329 B.S.

Crossing the dock, I boarded the ship. I have boarded a ship several times on earlier occasions but each time I feel sort of hesitant in the beginning. This hesitation is not because of being among unknown people in unknown places. I feel the separation between the ship and my own life very deeply. The people who have built this ship, those who are sailing in it, they are the lords of this ship—I have just got a place here by purchasing a ticket. For generations so many sailors have left their invisible trail on the unmarked paths of this ocean; so many hundreds of deaths have repeatedly occurred to make this path gradually easier. That I can freely eat and move about in this ship during the day and sleep peacefully at night—can this reliability be procured only through money? Behind it lie so many layers of thought, so much accumulated courage, whereas we have nothing to offer yet.

When I see these English men and women playing on the deck, sleeping and gossiping, then I can see that they are not just only on the ship; they are also relying on the strength of their fellow beings. They surely know that what needed to be done has been done, and what needs to be done, will also be done; this is why their entire nation is so dedicated. For any life risk that might occur, they not only have the captain but the entire nation which, with its natural endeavor and untiring alertness, is prepared to fight against death till the last moment. Thus they are moving so freely and cheerfully on that firm ground without bothering to consider the waves on all sides. Here they are receiving what they have already given; and we, who have not yet given anything, are also taking it. Thus as we are crossing the ocean we are leaving debts behind us. That is why I feel hesitant to sit on the deck along with these English passengers.

On land we use a lot of foreign items but that does not cause a sense of poverty in our minds. On the ship it seems that we are taking even more. This is not just a factory—there are human beings in it. The people who are navigating the ship are doing it with their own bravery and strength; if we had the sense to realize how we are relying on their humanity, then the sound of money with which we had bought our tickets would also have blended with the sound of other values as well. Today I feel a sorrow in my heart because they are steering the ship with their hearts while we are travelling by just paying some money. How and when shall we be able to cross the great ocean that lies between the two of us? We have not yet begun; there are still so many human sacrifices to be made, so many ties to be broken, so many beliefs to be trampled upon. Whenever I think of this I understand that by making a few paper boats and blowing a few speeches on them will not lead us anywhere.

Severing ties with the shore we are now in the middle of the blue ocean. I feared that as inhabitants of the land I would not be able to tolerate the sway of the ocean but the seasonal turbulence of the Arabian Sea was yet to begin. Not that there is no disturbance at all; the westerly wind is blowing and the waves are lashing against the front of the ship. But this has not caused any revolt within my body. So my first encounter with the ocean has begun as an address of love; it has not shaken out and emptied the poetry out of the poet; the dance of my blood can keep good pace with the tune in which she is playing the beat. But I shall not be able to raise my head if she suddenly wishes to become violent and play the tune of destruction. But it seems in his trip she is not going to apply her great powers over this scared disciple.

So I spend my days holding on to the railing of the ship and looking at the water. Our journey began towards the end of the full moon cycle. The night over the ocean is just like the ocean itself; I stand still and watch the union of two infinite things; quietly listening to the union spread around the horizon—stasis with movement, silence with sound. I like to watch the way in which the waves fall and rise on both sides of the ship. It seems as if the ship is cutting through the core of a flower and the white petals are instantly spreading out on either side.

In this quiet night I have the deep sound of the ocean in front of me, while behind me is the constant fun and frolic and laughter of the passengers of the ship. Every time I have travelled in a ship I have felt that the passengers did not have a moment to look at the serene eternity that surrounds our little lives. Their attachment to life is so strong that even for a single moment they cannot cross the distance required to understand the truth of life. This is why their ceremony of worship is such a grand affair—as if they have to detach themselves from one place for a moment to reach the other. If this ship was full of Indian travelers, then even amid the day's work and pleasure we would have seen people pressing their palms together unashamedly and paying obeisance to eternity; even amidst petty laughter and gossip, they would very easily break into religious songs. The here and the eternal, man and god are all blended together. The idea that the union of both these elements results in complete truth is so easily ingrained in our minds that we do not feel any hesitation about it. But I cannot imagine that these English passengers would break into religious songs within the course of a small break in their merrymaking and while gambling on the deck, if they suddenly lift their eyes and see one of their fellow passengers sitting on a stool praying, then they will all be very disappointed and consider him out of his mind.

This is why we do not find the benign gleam of spiritual awareness in their lives; a one-sided fierceness reveals itself in their work and conversation instead.

This ship has such wonderful arrangements. We do not know the whole mystery behind the way she constantly fights her way through time and space. Day and night I can feel the beat of its hard iron heart going up and down. The great power and effort emanating from the burning of her stomach and the hot steam churning in her veins are hidden from our eyes. Up here amid a lot of leisure and laziness we are made aware of the timings for food and bath through the occasional sound of a bell. I keep on thinking about the place where they prepare the meals for all these hundred and fifty to two hundred passengers. That also takes place behind our eyes. We can neither hear their sound, nor smell anything. When we go and sit at the dining table then everything is decorated and ready; the food items are continuously served like the easy flow of a river.

What is really worrying is that while crossing such a huge ocean these people do not accept the least bit of inconvenience or any little shortage in food and pleasure. They are unwilling to accept any form of excuse and in all conditions want to keep their personal needs at the highest level. As a result, even their impossible requirements are met with. It is only people who do not have the courage to demand, people who somehow spend their days compromising with wants, believe that half of what they have should be given to pundits. As a result, even from that half, only the half is excluded and the pundits are engulfed in their own learning.

But if one thinks of taking all the advantages, then one has to carry a heavy burden. Every little arrangement for comfort takes up such a lot of space! They have the power to carry such weight and do not feel the slightest shame about it. In this instance I am reminded of our school system. There also arrangements have to be made to feed two hundred people four times a day. There is no dearth of effort but even then shouting continues from four in the morning to one o'clock at night. There is nothing more than bare essentials and though the arrangements are reduced as much as possible, the weight of the wastage does not decrease.

The confusion increases, garbage is accumulated, and no one knows what to do with the rice water, vegetable peels and the extra food. Gradually one stops thinking about it and somehow continues with the mounds of waste. We are unable to say with emphasis that this cannot be done because if you say that you will have to bear the burden. In the end, we go to the beginning and see that neither do we have the confidence nor the power to bear such burden. This is why we can bear only sorrow and inconvenience, but are unwilling to bear any responsibility.

A highly-placed railway engineer is travelling with us. He told me, "I have tried very hard to collect locks, keys and many other small essential items from our country for the railway department. But every time I see that they cost more and are not of good quality." The cost of merchandise and salary is increasing on the one hand but the products that are manufactured cannot compete with the market prices of the world. He further added that those factories that are run by European management have very little impact on the people of our country. Again, those under local management cannot extract full labor—most of them do not have the power to make people work with their maximum strength. This is why though the wages are low, the price of things cannot be reduced. The power generated is not equivalent to the number of people working.

Though it does not sound nice, this is the sight visible wherever you look in our country. All kinds of work have become difficult there and the only reason for it is that we do not get the complete man. Hence we have to work with more people and at the same time it is beyond our power to make them work in a regulated manner and satisfy them. This is also the reason why the paraphernalia of work becomes several times more important than the actual work; there is more waste than the arrangement and the holes in the boat go on increasing in such number that more labor is expended in spilling out the water than the actual rowing of the boat. Anyone who has attempted any sort of work in our country will vouch for it.

I asked that engineer, "Are not prices going down in your country because of joint business and quality factories?"

"It might be so," he replied. "But in any country we cannot say

758 that joint business comes first and development follows later. If men are inclined to joint business then it happens by itself." He added, "I have seen the rise and decline of many local joint businesses near Madras in South India. I have seen that no one has the loyalty to run such an organization; everyone only looks after his own individual needs. For this reason, nothing can be constructive. If this stern loyalty is expedited in our national character then all kinds of collaborative efforts are possible."

I liked his words. It is not true that prosperity comes through programs because at the very root of it we have man. Each work in our country begins by depending on one particular man but after that people who accept that same work depend a lot on it but do not turn out to be so dependable. This is because they do not look so much at the work as they do look after themselves. For every little thing their clenched fist becomes loose; instead of avoiding any impediment they try to leave it and run away while constantly thinking that given another situation they would have got better results. This is how things get scattered—from one it results in five pieces and all the five turn out to be failures. Until the time comes when people will accept both success and failure bravely and also complete their defined job with utmost loyalty, any attempt at joint business venture or group welfare project will be impossible in our country. This loyalty does not come from intelligence; it is generated from the heart, from life. With what strength does man carry himself in total failure? Calculating the profit and loss in one's life seems petty compared to the attraction of the entire life. If this was not true then man would have committed suicide to free himself of trivial reasons, trivial losses and trivial unhappiness. Thus, if we do not have some amount of respect for the work towards which we have dedicated our lives; if we are not attracted to it without feeling the sense of loss; if we cannot stand for it with due respect even when we are defeated; if we do not have the strength to hold the flag of success high even at the time of death; if we do not totally neglect the lesson by which we can come out of the magic circle as Abhimanyu did; then we shall not be able to create anything, nor protect it. In spite of all gain and loss, all defeat, first of all we need the strength to say, "This is ours, so this is mine." After that, some day or another, we shall be able to overcome the sea of impediments in whatever program we follow.

Nowadays even in the western countries we hear that European life is depleting itself by attempting too much of work; this allegation is not entirely false. I have mentioned earlier that Europe is determined not to accept any deficiency or drawback. She has unlimited faith in her own strength and the determination to express that strength in its full glory and achieve the impossible. But even then, there is a limit to power. We cannot say that we will light the candle very brightly and at the same time not let the wick burn. This is why the more the lifestyle demands increase in the western countries, the more they burn themselves. Determined not to compromise with comfort, their burden constantly grows larger and larger in size. This burden creates a pressure somewhere. Wherever this pressure is created, an equal amount of sadness is also being generated but without equal amount of compensation. In order to maintain equilibrium in this affected society, it therefore tries to raise its head intermittently like a volcanic earthquake. The constant increase in gadgets for the comfort of man is actually replacing man himself. Where is the end to this? Man is turning himself into a machine for fulfilling all his material wants. In which leisure moment will he find himself? He has got to put a full stop at any cost and say, "Here are my gadgets, now I must rescue myself. I will have to provide whatever is essential for me, but all these are unnecessary."

This means whenever the efforts of man go on at the same momentum, he reaches a point where he feels unsuccessful. The road to completion is not smooth. This is why what pains Europe today does not pain us. Europe has constructed her physical body and is trying to establish the spirit inside it. Our spirits have lost the body and are roaming fruitlessly around the earth like ghosts. Where is the external manifestation of that spirit? There is the religion of god in it, so it does not live without spreading its wealth. It wants to manifest itself in different ways —through the state, business, society, art, literature and religion. But where are the ingredients? Where is the control over those ingredients? I find that if we try to bind the body in one place, it becomes loose on the other—even if it remains dense for a moment, the next moment it evaporates. So today we must understand this body mechanism by whatever means possible; we must understand at any cost that a soul without a body is never true because the body is part of the soul. It gives us movement, power and death, but the soul gets its stability, happiness and eternity only along with it. It is this incompleteness of creating the body that makes the ugly soul of our country pine for it century after century. By distancing the external truth our internal spirit is constantly creating only dreams. It is losing its weight. This is why there is no proof or limit to its superstitions; this is why it sometimes plays with truth as if it is illusion; and sometimes takes illusion and tries to use it like truth.

1939
(From *Pather Sanchay*)
Translated by Somdatta Mandal

Travel

Red Sea
21 Jyeshtha 1319

Human beings were wild creatures once, and so were horses. Man could not run, but the horse could run like the wind. How graceful its movements were, and how unhindered its freedom! Man would watch with envy. If only I had two pairs of legs like those, capable of moving at lightning speed, he thought, faraway places wouldn't appear so remote, and in no time at all, I would conquer the furthest corners of the world. The joy of running, which danced swiftly through every fiber of the horse's being, aroused an intense craving in the heart of every human being.

But man was not born to languish in a state of yearning without doing something about it. "How can I acquire the horse's four legs?" he wondered, as he sat beneath a tree. Only humans are capable of conjuring up such strange ideas. "I am a biped who walks upright. How can I ever possess four legs? I must always walk slowly, one step at a time, while the horse races ahead at a tremendous speed. This law cannot be altered!" But man's restless spirit refused to accept this.

One day, he trapped the wild horse with a lasso. Grabbing its mane, he clambered onto its back and conjoined his body with the horse's four legs. It took him very long to bring those four legs completely under his control. He suffered many falls, many fatalities, but refused to be discouraged. He would rob the horse of its speed: that was his resolve. Ultimately, it was he who triumphed. Slow-footed man captured the element of speed and began to put it to his own use.

Traveling on land, man eventually found himself confronted with the sea. Now there was no way of moving forward. There lay the blue waters, their depth unfathomable, shores out of view. And countless waves, wagging their forefingers to warn the land-dwelling humans: "Take one step forward, and we will teach you a lesson. None of your coercion will work here." From the shore, man gazed at this boundless expanse of prohibition. But this negation also bore within it a great invitation. The waves were dancing in noisy mirth. The seashore had not succeeded in tying them down. Looking at them, one felt as if millions of children had been released from school. Shouting, leaping about, they could not have their fill of exuberance, it seemed. As if the world was a football that they wanted to kick into the air, tossing it up into the sky. At this sight, the human heart could no longer remain calm and inactive, there by the edge of the sea. The turbulence of the sea began to clash its cymbals within man's own bloodstream. Man now wanted to possess the freedom of that unrestricted expanse of water, stretching to the very horizon. He now began to covet the ocean's joy, which could conquer all distances. It was his desire to plunder the horizon, just like those waves.

But how could he satisfy an urge so bizarre? The shoreline marked the limit of human dominion. All human desire must end at this fullstop. But human desire surges and spills over, precisely where it is supposed to end. It refused to accept the obstacle as insurmountable.

Ultimately, one day, just as he had done with the wild horse, man seized the ocean-wave by its foaming mane and mounted its back. The angry ocean shook its back. There is no saying how many humans drowned, how many lost their lives. Finally, a time came when man succeeded in yoking even this disobedient ocean with himself. From its furthest shores, the entire ocean came and bowed its head at his feet.

761

What man becomes when linked to the vast ocean, is something we are experiencing on board this ship. We are small, humble creatures indeed, standing quietly in a corner of the vessel, but the remotest distances are connected with us. Standing motionless here, I have conquered even the faraway places of which not the faintest shoreline is visible. The very obstacle that separates us is bearing me forward on its back. The whole sea is mine, as if it is my own giant body, or like my own outspread wings. What obstructs us is precisely the thing we must transform into our chosen path, our means of liberation: that is the Almighty Ishwar's injunction upon us. Those who have followed this injunction are the ones who have attained freedom. Those who have disobeyed it have made this world a prison, fenced in by their own little village, tethered to their own little corner, their shackles clanking at every step.

We sailed on blissfully. I had feared that my body would not be able to withstand the ocean's roll. But that fear was dispelled now. The slight rocking movement seemed to caress rather than assault me. The sea was bearing me along, cradling me in her lap, as carefully as a father carries an ailing son. That is why, on this journey, the rigors of travel had not troubled me at all up until now. I was only relishing the joy of travel.

It was to savor this joy that I had set forth. For a long time, I had been feeling a desperate urge to travel like this, venturing out into the world. On many occasions, as I sat alone on the first floor balcony of our house at the ashram, gazing at the sky above the sal trees ahead, the sky had signaled to me, pointing at the remote distance. The sky was silent. But still, the call of all the unknown mountains, rivers and forests from faraway lands, welling up from every side, had suffused the blueness of the sky. Soundlessly, the sky carried all those distant murmurs, all that babble, to me. "Come, come, step outside!" it urged me constantly. The urge was not about travelling for some need, but about travelling for the sheer joy of it.

The heart wants to go on; that is its dharma. For unless it moves, it dies. Hence it keeps on moving, on the pretext of various needs and diversions. You've seen the flocks of geese on the alluvial sandbanks of the river Padma in early autumn, haven't you? Leaving their nests on the shore of some desolate lake encircled by impassable Himalayan peaks, flying incessantly for so many days and nights, they have descended on this Padma sandbank. In winter, the Himalayas, grown monstrous with mist and snow, drive out the geese, and they set out to change their habitat. So at that time, the geese indeed have a need to travel south. But still, there is something else, greater than that need. From this flight across the remote mountains and rivers, the inner spirit of these birds derives a sense of joy. Called upon frequently to change their abode, their entire life is shaken up, given a chance to become aware of itself.

I too had felt within me the call to change my abode. I must leave the bonds that kept me confined, and move elsewhere. Move on, move on, move on. Move like the waterfall, like the ocean waves, like the birds at dawn, like the light at sunrise. That is why the world is so vast, the earth so extraordinary, the sky so infinite. That is why dancing atoms and molecules fill the universe, and countless galaxies, carrying their own tents of light like wandering bedouins at the world's margins, traverse the sky without knowing where they are going. The universe does not decree at all that we should settle forever in one place and make our permanent nests there. That is why the call of death is nothing but the same call to change one's abode. Under no circumstances will it allow life to remain imprisoned within the walls of some tradition—death exists only to make life advance on the path to survival.

That is why I am travelling now. Like the fairy tale prince who suddenly set out one day for no reason to cross the seven seas, I have ventured forth into the outer world today. The princess has fallen asleep: she cannot be awakened from her slumber. A golden wand is needed. Remaining in the same place, the same system of practices renders life immobile and senseless, leaves it clinging only to its own bed, without any awareness of this vast world. Now it is time to seek out the golden wand, to voyage out to faraway places. Now there is a need for a consciousness that will constantly knock on the closed doors of our eyes, ears and hearts with sundry new versions of the new, shredding our threadbare veil to reveal the ever-new. How vast, how beautiful, how free is this world! What spirit, what light, what bliss! Having captured this world, how diversely man observes, contemplates and constructs it! There are no limits to the space where his spirit, emotions and imagination find full play. How endlessly and extraordinarily diverse is this human mental realm, which encircles the world! That's what this world of mine is all about. This is why my heart hears within it the call to circumnavigate this entire terrain, to witness it with my very own eyes.

No one has the means or the time to explore this immense diversity exhaustively. If one can only emerge with the aim of viewing the universe face to face, one can attain the fruits of such a vision. In a sense, the universe is everywhere. But still, only if one journeys forth, discarding languor, breaking old habits, opening one's eyes to the world, can our vision break free of its confinements and our soul be reborn, to feel the touch of the spirit that animates the universe. One who is immobile and lacking in initiative ends up losing what is absolutely near at hand. Hence, it is when we struggle to unearth the treasure close at hand that we succeed in grasping it at a very profound level. That is the real purpose of all our travel—to affirm at every step the existence of that which is always there, which can never be lost, to declare: "It exists, it exists, it exists!"—for our hearts too, constantly, in ever-new ways, touch the ancient and primordial as we move.

1939
(From *Pather Sanchay*)
Translated by Radha Chakravarty

Stopford Brooke

I don't think there is anything to be ashamed of if I feel happy because someone likes any of my works. As a matter of fact, there is nothing as arrogant as to say that one has not been happy about it. Whenever I have published a book, I have sent it forth with an ingrained hope that people will like it. If that is considered presumption then we can say that the publication of the book itself is a presumptive act.

Once, when I had some time to relax I had attempted to translate a few of my own poems and songs into English. I had never presumed that I would be able to write in English; hence I did not expect laurels for my English compositions. But to listen to my own emotions being expressed in a foreign language and the pleasure of finding it in its new guise possessed me. It was as if I was seeing the contents of my heart in a completely new garb.

After I came to England, when some of these translations reached my friend, he accepted them with special warmth and grace. He got a few copies of them made and gave them to a few men of letters. They liked my works in English written as they were by a foreign hand. One reason for this perhaps was that my control over English was not so perfect that it could annihilate the foreign essence from my writings completely.

A copy of these translations reached Stopford Brooke. That is why one day he invited me to dinner. He was by this time an old man, probably past seventy. A problem with his blood circulation had caused an inflammation in one of his legs; he was finding it difficult to move and would sit with that leg raised on a stool. Age overwhelms some people, befriends others. But in his case old age could neither affect his body nor his mind. His youthfulness was amazing. I kept thinking that when you can see such youthfulness in an old man, then you really see him at his best. This was because his youthfulness was his primary quality; it did not decay as the flesh and blood body had; on its own it had kept all disease and decay at bay. He had a huge body; his face was handsome, only his ailing leg reminded me of the Mahabharata episode where Arjuna strikes an arrow at Dronacharya's feet before the fight as a mark of respect to his master, so also to strike the first blow, old age had hurled the first arrow near this man's feet.

God had blessed him with a happy life—he was immensely enthusiastic about painting, poetry, nature's beauty, and the multitudinous aspects of human life in civilization. Age had not diminished his ability to enjoy the sensory world around him. The capacity to imbibe the world around him was proof of his youthfulness.

I had earlier read his religious treatises and criticism of poetry. That day I saw that he was enthusiastic about painting too. Many of his paintings of natural scenery lay stacked in the corner of his room. All these were drawn from his own imagination. My painter friend praised these paintings very much. These had been composed not for exhibitions or entertaining other people—they were merely expressions of the feelings within him. It occurred to me that although he was already quite old, had to write a lot, and was not fully healthy—yet these things did not curb his enthusiasm. The intensity of the life-force within him was such that he was able to find the time to indulge in play on the canvas despite so much work. Indeed we could get to know about the intensity of his life-force from such playfulness. The majesty of man lies in his ability to wrest some time for himself despite the necessities of life that engage him. I have noticed this desire for freedom in many people who have achieved fame in this country. Their lives are not confined by their profession or place of work; there is always some empty space that they find enabling them to move about freely. I have seen a great scientist here whose chief hobby is Chinese painting. They have a significant amount of extra space in their life's storage for storing things other than what they are supposed to accumulate. For many of them, their vocation is just a part of their lives. The office is just one room in their establishment.

After climbing a lot of steps I met him in a small room upstairs. We had plenty of time to converse in private. From his talk I understood that though at some point of time there was the necessity for an external framework of Christianity—something that in English is called "creed" —this was now preventing the essence of pure religion from percolating among people. Whenever the mind of man outgrows its shelter, there is no greater enemy than that very shelter. The main reason why many people in this country have become adverse towards religion is because of its external manifestations. He told me, "Your poems don't smack of any religion or any creed and this, I believe, will make them particularly beneficial for the people of our country."

At one point during our meeting he asked me whether I believed in the idea of rebirth. I told him that I had no vision about a world other than the one we lived in and also did not feel it necessary to think about such a world. But I added that when I think about it all, then it occurs to me that it can never be that within the cycle of existence human life can be out of place—it was never so before, it will never be so later; this is the reason for which this life has expressed itself in a specific form, the same reason that helped it to begin in the first place will also completely end it too. It seems possible that the reincarnation of the body over and over again leads it towards a kind of wholeness. But I can neither believe that in his earlier birth man was an animal nor that in the next birth he will also have an animal body again. This is because nature has a rhythm of its own and it is unlikely that its harmony will suddenly be disrupted. Stopford Brooke said that he too believed in rebirth; his belief is that after various births when we will complete a cycle of life, then the complete memory of our earlier births will revive. His words impressed me. I felt that after we finish reading a poem, a mood similar to the mood in which it was written occurs in our minds, and if we do not come to its conclusion, then we will not be able to get its essence. Each of us weaves a distinct cycle of life for distinctive reasons, but even after the stringing of the beads is over, it is not the case that everything has been concluded. What we can only say is that an episode has been completed. It is then that we can comprehend everything clearly.

1939

(From "Stopford Brooke," *Pather Sanchay*)

Translated by Somdatta Mandal

The English Village and the Clergy

It is not always the case that a man is able to judge which profession will suit him the best. This is why the wheels of the work chariot groan so much as it moves along in the world. The man who should have opened a grocery store becomes a school teacher, the man who was born to be a police inspector has to work as a priest. Such discrepancies do not create much of a problem in other businesses but they certainly do so in the business of religion. This is because if a man cannot stick to the truth as far as religion is concerned, then not only does he invite failure, but he also creates misfortune.

There is a great discrepancy between the ideals of Christianity and the nature of the people of this country—the norms of total humility and charity laid down in the Christian scriptures do not seem to go with the people here. Right from ancient times, the urge to fight with nature and other human beings and the excitement of winning battles has been flowing in their veins through generation after generation. This is why when those who should have been enrolled in the army are appointed as clergy, the color of religion, instead of being white, turns crimson. This is also why we do not find the clergy in Europe always on the side of peace or totally committed to the welfare and justice of all mankind. During times of war they especially make god their commander and make the worship of god an occasion for bloodshed.

It is often seen that clergymen are unable to deal justly with those people whom they consider to be heathens. They feel as if these people have been created by some other god who is opposed to the Christian god. Hence they give the impression that by humiliating these people they will increase the glory of their own god. This hostility, this naked rivalry, has been always used by the clergy to torture people from other religions. Just like soldiers with weapons, they have tried to triumph by hurting other people.

This is the reason why we Indians have such a negative feeling about the clergy. We have always felt that they are totally different from us. They are ready to convert us into Christians but not prepared to be one with us. They will conquer us but will not ever treat us as their equals. They should have taken on the responsibility of uniting one nation with another. It should have been their duty to build bridges between men so that one race could maintain good relations with another and also do justice to one another. But the opposite has proved to be true. The Christian clergy have depicted a distorted picture of non-Christians and have portrayed their religion, society and customs in the worst possible light to their own countrymen. Surely every nation can be treated in such a way that either its meanness or greatness is made to stand out. But certainly every nation should be judged by its superior qualities. Vanity and the lack of love in the hearts of these people are the chief obstacles preventing them from exercising true judgment. It was to be expected from the people who had given themselves to the love of god that they would overcome such impediments. But demeaning other races, and creating a big divide between Christians and non-Christians, these clergymen have created a great gulf of suspicion between people to an extent hitherto unimaginable. They have put on communal dark glasses to view other people in their bid to spread their religion. There is always a big difference between the ruler and the ruled and this is the pride that comes from being powerful. This acts as a big impediment preventing human interaction. The clergy have made this pride even larger than religion and maintain the status quo. Thus even Christianity has become a handicap for our union; in fact, it has kept us from displaying the best in us.

However, I have found proof that we cannot generalize about any sect. I have met a Christian clergyman after coming here who is less of a clergyman and more of a Christian—someone in whom religion has not asserted itself aggressively as a business proposition but has blended and revealed itself through his whole life. He is a person about whom no one will think, "He doesn't belong to us, but to another group." He has made me believe whole-heartedly that he is a person who is happy to see truth and well-being prevail in all men and does not feel envious because it is not an exclusively Christian attribute. What is even more surprising is that his workplace is India. There is a great obstacle for any Christian in India wanting to remain a true Christian since he is the king there. Politics there is the spouse of religion. Often, it is the Queen Bee. This is why the clergy in India have not been able to empathize with Indian life. There is an intense conflict between their national interests and ours and at one point they are not able to listen to their Guru and will not lower their heads. He had asked his followers to conquer the world with humility, but that apparently is a law meant for another world. These people are the gods of this world.

The person whom I am speaking of is Reverend Andrews. The people of India know him well. He has earned the heaven-sanctioned right to be one with us by completely suppressing the regal attitude that his Englishness had given him. I consider myself privileged to have been a witness to the way in which the loveliness and liberal ideas of Christianity have become so clearly a part of his life. One day he said to me,

"Before going back to your country you should go and see the house-holds here. A lot of transformation has taken place in the cities so you will not get the true picture of domestic life unless you go to the villages." Mr. Andrews arranged for my stay for a few days with one of his friends who worked as a priest in a village in Staffordshire.

      The month of August in this country is considered to be part of the summer season. During this time the people from the city become impatient to breathe country air. In our country we interact freely with nature because the sky and the sunlight are so easily available to us. We do not have to make any special arrangement to come into contact with them. But here people are always eager to unveil the beauty of nature and their desire to possess it is never satiated. On every holiday they form groups and rush to wherever there are open fields; leaving the city and going out on long vacations. This is how nature always keeps them moving and does not allow them to settle down anywhere. The holiday trains are full of people and seats are impossible to find. Blending with the flock of city-bred people, I too left for the countryside.

      Our host was waiting for us at the station with an unhooded car. The sky was overcast when we boarded the car. The village revealed itself to us that canopied morning amid the pale covering of the sky. En route, it had started to rain. When we reached the house, his wife took us to her sitting room where the fireplace had been lit. It was not an old parish home but had been newly built. There were no ancient trees in the adjacent garden narrating the chronicles of forgotten human memories through their murmuring leaves. The garden was new, and had been probably created by the present owners. With multi-colored flowers blooming amid the dark green grass, it offered a feast for the eyes. I had never seen so much beauty and such abundance of trees and flowers this English summer elsewhere. It is really difficult to convey in words the density and the beauty of the dark green color of the grass; one had to see the scene to believe it.

      The rooms in the house were neat and tidy; the library full of readable books; there were no signs of neglect both inside and outside. This aspect of all civilized English houses strikes me as distinctive. Compared to us they use many more things for comfort and decoration of their houses but the owners take good care of even the smallest thing in each room. They understand quite well that being slack in one's affairs actually means demeaning oneself. This consciousness affects all their work, whether big or small. They do not demean the dignity of man and hence they make their houses of use in all respects; attempting to make their own surroundings, their society and their country fine in all respects. They are not willing to pardon lapses anywhere and for whatever reason.

Our host Mr. Outram took me out for a walk in the late afternoon. By then the rain had stopped but there was no dearth of clouds in the sky. Just as the men here always move around in black hats and grey clothes, the gods here seem to don very somber and formal clothing. But the beauty of the countryside was not covered up by these somber overcast shadows. My eyes were filled with the soothing sight of deep green undulating fields divided by fences made of creepers. Though hilly, the place was devoid of sharp folds. The undulating hills sloped down and met one another just as the melodious tunes of a soft raga of our country meld harmoniously into one. It seemed as if some god was silently playing the lyre of the earth in raga meghamallar. The glorious pride of the lofty mountains in the hilly states of our country was not on view here. Looking around on all sides, it seemed as if one could see wild nature completely tamed here; just as instructed by the dictates of Shiva's disciple Nandi, his favorite bull bowed down its horns and silently laid his soft and smooth body at the feet of his master, scared to raise his voice and disturb his meditation.

On the way Mr. Outram discussed something important with a man he had met on the way. The topic they were discussing was the following: to encourage farmers to build gardens around their houses, a committee had been formed to judge the best garden and award a prize for the same. The competition had ended a few days ago and this man had won the prize. Mr. Outram took me to see a few homesteads of the farmers of the village. Everywhere the farmer had taken great pains to grow flowers and vegetables all around his house. These people work in their gardens in the evening, having labored the whole day in the fields. In the process, they had become so attached to these trees and plants that they did not mind putting in the extra labor. Another good effect of this craze for gardening was that it kept the addiction to drinking at bay. The attempt to enhance external beauty gradually develops internal peace in one. I saw how Mr. Outram was also involved in other developmental activities of these villagers and realized how wonderful such a life devoted to the welfare of others could be. His service to God made him as mellow as a sweet ripe fruit. His house was lit by the lamp of humanity; studies and meditation cleaned it everyday. I will never be able to forget how simple and beautiful his hospitality was.

I now clearly saw how each of these clergymen had become the pivotal point of a few of these villages. This attempt to encapsulate the remote villages within the countrywide development schemes testifies to their spirit of growth and welfare. This is how religion is spread all over this country. Thus by such immense initiatives all the villages in this country are strung together in the manner of a necklace. Only those of us who see but cannot avail the fruits of such collective endeavor can know how beneficial such initiatives can be.

Man has not been able to build a system so perfect that it can ward off spuriousness or corruption permanently. Everyone in this country is aware that in an age of enlightenment some gaps have opened up between religious theory and practice. I have heard from several good people here that they find it impossible to go to church. They do not want to commit the sin of trying to believe in things that they can accept without questioning. In this way they have totally abandoned their faith in a religion that has become worn out in various ways. It is during such times that some wily old men have taken refuge within the folds of religion to corrupt it even more. Nowadays there are surely many clergymen who preach things that they themselves do not believe in; these men fool even themselves by attempting to believe what they preach. There is no doubt that such forms of corruption are harming society in different ways. Always, holding on to the form of religion blocks its main door in such a manner that only small and petty things are able to enter within and great things are left lying outside. This is the reason why all intellectually agile and humane men of Europe have fallen outside the purview of European religious rule. Such a situation can in no way ever serve humanity.

But Europe is protecting her soul. It does not get stuck anywhere. Movement is in its nature and so is hitting against all obstacles on its way and denuding them. Christianity has constrained itself and the manner in which it is providing an impediment to the flow of things needs to be altered by hitting back and widening its path. This process is going on daily; what the great thinkers define as true Christianity is something that has at last done away with its crude external covering. They do not believe in the Trinity and do not accept Jesus as a prophet or believe in the unnatural miracles described in the holy book of Christianity. They do not seem to them capable of mediating through the tangle of the present. In Europe at present there is a great upheaval in matters religious. It is certain that it will never allow its traditional religious beliefs to lag behind its total developmental plans or burden itself permanently.

773

In any case, the clergy have bound up the entire nation within the net of religious ideals, but despite sometimes creating impediments to prevent the development of the country, there is no doubt that they have also managed to vibrate the finer strings of the country in the most effective way. The Brahmins in our country also had this sort of work as their goal but because their work was tied to their caste consciousness, they inevitably lost sight of their responsibilities. The higher the goal a particular Brahmin sets for himself the more he will have to rely on his unique capabilities and special skills. But whenever this responsibility is thrust on a particular class for generations, such idealism gets curbed considerably. A man can be a Brahmin only if he is born in a Brahmin household—this simple and unnatural falsehood has been followed blindly in our society and hence the religion has turned moribund and is beset by superstitions. The Brahmin whom we are forced to respect by society is a person who does not consider it necessary that he should earn respect for himself by his deeds. What he does try is to rule society with the whip of his sacred thread but in doing so he keeps debasing it although, because of the blindness induced by custom, we do not manage to understand that this is what is happening. I do not believe that all the clergymen here have accepted the ideals of true Christianity and practice it perfectly in their lives devotedly; but because they are not clergymen by birth they are answerable to society and therefore cannot afford to stain their character. Thus, at the very least they try to display to the nation a purity of character and their devotion to their faith. Whatever our own scriptures might say, our people do not feel ashamed to undergo religious ceremonies done by impious Brahmins. This leads to a big gap between our religious beliefs and our acts; consequently we keep getting debased everyday. Here in England however, society will never forgive an immoral clergyman; he may not be very religious but he has to be seen as morally upright. It is through this means that society here is able to affirm its humanity and needless to say, it is thus that it has been able to develop its human resources.

That is why I was saying that the clergy here has managed to come up with a system of religious morality for the whole country that depends on plain living and plain thinking. But this is not sufficient in many cases. Again and again, when this country faces religious problems, the clergy do not try and solve them through Christ's message. Here I find them deviating from the responsibility they have undertaken of establishing Christ in the heart of their countrymen. How did all the clergy of this country view the Boer War when it broke out? Why are the clergymen quiet, now that two fat European ladies are attempting to divide Persia into two halves? Much injustice is done in India in relation to the recruitment of coolies, the system of employing them, in the administrative system there, and in the manner in which the English misbehave with the natives. Is it not the case that there are many instances of abuse which necessitate these people to follow Christ and stand next to weak and humiliated people? Have we ever witnessed such heavenly sights? There is a saying in English, "Penny wise, pound foolish." In matters of religion we see the same thing everyday in all big Christian nations— they want to be secure in their personal moral values, but elsewhere the entire nation gets together and shamelessly commits major sinful acts resulting in a lot of intolerable suffering in faraway countries. I have seen many noble-hearted people of this country stand up against this collective weakness, but how many clergymen are there among them? In fact,

774

if we conduct a survey amongst them, it will be revealed that most of them do not have faith in the way Christianity is practiced. On the other hand, if there is the slightest deviation from the traditional rites practiced in the Church, the entire clergy create a ruckus. Was this the reason why Jesus shed his blood? What positive message do the clergy of all these Christian nations spread when they keep holding on to their own petty religious funds while remaining oblivious of big shareholdings of the company going down the drain? I can see everyday that they value their god as they would a farthing but can also humiliate him for the sake of a sovereign. There are a few gentlemen among the clergy who are true friends of the world, but that is due to their own magnanimity. But if you look at them as a whole and entrust them with your religion then you are sure to be trodden to some extent. This creates a kind of caste system and though it is in many ways much better than the heredi-tary caste system, it also retains some of the poisons of the system. Be-cause religion liberates man it should be kept completely open. But if re-ligion is confined within the barriers created by a group, then gradually its meaner side becomes more well-known than its prominent side; exter-nal elements begin to enshroud internal ones, and temporal issues keep plaguing it on a daily basis. This is why, in spite of the country being full of clergymen, political leaders do not hesitate to resort to loot and mur-der. The clergy do not have that sacred halo which would allow them to get rid of the scar of evil from spreading publicly and taking a monstrous shape.

1939
(From *Pather Sanchay*)
Translated by Somdatta Mandal

From *Journey to Japan*

Yesterday two Japanese women came to demonstrate the indigenous art of flower arrangement. The preparation, thought and skill that goes into this activity is indescribable. One must concentrate on every leaf, every branch. I realized yesterday from the handiwork of these two Japanese women that the rhythm and harmony of the eye is vibrantly visible to them.

I had read in a book that the famous warriors of old would discuss the art of ikebana in their spare time. They believed that this enhanced their martial skills and heroism. Clearly, the Japanese do not take their aesthetic sense lightly; they know it is profoundly empowering for mankind. At the root of this empowerment is peace. Where the enjoyment of beauty signals bliss without attachment, it prevents the erosion of the life-spirit, and this aesthetic sense calms the excitability that can cloud human thoughts and emotions.

The other day, a wealthy Japanese gentleman invited us to a tea ceremony at his house. You have read Okakura's *Book of Tea* where this ritual is described. Observing it that day, I clearly understood that for the Japanese, this ceremony is comparable to a religious ritual. It is one of their national endeavors. From this, one can distinctly infer the nature of the ideal they have in mind.

After a long car-ride from Kobe, we first entered a garden—a garden replete with shade, beauty and tranquility. The people here understand what a garden is all about. You only have to step into a Japanese garden to realize that gardening is not merely about scattering some gravel, planting some trees and drawing geometrical designs upon the earth. Japanese eyes and hands have been initiated into beauty by Nature; they are conditioned to see, and to create. The shaded avenue leads to a place where clear water fills a hollowed-out rock beneath a tree. We wash in that water, each one of us. Then, leading us into a small chamber, they spread small round straw mats on benches, for us to occupy. We were supposed to remain there in silence for a while. One did not immediately encounter the host as soon as one arrived. To calm the mind and stabilize it, one was invited there gradually, in stages. Slowly, after pausing for rest in two or three rooms, we ultimately arrived at our final destination. The entire room was silent, as if shaded by an eternal twilight. No word passed anyone's lips. The enchantment of this shadowy, silent stillness began to overshadow the mind. Finally, the owner of the house walked in slowly, and greeted us with folded hands.

The rooms were virtually bare, yet one felt as if they were full of something, and resonant. There might be a single picture or just one vessel, placed somewhere in the room. The invitees would view the object carefully, and derive satisfaction from it. Something truly beautiful requires a vast, empty space around it. To crowd valuable objects together is to insult them—like forcing a loyal spouse to live with a co-wife. How radiant a few lovely items appear when revealed gradually, after periods of waiting, after stillness and silence have whetted one's mental appetite! This was something I realized after coming to this place. I remembered that in the ashram at Santiniketan, when I presented everyone with a newly composed song each day, the song would bare its heart to all who heard it. Yet the same songs, when offered as a bouquet to an assembly of friends in Kolkata, withheld their true beauty. There was clearly a lack of space around the songs when performed in a Kolkata house—the crowds, the daily routine of housework, and the attendant confusion, had impinged upon the music. Missing was the backdrop of the open sky, against which the true meaning of a song might be felt.

777

Now the master of house came and announced that tea was ready, and that for special reasons, he had assigned his daughter the task of serving it to guests. She came and greeted us, and began to prepare the tea. From her entry, through all the stages of the procedure, a poetic rhythm infused every step of the ritual. Washing and wiping, lighting the fire, removing the tea-cozy, taking the pot of hot water off the fire, pouring cups of tea, handing them out to guests—the restraint and grace of the entire process must be seen to be believed. Every piece of this tea service was rare and beautiful. It was the duty of the guest to view these vessels very carefully from every angle, turning them this way and that. Every piece had its own separate name and history. The care they deserved was indescribable.

That is the essence of the matter: to restrain the mind and body and absorb the beauty of these things into one's inner nature, in a calm and detached frame of mind. This is not the intoxication of the sensualist; there is no sign of the slightest excess. To withdraw from the mind's surface, which is ever-susceptible to sundry interests and needs, and to immerse oneself in the depths of beauty—that is the significance of this tea ceremony.

1919

(From *Japan Jatri*)
Translated by Radha Chakravarty

778

Letter to Pratima Devi

Dago. Bandung. Java.
26 September, 1927

Dear Bouma

We have come to a wonderful place. It's on a hill, five thousand feet high, we're told. There's quite a nip in the air. But this is nothing compared to the cold encountered on a Himalayan hill of similar height. Here we are the guests of a gentleman called Deemont. He has put us up. His wife is an Austrian, she hails from Vienna. Their beautiful house set in a girdle of gardens is perched on the hill. From here we can see the blue hill-girt city of Bandung right before our eyes. Not so long ago, there was once a lake in the hollow where Bandung sits now. Later, at some time or the other, the surrounding hillsides crashed down in a landslide and the lake water drained away. I'm really feeling very comfortable here in the quiet house in this beautiful, secluded place after all the recent hectic travels.

The man who has been tirelessly, enthusiastically accompanying us all along ever since our arrival in Java is called Samuel Copperborg, which basically means a mountain of copper. Taking his cue from this meaning Suniti has translated his name into Sanskrit as Tamrachuda. And Samuel is delighted that the sobriquet has been accepted in our circle. But you would really like to call him Swarnachuda, the golden pinnacle, instead. With extraordinary care and alacrity he has always anticipated even our smallest needs for comfort and convenience and striven manfully to fulfill them. He is a genuine and sincere friend. He's of a diminutive stature, but exquisitely large-hearted. We have seen so much of him on so many occasions all these days, but never noticed any insolence or meanness or vanity in him. We have also seen that he always puts himself last. He is frail and weak, yet he has never claimed any special privilege for that reason. He satisfies his needs with whatever is left after everyone else's needs have been satisfied. He has had to put up with the bluster of so many people, but I have never heard him complain about it or run anyone down. He can't speak or understand English well, nor is he quick on the uptake. But he makes up for this deficiency in words by exerting himself fourfold. At first he would accompany us in the car on trips to different places; however, the moment he saw that it was difficult for us to converse with him, he stepped aside and made way for English speakers to accompany us. But now it not only becomes inconvenient if he does not happen to be with us, I positively feel ill at ease, as well. He has so completely devoted himself to ensuring our dignity, position, comfort and happiness that we miss him a great deal even if he withdraws ever so little. He's a great friend of children everywhere—and this is one characteristic of this large-hearted soul of which I'm very fond. For their part the children think he's just one of them and of their age. The fact that he has so consummately taken to the people of Java is further evidence of his large-heartedness. He does his utmost to keep alive Java's cultural heritage of dance, music, fine arts, history and so on. An association called the "Java Society" has been established to discuss these issues and managing the affairs of this society claims all his time and energy. From my account you can imagine that we've fallen in love with this self-sacrificing man.

For you I have copied out on the other page the poem I wrote on Borobudur. This is all.

1929

(Letter no. 18, *Java Jatrir Patra*)

Translated by Subhransu Maitra

779

From *Letters from Russia*

Bremen Steamer
Atlantic
3 October 1930

After returning from Russia, I am today sailing towards the shores of America. Yet even now memories of Russia wholly occupy my mind. The main reason being that none of the other countries I have visited stir up the mind so totally. Their endeavors are in different spheres. Sometimes in politics, sometimes a hospital, sometimes a university, sometimes a museum—experts are carrying on their work in those particular areas. Yet here, the entire country, keeping only one purpose in mind, interweaving every working department into a single network of nerves and sinews, has created a mammoth body which has assumed the shape of one vast unique personality. Everything has been integrated and assimilated into this one sovereign endeavor to achieve a difficult goal.

In countries where money and power are sustained by dividing wealth for personal interests, such a deeply unified mindset is absolutely impossible. During the five year war in Europe, perforce most of the region's thoughts and actions had been controlled by a single conscience; this was however a temporary phenomenon. But what is happening in Soviet Russia today is of the very same nature—in the name of working for the common man, common mind, common right to possession, they have begun to create an uncommon entity.

One saying of the Upanishads has become extremely clear to me since I came here—Do not be greedy. Why should one not be covetous? Since everything is pervaded by one truth, personal avarice impedes the attainment of whatever is coming from that source. One who relinquishes his own rights is ultimately the one who really enjoys whatever is acquired from that one source. They say this solely from the economic point of view. They alone in the whole of mankind consider this one incomparable human truth to be the most important. They say that whatever is produced through that one source should be equally enjoyed by everybody. No one has ever gained anything through avarice. Therefore, do not envy another's wealth. Yet, if there exists individual division of wealth, envy will automatically arise. So by removing this division they want to say, the one who forsakes his own rights will enjoy the fruits the most.

In all the other countries of Europe the arduous endeavor is all towards personal gain and personal enjoyment. This has caused a huge churning and upheaval and as in the churning of the ocean by gods and demons in the Hindu mythology of the Puranas, from it has emerged both poison and nectar. However, the share of nectar is going only to one section, most of the people are not getting it at all—due to which there is no end to unhappiness and unrest. Everyone had earlier accepted this as inevitable; they said that greed is intrinsic to human nature, and it is the role of greed to create inequality in the sharing of enjoyment. Therefore, rivalry and competition would continue, and one should be always prepared for conflict. But from what the Soviets seem to be saying, we must understand that within mankind the only truth is unity; division is the illusion. The moment we deny the separateness of men, through collective thinking, collective enterprise and effort, by all the means available —the minute man as an individual is denied—that very moment, divisions will vanish like a dream.

This effort to deny the self is a movement the entire country of Russia is greatly involved in today. Everything is now included within this one effort. As a result, by coming to Russia, I was touched by one great big heart. Nowhere else have I seen a festival of education celebrated to such an extent. That is because, in other countries only those who are educated are the ones who reap its benefits—they alone enjoy the feast of milk and rice. Here, in each person's education lies the education of all. Any lack of education in one individual will reflect a collective lack in the others. That is because, through collective education, they hope to influence the collective mind to work for the success of all humanity. They are like the heavenly architect "Vishwakarma"; hence it is mandatory for them to become universal in their outlook. Therefore, it is they who realize the true spirit of university education.

1931
(Letter no. 7, *Russiar Chithi*)
Translated by Nandini Guha

From *In Persia*

Then I came outside and saw a war dance. Brandishing poles, guns, swords, shouting and moving in circles energetically: such was their frenzy. The women cheered them on from the doorway of the inner chambers. It was past four o'clock when we set out on our return journey, accompanied by our host.

These are the hardy children of the desert; they grapple with life and death on a daily basis. They do not expect any latitude from anyone for the earth has never pampered them. Biology speaks of natural selection. There has been a stern selection of the fittest through the most difficult tests of life. The weak have been weeded out. Among those who survive is this race. Death has tested them rigorously. The various tribes are extremely close-knit. They have inherited a small portion of their motherland; the few, hard-won fruits of their perilous lives they share equally. Their meals are served on a big common platter—there is no room for fastidious tastes. As they break and share the coarse unleavened bread, they seem to pledge to protect one another with their lives. I am a son of Bengal, a land of many rivers. As I eat I realize that in front of me sits a being of a completely different order. However, the language of humanity's deepest utterances is one that we both recognize. Thus when the uneducated Bedouin leader says, "Our ancient sage has said that the person whose words and actions do not threaten anyone is a true Muslim," I am startled. He claims that the seed of hatred among Hindus and Muslims in India lies in the minds of the educated. "Sometime earlier, some educated Indian Muslims had tried to preach violent communal divisions in the name of Islam here. I did not trust them," he says. "I refused their invitation to dine. They have no support amongst the Arabs, at least." I told him that I had written in one of my poems, "O that I were an Arab Bedouin!" Today I have come very close to the Bedouin heart. I have broken bread with them.

Then as our motorcar starts, the horsemen display their skills on either side in the two adjoining fields. It is as if the desert whirlwind has taken human form.

I think my travels have ended with the Arab Bedouin. There are still a few days left before I leave for home, but I am too tired to contemplate any further travel. That is why I find it satisfying to conclude my travels with these desert friends. I tell my host that I have experienced Bedouin hospitality, but without the experience of Bedouin brigands my journey will be incomplete. He laughs and says that poses a problem: "Our brigands do not harm old and learned people. Thus when the traders bring merchandise through our desert, they often dress up a wise-looking old man, place him on a camel and pretend that he is the leader." I tell him that on my travels to China I had told a Chinese friend, "I wish I could add some thrills to my travels by being caught by a Chinese bandit." My friend had said, "Our bandits would never harm an old poet like you. They respect ancient things." One cannot undergo youthful challenges at the age of seventy!

My travels in various places are now over. I return with my foreign friends' love and respect. And I hope I shall have the opportunity to savor peace after much toil. Youth battles youth, and in that conflict the stream of life is cleansed. When the brigand reveres the old man, he removes him from his world of violence. The brigand's test of strength is with youth; in that conflict, strength is all. Thus, under the mask of reverence, they seem to be saying, follow the ancient scriptures and retire to the forest after fifty.

1932
(From *Parasye*)
Translated by Shormishtha Panja

1861   Born on 7 May 1861 in the family home in Jorasanko, Kolkata, the fourteenth and youngest child of Sharada Devi and Debendranath Tagore.

1867   After being tutored at home, goes to the Oriental Seminary and then to another institution called Normal School. Continues with formal schooling for a few more years but is eventually educated at home.

1868   Writes his first poem and gets the reputation of being a child prodigy.

1875   Sharada Devi dies on 8 March.

Tagore recites a patriotic poem in a festival and has the poem published in the *Amrita Bazaar Patrika.*

Composes first song for his brother Jyotirindranath's play *Sarojini.*

1877–
1878   Begins writing his first novel, *Karuna,* which will be serialized in the periodical *Bharati.*

1878   Older brothers Jyotirindranath and Dwijendranath start a literary magazine called *Bharati* to which Rabindranath becomes a frequent contributor.

First book of verse, *Kabi Kahni,* is published.

Leaves for England in September 1878 with brother Satyendranath.

Admitted first to a school at Brighton and then to University College London.

1880   Abandons studies in England and returns to India without a degree or any professional qualification.

Helps brother Jyotirindranath set up Saraswat Samaj, which becomes the Bangiya Sahitya Parishad ten years later.

786

1881   Writes musical drama called *Valmiki Prathibha.* When the play is staged acts the role of the protagonist Valmiki. Henceforth, devotes himself to writing poems, plays, and prose.

1883   Publishes the novel *Bou-Thakuranir Haat.*

Composes the poem "Nirjharer Swapnabhanga," widely acknowledged as his moment of poetic awakening.

Marries Mrinalini Devi.

Becomes secretary of the branch of the reformist sect of the Brahmo Samaj founded by his father, called Adi Brahmosamaj.

Publishes first collection of nonfictional prose, *Vividha Prasanga.*

1884   His sister-in-law Kadambari Devi commits suicide. He is overwhelmed by grief, and her memory continues to haunt him all his life.

1886   The first of his five children, Madhurilata, is born.

1890   Leaves for England along with Satyendranath but returns after a month. Publishes his first book of travel based on his experience of England, *Europe Jatrir Diary.*

Takes charge of the family's estates in Shilaidaha, Kushtia, and other parts of East Bengal. Comes into direct contact with the East Bengal countryside and rural life, with profound consequences for his work.

1891   Founds the literary journal *Sadhana* and contributes a spate of short stories, essays, and poems.

1894   Becomes vice president of Bangiya Sahitya Parishad, the Academy of Bengali Letters.

First collection of short fiction, *Chhoto Galpa,* published.

1896   Inaugurates the session of Congress held in Kolkata in 1896 by singing "Vandemataram" and is increasingly immersed in the nationalist movement.

Writes anti-British essays and stresses self-reliance.

1901   Founds school in Santiniketan, West Bengal, to teach children in a manner that goes against the conventional system of education.

1902   Suffers a series of personal tragedies, beginning with the death of his wife in 1902. His daughter Renuka dies in 1903, his father in 1905, and his son Samindranath in 1907.

1905   Bengal is partitioned. He joins the nationalist and anti-British movement and composes many patriotic songs for it. However, he is soon disillusioned by the violence and the parochialism he witnesses and withdraws from the movement.

1909   Begins writing his epic novel, *Gora*.

1911   Writes *Dak Ghar* [*The Post Office*], one of his best-known plays. It is performed in many countries in the years to come.

1912   His fiftieth birthday is celebrated belatedly but on a grand scale on 28 January, indicating his preeminence in Bengali letters.

Decides to visit England for the third time but falls ill on the eve of his departure, scheduled for 19 March. In convalescence he begins to translate some of his songs into English.

Reaches England in June. Hands over translations to the painter William Rothenstein, whom he had met in Kolkata in 1911. Rothenstein shares the poems with W. B. Yeats, Ezra Pound, and other leading English intellectuals.

The India Society publishes the English *Gitanjali* in a limited edition in November to mostly enthusiastic reviews.

Travels to the United States from England to visit his son, who is graduating from the University of Illinois.

1913   Lectures at the University of Chicago, Harvard, and other institutions. The lectures are published as *Sadhana: The Realisation of Life,* his first collection of English prose. Its publisher, Macmillan, also reprints the English *Gitanjali*. Other collections of poems, essays, and plays appear in English in quick succession in subsequent years.

Returns to India in October. In November learns that he has been awarded the Nobel Prize in Literature.

1915   Knighted by King George.

1916   Travels to Japan, Canada, and the United States.

Lectures on nationalism and the evils of materialism, as well as other subjects.

1918   Lays the cornerstone of Visva-Bharati on 18 December, intending to build a university that he conceives as an "international center of humanistic studies."

1919   Resigns his knighthood in protest against the Amritsar Massacre.

1920   Embarks on fifth foreign tour in May, visiting England and the United States and Europe mainly to raise funds for his university, and returns to India after a year.

1921   Sets up Sriniketan to promote rural development and self-reliance among villagers.

Dedicates Visva-Bharati to India in a formal ceremony and sets up Visva-Bharati Society.

1922   Travels to Sri Lanka.

1924   Sets up Sikshashastra, another educational scheme, to impart vocational education to students. This would later be merged with Sriniketan.

Travels to China and Japan in March and April and then to South America, responding to an invitation to visit Peru. However, he becomes ill en route and pauses to recover in Argentina, where he meets Victoria Ocampo in Buenos Aires. Recuperates in her home for three months and becomes close to her.

1925   Visits Italy on his way back from South America.

1926   Takes an extended tour of Europe, visiting fifteen countries in seven months.

1927   Travels to Indonesia.

1929   Begins to paint, extending his hobby of doodling and drawing in his manuscripts.

1930   Visits Paris, where an exhibition of his paintings is held. Moves on to England to deliver the Hibbert Lectures at the University of Oxford in May.

Travels from England to Germany, Denmark, Switzerland, Russia, and the United States.

1931   His seventieth birthday is celebrated countrywide. *The Golden Book of Tagore* is published, containing tributes and messages from distinguished admirers from all over the world.

1932   Visits Persia and Iraq. Accepts a professorship at the University of Calcutta.

788

1934   Visits Sri Lanka.

1936   Composes *Chitrangada,* the first of a number of dance dramas he wrote in this decade.

1940   Falls ill in Kalimpong. His health begins to deteriorate.

1941   Writes *Crisis in Civilization,* his last testament for humanity, read out on his eightieth birthday.

Dictates his last poems from his deathbed. Dies on 7 August 1941.

NOTES

1. AUTOBIOGRAPHY

1. Irabati (1861–1918), daughter of Saudamini Devi, eldest daughter of Debendranath Tagore.

2. LETTERS

1. Tagore contributed a series of important articles to the journal *Sadhana.*

2. At the beginning of each letter is the place and date from which the letter was sent, and at the end is the place and date marking its arrival. Italicized words appear in English in the original letters.

3. Tagore sometimes uses the initials "BB" in Bengali to address his niece in these letters.

4. Myron H. Phelps (1856–1916) was a lawyer who practiced in New York.

5. After several positive reviews of the English *Gitanjali,* Tagore read a piece in the *Athenaeum* (16 November 1912) expressing the reviewer's feeling that the poems are bafflingly different from English poetry, possessing a value that could be better appreciated if accessed in the original Bengali.

6. *Naibedya* (Offerings), *Rabindra Rachanabali,* VIII, Visva-Bharati, p. 64.

7. Tagore wrote several poems on themes from the *Ramayana.* Two well-known ones are "Ahalyar Prati," *Manashi,* and "Patita," *Kahini.*

8. Tagore wrote this letter a few months after Bridges expressed a desire to modify a poem in the *Gitanjali* to include it in his anthology *The Spirit of Man* (1916). Tagore refused at first, and gave in only after Yeats interceded on behalf of Bridges.

9.   James Drummond Anderson served in the ICS in Bengal for twenty-five years. After he retired in 1900, he became a lecturer in Bengali at the University of Cambridge. He took great interest in Tagore's writings and exchanged ideas about translation with him.

10. "Chander artha," published in *Shabuj Patra* (March–April 1918).

11. In March 1919, Gandhi launched a nationwide campaign of passive resistance to protest the repressive Rowlatt legislation. This led to the massacre by the British of nearly 400 unarmed protesters and the wounding of another 2,000 in Amritsar's Jallianawala Bagh. British repression in the Punjab continued, even after Gandhi called off the campaign of passive resistance on 18 April 1919. When he failed to muster support from politicians, Tagore felt compelled to register a lone protest. On 31 May, he wrote a letter to the viceroy, rejecting his knighthood. Published on 2 June, this is perhaps Tagore's most famous letter.

12. In 1921, Tagore, after much introspection, opposed the Noncooperation Movement spearheaded by Gandhi. For this, he faced strong criticism from the Bengali community.

13. See *Gitanjali* (60).

14. See Rathindranath Tagore, *On the Edges of Time,* 2nd ed., Kolkata, 1981, pp. 62–64.

15. *Bara Dada:* Dwijendranath, Tagore's eldest brother, was one of Gandhi's early supporters in Bengal.

16. Tagore's father Debendranath offered to give up all his property to settle family debts after his father's company crashed in the 1840s.

17. Edward John Thompson published his short biography, *Rabindranath Tagore: His Life and Work,* in Kolkata in 1921. He sent a copy to Tagore, whose reactions are expressed in this letter.

18. Ajit Kumar Chakravarty, teacher and literary critic in Santiniketan.

19. Tagore's verse letter to Kazi Nazrul Islam (1899–1976), Bengali poet, musician, and revolutionary, dated 24 Sravan 1329, was included in *Dhumketu,* edited by Nazrul; in the first edition published on 12 August 1922; and in successive editions, reproduced in Tagore's own handwriting.

20. Tagore left Kolkata for China on 21 March 1924.

21. In the second volume of his memoirs, *Men and Memories* (1932), Roth-

enstein recalls Robert Bridges's wish to alter a *Gitanjali* poem, and refers to the popular view in India that the success of *Gitanjali* was mainly due to Yeats's revisions of Tagore's English version. This is Tagore's reply to a letter from Rothenstein (4 Nov. 1932) in which the same issues are discussed.

22. The Bauls, whose songs were of special interest to Tagore.

23. Boyd W. Tucker, an American Methodist, who remained in Santiniketan from 1927 to 1934.

24. "The Sacred Touch," *Harijan,* 25 March 1933.

25. Mahadev Desai was Gandhi's secretary. This letter is Tagore's response to Desai's request that he clarify his views on the conversion of Harijans to Sikhism.

26. "O My Unfortunate Country," *Gitanjali.*

27. Nanda Lal Bose, who at Gandhi's request decorated the exhibition at the annual Congress session in Faizpur village in December 1936.

28. Sufia Kamal met Tagore for the first time in 1928. In more than one letter, he expressed his admiration for her skills as a poet. His undated verse letter to her appeared in the journal *Jayashri* in 1355 (*c.* 1948). From the reference to Almora at the beginning of the letter, analysts surmise that it must have been written around May/June 1937, when he was at the hill station for a period of rest.

29. Tagore composed the song "Janaganamana" in 1911. In December that year, it was sung at the twenty-sixth session of the Congress in Kolkata. A song written by Tagore's niece's husband, Rambhuj Chowdhury, in welcome to His Majesty King George V, followed Tagore's song. This caused confusion, compounded by some Anglo-Indian newspapers, such as *The Statesman,* who deliberately or otherwise mixed up the two songs.

   The Pulinbehari letter was written in November 1937. That year the Congress appointed a subcommittee, including Maulana Azad, Nehru, Subhash Bose, and Narendra Dev, to consider the question of a national anthem for India. There was a controversy regarding the relative values of "Vandemataram" and "Janaganamana." Votaries of the first song fabricated a scandal about the second. It is in the context of this that Tagore wrote to Pulinbehari. The letter was published in *Bichitra* in 1937.

30. The house called Miralrio, overlooking the River Plate at San Isidro.

31.   Reference to *Purabi*.

32.   Shortly before Tagore's death, Eleanor Rathbone, a member of the British Parliament, wrote an open letter to Indians, seeking their support in the fight against fascism. Tagore responded with a strong statement, accusing the British of betraying the trust of Indians in the name of safeguarding their welfare. On 14 June 1941, Rev. Westcott, the bishop of Kolkata, wrote to Tagore in support of Rathbone's plea. Tagore's answer to Westcott expresses his final views on British rule in India.

793

3. PROSE

1.   Compare with the "Brahmin," "Bharatvarsha," *Rabindra Rachanabali,* vol. 4.

2.   *"Rashtraniti aar Dharmaniti,"* the original title of this essay, is semantically multi-layered, playing upon varied ideas such as virtue, wisdom, philosophy, logic, legality, and so on. In their original, the words encapsulate a way of life and thought, the essence of an ancient civilization. This English translation, "Statecraft and Ethics," tries to capture the quintessence and spirit of those words.

3.   "Svābhāvikī jnāna bala kriyācha."

4.   Ānandādhyēva khalvimāni bhūtāni jāyantē, ānandēna jātāni jīvanti, anandamprayan-tyabhisamvicanti.

5.   Ānandarūpamamritam yadvibhāti.

6.   Adharmēnaidhatē tāavat tatō bhadrani pacyati tatah sapatān jayati samūlastu vinaçvati.

5. POEMS

1.   There is a pun here: the word for sun in Bangla, *rabi*, is also part of the poet's name.

2.   An account of the background to this poem can be found on page 103 of Krishna Kripalani's *Rabindranath Tagore: A Biography* (Kolkata: Visva-Bharati, 1980):

> [Rabindranath had recently taken up residence in a house in Sudder Street, Calcutta, with his brother Jyotindranath and his sister-in-law Kadambari.] It was in this modest house in the very heart of the new metropolis that the young poet had his first deeply felt

spiritual experience which burst upon him with the force of a vision and which he has described at length, both in his reminiscences and later in the Hibbert Lectures at Oxford University in 1930. Early one morning as he was standing on the balcony of the house watching the sun rise behind the fringe of trees at the end of the lane, "all of a sudden a covering seemed to fall from my eyes, and I found the world bathed in a wonderful radiance, with waves of beauty and joy swelling on every side." All the gloom and despondency which had weighed over and oppressed his spirit, forcing it to turn upon itself in a morbid relish of its own disease, fell from him like a garment stripped from end to end. Nothing in the outside world seemed trivial any more. "The invisible screen of the commonplace was removed from all things and all men, and their ultimate significance was intensified in my mind."

Kripalini goes on to record that this experience went on for four days "during which he saw and heard everything not only with his eyes and ears but with his entire being," but that on the first day he wrote this poem, which came to Rabindranath in a flow.

3. The poem was written heralding the first day of spring and is dated 2 Phalgun 1302 (1895) in *Sanchayita*. In Bengali, the poem is titled "The Year 1400" (1993).

4. Krishna is of course divine. The word is also used to refer to someone with a dark complexion, however. "Krishnakali" is a plant and also its flower, dark in hue.

5. There is an allusion here to an *apsara*—a celestial nymph—disturbing the meditation of the god Shiva.

6. About the genesis of the poem, Rabindranath has this to say: "I wrote this poem while in Srinagar. I used to live in a boat on the Jhelum river then. One evening darkness was descending gradually on the river water. I was on the roof of the boat. The other side had become completely dark, the tide seemed to be dark too, and not a sound anywhere. Then, a flock of wild geese suddenly flew by. I had been similarly amazed by the flapping of wings that sounded very much like loud laughter while on board my boat on the Padma." As Krishna Kripalini notes in his biography of the poet, "the flight symbolizes for him the latent motion in all motionless things, the passage of the time-spirit, the unending quest of life and of the soul, the eternal cry in the heart of the universe: 'Not

here, not here, but somewhere else'"; see *Rabindranath Tagore: A Biography* (Kolkata: Visva-Bharati, 1980, 254).

7. This is one of the few prose poems that Tagore wrote at this stage of his poetic career.

8. The fictitious name of a heroine in a novel by Sharatchandra Chatterjee. He had created no such heroine, neither did he write a novel titled *A Garland of Shriveled Flowers.*

9. The Bengali word for the jasmine flower.

10. The name of a mythological character, celebrated in classical Indian literature for her suffering.

11. There is a pun here: the Bengali word *bar* means "husband" as well as "boon."

12. This was Tagore's last poem, dictated from his deathbed.

6. PLAYS

1. (Translator's note) The normal Anglicized spelling for the play is *Rakta-karabi* or *Rakta-karavi*, but this does not convey the correct Bengali pronunciation. This is because the "a" in the first syllable sounds the same as in "wrack" at the expense of the "o" sound; and the "a"s in *-karabi* also sound incongruous. *Roktokorobi* comes closer to the Bengali pronunciation. The word contains its own dramatic resonance, and I prefer it to the translated *Red Oleanders,* notwithstanding the fact that Tagore chose the latter for English audiences. If the original usage makes it more exotic—so much the better!

2. Morol, or Headman.

3. The original mentions the character as *Saudagarputra,* which translates as the "son of the Merchant"; to keep the appellation more readable, the present translation mentions him simply as the "Merchant."

4. Patralekha, used as a proper name here, literally translates as the woman-writer of letters but perhaps epitomizes the idea of a Muse.

5. *Navin* means new, fresh, even youthful; the feminine form *navina* is used here.

6. Though, in the West, "Queen-mother" usually denotes the mother of

the reigning monarch, the term is used here not only because the Bengali original reads *Rajmata,* but also because it helps to distinguish her from the Queen of the Cards (who is later referred to as simply the "Queen").

7. This is supposedly timber of inferior quality that can't be used for anything much.

8. The original has *ajatasasru,* which literally translates as "one who is yet to sprout a beard."

9. They proudly mention their names, being Six and Five among the cards, while their respective surnames signal that they belong to a higher social caste.

10. Tiri is Three and Duri is Two among the cards; also, their surnames indicate they are of a lower social order in the Hindu caste system.

11. The Bengali word for "yawn" is *hai* (pronounced like the English "high"). There is an obvious pun here on the Bengali sense and the English pronunciation of the word (*hai/high*), which would be adequately available only in performance.

12. These are Indian names for the four suits of the cards: Iskaban is Spades, Ruhitan is Diamonds, Haratan is Hearts, and Chiretan is Clubs.

13. The original uses the term *kulin,* which denotes high birth and hence high social ranking.

14. Once again, the original text quibbles on the words *mukhya* (primary) and *mukh* (mouth).

15. Used as a proper name for the poet, the name is suggestive of his deftness in the art of poetry.

16. The original reads *char prahar* (four prahars). In the ancient Indian system, twenty-four hours consisted of four prahars of the day and four prahars of the night (a total of eight prahars).

17. This is just a nonsensical word, deployed here merely to parody the blind following of rituals.

18. Once again a parody of the ludicrous rituals often followed by religious communities.

19. *Golam* is the Indian equivalent of the Jack among the cards; he belongs to the superior order in the society of cards.

20. In the original, Brahma is designated as *Pitamaha* (meaning grandfather). This is his customary epithet because as the Creator he is one of the oldest gods in the Hindu pantheon. The English "Grandfather" is used here to underscore the irreverence in the Merchant's words.

21. The pun on the term *nasaka* (as used in the original) plays upon the double sense of "being born out of the nose" as well as "being destructive"; because the simultaneous presence of both senses would be lost in translation, the original term has been retained here.

22. *Tekka* is the Ace and *Golam* is the Jack in the deck of cards; in the play, they evidently belong to a higher social order among the cards.

23. To sing of victories *(jay)* was a typical stance in the Indian version of paeans and panegyrics.

24. This is the name given to the priest of the land. As the priest he bears the appellation *Goswami,* while *Nahala* indicates he is a Nine (in the pack of cards), and hence among the elite.

25. This is presumably the name of the paper he edits; the original reads *Tashdwip-pradip.*

26. The original mentions the female cards here as *Tekkakumari* (which literally translate as "Ace-maidens").

27. Because the female cards are called by their proper names, the original names of Tekkakumari and Bibisundari are retained here.

28. This scene consists of the female characters in the kingdom of cards; so the feminine forms of the card names are used (hence, *Iskabani* for the female Spades, *Tekkani* for the female Ace, *Chiretani* for the female Clubs).

29. The Ace of Hearts, here imagined as a feminine entity. Elsewhere she is called *Haratani* (the feminine form of Hearts); we have retained that name for the rest of the play.

30. The King of Diamonds. As elsewhere he is merely mentioned as *Ruhitan,* and as there is a separate King of the Kingdom of Cards, we shall subsequently use only *Ruhitan* to designate this character.

31. The original text reads *garabumandal,* presumably a concocted term used by the dramatist to suggest pomposity.

32. This exit is not marked in the original text. But since they are said to "re-enter" after the following song of the card-maidens, it may be assumed

797

that they are meant to leave the stage here, and so the "Exit" has been inserted here.

33. *Dahala* is Ten (of one of the card-suits) and *Pundit* suggests that he is a scholar (probably one of the Brahmins, the traditional scholars in the Hindu society). In either capacity, he belongs to a higher social station.

34. The Hindu god of the winds; hence the idea of everything going topsy-turvy in strong gusts of wind.

35. The reference is to Hanuman, who, though supposedly a langur, is depicted as a heroic figure in the Indian epic, *Ramayana*. The original text uses the term *Mahavir*, which means a great hero and is also an appellation of Hanuman.

36. A euphemistic description of the ape-family. A section of Hindus also worship Hanuman/Mahavir as a god.

37. The name of an Indian game of cards; this is like calling a bird (here, dove) whist or poker or rummy.

7. STORIES

1. "She whose speech is sweet."

2. "She of the beautiful hair" and "She of the beautiful smile," respectively.

GLOSSARY

adharma impiety; sinful act

Akbar Mughal emperor of India, 1556–1605

Alakshmi goddess of misfortune; woman who brings misfortune or misery

ananta a medicinal plant

Asadh first of the two monsoon months, equivalent to the middle of June

Ashwin sixth month of Bengali calendar; mid-September–mid-October

Asoka emperor of India, c. 270–c. 232 BC

aush-rice paddy that ripens early, in the rainy season or in autumn

babus Hindu gentlemen but often used disparagingly to indicate a class of people who affected English manners

Baikuntha celestial abode of Hindu deity Vishnu

bakul a large evergreen flowering tree or its small, white, sweet-scented flowers

behag a raga in Indian classical music

bhishti a water carrier who uses a leather bag to transport water

Bholanath another name for Shiva, one of the three principal Hindu gods (who is primarily entrusted with the task of destruction); also means an utterly forgetful person

Brahma Hindu god of creation; one of the Trimurti, the others being Vishnu and Shiva

brahma-vidya the branch of learning imparting knowledge of God

Brahmin first of the four classical Hindu castes or "varnas"; the "priestly caste" in Hindu religion

799

Brahmo a follower of Brahmoism

bouma This is how an elder affectionately addresses his/her daughter-in-law.

Bushido the code of the Japanese samurai, which stresses self-discipline, honor, bravery, loyalty, and a simple way of life

chadar a sheet of cloth worn over the body like a shawl; often used in winter

800

Chaitanya Bengali mystic (1485–1533) who founded Vaishnavism

chakor a legendary bird said to thirst for the moon

champak name of a flower

chandan paste made from sandalwood smeared ritually on the forehead

Chandidas Bengali poet

chire and paramanna popular rice preparations in Bengal

crore a unit in the Indian numbering system equal to 10 million

Damayanti Famous star-crossed lover in mythology whose relationship with Nala is narrated in the *Mahabharata*. It is believed that when Nala, king of Nishada, first heard of Damayanti's beauty, he sent a swan (whose life he had once saved) to search her out.

dharma in Hinduism, a principle of law that orders the universe and individual conduct in line with sacred law

doyel a bird

Dushyanta King of India, the story of whose love with Shakuntala is the subject-matter of Kalidasa's dramatic masterpiece *Shakuntala*. The greatest of the dramatists in the Sanskrit language, Kalidasa is placed by scholars anywhere from the first to the fifth century AD.

gaab a tree; mangosteen

gamchha a handwoven napkin or towel

ghat a landing-stage, as of a river or pond

golam a slave or servant, but in cards, the knave

goonda a thug

Gurkha Brigade British army unit composed of Nepalese soldiers

Guru Govinda (Gobind Singh) (1666–1708) tenth and last guru of the Sikhs

Hemanta late autumn

Hari divine manifestation of the Hindu deity Vishnu

Indra the king of gods and goddesses in Hindu mythology

jambu a tree of the rose family widely distributed in temperate regions that bears small, juicy, dark edible fruits with seeds in them

jatra or yatra a form of Bengali folk theater

Kabir a mystic poet (1440–1518) whom Tagore admired and had translated into English

kadamba a flowering tree; a mythical tree believed to be the Tree of Buddhism and thought to reunite separated lovers; also popularly associated with Krishna and Radha

Kailasa the mountain where Shiva dwells with his consort Durga

kajal lamp-black; collyrium; a thick black ointment made of ground lead sulfide or antimony sulfide that is used as an eye liner

Kalindi the river Jamuna/Yamna

kalomegh a bitter medicinal plant

kanchan the name of a flower

Kanwa chief of the hermits and foster-father of Shakuntala in Kalidasa's *Shakuntala*

keka call of the peacock

kheyal a form of Indian classical vocal music

khichri rice and pigeon-peas boiled with spices and oil; hotchpotch

kinshuk the name of a flower

koyel a bird

kuhu call of the cuckoo

Lakhima Devi One of the many wives of King Siva Simha. She is invoked most frequently in the songs of Vidyapati. Here is an example: "Says the poet Vidyapati: In this universe of three worlds, there is none like him. Raja Siva Simha, god-like in form, is the husband of Lakhima Devi."

Lakshmi the Hindu goddess of wealth and prosperity and the consort of Vishnu; fortune; beauty; grace; a term of endearment for the ideal woman *madhavi* an evergreen creeper; myrtle

Magh tenth month of the Bengali calendar (January–February)

mahajati the mighty race

malati a kind of jasmine; nutmeg

mallika a variety of jasmine

Marwari a member of a prosperous merchant community originally from Marwar in Rajputana, but subsequently spread throughout India

maund a unit of weight in India

maya illusion

Nanak founder of the Sikh religion, (1469–1539)

Nandi and Bhringhi the two chief attendants of Shiva; mischievous flatterers, undesirable lieutenants or associates

Narayan the common name for Vishnu

nautch girl a professional dancing girl

neem margosa

nupur ornament for the toes and ankles, often used in dancing

paan betel leaf stuffed with condiments, usually eaten after a meal

palash tree with beautiful red flowers; *Butea monosperma*

Pavandev in Hindu mythology, the wind-god

Phalgun the eleventh month of the Bengali calendar (February–March)

prabhu lord

pranam salute, especially in rituals

puja prayer

Puranas, Puranic collection of Hindu legends and religious instructions; pertaining to the Puranas

purdah The system of veiling women from the sight of strangers, traditionally practiced among Muslims as well as Hindu women

raga, ragini traditional melodic pattern or mode of Indian classical music *rajanigandha* the name of a flower

Rama a hero in Hindu mythology; an avatar of Vishnu

Ramanuja Indian philosopher (1017?–1137) associated with the concept of visishtadwaita or qualified non-dualism

rangan the name of a flower

rasa a concept in Indian aesthetics having to do with the quintessence or disposition of things

Rudra Hindu god; fiery

Santal name of indigenous people inhabiting parts of the Indian subcontinent, especially in Bengal

sarangi a violinlike musical instrument

Sarawsati Hindu goddess of music, learning, and poetry

sattwa, rajah, and tama excellence, essence of activity and lowest attributes

Shakuntala daughter of the sage Viswamitra and the nymph Menaka, foster-child of the hermit Kanwa in Kalidasa's *Shakuntala.*

Shankara an Indian philosopher (700?–750?) associated with the Advaita (non-dualistic) Vedanta stream of thought

sharad early autumn

shiuli a variety of the harsinghar, a white, fragrant autumnal flower

Shivaji an Indian ruler of the seventeenth century, famous for his military exploits

sindur vermillion applied on the forehead or hair parting of a married Hindu woman

Siva Simha the king of Mithila, India, from 1402 to 1406

Sravan the fourth month of the Bengali calendar (July–August)

Sudra the lowest of the Hindu castes; traditionally laborers, cultivators, fishermen, and servants

tabla a drumlike musical instrument

tamal a type of tree

tanpura or tambura a musical instrument used as a drone

tappa a light classical vocal form of Indian classical music

Uchchaisrava the mythical horse owned by Indra

Vandemataram hymn to mother India; penned by Bankim Chandra Chattapadhyaya and set to music by Tagore in 1896

804

Vasanta spring

veena a musical string instrument

Vidyapati Vidyapati Thakur, a friend and court poet of King Siva Simha. He was born in 1352 AD in Bispai, a village on the eastern side of Bihar. Known for his sensuous love songs, he wrote them in the Maithili dialect and addressed many of them to King Siva Simha.

Vikramaditya Literally, "the sun of heroism." Although the title was assumed by many Indian kings, historians agree that Chandragupta II, who ruled India from 375 AD to 413 AD and had strong literary inclinations like his father, the "poet-prince" Samudragupta, has the strongest claim to this title.

Yaksha a kind of demigod, attendant to Kuvera, god of wealth

Yama Raja Hindu god of death

yojana a measure of distance, usually about five miles

zamindar or zemindar a landlord or collector of revenue of land empowered to do so by the colonial government of British India

GENERAL SOURCES

To appreciate the magnitude of Tagore's achievement, it is necessary to situate his works in relation to their socio-historical contexts. For those who wish to know about Tagore's family background, *The Tagores of Jorasanko,* by Hironmoy Banerjee, translated by Biplab K. Mazumdar (New Delhi: Gyan Publishers, 1995), offers a useful introduction. For a study of the Brahmo Samaj, see David Kopf, *The Brahmo Samaj and the Shaping of the Modern Indian Mind* (Princeton: Princeton University Press, 1979). Colonial politics and nationalism in India are explored in Sumit Sarkar's *Swadeshi Movement in Bengal, 1903–1908* (New Delhi: People's Publishing House, 1973), Partha Chatterjee's *Nationalist Thought and the Colonial World: A Derivative Discourse?* (London: Zed Books, 1986), and *Partition of Bengal: Significant Signposts, 1905–1911,* edited by Nityapriya Ghose and Ashoke Kumar Mukhopadhyay (Kolkata: Sahitya Samsad, 2005). Caste and communal conflicts are discussed in *The Bengal Muslims, 1871–1906: A Quest for Identity,* by Rafiuddin Ahmed (New Delhi: Oxford University Press, 1981); *Social Conflict and Political Unrest in Bengal, 1875–1927,* by Rajat Kanta Ray (New Delhi: OUP, 1994); and *Caste, Culture and Hegemony: Social Dominance in Colonial Bengal,* by Sekhar Bandyopadhyay (New Delhi: Sage, 2004). Gender issues are historically contextualized in *Reluctant Debutante: The Response of Bengali Women to Modernization, 1849–1905,* by Ghulam Murshid (Rajshahi: Rajshahi University Press, 1983); *Recasting Women: Essays in Colonial History,* edited by Kumkum Sangari and Sudesh Vaid (New Delhi: Kali for Women, 1989); *Women in Modern India,* by Geraldine Forbes (Cambridge: Cambridge University Press, 1996); and *Hindu Wife, Hindu Nation,* by Tanika Sarkar (New Delhi: Permanent Black, 2001).

Tagore's most prolific biographer in Bengali is Prashantakumar Pal, whose *Rabijibani* (*The Life of Tagore*) (Kolkata: Bhurjapatra, 1982–2003) runs into nine volumes and remains an invaluable resource for researchers. *Rabindrajibani O Rabindra-Sahitya-Prabeshak,* in four volumes, by Prabhatkumar Mukhopadhyay (Kolkata: Visva-Bharati, 1933–1956), is also a useful series. In English, Edward Thompson's *Rabindranath Tagore: His Life and Works* (Kolkata: YMCA, 1921; rpt. 1961) is well known for the disagreement that it sparked between the biographer and his subject, an exchange documented in E. P. Thompson's *Alien Homage* (Oxford: Oxford University Press, 1993) and *Colonial Transactions: English Literature and India,* by Harish Trivedi (Manchester: Manchester University Press, 1993). "Rabindranath Tagore: A Chronicle of Eighty Years, 1861–1941," compiled by Prabhatkumar Mukhopadhyay and Kshitis Roy in *Rabindranath Tagore: A Centenary Volume, 1861–1961,* ed. S. Radhakrishnan (New Delhi: Sahitya Akademi, 1961); *Introduction to Tagore* (Kolkata: Visva-Bharati, 1983); Krishna Kripalani's *Rabindranath Tagore: A Biography* (New York: Grove Press, 1962); *Rabindranath Tagore: The Myriad-Minded Man,* by Krishna Dutta and Andrew Robinson (New Delhi: Rupa, 1995); and *Rabindranath Tagore: A Biography,* by Uma Das Gupta (New Delhi: Oxford University Press, 2004) are other important biographical studies. See also Fakrul Alam's entries on Tagore in *Dictionary of Literary Biography* (DLB) in *South Asian Writers in English,* vol. 323 (Detroit: Thomson Gale, 2006): 378–392; and in *Nobel Prize Laureates in Literature, Part 4: Quasimodo-Yeats,* vol. 332 (Detroit: Thomson Gale, 2007): 436–453.

For the most exhaustive bibliographical account of Tagore's works, we must turn to the writings of Pulinbehari Sen, the indefatigable editor and bibliographer who compiled Tagore's writings in the volumes of *Rabindra Rachanabali,* added the *Granthaparichay* section containing publication details and annotations, and among other things, published listings of Tagore's English writings and translations. For readers in English, the bibliography in *Rabindranath Tagore: A Centenary Volume,*

806

1861–1961, compiled by Pulinbihari Sen and Jagadindra Bhaumik, is very useful (504–520).

Katherine Henn's *Rabindranath Tagore: A Bibliography* (ATLA Bibliography Series, 13; London: The American Theological Library Association, 1985) is a valuable listing of Tagore's works in English translation and secondary sources in English. In Bengali, Meera Chattopadhyay's *Rabindra Rachanar Ingrezi Anubad Itibritta* (2 vols.) (Kolkata: Sriguru Prakashan, 1993) lists translations of Tagore's work into English alphabetically in the first volume; the second contains descriptive essays on significant translations. Anuttam Bhattacharya's *Rabindrarachanabhidhan,* a series in Bengali of which nine volumes have been published in Kolkata by Deep Prakashan between 1998 and 2009, is an invaluable resource for scholars searching for information about Tagore's individual works across genres.

Tagore's evolving international reputation is a fascinating trajectory to follow. *The Golden Book of Tagore* (Calcutta: The Golden Book Committee, 1931), published on the occasion of Tagore's birthday, contains letters and felicitations that demonstrate his stature as a world figure during his own lifetime. Alex Aronson, in *Rabindranath Through Western Eyes* (Kolkata, 1943) analyzes Anglo-American responses to Tagore after he won the Nobel Prize. Useful information on this subject may also be found in *Rabindranath and the British Press (1912–1941),* edited by Kalyan Kundu, Sakti Bhattacharya, and Kalyan Sircar (London: Tagore Centre, 1990); Ana Jelnikar's "W. B. Yeats's (Mis) Reading of Tagore: Interpeting an Alien Culture," *University of Toronto Quarterly* 77:4 (Fall 2008); and Sujit Mukherjee's *Passage to America: The Reception of Rabindranath Tagore in the United States, 1912–1941* (Kolkata: Bookland, 1964). *Rabindranath Tagore: A Centenary Volume 1861–1961* (New Delhi: Sahitya Akademi, 1961) contains tributes to Tagore by eminent intellectuals, addressing diverse aspects of Tagore's achievement. Humayun Kabir, in "Tagore Was No Obscurantist" (*Calcutta Municipal Gazette,* Tagore Birth Centenary Number, 1961, 122–125), argues that Tagore pioneered the ideas of federalism and nonalignment. For an account of Tagore's relationship with East Bengal, see Ghulam Murshid, *Rabindrab-*

iswe Purbabanga, Purbabange Rabindracharcha (East Bengal in Tagore's World and Tagore in East Bengal) (Dhaka: Bangla Academy, 1993); Bhuiya Iqbal, *Bangladeshe Rabindra Sangbardhana (Reception of Rabindranath Tagore in Bangladesh)* (Dhaka: Bangla Academy, 1993); Saifuddin Chowdhury, *Rabindranath O Purbabanger Kichhu Katha (Rabindranath and Some Topics on East Bengal)* (Dhaka: Bangla Academy, 2001); and Syed Abul Maqsud, *Purbabange Rabindranath* (Dhaka: Mowla Brothers, 2007).

808

Today, Tagore's intellectual and artistic legacy continues to attract the attention of intellectuals from around the world. Edward Said, in *Representations of the Intellectual: The 1993 Reith Lectures* (New York, 1994) describes Tagore as a postcolonial intellectual. Abu Saeed Zahurul Haque, in *Folklore and Nationalism in Rabindranath Tagore* (Dhaka: Bangla Academy, 1981), studies the links between folkloric elements and ideas about the nation in Tagore's writings. Martha C. Nussbaum cites Tagore's novel *Home and the World* in her critique of patriotism in *For Love of Country,* edited by Joshua Cohen (Boston: Beacon Press, 1996). In Bengali, *Arek Kalantarey (Reflections on Tagore's Socio-Political Essays),* edited by Ahmed Rafique (Dhaka: Bangla Academy, 1977) and Hayat Mamud's *Bhrami Bismaye (The Hypnotic Sojourn: Essays on Tagore)* (Dhaka: Bangla Academy, 1989) are collections of essays on contemporary themes. For an appraisal of Tagore's approach to education, see Kathleen M. O'Connell, *Rabindranath Tagore: The Poet as Educator* (Kolkata: Visva-Bharati, 2002). Jeanne Openshaw, in *Seeking Bauls of Bengal* (Cambridge: Cambridge University Press, 2002) relates Tagore to the Baul tradition.

In "Tagore and His India," reprinted in *The Argumentative Indian: Writings on Indian History, Culture and Identity* (London: Allen Lane/Penguin, 2005, 89–120), Amartya Sen locates Tagore in relation to the intellectual traditions of India. Nirad C. Chaudhuri's *Thy Hand, Great Anarch!* (London: Chatto and Windus, 1987) and Amit Chaudhuri's essays on Tagore in his book *Clearing a Space: Reflections on India, Literature and Culture* (Delhi and Ranikhet: Permanent Black, 2008) are important reappraisals of Tagore's significance for the modern world. *Tagore and Modernity,* edited by Krishna Sen and Tapati Gupta (Kolkata: Dasgupta and Co., 2006), is a useful collection of essays spanning Tagore's work across genres. Tagore's ideas on development and their relevance for today are analyzed in Kunja-Bihari Nayak's *Sustainable Development: An Alternative Approach in Rabindranath Tagore's Vision* (New Delhi: Serials Publications, 2008). The *University of Toronto Quarterly* 77, 4 (Fall 2008) is a special issue devoted to a reappraisal of Tagore's multifaceted genius. Ana Jelnikar's essay in the same volume, titled "W. B. Yeats's (Mis) Reading of Tagore: Interpreting an Alien Culture" relates Tagore's changing reputation in the West to his anti-imperialist stance.

Those interested in Tagore's experiments with the visual arts will enjoy *The Art of Rabindranath Tagore* by Andrew Robinson (London: Andre Deutsch, 1989) and *Rabindranath Tagore: Collection of Essays,* edited by Ratan Parimoo (New Delhi: Lalit Kala Akademi, 1989). For graphic images of Tagore and Visva-Bharati, Shambhu Shaha's *Faces and Places of Visva-Bharati: A Collection of Photographs* (Santiniketan: Visva-Bharati, 2000) is a wonderful source.

AUTOBIOGRAPHY

For extracts from Tagore's autobiographical writings arranged thematically, it is useful to read *Rabindranath Tagore: My Life in My Words,* edited by Uma Das Gupta (New Delhi: Penguin/Viking, 2006). Sisir Kumar Das's perceptive commentary in Bengali, *Atmajibani: Jibani O Rabindranath (Autobiography: Biography and Tagore)* (Kolkata, 2007), examines Tagore's autobiographical writings in the light of Tagore's claim that the life of a poet is manifest in his works, rather than in a factual account of external events. Some important autobiographical pieces are also to be found in the four-volume series *The English Writings of Rabindranath Tagore,* edited by Sisir Kumar Das (New Delhi: Sahitya Akademi). See also Amartya Sen's introduction to Tagore's *Boyhood Days,* translated by Radha Chakravarty (New Delhi: Puffin Classics, 2007; ix–xxiii).

LETTERS

Tagore's letters in Bengali are extensively anthologized in the *Chithipatra (Letters)* series published by Visva-Bharati. Additional volumes published by Visva-Bharati include *Chhinnapatra (Torn Leaves)* and *Chhinnapatrabali (Letter-Fragments)*, versions of the extraordinary letters that Tagore wrote from East Bengal, mainly to his niece Indira Devi; *Bhanusingher Patrabali*, a collection of his letters to the young Ranu Adhikari; and *Pathe O Pather Prante*, addressed to Nirmalkumari Mahalanobis, wife of the scientist Prashantakumar Mahalanobis. Bhuiya Iqbal's *Rabindranather Ekguchchha Patra (A Bunch of Letters by Rabindranath)* (Dhaka: Bangla Academy, 1985) is a collection of letters written by Tagore to eminent persons of East Bengal, now Bangladesh, with a commentary to contextualize the letters.

810

In English, the standard reference work is *Selected Letters of Rabindranath Tagore,* ed. Krishna Dutta and Andrew Robinson, 1997. Uma Das Gupta's *A Difficult Friendship* focuses on Tagore's correspondence with his biographer Edward Thompson. Other useful resources are C. F. Andrews's *Letters to a Friend* (London: George Allen and Unwin, 1928), Mary Lago's *Imperfect Encounter: Letters of William Rothenstein and Rabindranath Tagore, 1911–1941* (Cambridge, Mass.: Harvard University Press, 1972), and *The Mahatma and the Poet: Letters and Debates between Gandhi and Tagore, 1915–1941,* edited by S. Bhattacharya (New Delhi: National Book Trust, 1997). *The English Writings of Rabindranath Tagore,* edited by Sisir Kumar Das, also contains significant letters written in English.

PROSE

Buddhadeva Bose's "Tagore and Bengali Prose" in *Tagore: Portrait of a Poet* (Kolkata: Papyrus, 1962, 85–94) is an excellent introduction to Tagore's writings in this genre, situating them in the context of his other works and the evolution of Bengali prose. Uma Das Gupta's introduction to *The Oxford India Tagore: Selected Writings on Education and Nationalism* (New Delhi: Oxford University Press, 2009) is also useful. Stephen S. Jevaseela's *The Sky of Indian History: Themes and Thought of Rabindranath Tagore* (New Delhi: UBS Publishers' Distributors, 2010), contains a detailed prologue and a generous selection of Tagore's essays. *The English Writings of Rabindranath Tagore* also remains a significant source for this aspect of Tagore's oeuvre.

POEMS

Abu Sayeed Ayub's *Modernism and Tagore,* translated by Amitava Ray (New Delhi: Sahitya Akademi, 1995), attempts to assess Tagore's modernity. Buddhadeva Bose's *An Acre of Green Grass: A Review of Modern Bengali Literature* (Calcutta: Papyrus, 1948), positions Tagore in relation to modern Bengali poetry. In his *Tagore: Portrait of a Poet* (Kolkata: Papyrus, 1962), Bose, himself a leading poet, offers an excellent assessment of Tagore's poetry and locates it in relation to the rest of his work. The introduction to *I Won't Let You Go: Selected Poems,* edited by Ketaki Kushari Dyson (New Delhi: UBS Publishers' Distributors, 1992), is also quite helpful. Other important sources are Sankha Ghosh's introduction to *Rabindranath Tagore: Selected Poems,* edited by Sukanta Chaudhuri (New Delhi: Oxford University Press, 2004, 1–42) and Upendranath Bhattacharya's *Rabindra-Kavya-Parikrama* (Kolkata: Orient Books, 1998), which provides a detailed, volume-by-volume analytical account of Tagore's poetry.

SONGS

In *Of Love, Nature, and Devotion: Selected Songs of Rabindranath Tagore* (New Delhi: Oxford, 2008), Kalpana Bardhan has translated a substantial number of the songs and provided a detailed introduction, dates, and short introductions to all the selected songs, along with transliterations. The book also contains excerpts from some seminal essays on Tagore songs by leading critics and scholars. Another useful source is Edward Thompson's *Rabindranath Tagore: Poet and Dramatist* (Oxford University Press, 1994—originally published in 1926). See also Satyajit Ray, "Some Reflections on Rabindrasangeet" (171–175) and "Tagore and Einstein on Music: A Conversation" (175–176) in *Purabi: A Miscellany in Memory of Rabindranath Tagore 1941–1991,* edited by Krishna Dutta and Andrew Robinson (London: The Tagore Centre, 1991). Reba Som's *Rabindranath Tagore: The Singer and His Song* (New Delhi: Penguin Viking, 2009) is a helpful and readable introduction to Tagore's music. Som weaves biography with accounts of the evolution of Rabindranath's work.

In Bengali, Subhas Choudhury's *Gitabitaner Jagat* ("The World of *Gitabitan*"; Calcutta: Papyrus, 2004), offers almost everything one would want to know about the history of the songs and their musical aspects.

PLAYS

For an analysis of Tagore's plays, see Hirankumar Sanyal, "The Plays of Rabindranath Tagore," in *Rabindranath Tagore: A Centenary Volume, 1861–1961* (New Delhi: Sahitya Akademi, 1961, 233–242). Upendranath Bhattacharya's *Rabindra-Natya-Parikrama*, 6th ed. (Calcutta: Orient Book Company, 2008), is a knowledgable and detailed account of all Tagore's plays. Pramathanath Bishi's *Rabindranatyaprabaha*, 4th ed. (Calcutta: Orient Book Company, 2004), contains a discussion of all Tagore's plays, with details about stage versions.

STORIES

For an examination of ethical choice in Tagore's stories, see Mary Lago, "Modes of Questioning in Tagore's Short Stories," in *Studies in Short Fiction* 5, 1 (Fall, 1967): 24–36. See also Lago's essay "Tagore's Short Fiction," in *Rabindranath Tagore* (Twayne, 1976, 80–114), in which she describes these as the first "modern" short stories in Bengali. For recent translations, see *Rabindranath Tagore: Selected Short Stories,* translated and edited by William Radice (New Delhi: Penguin Books India, 1991); *Selected Short Stories of Rabindranath Tagore,* translated by Krishna Dutta and Mary Lago (London: Macmillan London, 1991); *Selected Stories,* edited by Sukanta Chaudhuri (Oxford Tagore Translations; New Delhi: Oxford University Press, 2000); and *The Return of Khokababu: The Best of Tagore,* edited by Sipra Bhattacharya (New Delhi: HarperPerennial, 2009).

NOVELS

Ashis Nandy, in *The Illegitimacy of Nationalism: Rabindranath Tagore and the Politics of the Self* (New Delhi: Oxford University Press, 1994), highlights Tagore's handling of political concerns, especially the issue of nationalism, in his novels. *Rabindranath Tagore's* The Home and the World: *A Critical Companion*, edited by P. K. Datta (Delhi: Permanent Black, 2003), offers a range of readings of one of Tagore's major novels, with valuable information about the socio-historical context of the work. See also Bertolt Brecht, *Diaries 1920–1922,* edited by Hertha Ramthun, translated by John Willet (London: Eyre Methuen, 1979), and Georg Lukács, *Reviews and Articles,* translated by Peter Palmer (London: Merlin, 1983, 9–11).

HUMOR

For this relatively underrated aspect of Tagore's genius, see Sukanta Chaudhuri's introduction to *Rabindranath Tagore: Selected Writings for Children,* edited by Sukanta Chaudhuri (New Delhi: Oxford University Press, 2002). See also two recollections of the writer by Indira Devi Chaudrani and Leonard Elmhirst in *Rabindranath Tagore: A Centenary Volume, 1861–1961* (New Delhi: Sahitya Akademi, 1961) and *The Land of Cards: Stories, Poems and Plays for Children,* translated by Radha Chakravarty (New Delhi: Puffin Classics, 2010).

TRAVEL WRITING

Santoshkumar Mandal's Bengali book *Rabindranather Bhramansahitya (Tagore's Travel Writings)* (Kolkata: Uddalak Sahitya Prakashan, 2003) contains a lot of documentary information, systematically organized. For an account of Tagore's relationship with Southeast Asia, see *Tagore and China,* edited by Kalidas Nag (Kolkata: Pranabeshchandra Sinha, 1945); Shakti Das Gupta, *Tagore's Asian Outlook* (Kolkata: Nava Bharati, 1961); Stephen N. Hay, *Asian Ideas of East and West: Tagore and His Critics in Japan, China, and India* (Cambridge, Mass.: Harvard University Press, 1970); and *Letters from Java,* translated by Indiradevi Chaudhurani and Supriya Roy, edited by Supriya Roy (Kolkata: Visva-Bharati, 2010). Tagore's artistic links with Japan are explored in Rustom Bharucha's *Another Asia: Rabindranath Tagore and Okakura Tenshin* (New Delhi: Oxford University Press, 2006). For the German response to Tagore, see Martin Kaempchen, *Rabindranath Tagore and Germany: A Documentation* (Kolkata: Goethe Institut, 1991). Readers interested in English translations of Tagore's travel writings may look for *Letters from Russia* translated from Bengali by Sasadhar Sinha (Kolkata: Visva-Bharati, 1960) and *Journey to Persia and Iraq: 1932* (Kolkata: Visva-Bharati, 2003). Tagore's visit to Argentina and his relationship with Victoria Ocampo are documented in Ketaki Kushari Dyson's *In Your Blossoming Flower Garden* (New Delhi: Sahitya Akademi, 1988). Kaiser Haq's *A Poet at Large: Selected Travel Writings of Tagore* (New Delhi: Chronicle Books, 2011) is another helpful source.

ACKNOWLEDGMENTS

It must have been a conjunction of the stars that brought together so many Tagore experts and enthusiasts in the giant collaborative effort that went into the publication of *The Essential Tagore*. Working on this book has been a great learning experience, and an immensely rewarding one. The process was as laborious and demanding as it was exhilarating, and although it is impossible to mention by name all the individuals who were associated with it at various stages, we wish to express our gratitude to all of them.

We must thank Kumkum Bhattacharya, Director of the Granthan Bibhag at Visva-Bharati, for inspiring us to edit an anthology of Tagore's writings to mark his sesquicentenary. We are also grateful to Sharmila Sen, Executive Editor-at-Large at Harvard University Press, whose commitment to our project facilitated fruitful collaborations between numerous key individuals and institutions without which the global publication of this historic volume might not have been realized.

In response to our queries, a number of scholars generously shared their expertise on Tagore. We appreciate the valuable input of all those who helped us with their advice, suggestions, and encouragement. In particular, we would like to thank Syed Akram Hossain of the University of Dhaka for providing a list of Tagore's writings as a starting point for our selections. Our thanks to M. Shakhaowat Hossain for organizing and collecting Fakrul Alam's translations of Tagore's poems and songs to aid the selection process, and to Syed Manzoorul Islam (University of Dhaka) and Farhad Bani Idris (Frostburg State University) for commenting on Fakrul Alam's contributions.

We are grateful to all our contributors for their enthusiastic participation in our project, and their patience and cooperation throughout the editing process.

Babul Prasad of the University of Dhaka has always been a pillar of strength. We thank him for helping us in innumerable ways, and especially for formatting the manuscript.

It is a privilege to have Amit Chaudhuri write the thoughtful foreword to this volume, and an honor to have Amartya Sen's endorsement of the idea behind our project. We thank our editors at Visva-Bharati and Harvard, especially Kumkum, Sharmila, Ian, Heather, and Kate for sharing our excitement and enthusiasm through all the stages of our work. We deeply appreciate the support of Rabindra Bhavana in organizing the illustrations, and thank Abhijit Nath for coming to our aid when we were really under pressure.

We would also like to acknowledge all those who kindly granted permission to reproduce some of the translations and illustrations in this volume. Sunetra Gupta provided translations of songs by Tagore from *Memories of Rain* (Grove Press, 1992). These are: "In traversing the lonely road"; "If you did not give me love"; "Your eyes have pleaded with me"; and "In the dense obsession of this deep dark rain." "You dressed him as a beggar" is from *Moonlight into Marzipan* (Penguin, 2002). All are copyright © Sunetra Gupta. Permission has been granted by Oxford University Press and Visva-Bharati to reprint Amitav Ghosh's translation of "Hungry Stone," and Supriya Chaudhuri's translation of "The Wife's Letter." Both were published in *Rabindranath Tagore: Selected Short Stories*, ed. Sukanta Chaudhuri (Delhi: Oxford University Press & Visva-Bharati, 2000). Oxford University Press and Visva-Bharati also granted us permission to reprint Supriya Chaudhuri's translations of poems: "The Restless One"; "Hymn to the Tree"; "I Saw in the Twilight"; and "They Work." They also kindly granted permission to publish Sukanta Chaudhuri's translations of "Voyage"; "Lord of Life"; "The Poet"; and "Woman Empowered." All are found in *Rabindranath Tagore: Selected Poems*, ed. Sukanta Chaudhuri (Delhi: Oxford University Press & Visva-Bharati, 2004). Penguin India kindly provided extracts from Radha Chakravarty's translations of *Boyhood Days* (2007), *Gora* (2009), and

816

ACKNOWLEDGMENTS

Farewell Song (2005), as well as the poem "The Invention of Shoes" from *The Land of Cards* (2010). Thanks are due as well to Srishti Publishers for an extract from Rimli Bhattacharya's translation of *Four Chapters* (Delhi: Srishti Publishers and Distributors, 2002).

Most of all, we thank our family members, without whose support and encouragement our book would not have seen the light of day.

FAKRUL ALAM
RADHA CHAKRAVARTY

817

CONTRIBUTORS

FAKRUL ALAM University of Dhaka

RIMLI BHATTACHARYA University of Delhi

ARUNA CHAKRAVARTI Independent writer and translator

RADHA CHAKRAVARTY Gargi College, University of Delhi

AMIT CHAUDHURI University of East Anglia

ROSINKA CHAUDHURI Centre for Studies in Social Sciences, Calcutta

SUKANTA CHAUDHURI Jadavpur University

SUPRIYA CHAUDHURI Jadavpur University

SANJUKTA DASGUPTA Calcutta University

CHANDANA DUTTA Independent translator

KALYANI DUTTA Independent writer and translator

AMITAV GHOSH Independent writer and translator

NANDINI GUHA College of Vocational Studies, University of Delhi

RUPENDRA GUHA MAJUMDAR University of Delhi

SUNETRA GUPTA University of Oxford

KAISER HAQ University of Dhaka

FARHAD B. IDRIS Frostburg State University

SUBHRANSU MAITRA Independent writer and translator

SOMDATTA MANDAL Visva-Bharati, Santiniketan

SYED MANZOORUL ISLAM University of Dhaka

SHORMISHTHA PANJA University of Delhi

SHAILESH PAREKH Independent writer and translator

RATNA PRAKASH Independent translator

RANI RAY Independent translator

ABHIJIT SEN Visva-Bharati, Santiniketan

NIVEDITA SEN Hans Raj College, University of Delhi

SUDEEP SEN Independent writer and translator

DEBJANI SENGUPTA Indraprastha College, University of Delhi

RUMANA SIDDIQUE University of Dhaka

REBA SOM Rabindranath Tagore Centre, Indian Council for Cultural Relations, Kolkata